AF394737

THE
IRISH FARM
IN COLOUR

MICHAEL B. BARRY

AND JOHN O'BYRNE

THE
IRISH FARM
IN COLOUR

GILL BOOKS

Gill Books
Hume Avenue
Park West
Dublin 12
www.gillbooks.ie

Gill Books is an imprint of M.H. Gill and Co.

9781804583135

By Michael B. Barry:
Across Deep Waters: Bridges of Ireland
Restoring a Victorian House
Through the Cities: The Revolution in Light Rail
Tales of the Permanent Way: Stories from the Heart of Ireland's Railways
Fifty Things to Do in Dublin
Dublin's Strangest Tales (with Patrick Sammon)
Bridges of Dublin: The Remarkable Story of Dublin's Liffey Bridges (with Annette Black)
Victorian Dublin Revealed: The Remarkable Legacy of Nineteenth-Century Dublin
Beyond the Chaos: The Remarkable Heritage of Syria
Homage to al-Andalus: The Rise and Fall of Islamic Spain
The Alhambra Revealed: The Remarkable Story of the Kingdom of Granada
Málaga: A Souvenir and Guide
Hispania: The Romans in Spain and Portugal
Courage Boys, We are Winning: An Illustrated History of the 1916 Rising
The Green Divide: An Illustrated History of the Irish Civil War
An Illustrated History of the Irish Revolution, 1916–1923
Fake News and the Irish War of Independence
The Fight for Irish Freedom: An Illustrated History of the War of Independence
The Irish Civil War in Colour (with John O'Byrne)
A Nation is Born (with John O'Byrne)
1588: The Spanish Armada and the 24 Ships Lost on Ireland's Shores
The Emergency in Colour (with John O'Byrne)

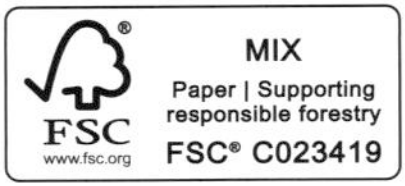

Colourising of photographs by John O'Byrne.

Designed by Padraig McCormack
Copy edited by Anna Kealy
Proofread by Heidi Houlihan
Indexed by Fergus Mulligan
Printed and bound by L.E.G.O. SpA, Italy
This book is typeset in 11.5pt on 16.5pt, Quinn Text

The paper used in this book comes from the wood pulp of sustainably managed forests.

A CIP catalogue record for this book is available from the British Library.

5 4 3 2 1

CONTENTS

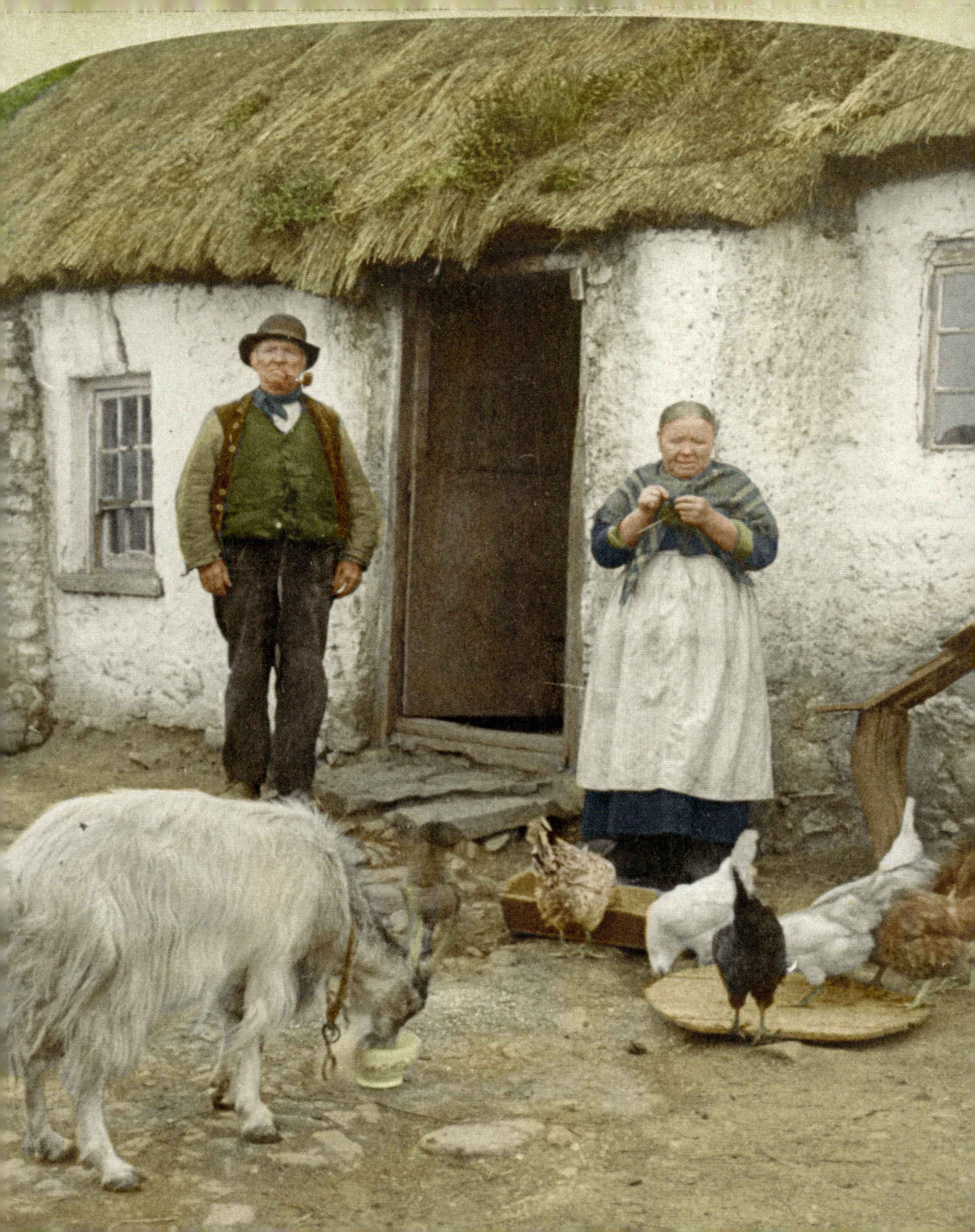

ACKNOWLEDGEMENTS

This work benefited from the help, insights and scholarship of many kind people.

Thanks are due especially to: Dr Brian Kirby, Irish Capuchin Provincial Archives; the Military Archives, Cathal Brugha Barracks; the National Library of Ireland; Eibhlin Colgan, Guinness Archives; Daniel Breen, Dara MacGrath, Cork Public Museum; Thomas Hall, An Garda Síochána Museum & Archives; Jim Dunleavy, ESB Archives; Jim Coughlan, *Irish Examiner*; Carlos García; Caitriona Morrissey; Philip Doyle; *Irish Farmers Journal*; and Ciaran Cooney, photo curator of the Irish Railway Record Society. Exceptional photographs (taken by his father, Garda Patrick Gahan, during the 1930s) were provided by Jim Gahan. We are particularly grateful to Caoilte Breatnach, who gave access to the remarkable Robert Cresswell Archive, which is part of the Kinvara Community Council's collection. Cathal McCarthy, ICMSA, smoothed our way in obtaining both agricultural knowledge and photographs. Niall Madigan of the IFA also kindly sent us photographs. We are especially appreciative of Alice Taylor, author of many books on Irish farming and country life, for kindly contributing the foreword to this book.

The following were very helpful: Professor Alan Matthews; Natasha Serne, RDS; Michael Talty, Clare Libraries; Saul Mitchell, PRONI; Stephen Travers; Jeanne Kelly and Niamh Thornton of Ornua; John Caffrey; Professor Siobhan Mullan, UCD; Donal Connolly; Michael Hinch; Edward Iliffe; Eveline van Wijmen and Niall McGauran, Lely; Bill Power; Dermot O'Doherty; Noel Campbell, Assistant Keeper at the National Museum of Ireland – Country Life. The team at Gill Books gave great encouragement and support: Patrick O'Donoghue with Iollann Ó Murchú and Kristen Olson. Last but not least, the authors are greatly appreciative of the support and help of, respectively: Paddy and Patricia O'Byrne, and Veronica Barry.

FOREWORD

Within the covers of this book you will walk back into the Ireland that nurtured all our roots.

In the first part I was introduced to an Ireland recalled by my parents, grandmother and old neighbours, and in the second half I walked back into an Ireland that I myself remembered. And both unlocked memory boxes full of hidden treasures. As I meandered through the pages, I recalled an old friend telling me that on his first reading of *To School Through the Fields,* he found himself looking out for his own memories, including minding chickens from the talons of the swooping hawk. And he smiled with appreciation as he told me how delighted he was to discover that I too had remembered the hawk. It was important for him that his memory was incorporated into my memories. And as you too go through this book you will find yourself looking out for remembered scenes or pictures painted for you by parents or grandparents. And they are all in here! In this book you walk into an art gallery where rare pictures of our past can be viewed and enjoyed. A treasure trove to be savoured in silence and later shared with appreciative friends.

The pictures of happy people, children and animals bring a smile to your face, but viewing the scenes of grinding poverty, evictions and the struggle for freedom chill your soul and bring an awareness of the price that our ancestors paid that we might now call this land our land.

Born in 1938 and growing up on a farm along the Cork–Kerry border, I absorbed a way of living that has now almost totally disappeared. Yes, there was hard work and long hours but also a closeness to nature with an unconscious absorption and appreciation of its blessings and beauties. Working with the earth, as many gardeners know, brings peace of mind and contentment, the value of which is now being recognised by modern therapists. I remember one evening when I was young, taking out a jug of tea with a wedge of brown bread to my father who had spent the day ploughing in a field at a far end of the farm. As I walked in the gap, the sun was setting behind my father, his horse silhouetting them against the skyline. I stood there transfixed, sensing that I had come on a scene beyond my understanding as the human, natural and divine blended harmoniously together.

To quote a now much-aspired-to ideal, we actually did then 'live inside the gate' as all our food was grown on the farm, and in the coming together to save the hay, cutting the corn and going to the bog and the creamery, the neighbours met and gathered in the *meitheal* system which created a 'bonding' when we did not even know the meaning of such a word. Neither had we heard the term 'organic farming' but that is exactly what was going on. Although the work was physically demanding, the way of life was kind to the natural world.

Every spring we waited for swoops of swallows to wing into the stable, piggeries and cow stalls, and begin reclaiming their old nests. During summer the call of the cuckoo echoed along the valley and at night we went to sleep to the sound the corncrake. Before my father mowed the hay he inspected the high meadow grass for nests and then left an uncut patch until the nestlings had flown. He cautioned us back then about the need to care for nature and the wild life on the farm, warning, 'Wrong nature and we will pay a terrible price.' Prophetic words indeed.

Nature and the divine were interlinked and on Rogation Days in April my parents went out with a bottle of holy water and blessed their crops and as our turn came around, we held the Stations when the priest came to our house and all the neighbours gathered for Mass around the kitchen table. This was a blending of the human and divine as over the years we had worked, celebrated and maybe grieved together and now we came together in prayer. And it was good to see the Stations included in this book.

Each night my mother led us all in the family rosary, which introduced a calming mantra into our noisy kitchen, and during which any family member or neighbour in trouble was remembered in prayer.

My father enjoyed fishing, and in summer brought home bags of brown trout from the river that meandered along the valley at the bottom of our farm. Salmon came up here every autumn to spawn and he strongly objected to poaching. When one neighbour gave us the gift of a poached salmon, my father later opened it on the kitchen table where all the fish eggs spilled out, showing us the huge loss of fish life in the poaching of this one salmon.

Back then we children were part of the work ethic on the farm and in this book a child sitting on a seat of a mowing machine brought a smile to my face. As we saved the hay, long-legged frogs of many colours jumped ahead of us along the headlands. Weeks previously, we had inspected in deep dykes their prenatal quivering frog's croak and watched with anticipation as they formed into tadpoles. Now they were fully formed and high jumping along the meadow headlands. One of the pluses of walking to school through the fields was our daily inspection of the birds' nests along the way. Going barefoot in summer we jumped with relish into muddy gaps and warm cow dung to later wash our feet in the tumbling water of a nearby stream. Could this have been the forerunner of reflexology? We harvested our way home on blackberries, haws and sloes, and sometimes buried sloes in glass bottles in an effort to make our own sloe wine. Come Halloween we climbed what we called 'nut trees' in a nearby field and brought home tin gallons full to later be cracked with a stone on the flag stone in front of the fire. Apple trees that my father had planted as a young man provided an ample supply for the jaw exercising pursuit of 'snap apple' that was then the Halloween entertainment. And around the apple trees which were fenced off from the marauding pigs were dozens of beehives, so honey was part of our daily diet. The land was good to us and gave us our daily bread and we in return were kind to the land.

A picture is worth a thousand words and this book speaks volumes, which will hopefully engender in the present and future generation a respect and appreciation of the gift that our ancestors preserved and handed on to us.

Alice Taylor

INTRODUCTION

Why a book on Irish farming? Despite increasing urbanisation, most Irish people are only a generation removed from the land.

Farming remains a powerful part of our national identity, shaping not just the countryside but also the culture, traditions and rhythms of daily life. The influence of rural Ireland is deeply embedded in our history and continues to define us as a people.

This book is not a technical tome but rather an attempt to capture the essence of Irish farming – its rhythms, its resilience and its deep connection to the land. Using imagery, history and storytelling, we seek to bring the sights, sounds and spirit of farming to life through a visual journey through the world of Irish agriculture. Alongside the photographs, we provide a broad historical perspective, tracing the evolution of farming in Ireland while also considering its present and future.

Agriculture has been our nation's lifeline: Ireland, an island without significant mineral resources, remained largely untouched by the Industrial Revolution, which transformed its coal- and iron-rich neighbour. With little industry to speak of, agriculture was, throughout the nineteenth century and for much of the twentieth, the nation's only means of keeping body and soul together.

Part One of the book makes reference to the Neolithic era, the transition from a hunter-gatherer lifestyle to settled agriculture, marking a major shift in human history. Then we arrive at rural Ireland during the mid-nineteenth century, when photographs began. The introduction of the potato – once a symbol of agricultural abundance – had devastating consequences during the Great Famine. In the following 60 years, under British rule, Ireland lost half its population, leaving ruined cottages as silent witnesses to depopulation. There are many photographs of peasants depicted living in basic conditions, generally along the Atlantic seaboard. Yet those on the land in more prosperous rural communities lived a better life. This was particularly evident in the photographs we see of the Anglo-Irish gentry (and their servants). Towards the end of the nineteenth century, the countryside was also the stage for radical change: the land agitation movement, spearheaded by the National Land League, brought about the end of the landlord system. By 1910, two-thirds of tenant farmers owned their land, with the remainder following suit by the 1920s. Ireland had finally moved beyond the days of forelock-tugging servitude. It was a game-changer in land ownership – by contrast, even in Britain today, a third of farmland remains rented from landlords.

Part Two delves into the early twentieth century, a time of war, independence and societal transformation. The War of

Independence and Civil War played out largely in the countryside, while after independence, the new Cumann na nGaedheal government maintained Ireland as Britain's 'larder', with nearly 90 per cent of exports, primarily agricultural, going to the neighbouring island. The Economic War that followed devastated prices, and during World War II – the Emergency – our dependence on the land became starkly clear, with turf replacing imported coal as the nation's primary fuel source.

Part Three examines the transition from horsepower to tractors, while the final section, Part Four, brings us into the modern era. Ireland's economy has changed dramatically, moving from an agriculture-dominated society to one shaped by multinationals, principally in the information technology and pharmaceutical sectors. Recent developments have reminded us that the multinational sector is vulnerable, yet agriculture will always be with us – it remains a central part of our economy. As the nation entered the European Economic Community, it moved from basic commodity production to high-value, premium food exports. The Common Agricultural Policy and, more recently, climate change policies have further reshaped the sector. While agriculture, forestry and fishing now account for around 1.2 per cent of gross national income – compared to nearly 40 per cent in 1922 – the core of Irish farming life remains. The cow still grazes, the farmer still tills the land and the rhythms of the countryside continue much as they always have.

For this book, we have drawn upon a wide range of photographic collections, and we are grateful for the support of the kind people who curate these. In particular, we appreciate the generosity of the Kinvara Community Group in granting access to the archive of anthropologist Robert Cresswell, which provides a unique window into Irish farm life in the County Galway of the 1950s. We are also honoured to have Alice Taylor, the celebrated author of *To School Through the Fields*, writing the foreword for this book. Her work has beautifully captured the heart and soul of rural Ireland, and it is a privilege to have her lend her voice to this project.

The debate over colourisation of historical photographs has largely moved on, with most people appreciating how it brings the past to life. While artificial intelligence continues its march forward, we remain committed to the art of hand-colourisation, which adds depth and richness to the images. Just look at the eviction photograph on pages 32–3, where John O'Byrne's expertise allows us to distinguish the gradations between military and police uniforms of the era.

To a large extent – though not entirely – Ireland has moved beyond its role as Britain's larder. While we still export around a third of our agri-food products to Britain, we now supply premium-quality produce, from butter to beef, to discerning markets worldwide, including the United States and Germany. Ireland is blessed with rich, green pastures – though, of course, that vibrant landscape comes at the cost of our famously frequent rain. Whenever I see Spanish cows grazing on the few tufts of grass in the sparse fields common across much of the Iberian Peninsula, I can't help but wonder if there's a cow heaven – how these animals would react at the sight of the lush and verdant fields of Ireland.

Farming is not an easy life, and the

landscape is changing: small family farms are disappearing, while farm sizes continue to increase. Many farmers are asset-rich but cash-poor, facing tight margins and economic uncertainty. Yet there are rewards. For those with an agricultural heritage and a connection to the land, farming offers independence – an ability to be one's own boss, to work in the open air. At the same time, Irish farmers face growing pressure to balance food production with environmental sustainability. Agriculture is Ireland's largest contributor to greenhouse gas emissions, largely due to methane from cattle and nitrous oxide from fertilisers. As climate targets tighten, the sector must adopt new strategies to reduce its impact. Though challenging, these changes are essential – not only to meet present commitments, but also to secure the long-term viability of farming.

Farmers have a strong foundation with their grass-fed, high-quality produce, but the future lies in adding value and improving efficiency. Expanding into premium markets with verified sustainability credentials – such as carbon-neutral dairy – can open new opportunities. Technology, including robotic milking systems and precision farming, is already helping to reduce labour costs and improve soil management. Renewable energy, particularly wind, offers an additional income. EU and Irish government funding is available to help farmers transition toward a more sustainable and efficient future.

John O'Byrne and I hope you enjoy this book. Both of us were raised in small towns and have a deep appreciation for rural Ireland. Within these pages, we present a visual journey through Irish farming and country life from the mid-nineteenth century to today. The colourised images allow you to see the past as people of the time experienced it. Together with the detailed and granular captions, we present the story of Irish farming, while at the same time capturing the nuances of country life. As you turn the pages, we hope you will join us in celebrating the resilience, heritage and enduring spirit of Irish farming.

Michael B. Barry

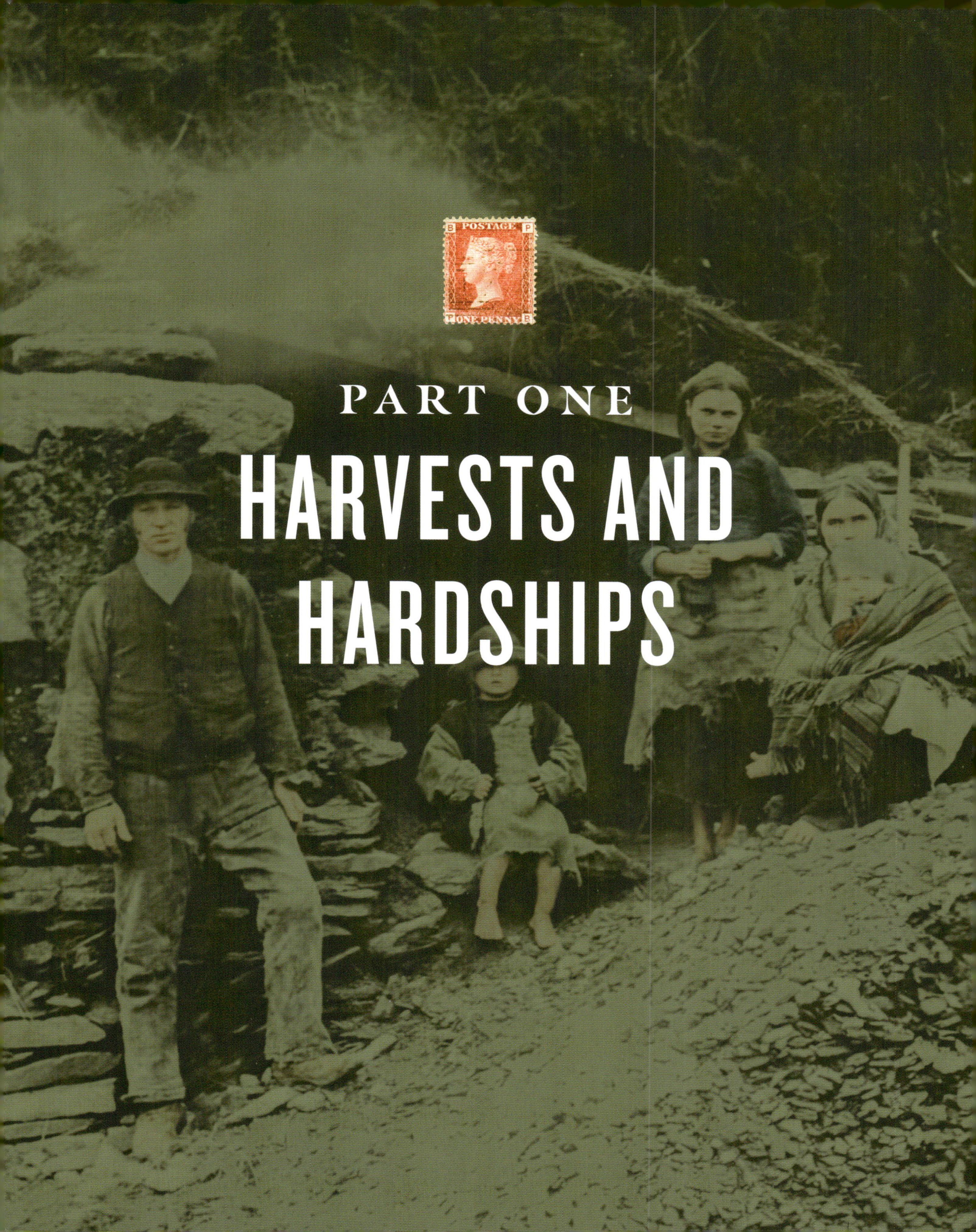

PART ONE

HARVESTS AND
HARDSHIPS

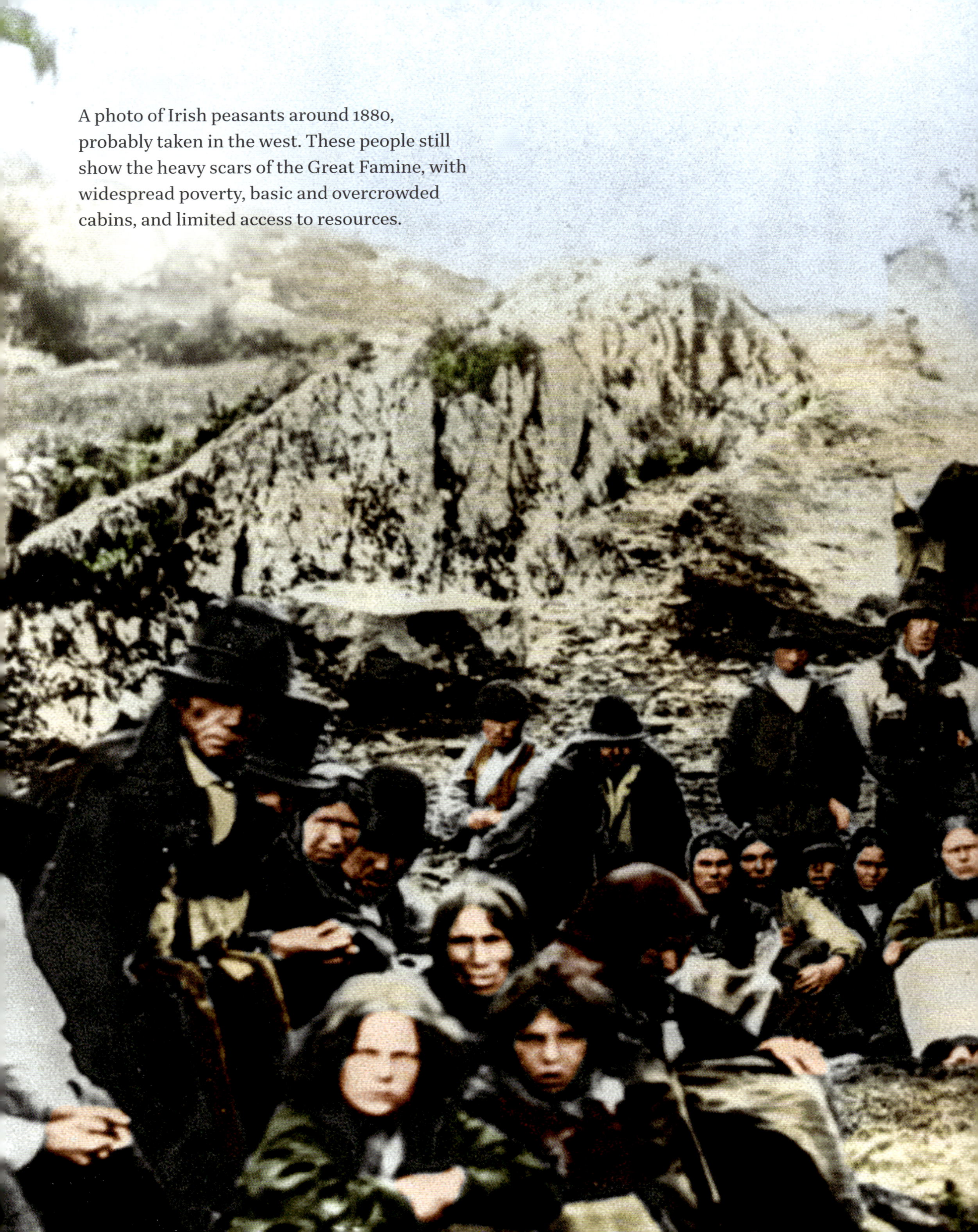

A photo of Irish peasants around 1880, probably taken in the west. These people still show the heavy scars of the Great Famine, with widespread poverty, basic and overcrowded cabins, and limited access to resources.

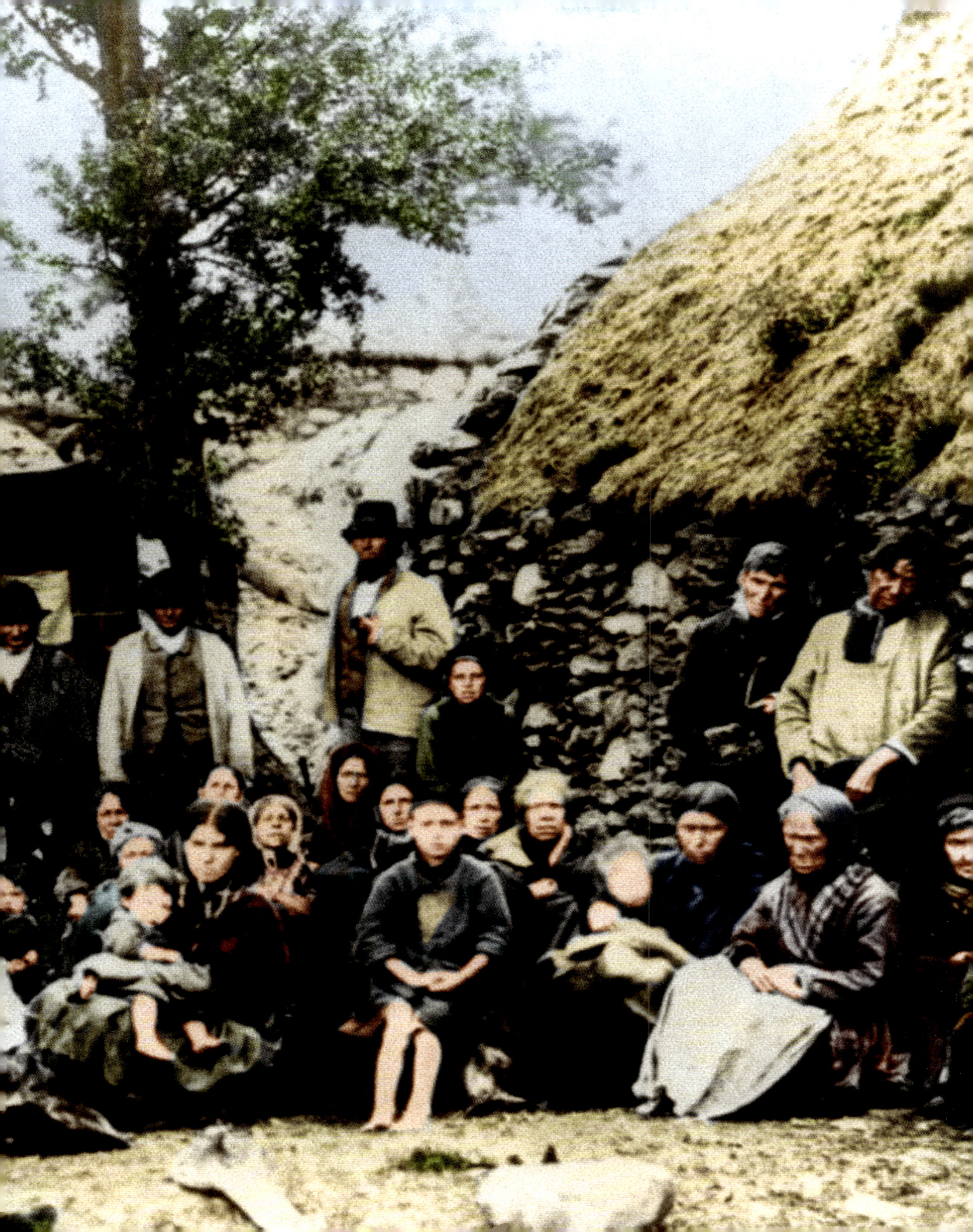

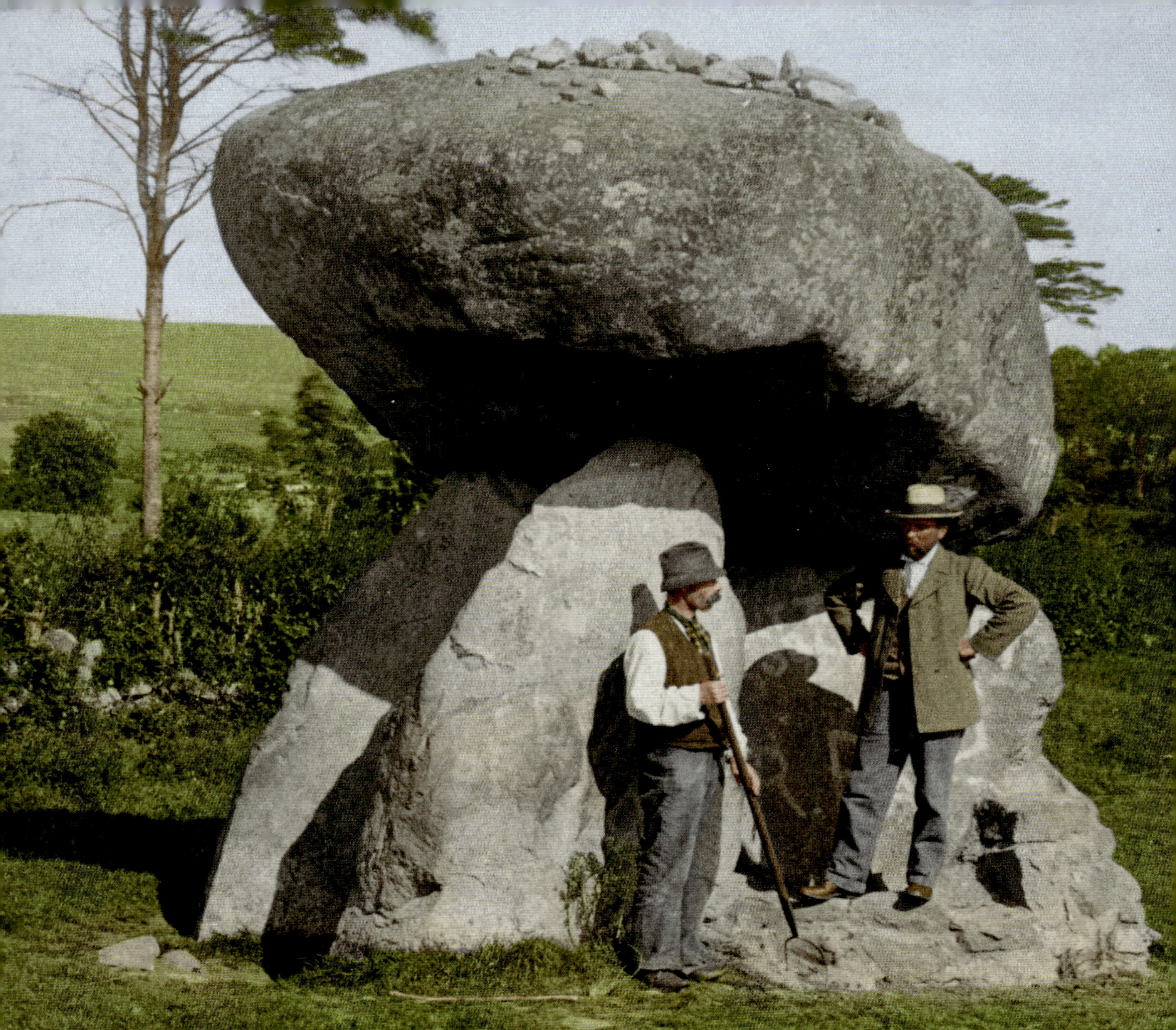

The Proleek Dolmen, a megalithic tomb from the Neolithic period, located near Dundalk, County Louth. Neolithic settlers came to Ireland around 4000 BC, attracted by fertile land and the relatively mild climate. They settled in lowland areas and river valleys. These settlers introduced crops like wheat and barley and domesticated animals like cattle, sheep and pigs.

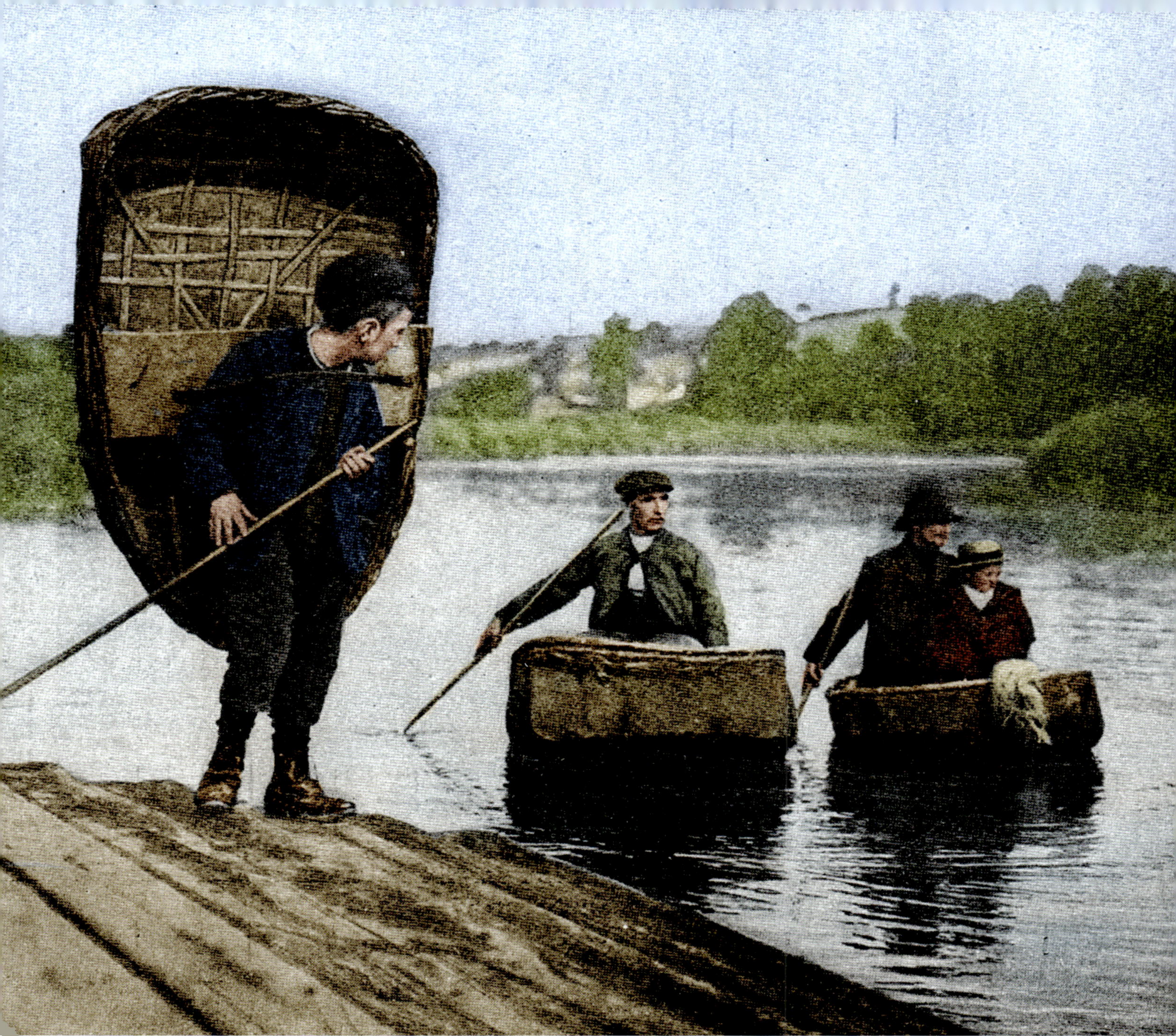

Nineteenth-century coracles. It is thought that the Neolithic settlers travelled to Ireland in dugout canoes (made by hollowing out large trees) or in coracles, wooden-framed boats covered in animal hides. Early settlers are thought to have come from the neighbouring island, with others (validated by genetic traces) having travelled along the western Atlantic seaboard from Iberia and the Mediterranean.

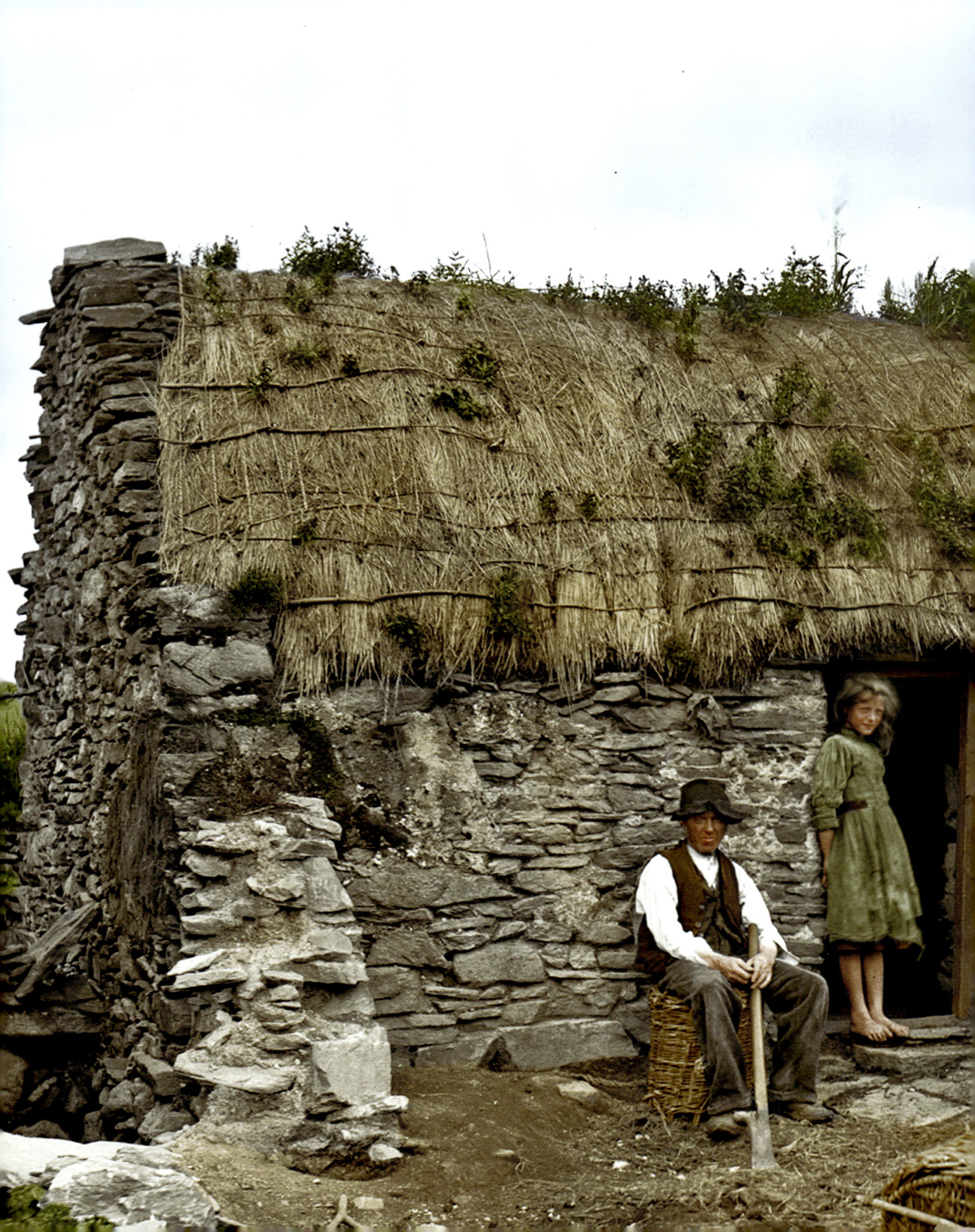

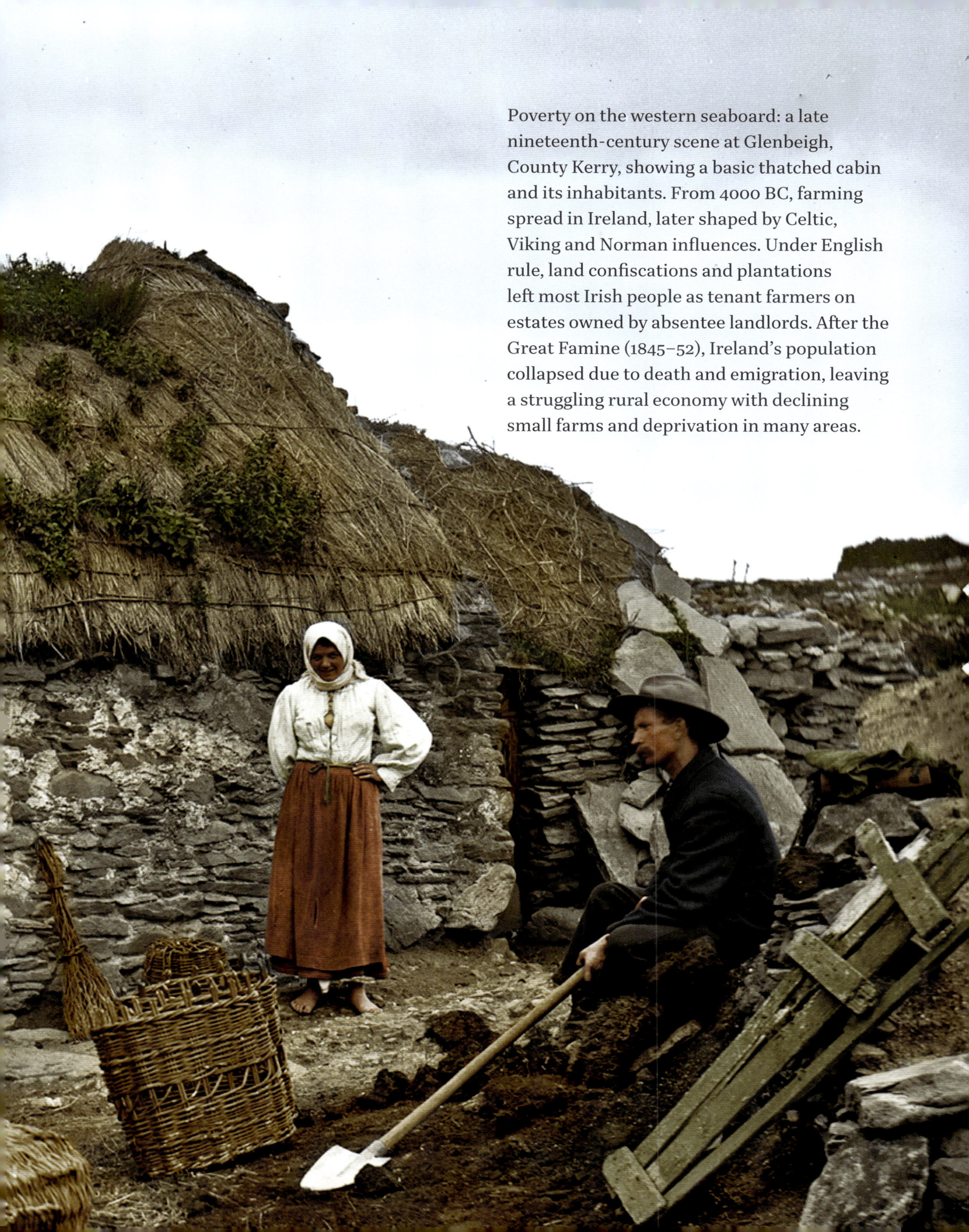

Poverty on the western seaboard: a late nineteenth-century scene at Glenbeigh, County Kerry, showing a basic thatched cabin and its inhabitants. From 4000 BC, farming spread in Ireland, later shaped by Celtic, Viking and Norman influences. Under English rule, land confiscations and plantations left most Irish people as tenant farmers on estates owned by absentee landlords. After the Great Famine (1845–52), Ireland's population collapsed due to death and emigration, leaving a struggling rural economy with declining small farms and deprivation in many areas.

A sled cart. Basic technology, simple and cheap, these were horse-drawn sledges made of two long wooden runners that dragged along the ground, with a platform or framework on top for carrying loads. They were common in poor western districts with equally poor terrain, especially on rocky or boggy land where wheels were impractical.

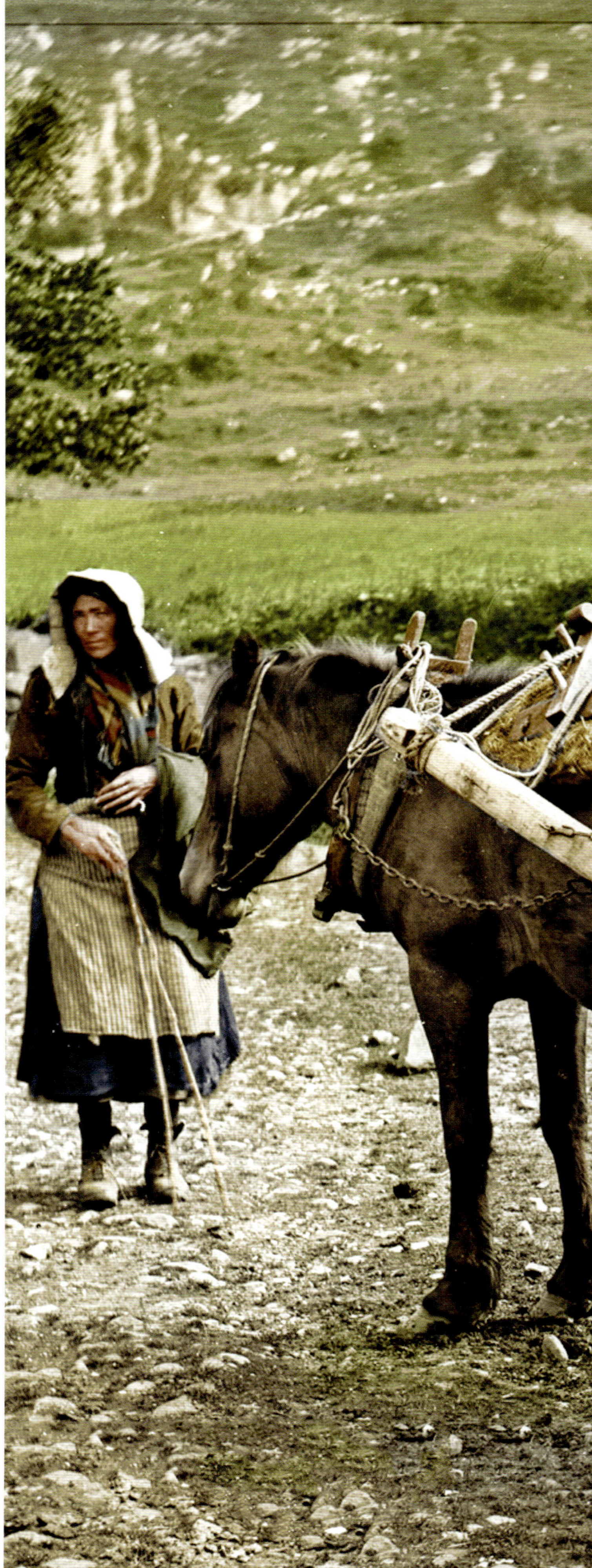

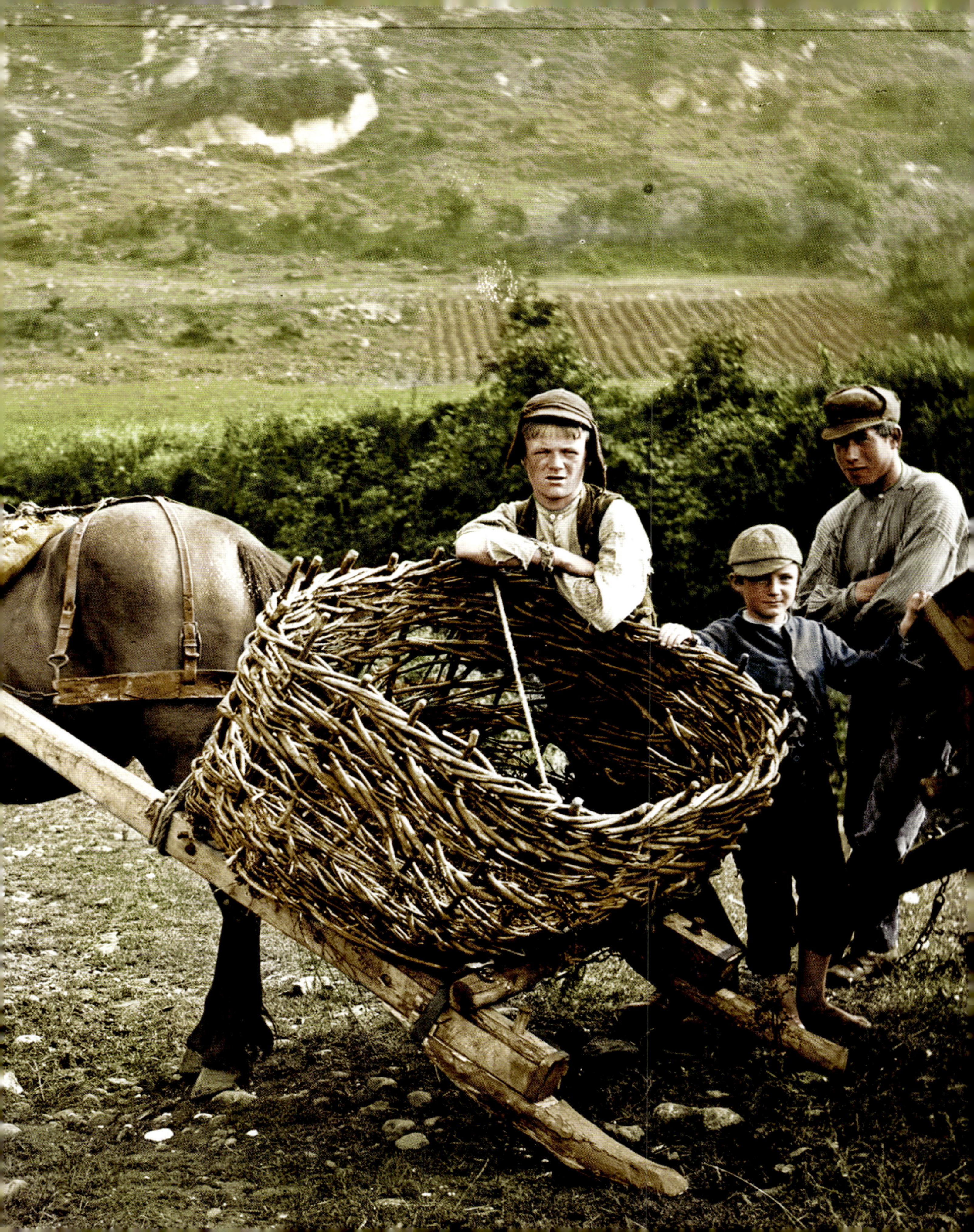

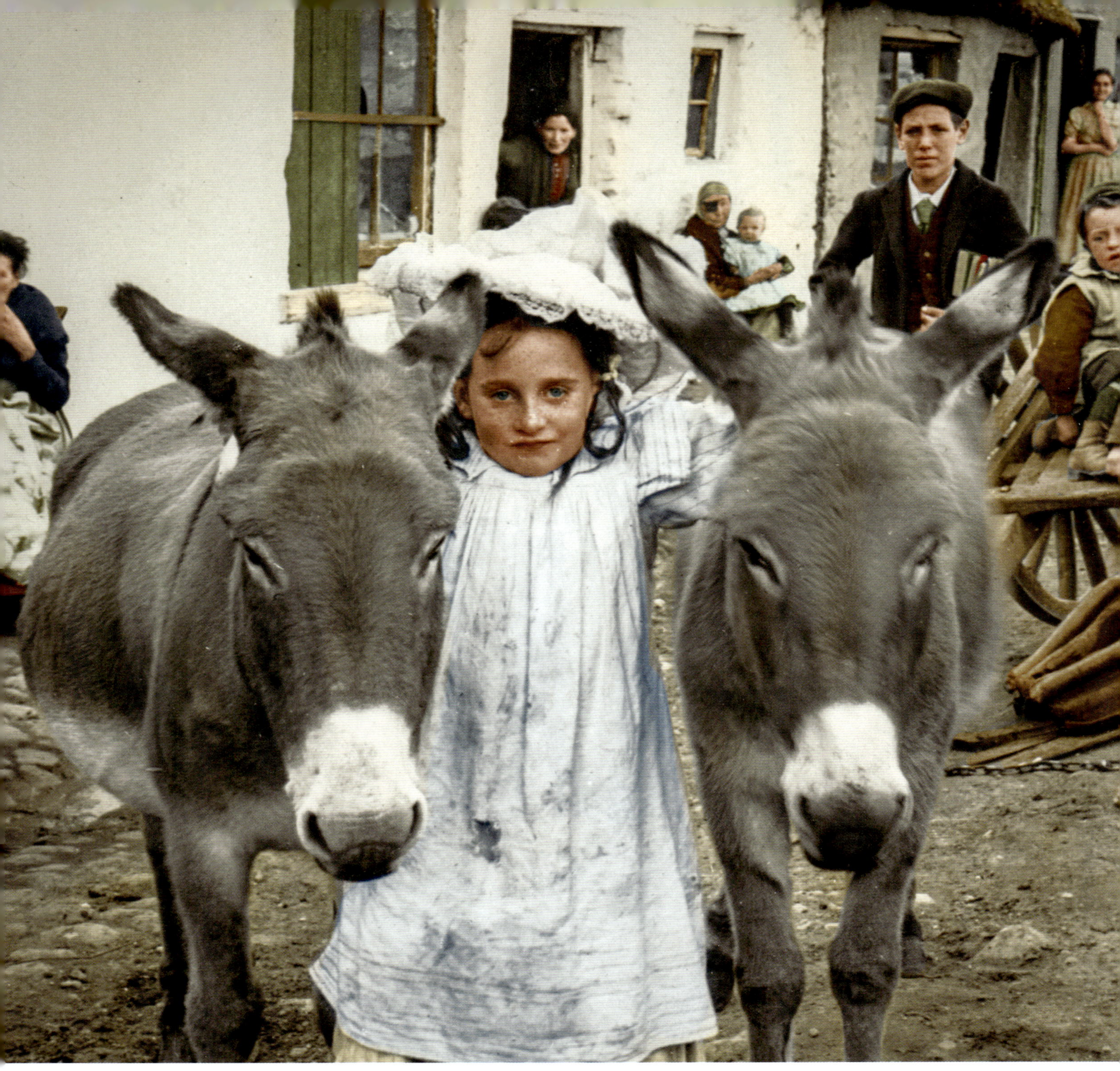

Donkeys were not only invaluable for navigating rough terrain, but also served as charming subjects for nineteenth-century photographers seeking picturesque scenes, such as this one featuring a winsome young girl.

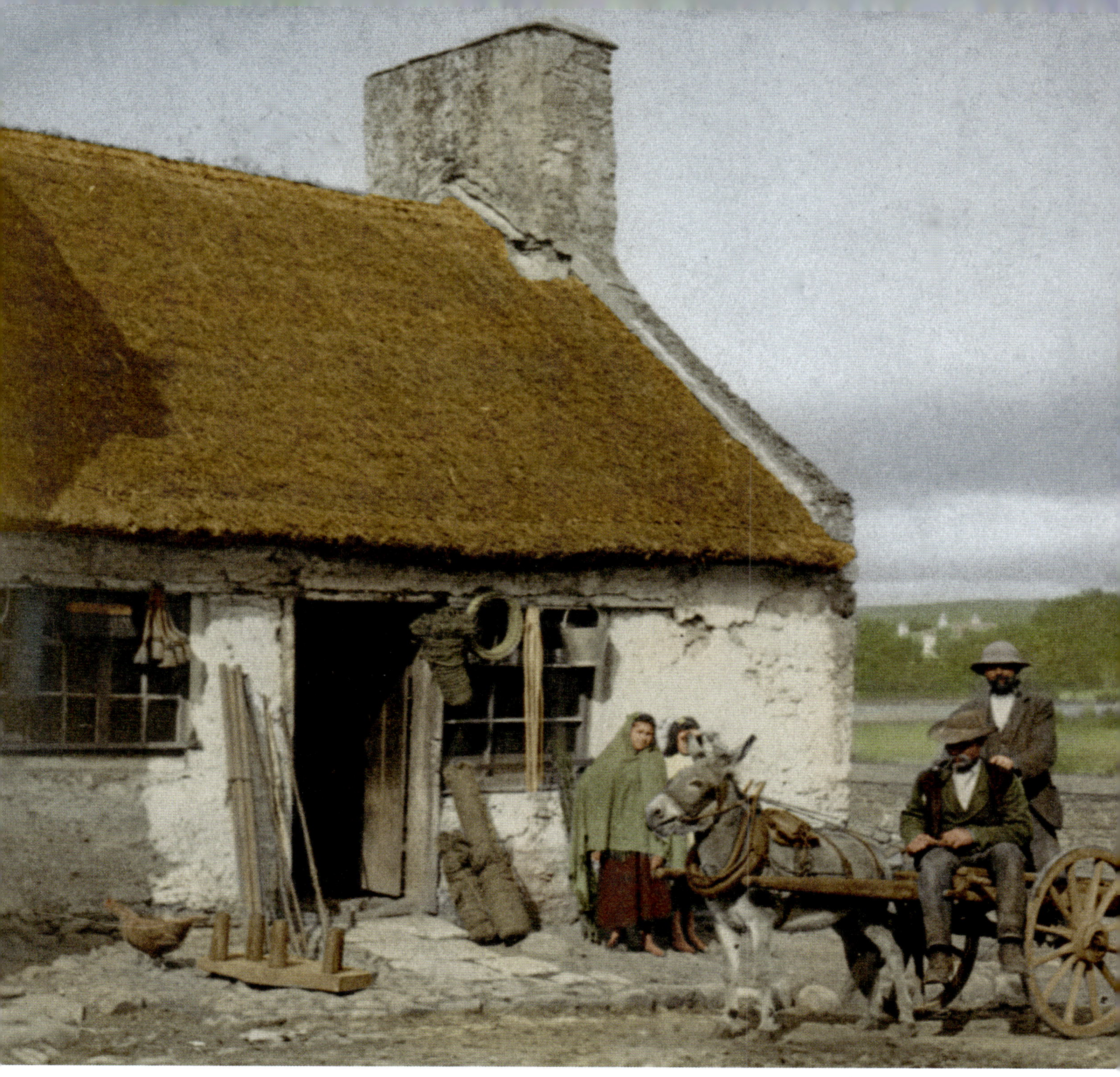

A general merchandise store in Killorglin,
County Kerry. This rudimentary store displays
utilitarian items: what look like handles for
shovels or spades, a hay rake, buckets and
brushes.

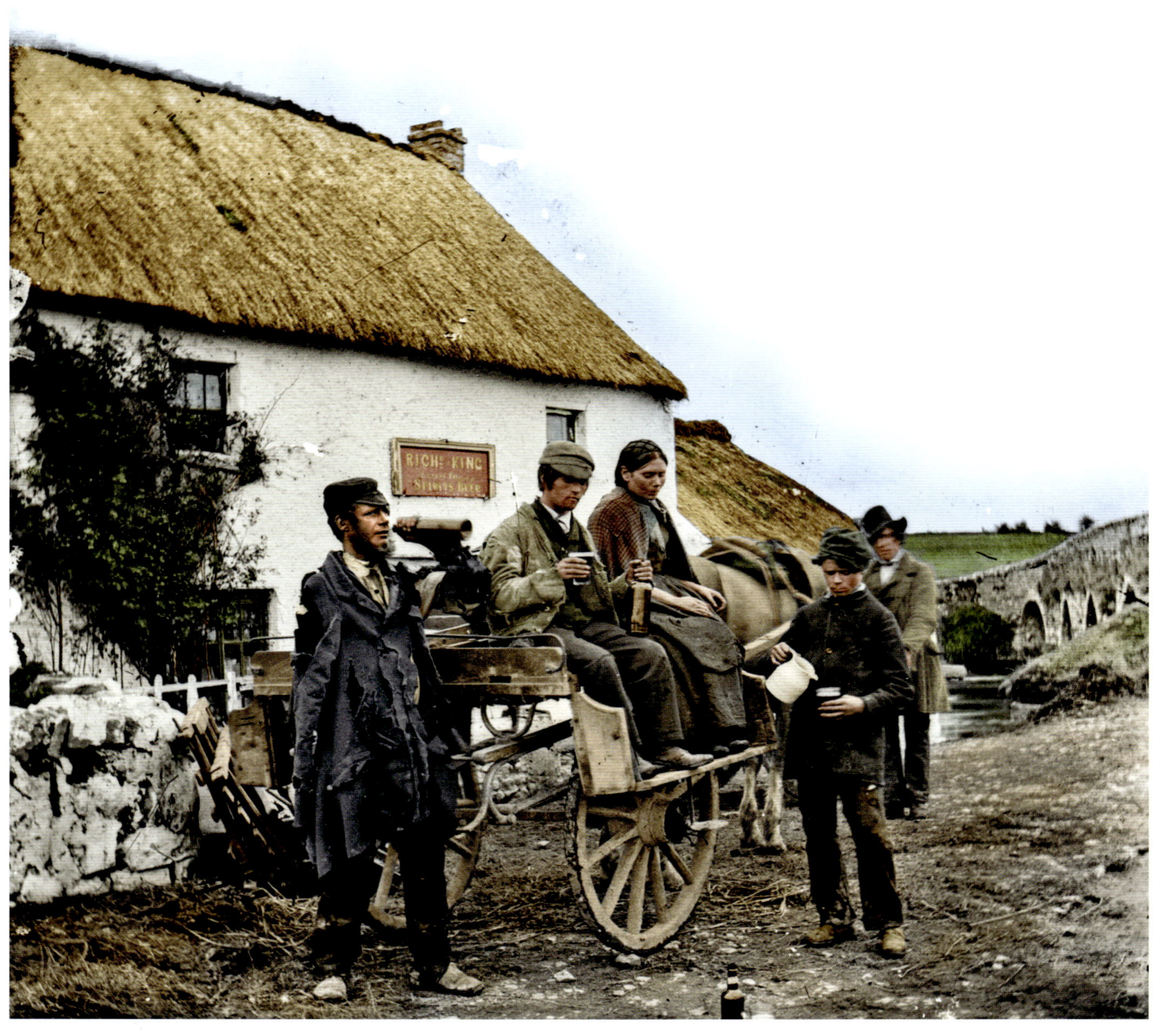

Top left: Father Theobald Mathew's temperance crusade had seemingly little effect in some places, as seen in this photo of men determinedly drinking outside Richard King's licensed premises in County Kerry.

Right: Life was hard for women on Irish farms. However, they were supremely tough and resourceful, learning to make do with what they had. They were skilled at handling the demands of farming, cooking, cleaning and child-rearing, invariably working long days.

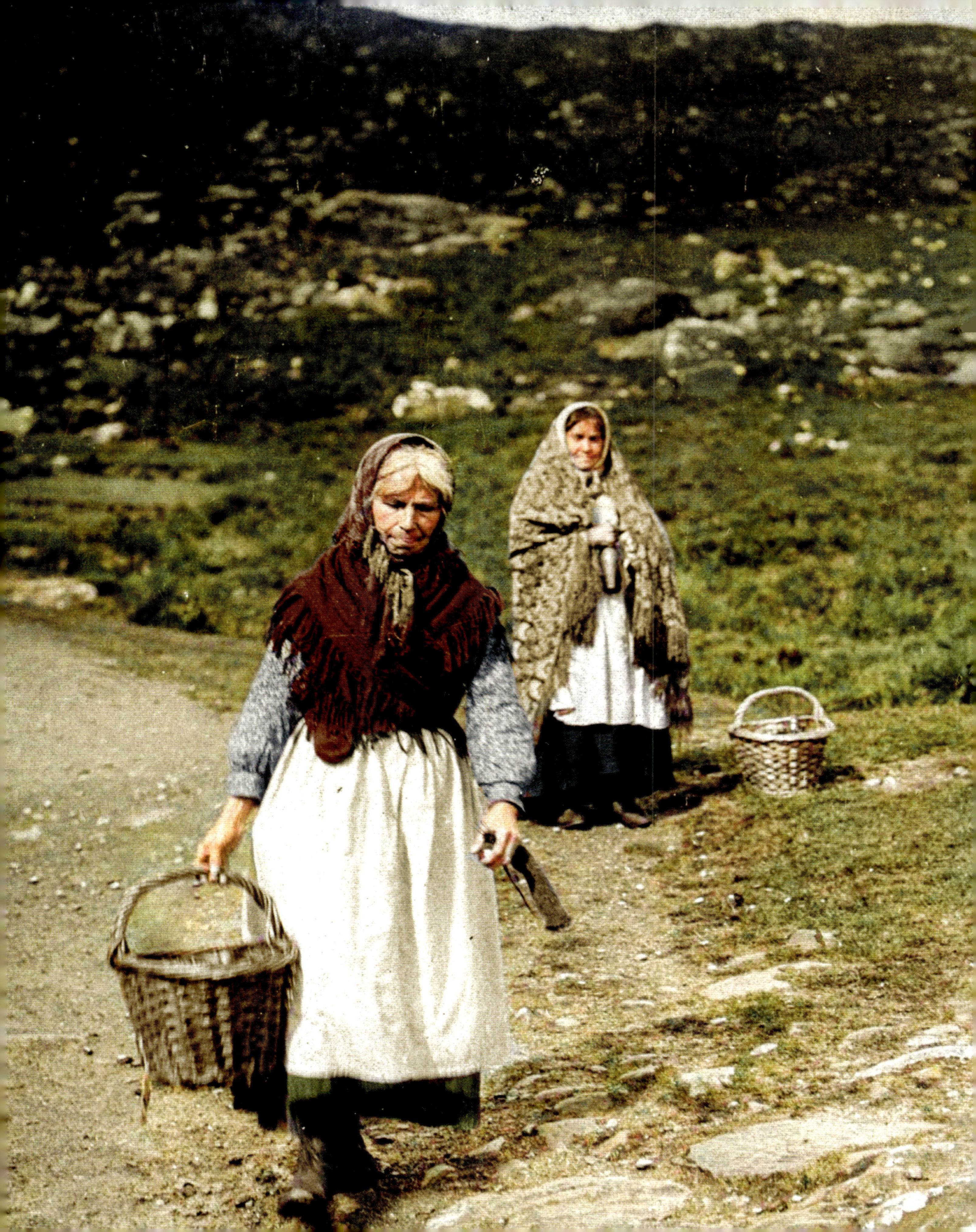

In a time before modern conveniences, a mother, accompanied by her children, is seen washing clothes by the river at Ballyshannon, County Donegal. It shows a quiet moment of everyday life, where women played a vital role in keeping the household running in rural Ireland.

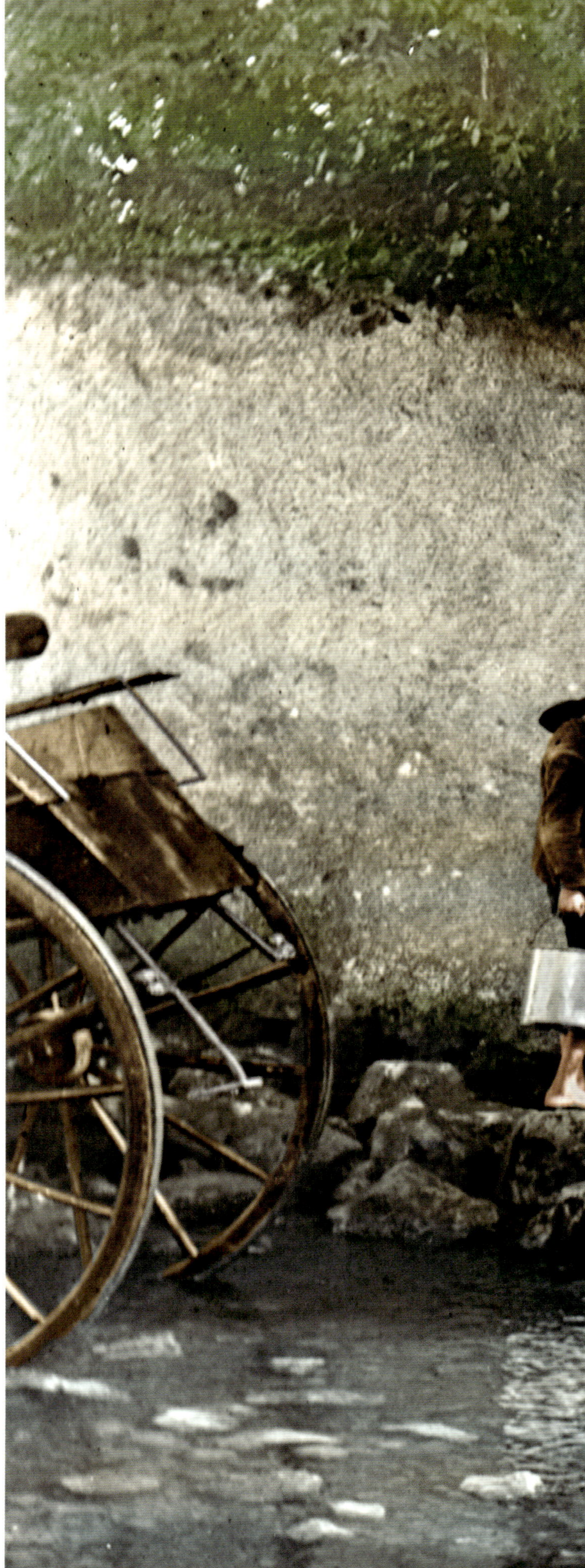

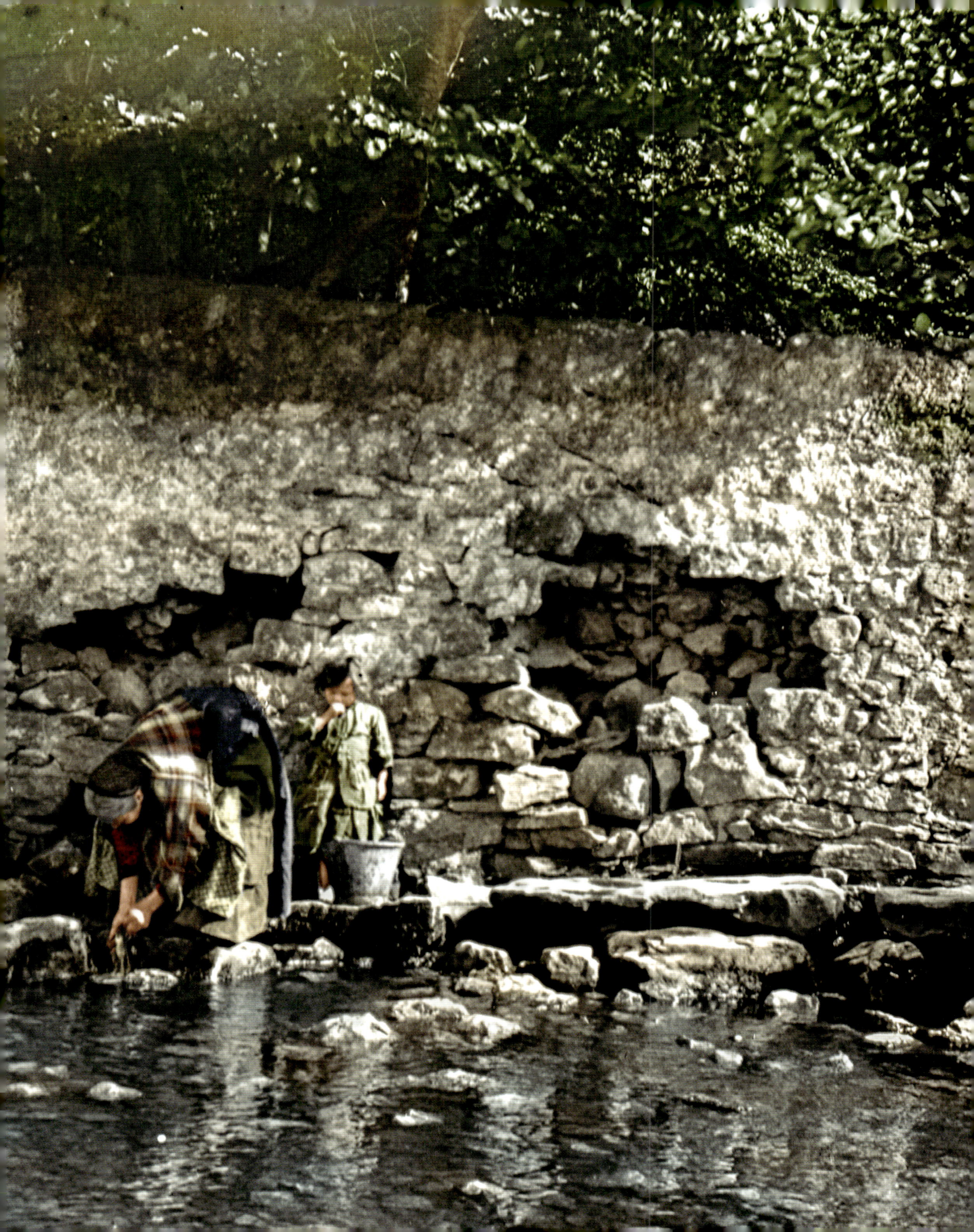

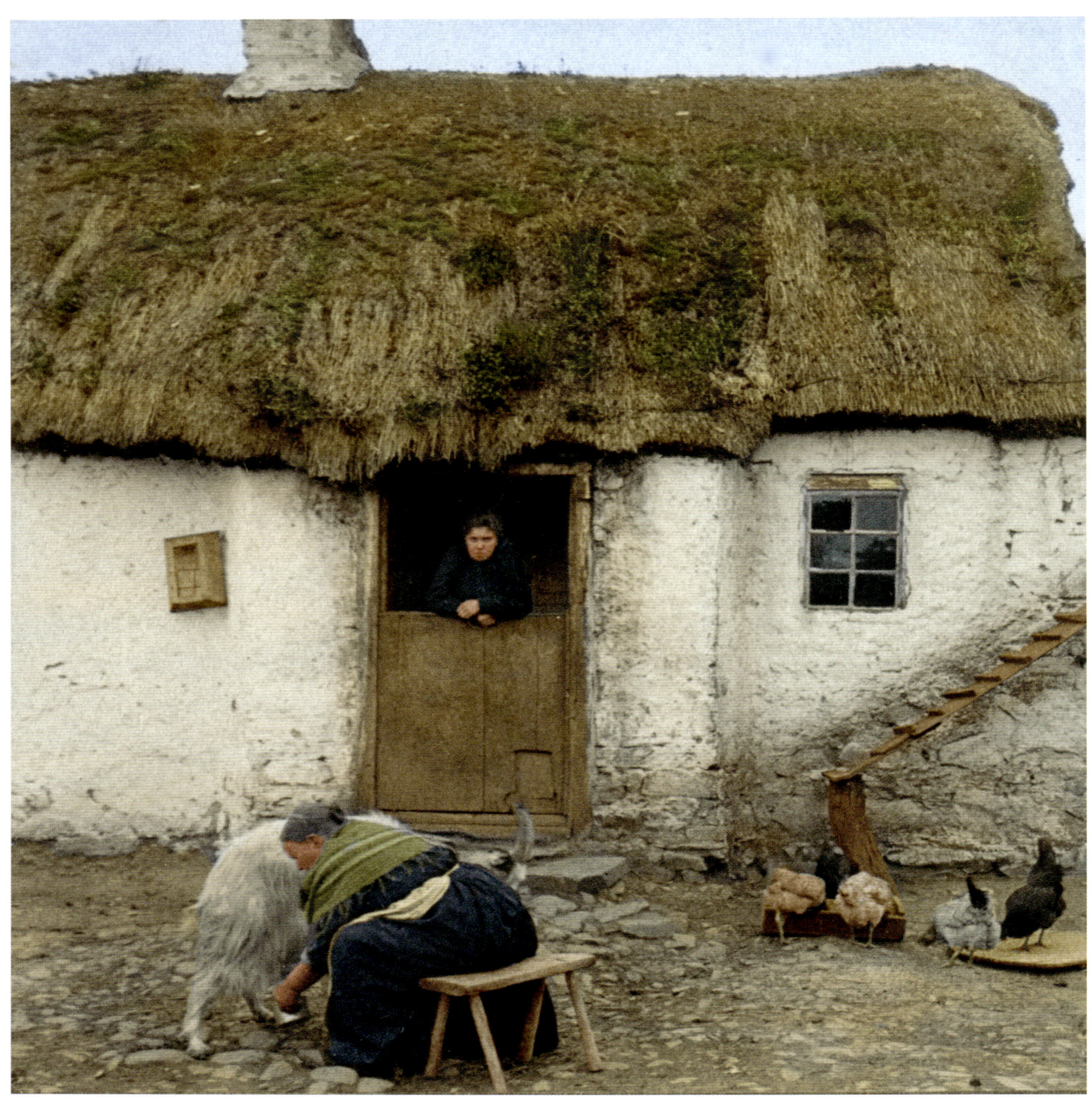

Top left: A woman milks a goat, an invaluable asset to families in rural Ireland. Goats thrived on the rough land of marginal areas, providing essential milk in regions with poor soil and limited resources.

Right: A woman at work at her spinning wheel. In Ireland, women often used traditional skills like spinning to contribute to the farm's income.

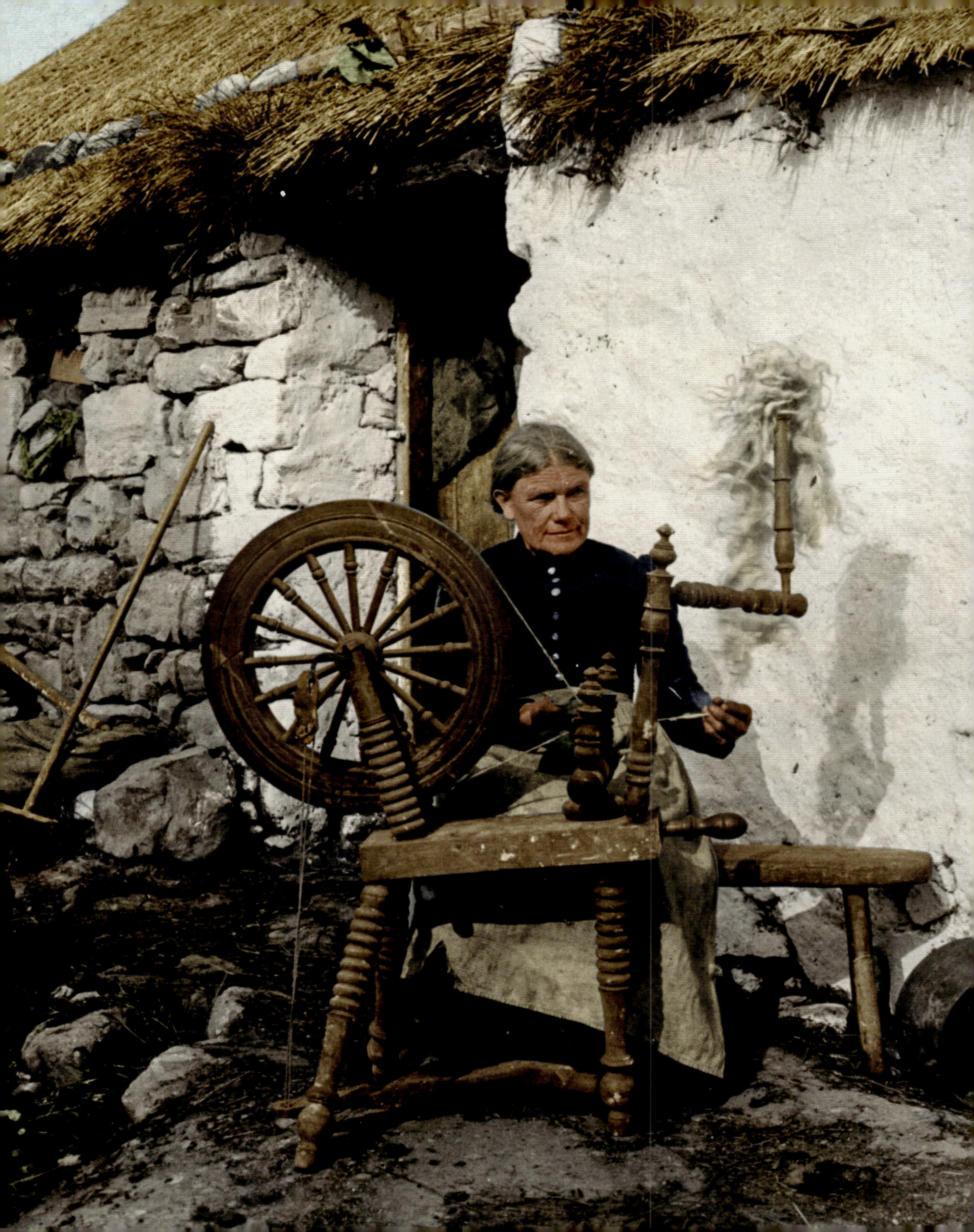

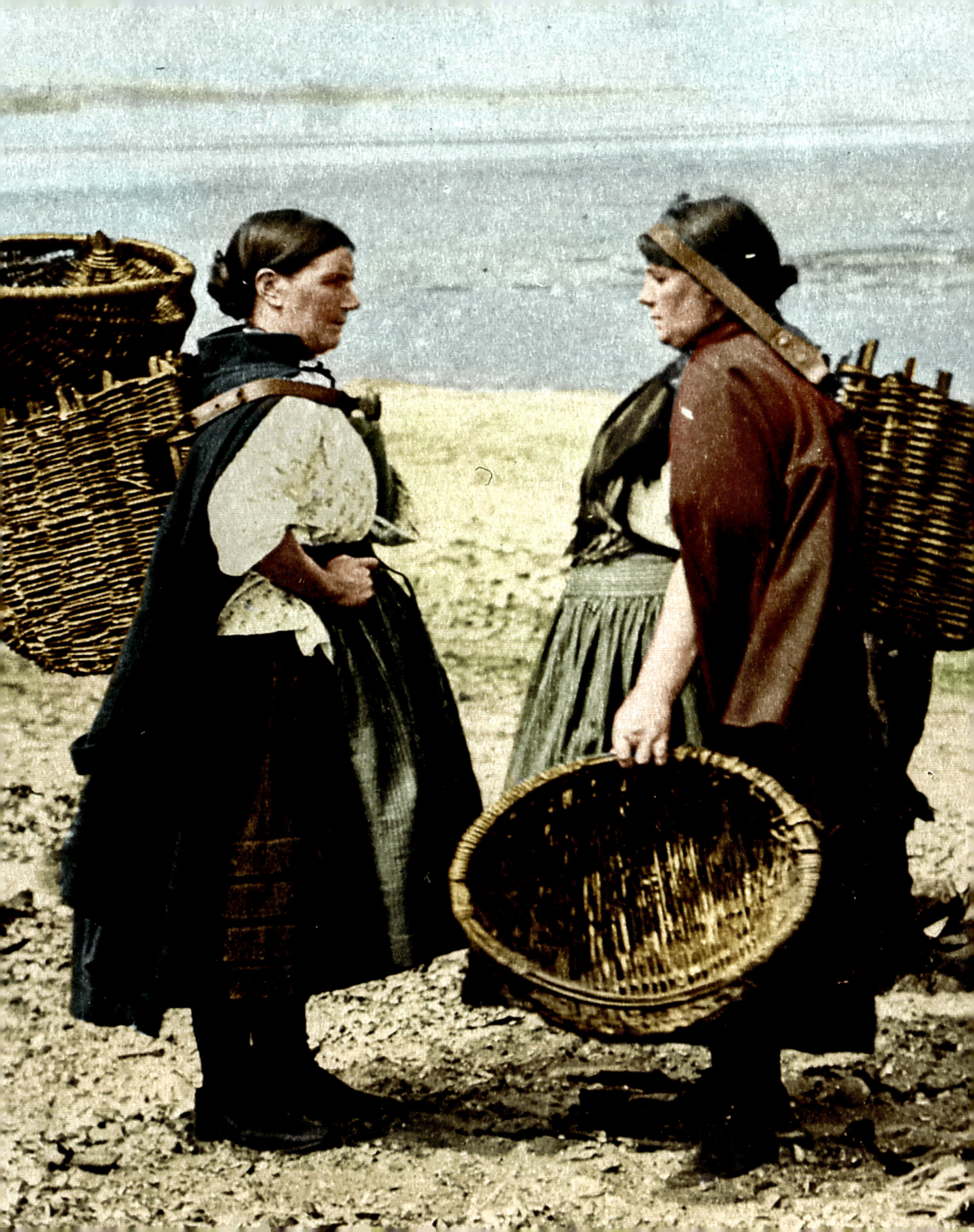

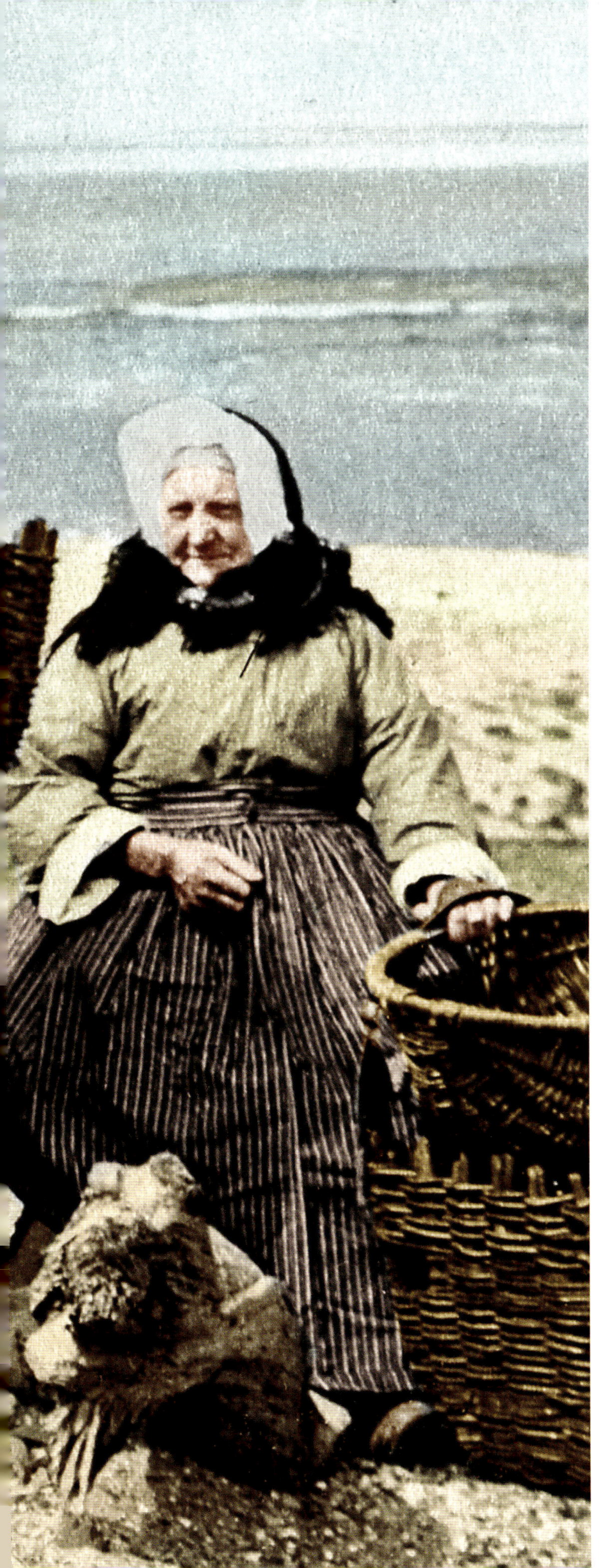

Three women with multiple baskets stand by the coast, *c.*1900, in a scene depicting the practice of cockle picking along Ireland's shores. This labour-intensive work was an essential source of food and income for many coastal families, particularly women and children. At low tide, the beaches would be exposed, allowing access to the cockles buried in the sand. The women would search the wet sand with their hands or tools, gathering the shellfish to sell in local markets or perhaps save some for their own sustenance.

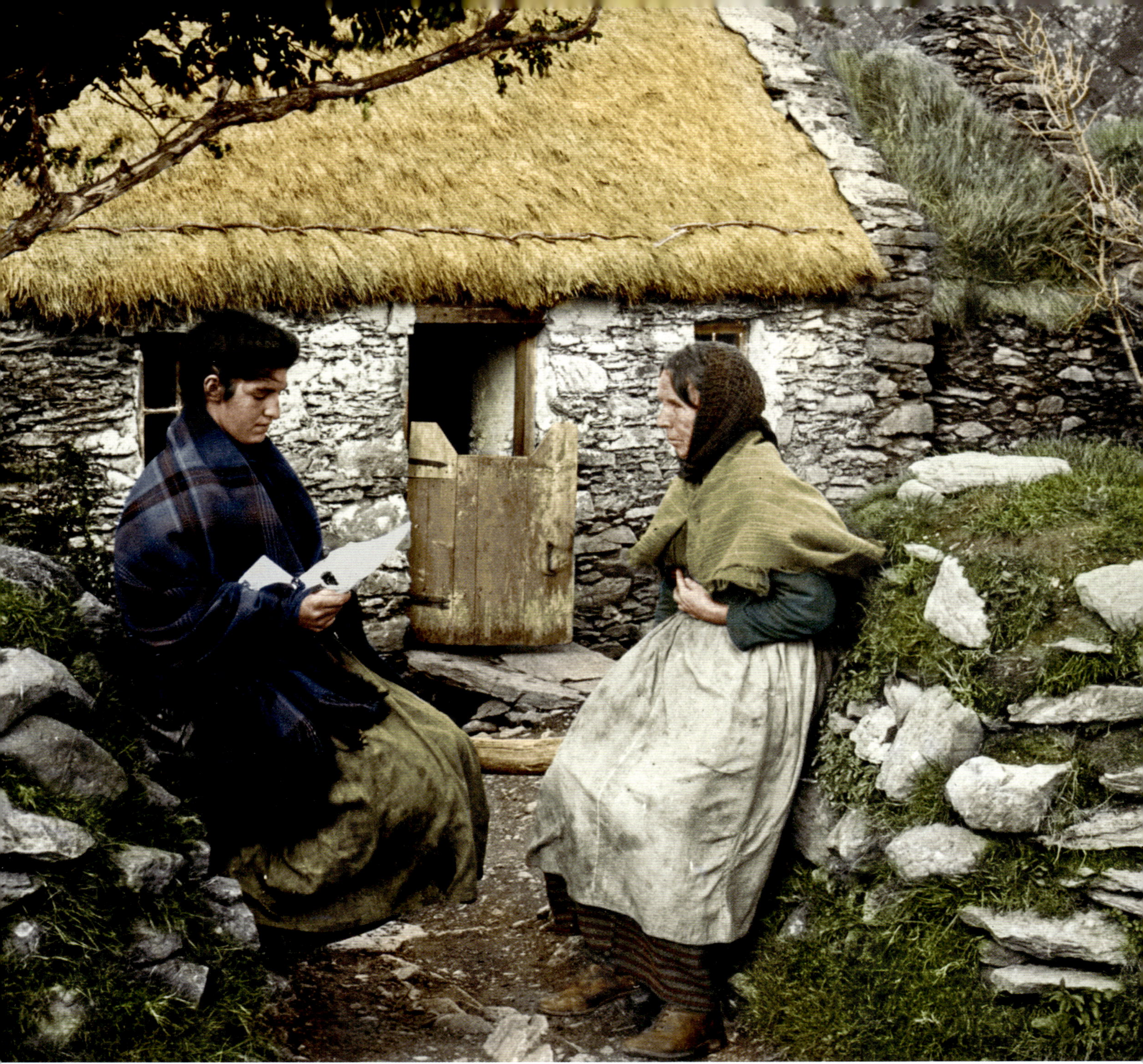

The 'Letter from America'. A woman reads a letter, a connection to family members who had emigrated following the Great Famine in search of better opportunities. Letters like these, carrying news and usually including money, were an important lifeline for many rural Irish families from the mid-nineteenth century onwards.

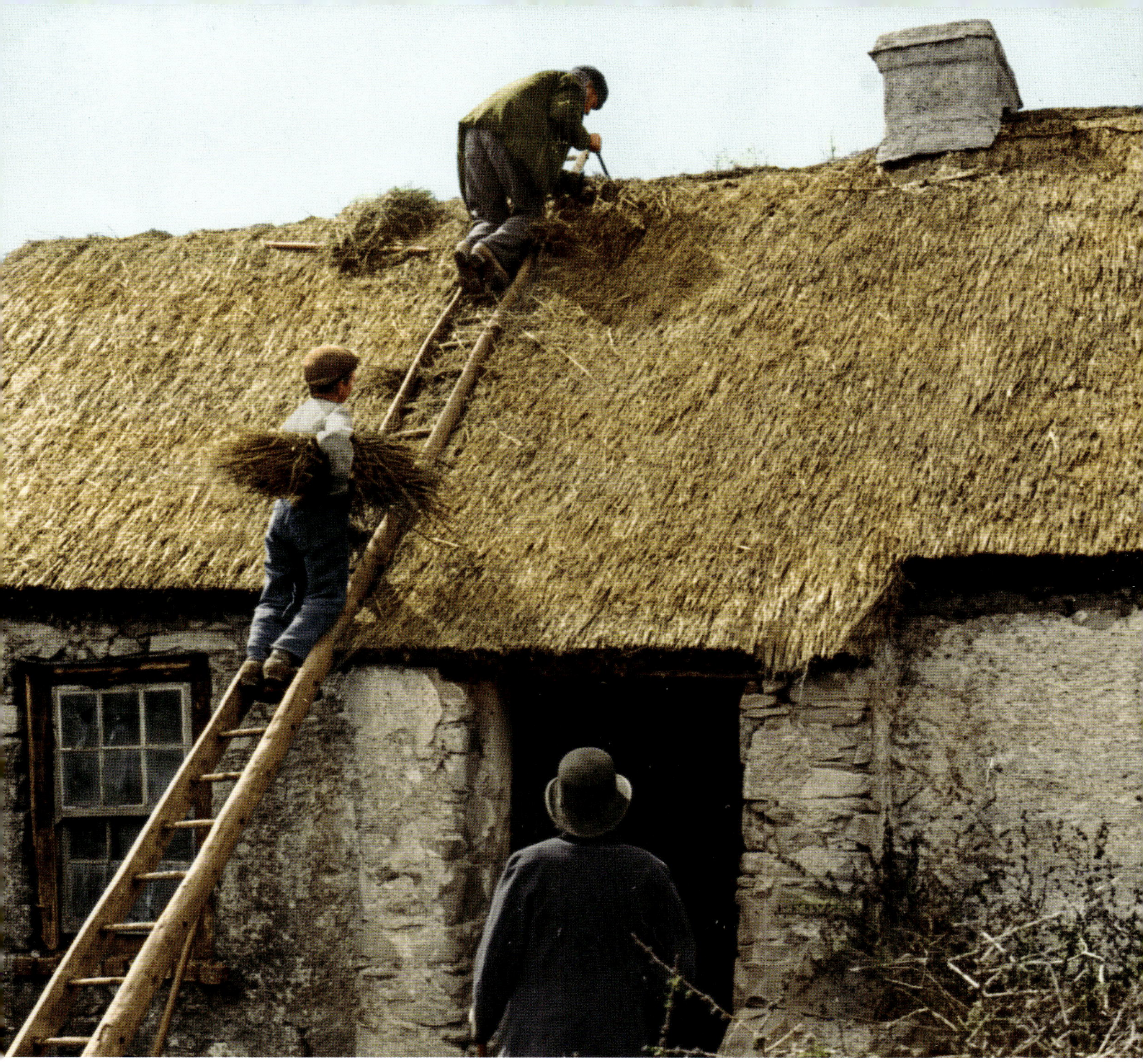

A man and his young assistant work on thatching the roof of a cottage in County Monaghan. Using locally sourced materials like straw or rushes, they carefully layer the thatch to create a weatherproof covering, continuing an age-old craft that was common for rural homes across Ireland.

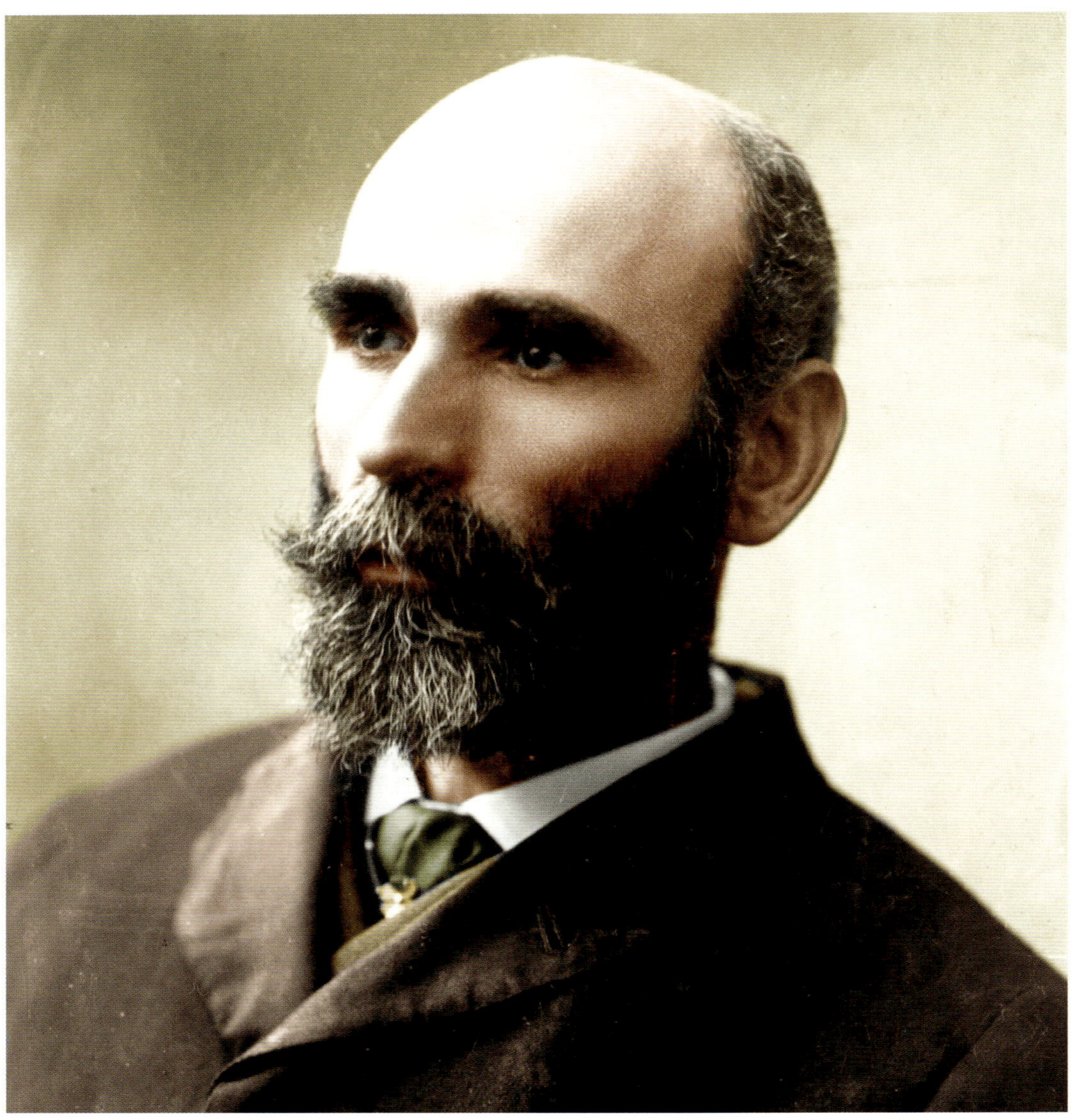

Top left: Michael Davitt, a founder of the Irish National Land League (1879), led the fight for tenants' rights and land reform in Ireland. A former Fenian prisoner, he championed the Land War (1879–82), organising rent strikes, boycotts and protests against landlord oppression. The League's efforts led to government crackdowns, and the imprisonment of Davitt (and Parnell) in 1881.

Right: Charles Stewart Parnell, leader of the Irish Parliamentary Party, himself a landlord, was the driving force, with Davitt, behind the Land League. From his role in securing tenants' rights, such as fair rents and fixity of tenure, to his imprisonment in 1881, Parnell's leadership brought Ireland's land crisis to the forefront of British politics. Known for his unwavering commitment to Home Rule, Parnell's political skill and determination made him the most influential Irish leader of his time.

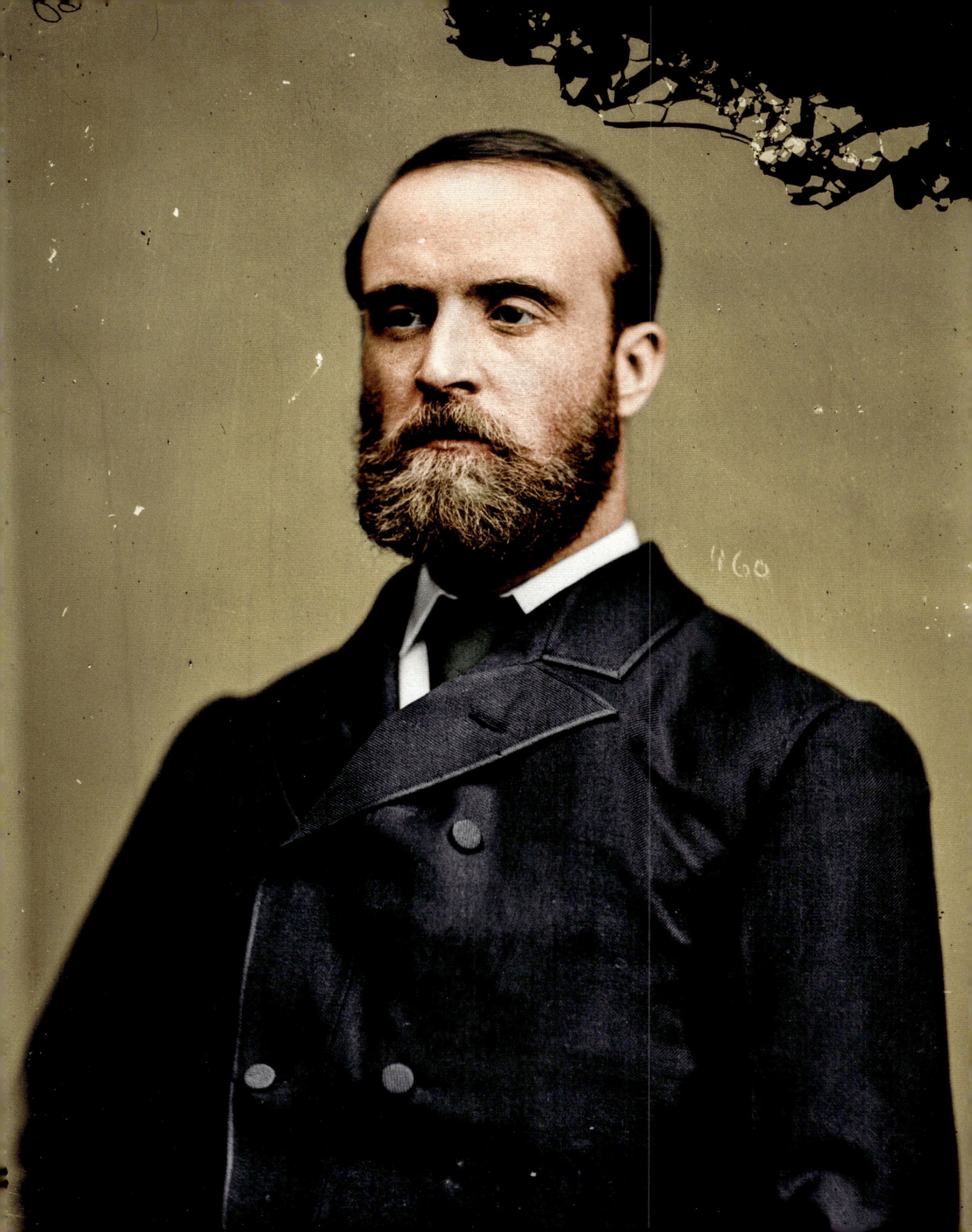
1860

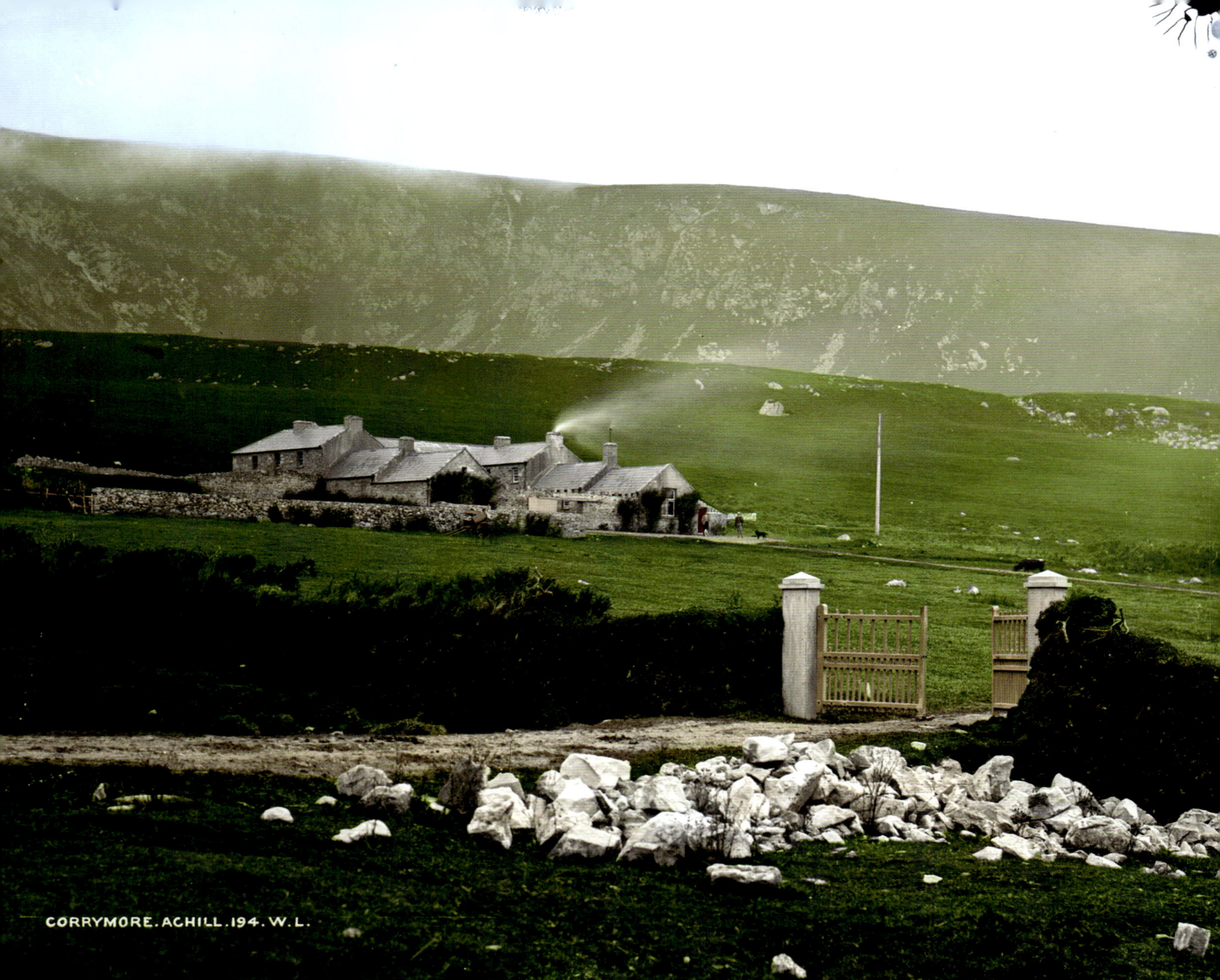

After retiring from the army, Captain Charles Boycott had settled here at Corrymore House in Achill, County Mayo for a period. He later moved to Lough Mask House (near Ballinrobe) where, as land agent for Lord Erne, Boycott enforced harsh rent demands on struggling tenants, refusing to lower rents despite widespread poverty. In response, local Land League activists organised a campaign against him in 1880. Tenants, workers and merchants in the area refused to work for or trade with Boycott, isolating him economically. This approach of non-violent resistance drew national attention and was so effective that Boycott sought military protection to carry out his work. This powerful tactic of non-co-operation became known as the 'boycott'.

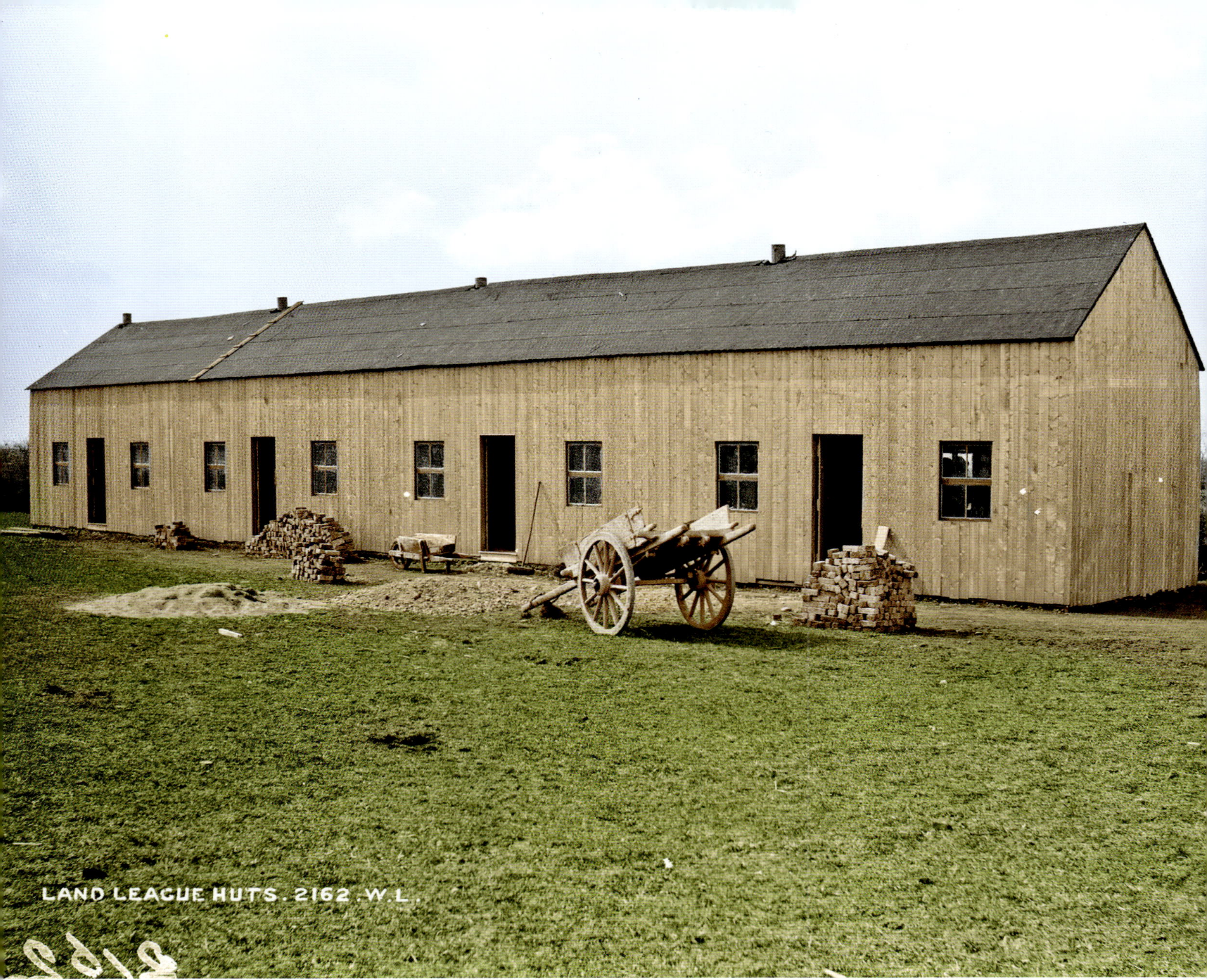

These timber huts were built by members
of the Land League during the Land War
in the late nineteenth century. Erected in
areas where tenants faced evictions or harsh
treatment by landlords, the huts served as a
place of refuge for those affected.

The photograph captures the arrival of British troops (with fixed bayonets) alongside the Royal Irish Constabulary (RIC) at the home of John Flanagan in Tullycrine, County Clare, one of a series of evictions on the Vandeleur estate in 1888. Note the solid construction of the house and the fine slated roof.

Unlike the thousands of uncontested evictions that had taken place in Clare in the wake of the Great Famine, these evictions were markedly different. The tenants, relatively well-off farmers with generally well-built farmhouses, had legal representation and chose to resist. As the first eviction began on 18 July, the chapel bell was rung. Large crowds turned out to witness the events, along with members of the press and photographers, highlighting the growing tension between tenants and landlords during this time of the ongoing Land War.

The evictions were set against the backdrop of the Plan of Campaign (organised by the Irish National League), launched in 1886, a strategy in which tenants collectively offered reduced rents in response to economic hardship. If landlords refused, the tenants redirected payments into an estate fund to support those evicted.

Following the death of the family patriarch in 1881, his successor, Captain Hector Vandeleur, distanced himself from the Vandeleur estate in Kilrush and rarely resided there, further straining relations. Poor weather, falling farm prices due to American competition and economic hardship led the Vandeleur tenants to seek rent reductions. No agreement was reached, and by early July 1888, a major confrontation was imminent. In response, detachments of the Crown forces, accompanied by magistrates, were dispatched to enforce the evictions. The tenants usually resisted, but the bailiffs, working with crowbars or a battering ram, would gain entry.

There were 23 evictions, which took place in the period 18 July to 2 August 1888 – all were extensively reported in the Irish and British press.

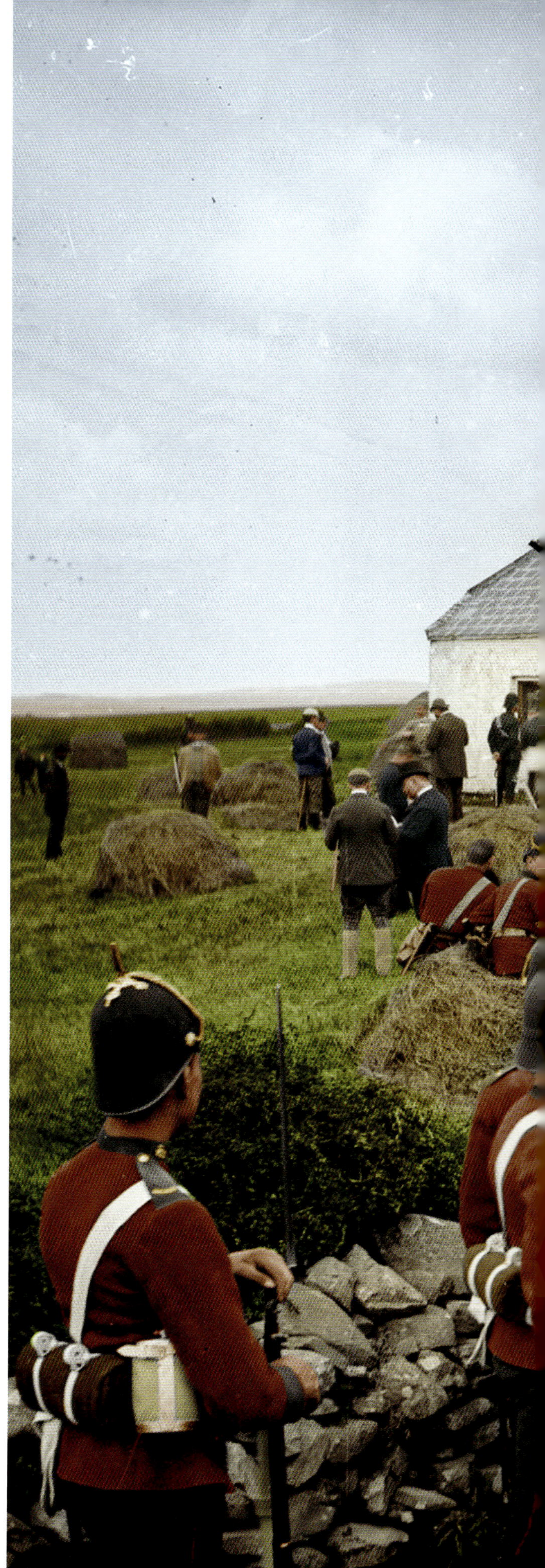

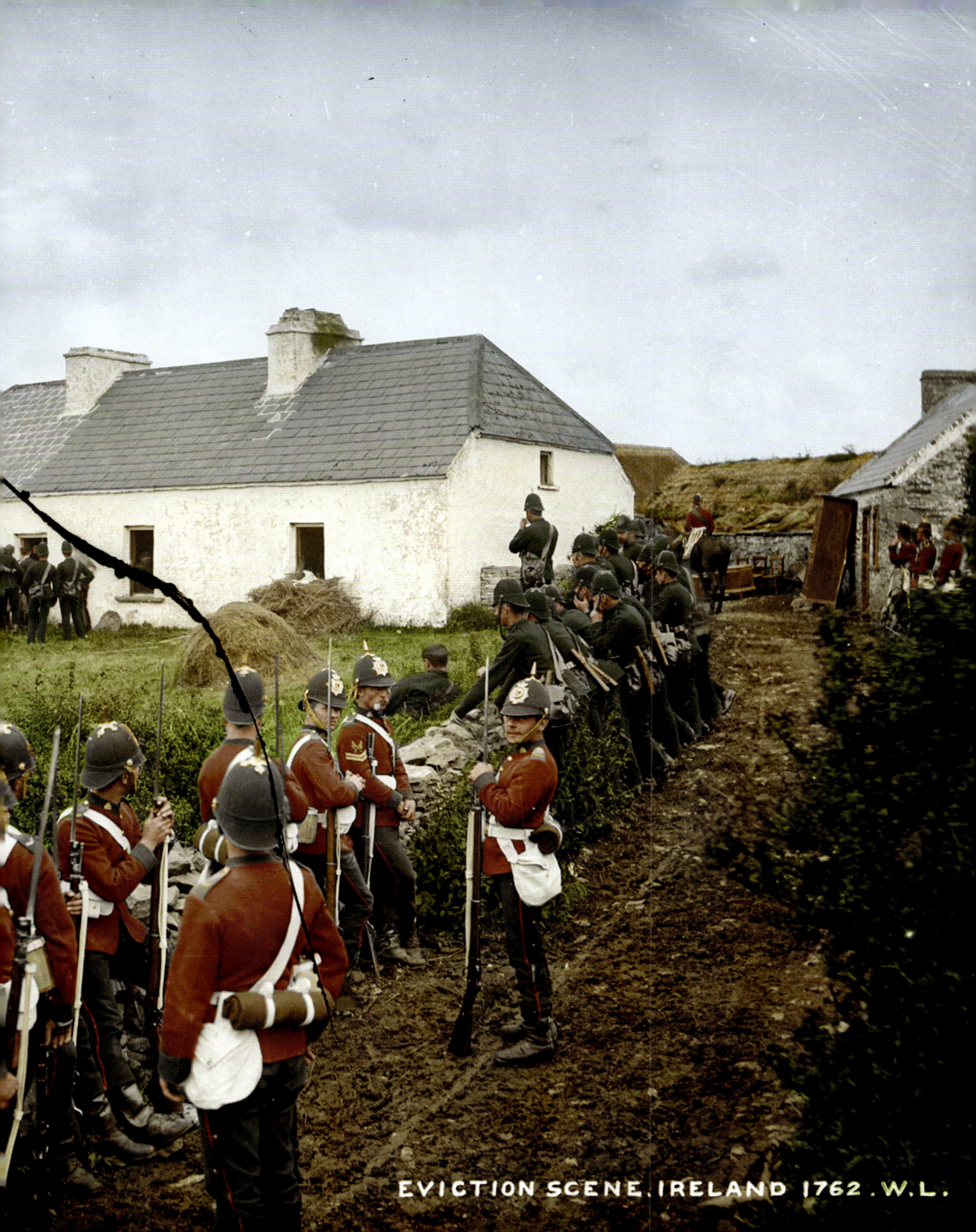
EVICTION SCENE. IRELAND 1762 .W.L.

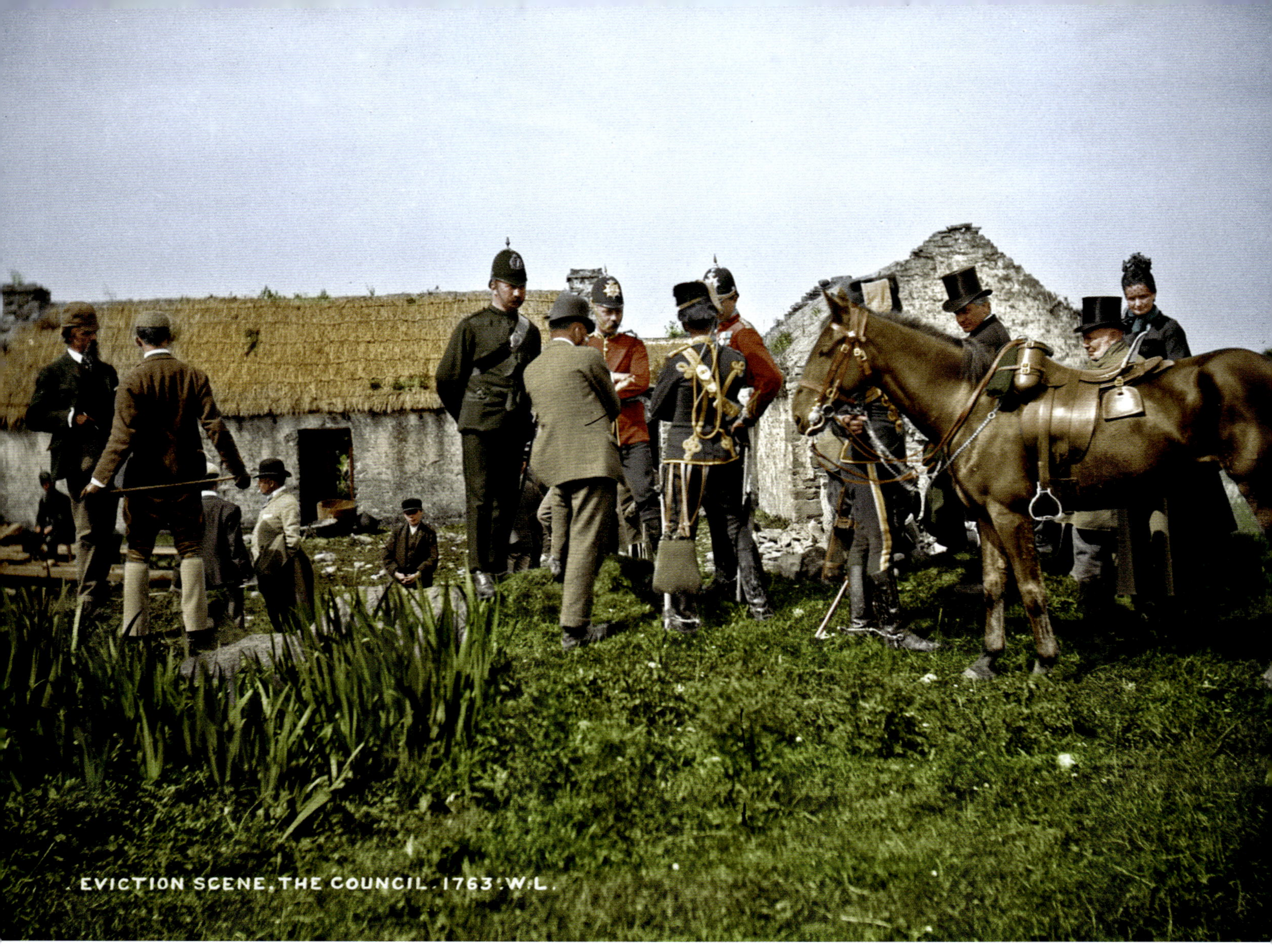

The Vandeleur evictions were organised on military lines. In
this gathering, important arrangements are clearly being made.
The grouping is thought to include, as well as army officers,
the landlord's agent, a Resident Magistrate and an RIC Acting
County Inspector. There may be ongoing negotiations with a
solicitor representing the tenants on behalf of the National
League. The tall man in the top hat on the right is thought to
be a priest, an advocate for tenants' rights. A total of 170 British
soldiers (made up of the Sherwood Foresters, the 3rd Hussars
and the Royal Berkshires) and 120 RIC were deployed for the
eviction exercise.

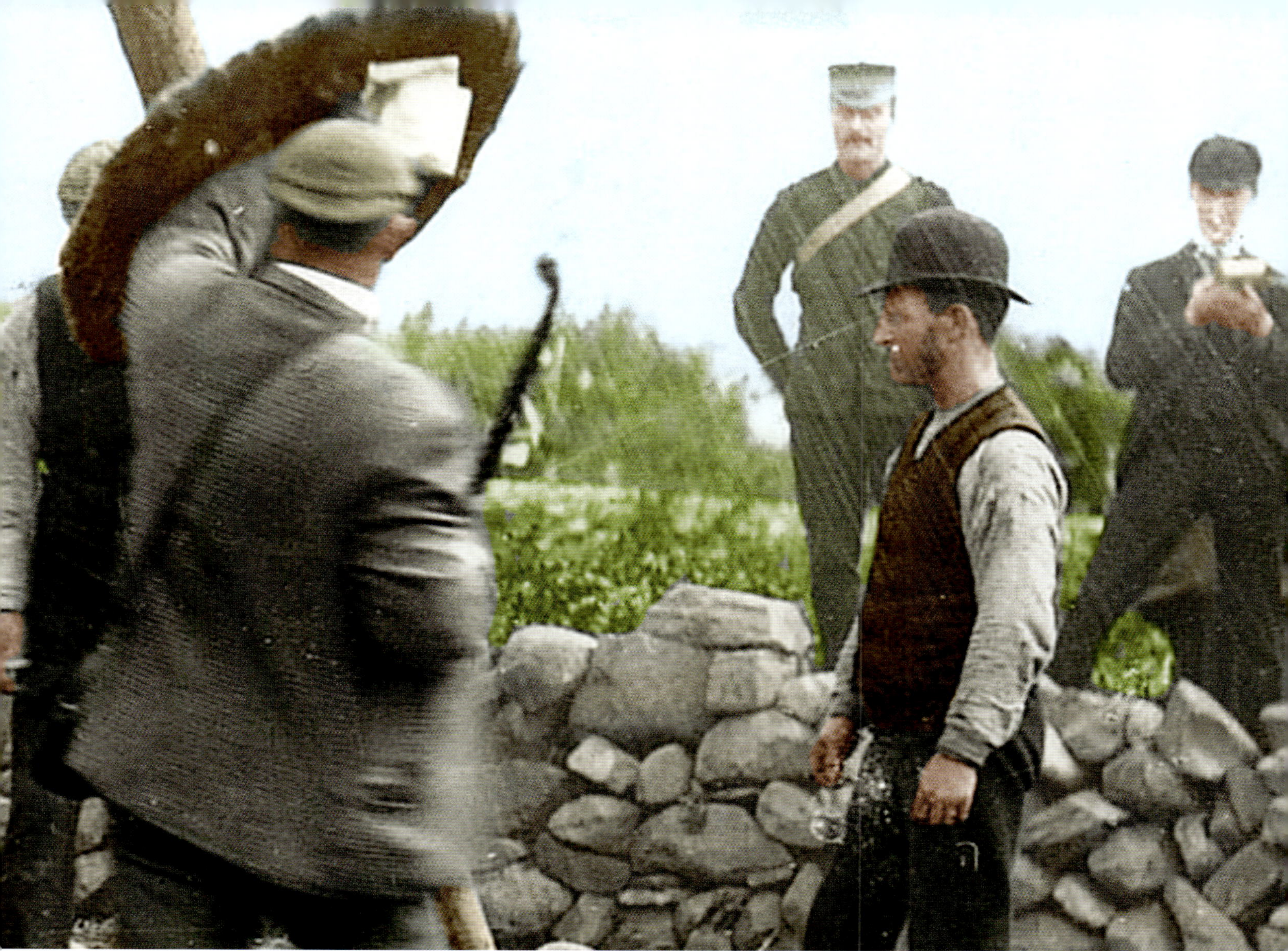

A scene from one of the last evictions, that of
Thomas Bermingham on 2 August 1888. As he
stands by a leg of the battering ram tripod, one
of the eviction party, possibly a bailiff, uses a
wicker-work shield to protect himself against
boiling water. Tenants at the Vandeleur estate
had been in preparation for evictions and had
barricaded their houses for over a month.
However, despite the throwing of buckets
of boiling water or stones, ultimately the
battering ram prevailed.

Many, like the elderly and affluent-looking couple on the left, gathered to watch the spectacle of the evictions. This photo shows the eviction at Thomas Bermingham's thatched house in Moyasta. Here, the battering ram (a timber beam of around 10m, with an iron tip) has swung into action, operated by a squad known as the 'Emergency men'. The leading men wield shields to protect against boiling water thrown by those inside. When the breach was created, the RIC and bailiffs could dash through and eject those inside. The house was then razed to the ground.

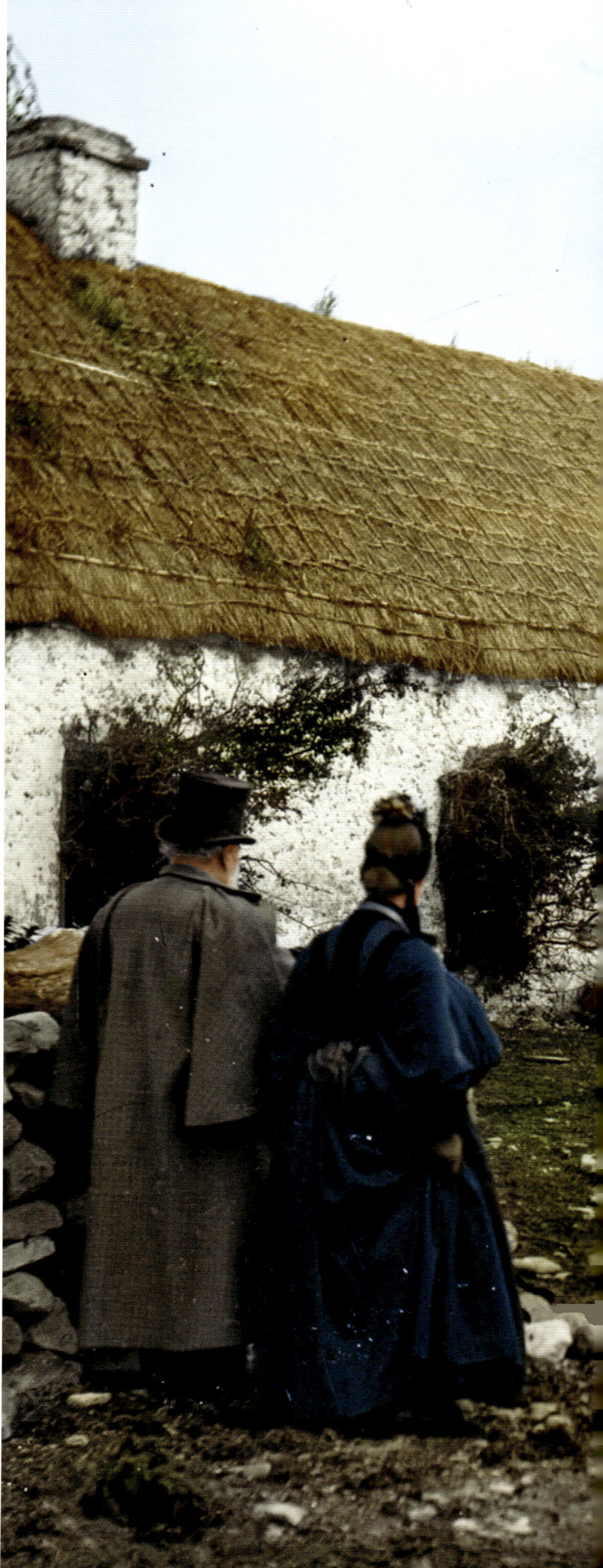

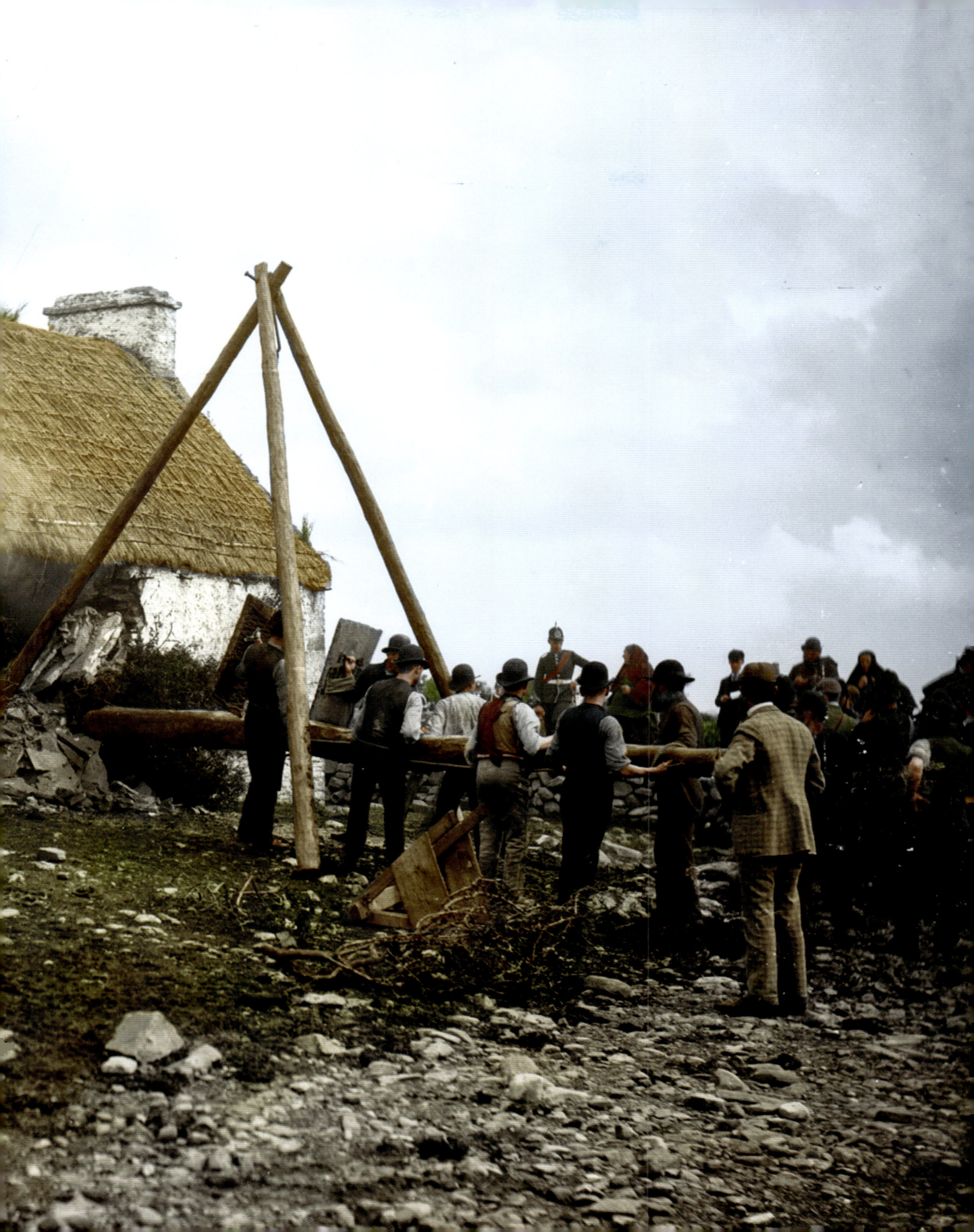

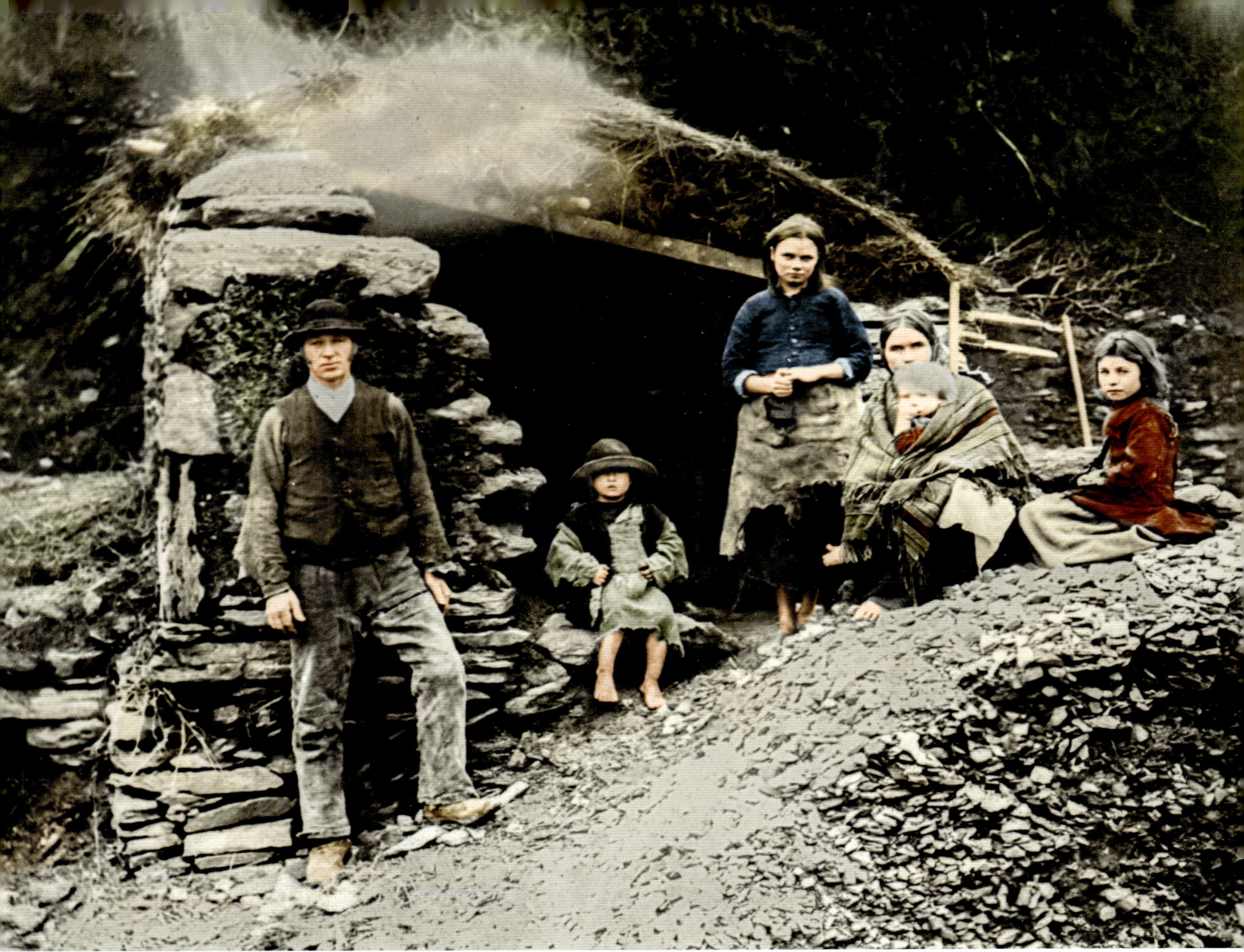

The Vandeleur evictions of July 1888 garnered widespread publicity and questions were asked in the House of Commons. It is reported that eventually a settlement was reached and the tenants were allowed back to their holdings. However, evicted tenants in other parts of the country were not so lucky. Many had to secure refuge where they could find it, such as this family in County Donegal outside their makeshift hut.

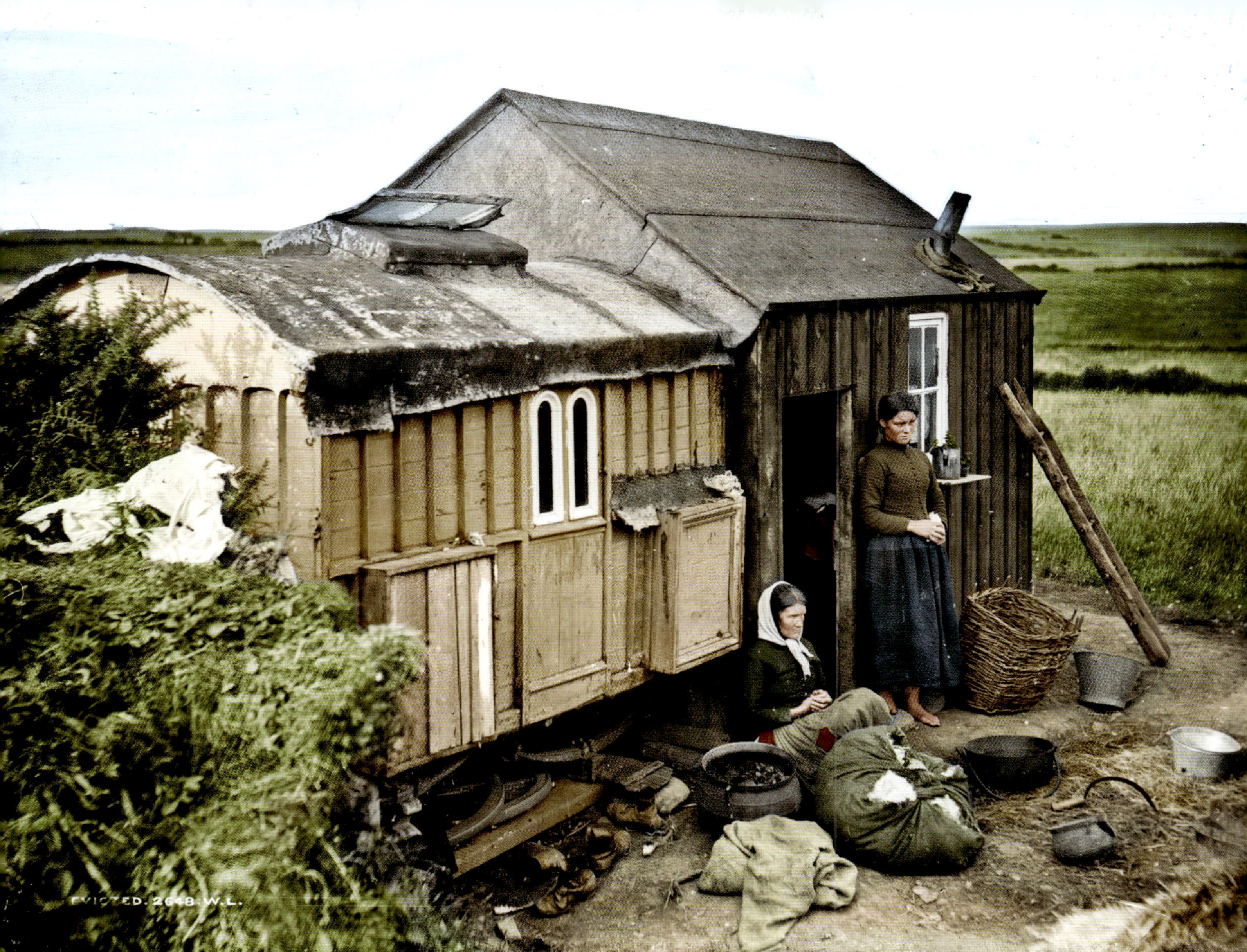

This photograph from the Lawrence Photograph Collection shows two evicted women, who have devised an innovative and effective solution to their quest for immediate shelter – a rudimentary timber shack augmented by what looks like the recycled body of a small wagon or carriage (with the leaf springs of the suspension still attached).

The Arcade at New Tipperary, with an array
of butter firkins. Most of Tipperary town was
owned by landlord Arthur Smith-Barry. In
response to mass evictions carried out at the
end of 1889, volunteers came from all over
Munster to build 'New Tipperary' on the
western outskirts of the town – there was
widespread political support, and funds came
from Australia and the USA. Featuring two
main streets, New Tipperary housed evicted
families, shops, a butter market and even
its own Gaelic team. There were challenges,
including the fallout from the Parnell scandal,
and by late 1891, many tenants settled with
Smith-Barry to return to their original homes.
While the Arcade has been demolished, the
two streets of New Tipperary still stand today.

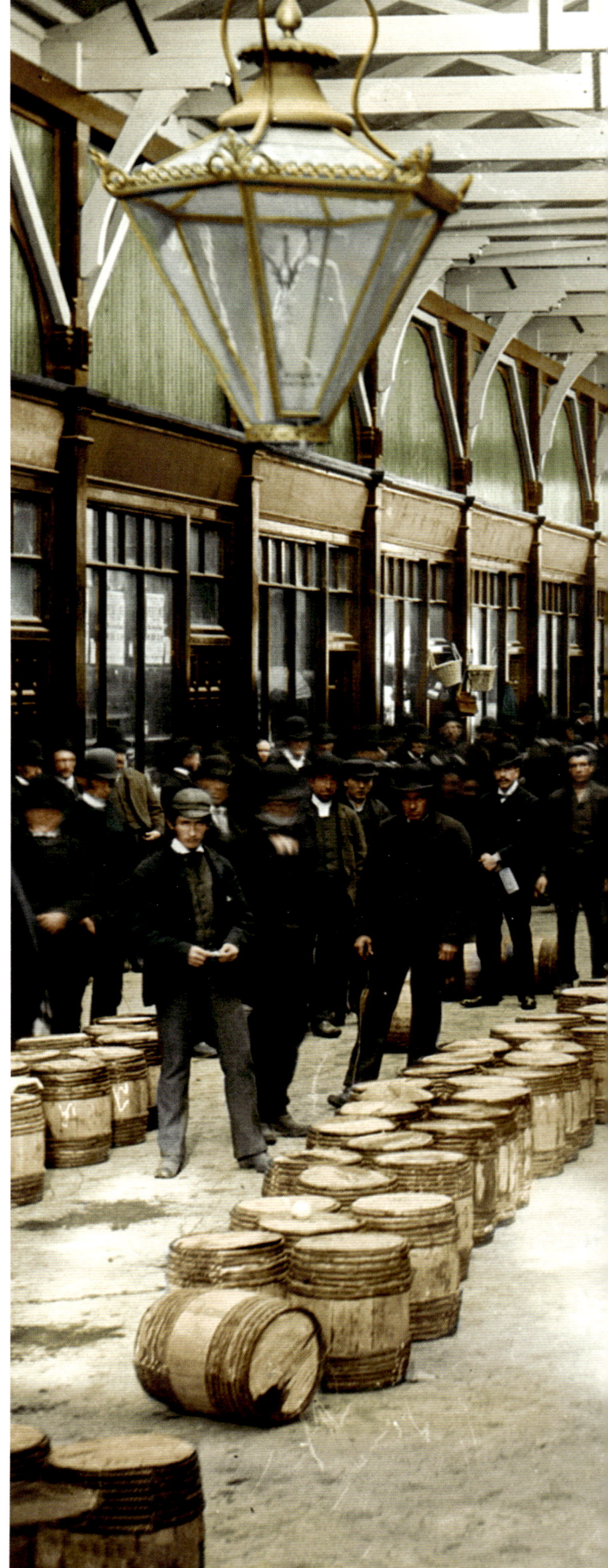

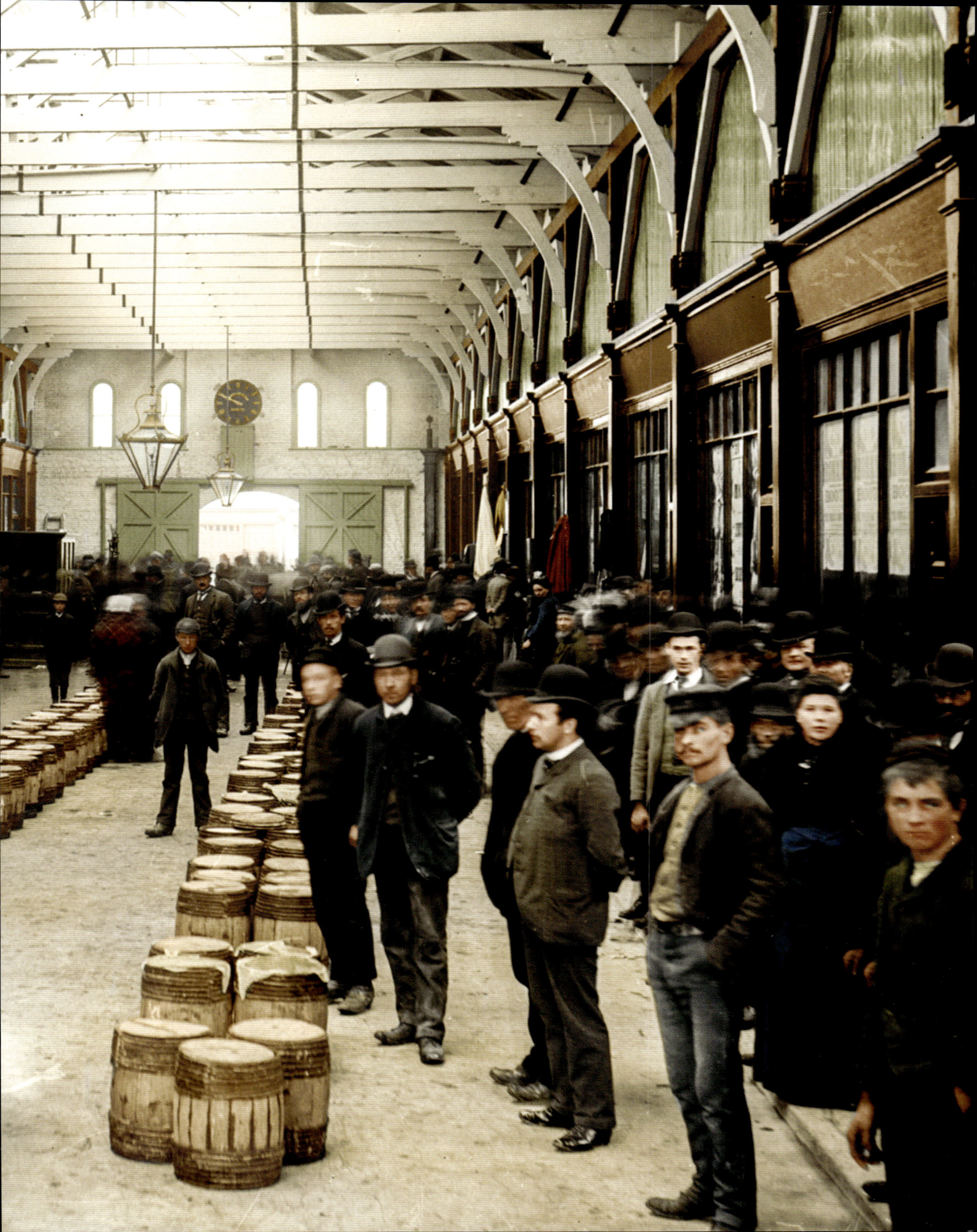

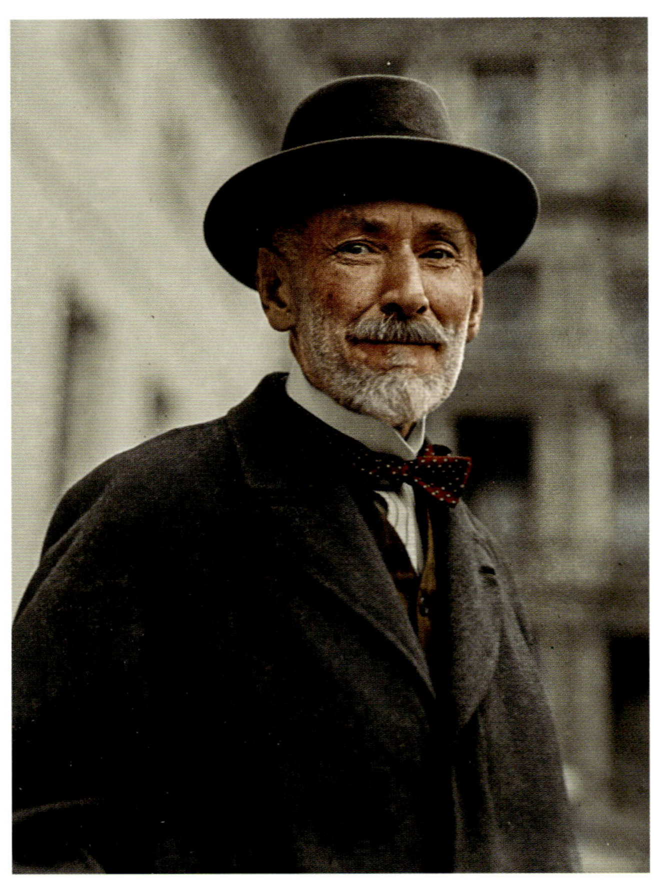

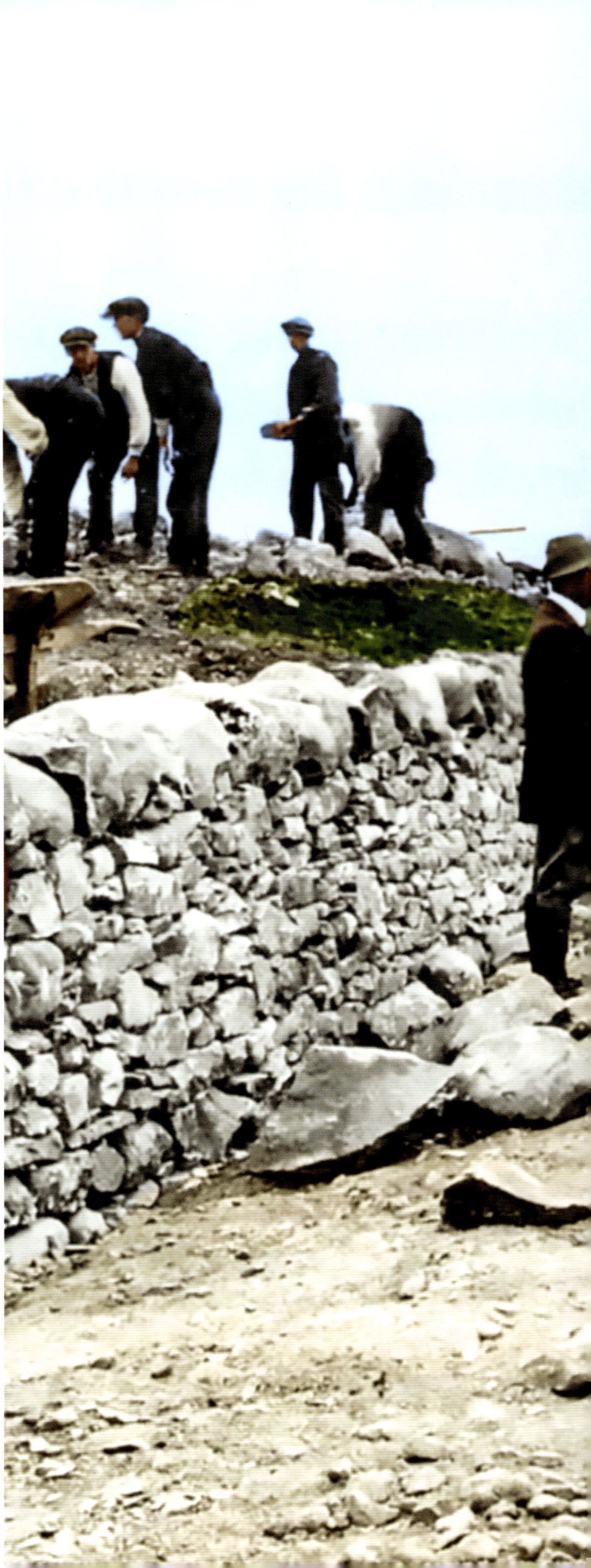

Top left: The Irish Land War led to significant legislative reforms aimed at resolving tenant grievances and progress towards ending landlordism. Early acts like the Land Law (Ireland) Act 1881 addressed rent and tenure issues, while later acts facilitated tenant ownership. As land reform measures were put in place, the focus switched to addressing rural poverty through agricultural reform and co-operation. One of the most outstanding pioneers in this was the Anglo-Irish agricultural reformer, co-operative pioneer, and politician, Horace Plunkett. He promoted co-operative creameries and founded the Irish Agricultural Organisation Society in 1894, aiming to improve farmers' livelihoods in a post-Land War Ireland.

The Congested Districts Board (CDB) was established by
Arthur Balfour in 1891 under the Purchase of Land Act
to address severe poverty in Ireland's most overcrowded
regions. It aimed to improve rural living conditions by
redistributing land, purchasing large estates, facilitating
migration to more viable farms and promoting agriculture
and industry. The photo shows men building a road
under a CDB scheme. There had been earlier 'make-work'
schemes during the Great Famine and this temporary
measure aimed to create useful infrastructure while
providing income in Ireland's most impoverished regions.

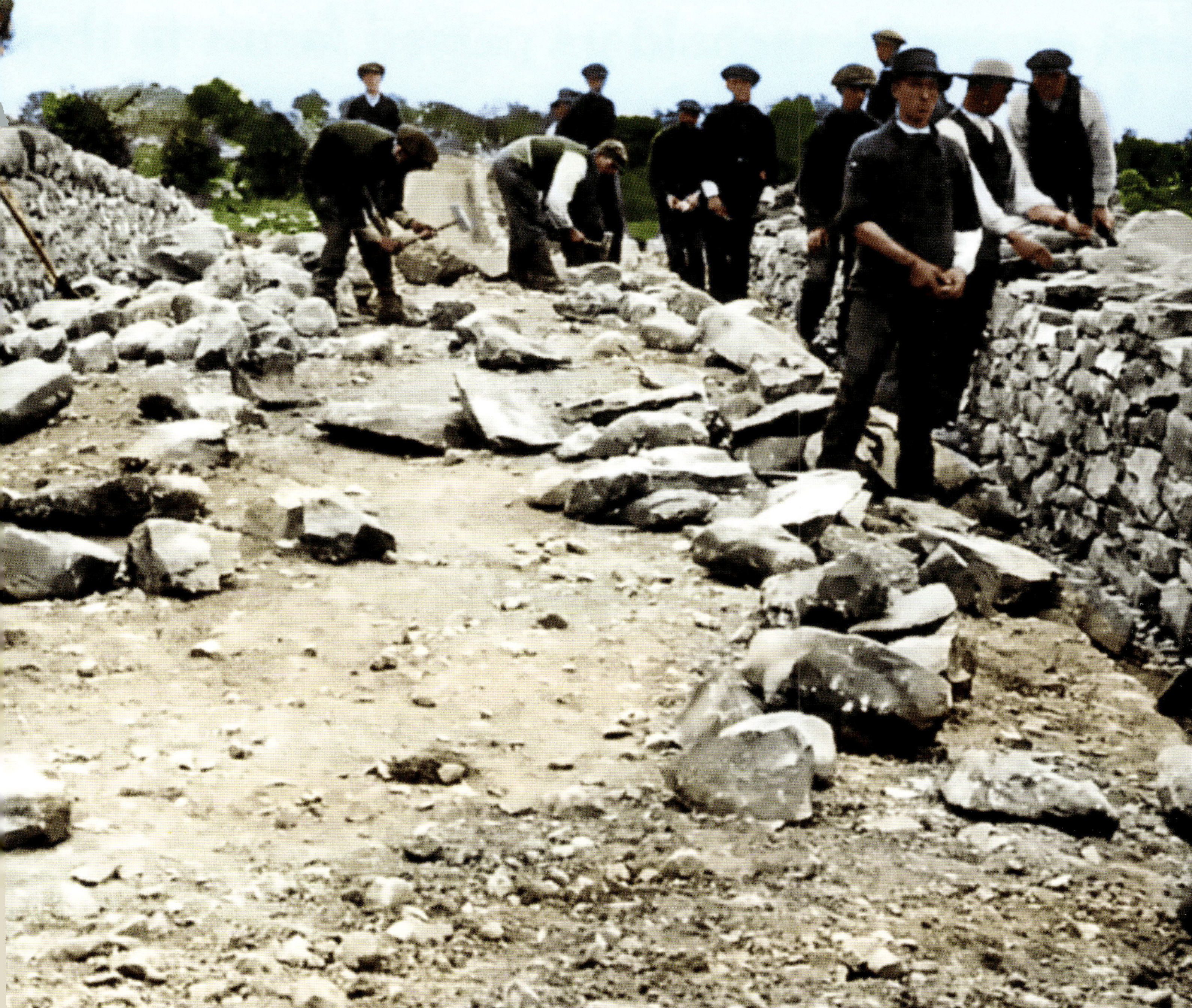

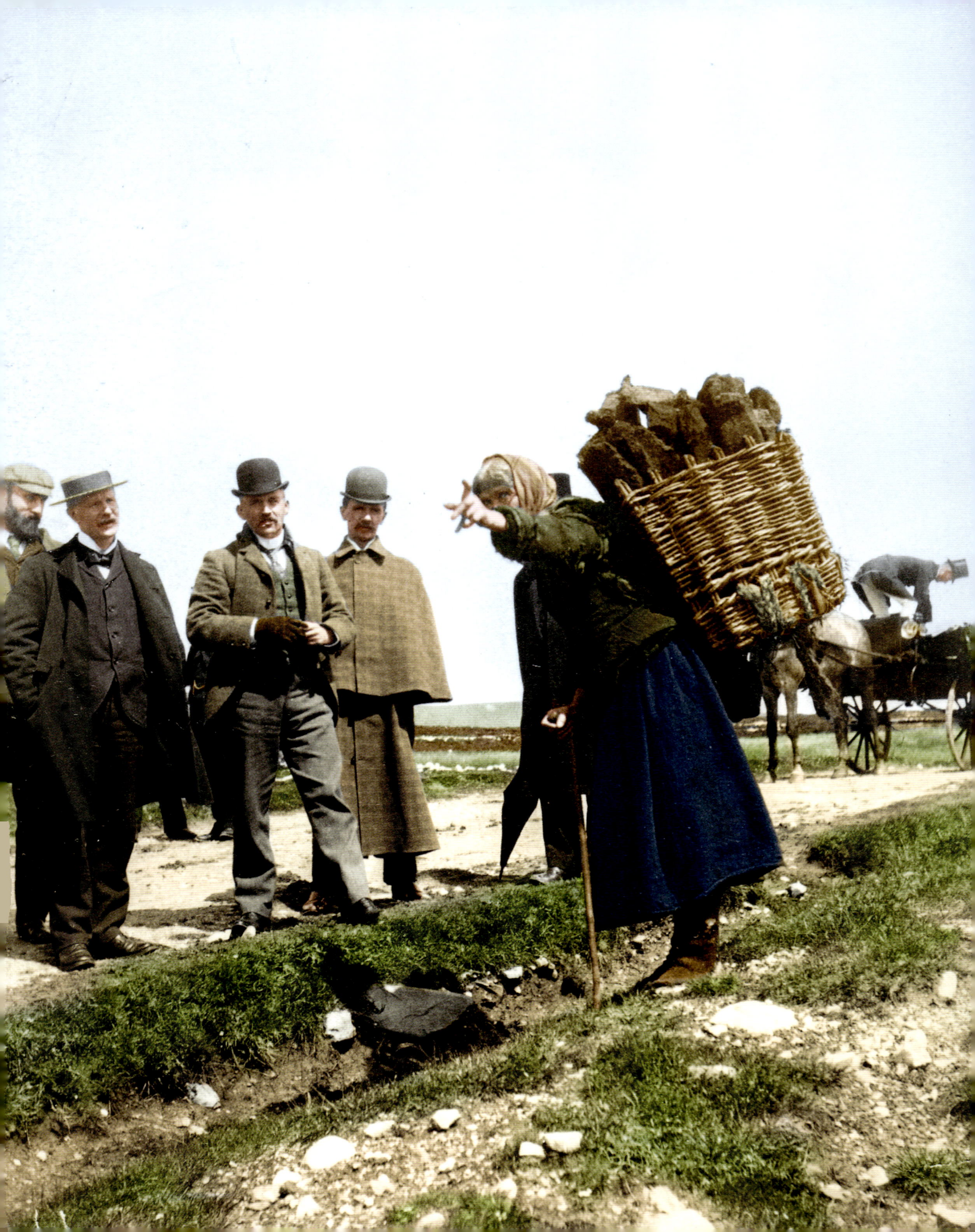

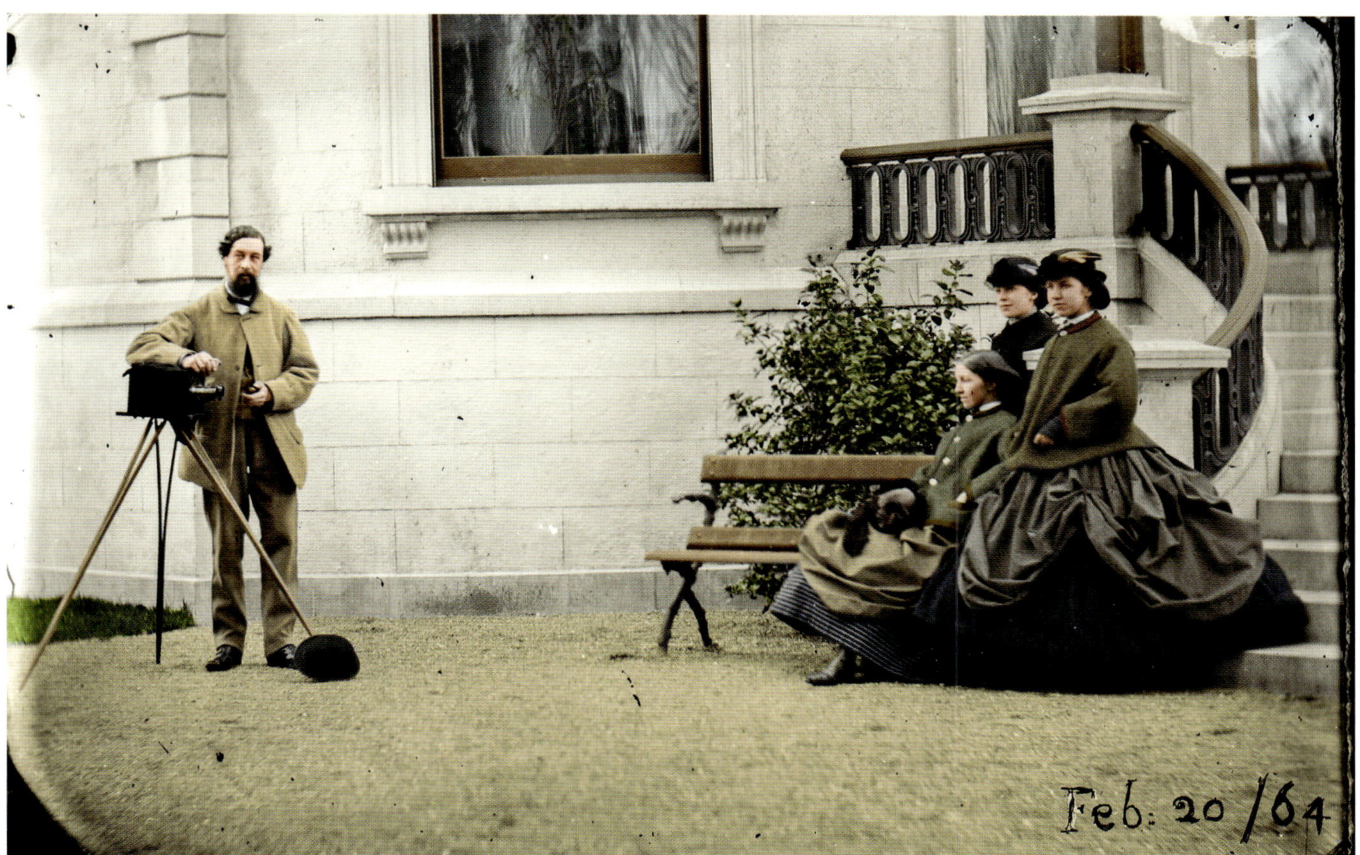

Left: Into the west: a woman gives directions to a CDB delegation during the early 1900s. The CDB made limited and slow progress in alleviating rural poverty by improving roads, drainage and piers (although some proved to be uneconomic) and with partial land redistribution. Dissolved in 1923, its land distribution functions were absorbed by the Irish Land Commission under the new Irish Free State.

Top right: In contrast to their tenants, many of the landed classes in Ireland could afford the latest trend-setting devices. Here on 20 February 1864 at the Georgian-era Clonbrock House, in eastern County Galway, Richard Somerset Le Poer Trench, Earl of Clancarty, from a neighbouring estate, poses with his novel stereo camera. The photograph was possibly taken by Luke Dillon, 4th Baron Clonbrock, and the scene includes his three sisters. We are fortunate that Dillon and his wife were avid photographers who built a studio on the estate. The Clonbrock Collection of over 2,000 glass plates, now preserved at the National Library of Ireland, offers a fascinating insight into life on a great estate over the second half of the nineteenth century.

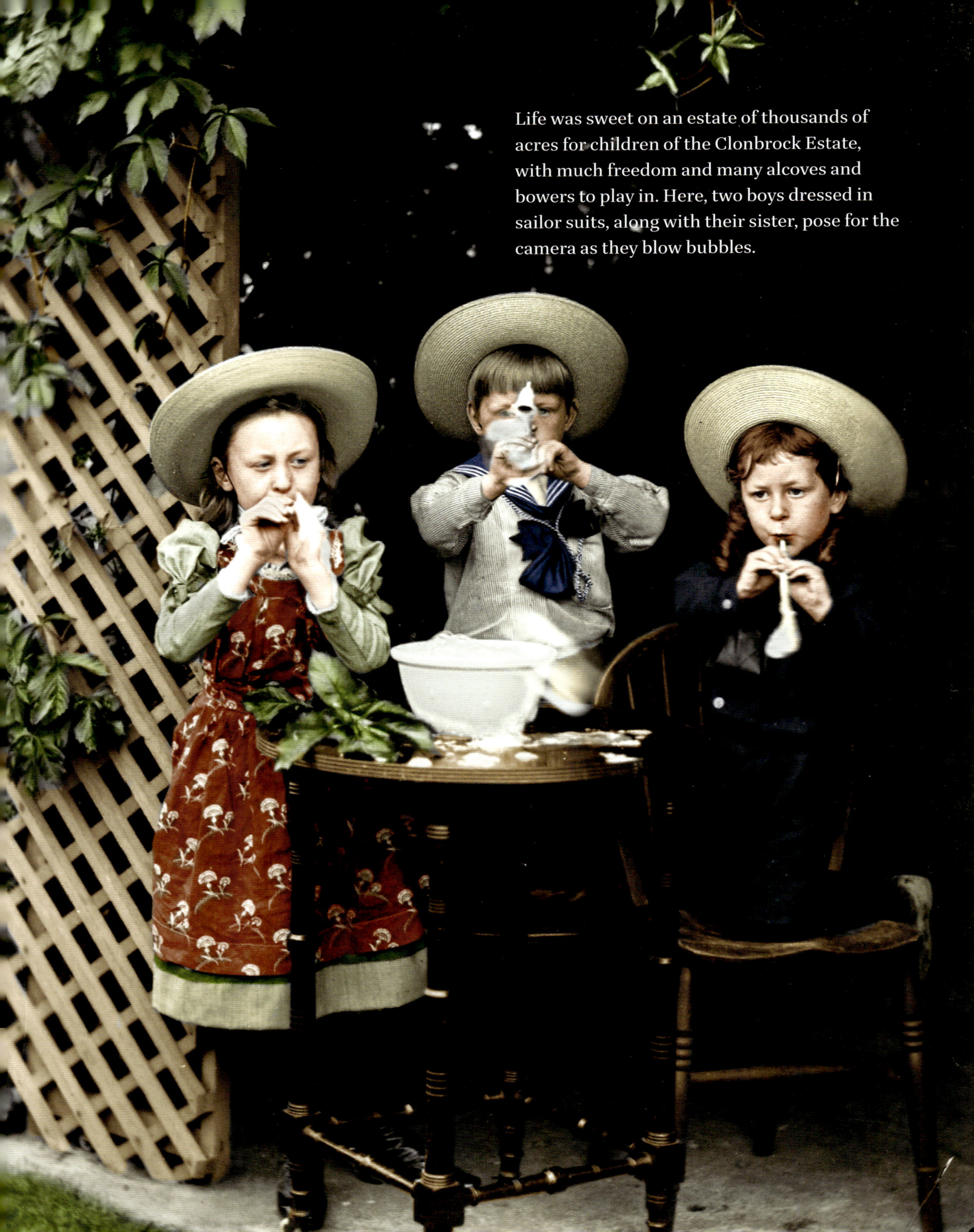

Life was sweet on an estate of thousands of acres for children of the Clonbrock Estate, with much freedom and many alcoves and bowers to play in. Here, two boys dressed in sailor suits, along with their sister, pose for the camera as they blow bubbles.

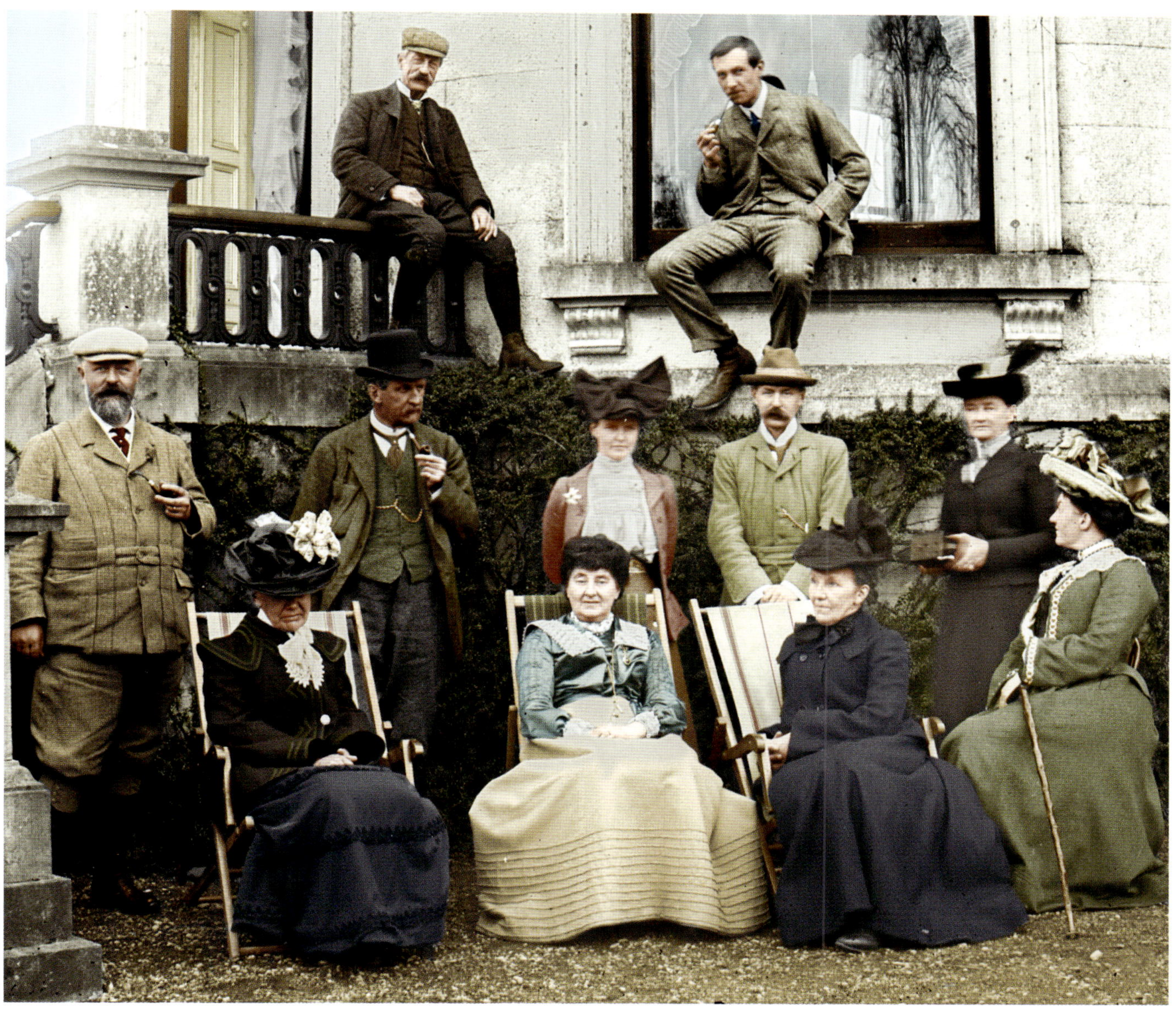

Some of the gentry can manage to effortlessly emanate an insouciant air of privilege and ennui. A group poses just outside the entrance to the ballroom in Clonbrock House at the beginning of the twentieth century.

The Dillons of Clonbrock were a long-established family, tracing their lineage from the Anglo-Normans. Their estate was one of the largest in County Galway. The Dillons gained a reputation as good landlords, avoiding mass evictions, and in addition, they ran a well-managed demesne.

The Wyndham Act of 1903 proved advantageous for landlords to sell their land, as well as for tenants to purchase it. By the start of World War I, the Dillons had disposed of most of their tenanted land. Members of the family continued to live at Clonbrock House up to the mid-1970s. The house has now been restored following a major fire in 1984.

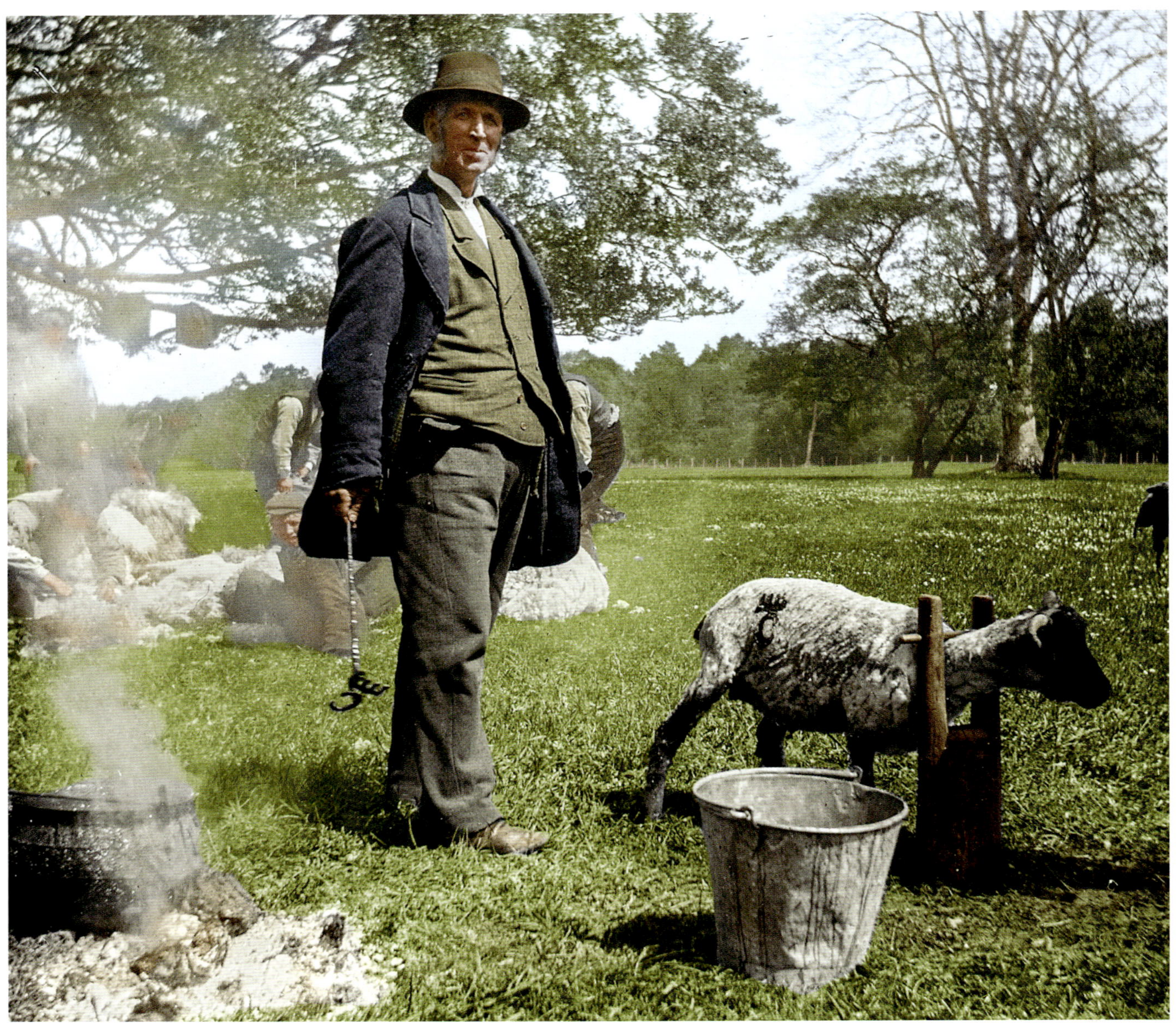

Top left: We are fortunate that the Clonbrock photo collection captures the intricate details of farm life. This scene shows the branding of sheep *c.*1900, with Mr Carroll having just marked the animal, held securely in place, using a branding iron with a bold 'C' and 'E' positioned 180 degrees apart.

Right: Tenants at Snowhill Estate, County Kilkenny, 1900–10: the tenants, wearing their best clothes, are gathered under a grand tent for a celebratory meal hosted by the Power family. Despite the Powers' reputation for good relations with their tenants, those sitting at the table are clearly on their best behaviour and sit frozen for the camera. The Powers, prominent Catholic landlords, lived in Power Hall, a grand Georgian mansion.

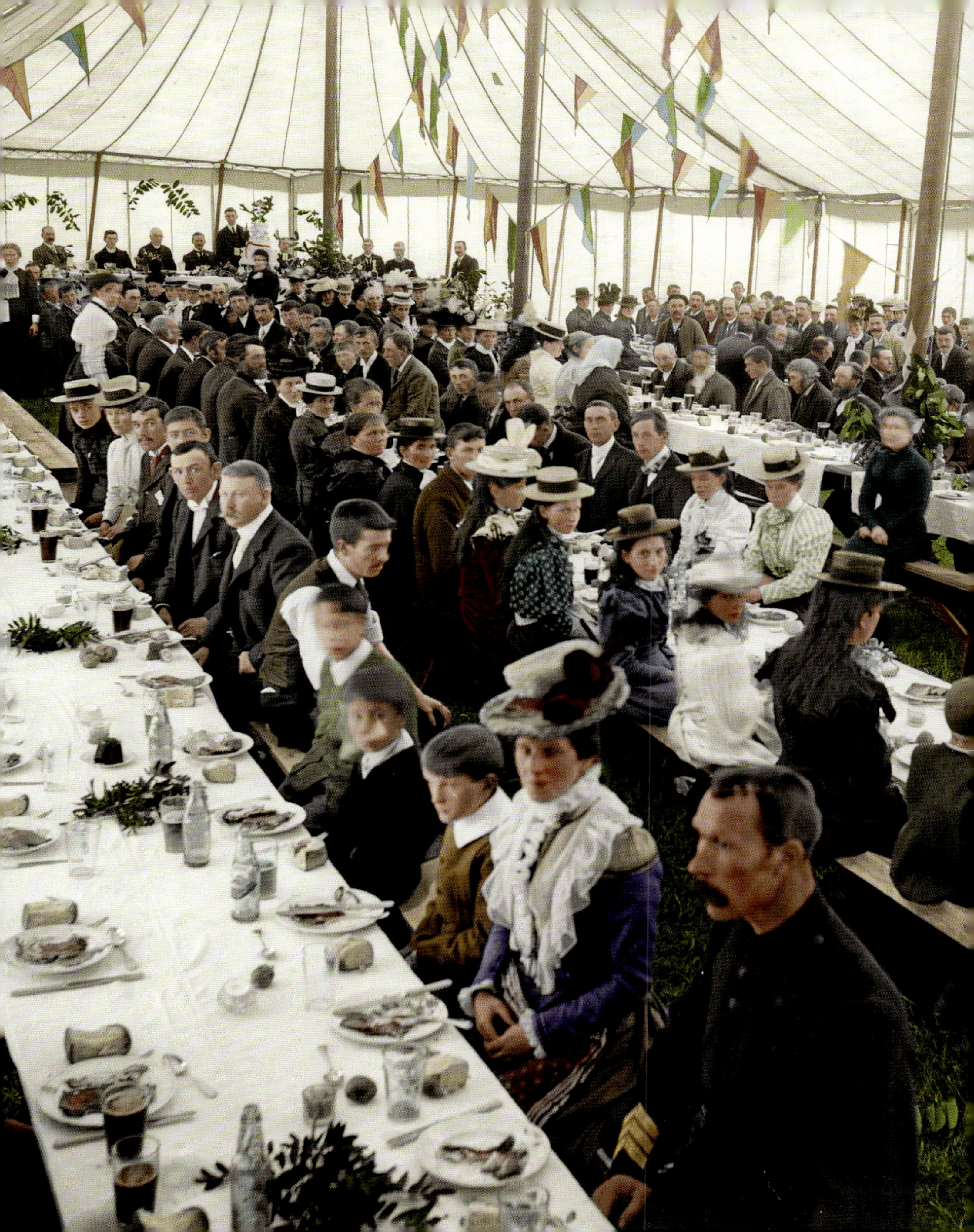

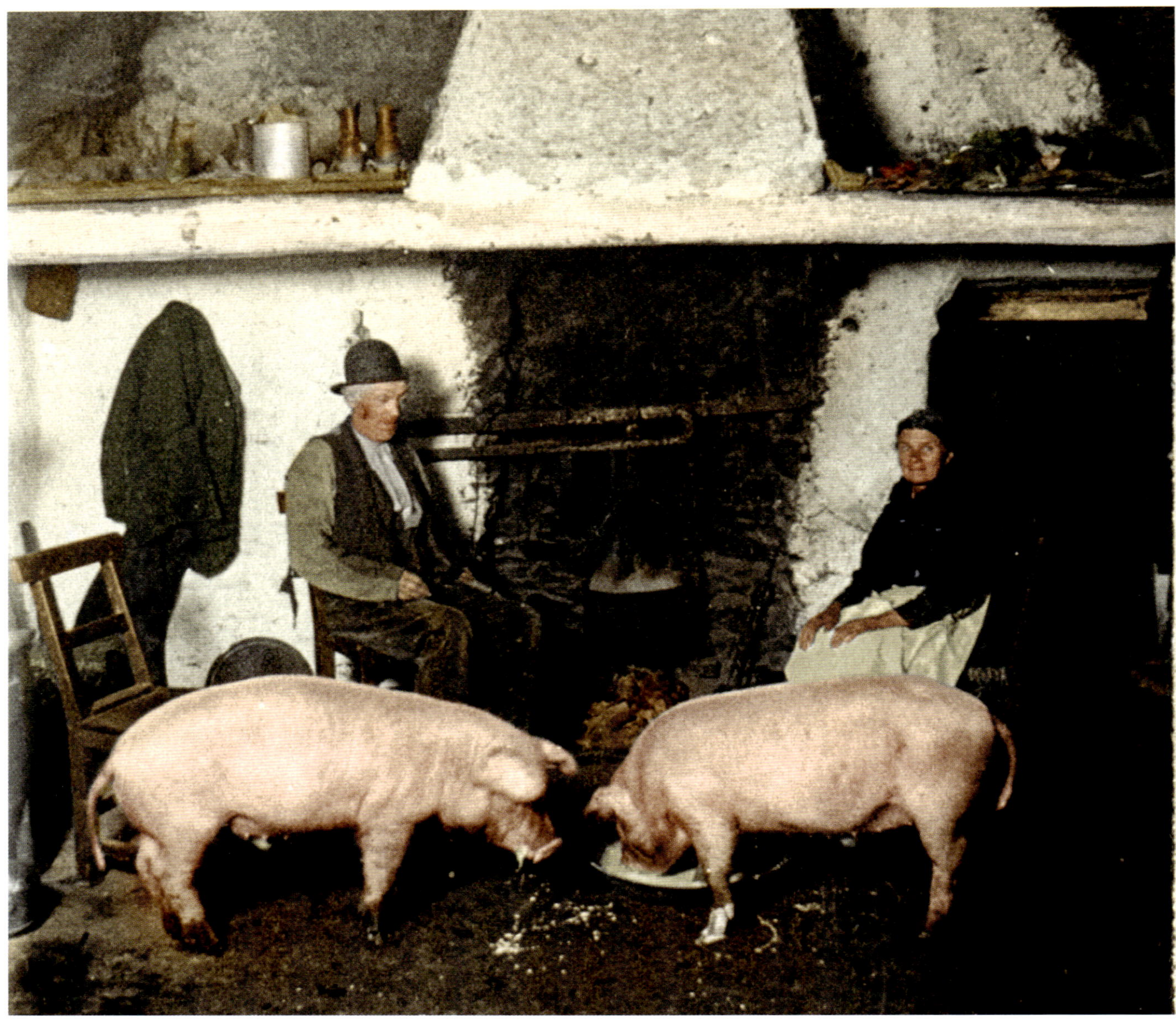

Top left: 'A fireside scene, Co. Kerry'. At the turn of the twentieth century, US photographers travelled to Ireland to produce stereographs depicting rural life, often reinforcing stereotypes of Irish poverty and primitiveness. These images, accompanied by commentary reflecting East Coast American prejudices, romanticised hardship and catered to a market eager for 'picturesque' views of Ireland.

Right: Continuing the stereotyping of Irish life, US stereograph publishers often paired their images with captions mocking Irish accents and culture. This example, by the firm of Underwood & Underwood of New York (one of the largest publishers of stereoscopic images in the world), shows a couple at the entrance to their cottage and is titled 'A raal convanience – a woife'.

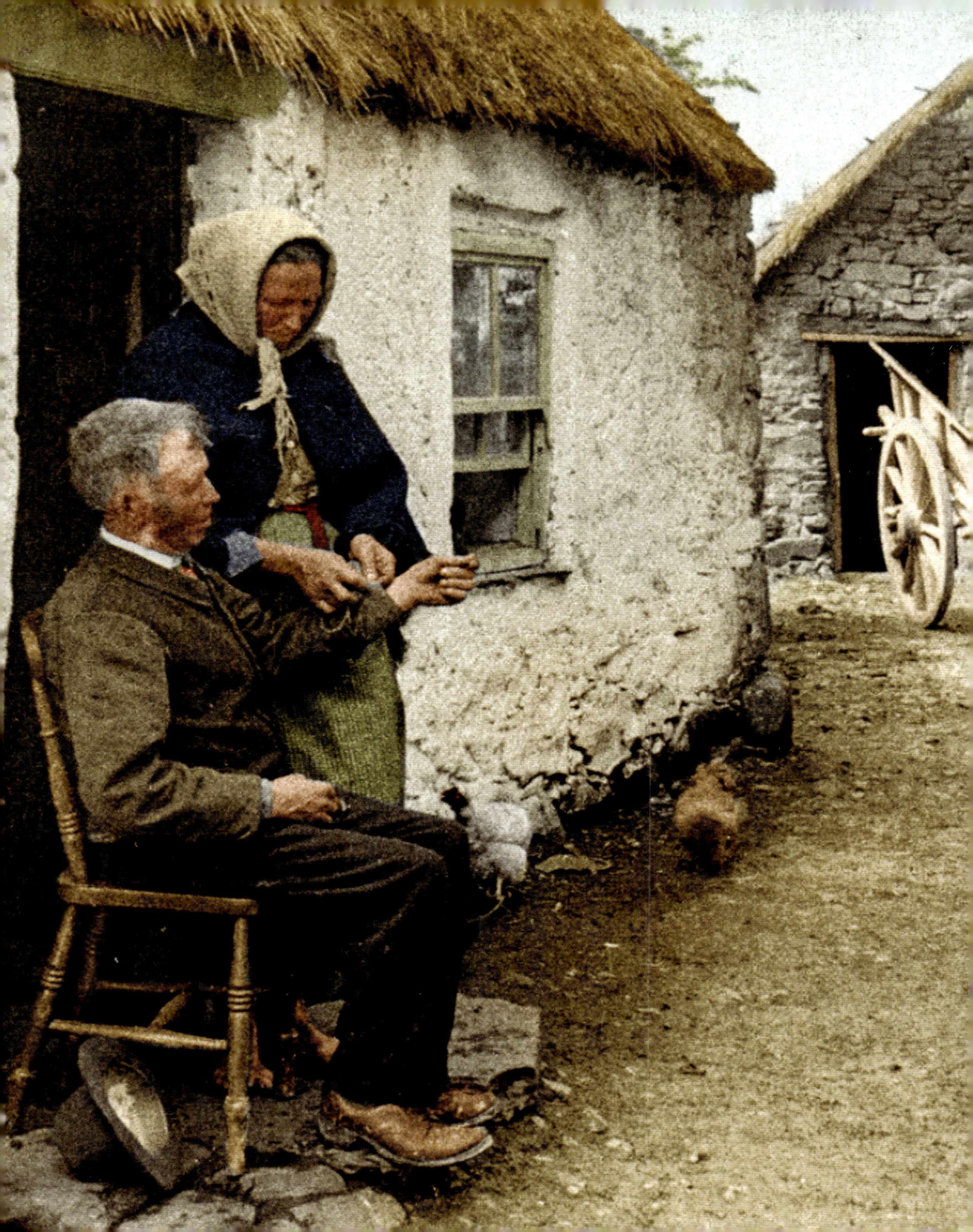

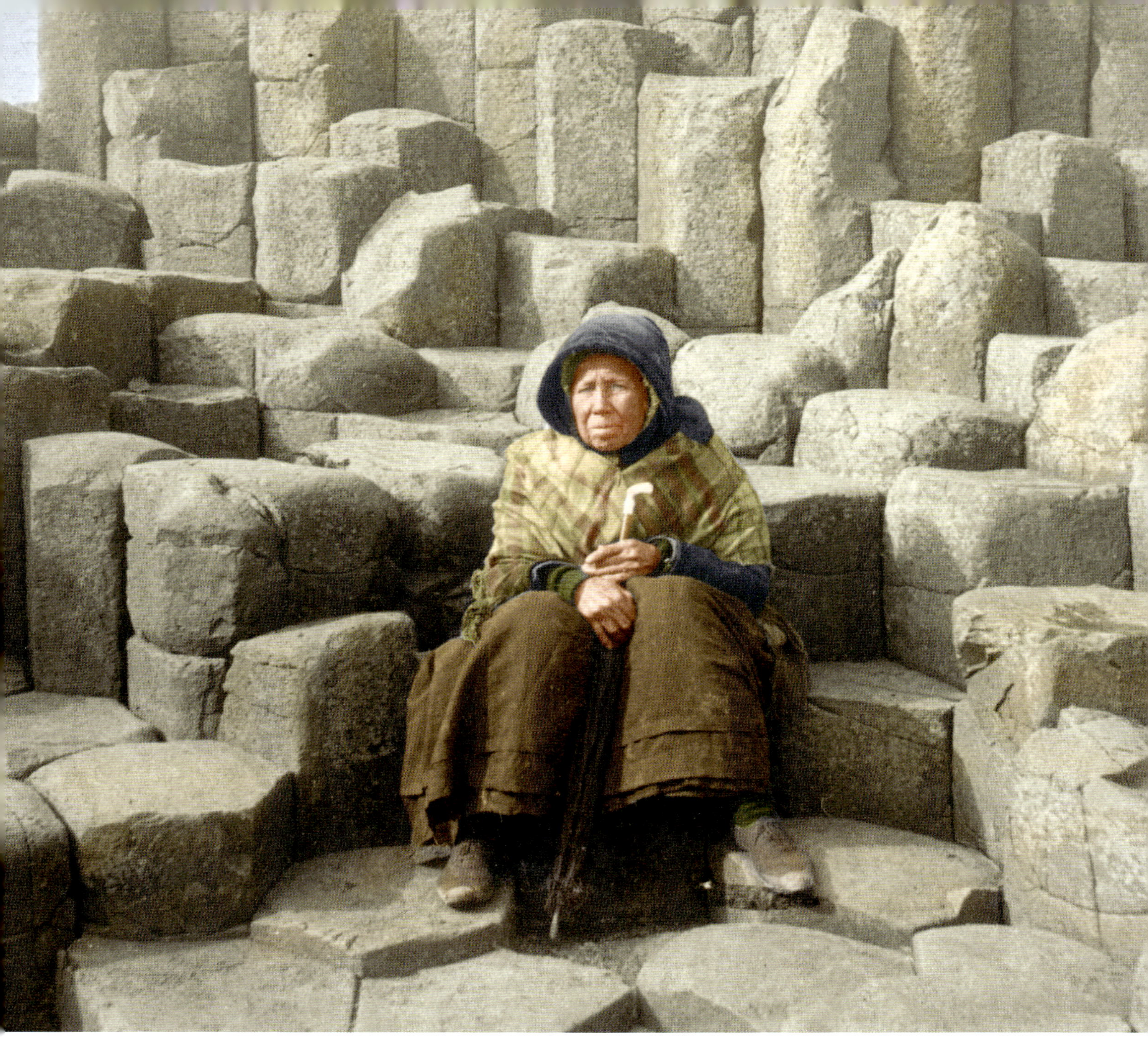

Continuing the American photographers'
search for the 'quaint', this *c.*1900 stereograph
shows an elderly woman seated at the basalt
Wishing Chair at the Giant's Causeway.

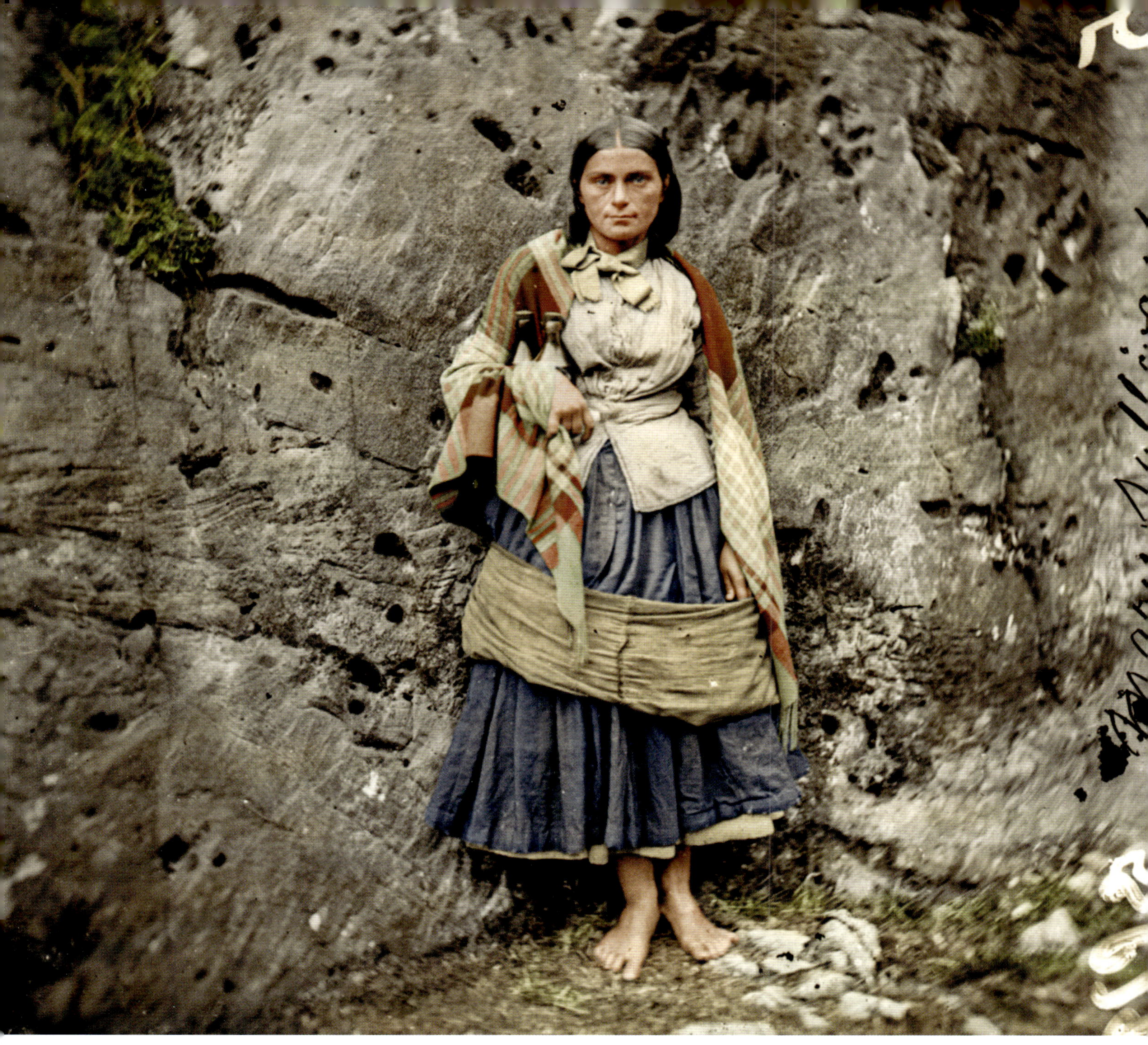

Poignant amidst the picturesque. A photograph of a
barefoot local woman, her hard life imprinted on her
face; one of a series taken of women posing by this
rock face at the Gap of Dunloe.

This photograph from the end of the nineteenth century captures a group of men (with two children along for the spectacle). Several wield two-tined turf forks, and one man holds what looks to be a *sleán*. They are saving the turf, a practice that was vital to rural life in Ireland at the time.

Turf (peat) is formed over thousands of years from decayed plant material in waterlogged bogs, which cover around one-sixth of Ireland's surface. It has served as a primary fuel source over the millennia for heating and cooking, in an island with few coal reserves and where woodlands had long been depleted. Although it has low calorific value (in comparison to coal), and despite the back-breaking labour of harvesting, it was cheap and locally available.

To make turf usable as fuel, bogs must be drained. Turf is traditionally cut using the spade-like tool called a *sleán*. This process involves slicing rectangular sods from the bog face. The freshly cut turf sods are left to dry on the bog surface. This drying process takes many weeks as the high water content evaporates. Once dried, turf is transported to homesteads and stacked into piles for later use as fuel.

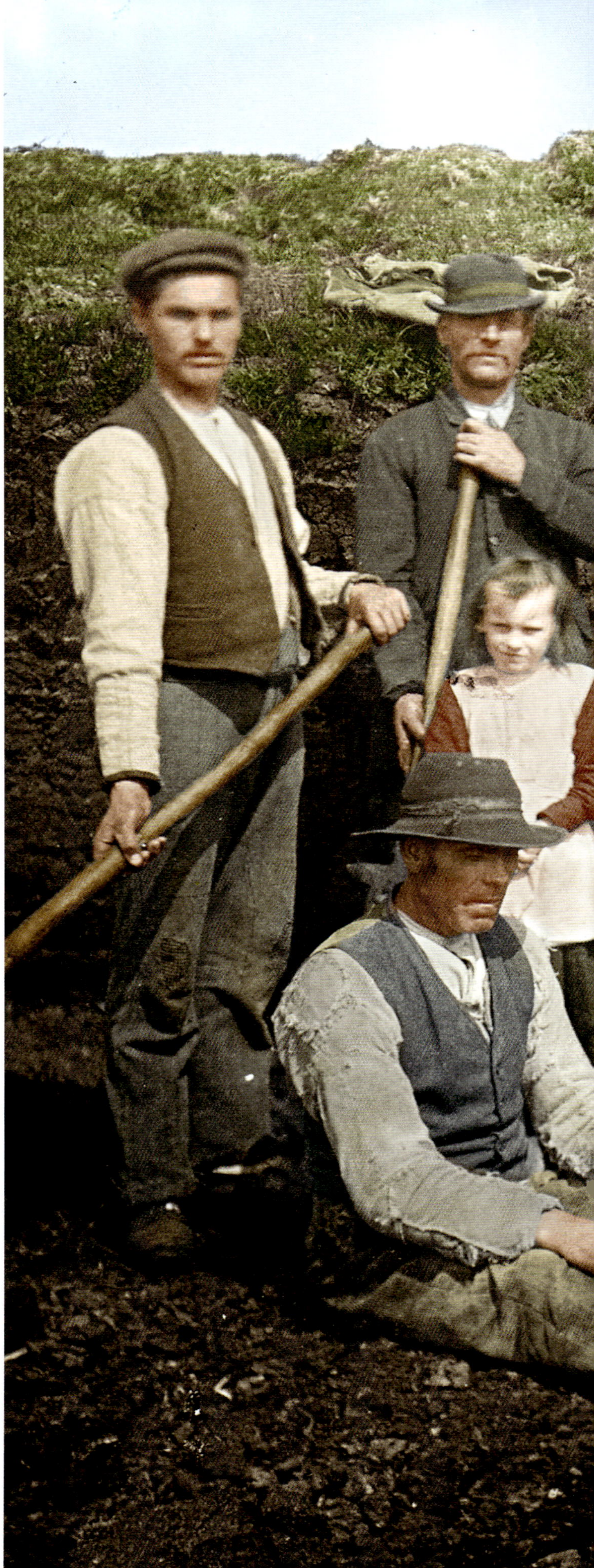

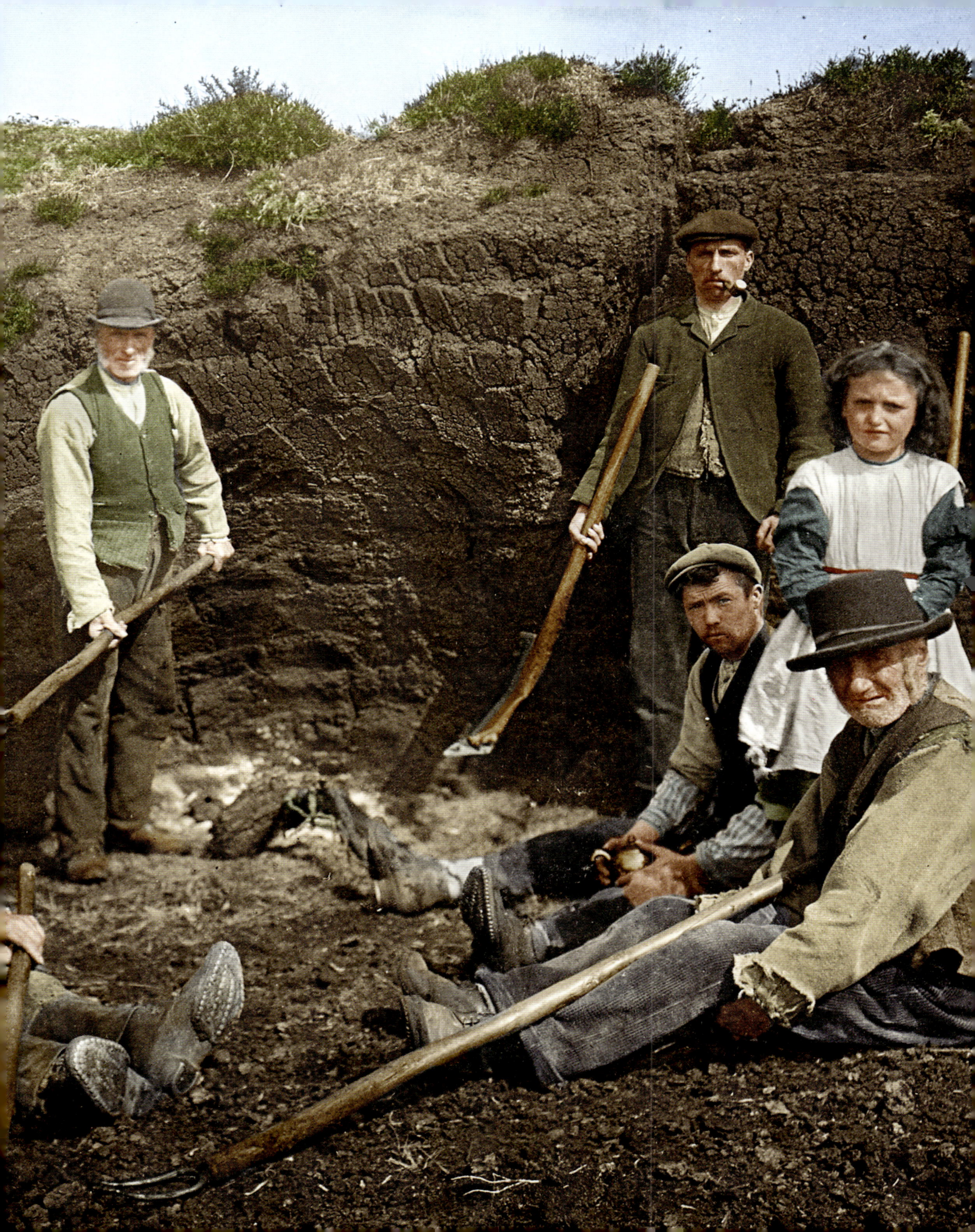

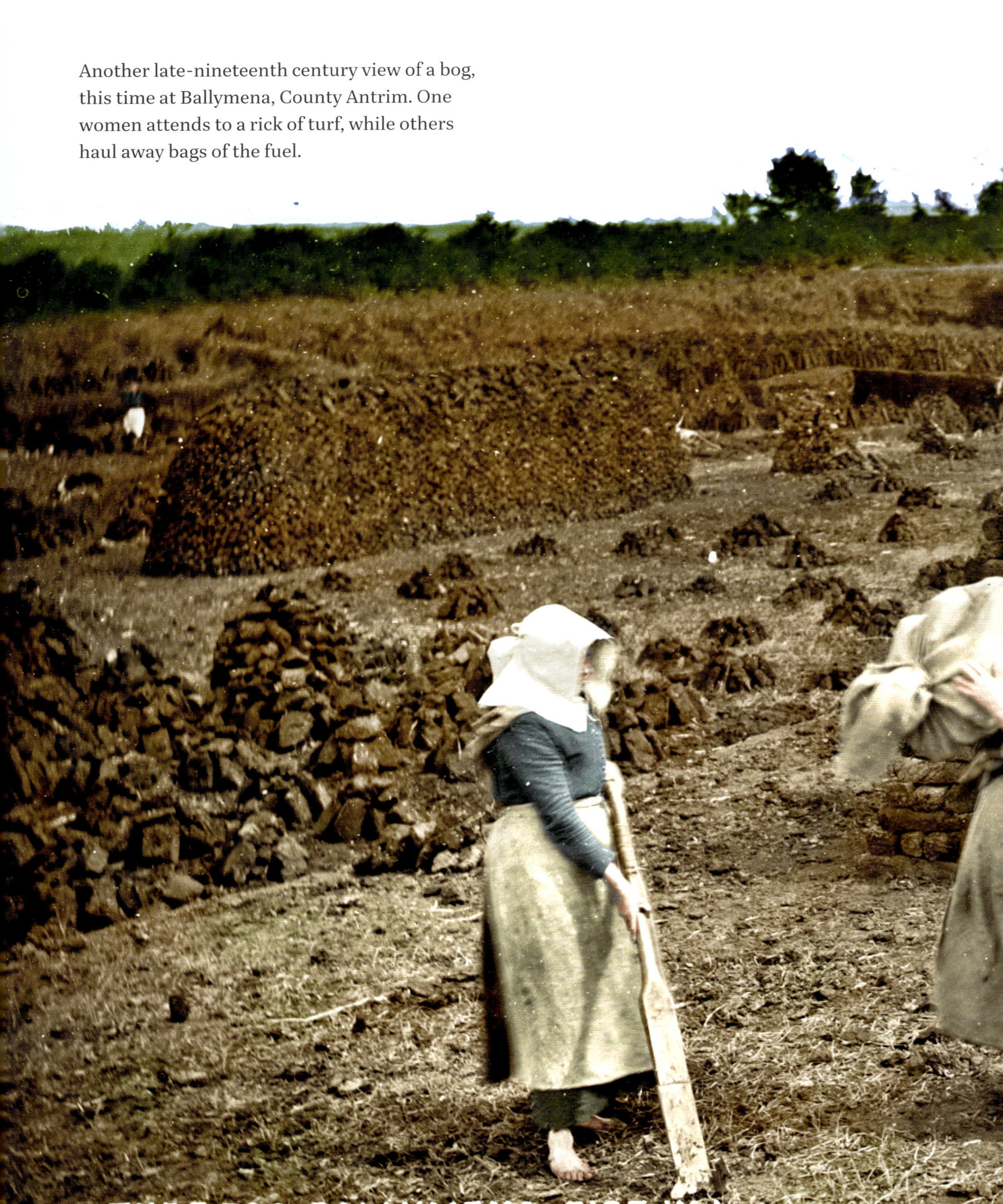

Another late-nineteenth century view of a bog, this time at Ballymena, County Antrim. One women attends to a rick of turf, while others haul away bags of the fuel.

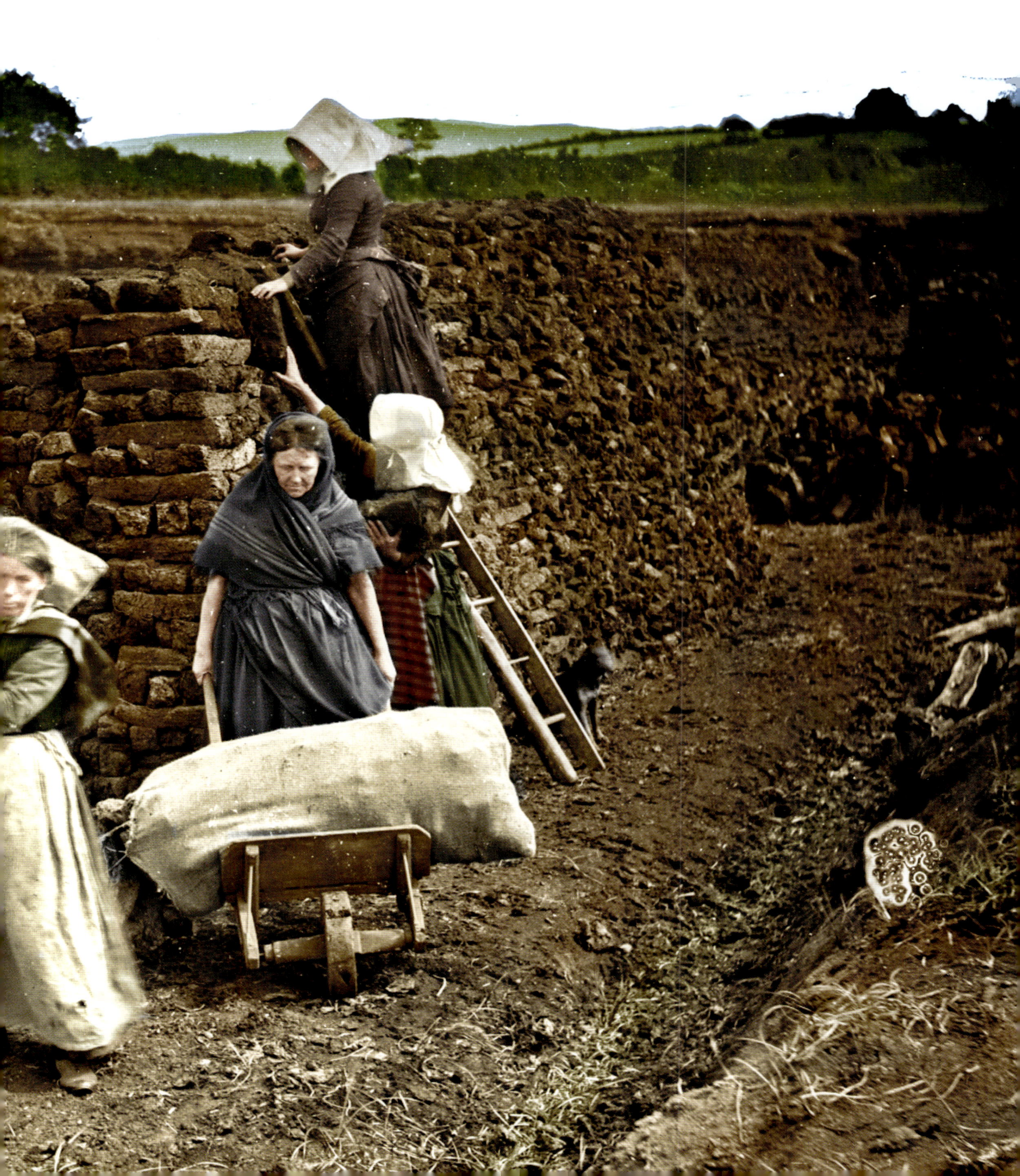

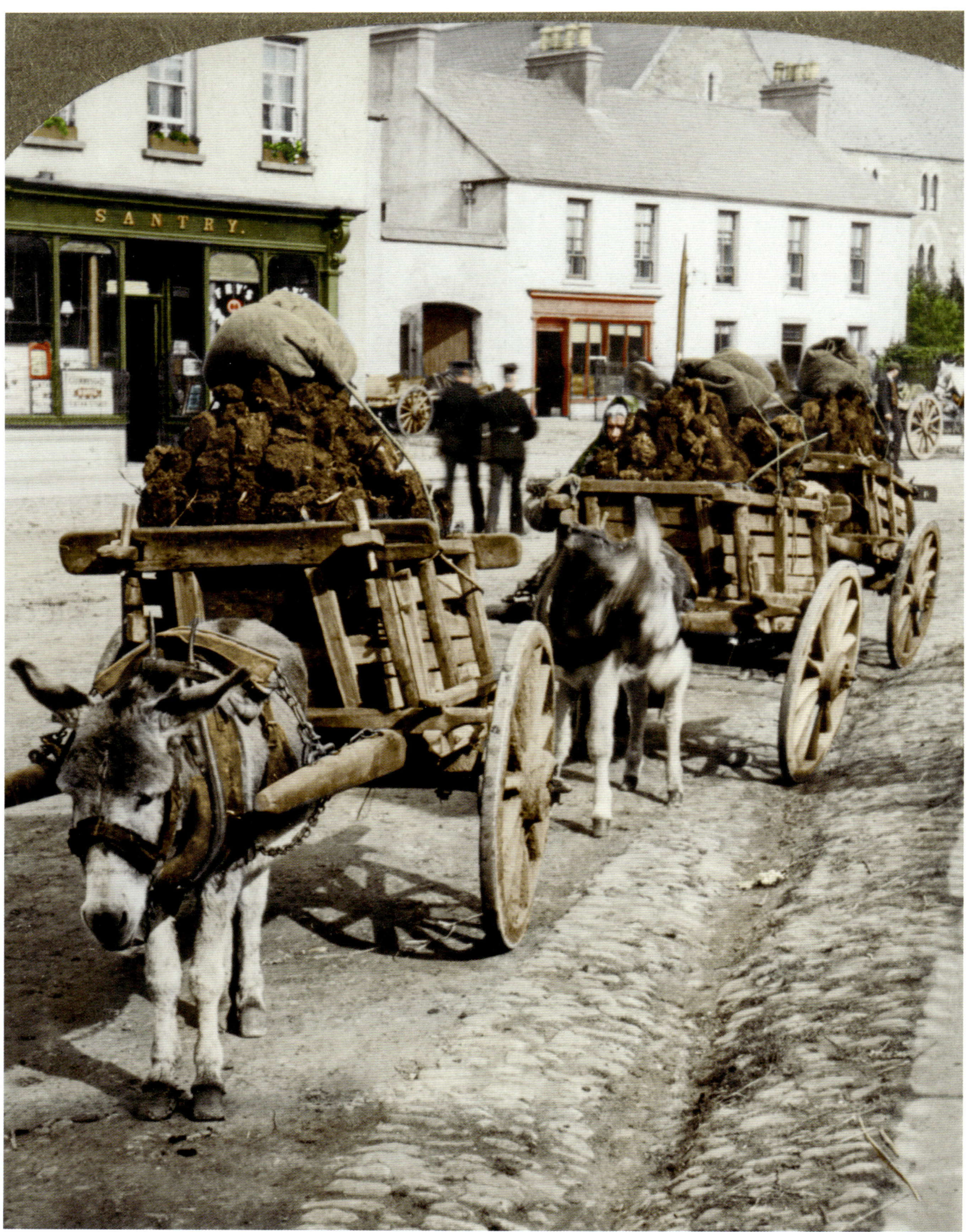
SANTRY.

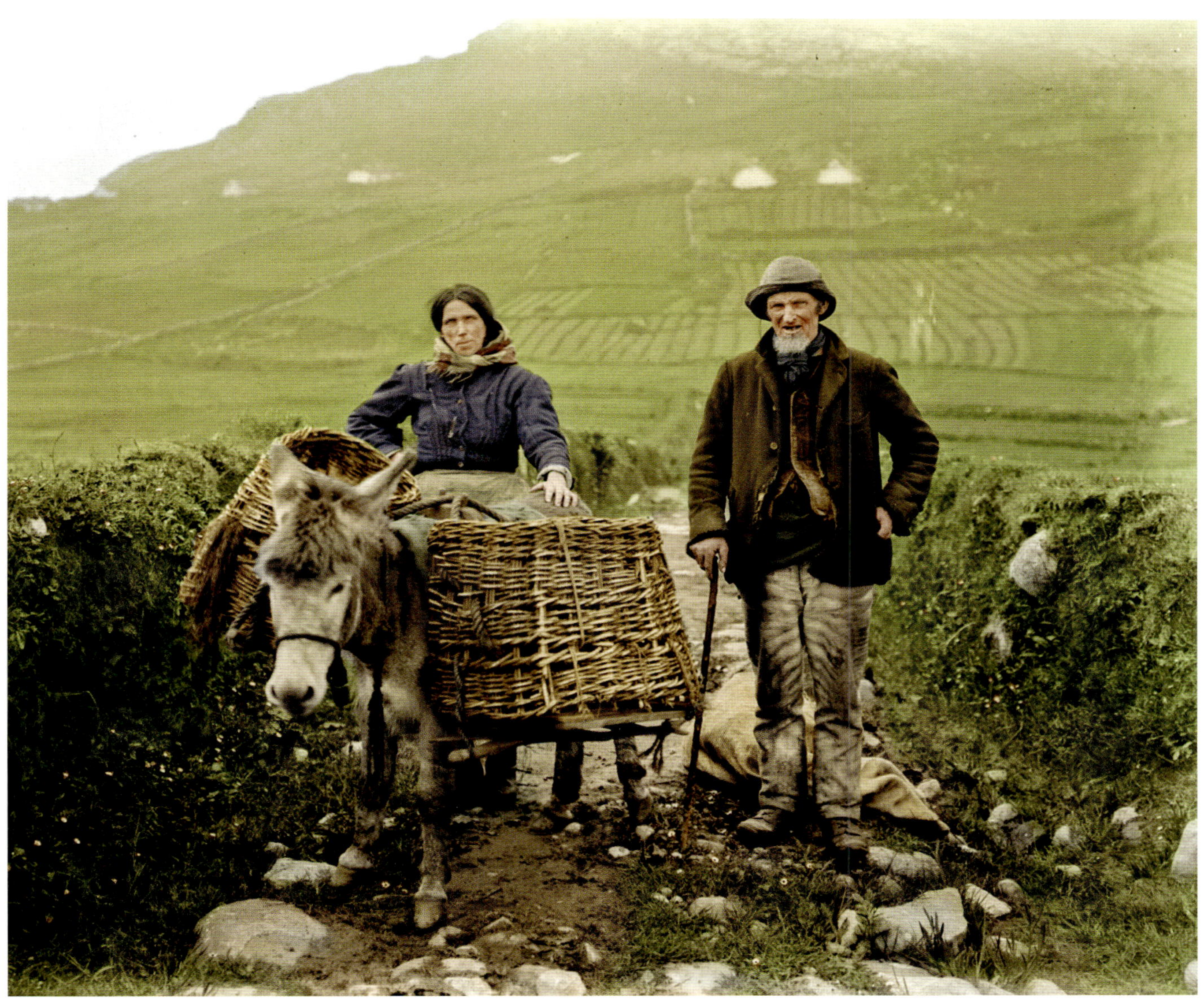

Left: Donkey carts piled high with turf are pictured at a street in Killarney, County Kerry. For rural communities, turf was not only essential for their own use but also held economic value, as it could be sold to town dwellers who lacked direct access to bogs.

Top right: A man and woman stand with their donkey, its creels empty as they pause on a rugged boreen. In remote rural Ireland, donkeys played a vital role in daily life, carrying goods like turf, seaweed or potatoes. Their ability to traverse uneven tracks, like the one pictured here, made them an essential part of the rural landscape.

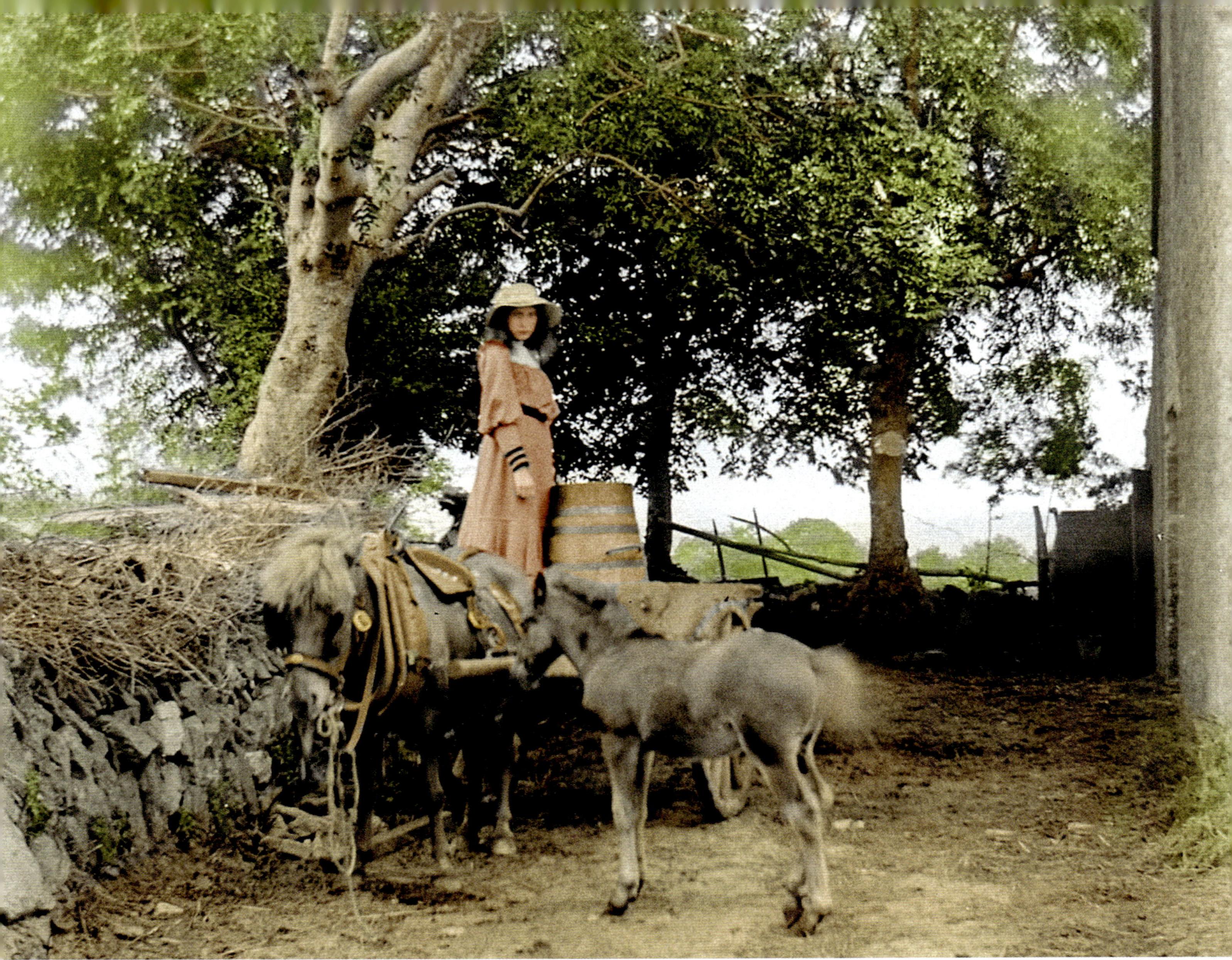

A sylvan scene at a mare and foal farm at
Rochestown, County Cork. For farmers in
those days, animal power was the only option,
but was also cheap to run and maintain.
Additionally, these beasts of burden offered an
advantage: the gift of offspring, a renewable
source of labour.

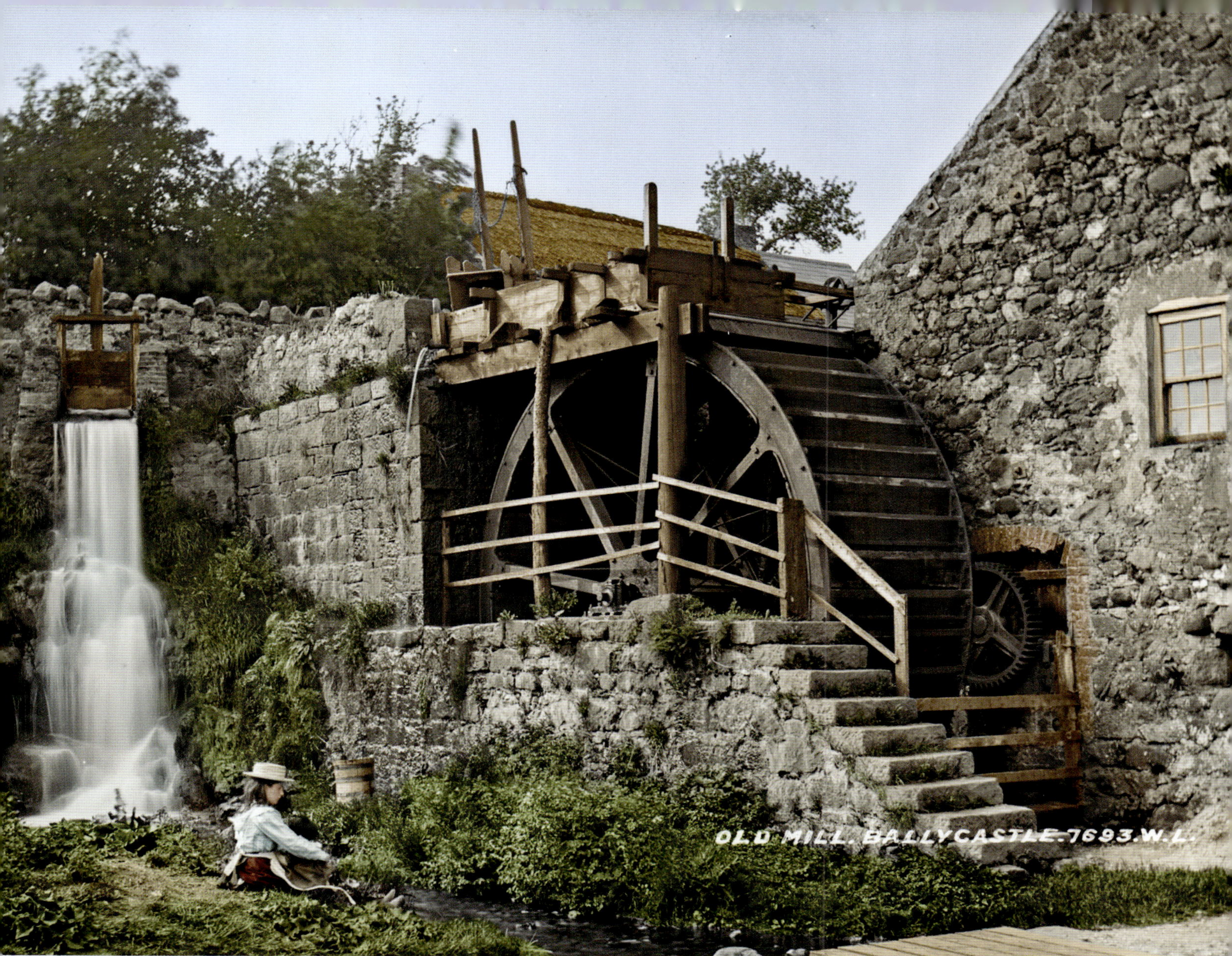

From the earliest times, animal power had been used on farms. In addition, man had succeeded in making use of water power over the millennia – in Ireland, remains of water mills have been found, the earliest dating from the seventh century AD. This is a photograph of the Old Mill at Ballycastle, County Antrim: a reminder of how water mills harnessing the energy of local rivers were dotted all over the Irish countryside and, up to the early twentieth century, served as useful local centres for farmers where they could bring their corn or wheat to be milled.

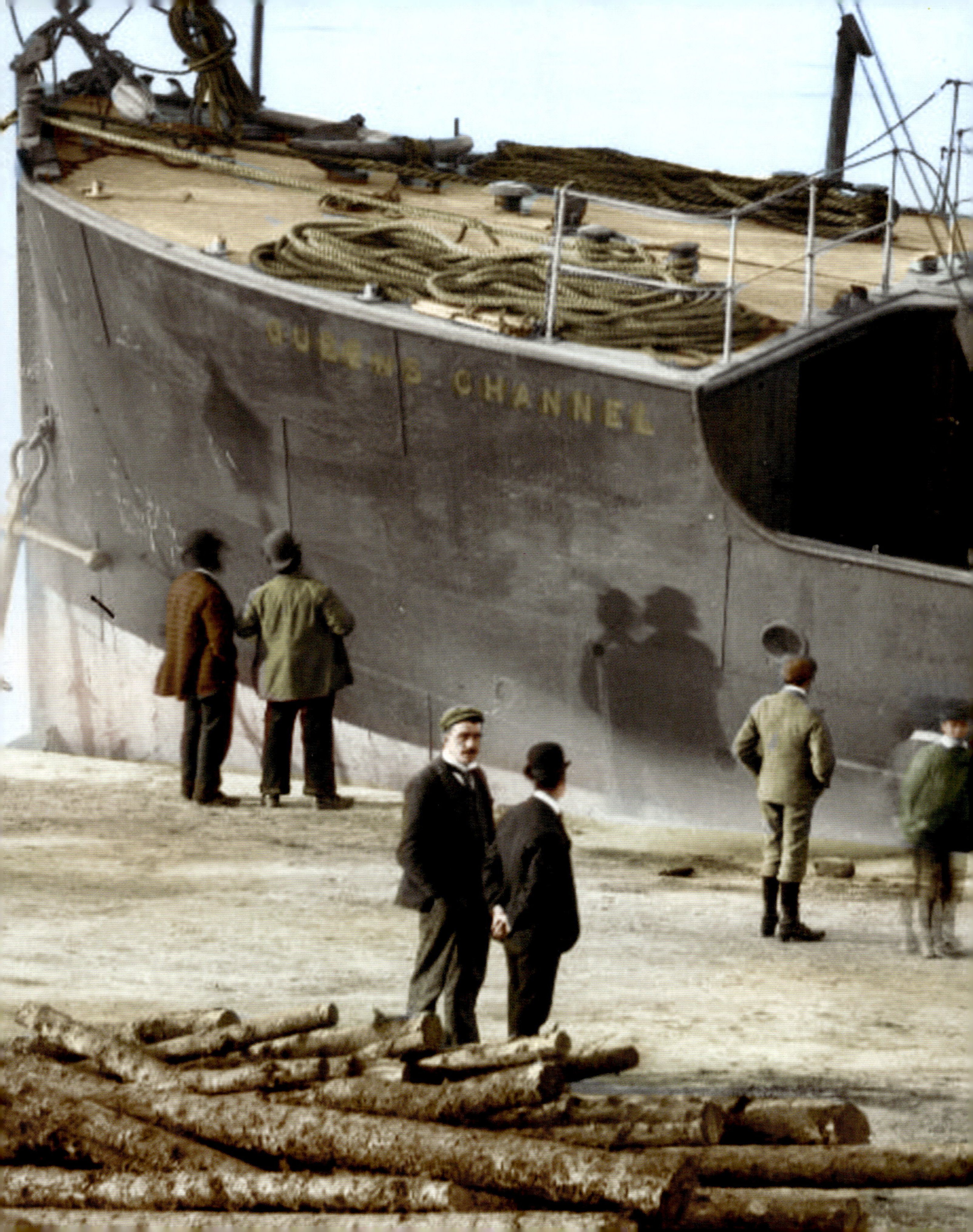
QUEENS CHANNEL

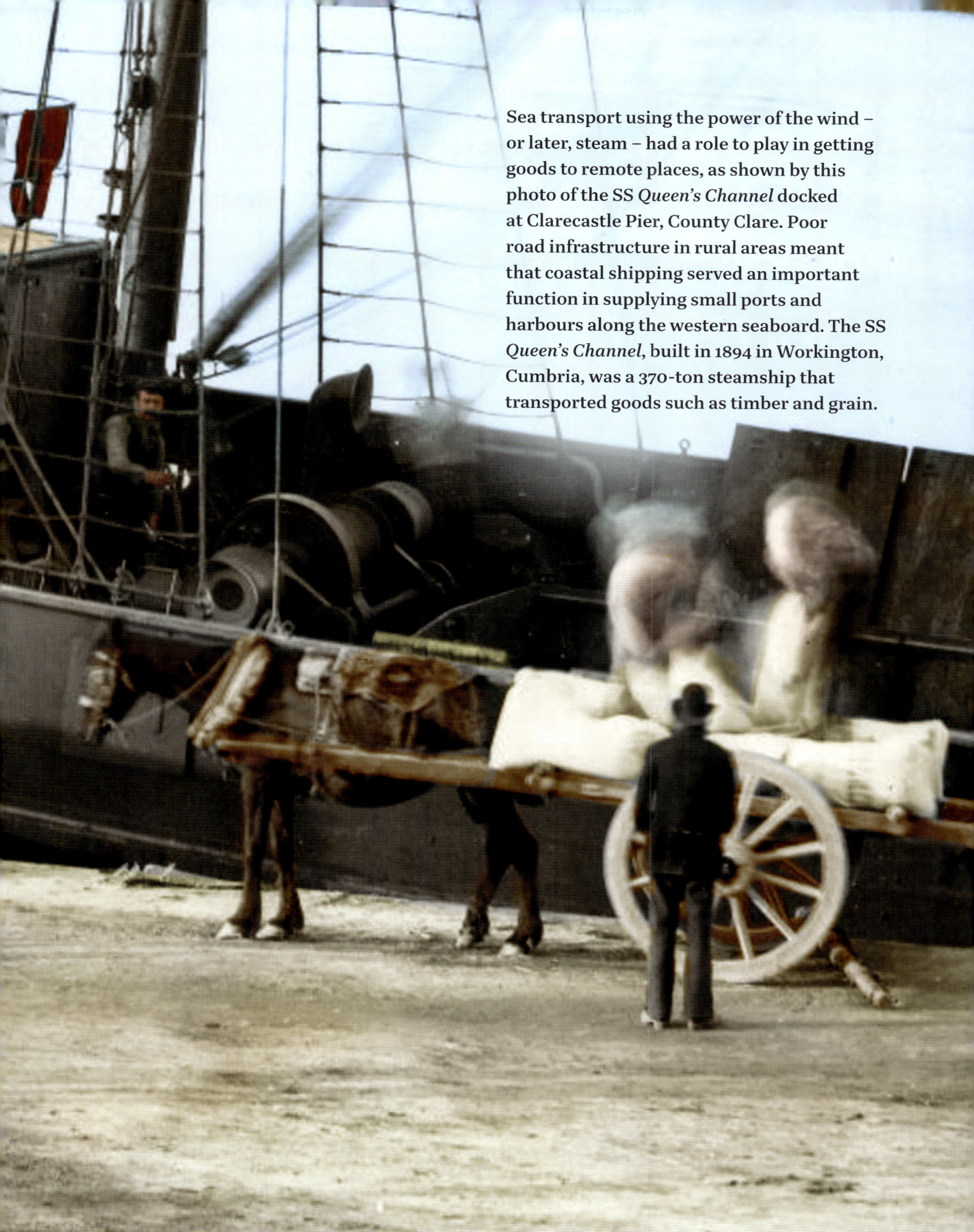

Sea transport using the power of the wind – or later, steam – had a role to play in getting goods to remote places, as shown by this photo of the SS *Queen's Channel* docked at Clarecastle Pier, County Clare. Poor road infrastructure in rural areas meant that coastal shipping served an important function in supplying small ports and harbours along the western seaboard. The SS *Queen's Channel*, built in 1894 in Workington, Cumbria, was a 370-ton steamship that transported goods such as timber and grain.

The revolution wrought by the introduction of railways, powered by steam, changed the economic landscape of Ireland. This is the impressive twelve-arch viaduct of the Schull and Skibbereen Light Railway at Ballydehob, County Cork, built in 1886, one of a series of light railways built around that time.

By 1880, Ireland's railway network amounted to 3,200km of standard Irish gauge (1,600mm) and most major towns were connected, driven by the railway boom of private investment seeking profitable returns. One benefit was that farms could send their produce (animals or crops) to faraway markets rapidly and cheaply.

However, in that decade attention turned to rural and remote areas, particularly in the west and north, where low population densities and challenging terrain made standard-gauge railways unprofitable. To address this, light railways with narrow gauges (typically 914mm) were introduced as a cheaper alternative. These railways required less land and lighter materials and could navigate tighter curves, reducing construction and operational costs.

Subsidies under the Tramways (Ireland) Act of 1883 and the Light Railways (Ireland) Act of 1889 included baronial guarantees funded by local ratepayers and direct government grants. Notable examples include the Schull and Skibbereen Light Railway seen here, the West Clare Railway, the Tralee and Dingle Light Railway, the Cavan and Leitrim Railway and various Donegal light railways.

By 1910, the number of railway lines had reached its apogee in Ireland. There was a total track length of around 4,700km in 1,600mm gauge, plus around 800km in narrow gauge.

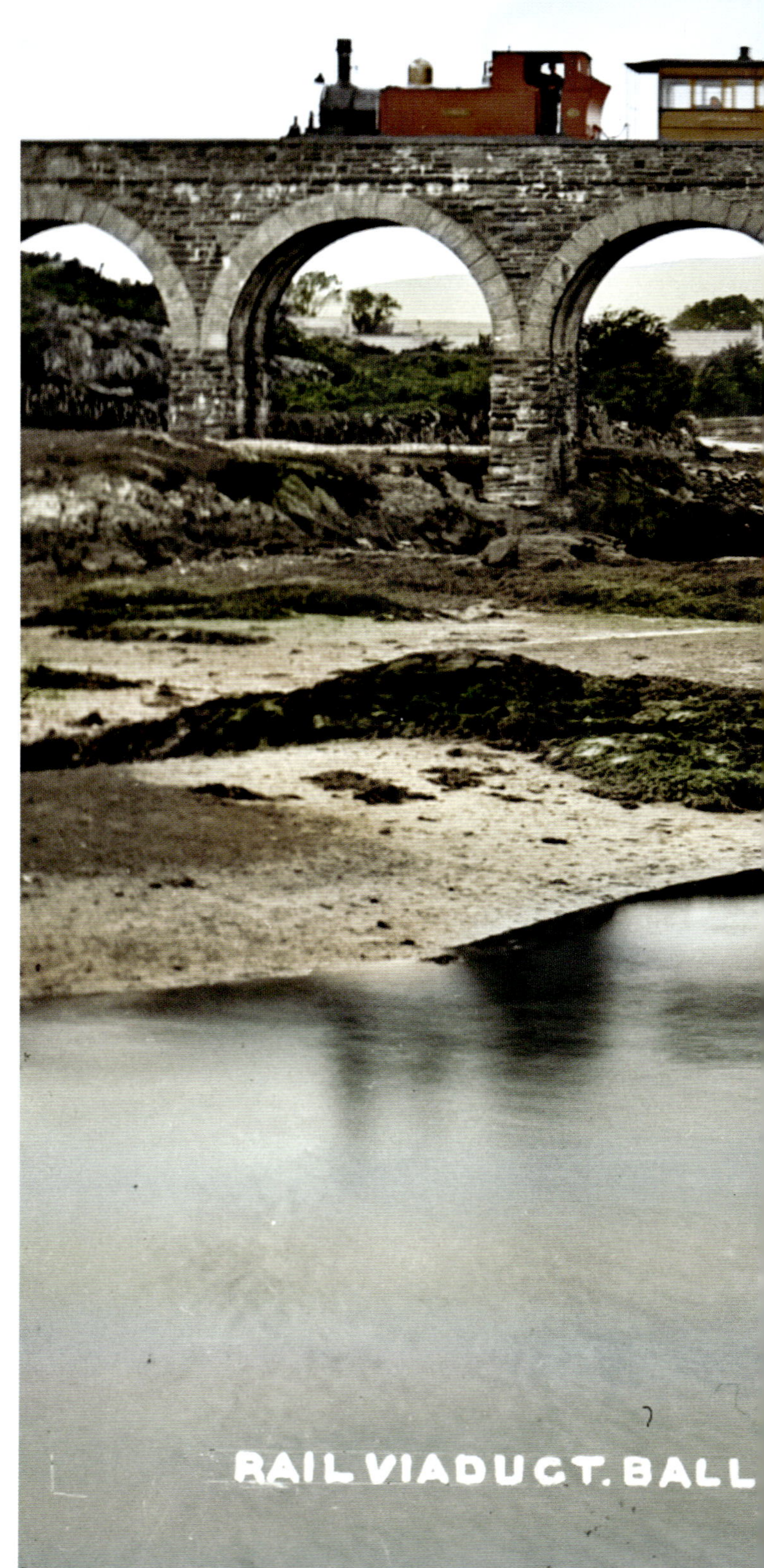

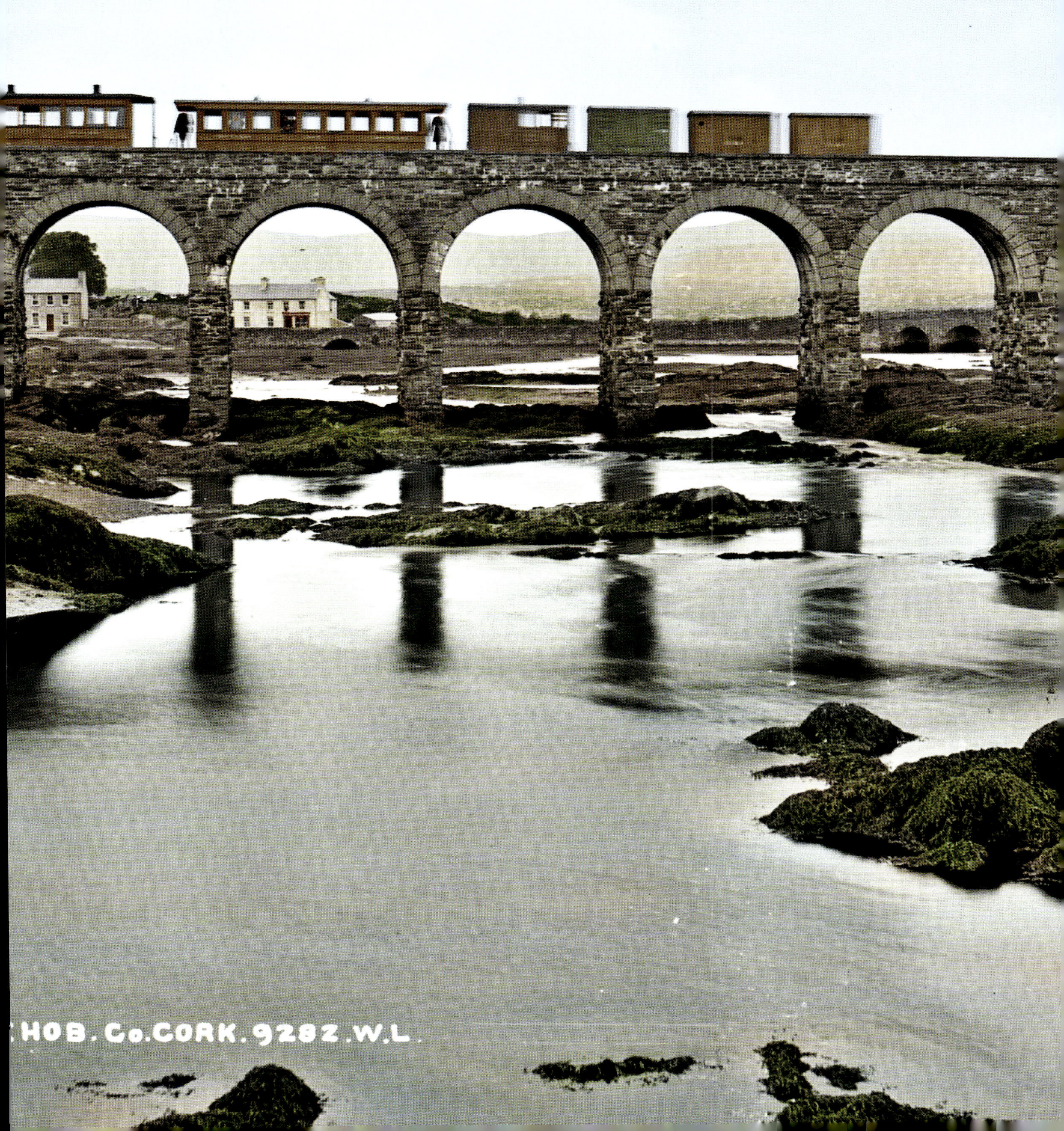
HOB. Co. CORK. 9282. W.L.

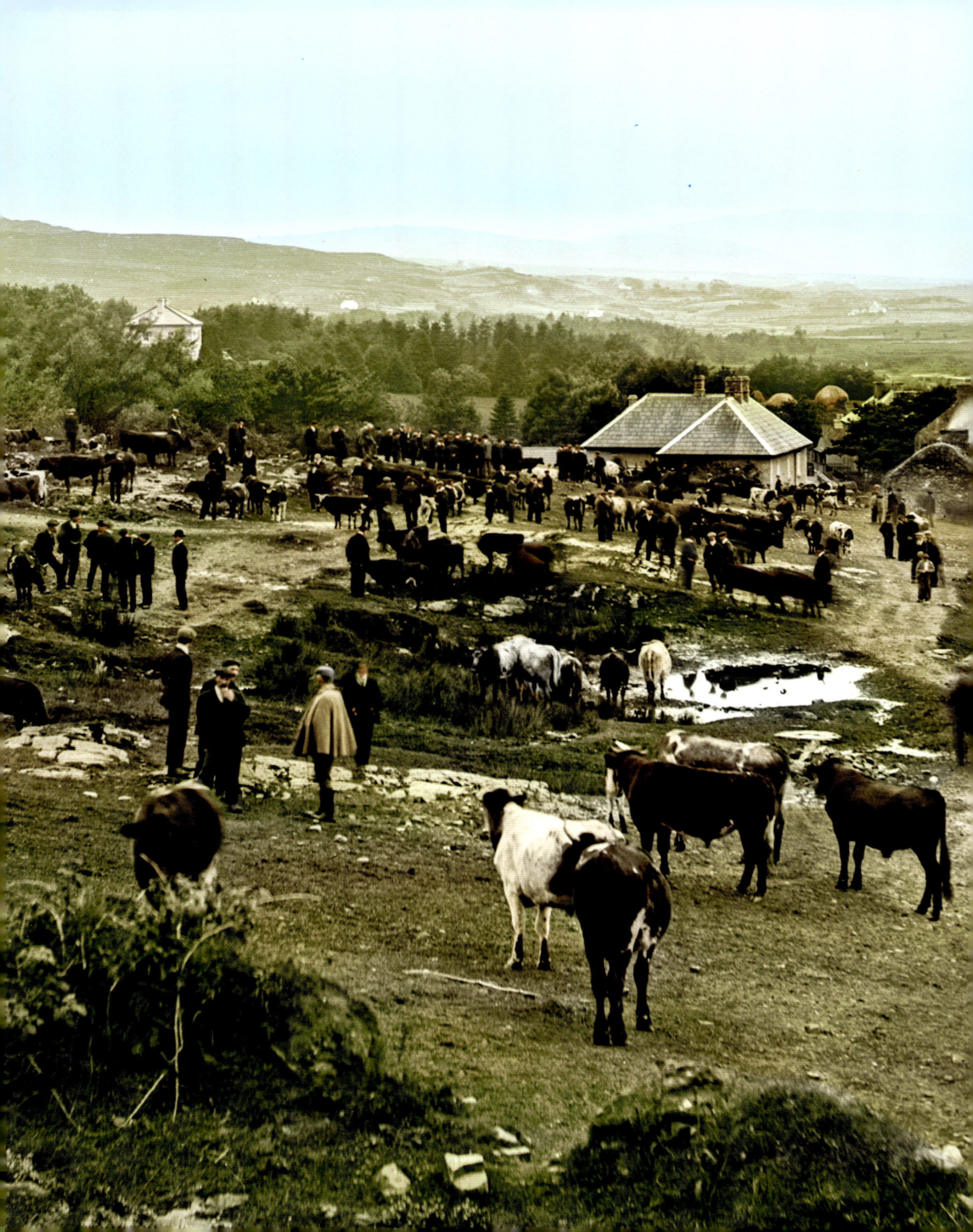

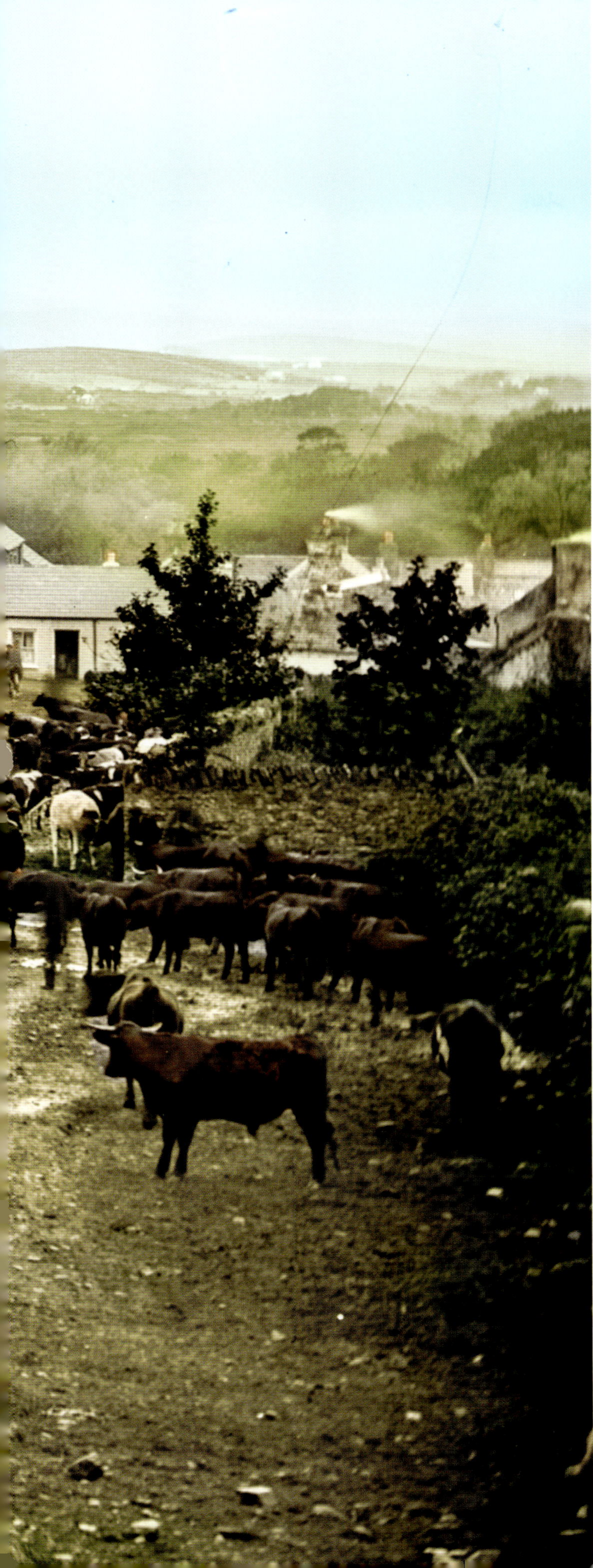

Cattle at the Harvest Fair at Glenties, County Donegal. Cattle have been central to Irish agriculture and society since farming first began on the island over 6,000 years ago. In early Ireland, wealth and status were often measured in cattle, and they played a crucial role in the economy, diet and culture. From ancient Gaelic laws that detailed cattle ownership and grazing rights to their prominence in Irish folklore and traditions, cattle have been deeply embedded in Ireland's rural life for millennia.

In general, Ireland's mild, wet climate and natural grasslands make it well-suited to cattle farming, particularly in regions with fertile, well-drained soils. The best areas for beef and dairy farming include the Golden Vale (Tipperary, Limerick, Cork), the Midlands, and parts of the south-east, where limestone-rich soils provide excellent pasture. In contrast, western coastal regions, bogland areas and mountainous terrain – such as much of Donegal, Connemara and Kerry – tend to have poorer, wetter soils and rougher grazing land, making large-scale cattle farming more difficult.

The land around Glenties falls into this category, mainly characterised by rugged hills, peat bogs and high rainfall. These conditions are less suited to intensive cattle farming, and many farmers historically kept sheep instead. However, despite the marginal land, cattle were still raised throughout Ireland, including in Donegal, where hardy breeds that could thrive on rough grazing were preferred. Cattle fairs like this one played an essential role in rural life, providing a place for farmers to buy and sell livestock.

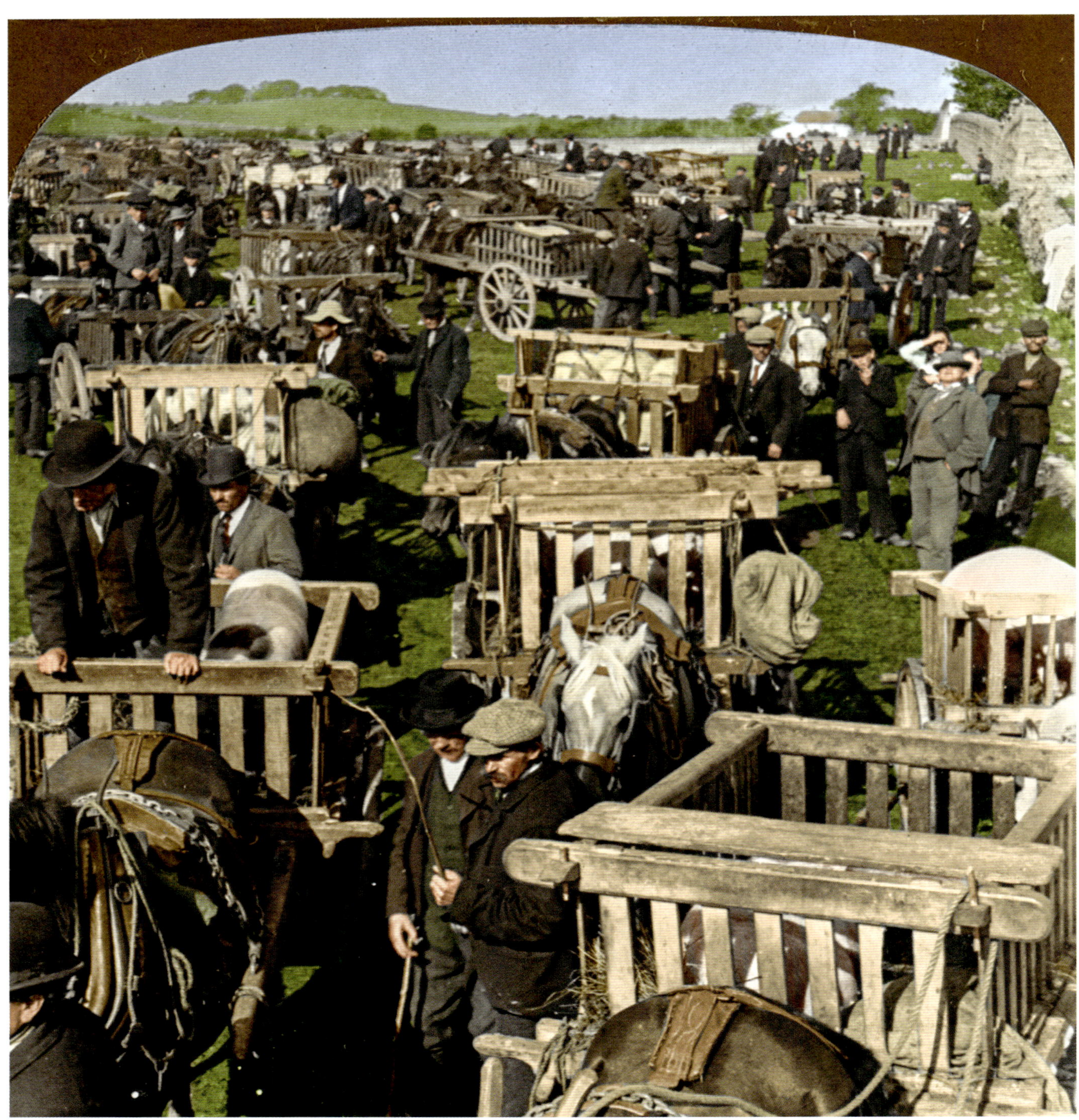

The market at Kilrush, County Clare. A mass of high-sided carts fills the field. These carts are just large enough to carry a pig or a calf and are therefore suited to the small-scale farms of the area. Farmers converse, inspect the livestock and strike deals.

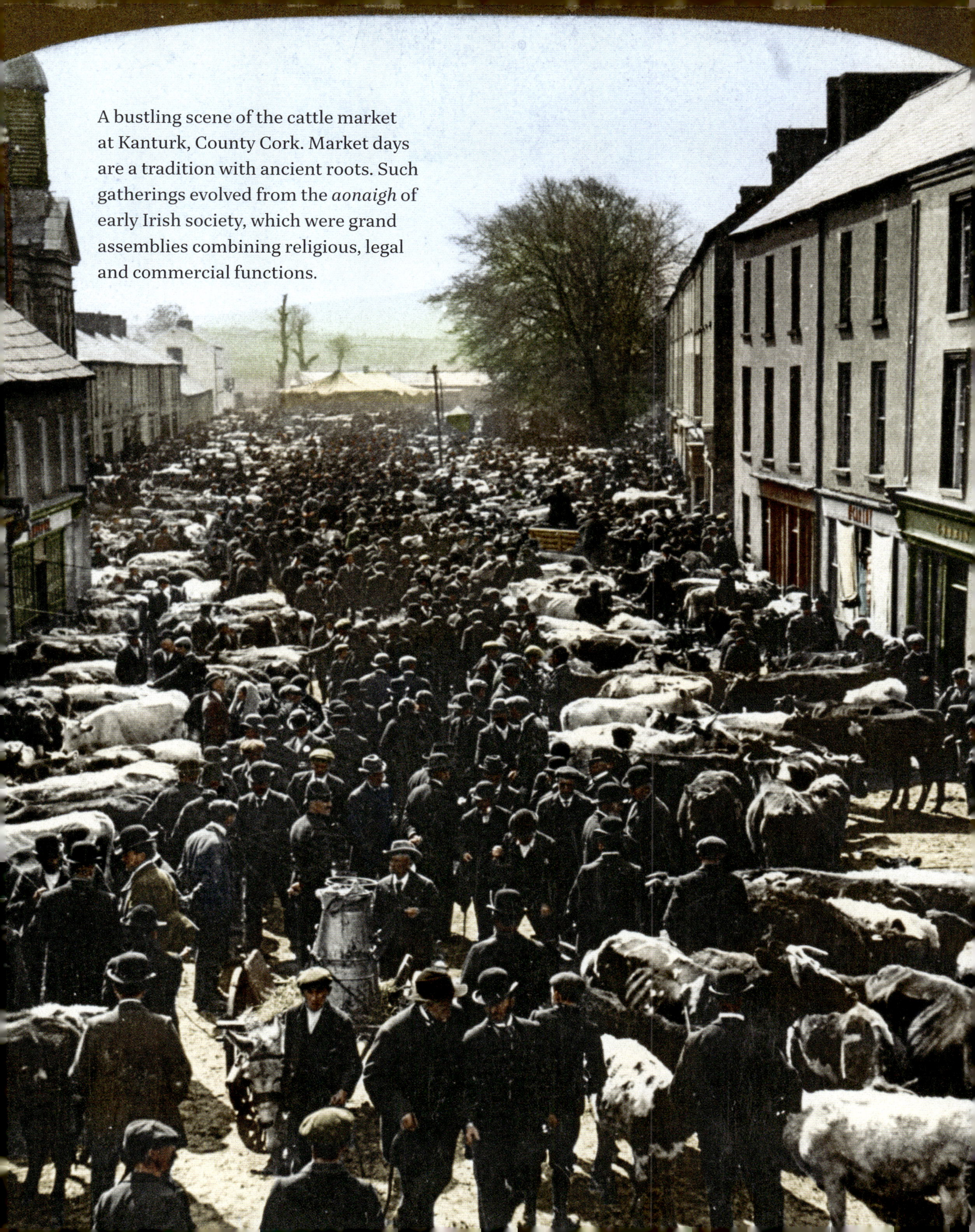

A bustling scene of the cattle market at Kanturk, County Cork. Market days are a tradition with ancient roots. Such gatherings evolved from the *aonaigh* of early Irish society, which were grand assemblies combining religious, legal and commercial functions.

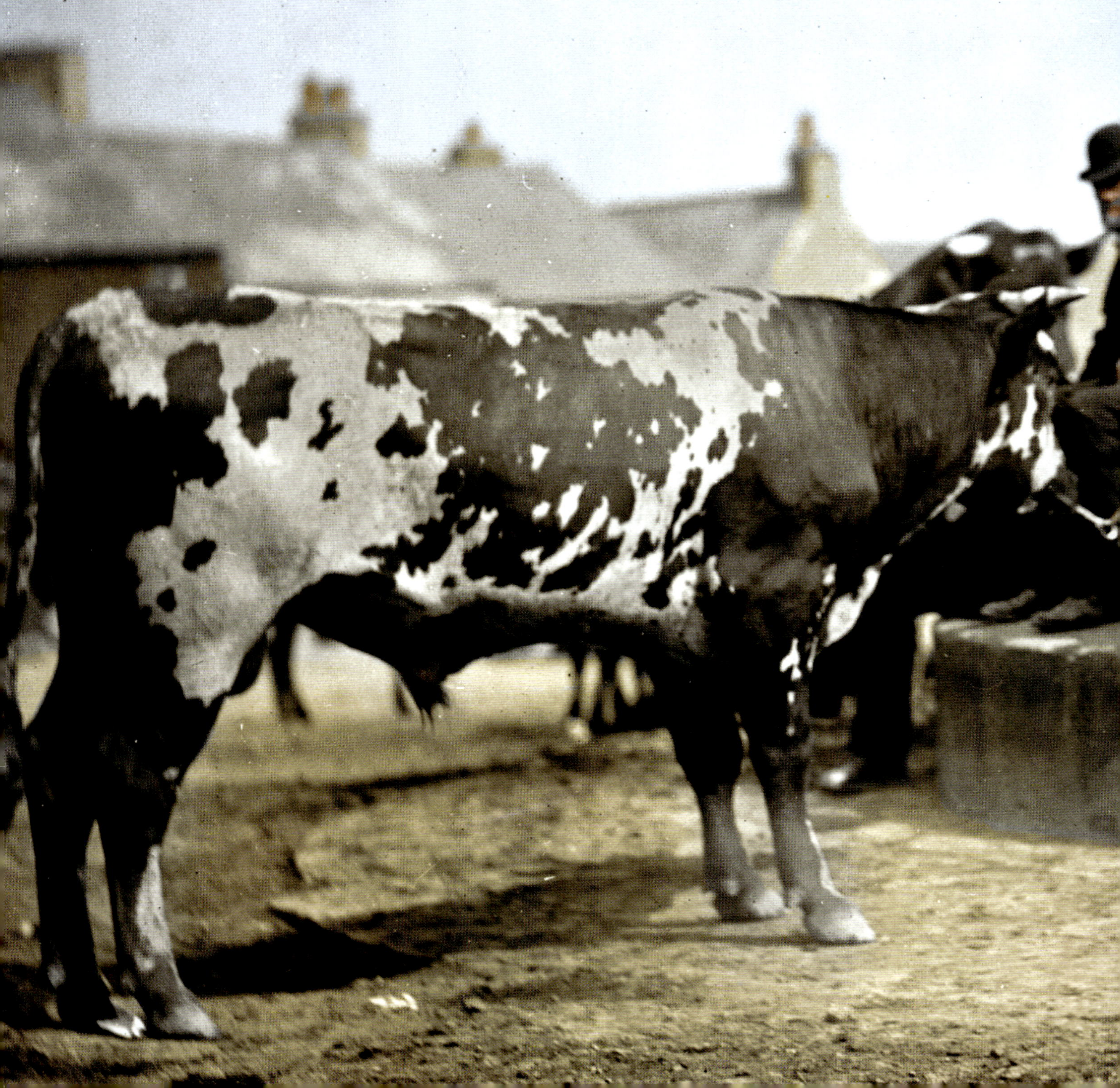

Time to take a break at Ballybricken Fair, Waterford. At these events farmers sold to one another, but cattle dealers also featured strongly. These would often travel from fair to fair, buying livestock to sell on to butchers, other markets or for export.

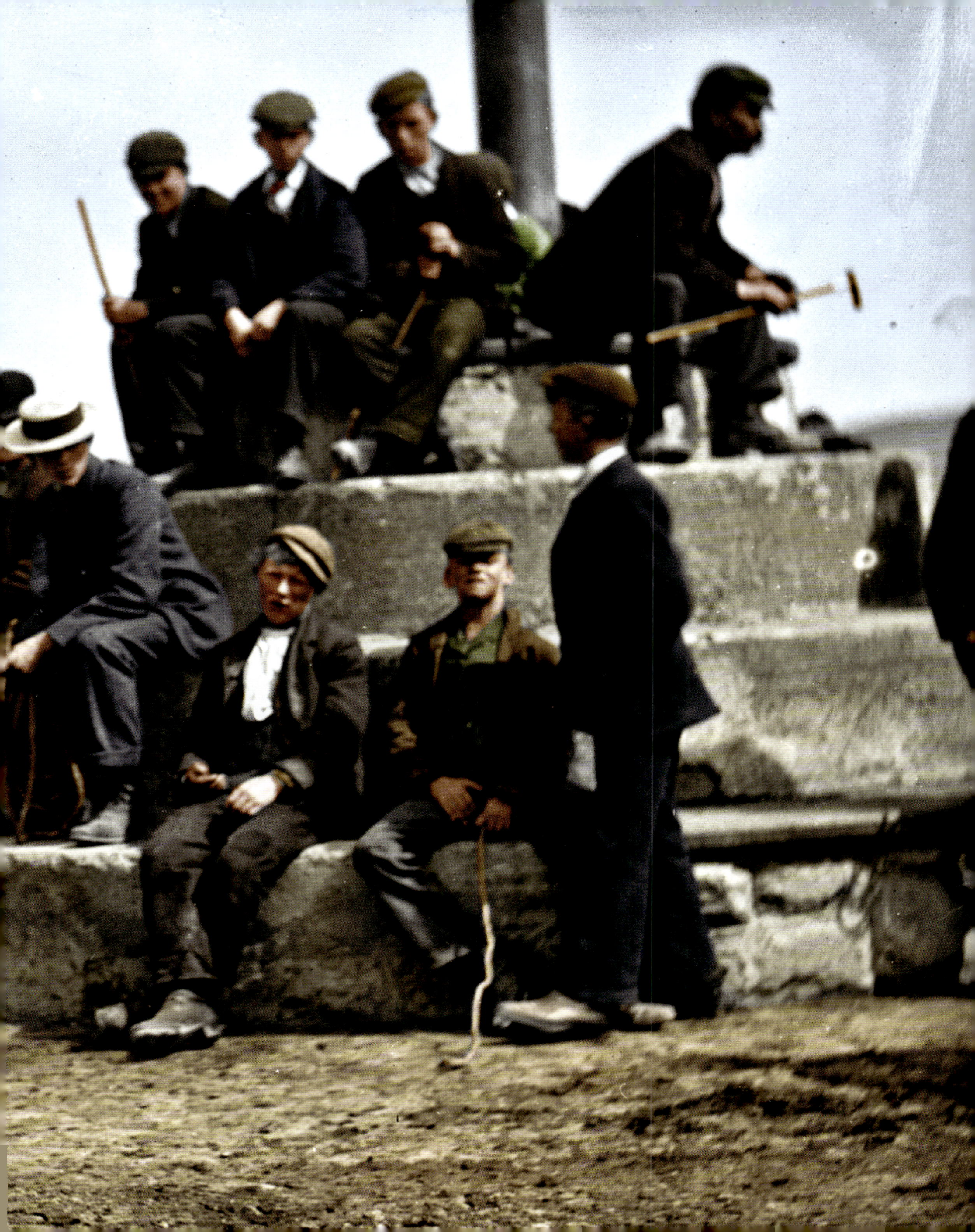

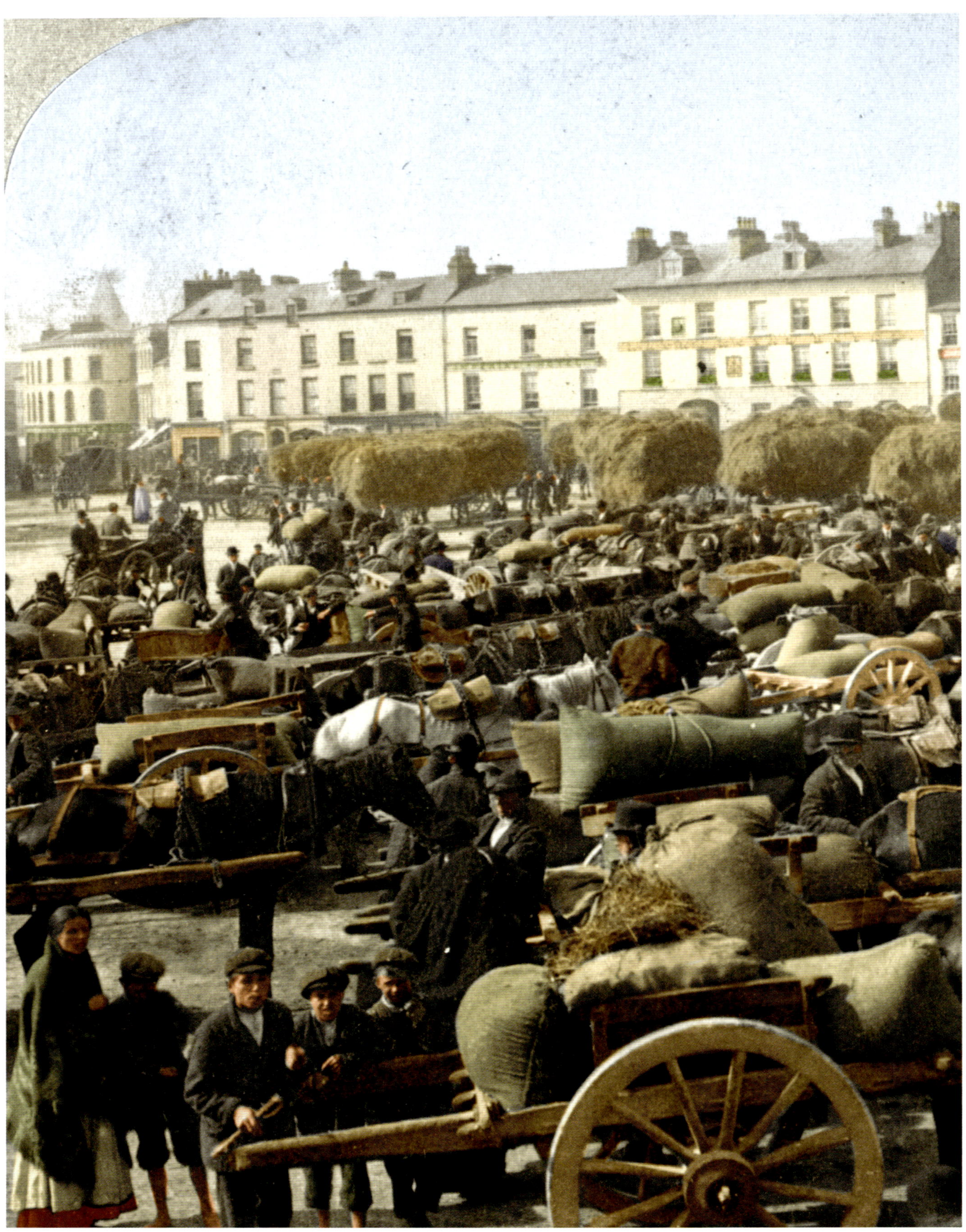

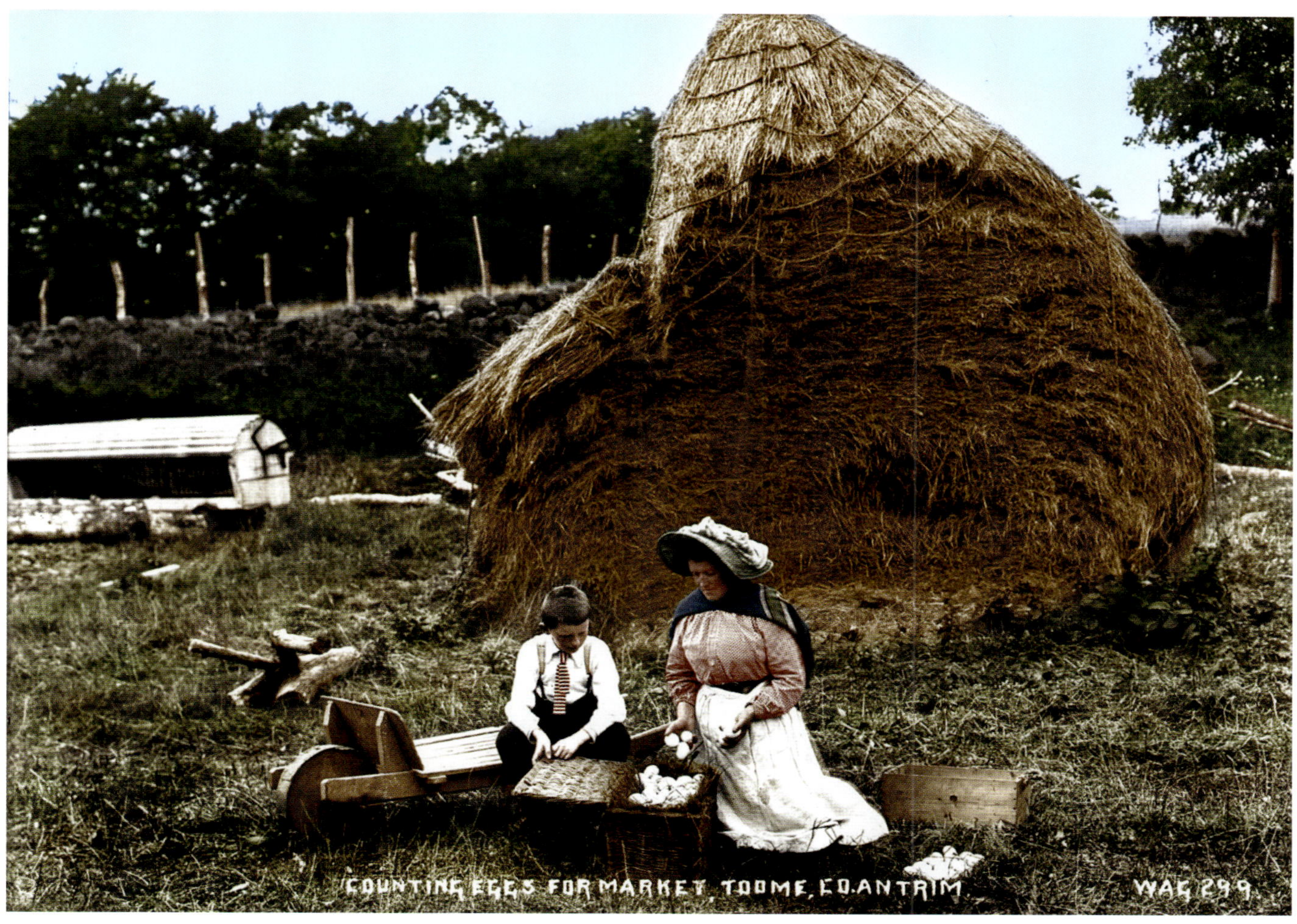

Left: The hay market at Galway, with carts piled high dominating one side of the square. Farmers from the surrounding countryside converged to trade hay and other goods vital to the agricultural economy. The market square buzzed with activity, as money changed hands and news was exchanged.

Top right: Getting ready for market: counting the eggs at Toome, County Antrim.

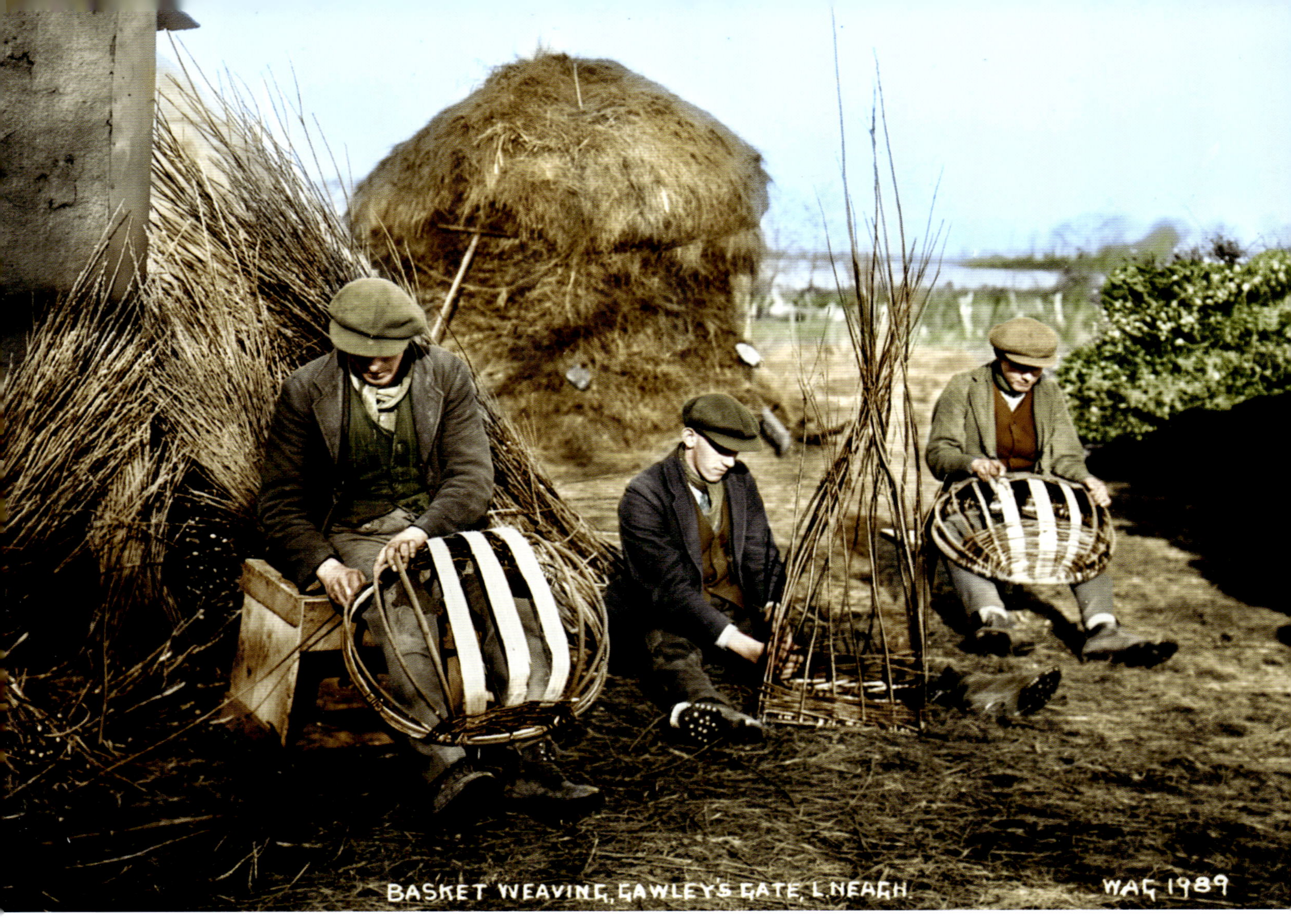

Also getting ready for market: weaving baskets at Gawley's Gate on Lough Neagh – the area was known for its basket-making tradition. This craft has a long history in Ireland, with different regions developing their own distinctive styles. One such basket, the creel, was commonly used for carrying turf or potatoes, while the *sciob* was a kitchen basket, typically used for straining boiled potatoes. Willow (or sally) was the most common material, and farmers often grew it in 'sally gardens'.

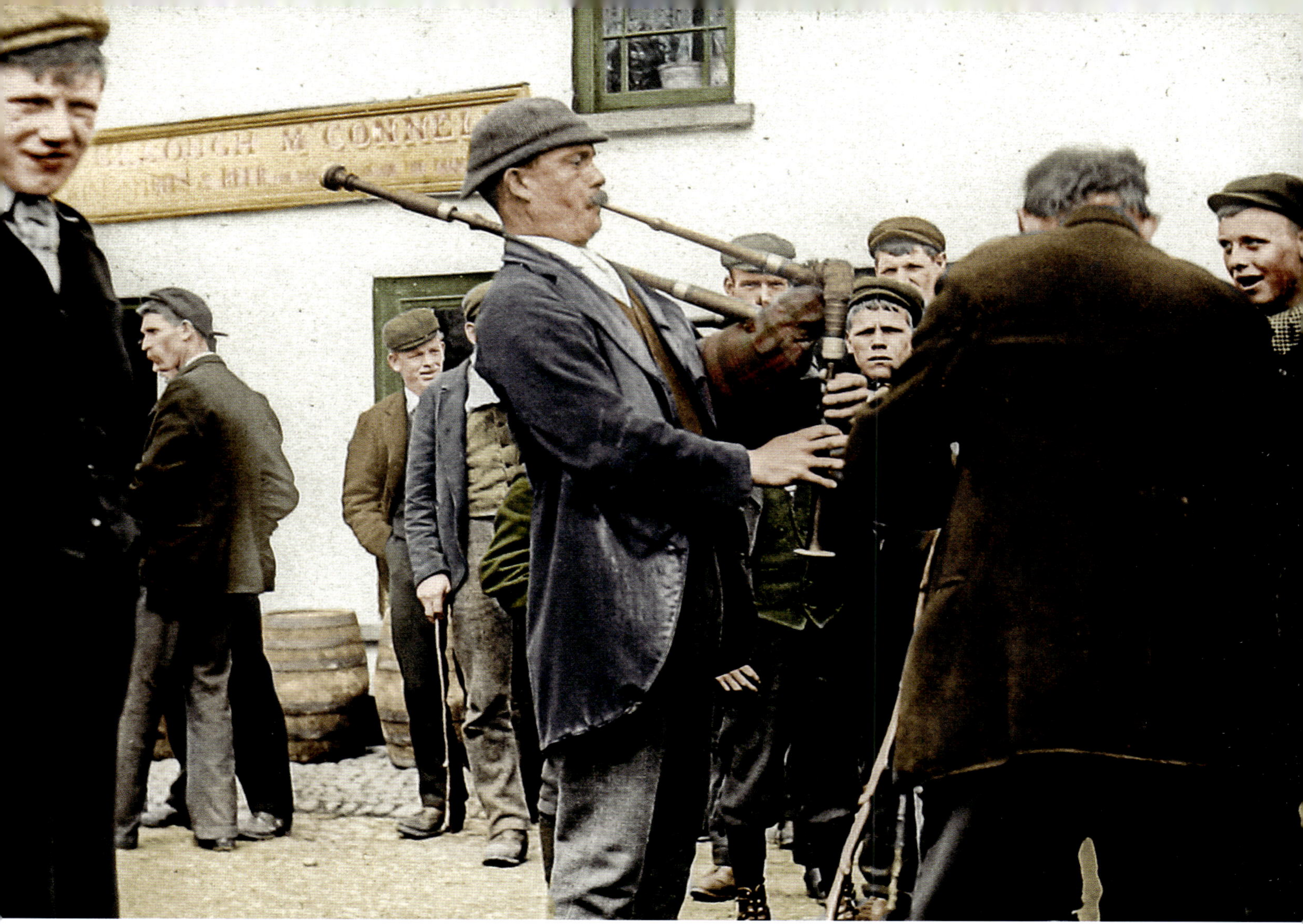

Musicians, performers and storytellers
travelled from town to town, bringing life
and energy to fairs and markets. Here a
piper plays a lively tune at the Ballyclare
May Fair in County Antrim, an event with a
tradition dating back over 300 years. Once
centred around livestock markets, the fair has
transformed over the years. Today, it is held
as a celebration of local culture, with many
carnival rides, parades, market stalls and
community gatherings.

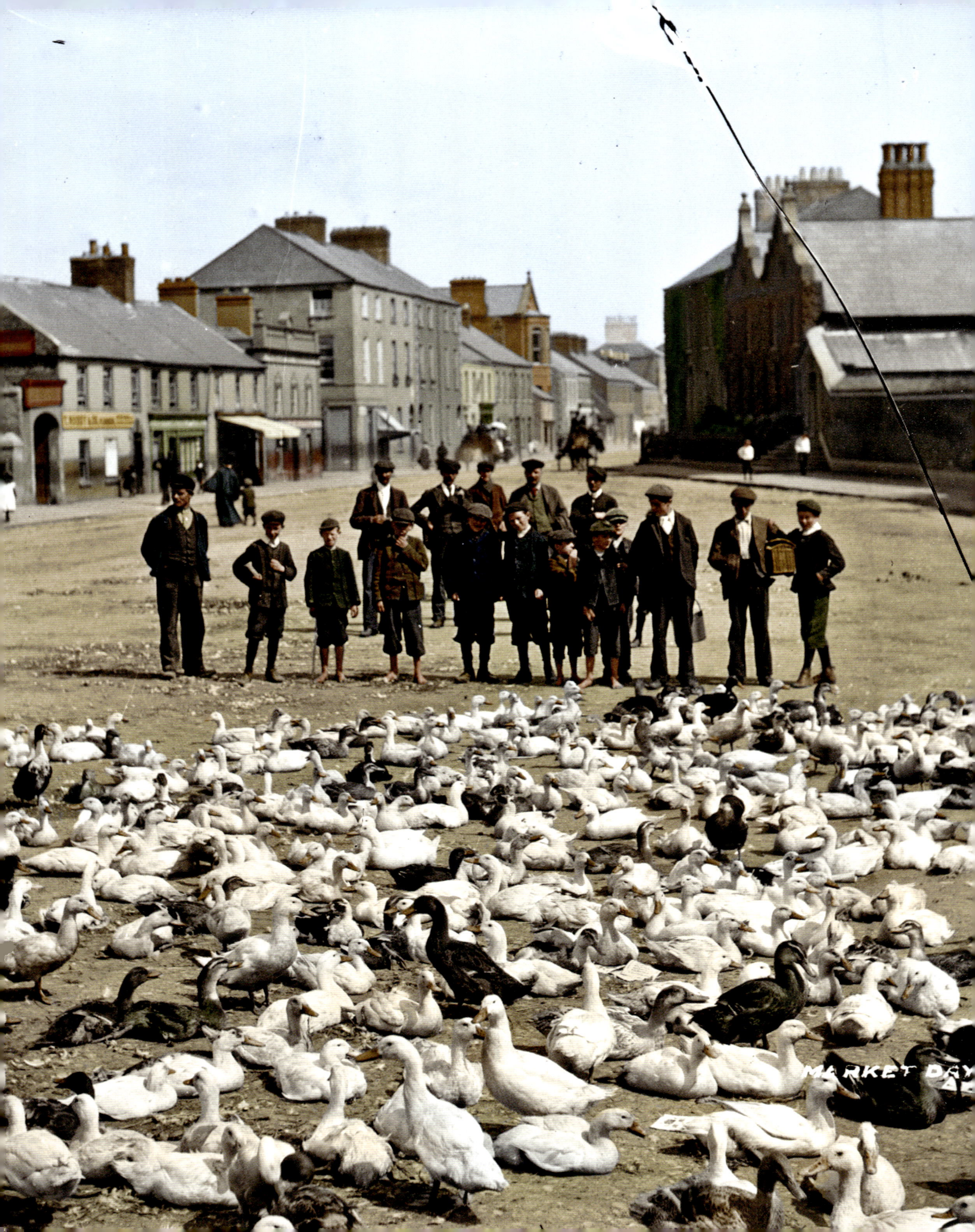

MARKET DAY

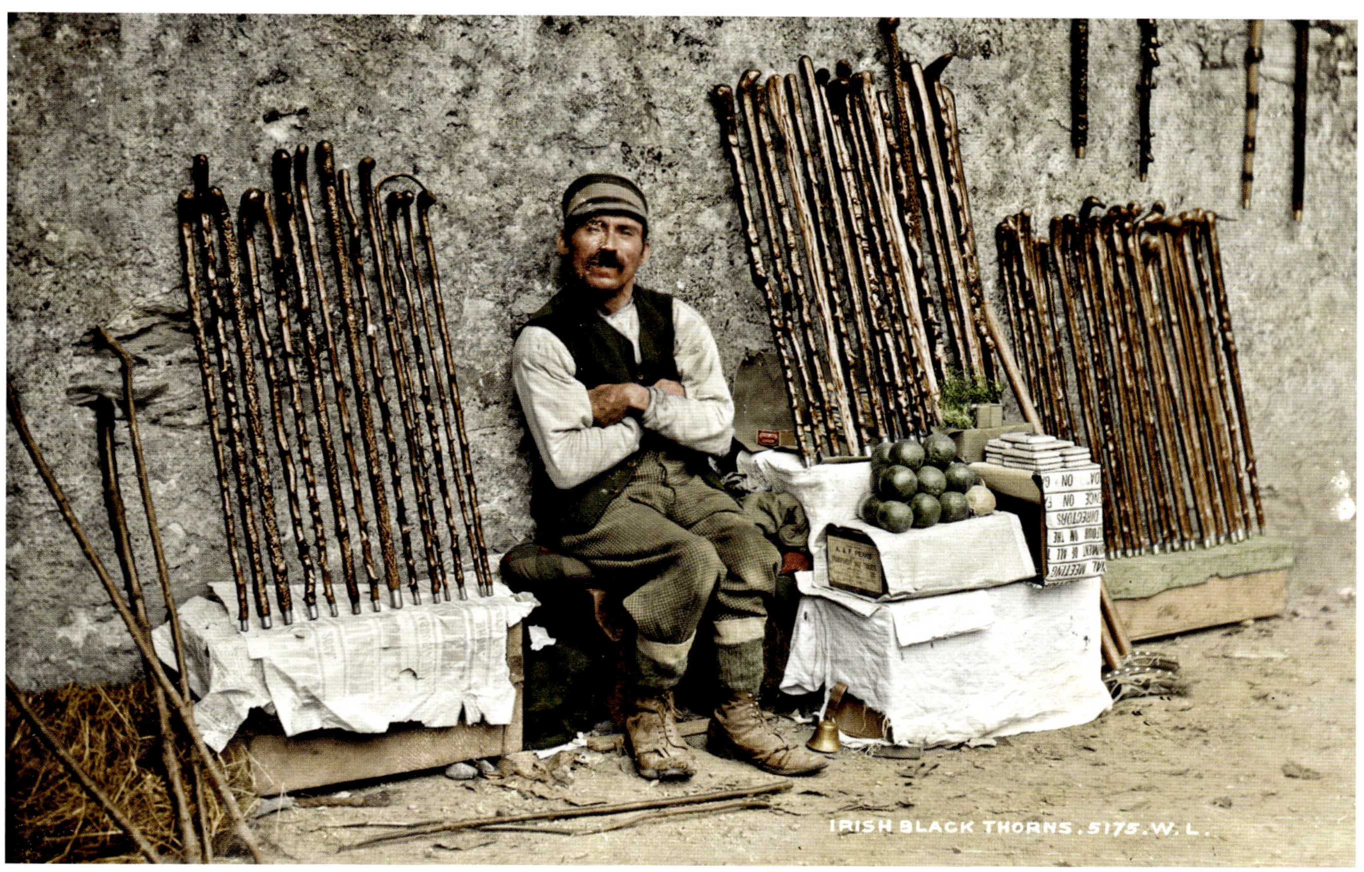

Left: A large gaggle of geese and ducks adds a lively touch to a Dundalk street on market day, reflecting the town's market tradition, which dates back to at least the medieval period, when its fairs and markets were central to the local agricultural economy.

Top right: Late nineteenth-century Irish fairs and markets bustled with activity, attracting traders and sellers of all kinds, covering the essential business of trading livestock or farm produce to the sale of more humble wares, like those of this patient blackthorn stick seller.

The making of blackthorn sticks in Ireland is a traditional craft that involves carefully selecting and seasoning dense blackthorn wood, often for years, before skilfully shaping it into durable walking sticks.

Puck Fair is among Ireland's oldest
and most distinctive festivals, taking
place every August in Killorglin, County
Kerry. Records show that King James
I granted it official recognition in 1613.
However, many believe the tradition
dates back much further, possibly to
pre-Christian times and the Celtic
festival of Lughnasa.

At the heart of the festival is the
crowning of a wild mountain goat as
'King Puck' for the duration of the
fair. A wild goat is captured from the
mountains and brought to the town,
where it is crowned King Puck by the
'Queen of Puck,' a role traditionally
given to a local schoolgirl. A parade
featuring King Puck and the Queen
moves through the town, then the goat
is placed in a cage atop a high platform
in the town square, as seen here. Over
the following days there is a horse fair,
festivities and entertainment.

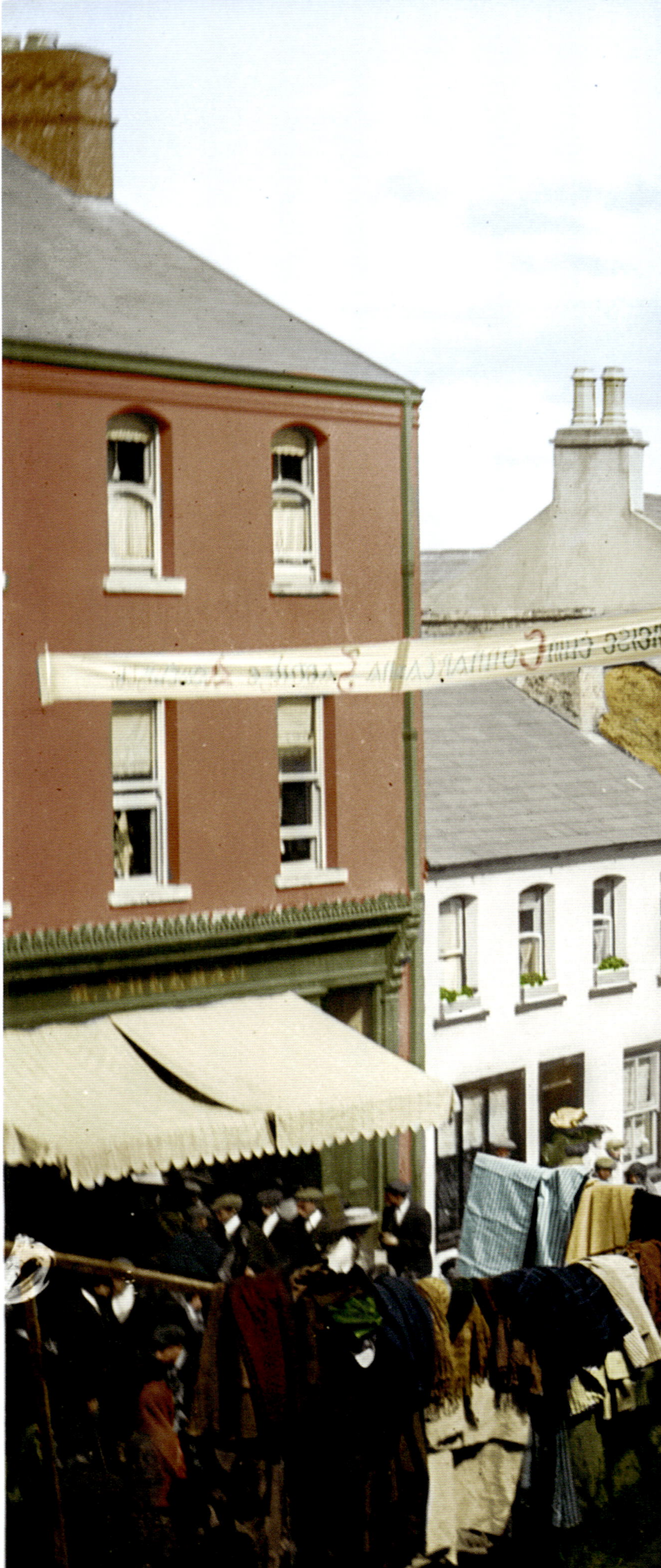

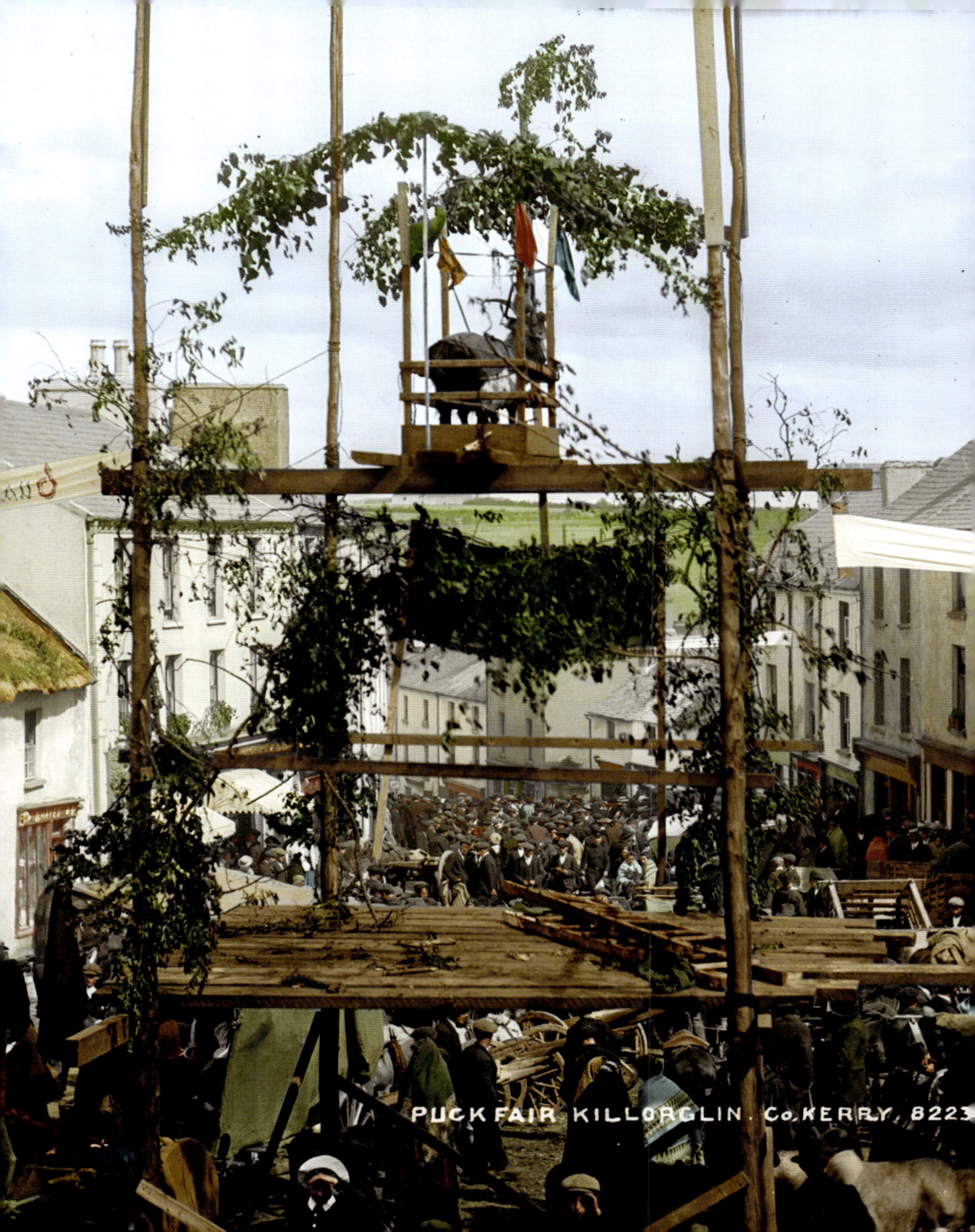

PUCK FAIR. KILLORGLIN. Co. KERRY. 8223.

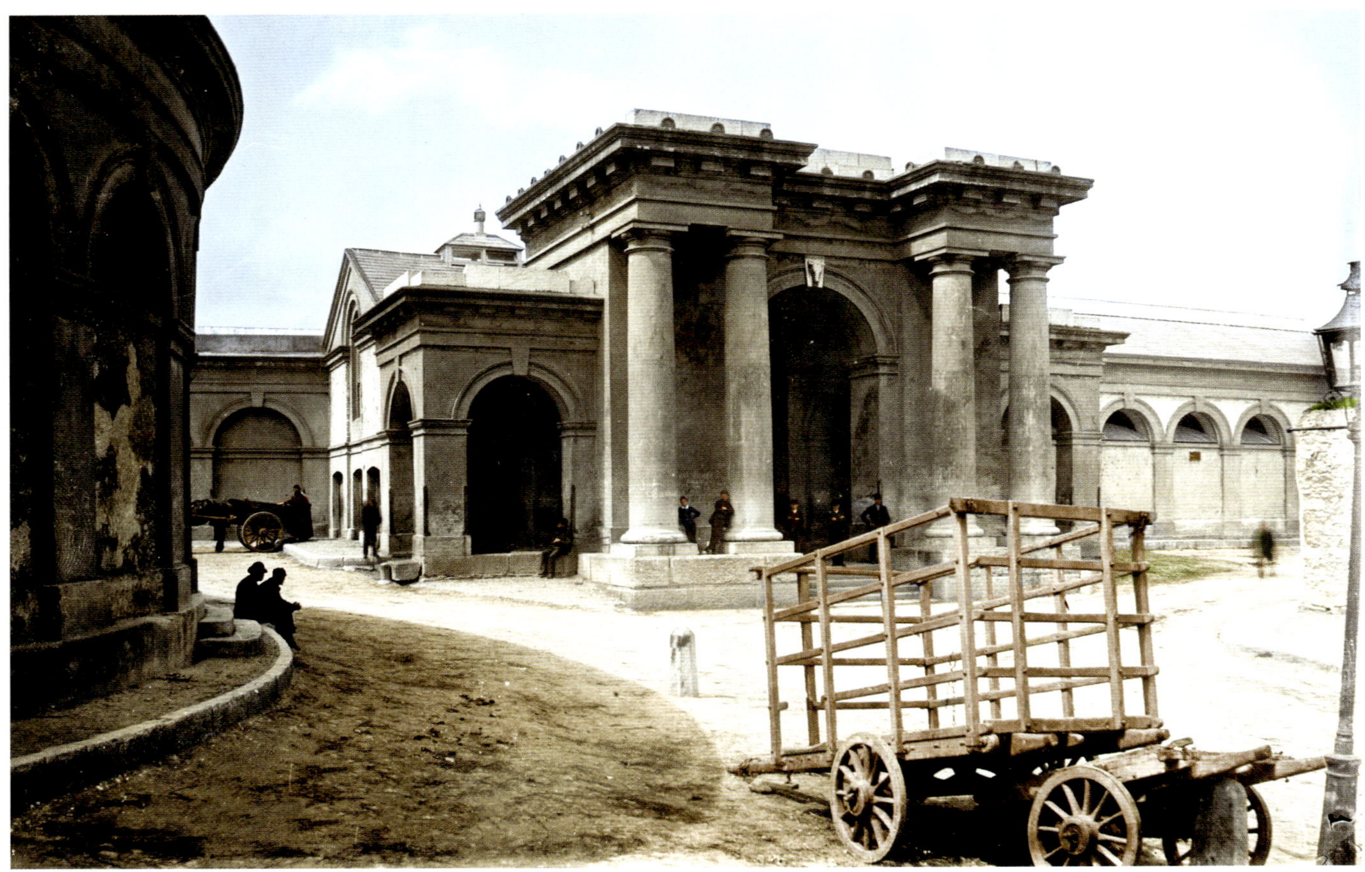

The Cork Butter Market, established in 1770 near Shandon, was once the world's largest butter market and global price setter. This historic institution capitalised on Cork's extensive dairy farming hinterland.

Farmers from across Munster transported their butter to the market. The journey was often arduous, with farmers travelling long distances along what were called 'butter roads'. The butter supply extended to West Cork and Kerry, where farmers would make the long journey to Cork, often travelling through the night to reach the market by its 6 a.m. opening.

The market's Committee of Merchants, formed in 1769, played a crucial role in regulating trade and setting butter prices – not just in Ireland, but around the world. Their rigorous quality control system, which graded butter into five categories, contributed significantly to Cork butter's global reputation.

Cork butter was exported worldwide, with the port of Cork controlling two-thirds of Irish butter exports to the continent and 80 per cent to America by 1774. The British navy and army were major customers for Cork's butter exports, along with various British colonies. At its peak in the late 1870s, the market traded 400,000 firkins annually, supplied by 70,000 to 80,000 farmers.

However, the market's dominance began to decline in the mid-nineteenth century. Increased competition from continental Europe and new technologies like the cream separator eroded Cork's position. Despite attempts to adapt, including switching from firkins to butter boxes, the Cork Butter Market eventually ceased trading in 1924.

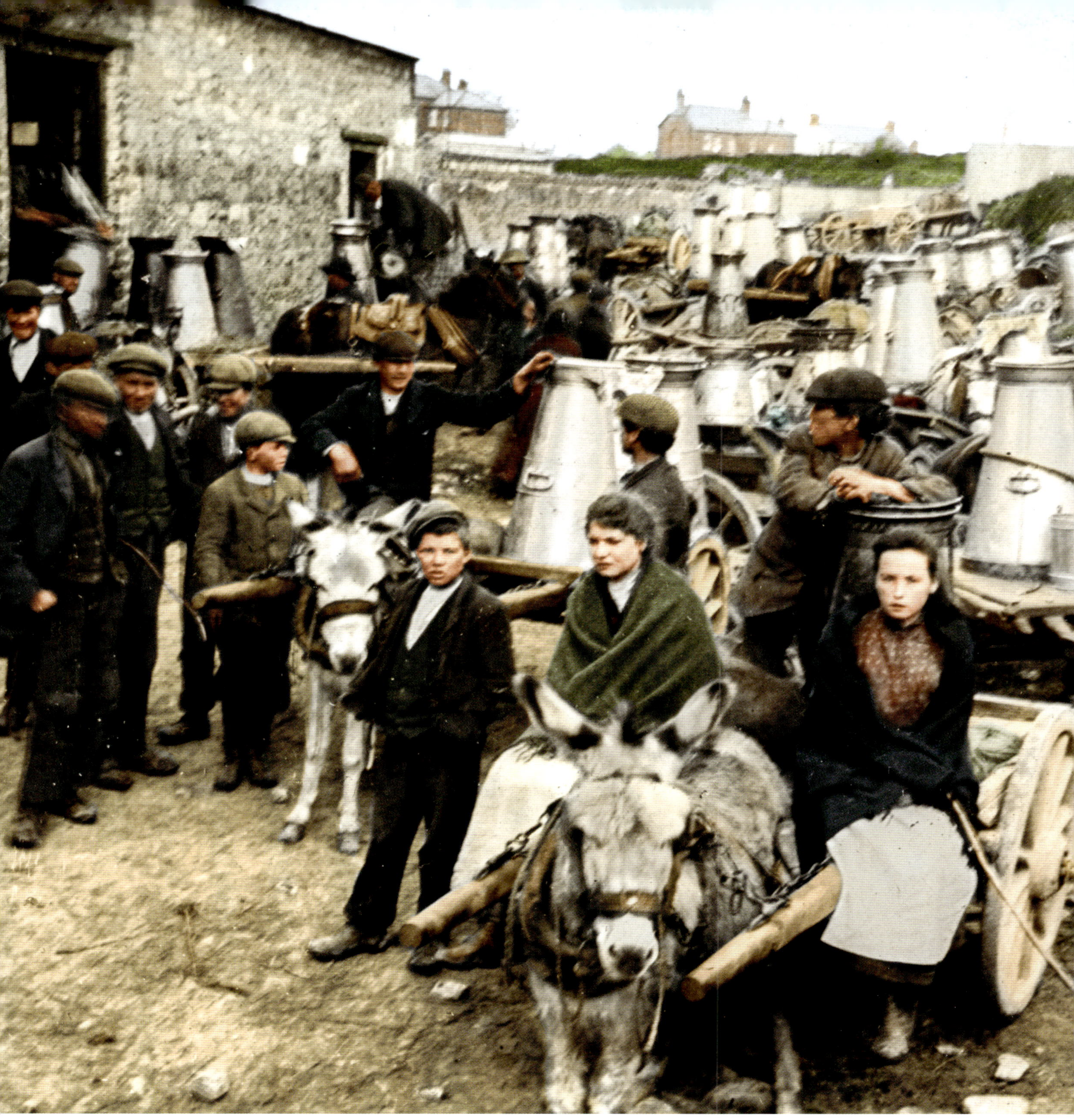

A busy scene – bringing churns of fresh milk to a creamery in County Limerick during the early 1900s. The eastern part of the county is part of the famed Golden Vale. Renowned for its rich, lush pastures, this region was and is a hub of dairy production. The butter made here may well have found its way to the Cork Butter Market.

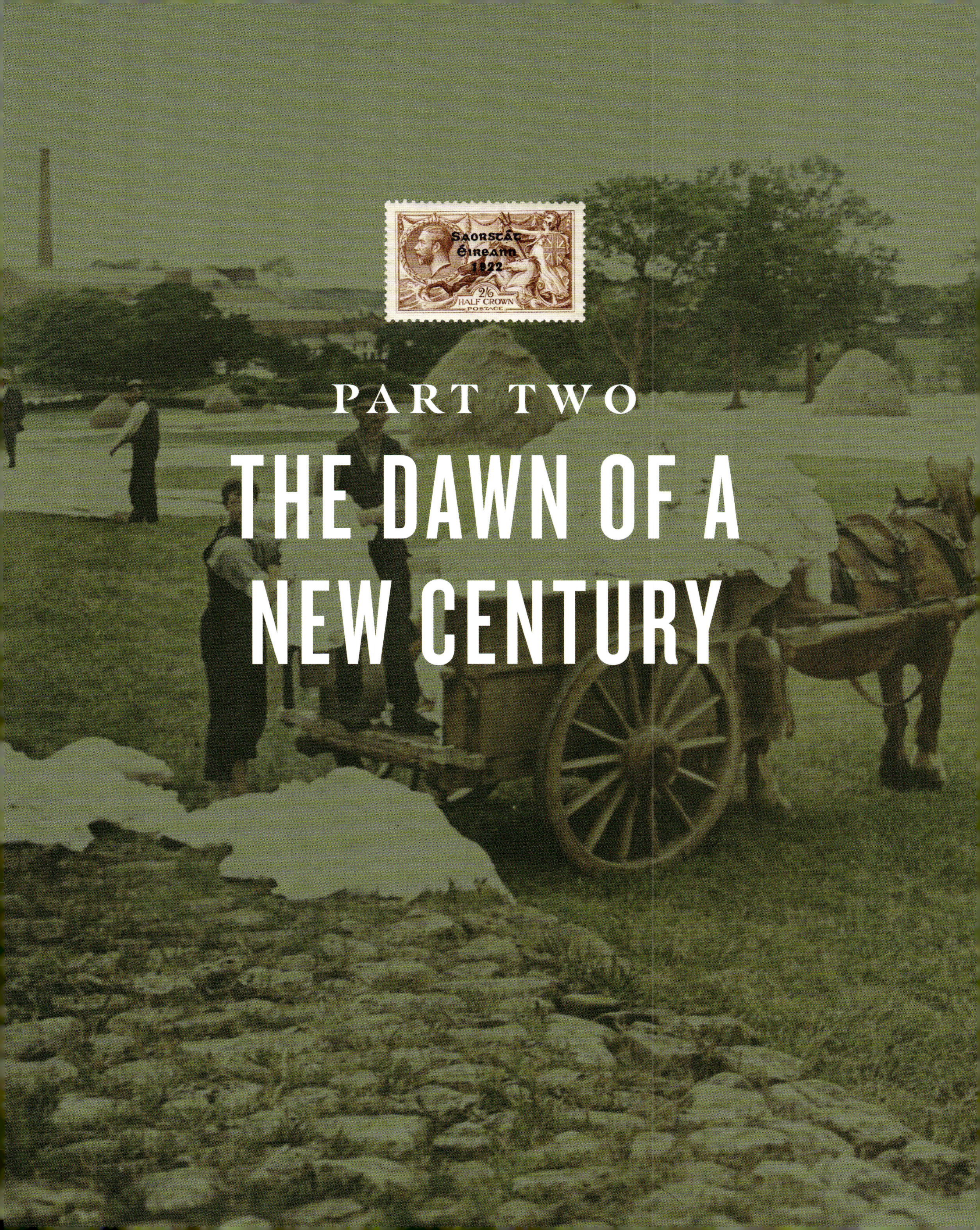

THE DAWN OF A NEW CENTURY

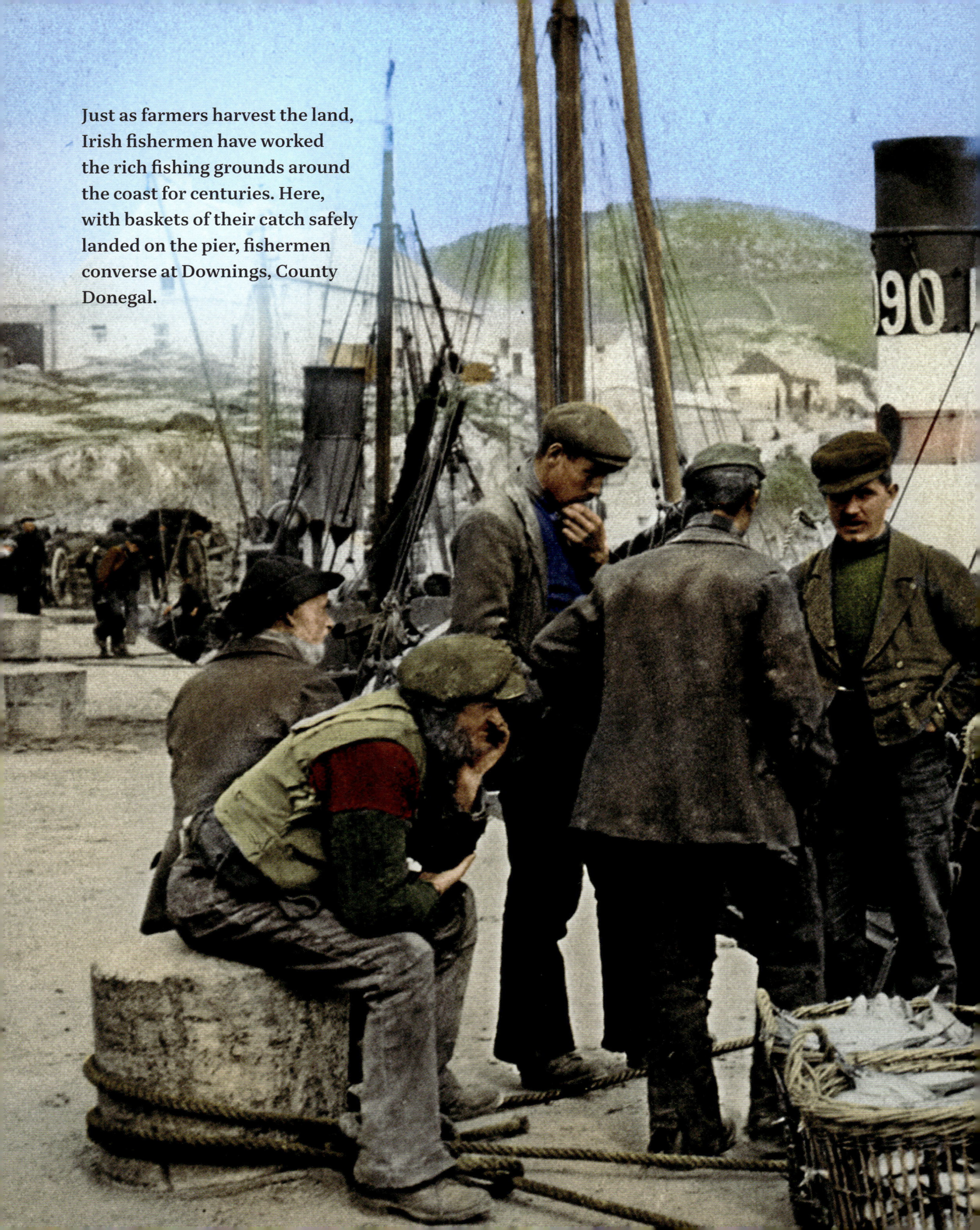

Just as farmers harvest the land, Irish fishermen have worked the rich fishing grounds around the coast for centuries. Here, with baskets of their catch safely landed on the pier, fishermen converse at Downings, County Donegal.

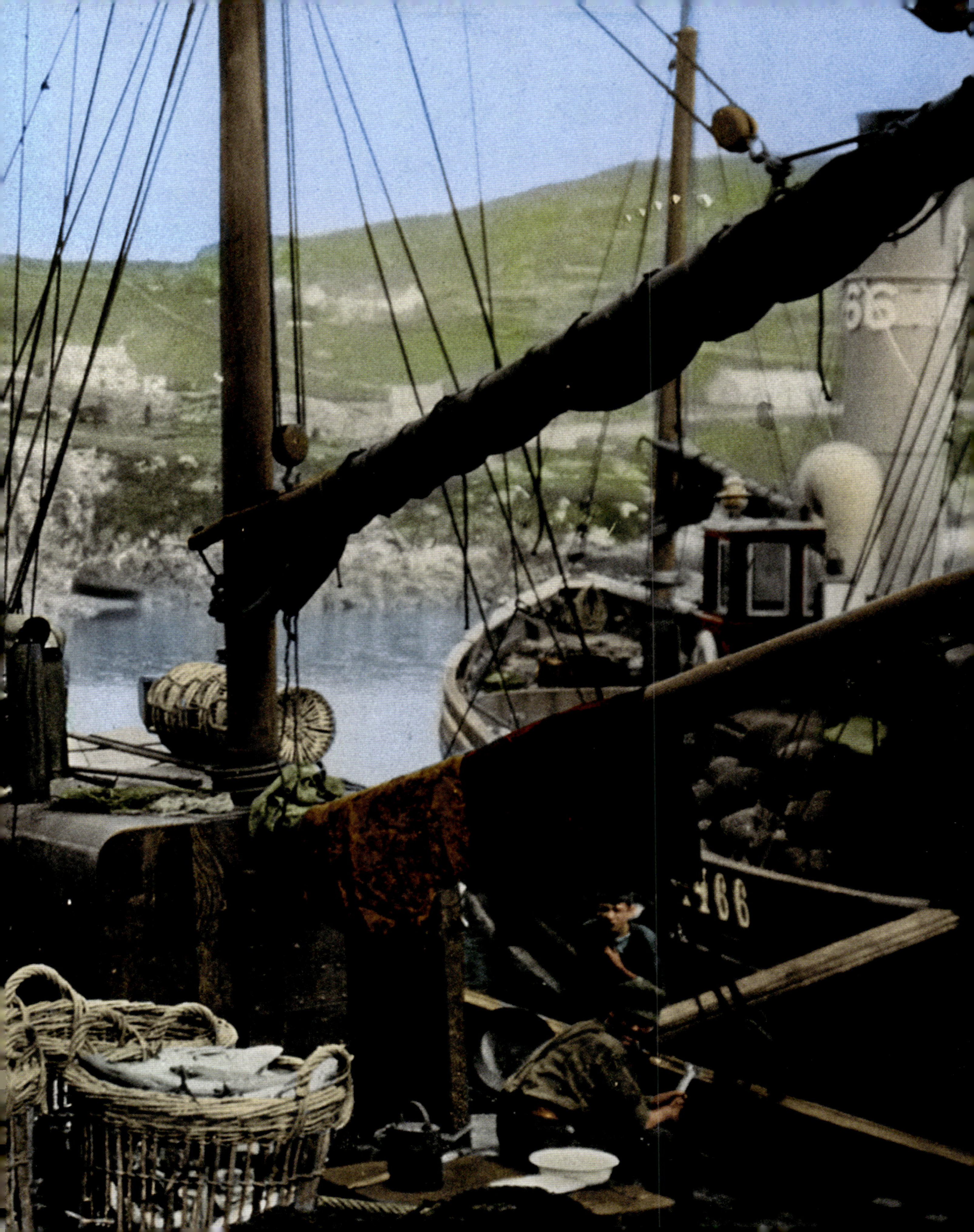

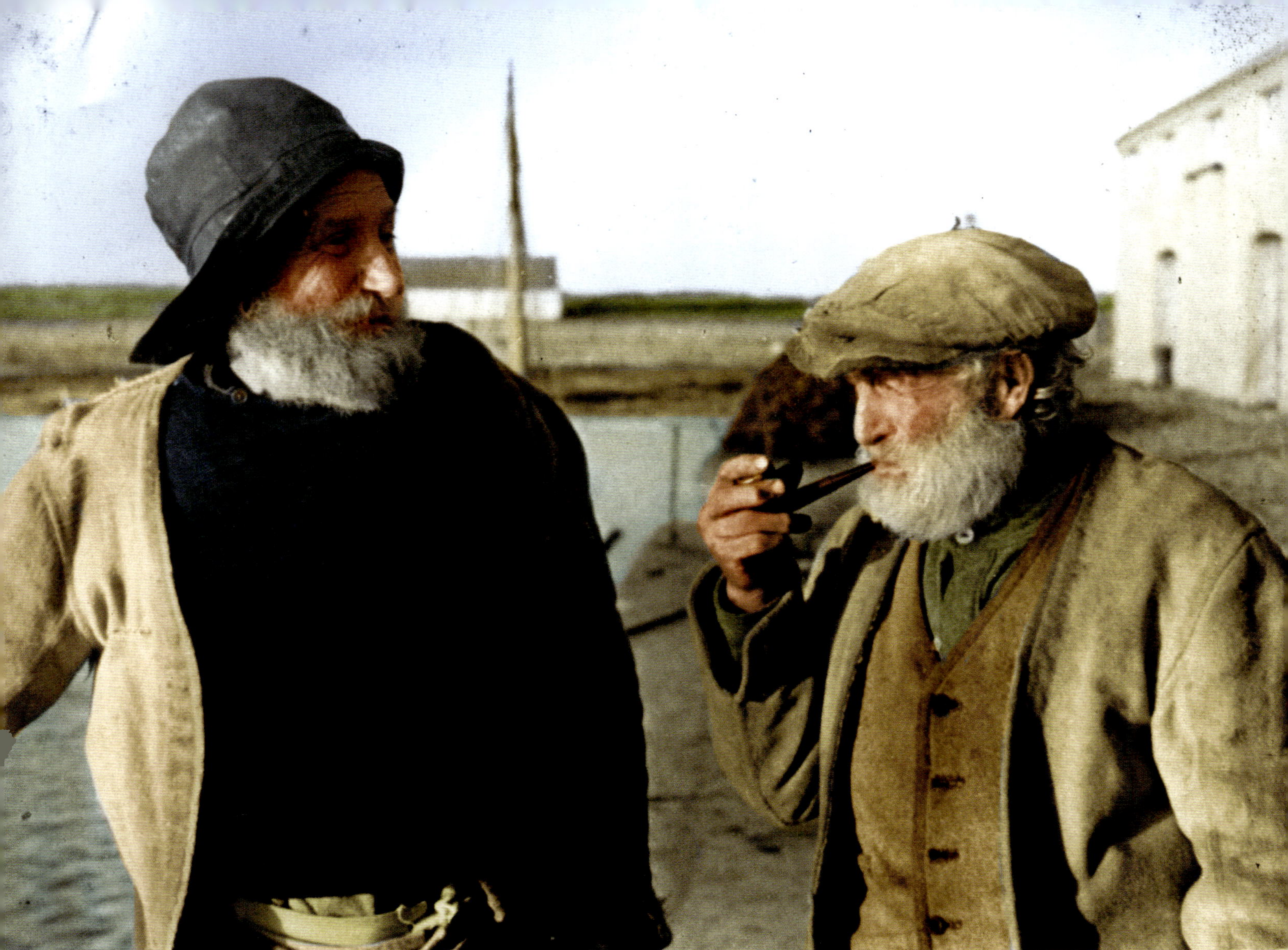

Two turf boat men seen on the Aran Islands, their faces etched with the marks of a life shaped by the sea and the Atlantic waves. They are a testament to the resilience and resourcefulness of life on these rugged, windswept islands.

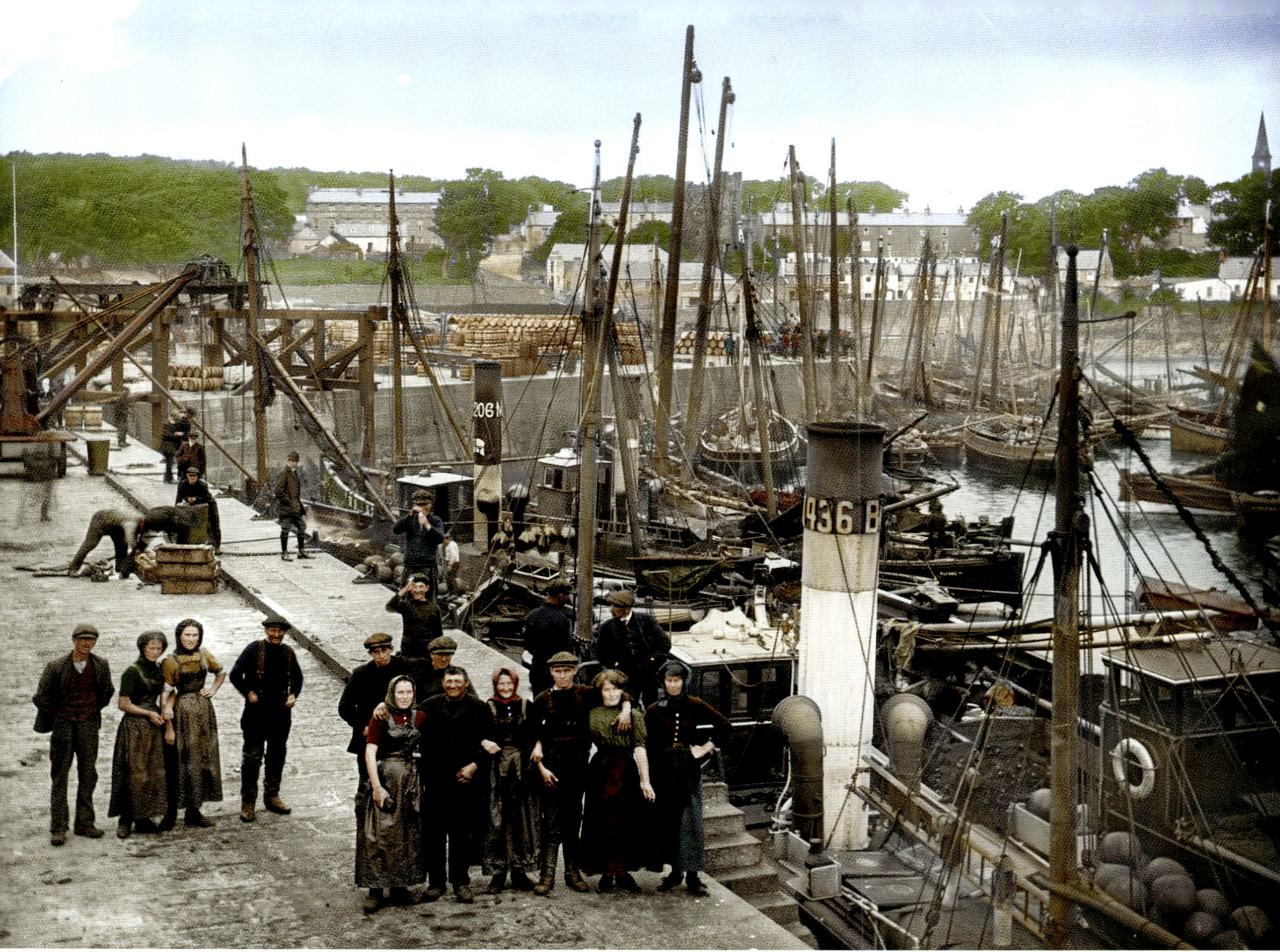

The bustling scene at Ardglass Harbour, County Down at the beginning of the twentieth century, where herring was king. In the foreground, fishermen and women in aprons engaged in fish processing pose for the camera. Moored alongside the pier are several fishing vessels, including three steam-powered trawlers with long funnels, accompanied by numerous smaller fishing craft. The small crane on the pier indicates a capacity for handling larger catches, as well as the heavy barrels.

The abundance of barrels in the background highlights the thriving herring-processing industry here. This labour-intensive work was primarily carried out by women from Scotland, known as 'Scots lasses', who travelled with the fishing fleet, as well as workers from Donegal. Working in crews of three – two gutters and one packer – these skilled women processed the herring using the 'Scotch cure' method. This involved gutting the fish, packing them in layers with salt in barrels and allowing them to cure for up to ten days. The barrels, made to strict specifications, were a crucial part of the industry, each holding a specific quantity of herring called a 'cran'.

Harvesting the bounty of the sea – and then salting it. This photograph, taken at the end of the nineteenth century, captures the thriving fish-curing industry on Clare Island, at the entrance to Clew Bay, County Mayo.

In the foreground, workers (mainly women) can be seen packing barrels with cured fish on the beach, while numerous filled barrels are stacked around the harbour area. Looming above the array of barrels is the imposing tower house known as Granuaile's Castle, once one of the strongholds of the O'Malley family and associated with the legendary pirate queen Grace O'Malley. All of this is observed by a delegation of tourists dressed in all their travelling finery.

This scene illustrates the economic importance of fishing to Clare Island at the turn of the twentieth century, which was encouraged by the Congested Districts Board (CDB), established in 1891. The CDB's mandate did not cover relatively developed areas, including ports such as Ardglass on the east coast. Its area of operations included land and agricultural reforms together with developing the fishing industry along Ireland's western coast, constructing harbours and piers to support fishermen. The CDB also provided instruction in fishing techniques and processing, as well as supplying many fishing boats.

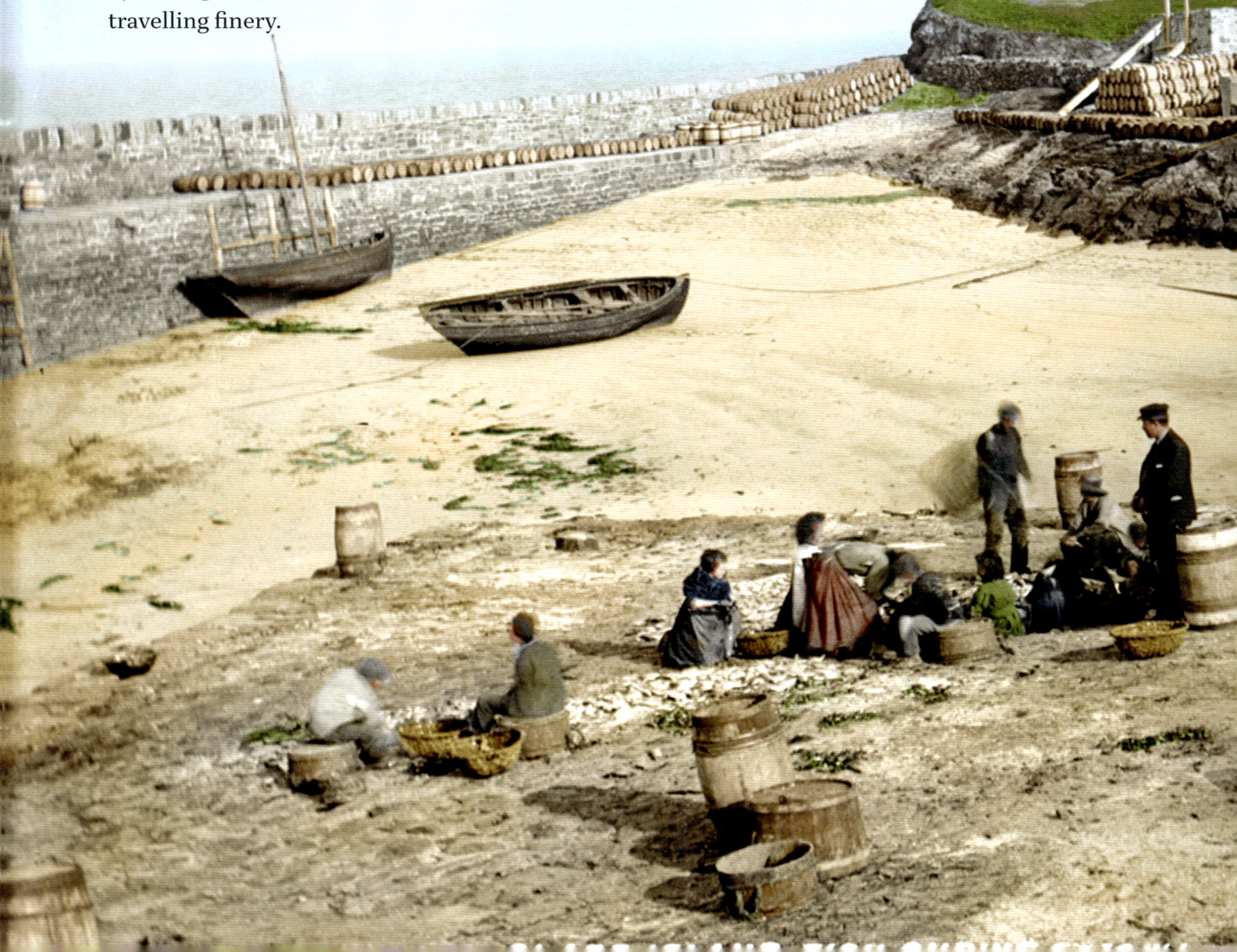

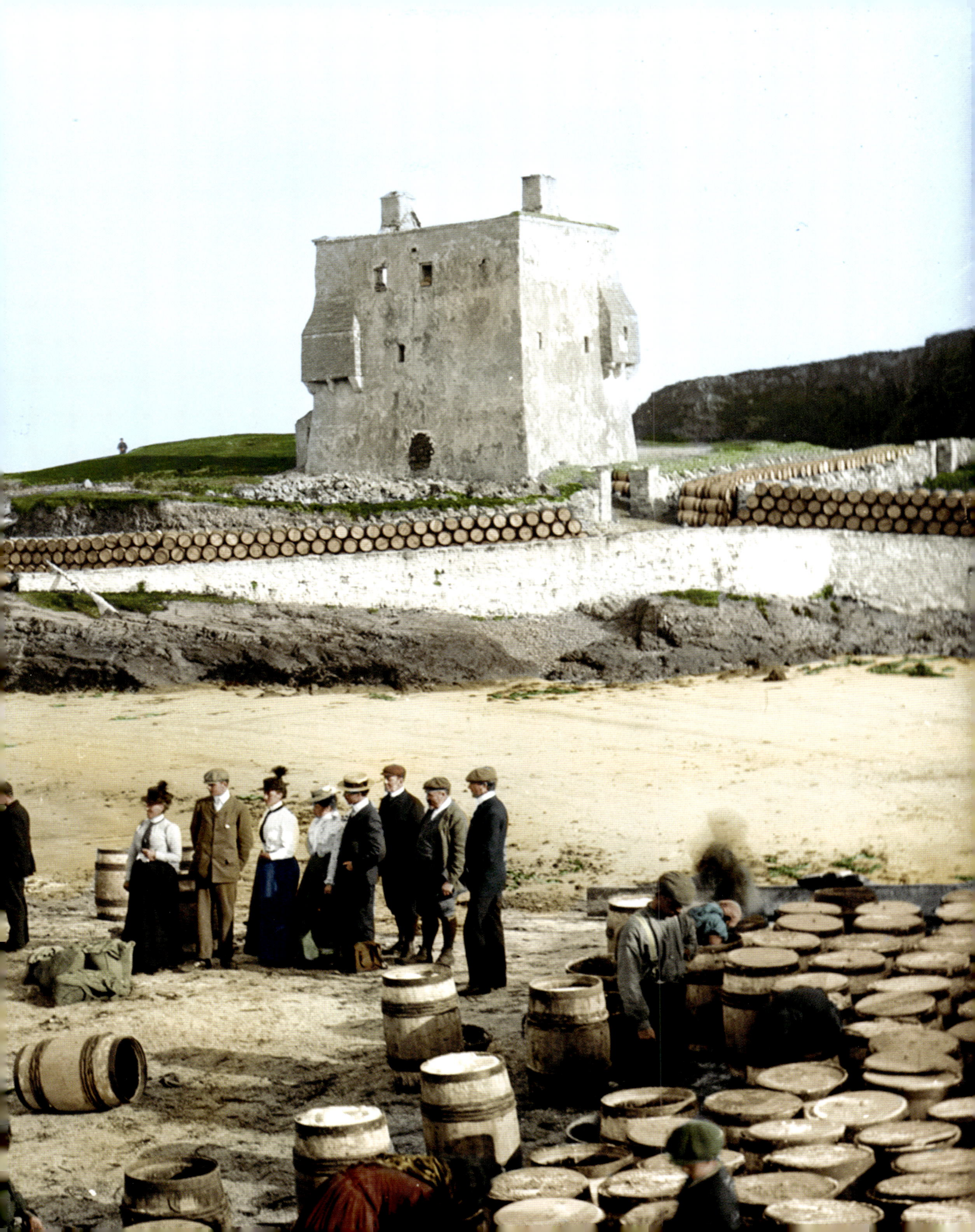

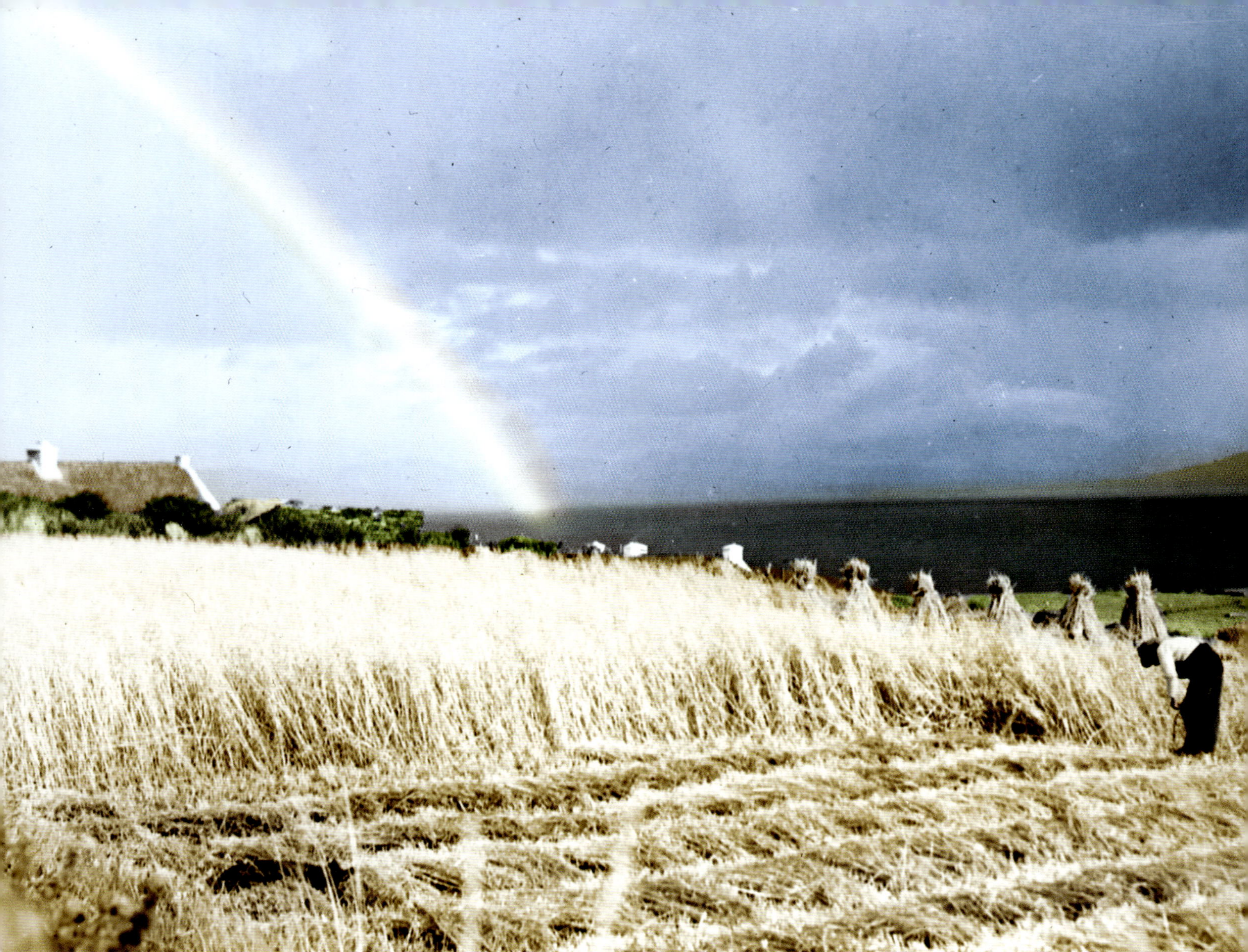

Man was also able to harvest the bounty of the land on Clare Island, as attested to by this harvest scene, with a rainbow and the majestic mountains of the Mayo mainland just visible in the distance. The photograph is part of a series by the photographer Thomas H. Mason (1877–1958) attributed as being from the island, now held in the National Library of Ireland.

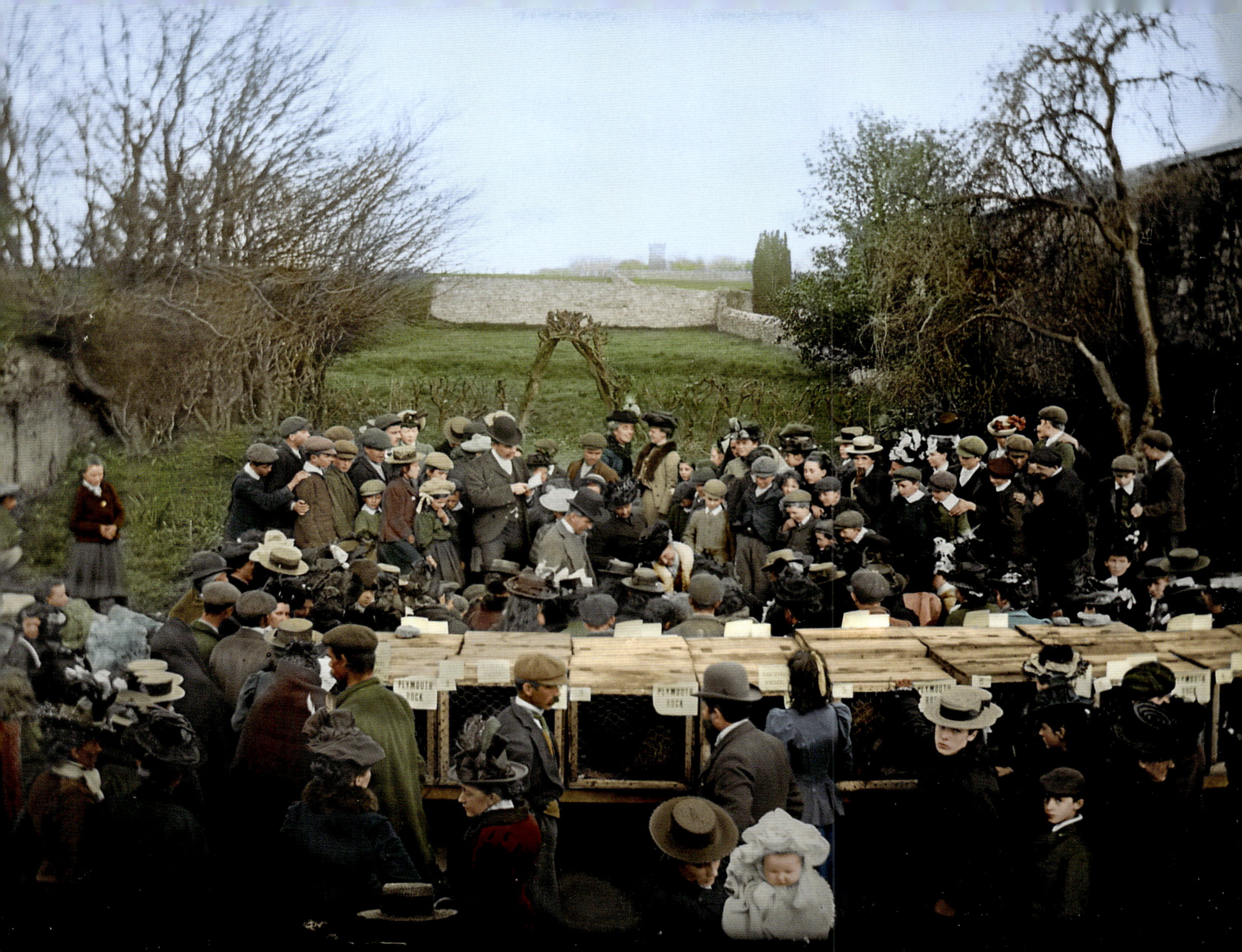

Crowds gather around poultry cages at the show of the grandly named
Clonbrock and Castlegar Co-operative Poultry Society – a photograph
courtesy of the Dillon amateur photographers mentioned on page 45.
Poultry farming was gaining in prominence – by 1902, Ireland boasted
nearly 19 million hens, with poultry societies like this one playing
a crucial role in improving breeds and practices. Women managed
much of this burgeoning industry, contributing up to a quarter of total
family income through egg and poultry sales.

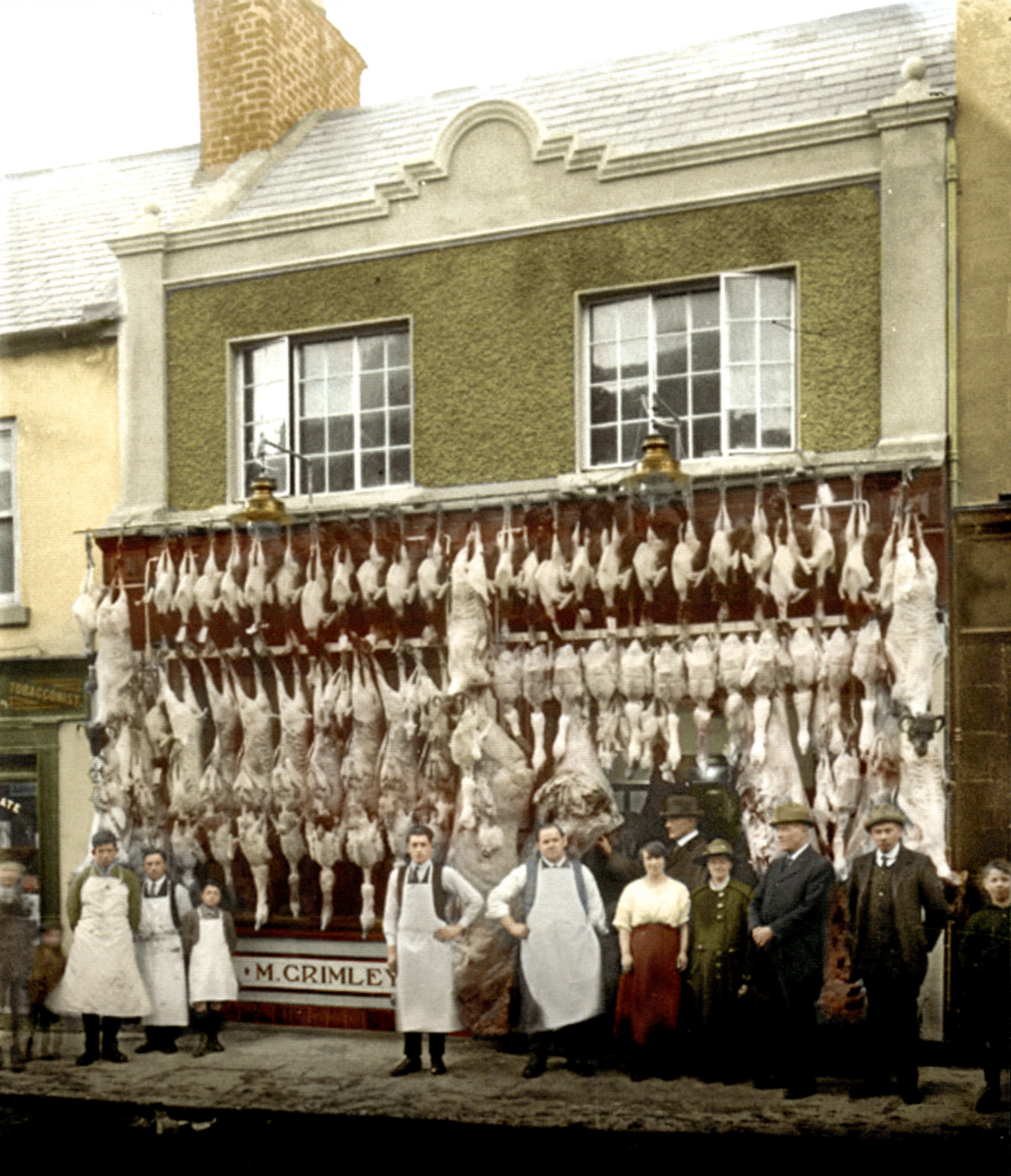
TOBACCONIST
M. CRIMLEY

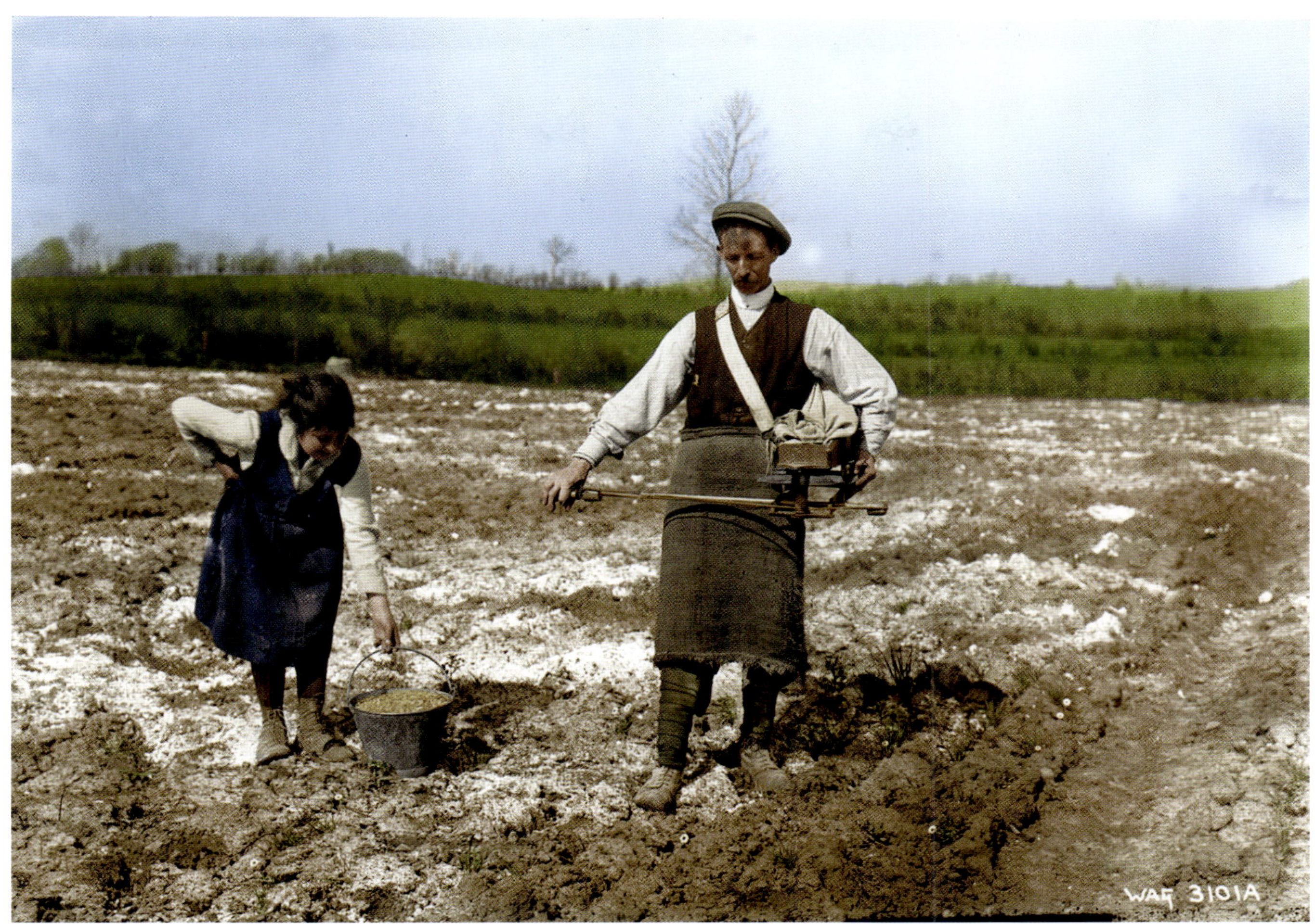

Left: The family and employees of M. Grimley, Butchers, pose outside their shop in Armagh. The popularity of turkey as a Christmas dinner option had been growing since the 1850s, gradually replacing goose. Typically raised free-range on small farms, the turkeys on prominent display highlight the bird's place as by now the festive meat of choice.

Top right: A man, aided by his young assistant with a bucket of grain seed, operates a 'fiddle sower'. This was a broadcast seeder, named for the fiddle-like motion used to scatter the seed. It featured a canvas seed bag within a small wooden frame and a rotating finned disc. As the farmer walked the field, pulling a leather-thronged bow back and forth, the disc spun, casting the seed in a broad, even arc.

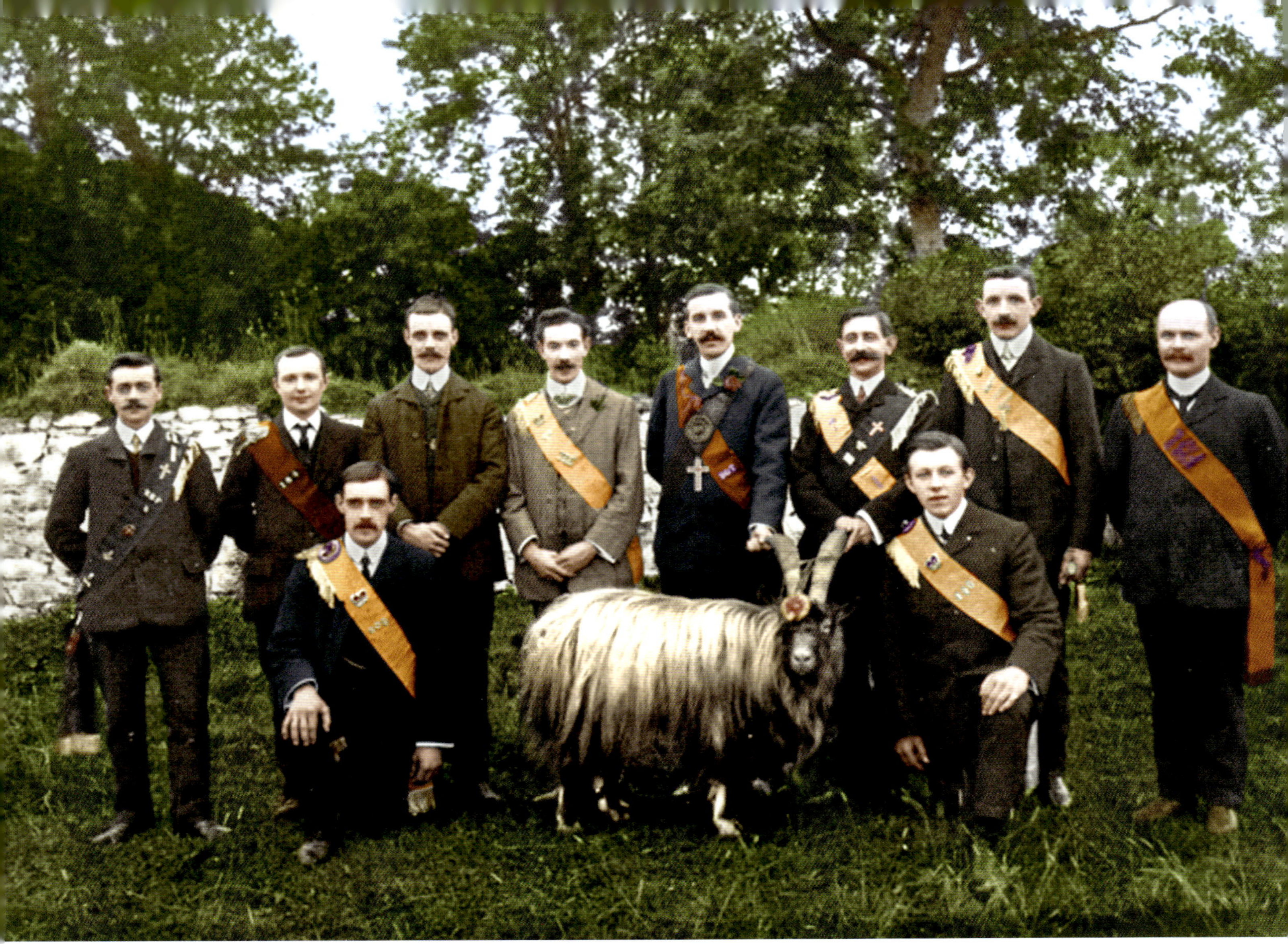

A rural scene: Orange Order members in their traditional sashes pose alongside a magnificently horned male goat adorned with a rosette. Founded in 1795, the Orange Order initially drew significant membership from Protestant farmers and rural communities. In 1880, during the Land War, Orangemen provided labour to harvest the crops of Captain Boycott, opposing the Irish Land League's campaign for tenants' rights.

However, there were instances of co-operation, albeit short-lived. In 1881, the Land League held a meeting in the local Orange hall at Loughgall, County Armagh, where Michael Davitt addressed both Catholic and Protestant farmers. This prompted the Grand Orange Lodge of Ireland to issue a manifesto claiming the Land League threatened property rights, Protestantism and the British constitution.

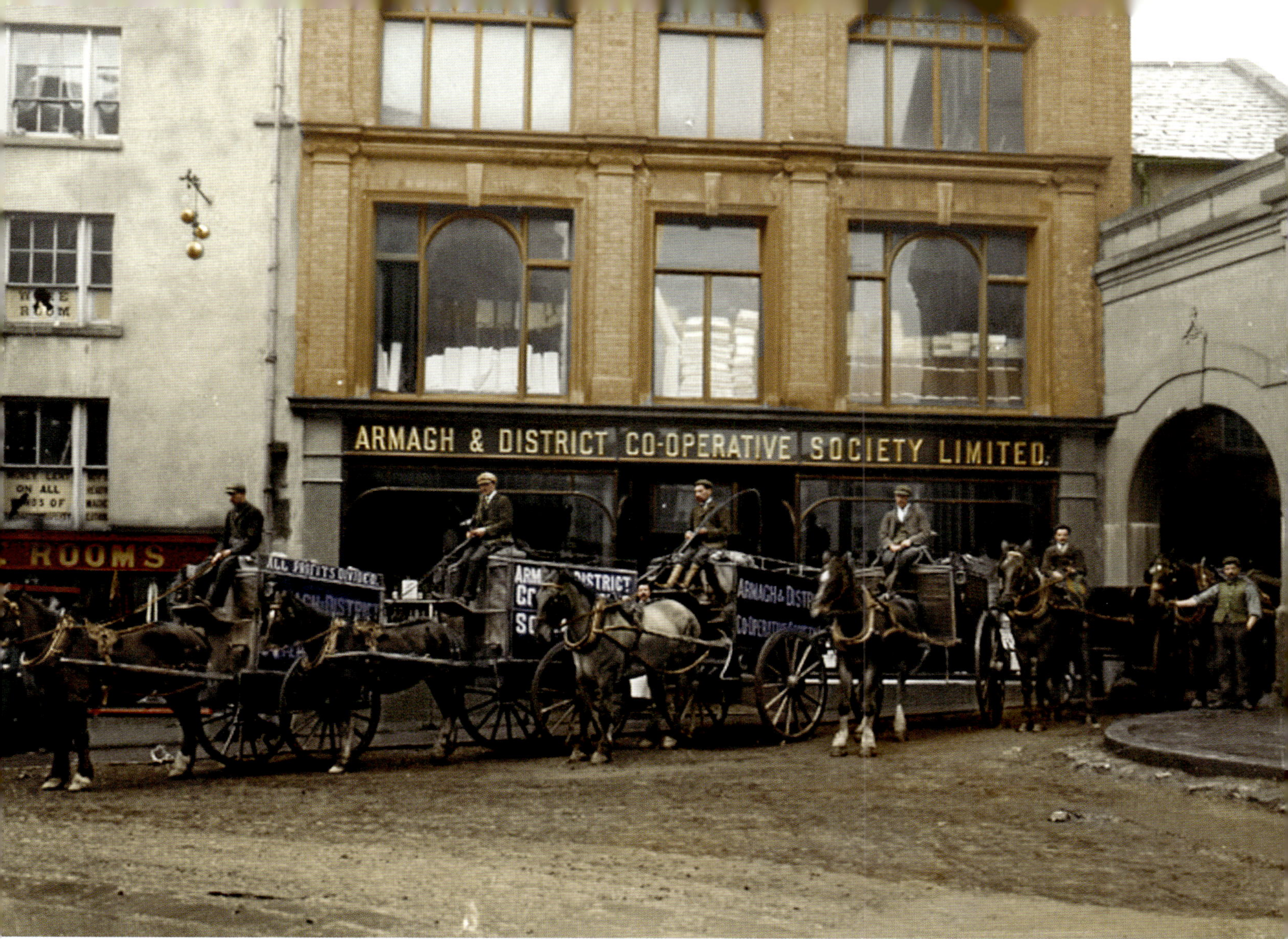

'All profits divided' runs the egalitarian slogan on one of the carts lined up outside the Armagh and District Co-operative Society premises. At the beginning of the twentieth century, the Irish co-operative movement had gained significant momentum, championed by Horace Plunkett and driven by local farmers and reformers – by 1910, there were well over 500. These co-operative creameries, agricultural stores and credit societies, spread across the country, helped modernise agriculture, create jobs, curb emigration and strengthen farmers' economic independence.

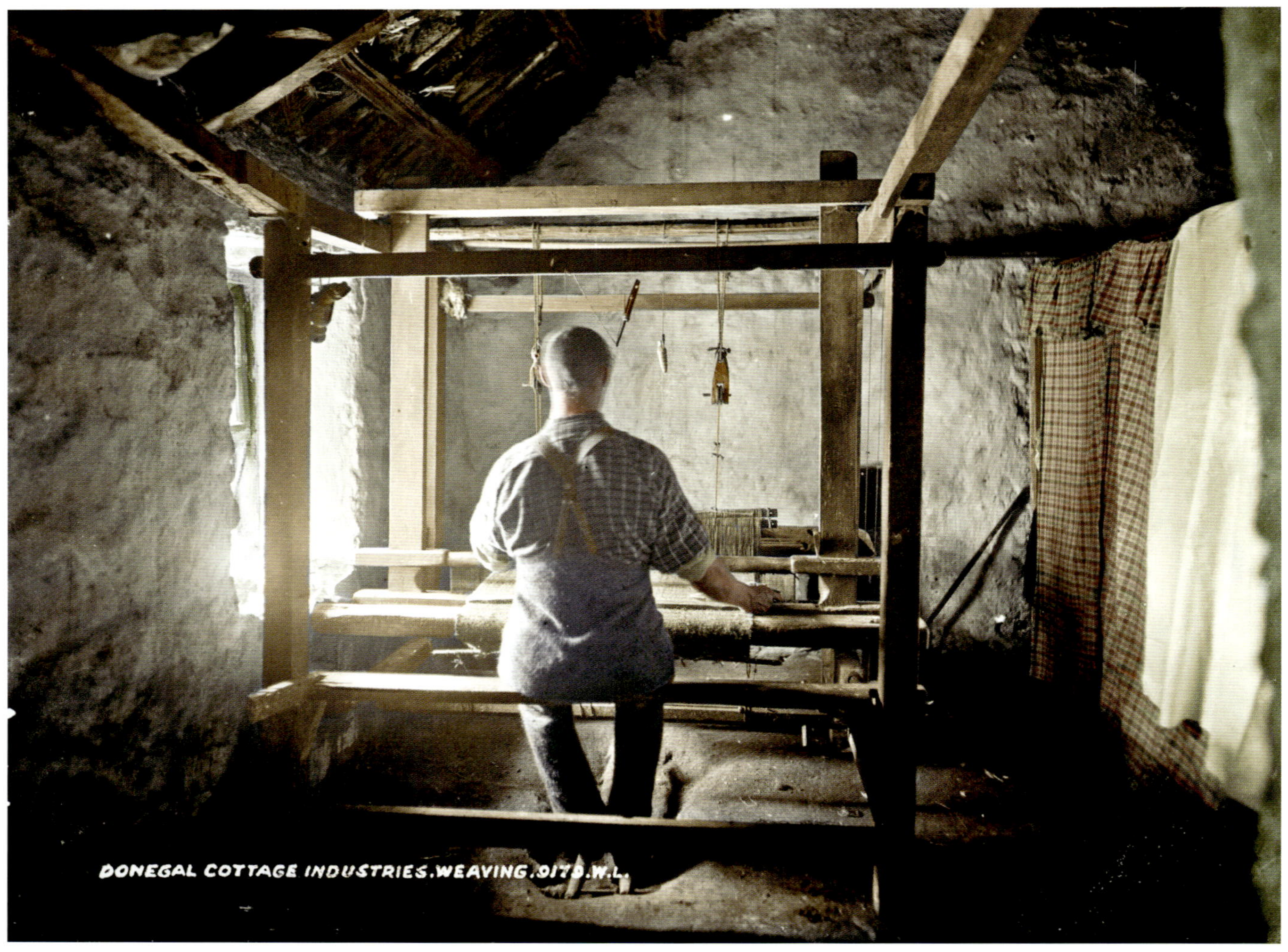

Top left: A Donegal weaver at work, part of a cottage industry initiative. Much like the co-operative societies, these endeavours were rooted in community effort and the concept of shared prosperity. At the end of the nineteenth century, the Congested Districts Board established lace schools in towns across County Donegal, promoting traditional crafts such as Donegal tweed, which grew to earn an international reputation.

Right: A bleaching field at Lisburn, with a linen mill in the background. Here, the fibres were spread out in the open to bleach. Kept damp and exposed to sunlight and air, the material gradually whitened – a process that could take weeks in Ireland's limited sunlight.

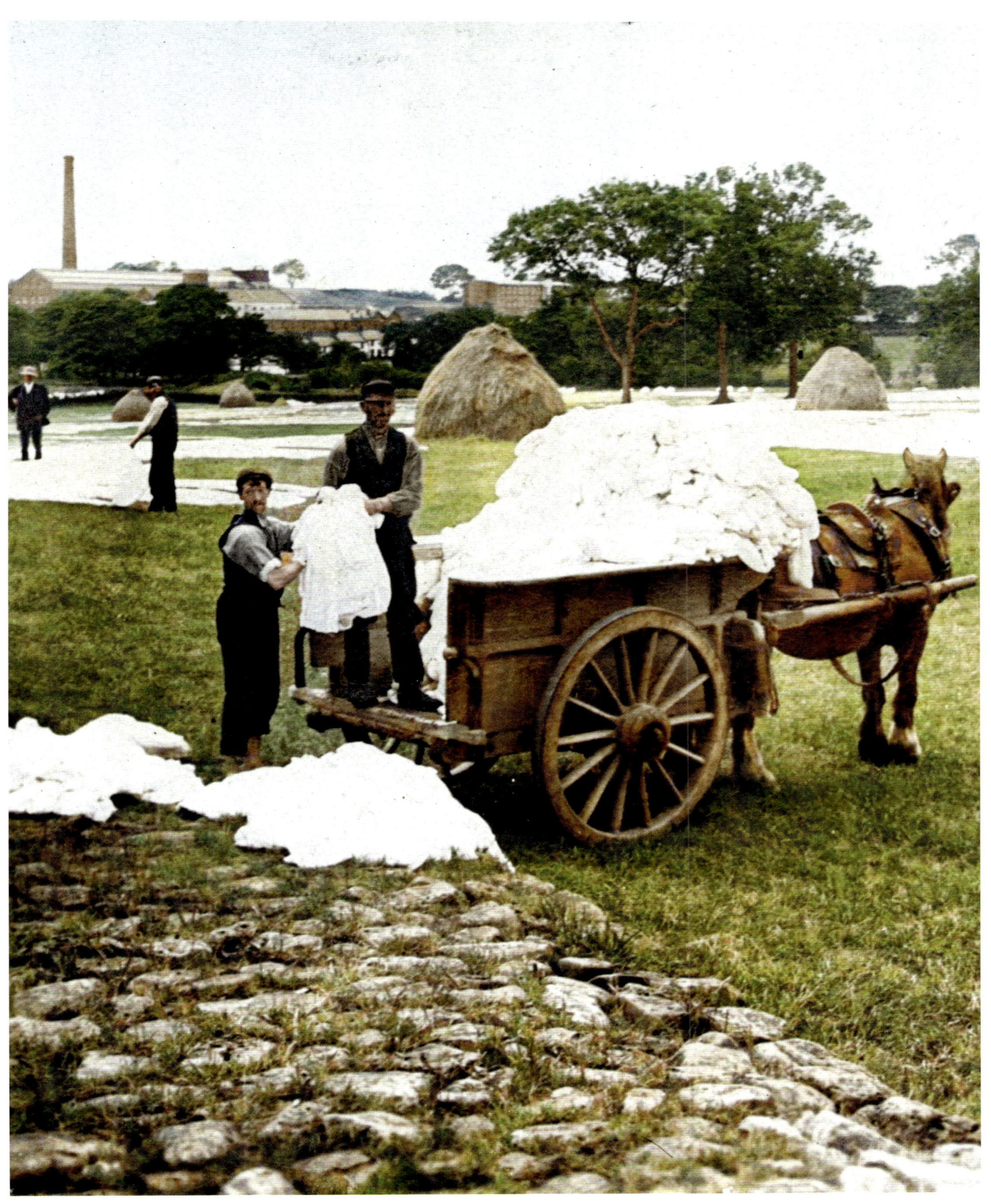

The massed machines at Ewart's Linen Works in Belfast. While flax was cultivated throughout Ireland, Belfast and its surrounding areas in the north-east rose to prominence as the centre of linen production in the nineteenth century. This industrial boom spurred Belfast's growth, enabling it to surpass Dublin in population by 1891. Belfast earned the nickname 'Linenopolis' and the industry's success was so remarkable that by 1915, the north-east of Ireland had become the largest linen-producing region globally, employing over 75,000 people and solidifying the reputation of Irish linen for excellence.

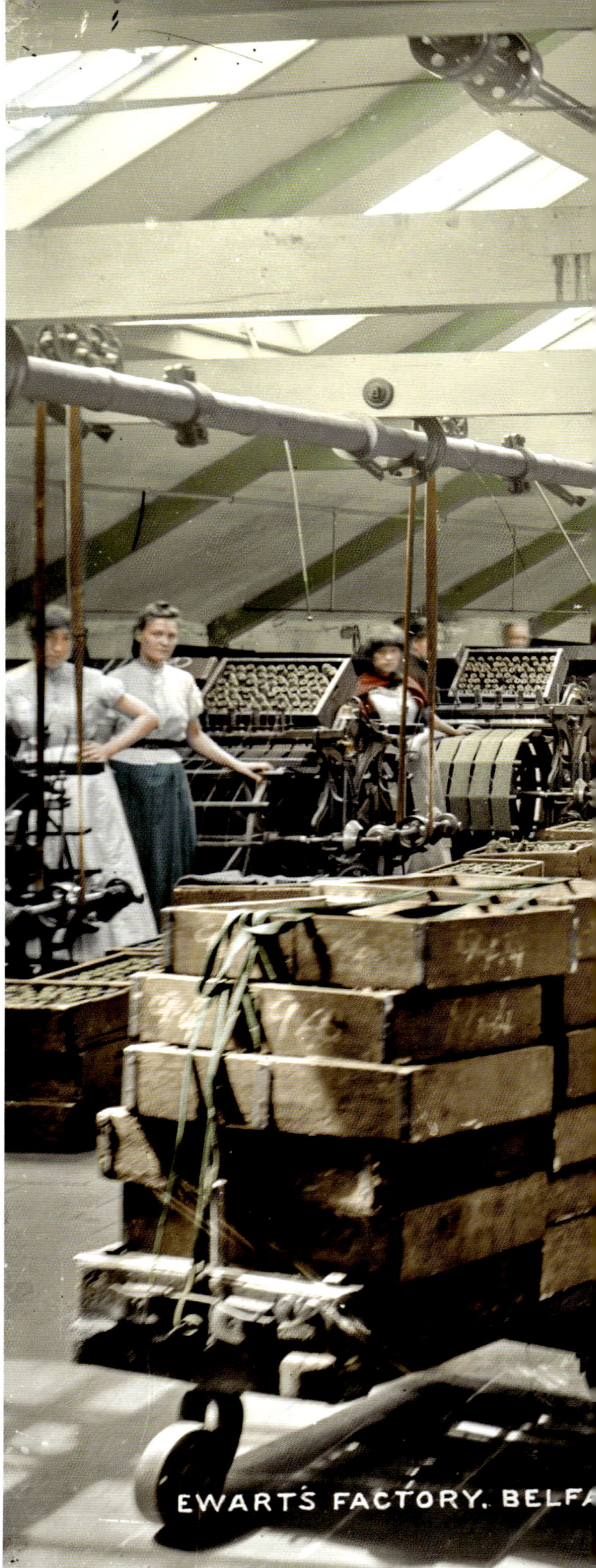

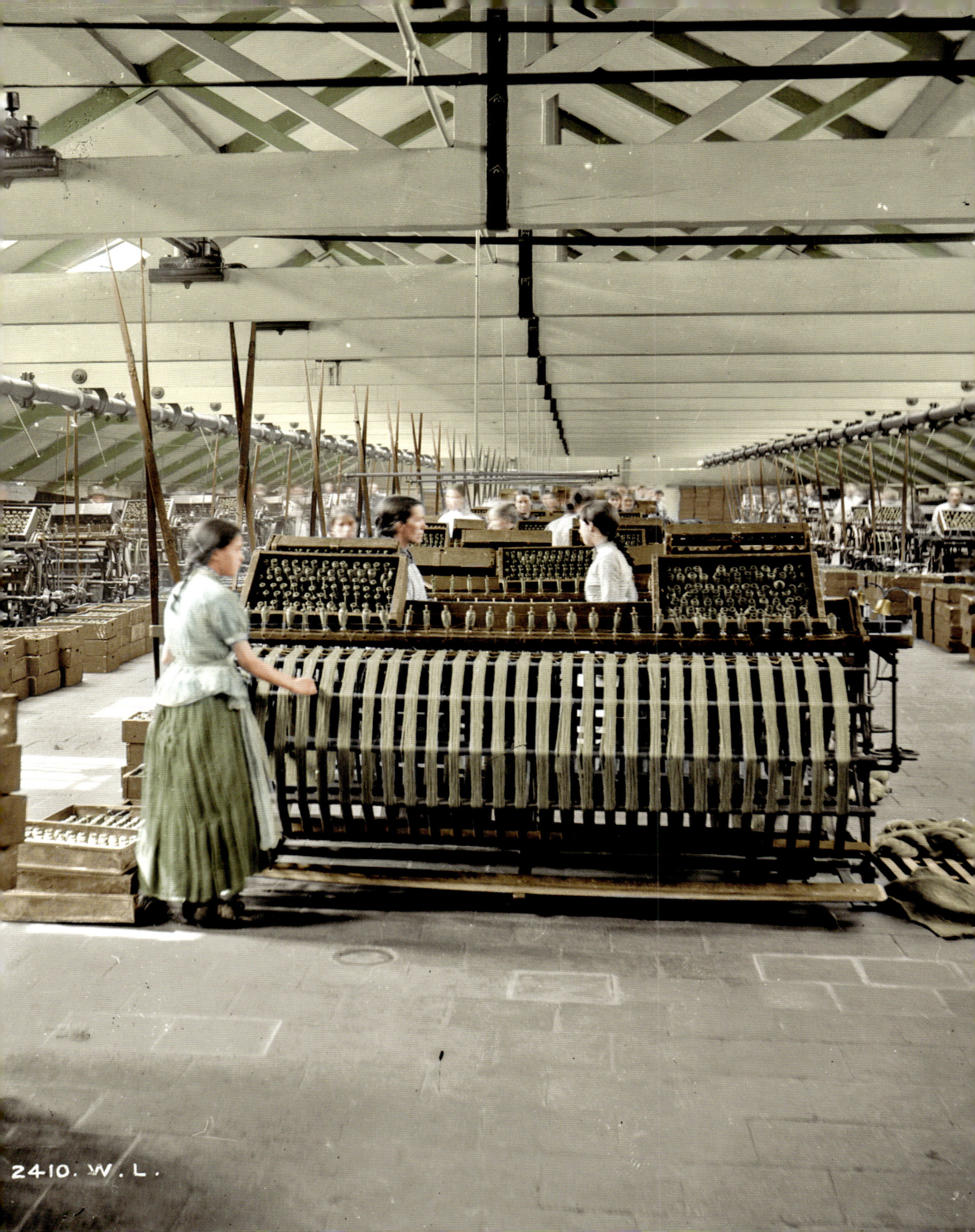

2410. W. L.

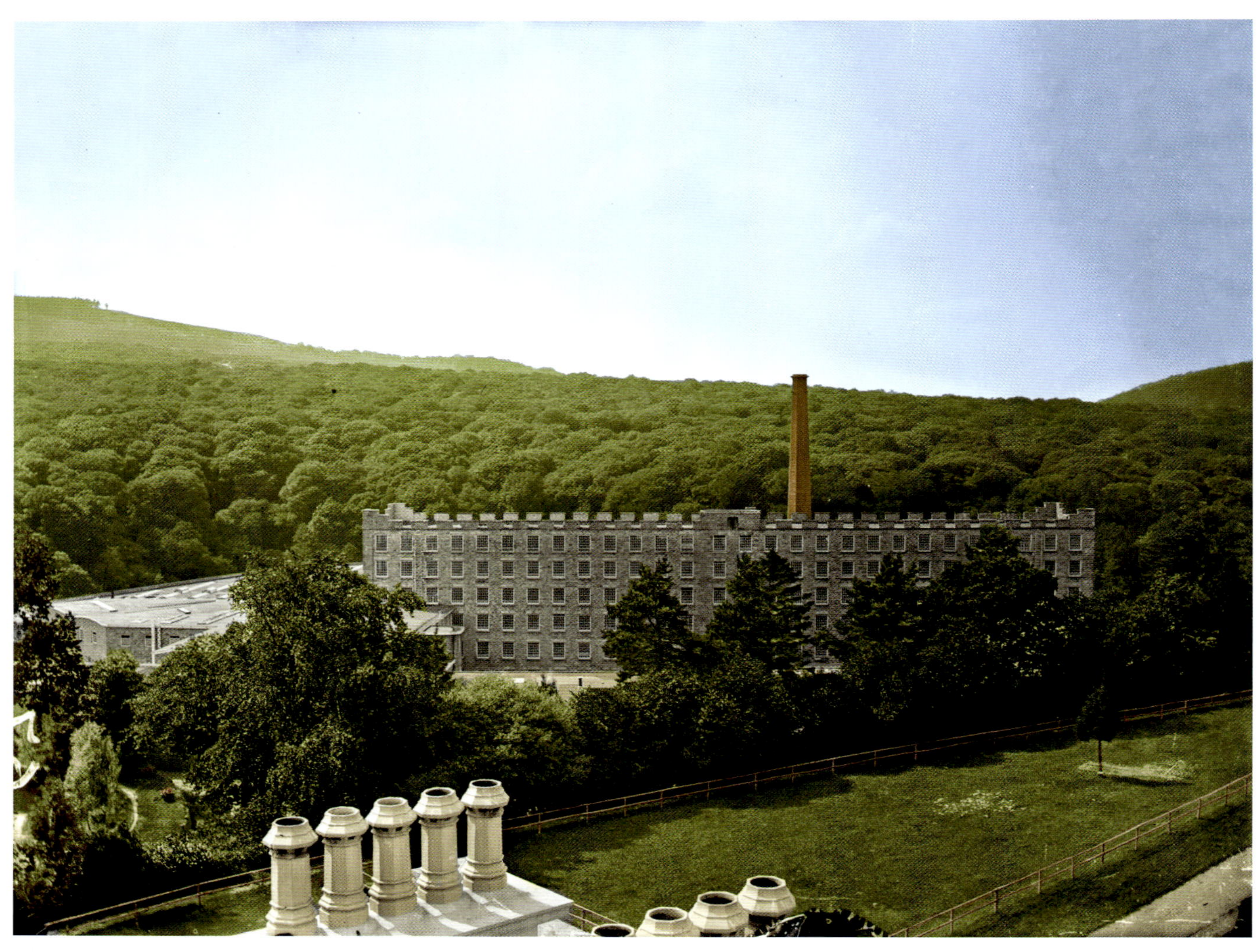

The imposing Portlaw Cotton Mill in County Waterford, a
notable exception to an Irish textile landscape dominated
by Ulster's linen industry. Established in 1825 by David
Malcolmson, it was once the world's largest single-span
building, employing 2,000 workers at its peak. Unlike the
thriving linen mills of Belfast, Portlaw's cotton industry faced
unique challenges. The American Civil War (1861–5) initially
disrupted cotton supplies, and the Malcolmsons were affected.
Post-war tariff increases and shifts in global cotton trade further
strained the industry. By 1904, the mill had ceased operations.

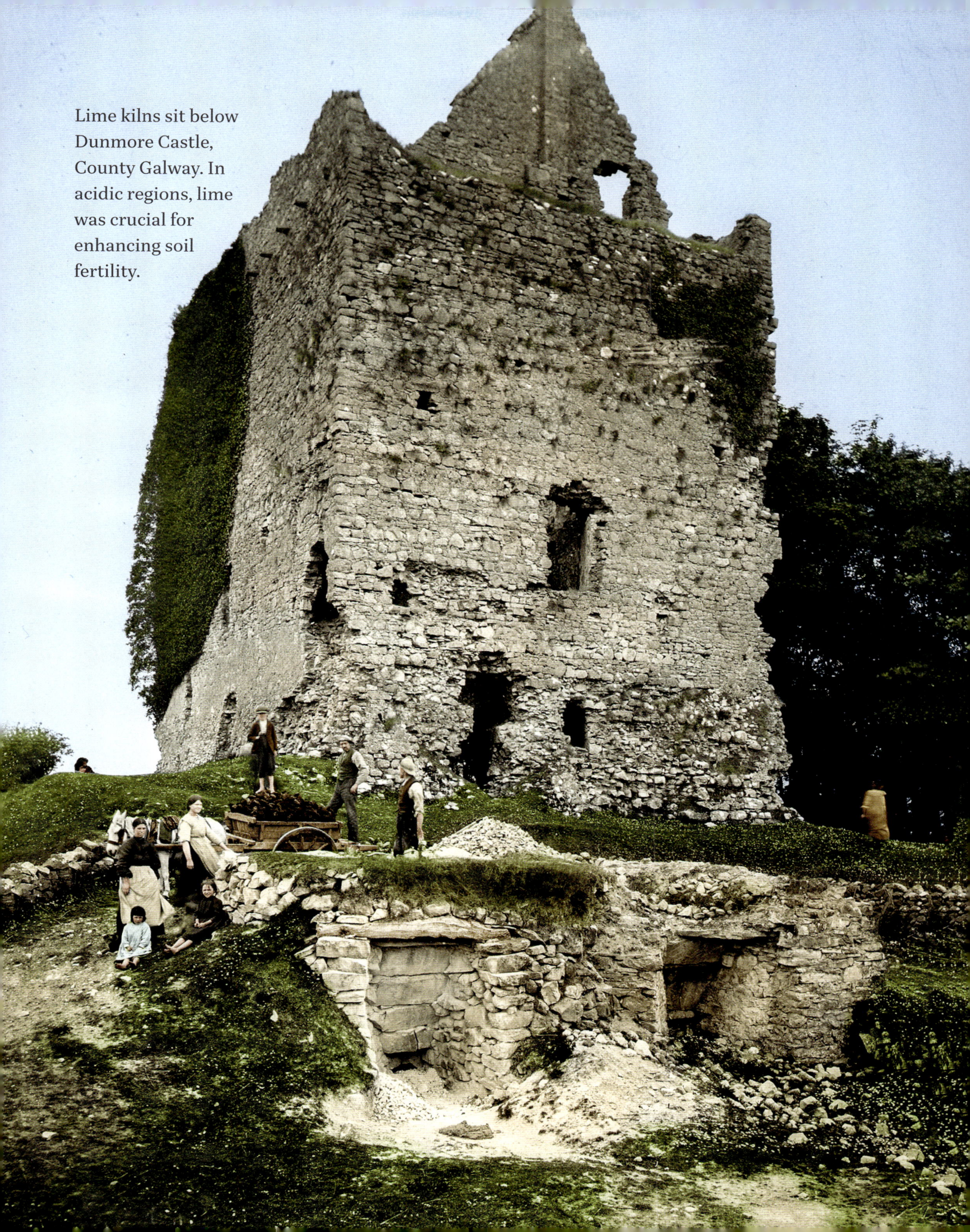

Lime kilns sit below Dunmore Castle, County Galway. In acidic regions, lime was crucial for enhancing soil fertility.

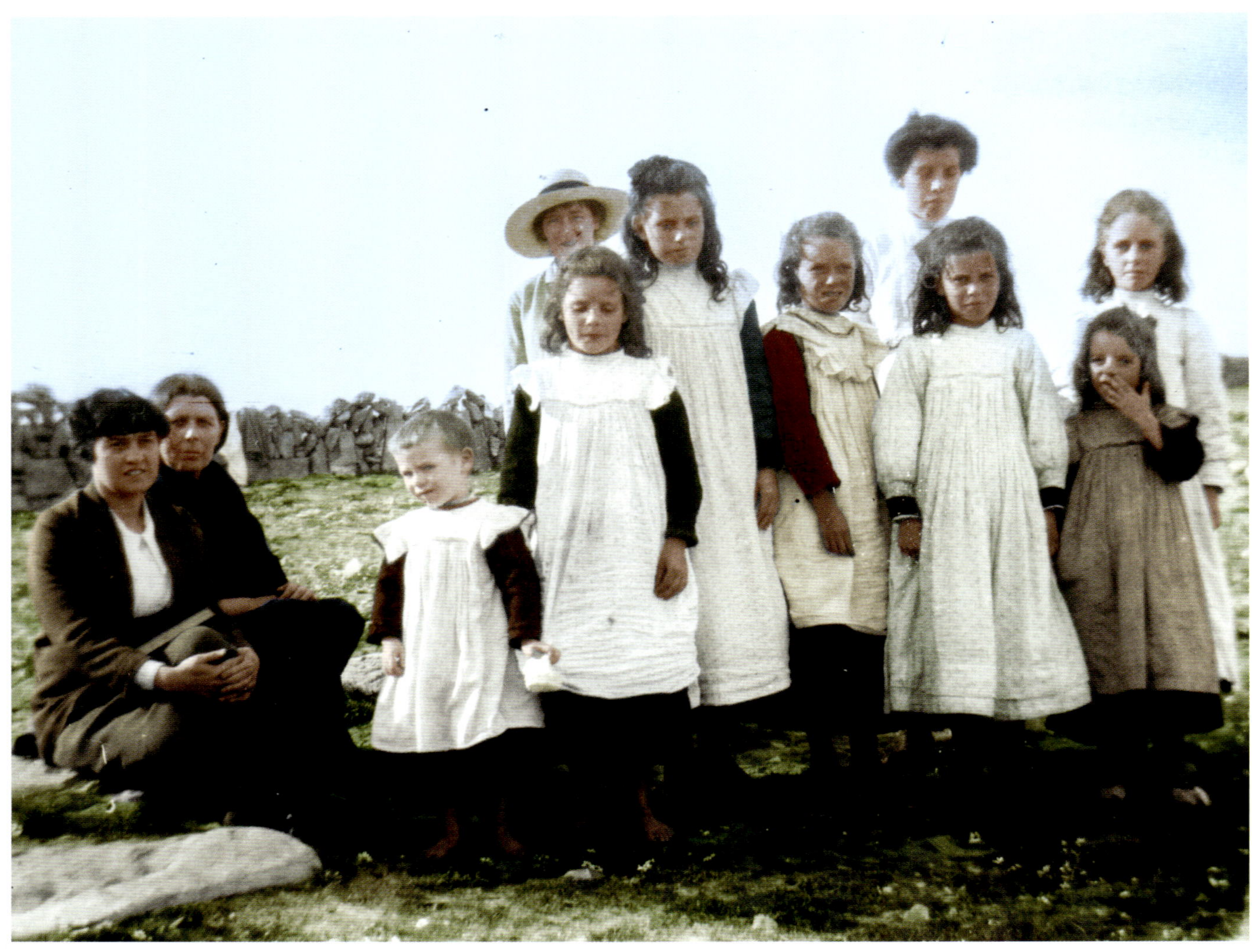

Schoolchildren are pictured at Inis Oírr, Aran Islands, in 1914. In rural Ireland, education was highly valued, as seen in the hidden hedge schools of the Penal Laws era, where wandering teachers provided lessons in reading, writing and classical subjects. A major step forward came with the 1831 Education Act, which sought to establish a state-funded national school system. However, its implementation faced significant resistance. Despite many obstacles, the national school system gradually expanded, and by the early twentieth century, literacy rates had risen significantly, marking a profound shift in educational access across Ireland.

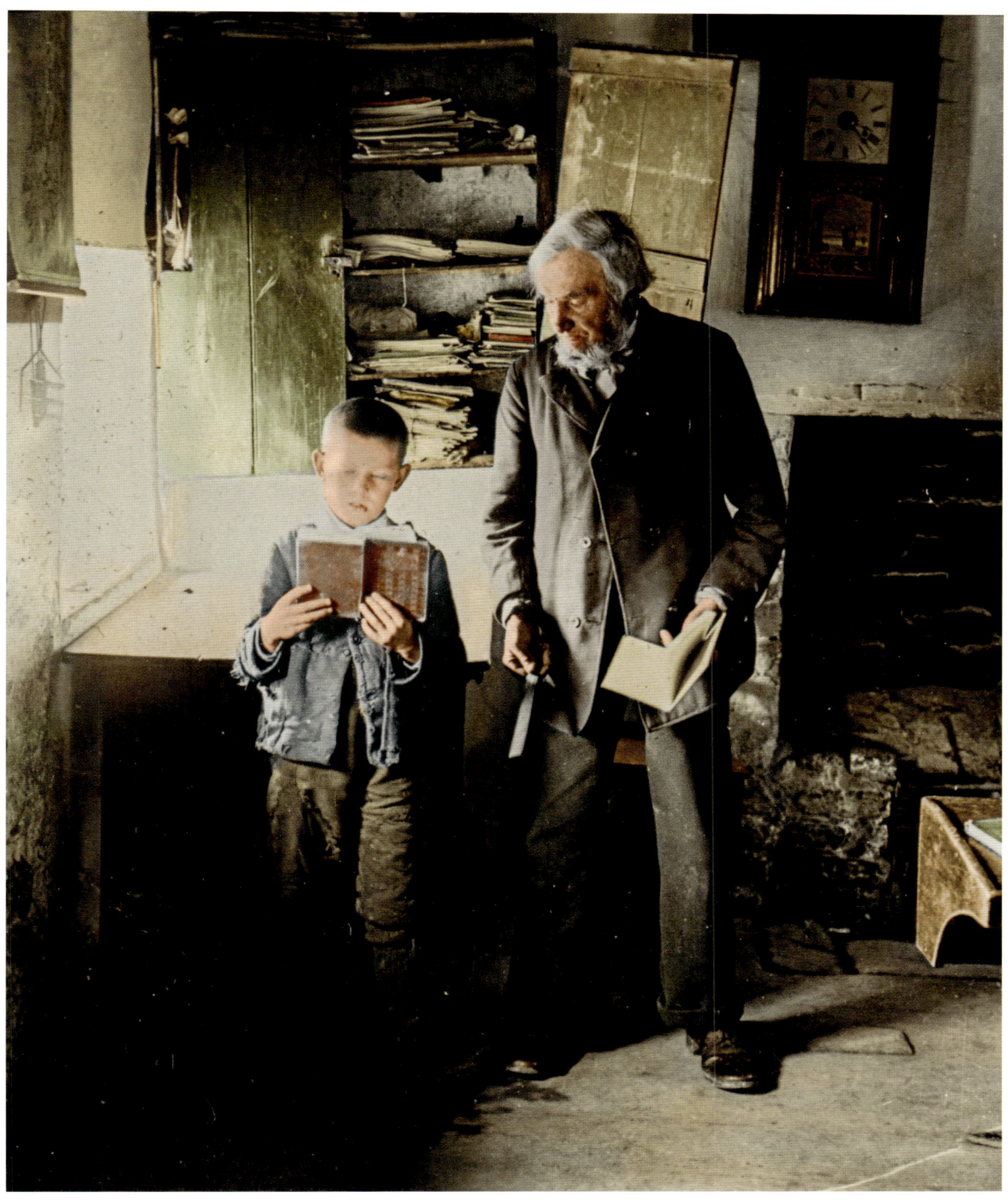

A Master – a figure of both knowledge and authority, respected by the community – stands, instructing his pupil.

This photograph captures the
Waterford Young Ireland Hurling
Club, well-worn hurleys in hand, in
1916, representing the early years of
the Gaelic Athletic Association (GAA).
Founded in November 1884 in Thurles,
County Tipperary, the GAA was
established to preserve and promote
traditional Irish sports and pastimes.

Over the decades, it has become an
essential part of rural communities,
where Gaelic football, hurling,
camogie, and handball are more than
just sports – they are key elements of
local identity, social gatherings and
community pride.

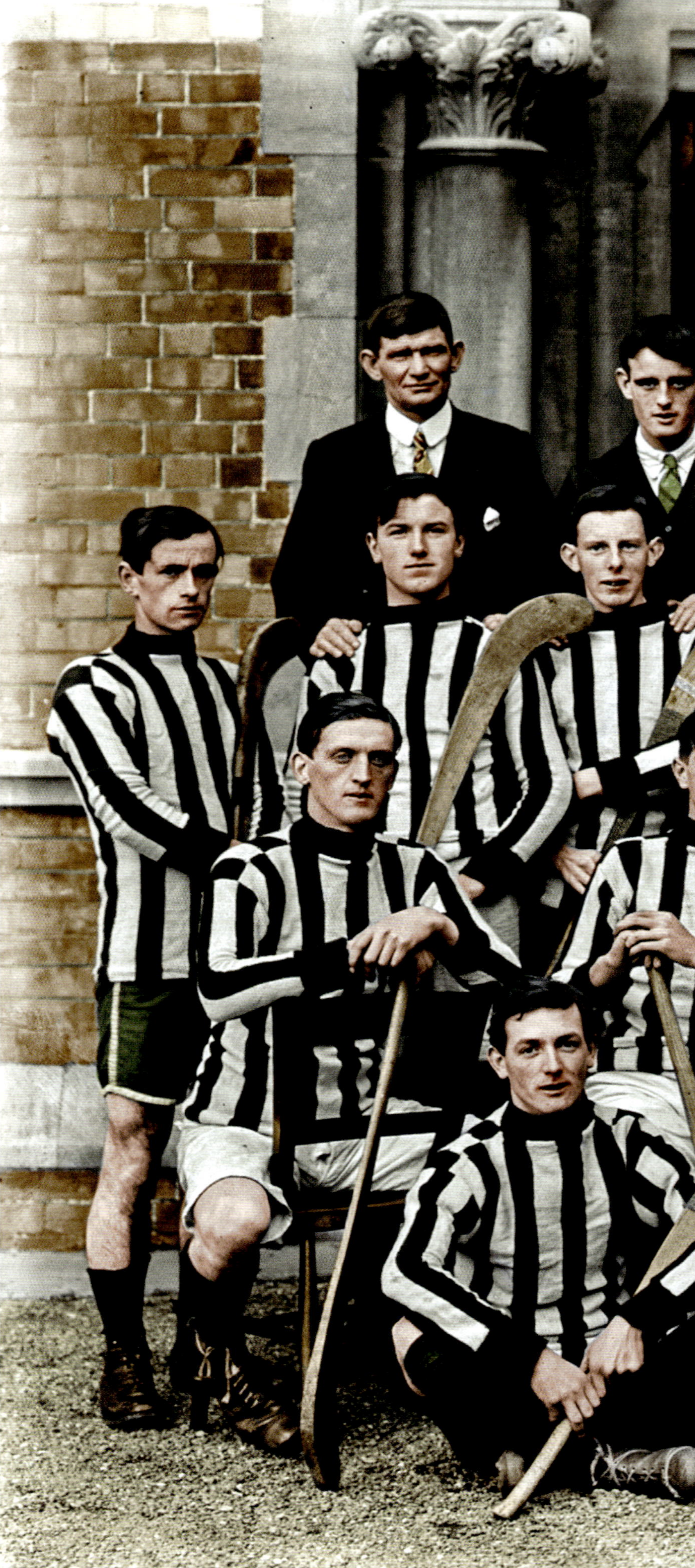

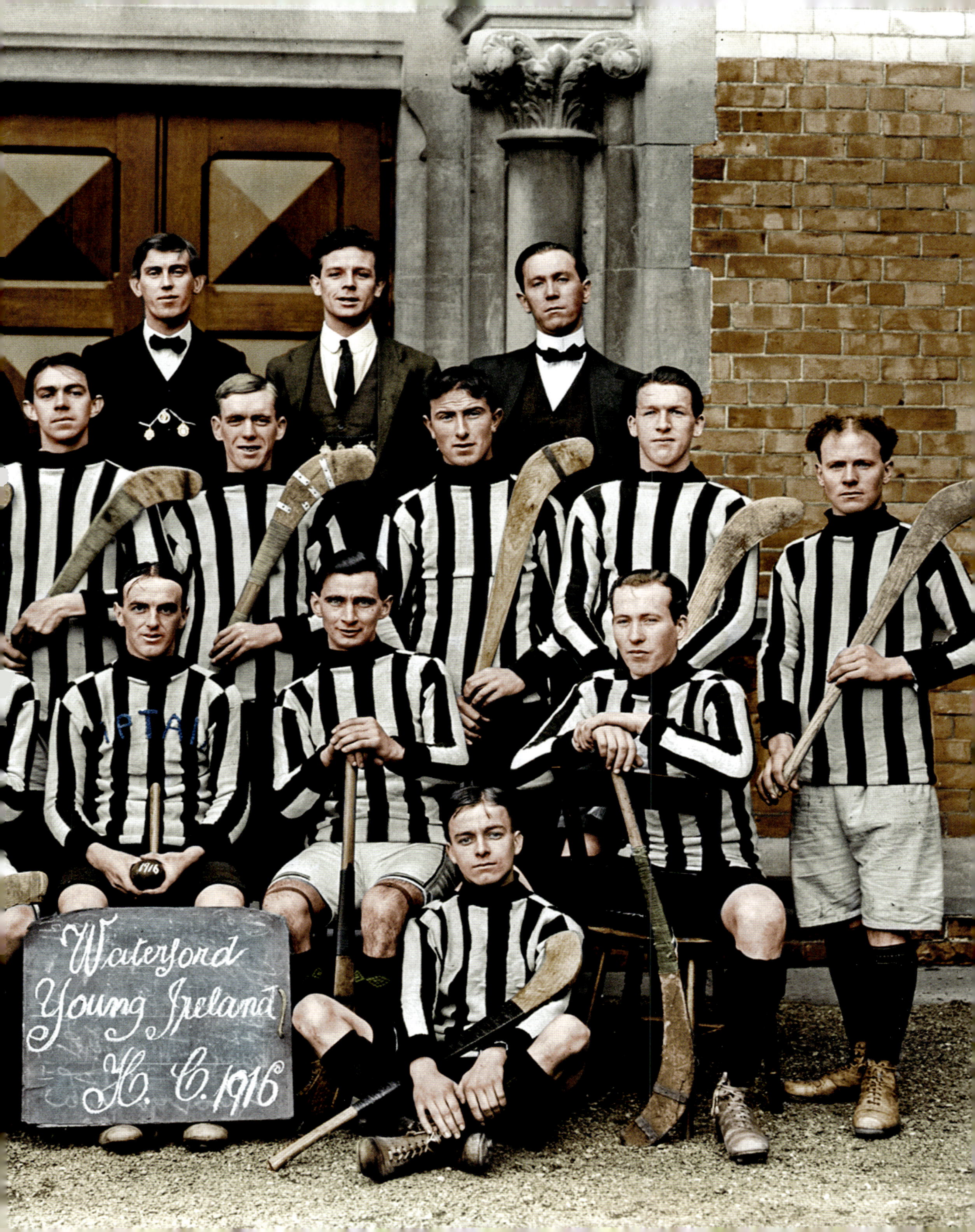
Waterford
Young Ireland
H. C. 1916

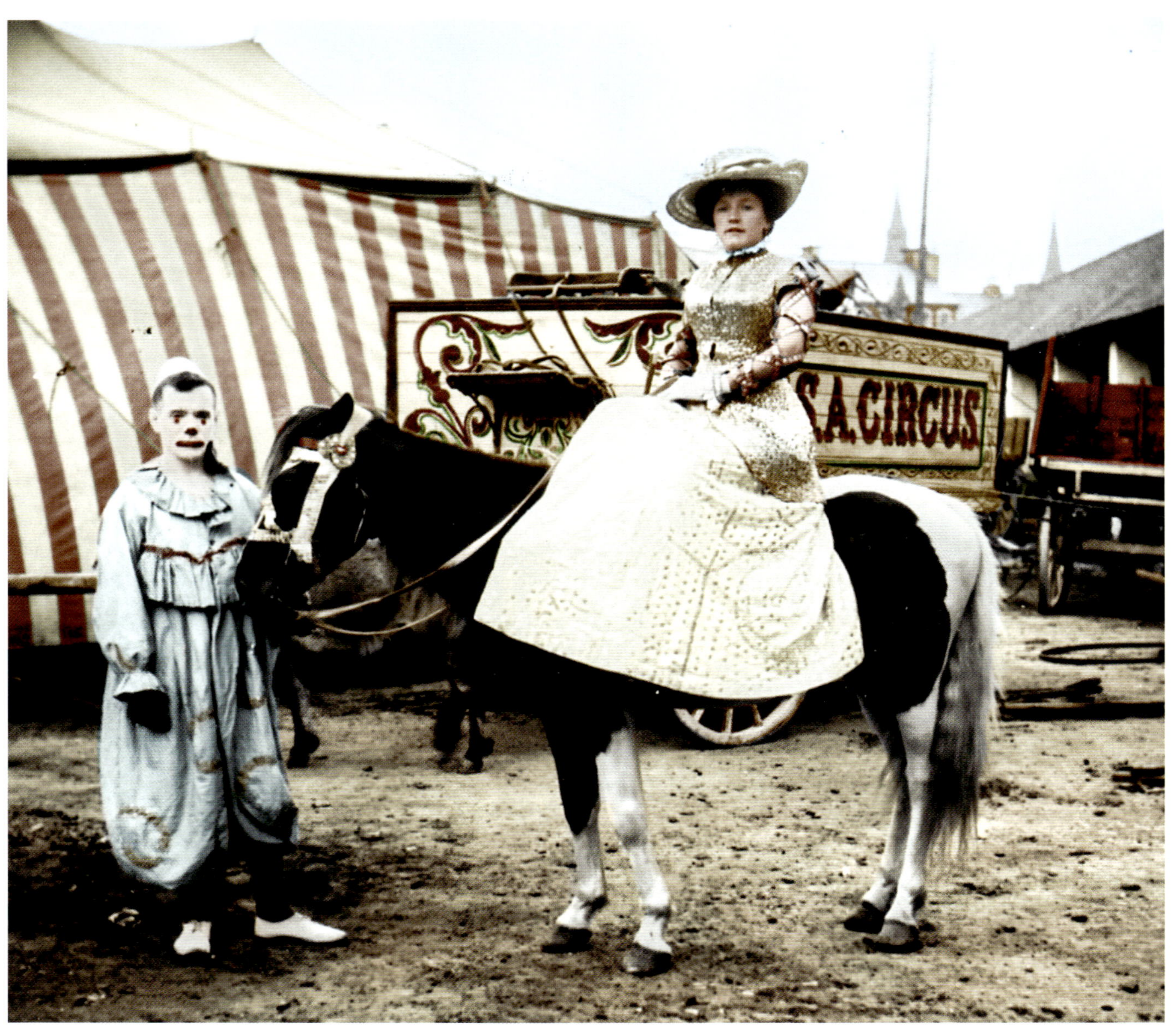

A woman on horseback and a clown, part of Buff Bill's American Circus, pose for a photograph at Strabane, County Derry, around 1910. Travelling circuses like Buff Bill's were highly popular in Ireland just before World War I, bringing novelty to rural towns across the country, offering a glimpse of the wider world. In that era, these shows offered families a rare opportunity to escape reality and enjoy a few hours of entertainment, featuring acts like acrobats, animal performances and Wild West-style demonstrations.

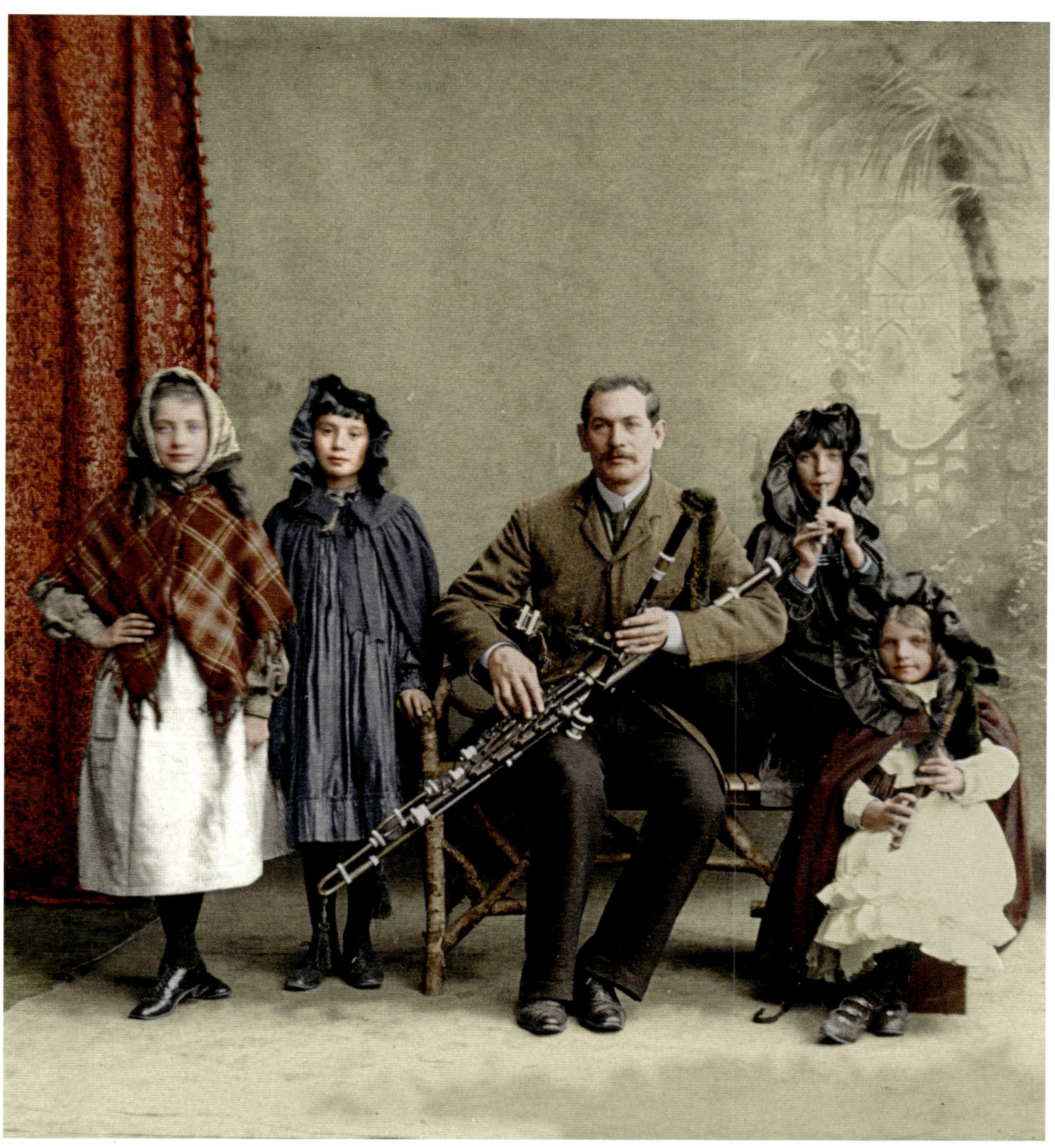

A family in Cork pose: the father playing uilleann pipes, two daughters with flutes, and two others poised to dance – music was then primarily played for dancing. Traditional music was deeply interwoven into Irish rural life, with performances often taking place in homes. Irish uilleann pipes differ from Scottish bagpipes with their softer tone and wider range, played seated using elbow-pumped bellows.

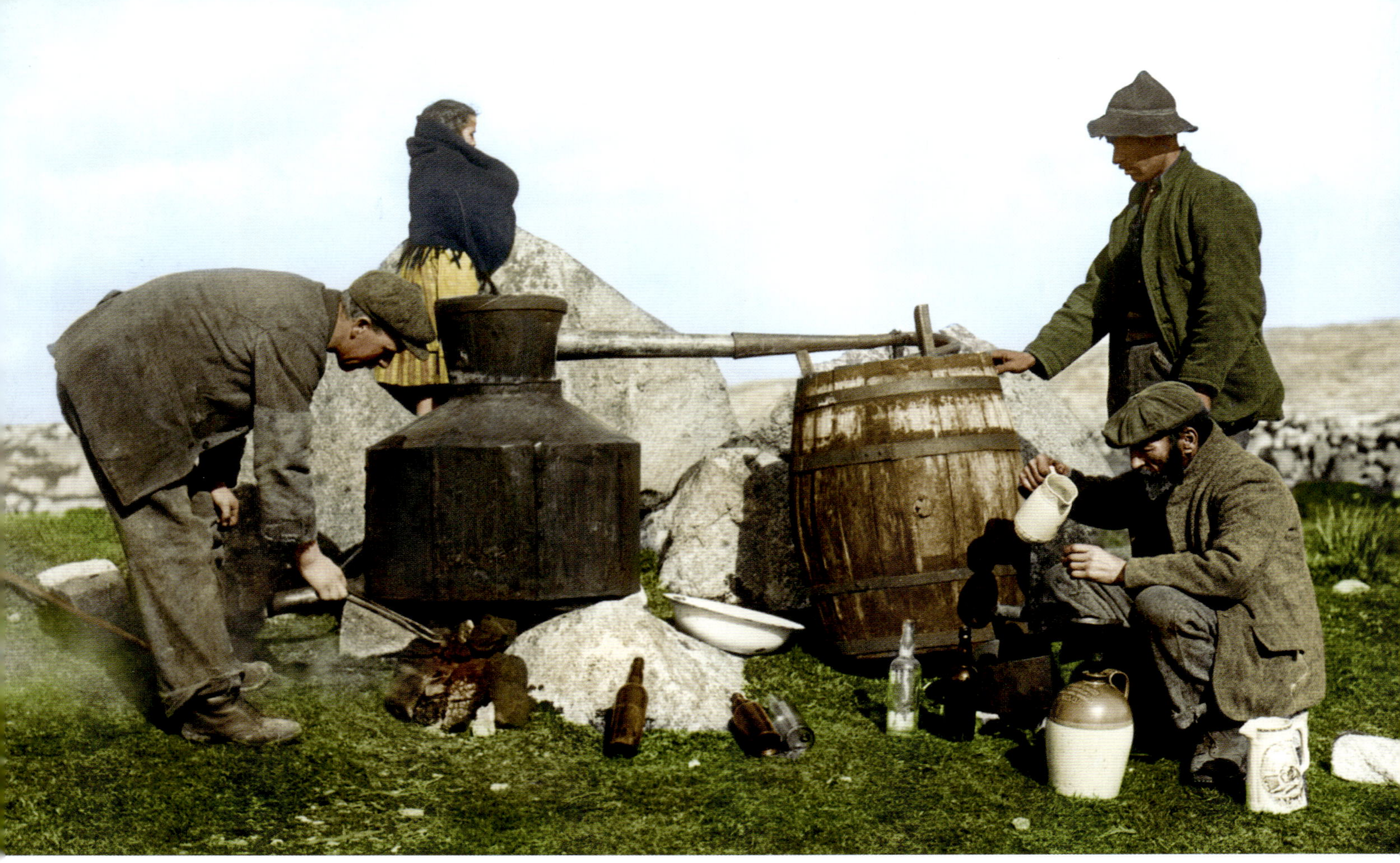

The lively social traditions of the Irish countryside were not limited to music and dance alone. Another form of socialising took place, where a different kind of spirit was shared. The potato harvest provided not only food but also the raw material for a spirited tradition. In quiet corners across the countryside, the humble potato was transformed into something far more potent: poteen.

In this image, several men are engaged in the clandestine craft of distilling poteen, a practice passed down through generations, while the woman in the background appears to be maintaining a lookout. Using simple yet ingenious equipment – a pot still, often homemade, and fermented potato mash – they carefully heat the mixture, capturing the vapours that condense into clear spirit, with a miscellany of jugs and bottles ready to be filled. The potency and quality depended on the skill of the distiller, and poteen was usually far stronger than commercially produced spirits. The process required skill, patience and secrecy, as poteen distillation was outlawed for centuries under strict revenue laws that aimed to control alcohol production and taxation.

Despite its illicit status, poteen remained a cherished part of rural Irish life. Distillers often worked under the cover of darkness, in remote bogs, hidden valleys or on lonely islands, evading the authorities and preserving a long-standing tradition. It was not only enjoyed as a drink, but also valued for its medicinal properties. Many swore by its ability to soothe aches and pains, rubbing it on joints to ease rheumatism or other ailments.

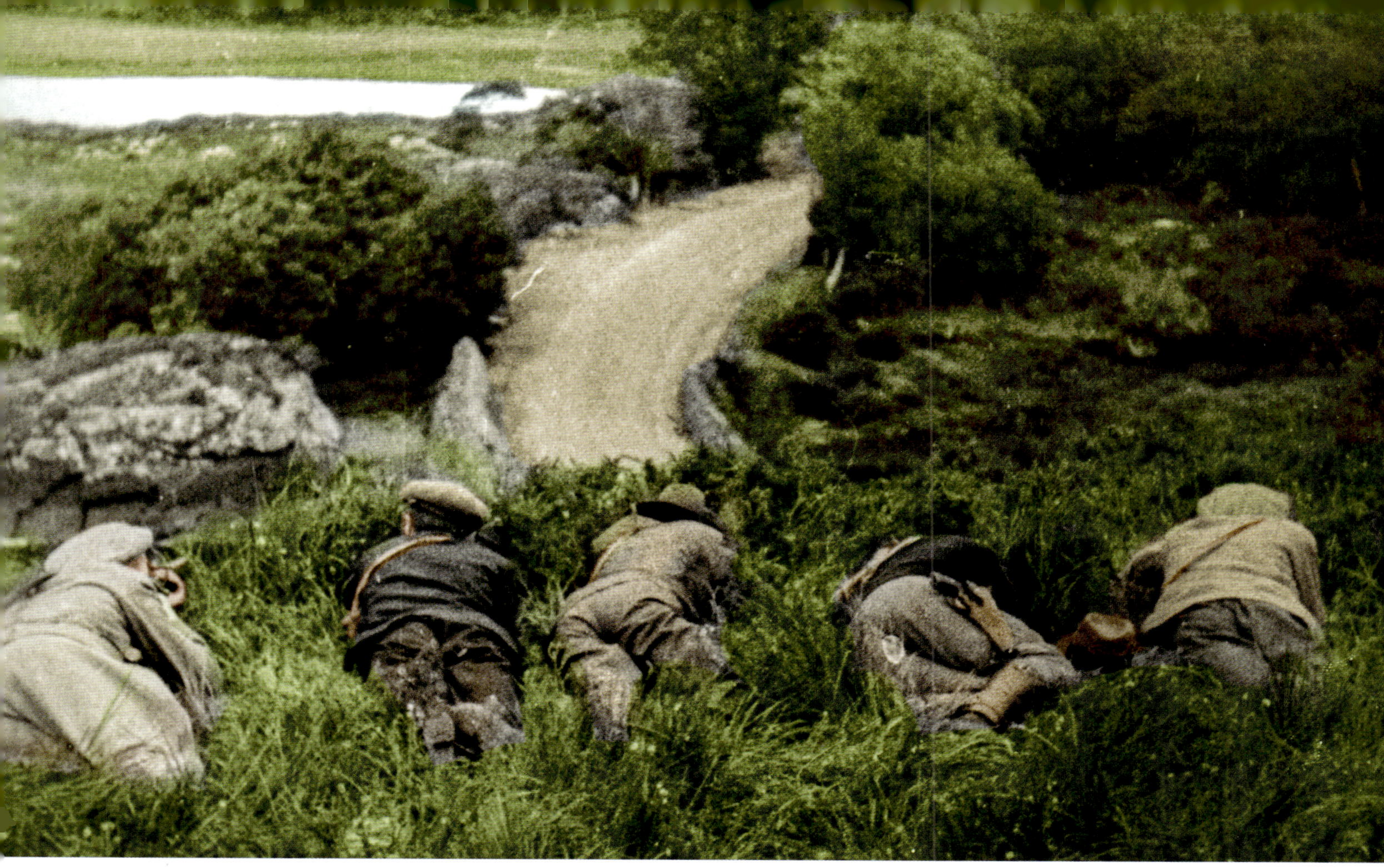

A typical Irish Republican Army (IRA) ambush in the countryside. Well-concealed men lie in wait at a commanding point above a bend in a road. In reality and given the vicissitudes of guerilla warfare, there are no photographs of actual IRA ambushes. However, this film still evokes a sense of how it might have been – it is from the first full-length Irish feature film with sound, *The Dawn* (1936), shot around Killarney using extras, many of whom were IRA veterans.

The Great Famine created a vast Irish exile population, many of whom harboured deep resentment toward British rule – which in time contributed directly to the Irish Revolution of 1916–23. The Fenians, founded in America, had embraced militant nationalism, and it was the veteran Fenian, Tom Clarke, who played a key role in planning the 1916 Easter Rising.

While the Rising occurred primarily in Dublin, the Irish War of Independence (1919–21) had a profound impact on rural life and farming across Ireland. With over half of IRA members hailing from rural backgrounds, many farms became guerrilla strongholds. Hedgerows became ambush sites and hillsides hid flying columns.

A tank was a visible manifestation of military might, thought appropriate for Ireland – by late 1919 a variety of tanks and armoured cars had been assigned around the country. Here Mark A. Whippet tanks are seen on patrol along a misty County Clare road in November 1919. Showing how people from the country adapt to whatever circumstances are presented to them, a man, unperturbed, carefully leads his pony and trap past the tanks.

However, relatively few armoured vehicles were deployed. Most patrols by Crown forces during the War of Independence were made up of convoys using the Crossley Tender light truck, which proved very vulnerable to IRA ambushes.

Towards the end of the war, Major Arthur Percival (Essex Regiment, based in Bandon, later as General would unconditionally surrender Singapore to the Japanese in 1942) developed an initiative, sending what could be described as 'flying columns' of British troops through fields and countryside, mirroring the IRA's own tactics. They slept in barns or tents and surrounded farmhouses at nightfall, closing in at daybreak. It increased mobility and unpredictability, while reducing vulnerability to road ambushes. Nevertheless, this tactic ultimately failed to defeat the IRA's flying columns, which continued to operate effectively throughout the war.

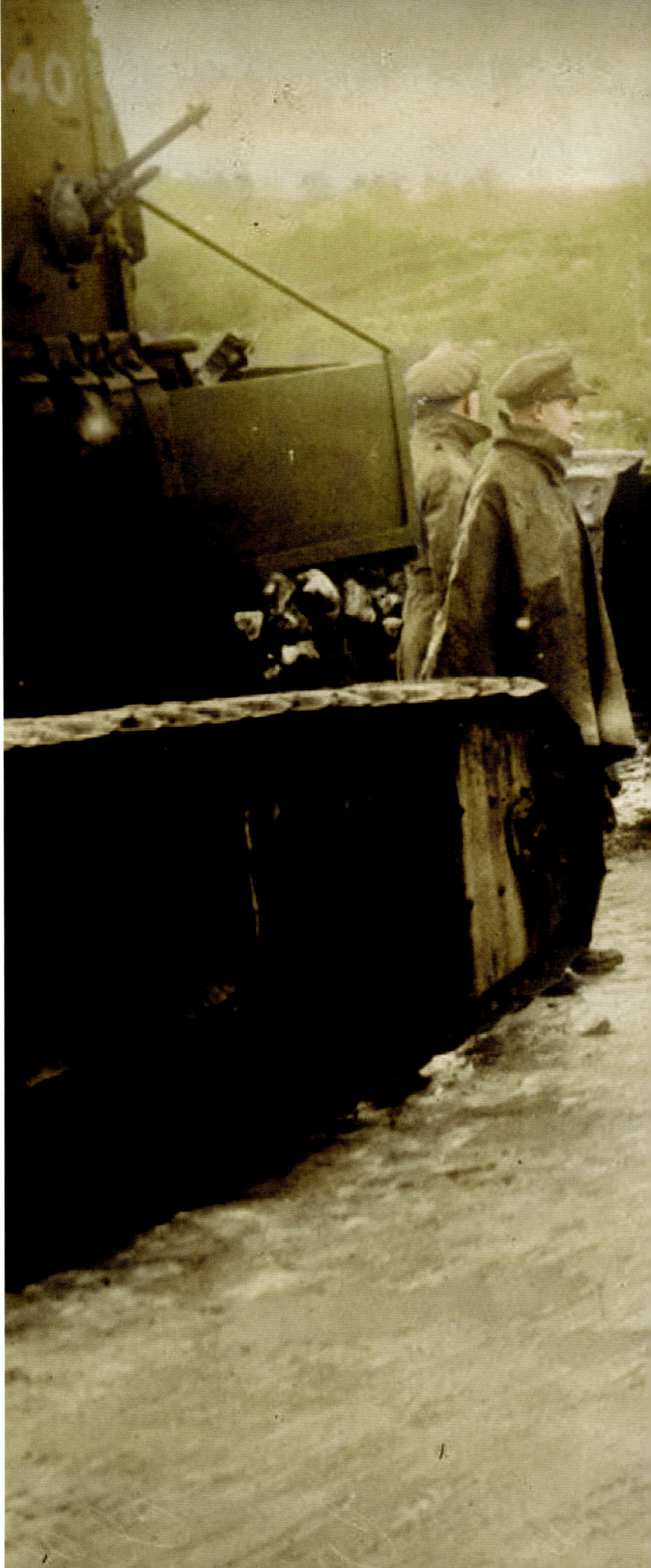

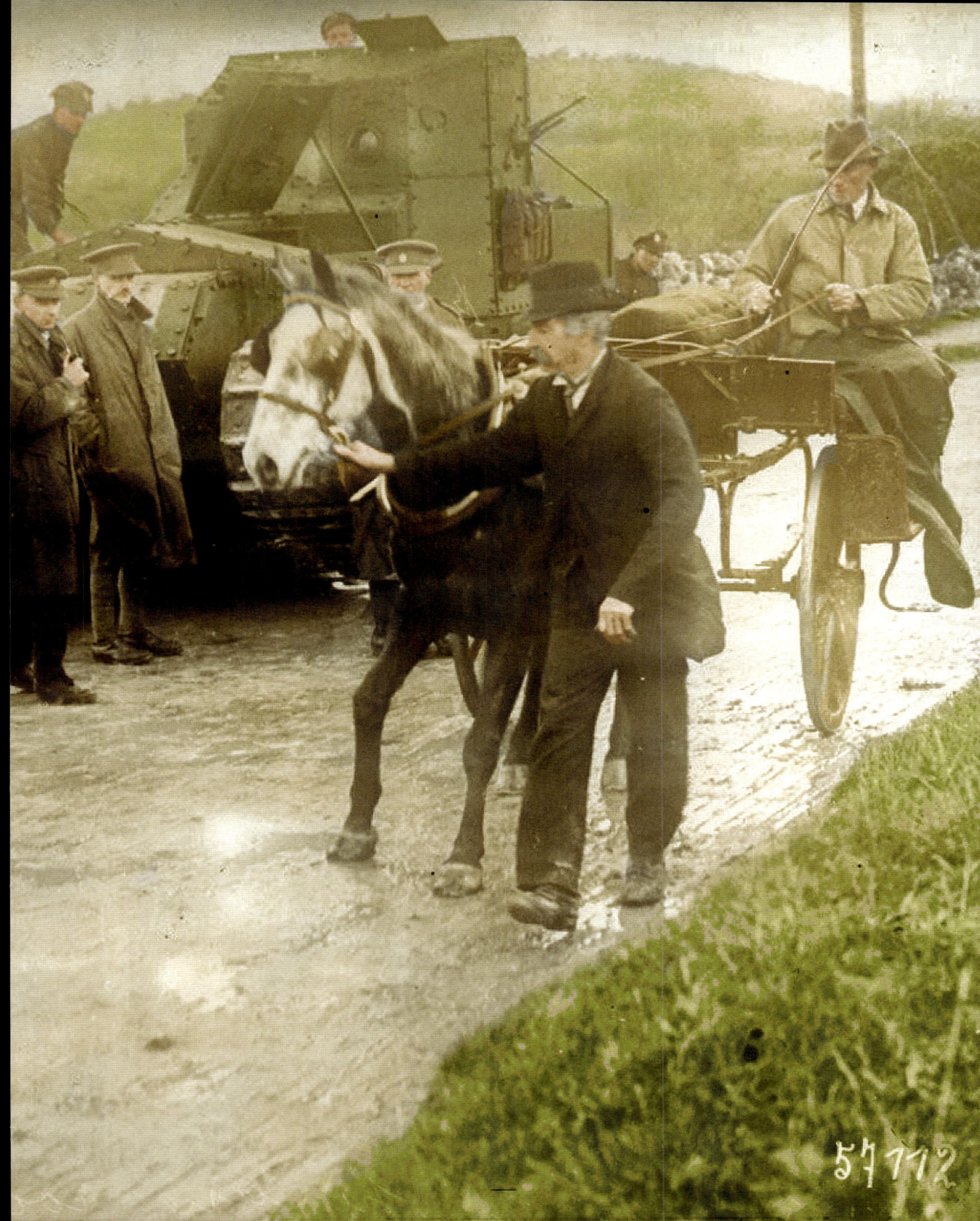
57112

The Lord Mayor and the Fordson. Henry
Ford had chosen his ancestral county,
Cork, as the place to build a large tractor
plant. This, Ford's first manufacturing
site for tractors outside of the United
States, opened at the Marina in July 1919.
Tomás MacCurtain became Cork's first
Republican lord mayor on 30 January
1920. However, his time in office was
cut short when he was assassinated by
Crown forces on 20 March 1920. This
photograph is likely to have been one of
the last taken before his death.

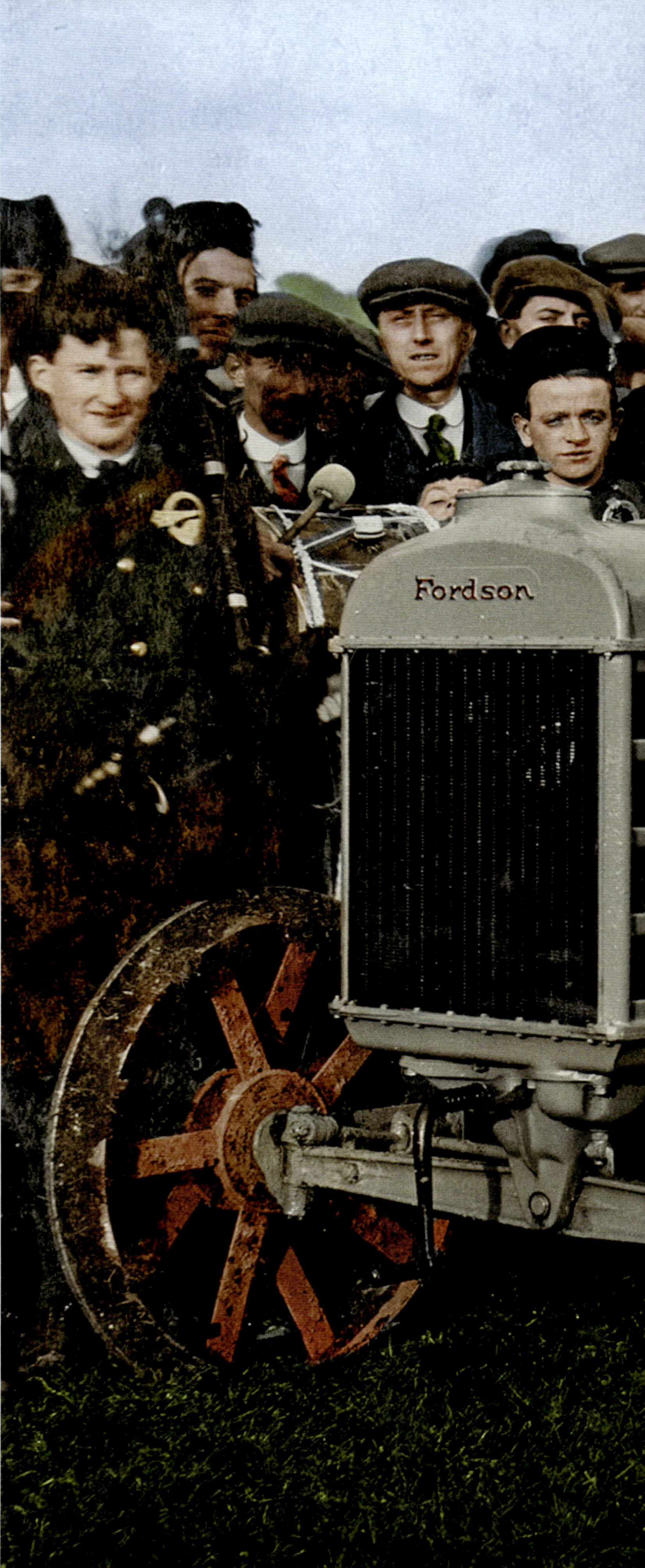

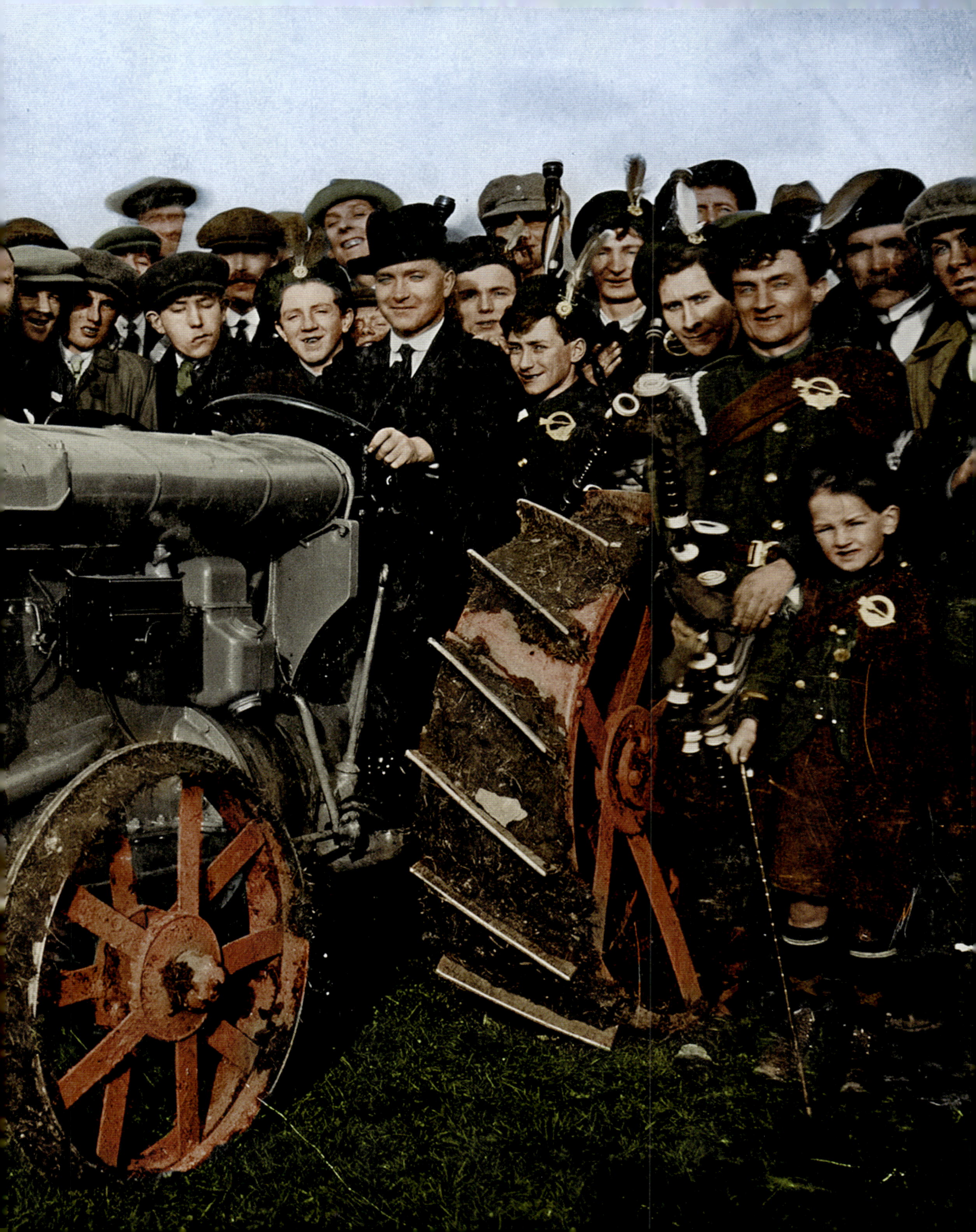

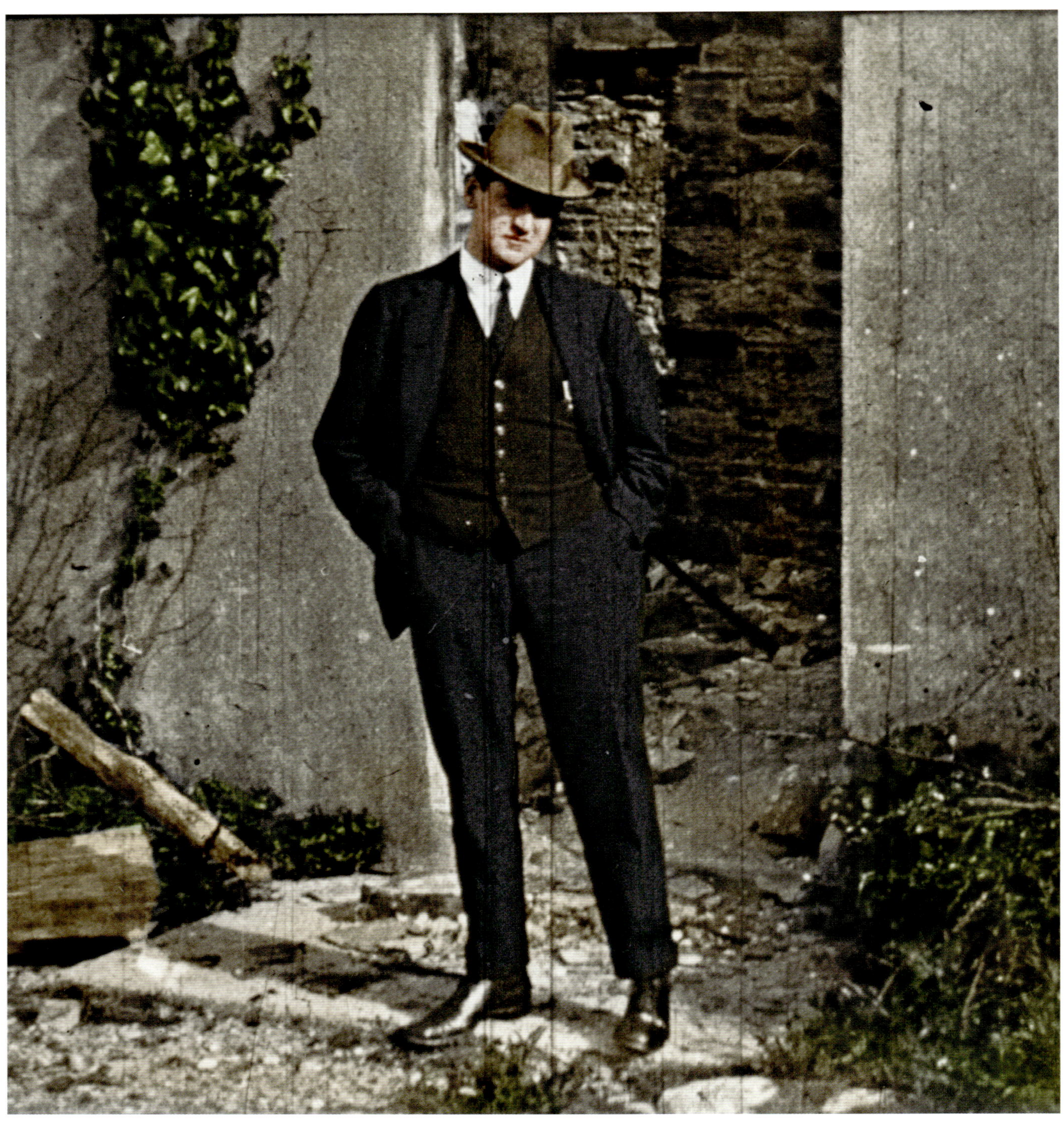

As the War of Independence raged on, reprisals by the Crown forces on towns, villages and farms became common. Here Michael Collins stands looking at the ruins of his home (built by the family in 1900) at Woodfield, West Cork, where the family ran a farm of 90 acres. The house had been burned down by soldiers of the Essex Regiment in April 1921. Upon learning of the destruction a few days later in Dublin, he is said to have remarked, 'They knew how to hurt me most.'

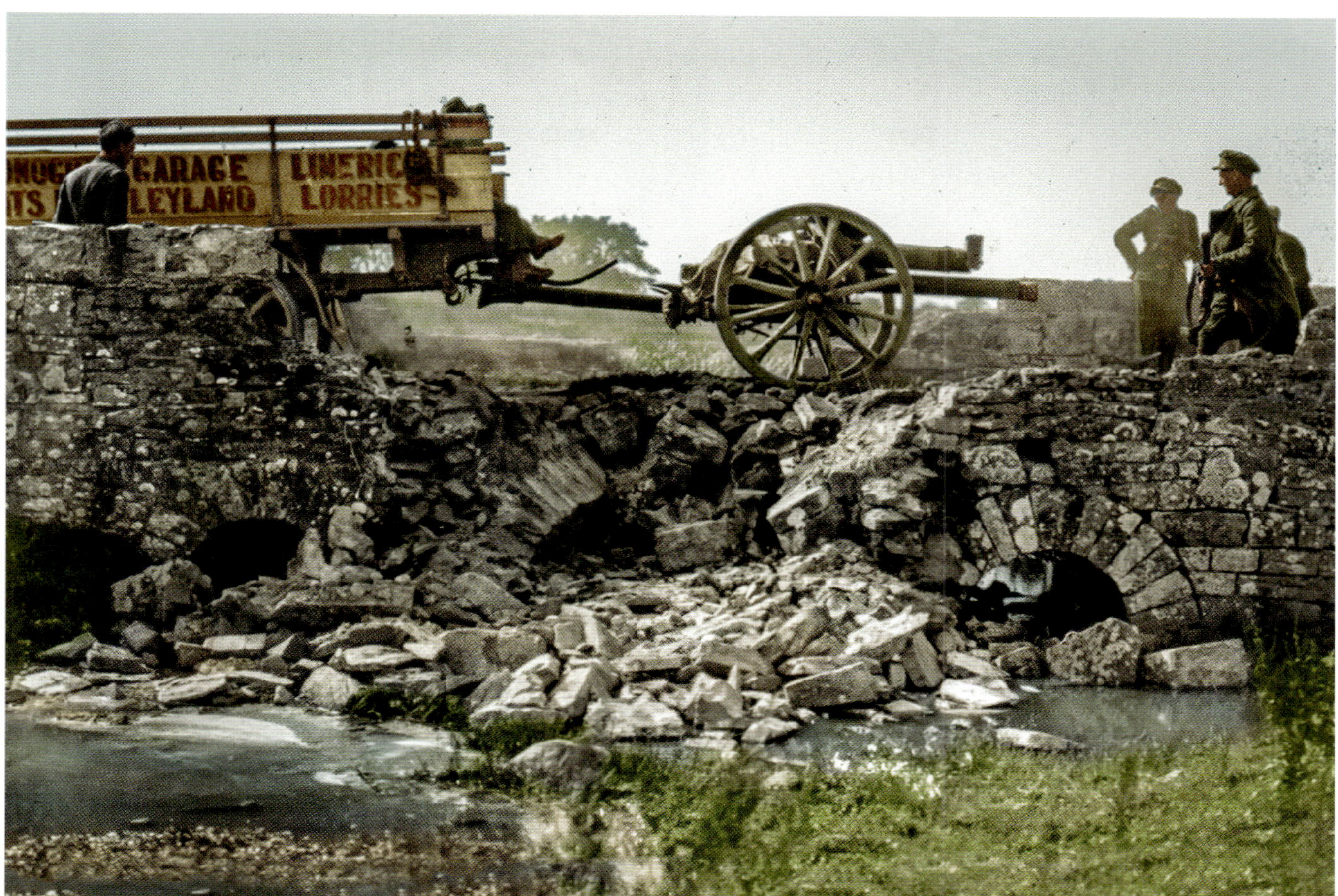

The Civil War emerged in the wake of the Anglo-Irish Treaty of December 1921, with hostilities beginning at the end of June 1922. After initial battles in Dublin, the war spread across the country. The first major encounter was the taking of Limerick City from the anti-Treaty side by Provisional Government troops. Following this, there was heavy fighting in the Kilamllock-Bruree countryside. This photograph, taken in what the press dubbed as the 'South-Western Front' shows a motley convoy of pro-Treaty troops, with a commandeered lorry towing an 18-pounder, paused at a partially destroyed bridge in County Limerick.

Over the course of the war, the anti-Treaty side – aiming to disrupt the movement of government forces – destroyed many road bridges and, in particular, targeted railway infrastructure on a large scale, including bridges, tracks, stations and locomotives. With communications severed, many rural communities faced shortages and serious disruption.

With ambush and retribution once again occurring across the roads and fields of the Irish countryside, it was a rerun of the War of Independence, the difference being that it was now a conflict between former colleagues.

It turned out that the new Free State government was willing to use the army to suppress labour unrest. In May 1923, following a slump in agricultural prices, large farmers in Waterford tried to reduce the wages of their farm labourers which led to a strike. In June the government dispatched 600 members of the Special Infantry Corps and East Waterford was put under martial law. The Corps escorted supply columns and protected farmers' property from attack. By early December the strike collapsed. Here in September 1923, soldiers stand guard at a threshing at a County Waterford farm, with what looks like the affluent proprietors centre stage.

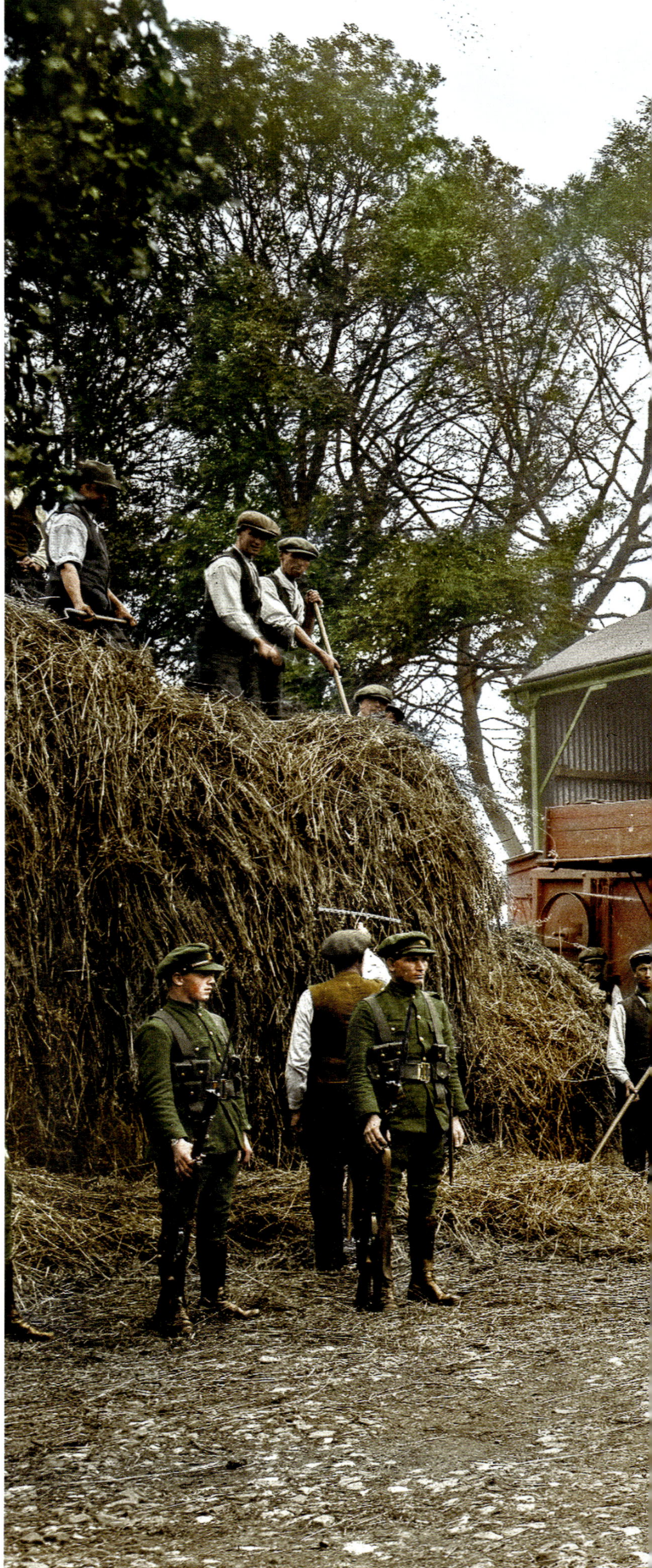

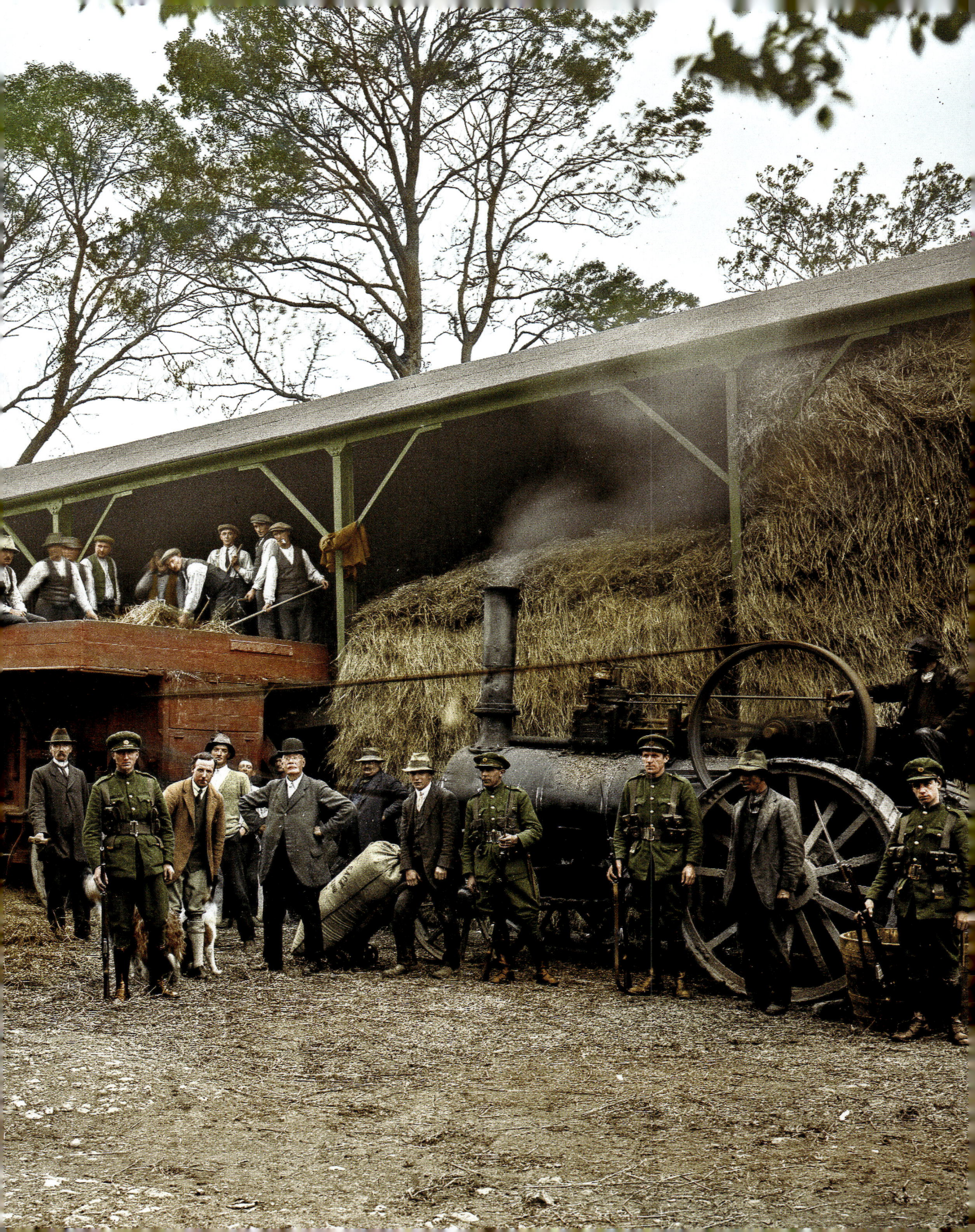

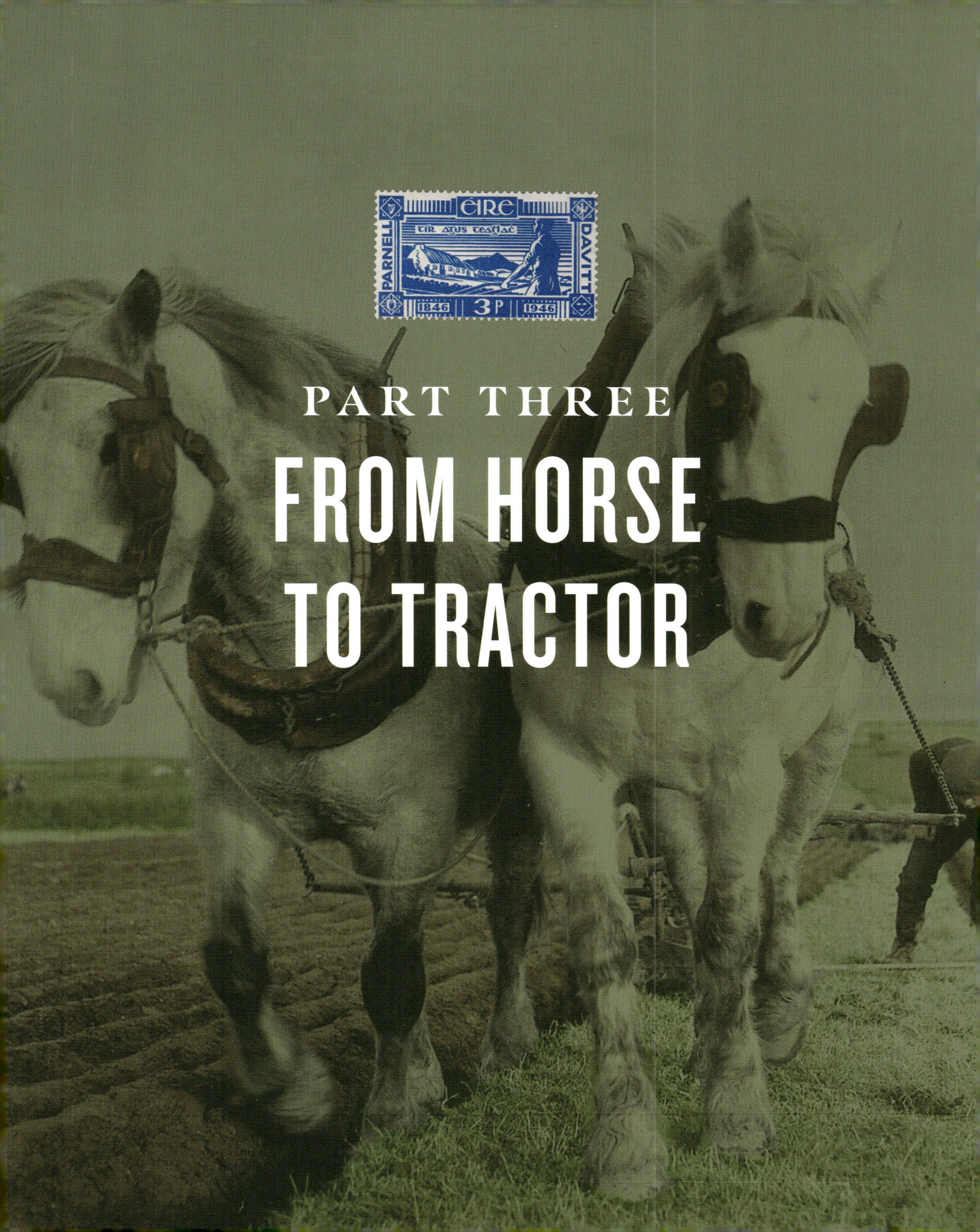

PART THREE
FROM HORSE
TO TRACTOR

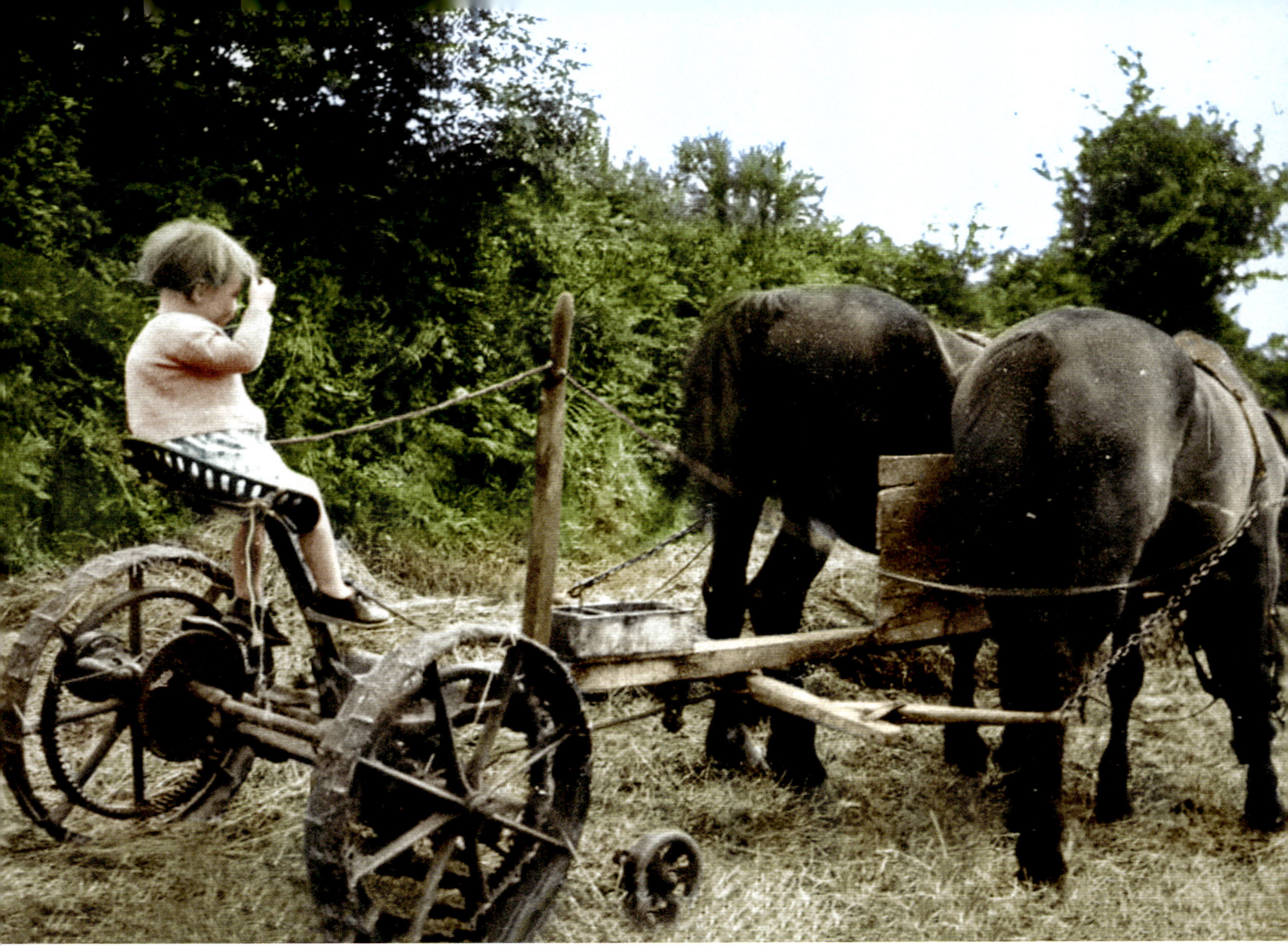

Photographed by her father, Patrick, Mary Gahan sits on the mowing machine at Rathcormac, County Cork in 1936. This machine was powered by a team of two horses, which pulled it forward to activate its cutting mechanism. As the horses moved, the left wheel rotated, driving a gearbox that powered a reciprocating scythe with sharp teeth on a cutting bar. These were hugely efficient when compared to manual methods of hay cutting – one estimate is that a mowing machine could cut as much hay in an hour as a man with a scythe could cut in seven to ten hours.

At the beginning of the twentieth century, there were many thousands of these machines in use in farms across Ireland; however, as the century progressed, there was a transition from traditional horse-drawn equipment towards increasing mechanisation.

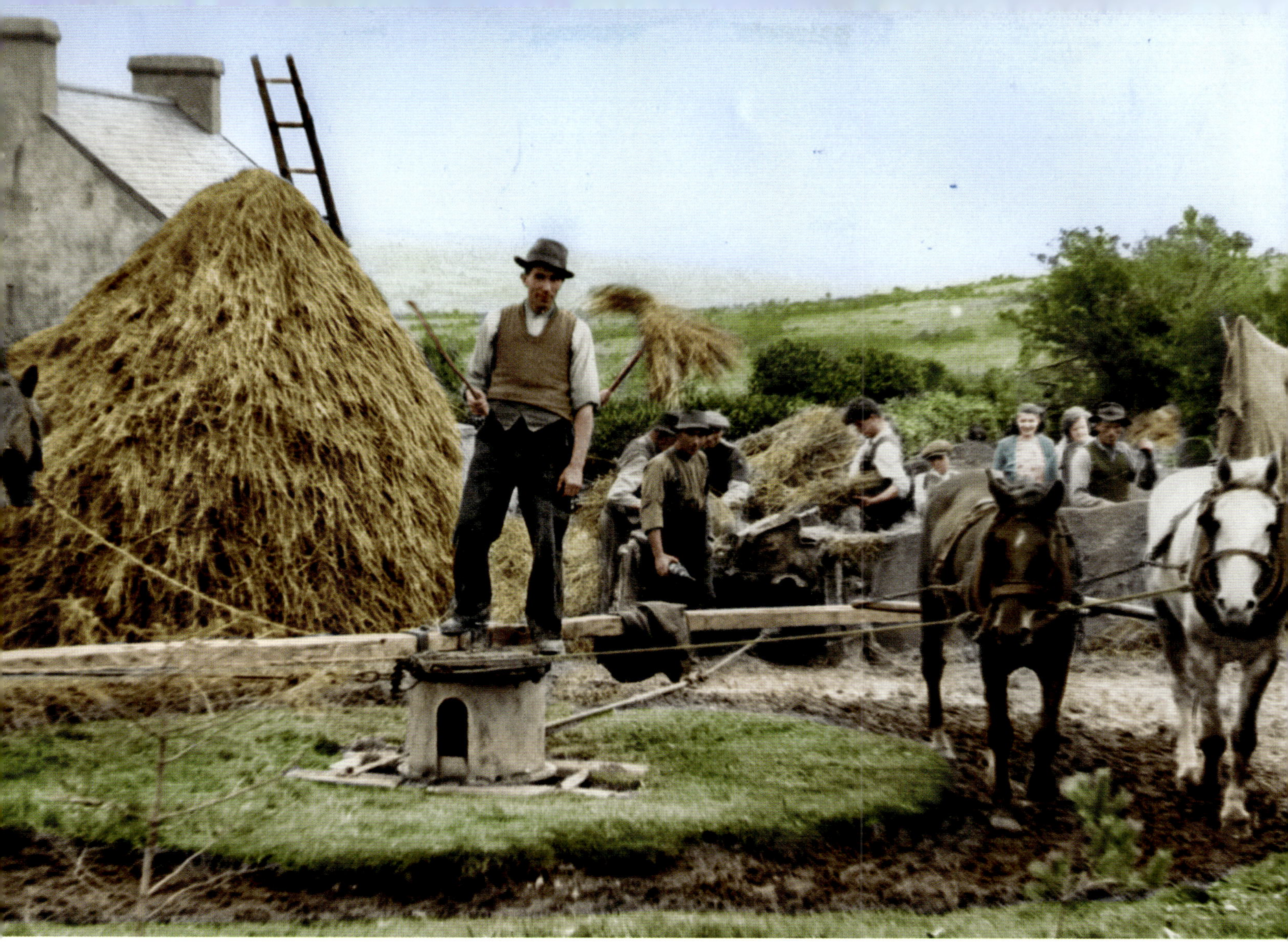

Once the hay was dry, it was transported back
to the farmyard. Here in another Patrick Gahan
photograph we see the next step, where the hay is
prepared for storage by running through a hay press.
A man poses atop the spindle, turned by several
horses. The spindle is connected to the press by an
iron rod that drives the mechanism that compresses
loose hay into compact bales. Several men, seen in
the background, work at the press, feeding in hay
and securing the finished bales.

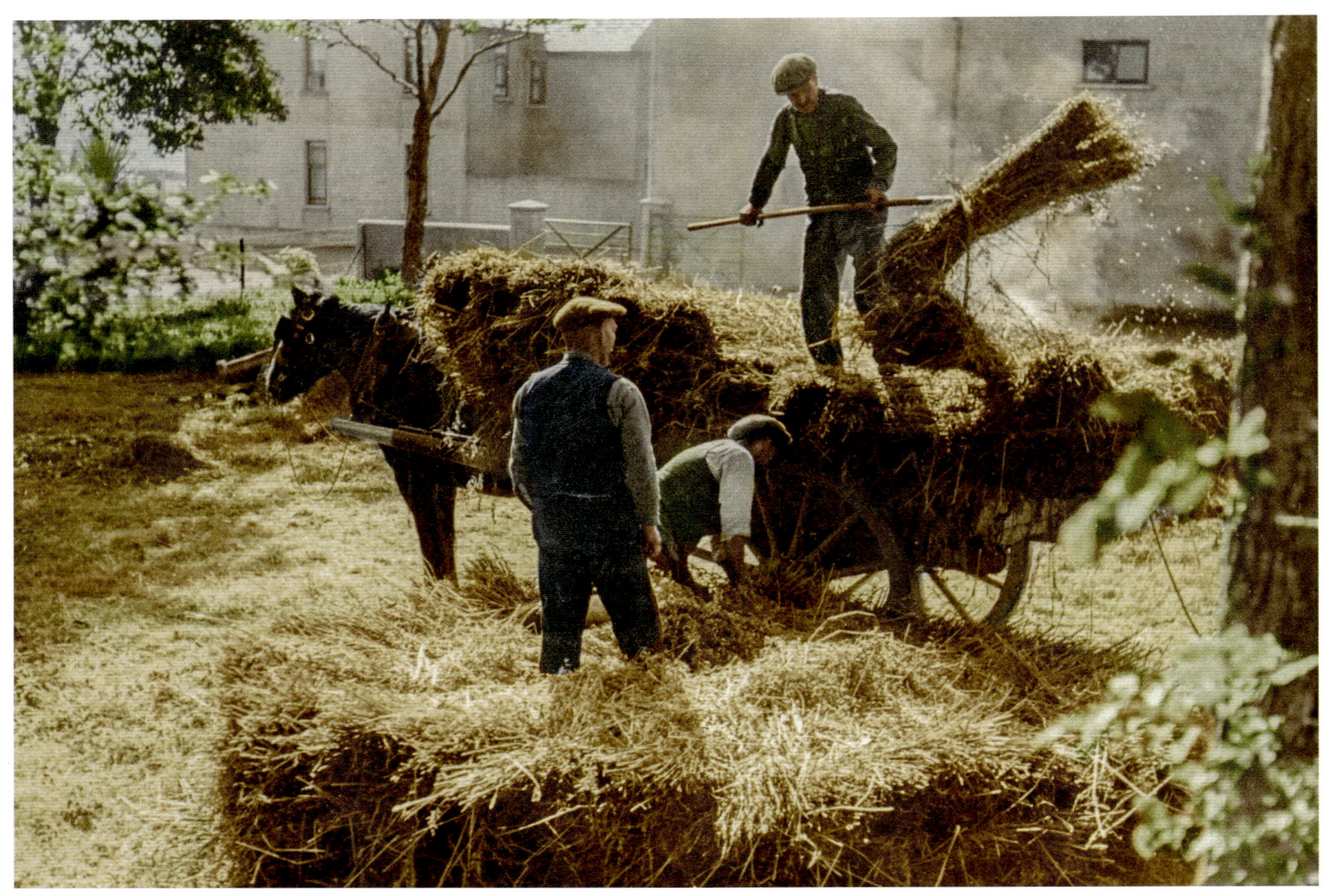

Top left: The golden days of the harvest – warm sun and the rhythm of hard work. An elegiac scene from the Fermanagh countryside from around 1945.

Right: Ireland's farming industry was not just about the land – it fuelled a network of skilled trades that kept it running. From blacksmiths to millwrights, each had a role. Here, a man dresses a millstone.

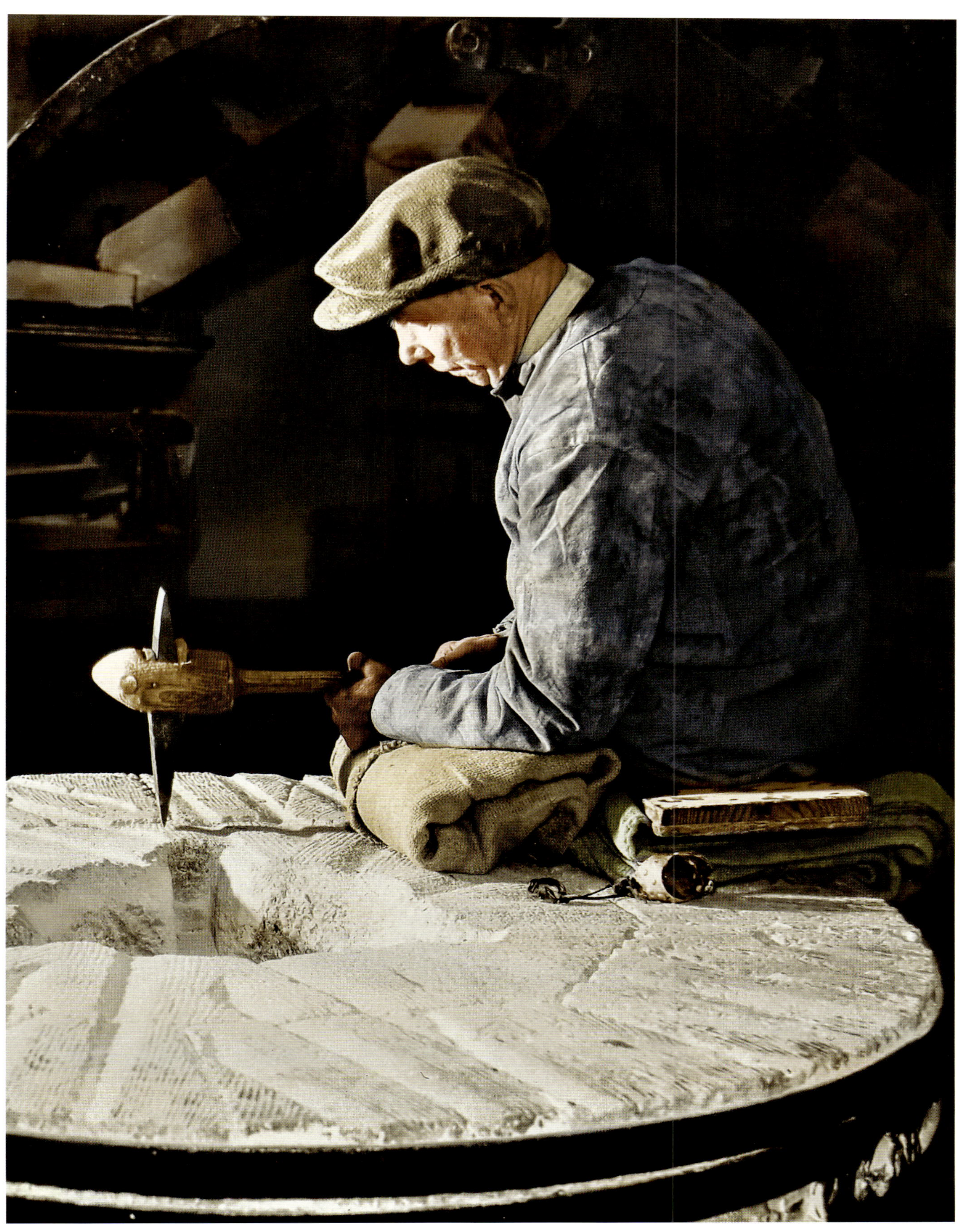

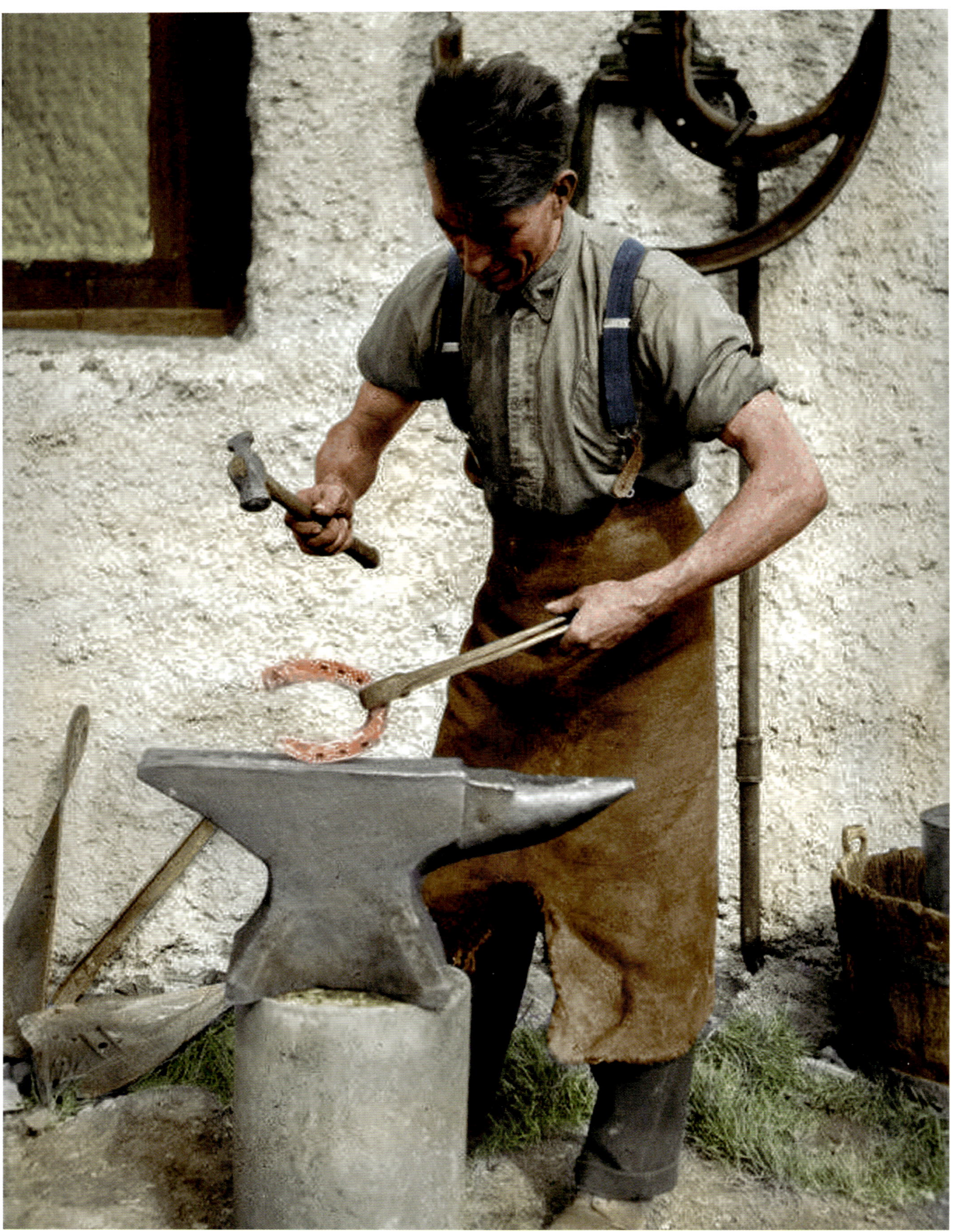

   THE IRISH FARM IN COLOUR

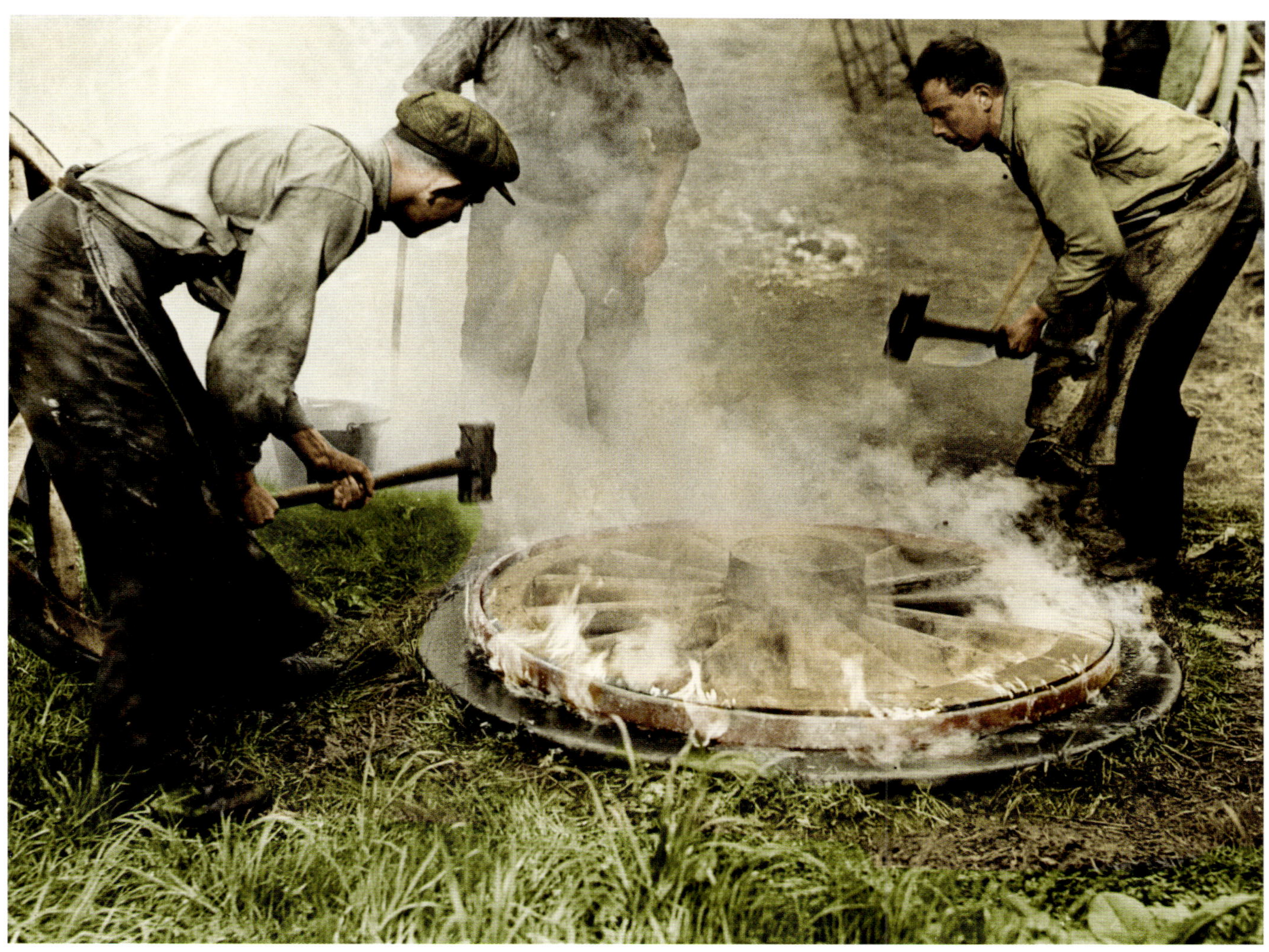

Left: The ring of hammer on anvil once echoed through every Irish village. Here, a blacksmith shapes a red-hot horseshoe, crafting the fittings that kept working horses steady and sure-footed.

Top right: Blacksmiths were crucial in keeping the wheels of rural Ireland turning, making much more than just horseshoes. Here, two blacksmiths work together to fit a red-hot iron tyre onto a cartwheel, a process that involved heating the metal, placing it on the timber rim, and then quenching it in water to shrink the tyre into a tight, secure fit. Beyond cartwheels, blacksmiths also repaired and crafted essential farm tools like ploughshares, horse-drawn mowing machines, farm carts and wagons.

A threshing is underway – always a great spectacle, as seen in this tableau of bustle and energy at Cloghroe, County Cork in 1928. A large steam tractor provides energy through a great wheel, on which a belt drives the machinery of the wood-clad threshing machine. Men stand atop the machine, feeding the bundles of wheat into the hopper or feeding chute. Once inside, oscillating feed rakes drag the wheat towards the threshing cylinder. This separates the grain from the straw, allowing the grain to fall through while the straw is expelled.

Belts, wheels and moving parts – it is not a scene that would pass today's health and safety criteria. For the men on top, caution was always necessary around the machine's moving components, as over the decades, fatalities or serious injuries like loss of hands or arms had ensued.

In the foreground, a woman stands alongside bags of freshly threshed grain, ready for storage or milling. This image demonstrates the efficiency of steam-powered machinery, which revolutionised farming by significantly speeding up the harvest process compared to traditional manual threshing methods.

Threshing machines were expensive pieces of equipment with limited seasonal use. As a result, in Ireland these machines were primarily hired out to farmers by agricultural contractors. While this was the predominant model, some larger estates or groups of wealthier farmers occasionally jointly purchased these machines.

There was a social aspect to threshing. The event itself required a lot of people: up to 18 or 20 could be needed for the various duties. In many instances, there was a meal on offer when the threshing was over. Frequently there was porter, and the bottle of whiskey would be produced.

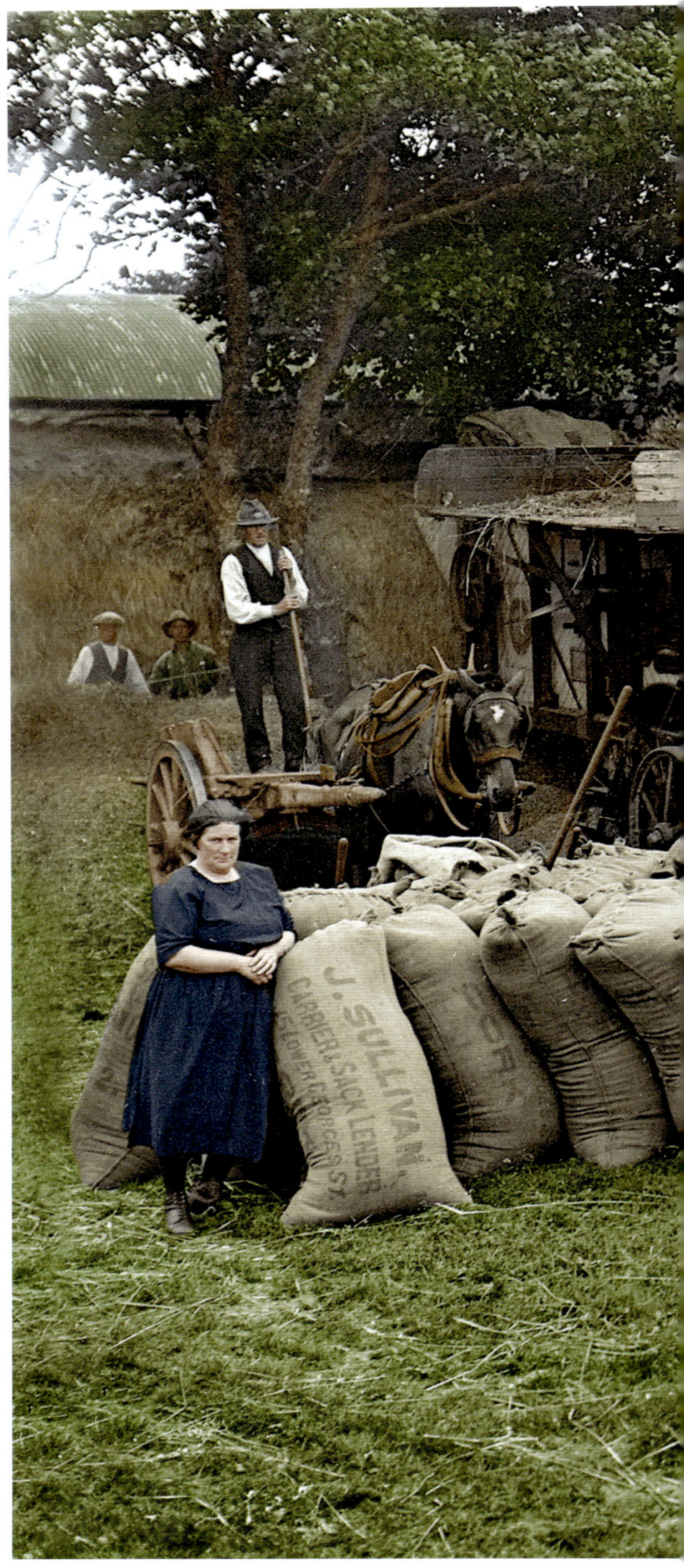

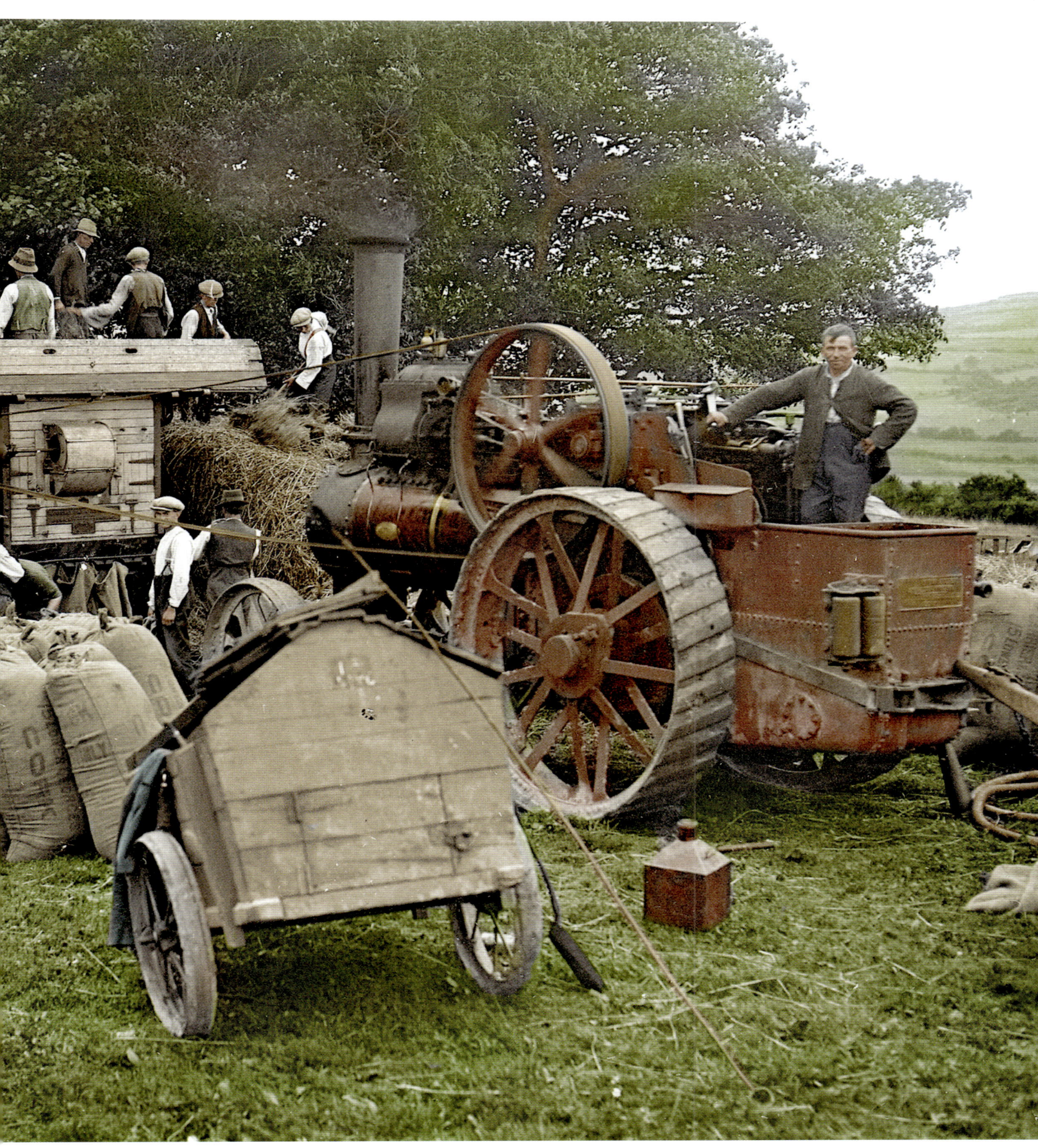

A 1946 scene of a threshing at Watergrasshill, County Cork. Many elements of the scene are similar to those of the previous photo. Men stand atop the threshing machine, feeding the hopper chute, while sacks of grain lie in the foreground. The difference is that now a compact tractor provides the power to the threshing machine, via the belt drive.

Diesel or petrol tractors offered many advantages over those powered by steam. This included greater mobility, higher fuel efficiency, consistent power output and improved safety. They required less maintenance and were easier to operate.

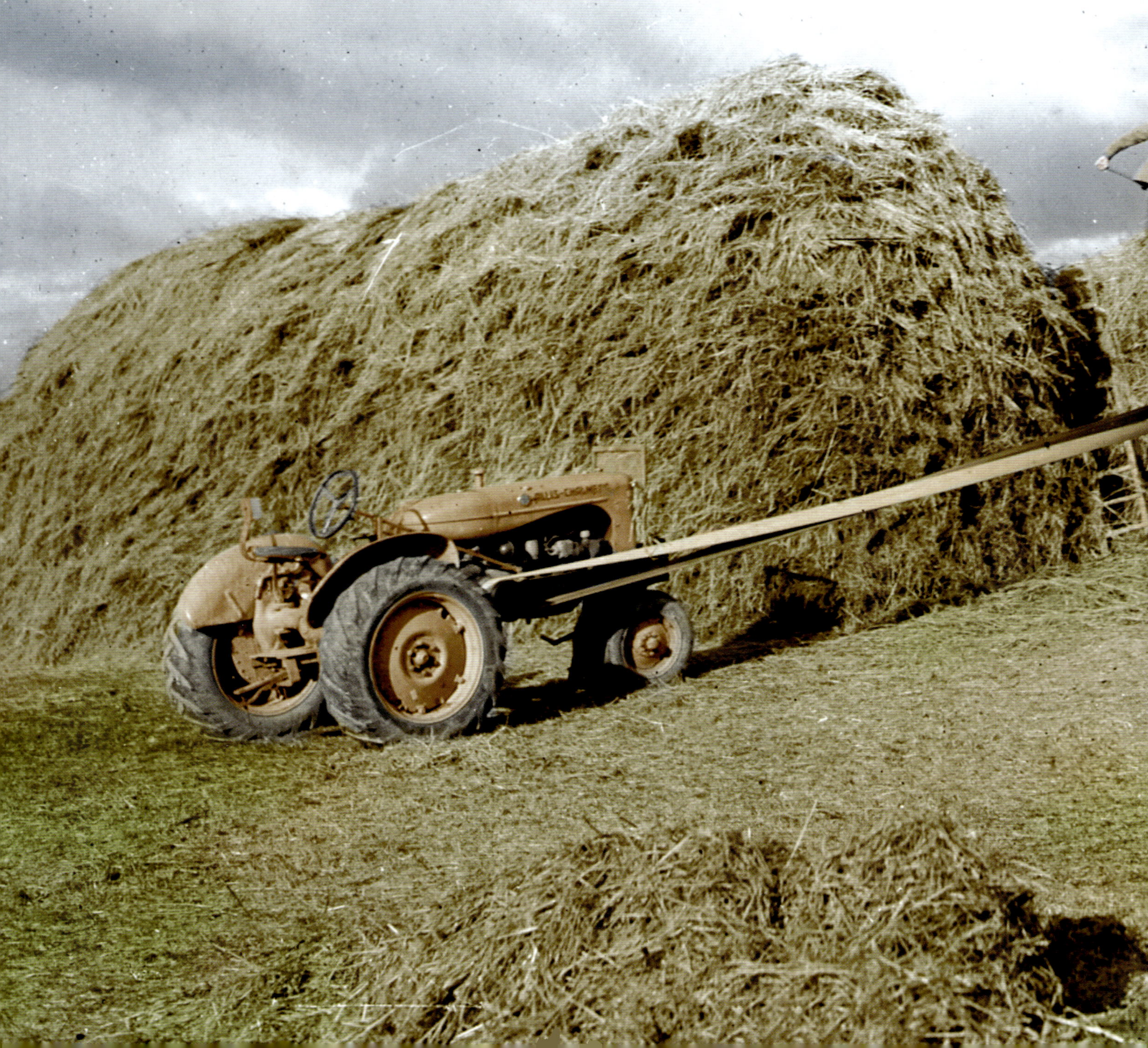

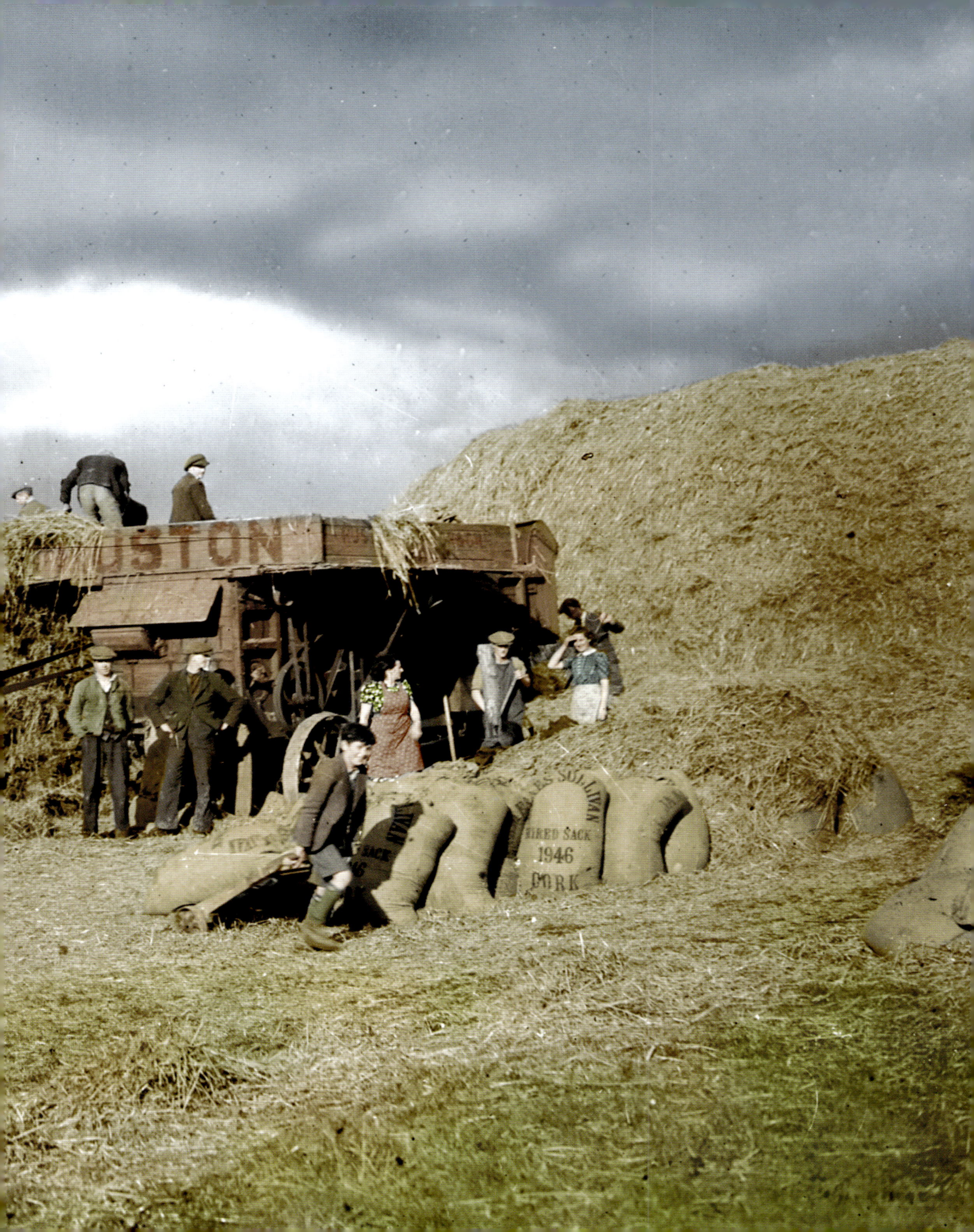

USTON
JAMES SULLIVAN
HIRED SACK
1946
CORK

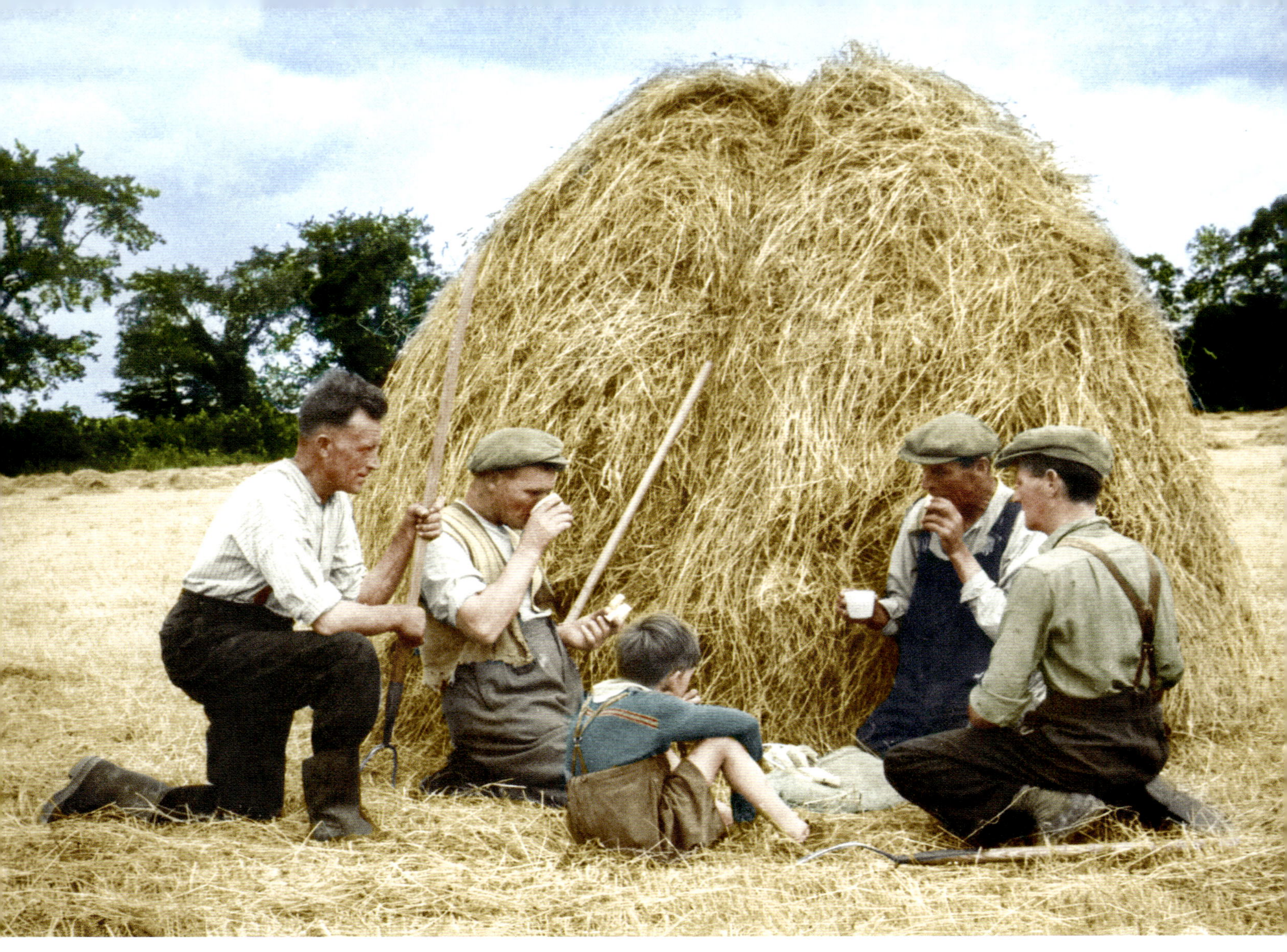

Time for a break when saving the hay, and so to set aside the pitchfork. With the scent of hay filling the air, the men along with a young boy sip their tea, possibly served from a sweet tin brought by the woman of the house. They can also savour the taste of homemade bread and, on occasion, enjoy such treats as currant cake.

Here, in the sunlit open meadow, the food would have tasted better, as seen in this nostalgic glimpse back to a simpler time now largely lost in an era of mechanised farming.

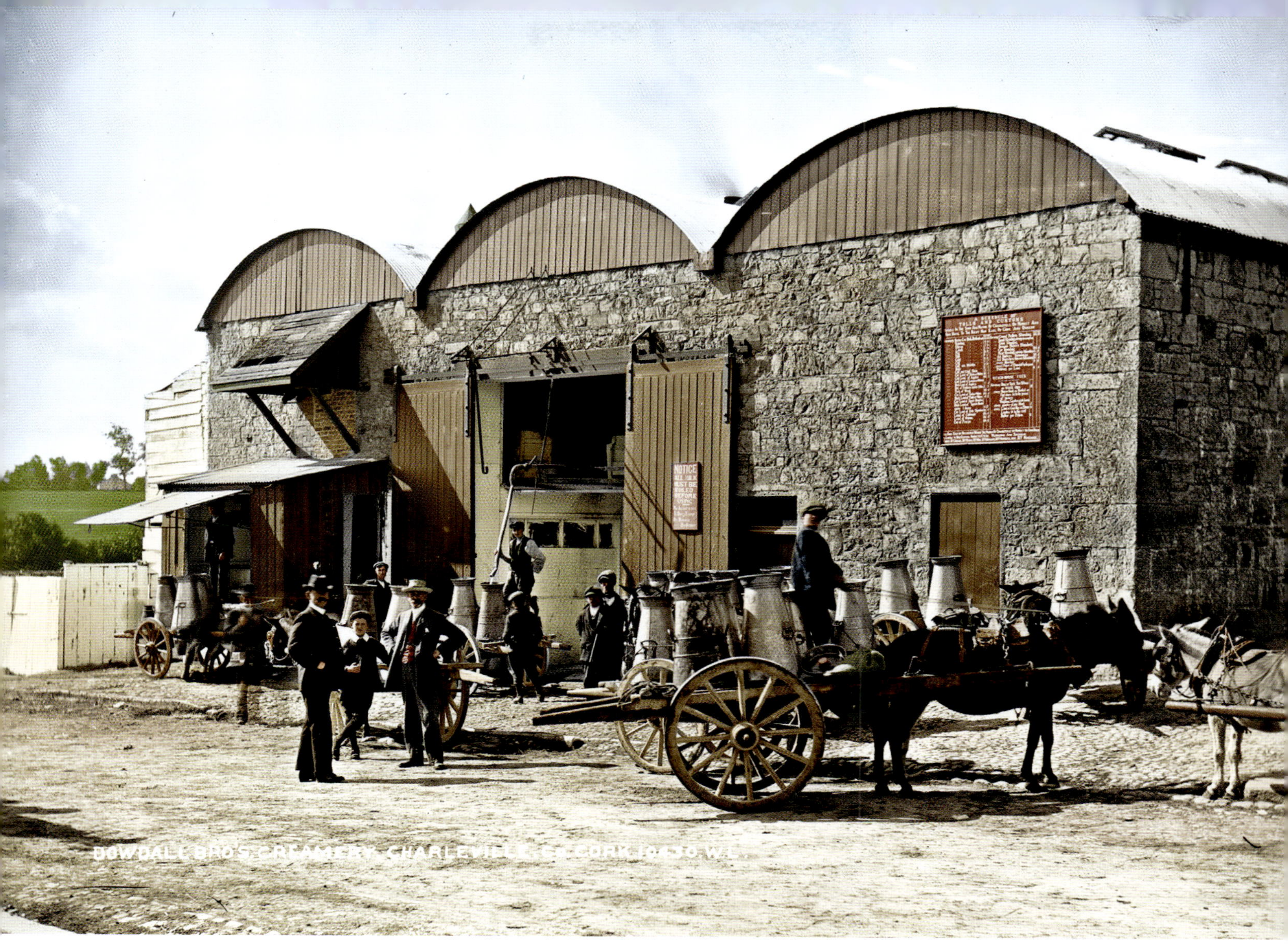

The horse was still king in this scene from the early twentieth century at Dowdall's Creamery near Charleville, County Cork. Just in case they had forgotten, a prominent sign on the wall informs the farmers of the taxes and tolls they have to pay to the Earl of Cork and Ossory. Here the farmers would arrive with their horse and carts, laden with milk in steel churns. They would unload the milk, which was measured and recorded. The milk was stored in holding tanks before being piped to a centrifugal separator, which separated the cream from the whole milk. The cream was cooled and then pumped to an industrial butter churn, where it was transformed into butter.

Skim milk can be seen filling a churn – this by-product was valuable for animal feed, particularly for pigs.

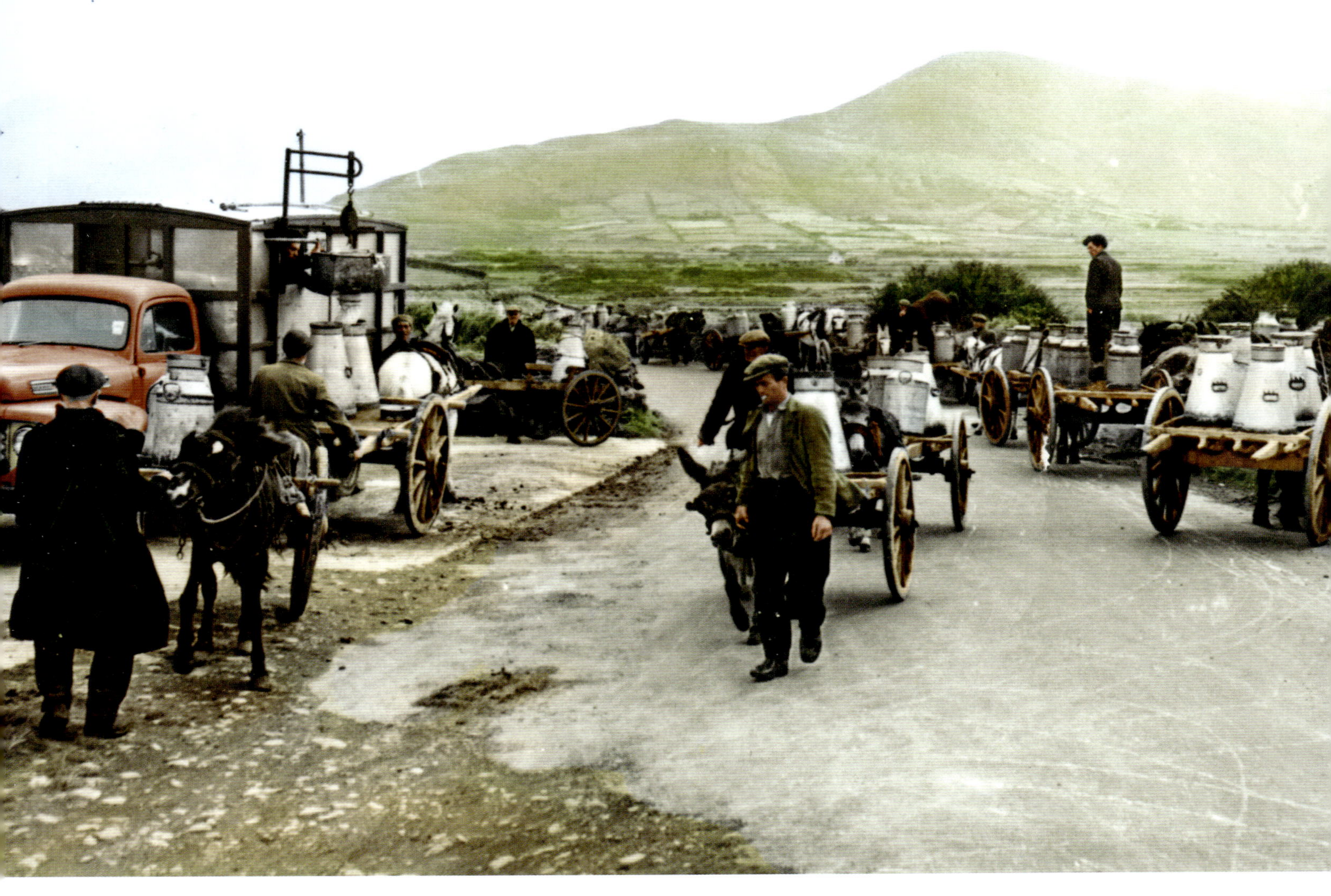

Five decades later, mobile creameries revolutionised life for farmers in remote areas by bringing milk collection closer to the farm. In this scene from County Kerry in 1967, horse power still transports the milk churns, while the travelling creamery operates from a truck instead.

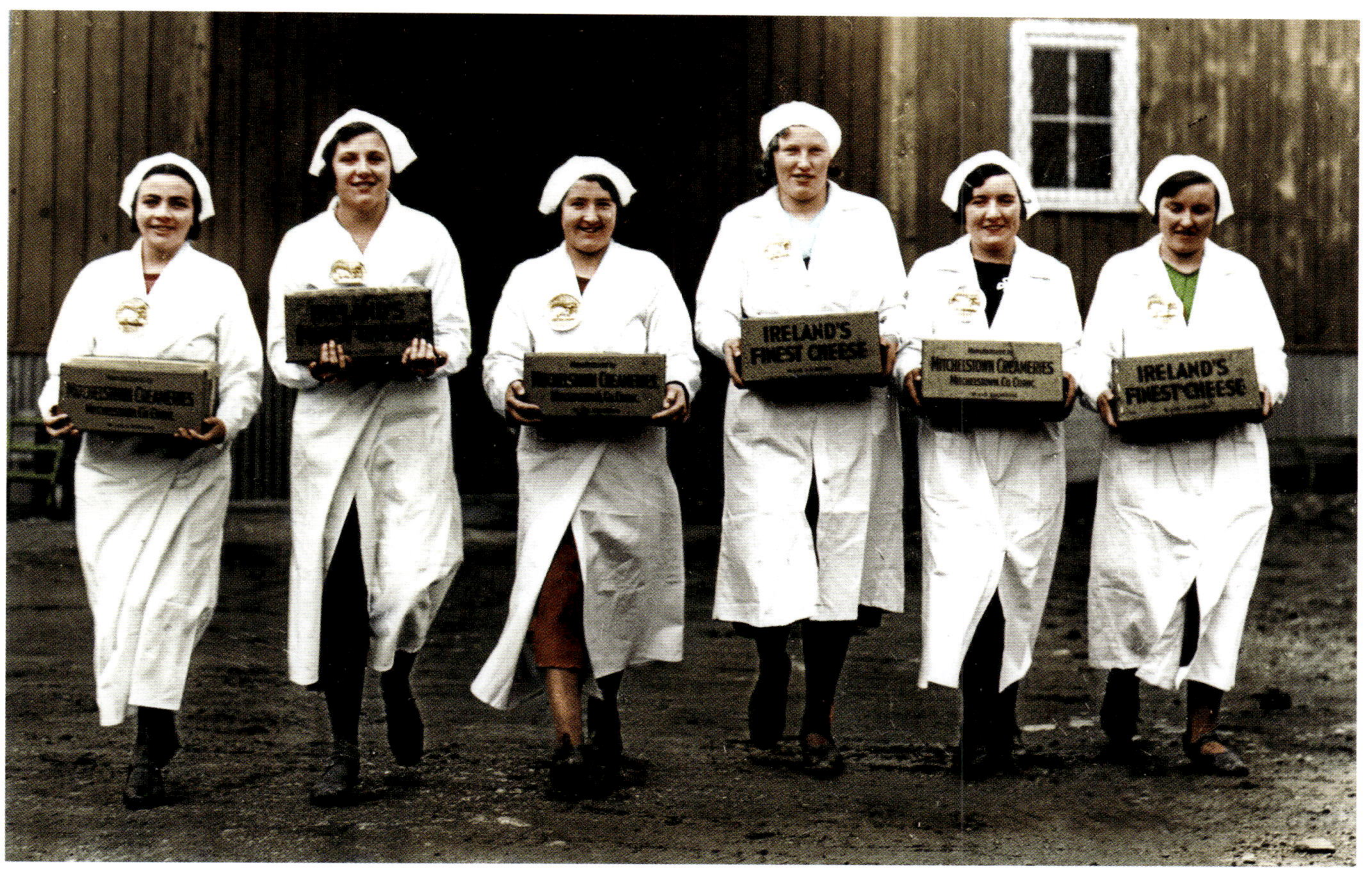

Today, Ireland boasts a vibrant cheese industry, with over 60 farmhouse cheese producers crafting a wonderful variety of high-quality cheeses. These are made from diverse milk sources – including cow, goat, sheep and even buffalo – and span a wide range of styles.

It was not always so. Younger generations may not recall the Ireland of the 1960s, when the market was dominated by just two processed, mass-produced cheeses: Galtee and Calvita (packs of six cheese triangles), both made by Mitchelstown Creameries.

This photograph captures an earlier era, showing five young women in white coats and hats carrying boxes labelled 'Mitchelstown Creameries' and 'Ireland's Finest Cheese'. These workers represent the thriving dairy industry in Mitchelstown, County Cork, during a time of significant growth for the local co-operative. Founded in 1919, Mitchelstown Co-operative Agricultural Society Ltd quickly became a powerhouse in Irish dairy production. In 1932, Mitchelstown obtained a government licence granting it a monopoly on the production and sale of processed cheese in the Irish market. By 1950, it was the country's second-largest employer, surpassed only by Guinness.

Mitchelstown Creameries, now part of Dairygold, continues to thrive in the dairy industry. Dairygold produces a range of premium dairy products, including rennet casein, demineralised whey, bulk cheddar cheese, speciality cheeses, milk powders and butter.

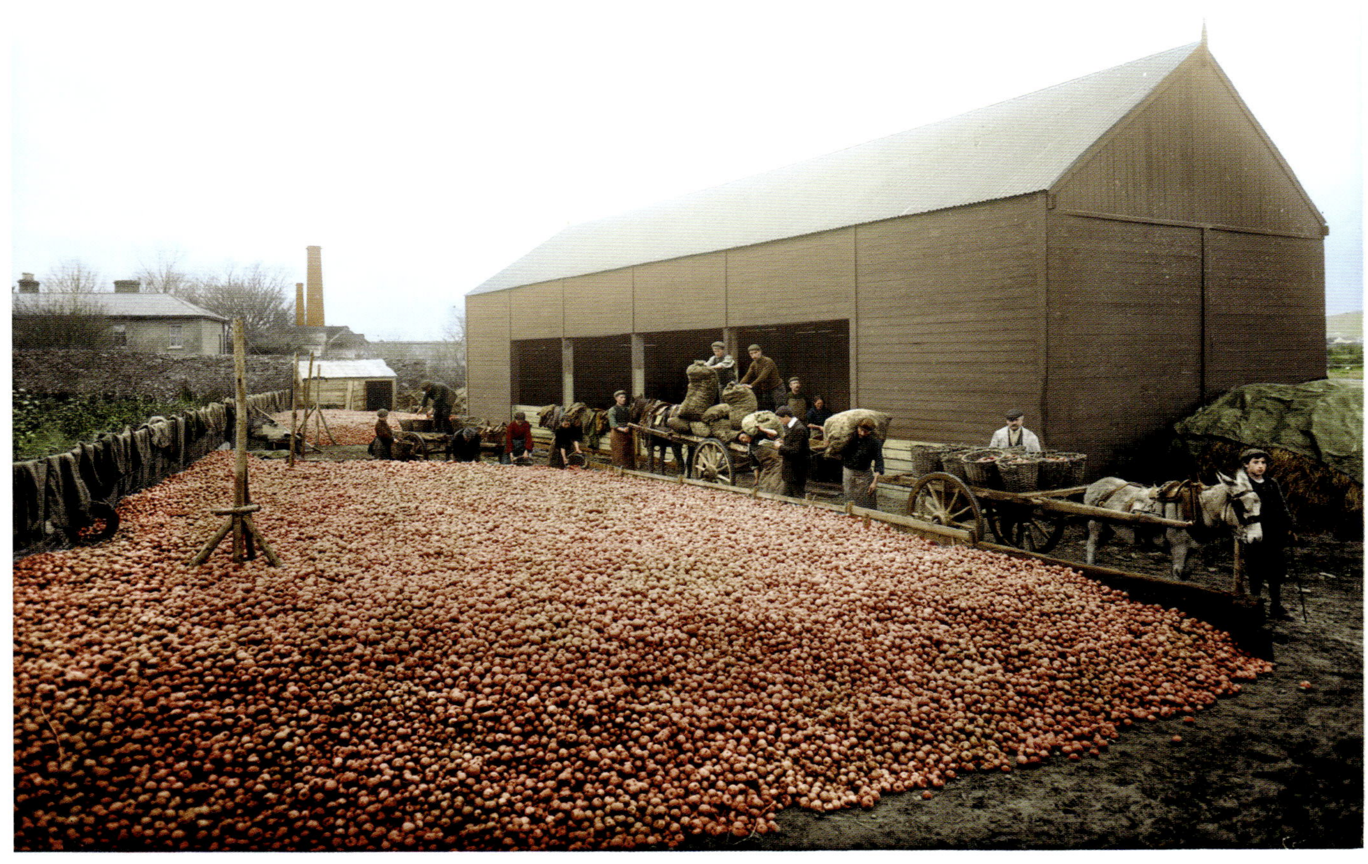

Top left: A red harvest: Thomas Power's cider factory in Dungarvan, County Waterford, was a notable player in the Irish market in the early twentieth century. The local climate and soil conditions, especially in Waterford, are ideal for apple cultivation. Cider production has been a part of Irish heritage for millennia.

Right: Taking a break during the barley harvest in County Wexford, *c*.1960. Men gather in front of the stationary harvester, some with bottles. In the foreground, one man with his sheepdog kneels in the field, holding his own bottle of Guinness – perhaps a fitting nod to the journey their barley will soon take from farm to brewery.

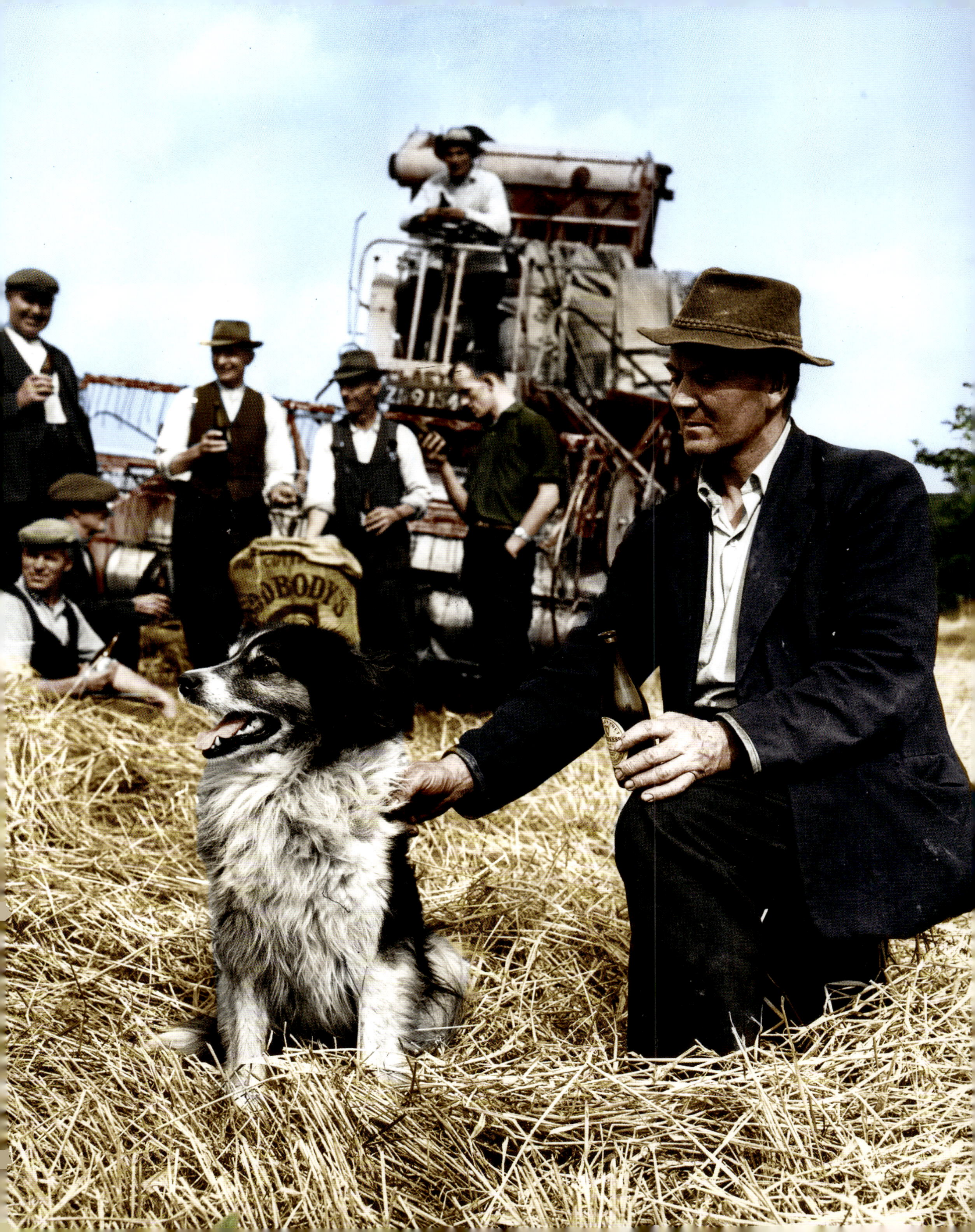
NOBODY'S

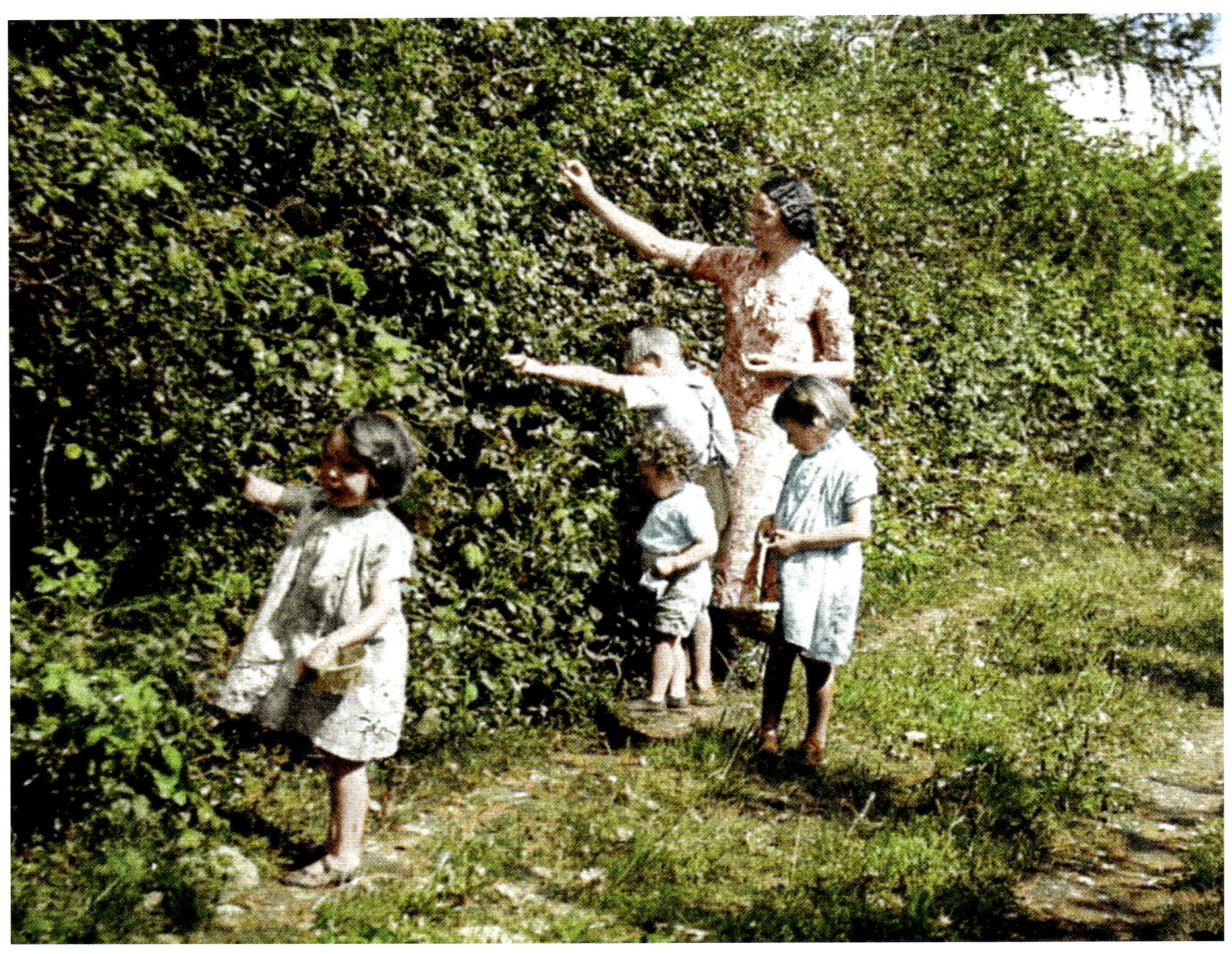

Top left: Children delight in the simple magic of blackberry picking – the joy of harvesting nature's bounty along byways and fields. These juicy berries are perfect for jams, pies or eating fresh on the spot.

Right: Harvesting along Ireland's coastline, rich with seaweeds that offer natural health benefits. A carrageen collector at Trá an Dóilín, Carraroe, County Galway gathers this valuable seaweed, traditionally used to thicken soups and desserts.

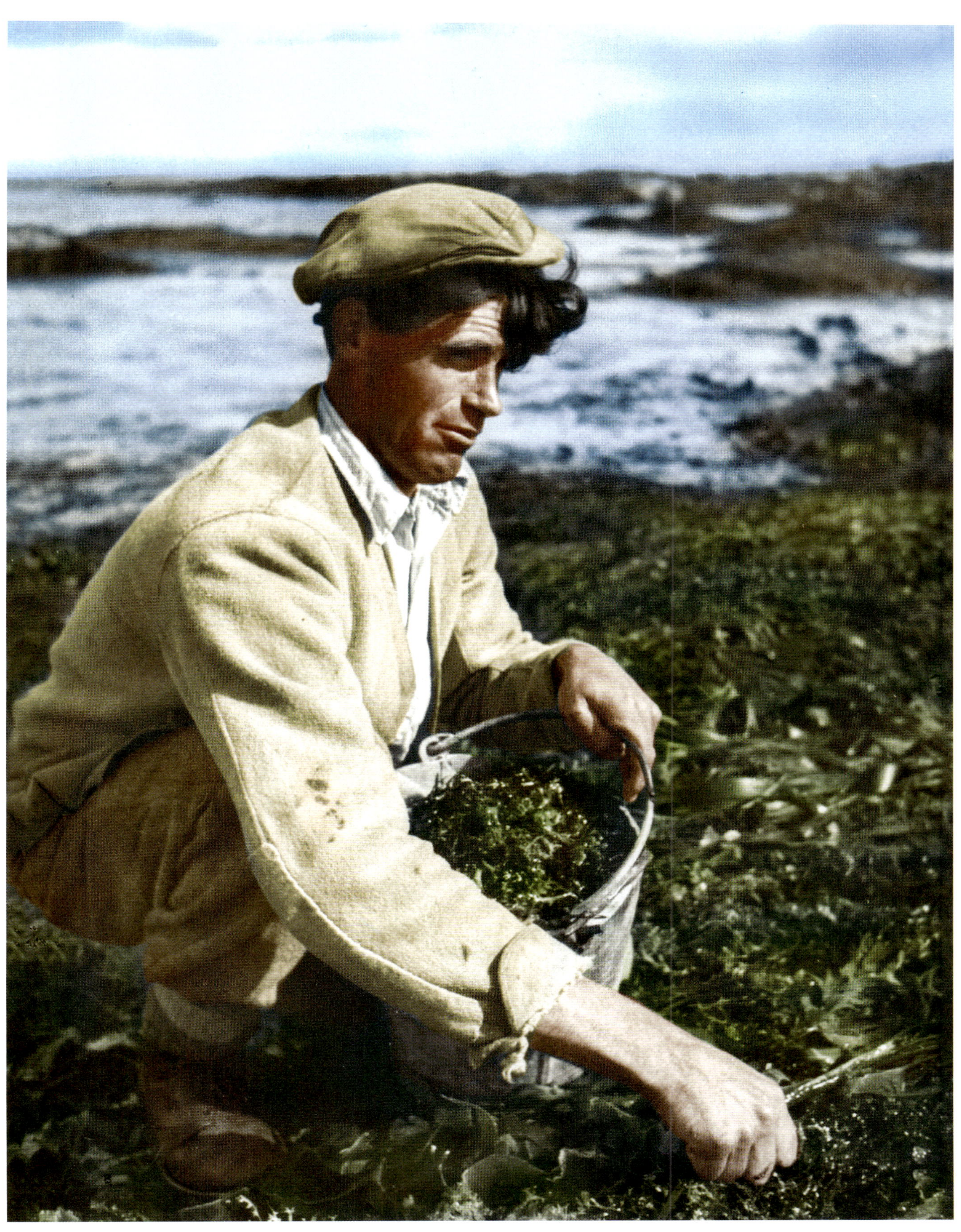

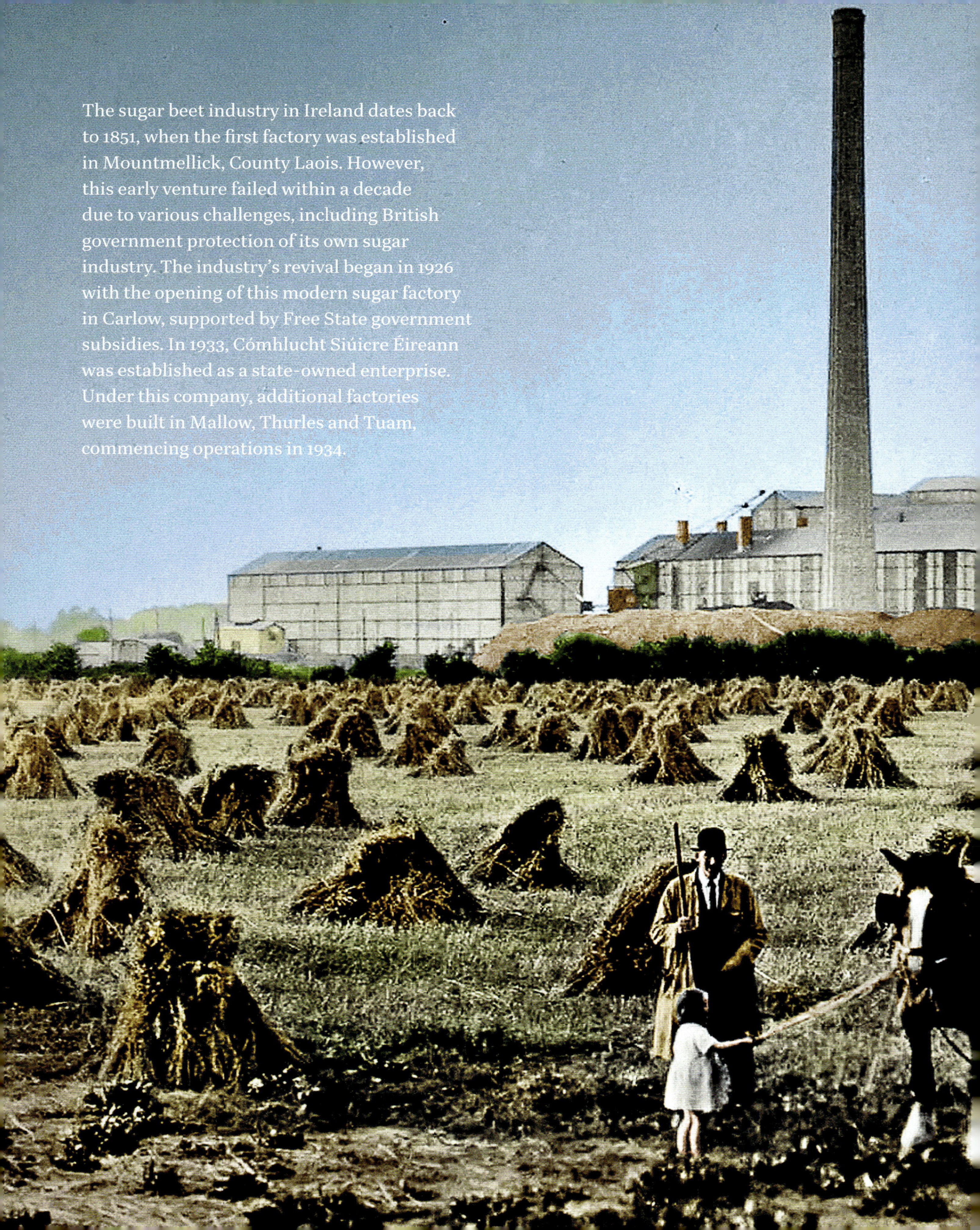

The sugar beet industry in Ireland dates back
to 1851, when the first factory was established
in Mountmellick, County Laois. However,
this early venture failed within a decade
due to various challenges, including British
government protection of its own sugar
industry. The industry's revival began in 1926
with the opening of this modern sugar factory
in Carlow, supported by Free State government
subsidies. In 1933, Cómhlucht Siúicre Éireann
was established as a state-owned enterprise.
Under this company, additional factories
were built in Mallow, Thurles and Tuam,
commencing operations in 1934.

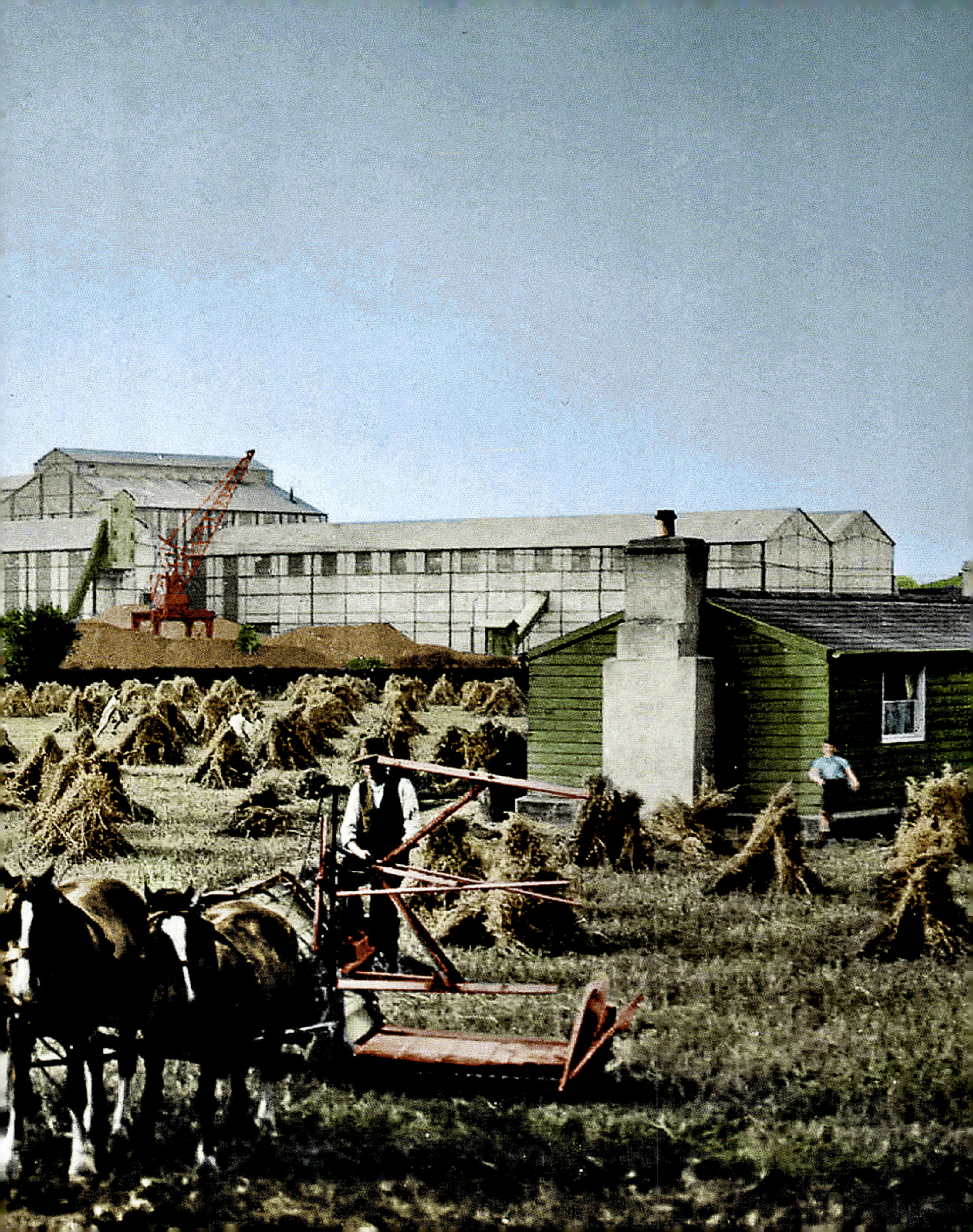

Tobacco workers pose at Rathmoylan, County Waterford, in 1933. This scene captures a brief resurgence in Irish tobacco cultivation, part of Fianna Fáil's efforts to promote economic self-sufficiency during the 1930s. While Ireland's soil and climate – particularly in the east and south-west – were suitable for growing tobacco, they were far less optimal than regions like the south-eastern states of the US, where the crop thrived. As a result, Irish tobacco struggled to compete economically, and by the 1950s, the experiment in self-sufficiency had effectively come to an end.

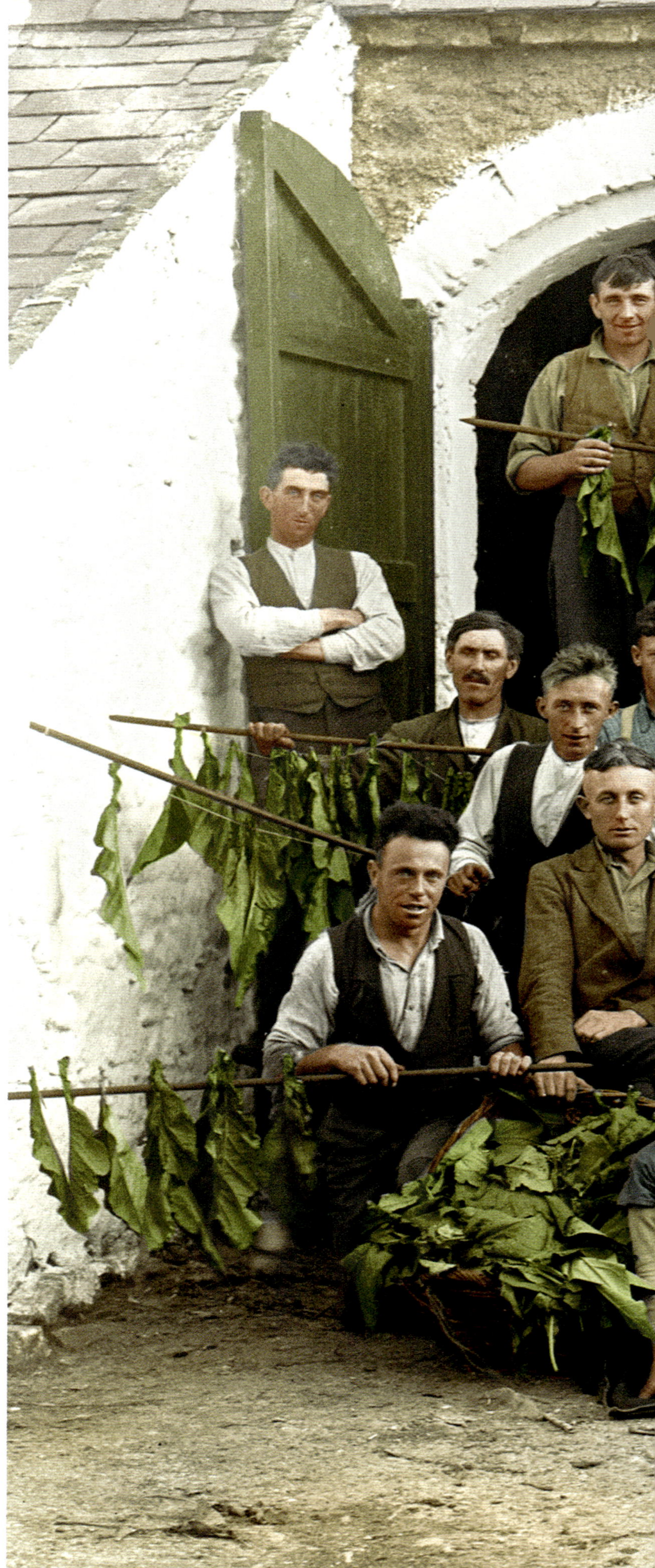

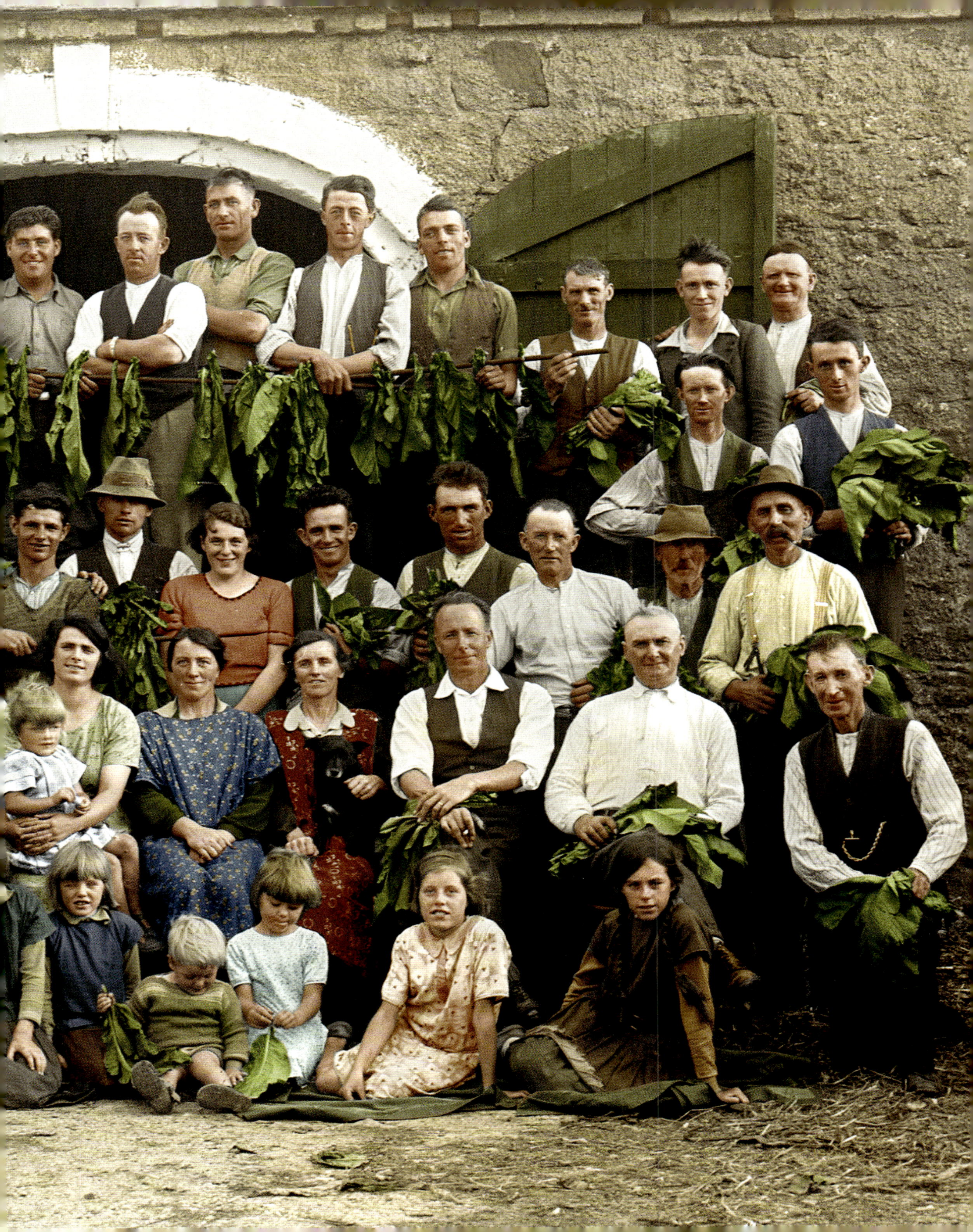

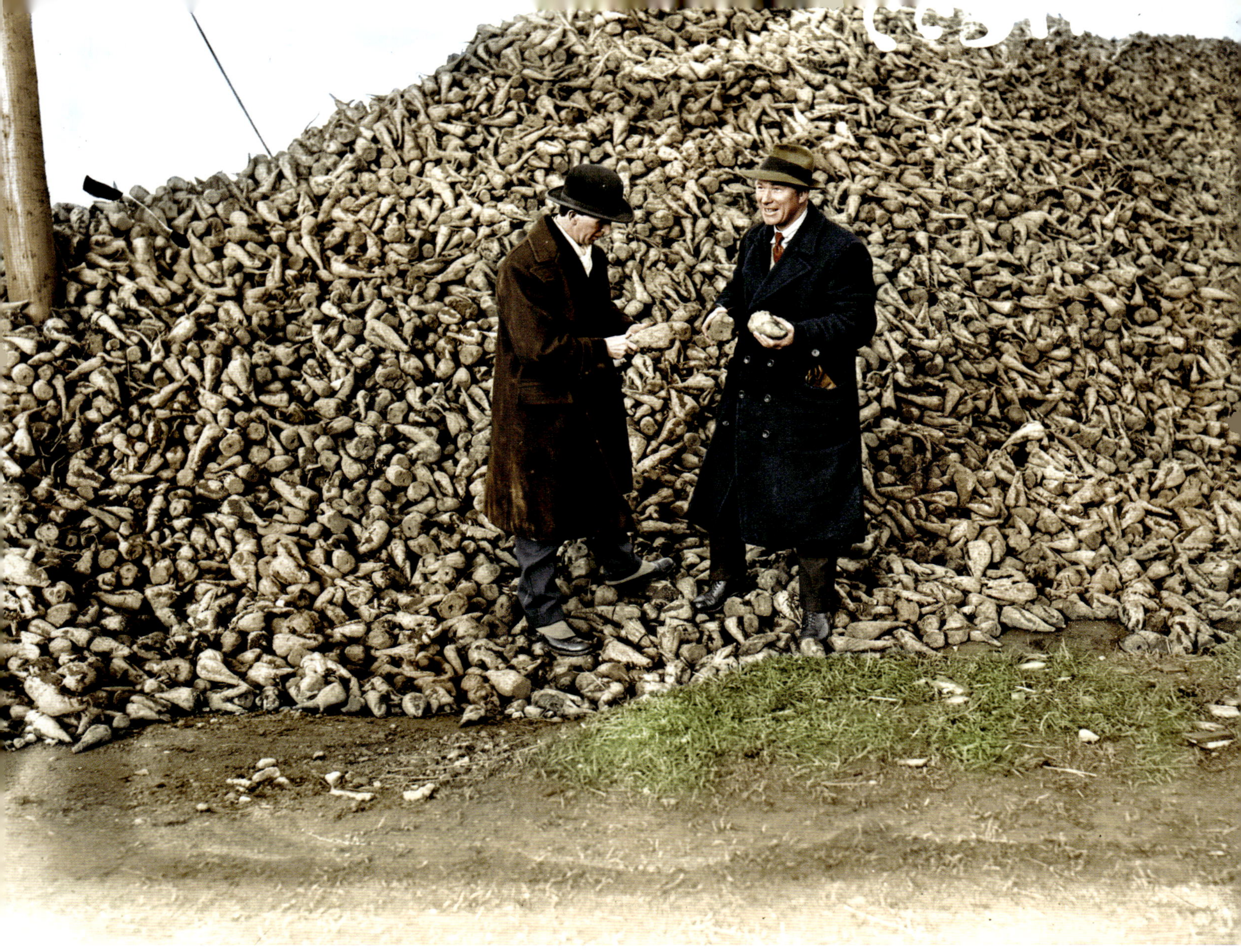

Men inspect beet at the Carlow factory. By 1936, almost 28,000 farmers were growing 500,000 tonnes of sugar beet in 22 counties nationwide and it provided a profitable cash crop for farmers. However, fast forward to 2006, when EU reforms slashed sugar beet prices by 36 per cent, and production was no longer viable in Ireland. Despite the historically high sugar content in Irish beet, the government accepted EU compensation to exit the industry, which led to the closure of the last sugar factory in Mallow.

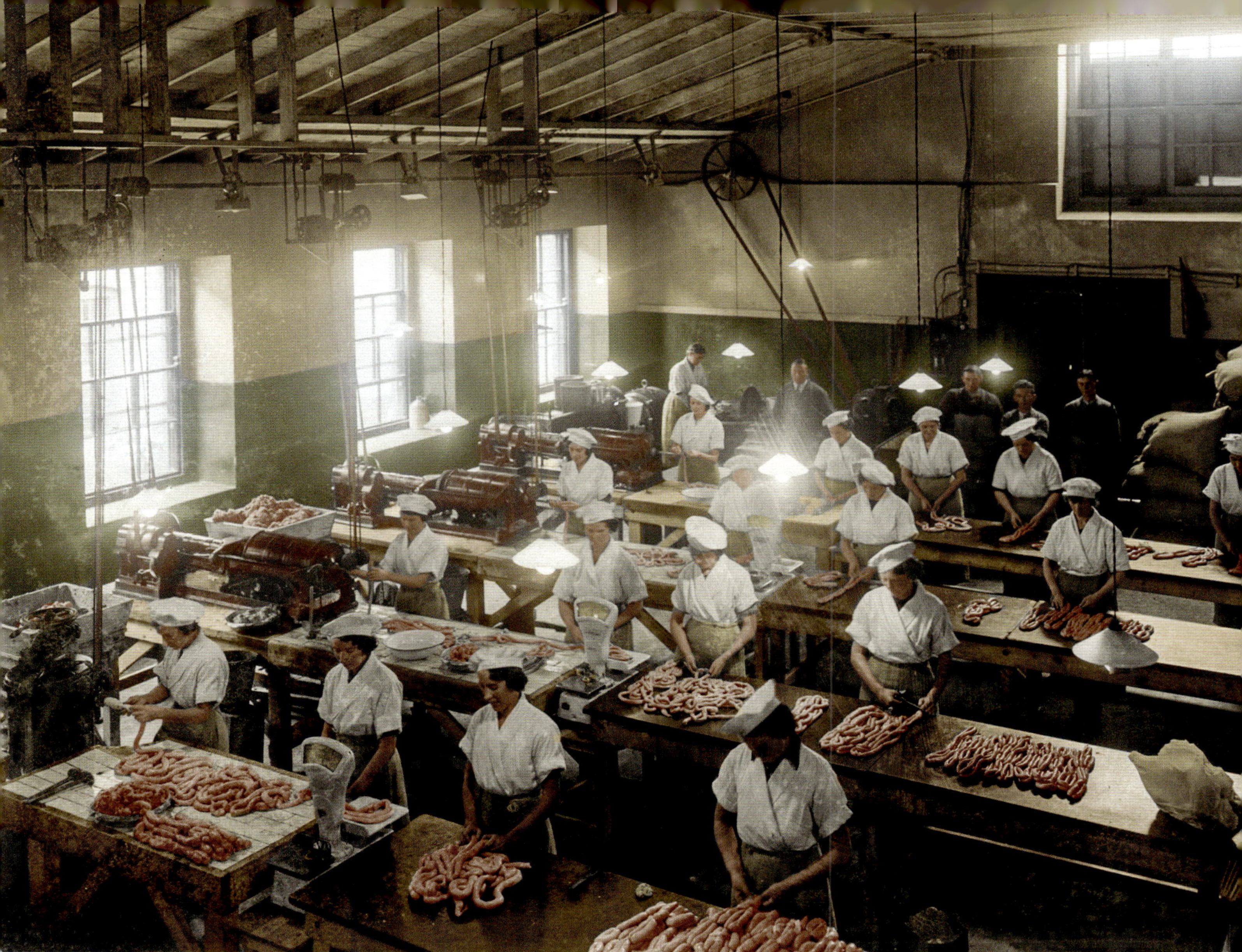

The sausage was, and still is, a key part of the Irish diet. Denny's Sausage Room, Waterford, seen here in 1937, shows women workers amidst tables piled with sausages. Henry Denny & Sons, founded in the 1820s, revolutionised the Irish bacon industry with advanced curing techniques. Their sausages became well known, even earning a mention in James Joyce's *Ulysses*, where Leopold Bloom contemplates his breakfast and plans his purchases at the butchers: 'And a pound and a half of Denny's sausages'.

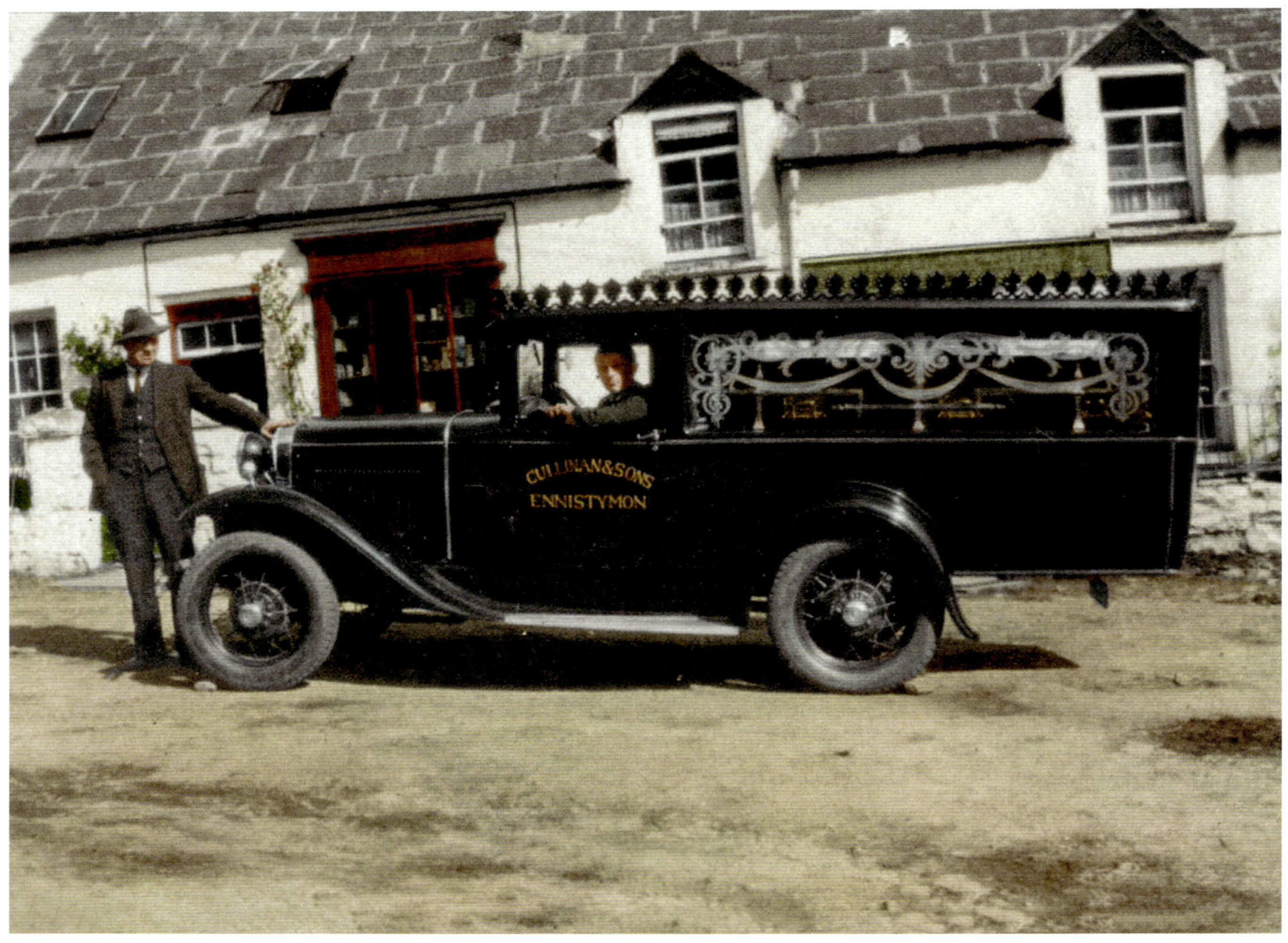

Top left: An impressive hearse from Cullinan and Sons, undertakers, seen here at Ennistymon, County Clare during the late 1930s. While the country generally held to its traditional funeral practices, this vehicle marks a shift from the time of horse-drawn hearses.

Right: Traditional Irish funeral processions carry the weight of both grief and community. The Arranmore disaster, in November 1935, saw 19 people drown when their boat struck a rock off the coast of Donegal. In this photograph the islanders, bound by sorrow and solidarity, carry the multiple coffins to the graveyard, led by a priest.

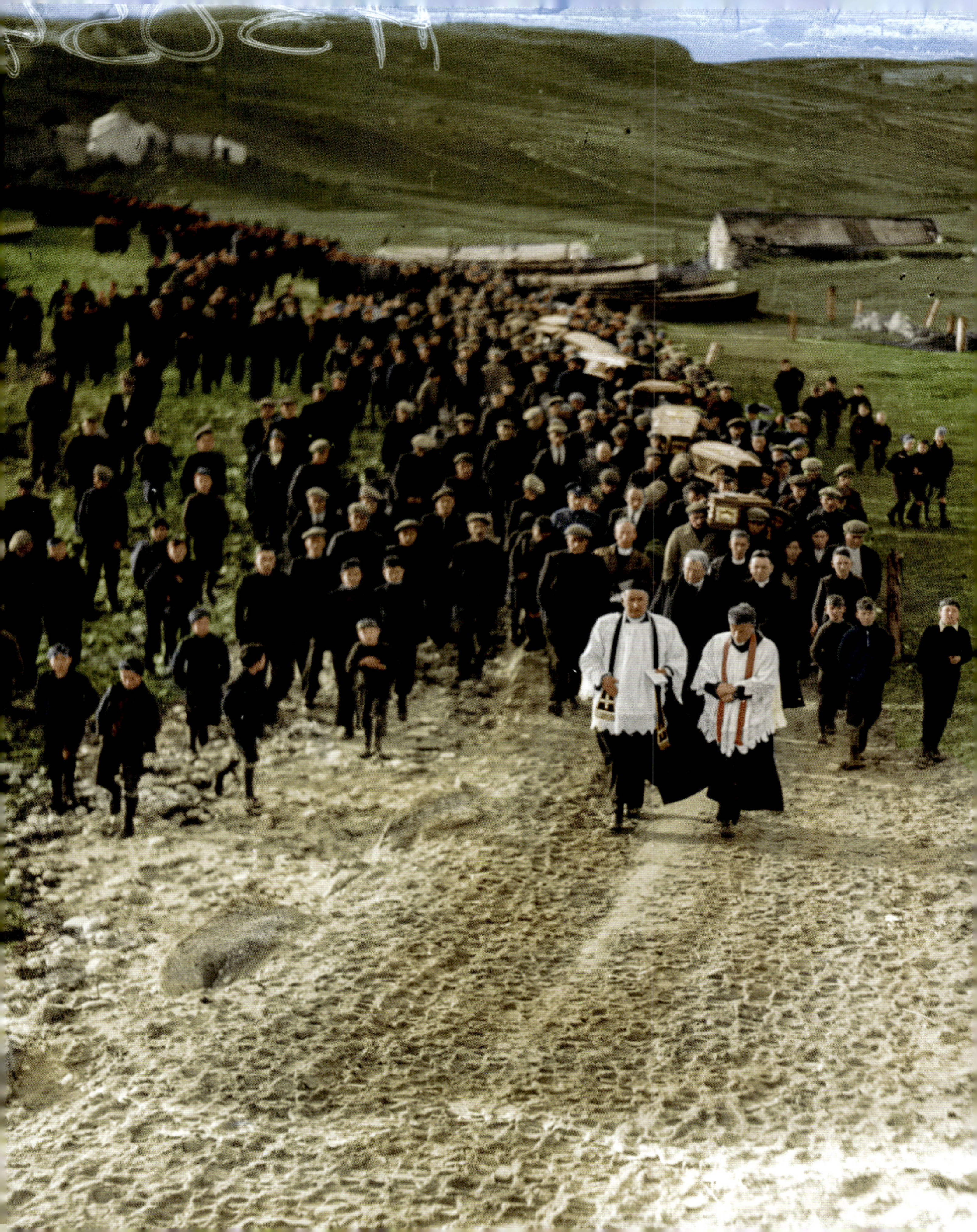

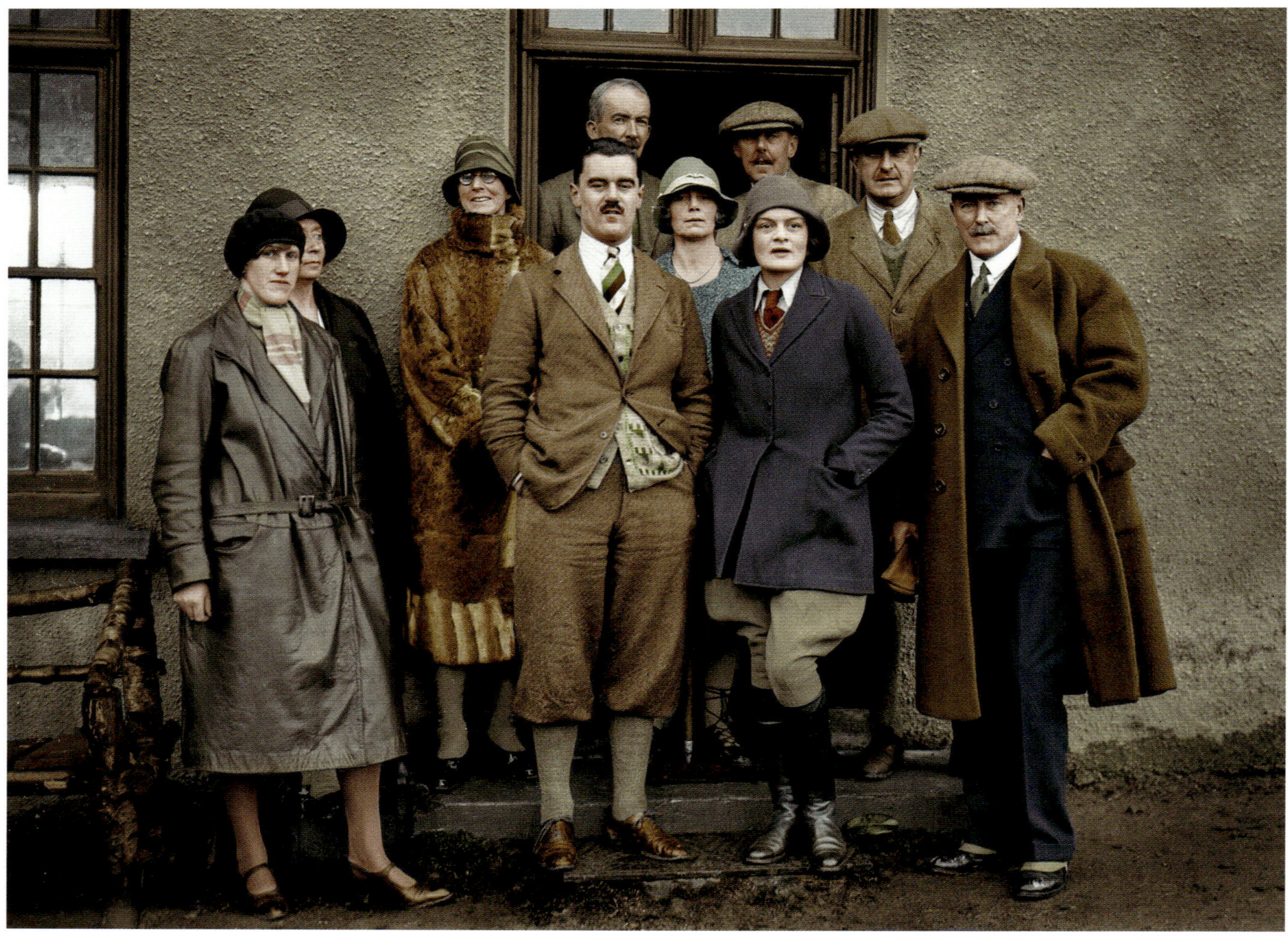

Percy Bernard, 5th Earl of Bandon, is pictured here with companions at a meet of the Carbery Hunt, an important social event bringing together members of the local gentry and aristocracy. The caption says this scene is at Castle Bernard in 1929. This is a little puzzling, as the building in the background looks to be in remarkably good shape – the castle had been burned down in June 1921, during the War of Independence.

Castle Bernard, like many of the great houses in Ireland, fell into decline in the wake of the War of Independence and the Civil War, with several estates burned out during this tumultuous period.

Percy Bernard was a prominent figure in the Anglo-Irish aristocracy. He inherited the earldom in 1924 and would go on to become an Air Chief Marshal in the Royal Air Force, serving with distinction during World War II.

By the time this photo was taken, the era of the Anglo-Irish ascendancy was fading, with families like the Bernards having to contend with the new political realities in Ireland.

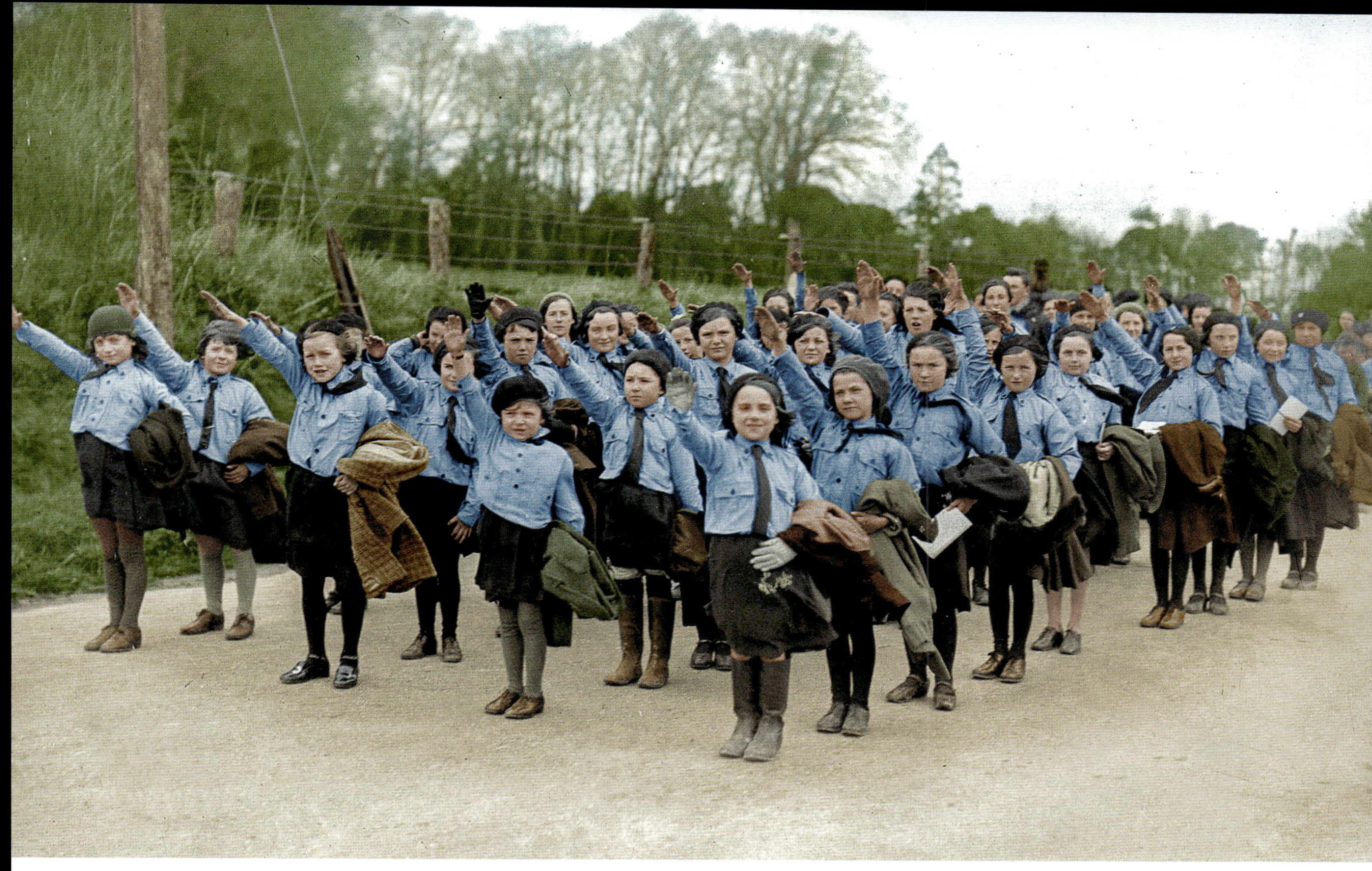

The Blueshirts, a paramilitary organisation founded in Ireland in 1932 as the Army Comrades Association, initially emerged in response to perceived threats from Republican mob violence. The movement shared some characteristics with contemporary fascist movements, advocating for corporatism and a patriotic reawakening. However, one prominent historian has suggested (perhaps unkindly) that 'Fascism was far too intellectually demanding for the bulk of the Blueshirts.'

Ostensibly, they were against the menace of communism – in a country that had perhaps the lowest number of communists per square kilometre in all of Europe. Very few were urban working class or small farmers. Many were large and medium-sized farmers on good land, hurting as a consequence of the Economic War.

The Blueshirts encouraged farmers to withhold payment of land annuities, leading to clashes with authorities, which culminated in a riot in August 1934, where Blueshirts rammed a truck into a Cork cattle auction, resulting in one death and several injuries.

In many cases, being a member of the movement was a family affair. In the Blueshirt heartlands, there were even equivalents to the Boy Scouts or Girl Guides – here at Charleville, County Cork, young girls give the fascist salute.

At its peak, the movement claimed up to 48,000 members. However, the organisation began to decline by 1935, with most members eventually backing the newly formed Fine Gael, which took a more moderate and democratic path.

Vets are critical for the care and management of Irish livestock. Aleen Cust was a pioneer, breaking barriers for women in the profession. Born in Tipperary in 1868, she trained at the New Veterinary College in Edinburgh, but was denied membership of the Royal College of Veterinary Surgeons (RCVS) in 1897 solely because she was a woman.

Undeterred, she managed to practise in Ireland, being appointed Veterinary Inspector for Galway County Council and tending to farm animals across rural areas. During World War I, she travelled to France, where she drove ambulances and assisted in the care of war horses. Following the passage of the Sex Disqualification (Removal) Act, she was finally admitted to the RCVS in 1922, officially becoming the first female veterinary surgeon in Britain and Ireland. She retired in 1924 and later moved to England, where she died in 1937.

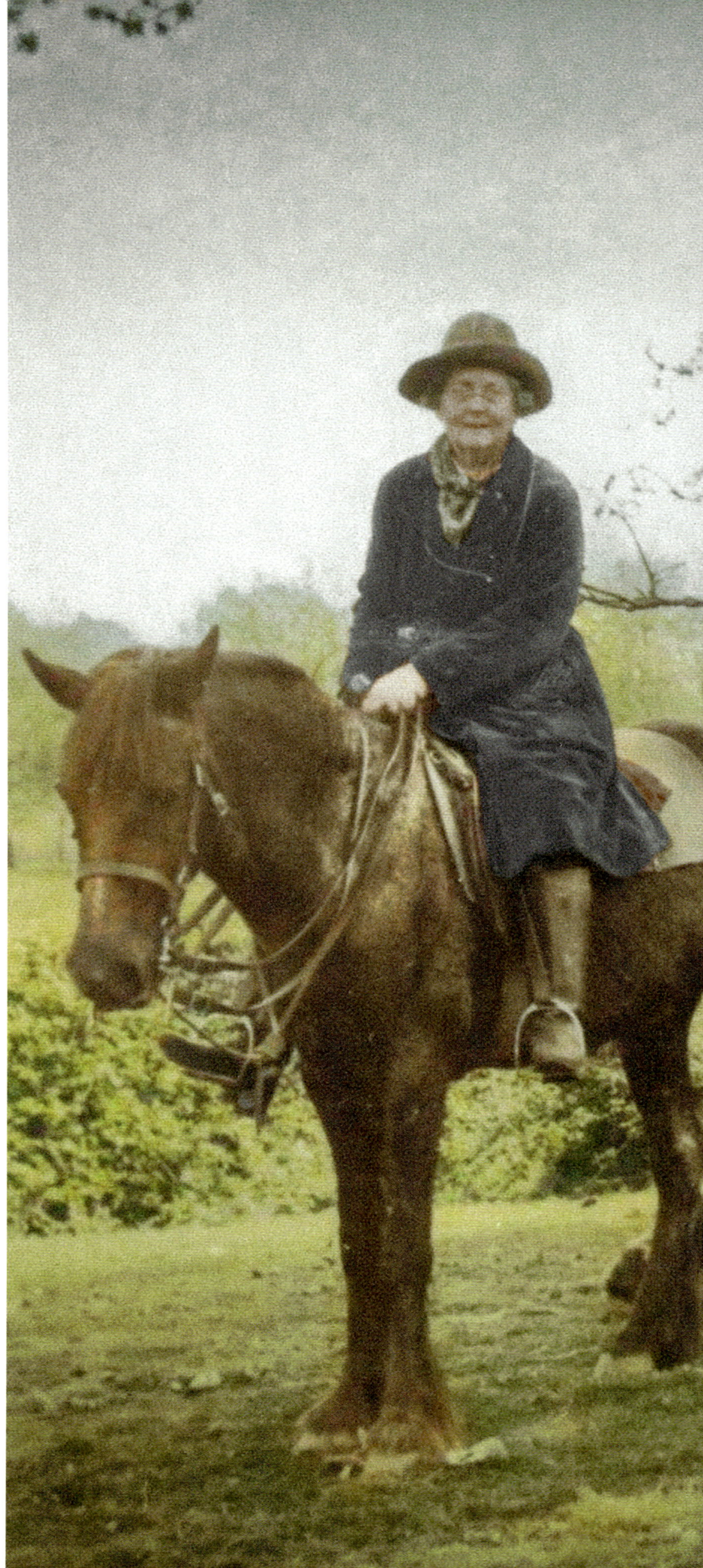

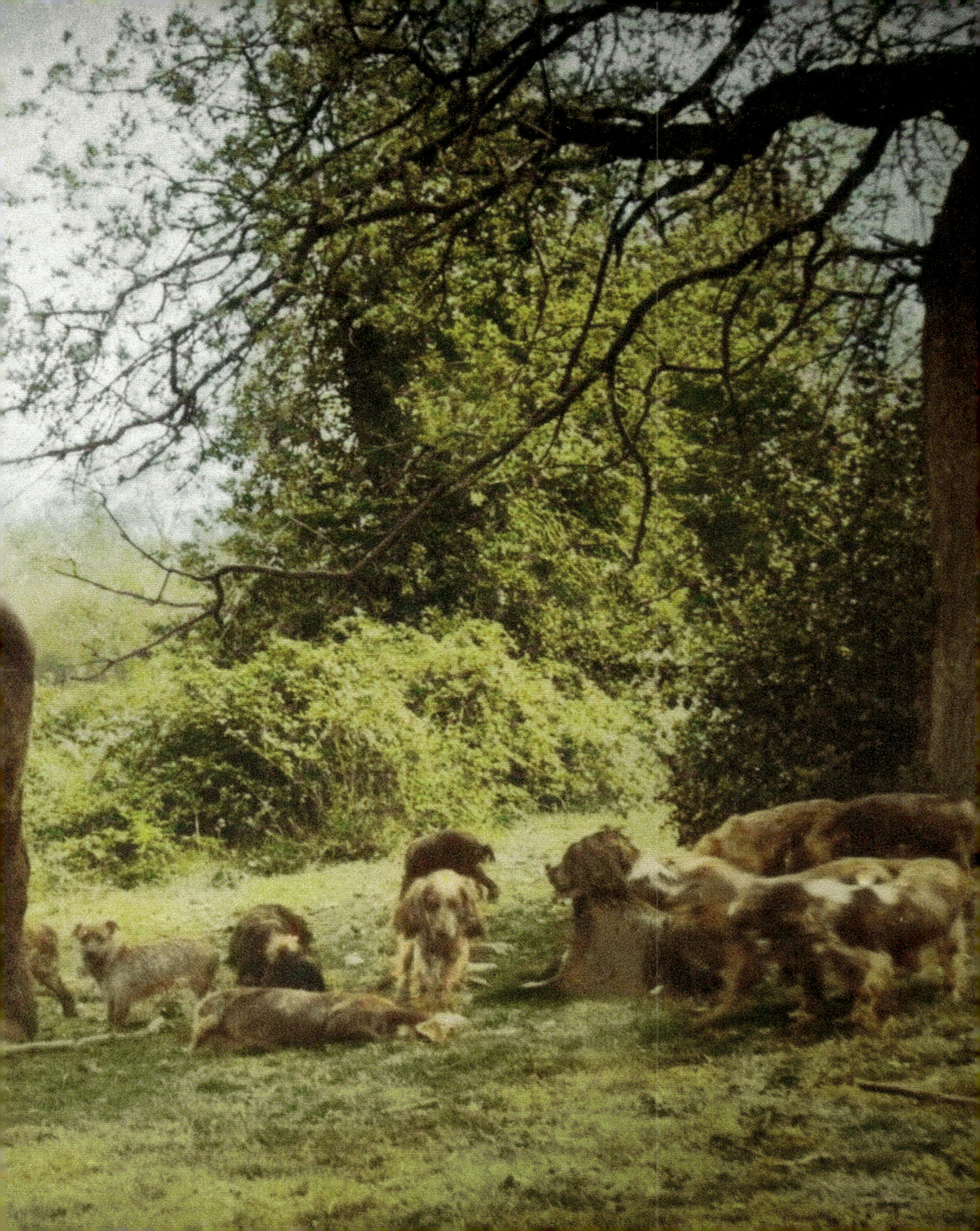

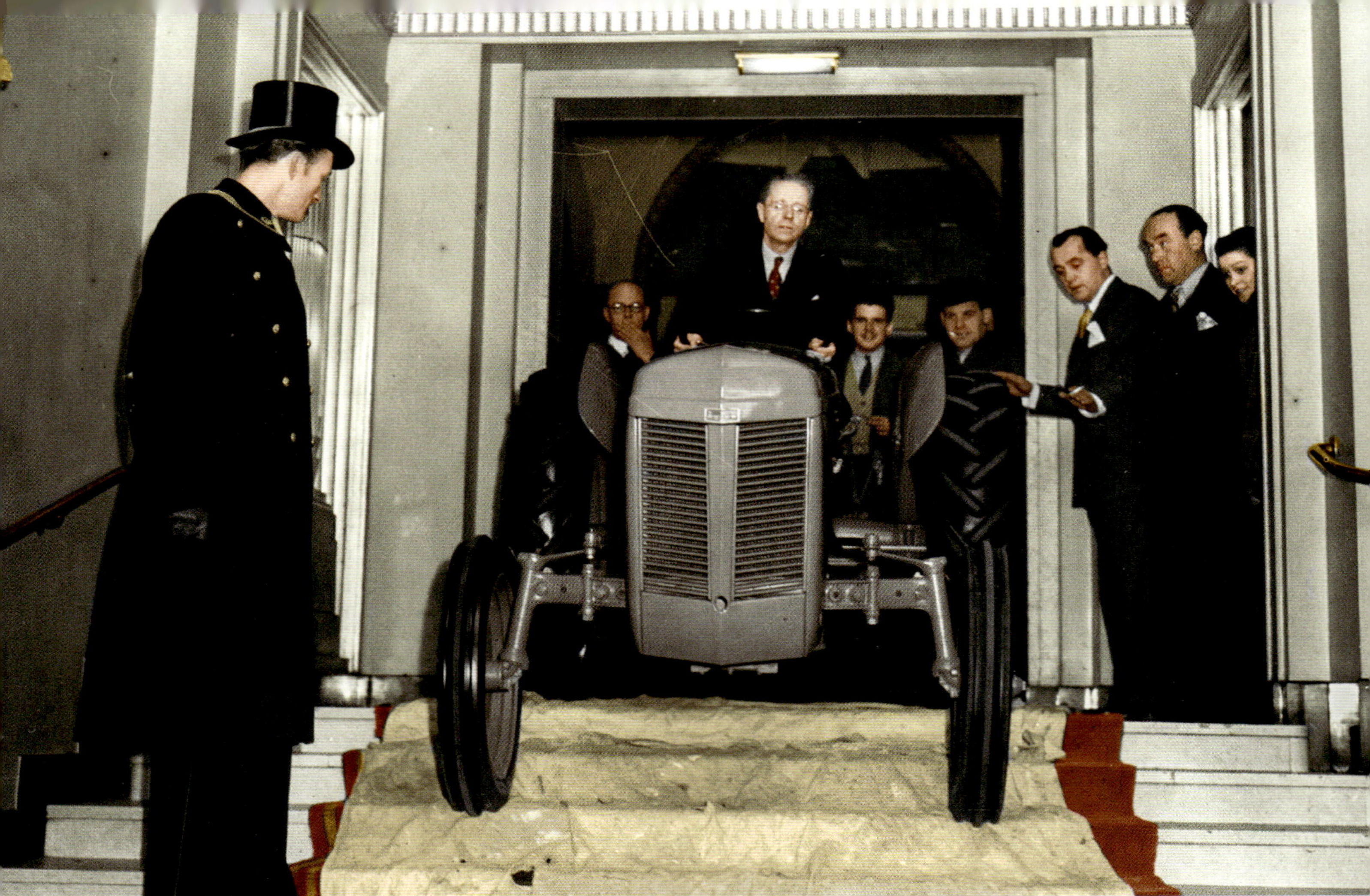

Harry Ferguson, a pioneer in agricultural engineering from County Down, demonstrated his TE 20 tractor's versatility in 1948 by driving it down the steps of Claridge's Hotel in London. He revolutionised farming with his groundbreaking three-point linkage system, which allowed implements to be more effectively mounted and controlled.

Tractor manufacturing had flourished for a period in Cork, where Ford had produced Fordson tractors until 1932. A few years later, in 1938, Ferguson and Henry Ford entered into a verbal 'handshake agreement' to collaborate on tractor production. Ferguson provided his innovative hitch system while Ford handled manufacturing, resulting in the launch of the Ford-Ferguson 9N tractor in 1939.

However, their partnership ended in 1946 when Ford unilaterally terminated the agreement. Ferguson later sued Ford for patent infringement over the 8N tractor, securing a $9.25 million settlement in 1952.

The Ferguson TE 20 tractor had been introduced in 1946, and soon became a ubiquitous sight on Irish farms. It was widely distributed around the world – by 1956, the Coventry factory had produced over a half million examples.

In 1953, Ferguson's company merged with Massey-Harris, a Canadian agricultural machinery company. Following the merger, Massey Ferguson tractors quickly became bestsellers, with models prized for reliability, fuel efficiency and ease of use on farms.

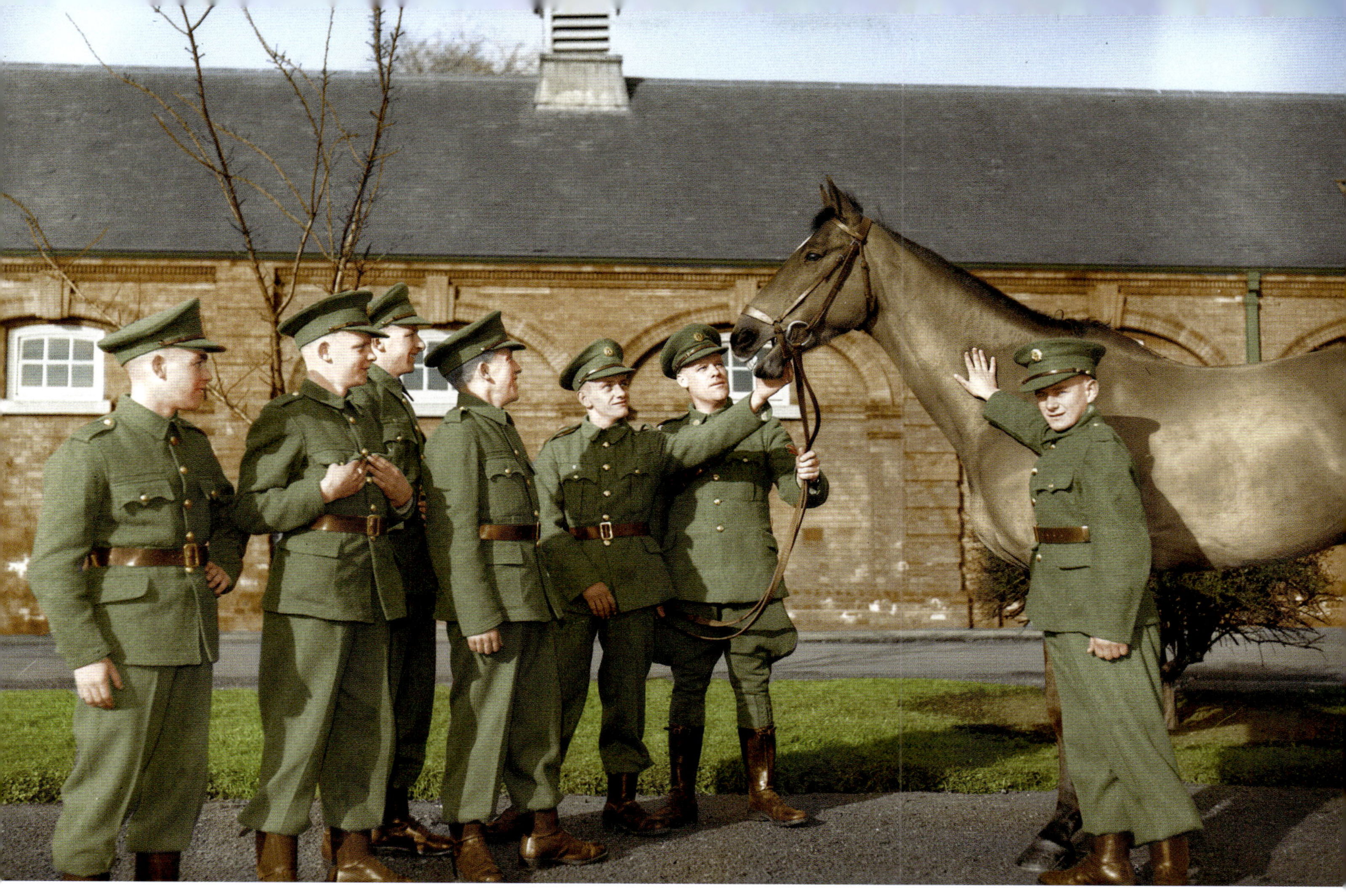

Soldiers with a horse at the Army Equitation School. Established in 1926, this has played a significant role in Ireland's show-jumping history and the promotion of Irish horses internationally.

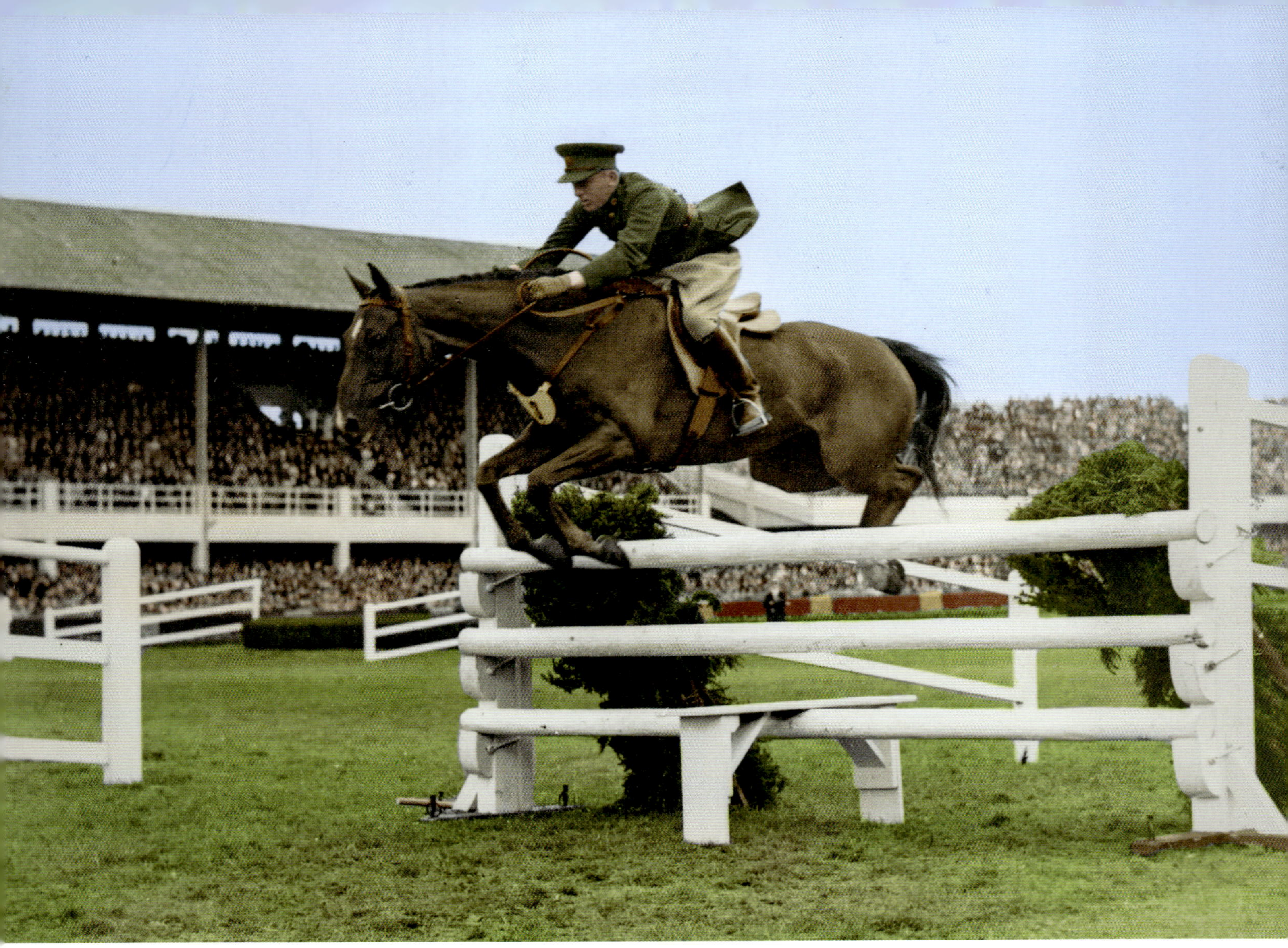

Top left: Captain Dan Corry clears a fence on Red Hugh during the 1939 Aga Khan Cup at Dublin's RDS. Corry led the Irish army team at the event, held just weeks before the outbreak of World War II.

Top right: When World War II broke out, Ireland (Éire) declared neutrality. As it turned out, the country's neutrality, during what became known as the Emergency, did not shield it from severe shortages. From 1941 onwards, British supply cuts meant rationing took hold, with food, fuel and essential goods in short supply. For farmers, as well as the general population, rationing made everyday life difficult – sugar, tea, flour and soap became scarce, while food prices soared due to shortages. However, Ireland experienced less severe rationing than Britain in some foodstuffs, particularly items like eggs and meat.

Fertilisers vanished, animal feed ran out and tractors stood idle without petrol. With private cars disappearing from the roads and mechanised farming grinding to a halt, horsepower – of the four-legged kind – once again became the backbone of

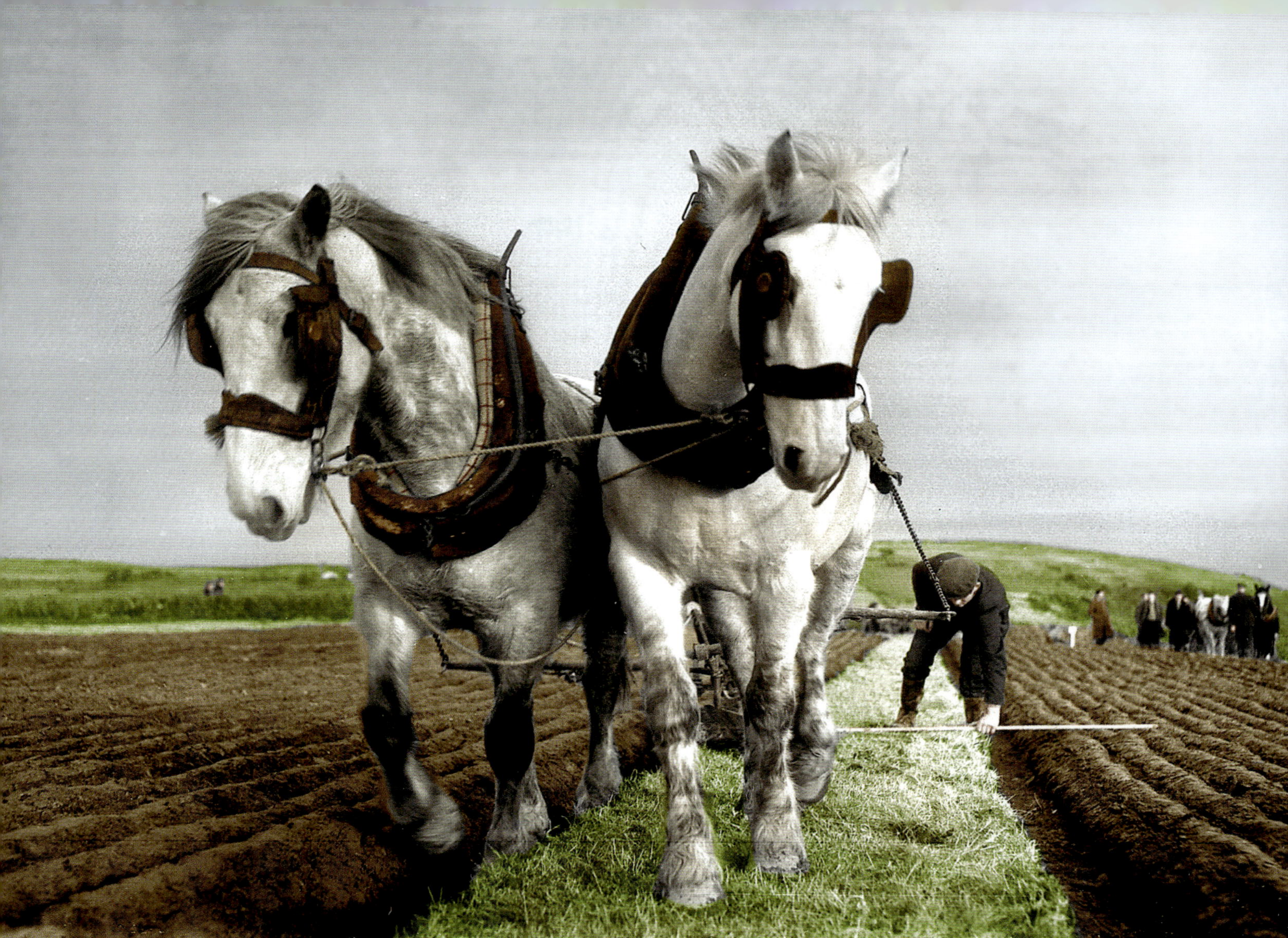

agriculture. Farmers relied once more on the horse to plough the land, as captured in this photograph.

The Fianna Fáil government had always been committed to a self-sufficient Ireland – and wanted to reduce the substantial imports of wheat and animal feedstuff. They wished to promote tillage as opposed to the prevalent practice of dairy and beef farming. The government introduced an obligation for the 1940 growing season that all farmers with more than 10 acres were to till one-eighth of their acreage (with exemptions for unsuitable land, like bog). There was opposition to this measure, with many dairy and cattle farmers being reluctant to plough up their land.

Despite these struggles, the war years saw a dramatic increase in crop production. By 1945, wheat output had surged by 124 per cent, and tillage expanded by 60 per cent, ensuring that Ireland remained largely self-sufficient in food. However, the toll on the land was severe. Without fertiliser, fields were in poor shape. As soon as restrictions eased, farmers eagerly shifted back to livestock, abandoning large-scale tillage in favour of the more sustainable mixed farming system that had been common in rural Ireland before the war.

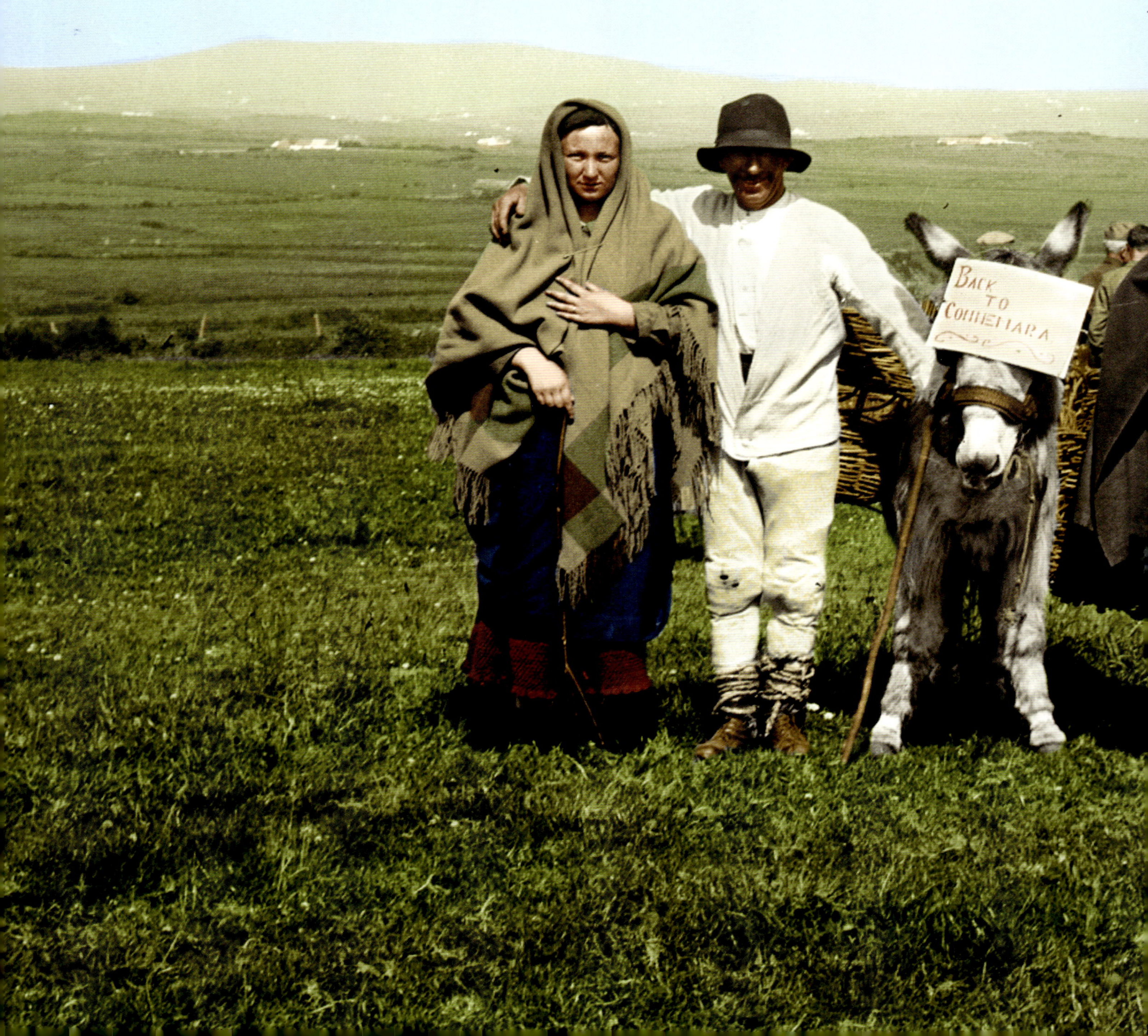

The Mullagh Carnival in County Clare, 1943 – a reminder that, despite the war, people could still come together and enjoy themselves. In a time of shortages and restrictions, the people of rural Ireland, accustomed to a life of self-reliance and resourcefulness, was better placed than those living in cities to weather the challenges of the Emergency.

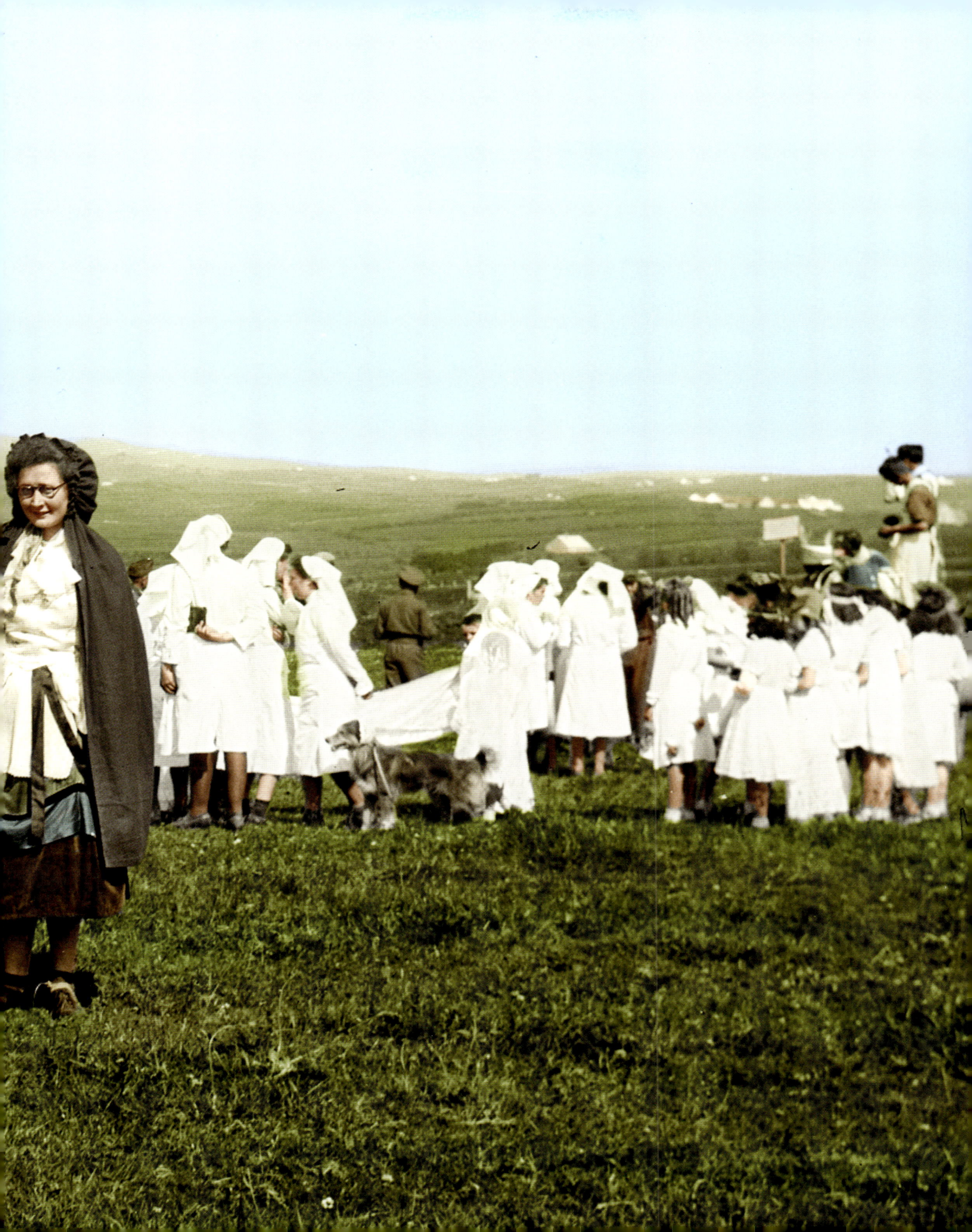

Coal has nearly twice the calorific value of turf (peat), making it a more energy-dense fuel. Prior to the war, coal had been the primary fuel in Ireland for trains, industry and domestic heating, particularly in towns. While there was some domestic coal production, Ireland depended mainly on imported British coal. From the beginning of 1941, the shortage of coal began to bite. The British government had reduced exports of coal (as well as petrol) to Éire at the end of 1940. With the shortage of coal now looming large, attention quickly reverted to the humbler fuel, turf.

This fuel, widely available and traditionally cut in rural Ireland, became a critical substitute for coal. Its availability across the country, especially in the bogs of the midlands, made it an essential resource in the face of wartime restrictions. The Irish government's strategy had been to encourage turf production, and now that policy was accelerated. The Turf Development Board, established in the 1930s, played a leading role and became the central body responsible for overseeing and organising large-scale turf production. A campaign was started that encouraged businesses and private individuals to cut turf. Local authorities were given powers to engage in turf cutting, and by July 1941, they employed around 30,000.

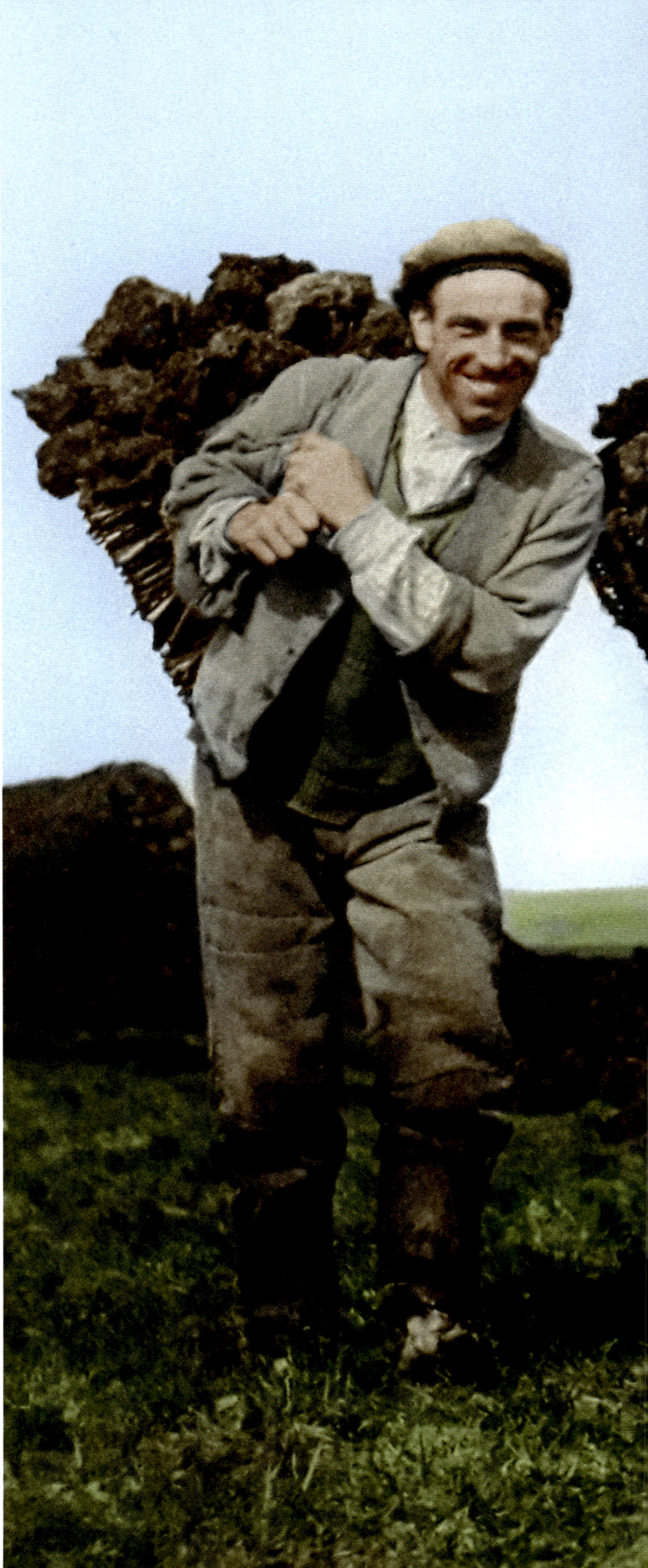

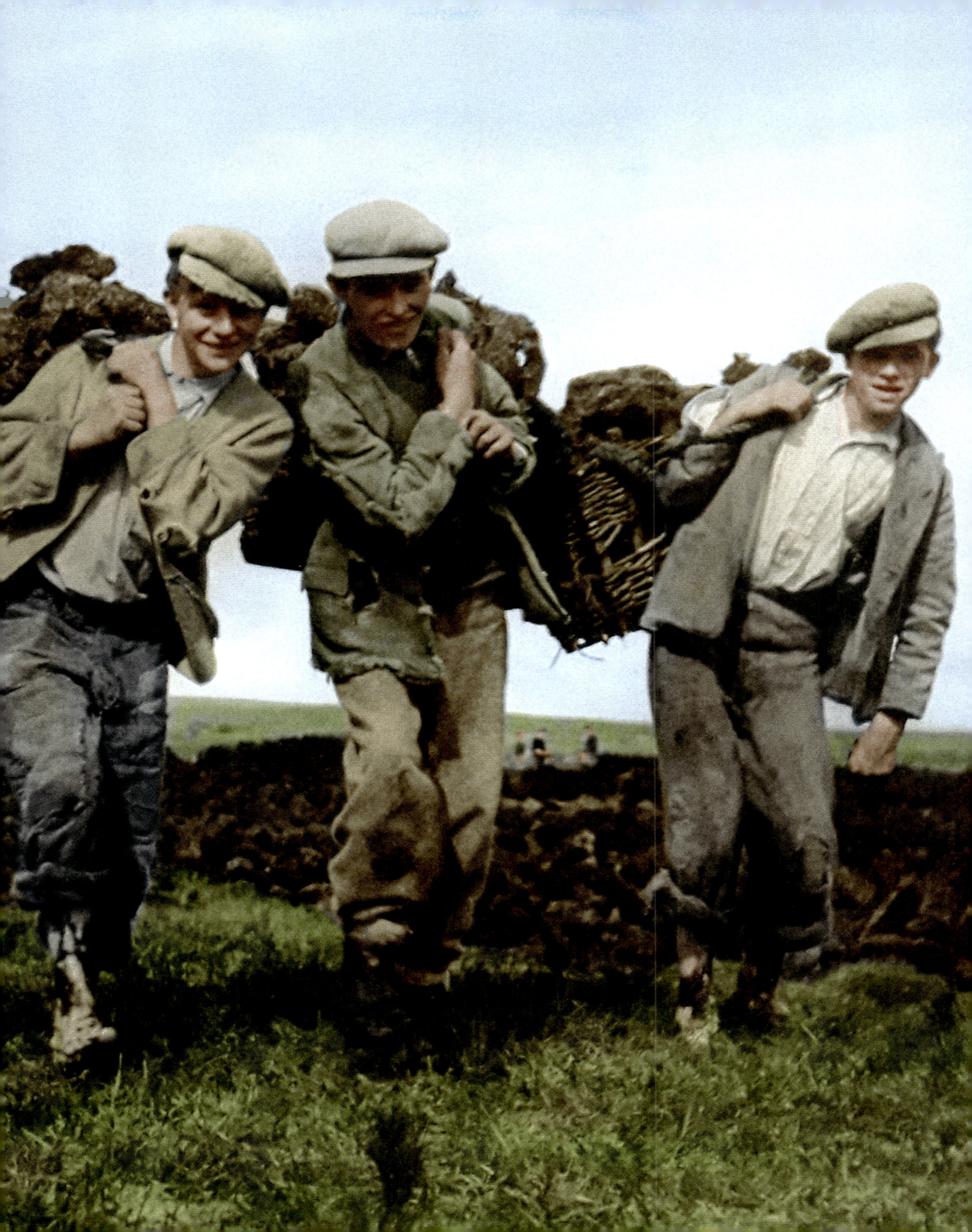

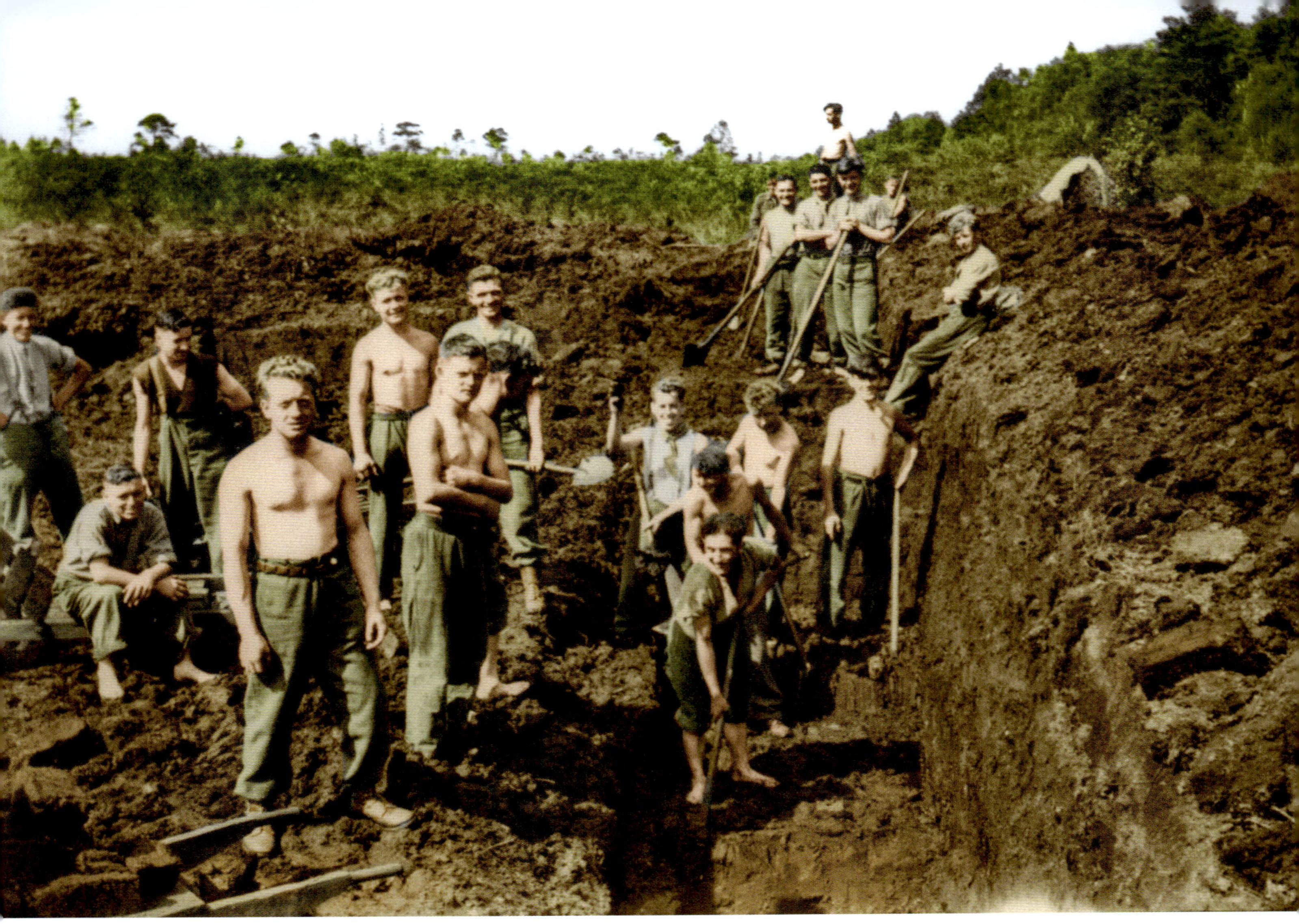

Hard at work: the Irish army was mobilised
to assist in the large-scale production of turf
during the Emergency. This initiative saw
soldiers deployed to peat bogs across the
country to cut, dry and transport turf. In one
example, at Nadd Bog in north Cork, over 2,000
soldiers participated, living in an area known
as 'the Camps'. They had to first develop the
vast bogland, creating drainage and roads,
before they could get down to cutting the turf.

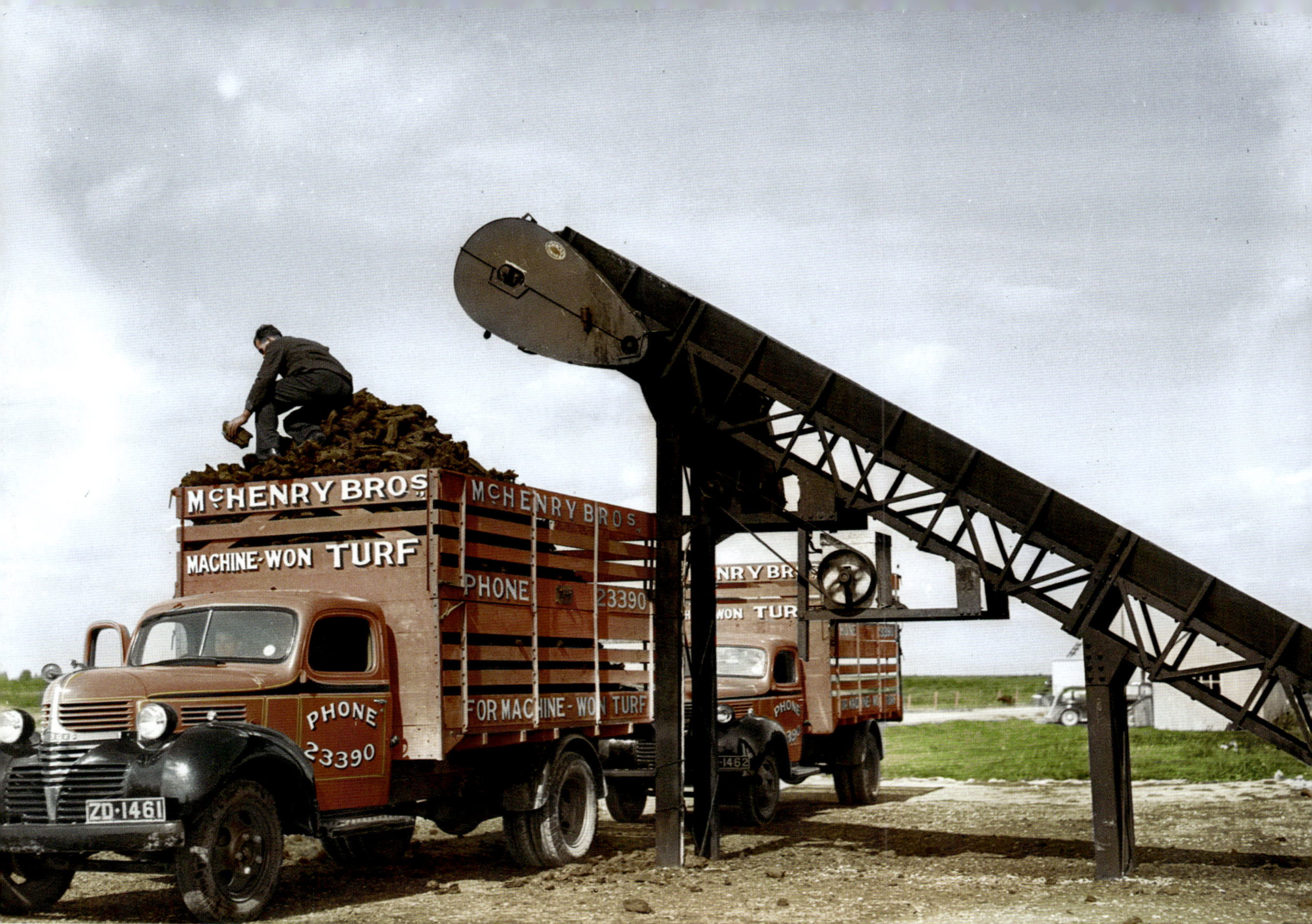

A McHenry Brothers truck is being loaded with turf for delivery in Dublin, 1945. During the Emergency, special turf trains were organised to transport the fuel from the Atlantic seaboard and the midlands to urban centres. As coal shortages hampered rail transport, the government also had to finance the construction of 29 horse-drawn barges to move turf along the canal system. Dublin's main stockpile was the turf piled in large ricks along the Phoenix Park's main thoroughfare, then dubbed the 'New Bog Road'.

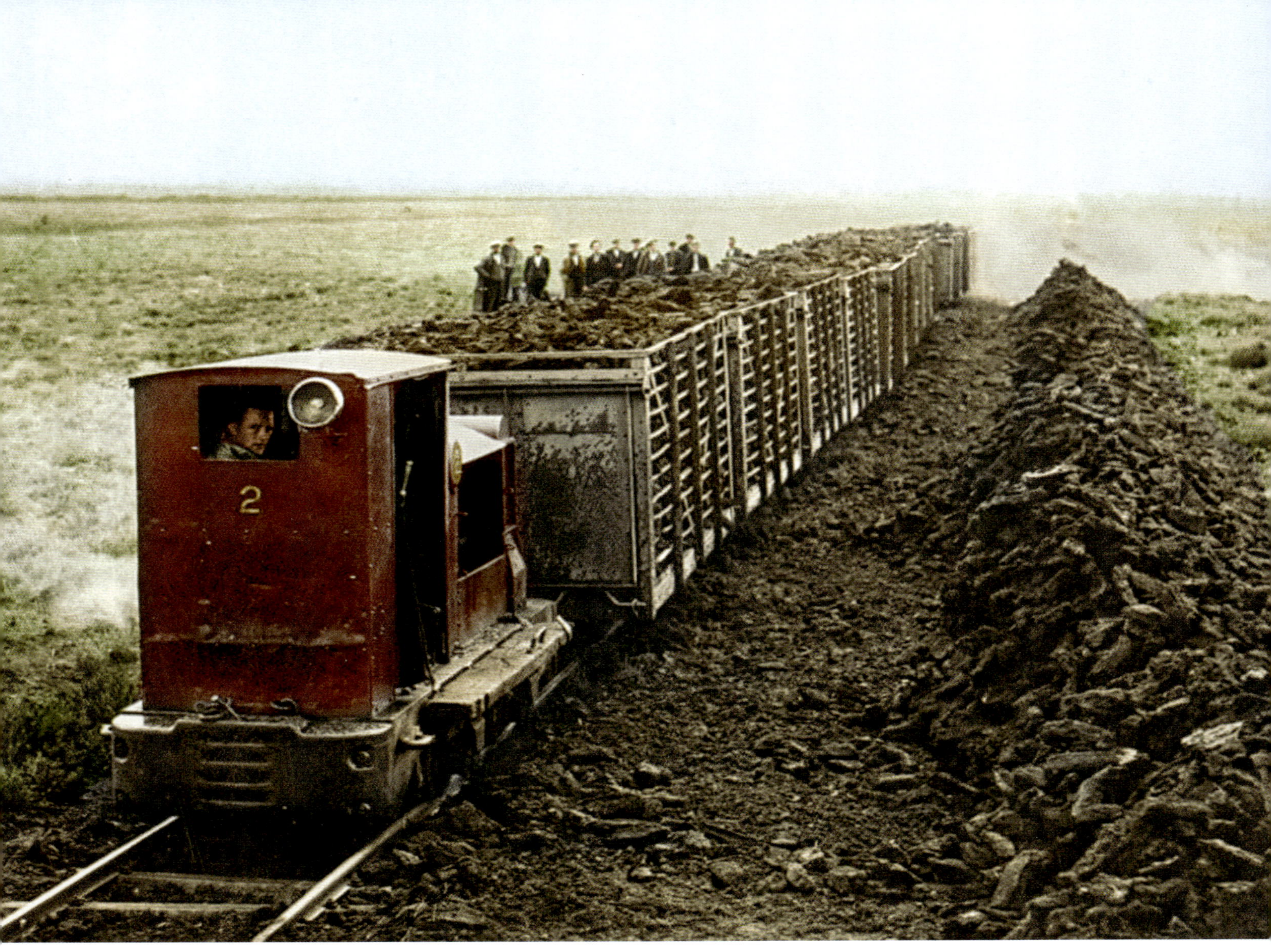

A Bord na Móna turf train in action, marking the shift from the wartime turf production efforts to a more structured development of Ireland's turf industry. The Turf Development Board's work during the Emergency paved the way for the creation of Bord na Móna in 1946. The company set up a network of narrow-gauge railways, operating primarily in the midlands, to transport turf from vast bogs like those in Offaly, Westmeath and Longford to power stations and urban centres. This infrastructure would play an important role in Ireland's energy supply in the post-war years.

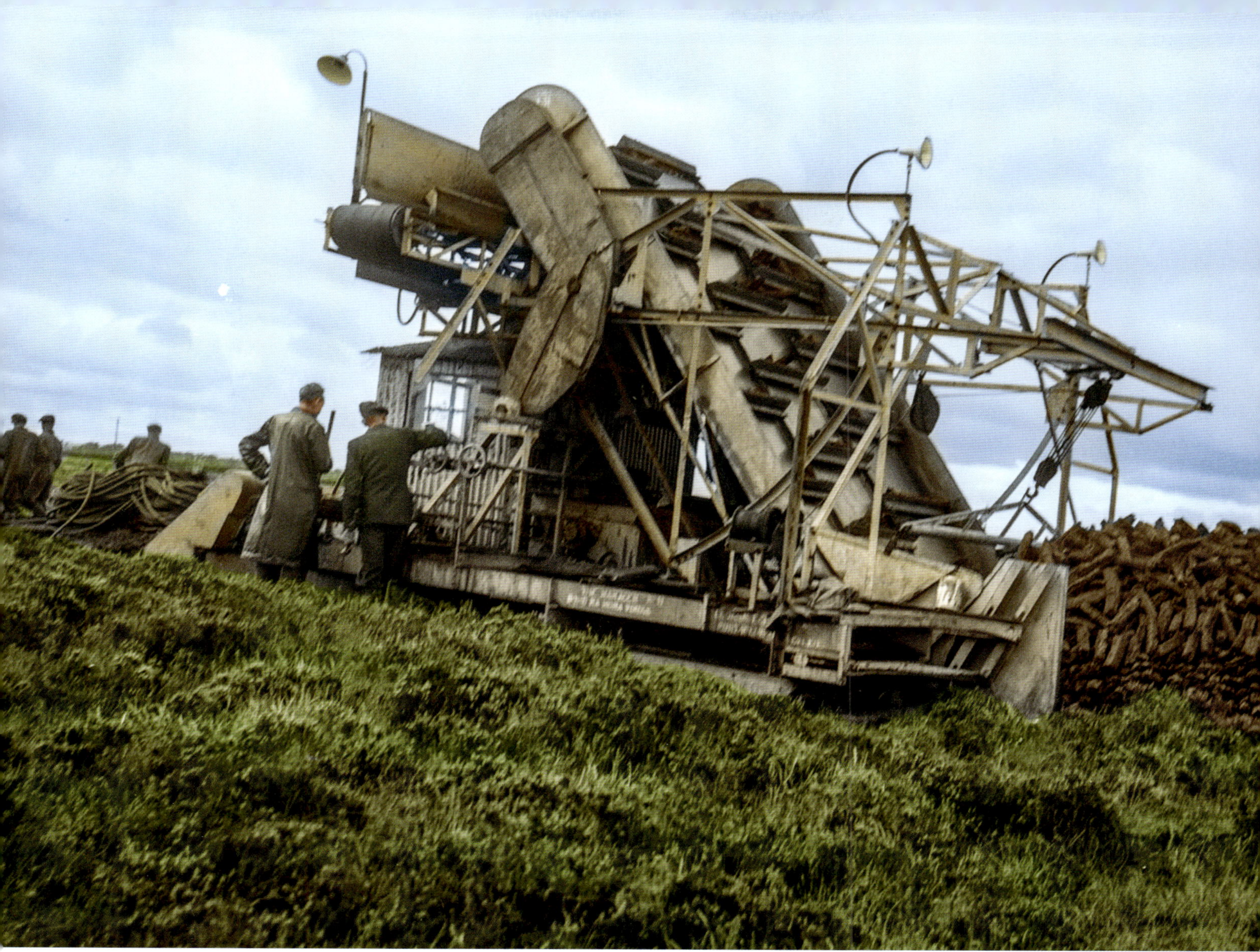

A large Bord na Móna machine. The Board's efforts to mechanise turf cutting marked a significant shift from manual labour to more efficient, machine-driven operations across their vast bogs. Their innovations over the years in machinery design and implementation set new standards for the peat industry worldwide.

No large machines were required on the Aran Islands to harvest the turf! Turf was the traditional fuel here where people lived a self-sufficient existence, much simpler than that on the mainland. The islanders relied on small-scale farming, seaweed collection and fishing to sustain themselves.

Young women and children pose on a beach, with the *Dún Aengus* ferry in the background. They are dressed in traditional clothing and reflect a way of life that remained closely connected to the land and sea.

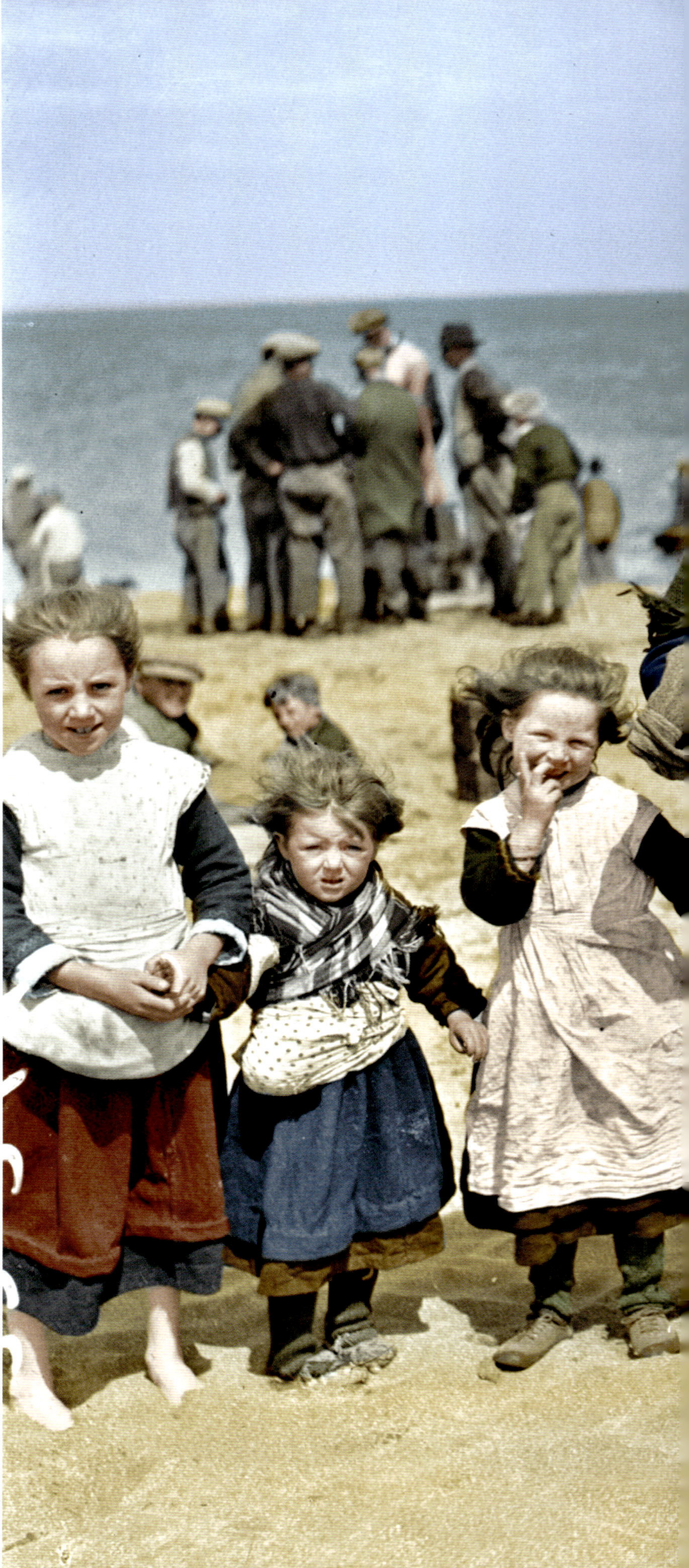

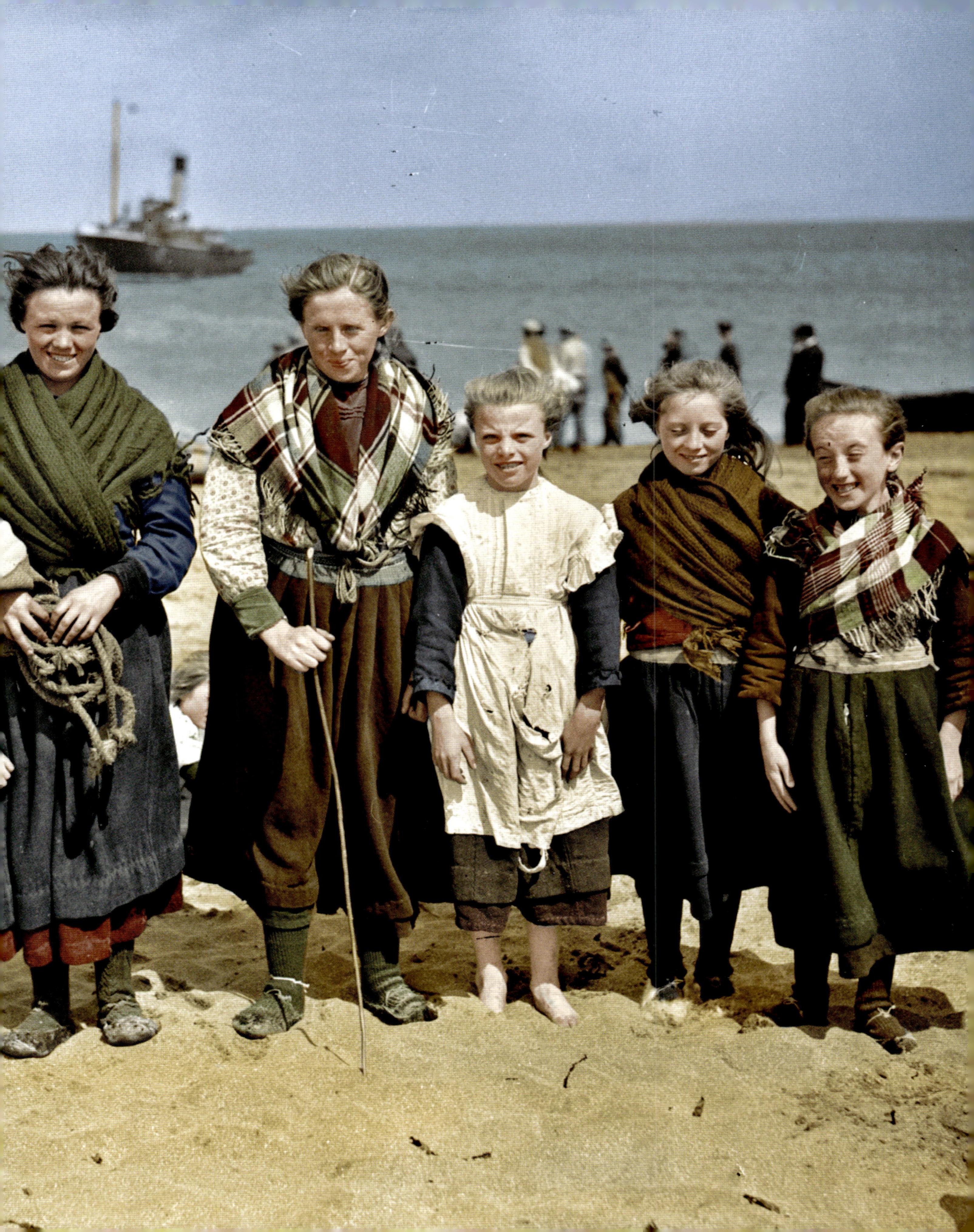

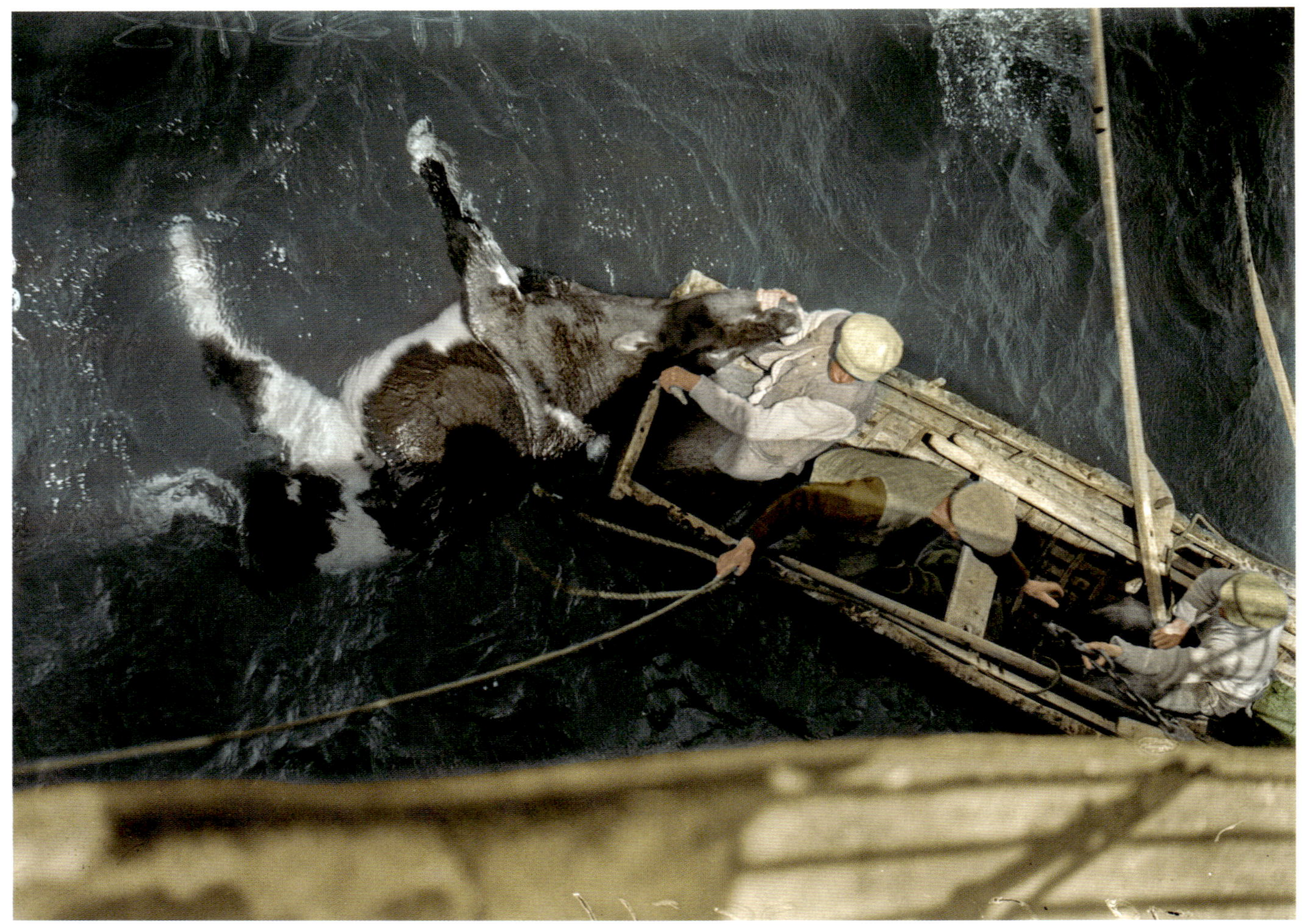

Top left: The steamboat *Dún Aengus* plied between the Aran islands and the mainland, carrying passengers, livestock and freight. She could dock at Cill Rónáin on Inis Mór, the largest island. However, she could not dock at the two smaller islands, Inis Meáin and Inis Oírr, and had to offload onto small boats. It was a complicated situation when cattle, horses or even elderly people had to be transferred. Cattle had to swim to the ship, towed by a currach. Here, looking down from the deck of the *Dún Aengus*, is a view of a bullock about to be hoisted on board.

Right: In October 1960, the remaining 24 inhabitants of Inis Airc, an island off the Galway coast, were evacuated. This photo shows a pupil, one of five at the primary school, just before evacuation.

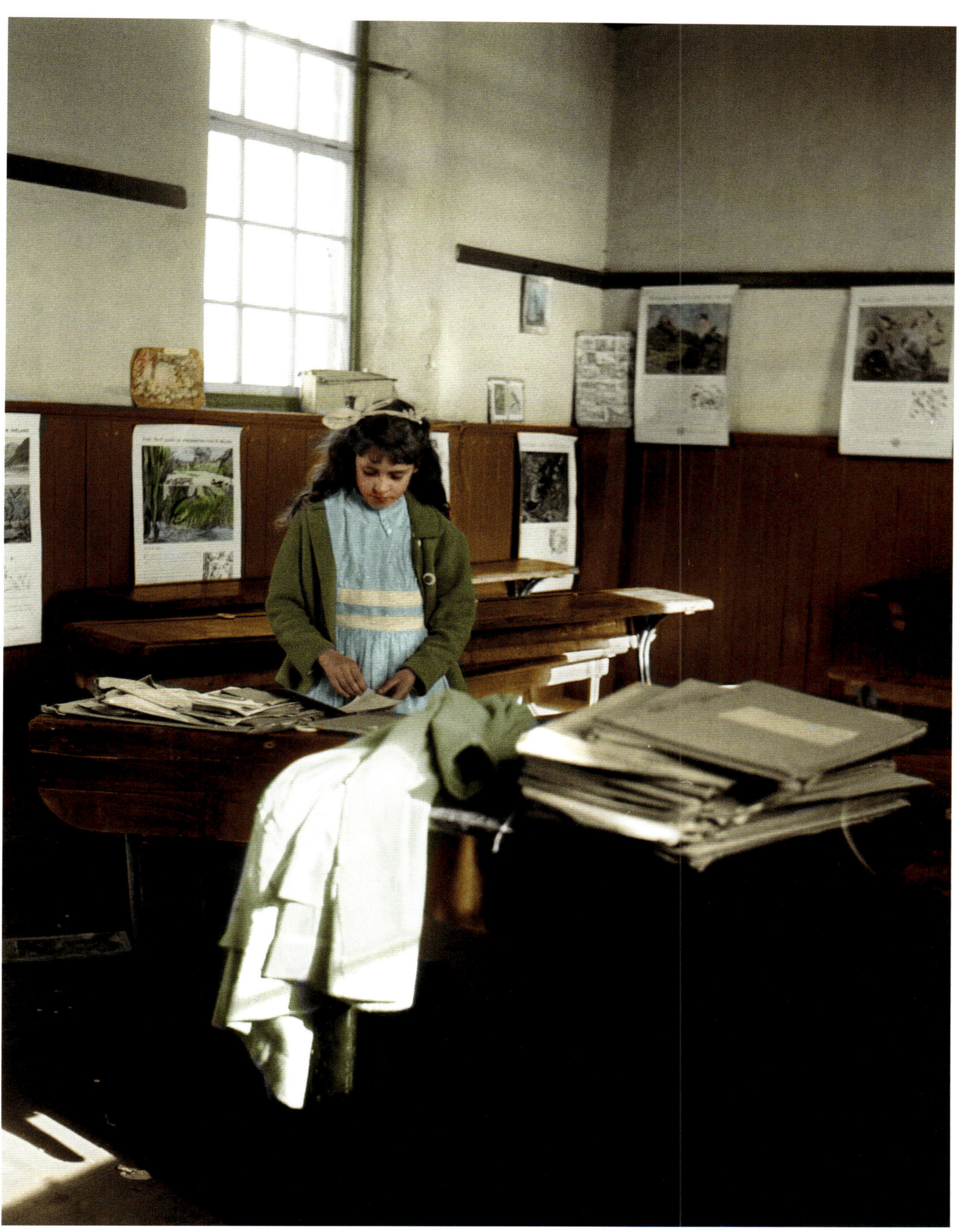

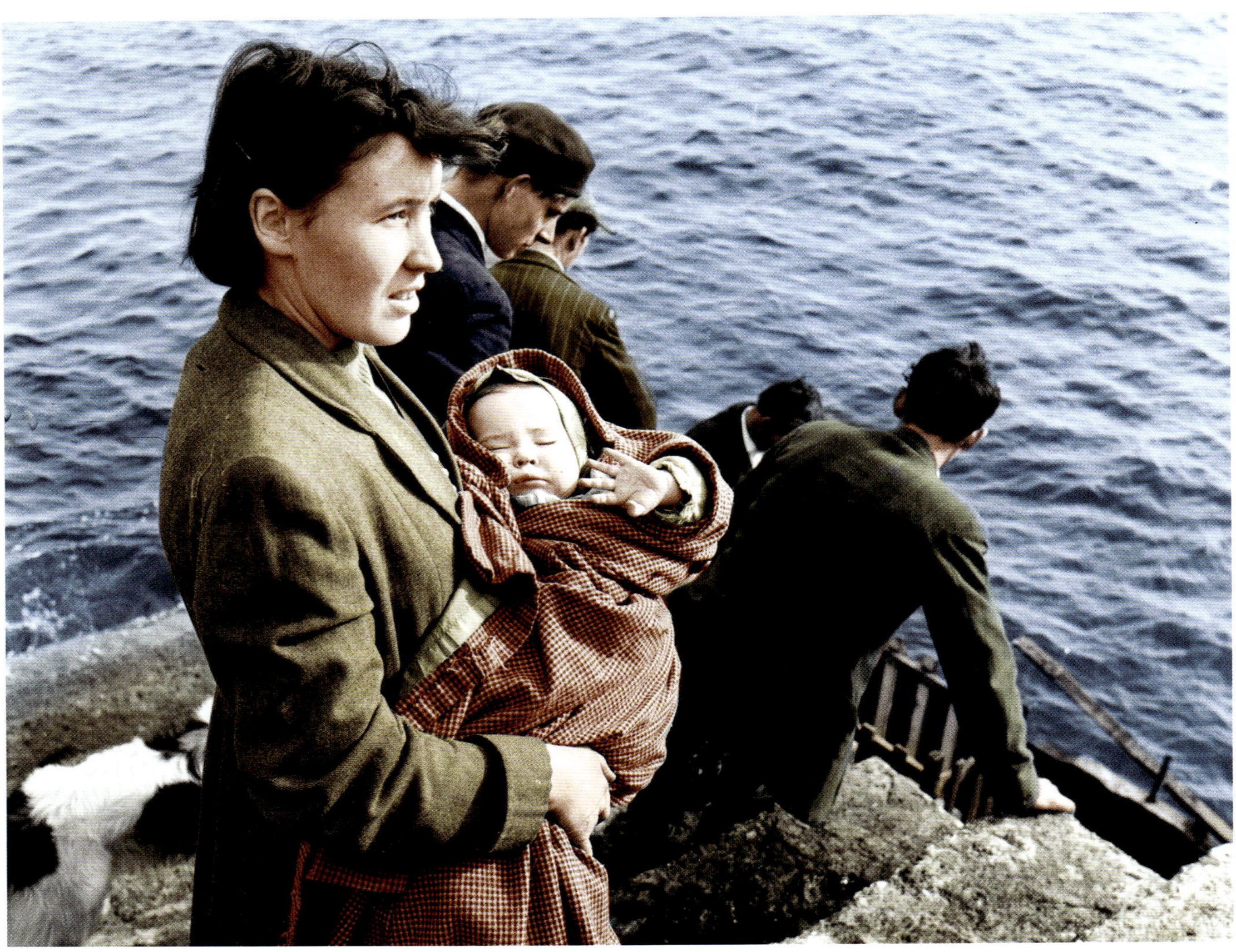

Top left: Facing an uncertain future – a mother and baby at the pier at Inis Airc prepare to leave.

Top right: Two men depart the island, their currach piled high with belongings, as Inis Airc's last residents abandon their home. Isolated and without modern services, the island's dwindling population had faced an uncertain future.

The tragic death of a young man in 1959, when rough seas prevented his evacuation for medical care, sealed Inis Airc's fate. Like the Blaskets before it and other islands to follow, Inis Airc's evacuation marked another step in the slow retreat from Ireland's offshore islands, as communities left behind a way of life that had endured for centuries.

While some resettled on the mainland, many had no choice but to emigrate, joining the long exodus of Irish islanders seeking a new life abroad.

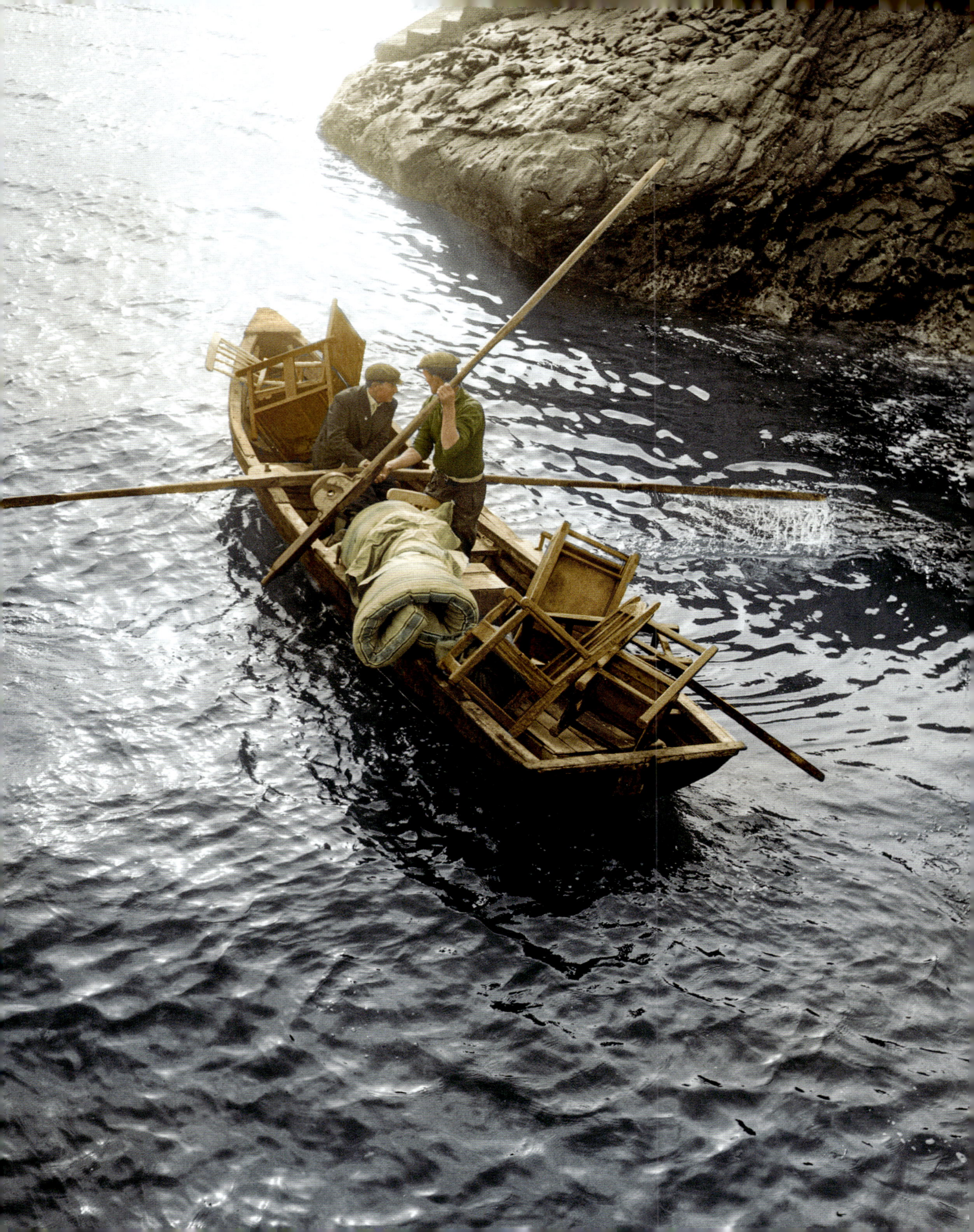

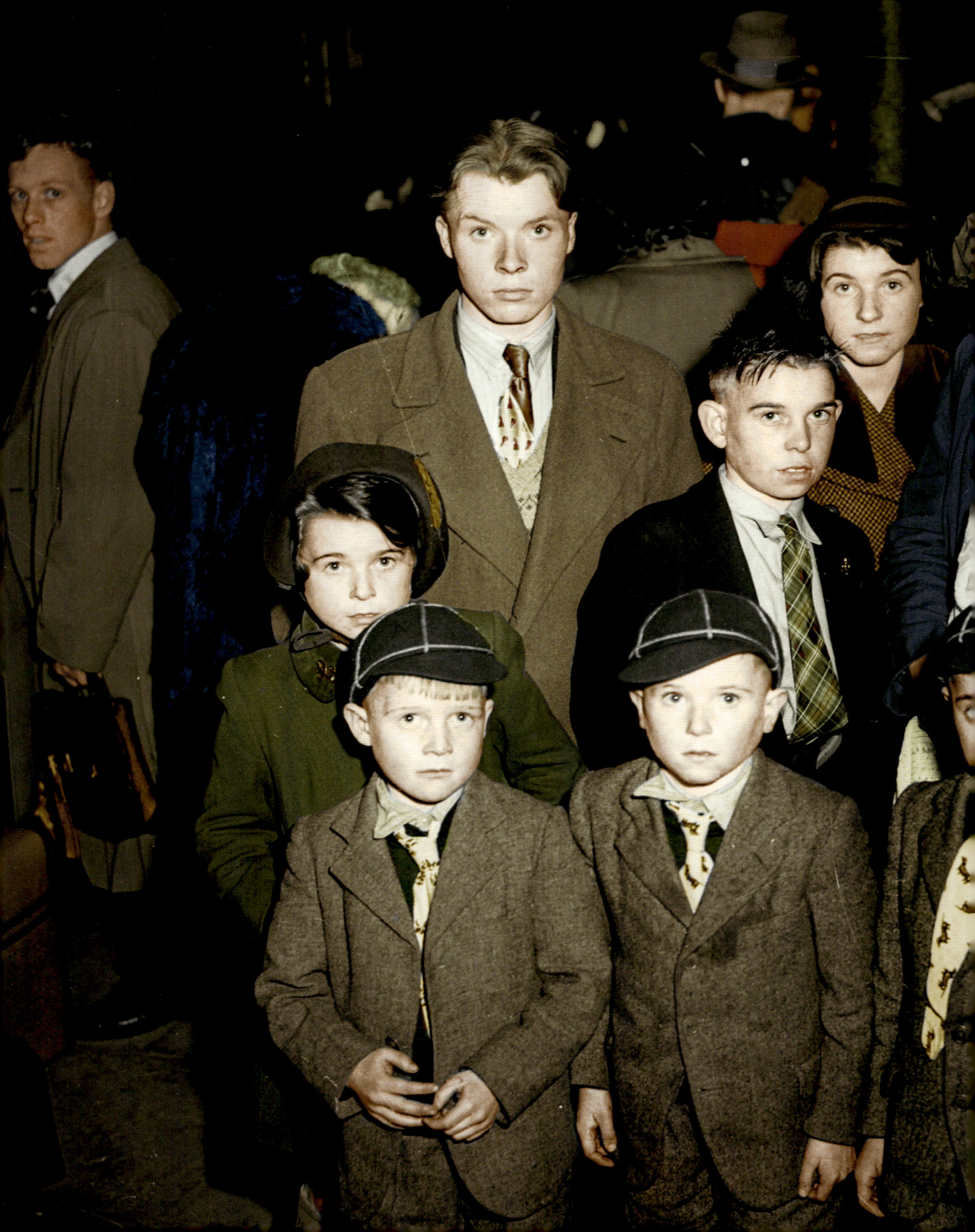

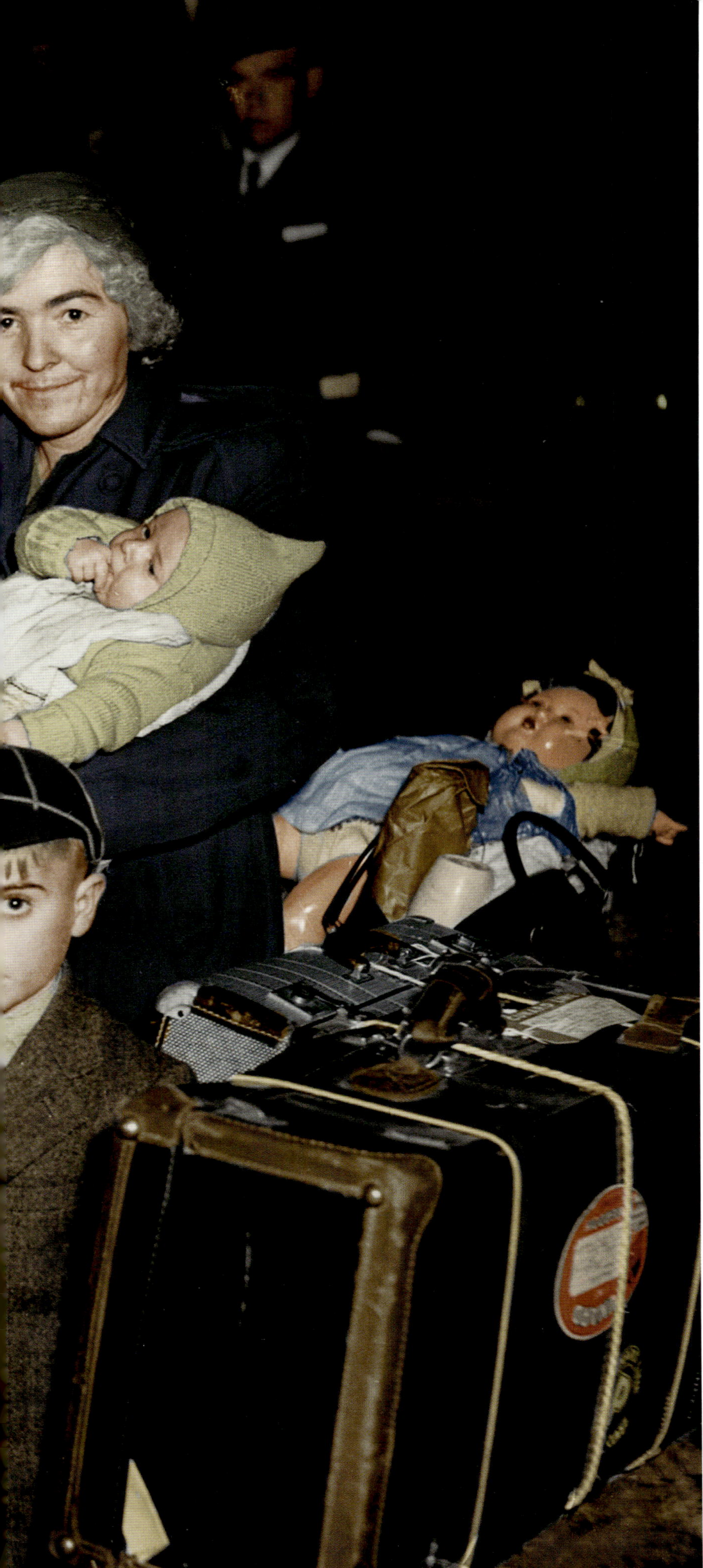

A glum prospect: a family stands at Cobh, lined up to board a ship bound for Canada, part of the great exodus that hollowed out rural Ireland. The 1950s saw over half a million people leave, driven by unemployment, failing farms and a lack of opportunity. Many emigrants sought new lives in Britain and North America; many never returned. In the west of Ireland, entire communities were left diminished, their young people gone, their homes abandoned.

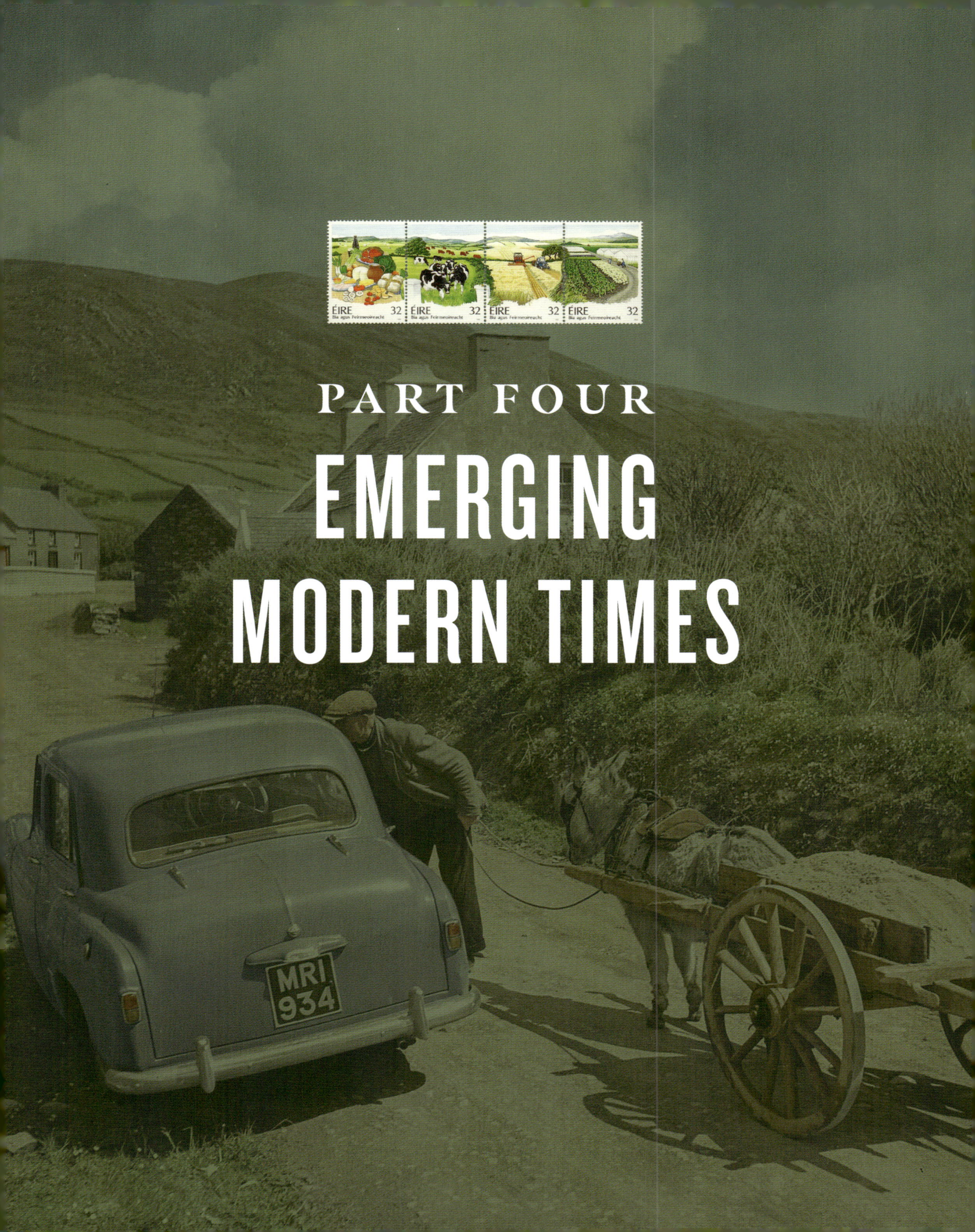

PART FOUR
EMERGING
MODERN TIMES

The personnel of Duffy's Circus at their winter
headquarters in Dunmanway, County Cork,
in 1936. With a young girl in the background
shyly observing the scene, the group poses
for the photograph, including a sitting clown
with (behind) men in tuxedos and top hats. A
performer in ornate Oriental dress stands, with
the band's instruments laid out on the grass – a
striking display of pageantry that must have
been quite a sight in a West Cork town.

Over many decades, travelling circuses
brought a sense of wonder to rural communities
across Ireland, offering a rare spectacle of
acrobats, clowns, exotic animals and thrilling
performances. These roving entertainers
transformed town squares and fairgrounds into
temporary worlds of colour and excitement.

Duffy's Circus, one of Ireland's oldest and
most renowned circus families, traces its
origins back to 1775, when Dublin-born acrobat
Patrick James Duffy founded the first iteration
of the circus. Over generations, the Duffy name
became synonymous with circus entertainment,
with various branches of the family carrying
the tradition forward. During the off season,
typically from autumn to spring, Duffy's Circus
made its home on Doheny Lane in Dunmanway,
where wagons were repaired, equipment
maintained, and performers and animals
rested before the touring season resumed. The
presence of the circus had a tangible impact
on the town, providing some employment for
locals in the care and maintenance of the circus,
while children of circus families attended local
schools.

However, times were changing – by the
late 1960s, new forms of entertainment like
television began to compete for audiences,
gradually reshaping the traditions of rural
amusements.

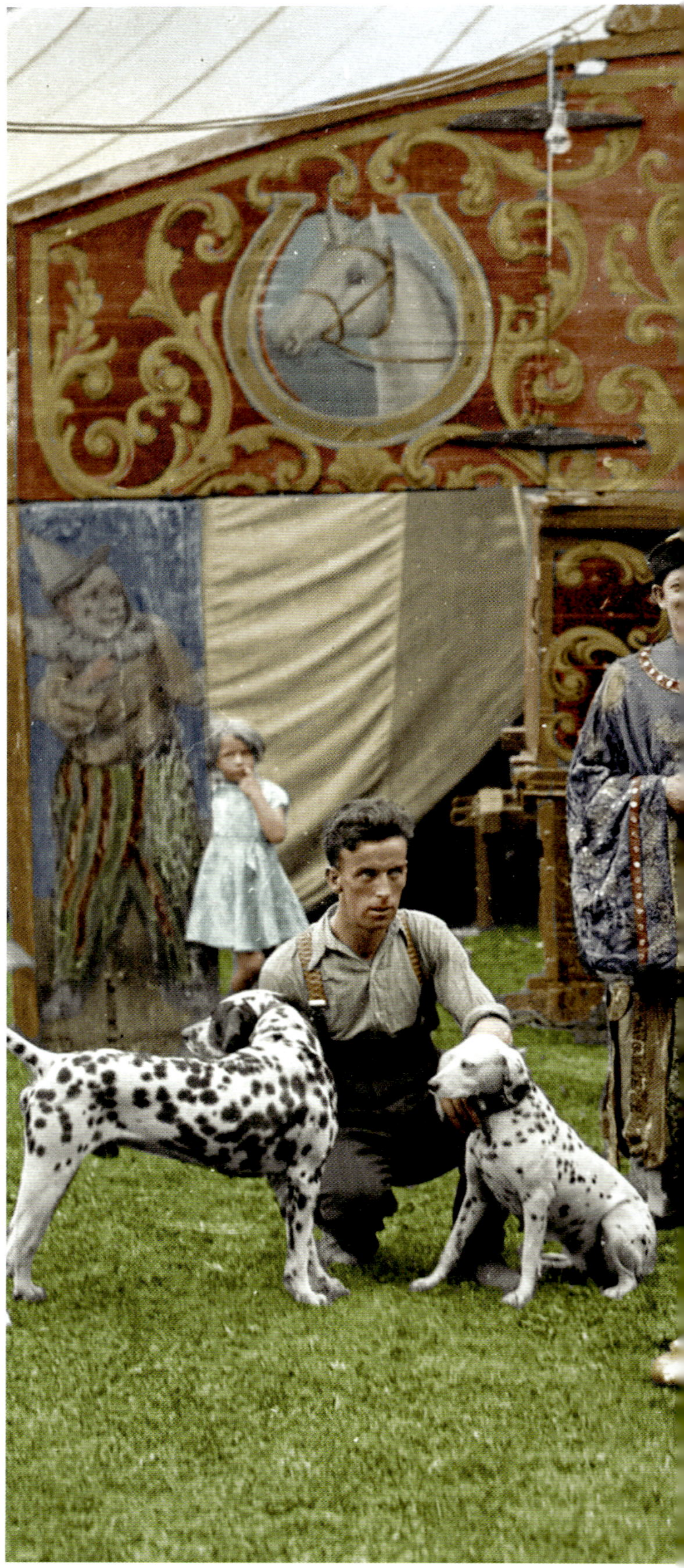

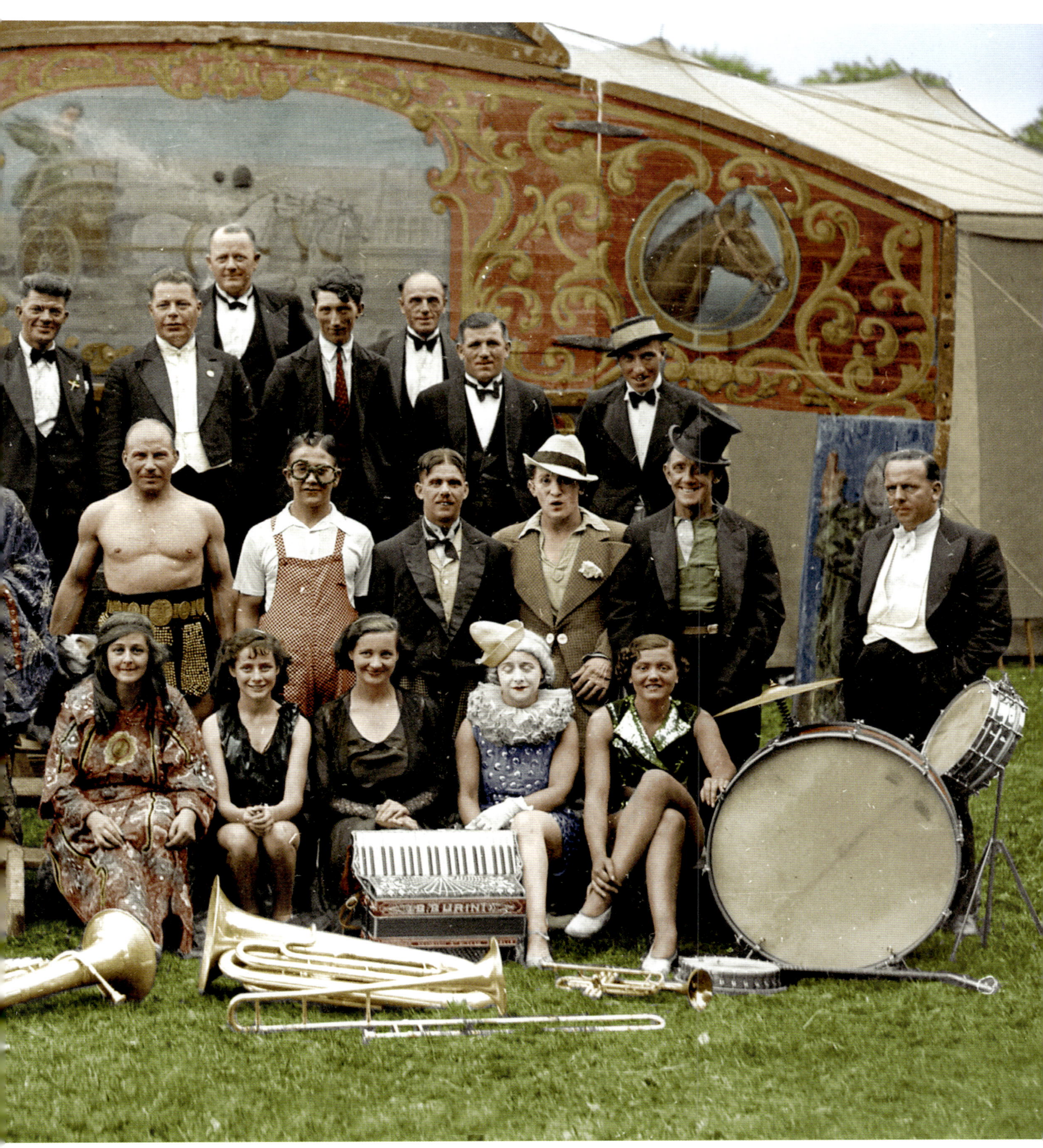

Times were changing not just for circuses but also for the Travellers, whose traditional way of life was increasingly challenged by a changing society. The photograph captures a family beside their caravan in County Clare in 1951.

With large families and a mobile lifestyle, the Travellers' presence had been a common sight in rural communities, where they provided useful services like tin smithing and horse trading. However, significant change began over the following decades, as mechanisation and new ways of working led to the decline of many traditional Traveller occupations, gradually eroding the symbiotic relationship between Travellers and settled rural people.

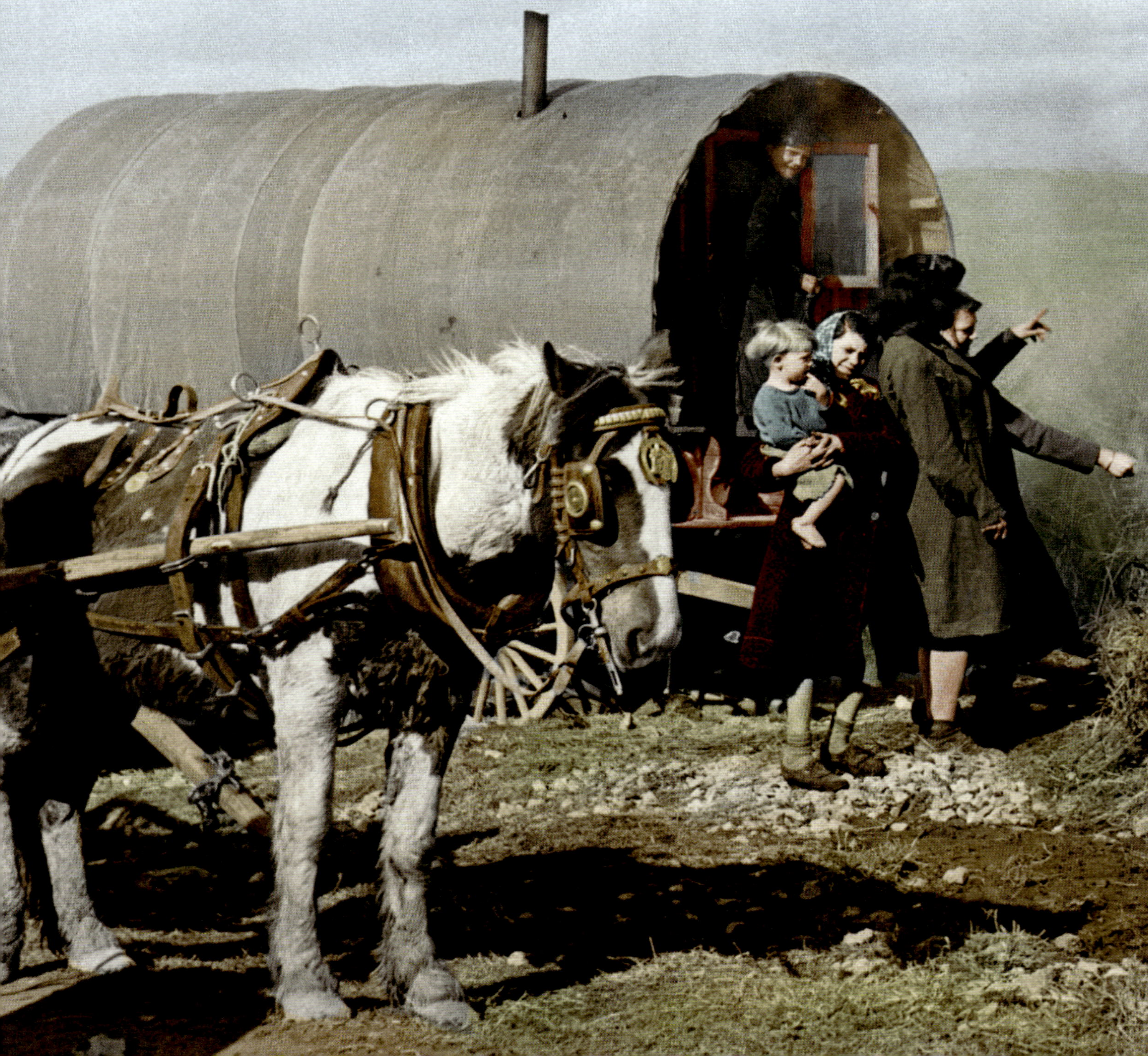

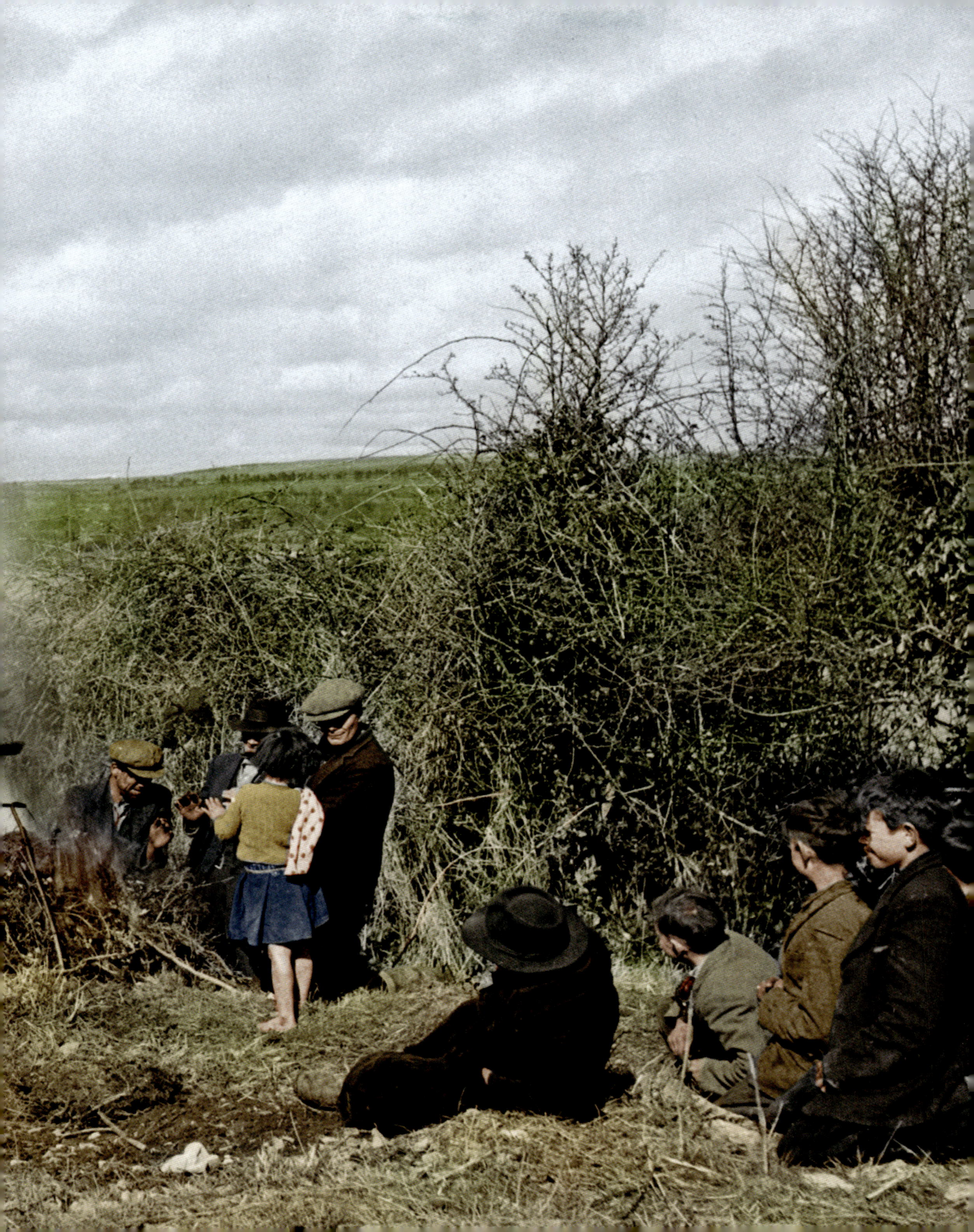

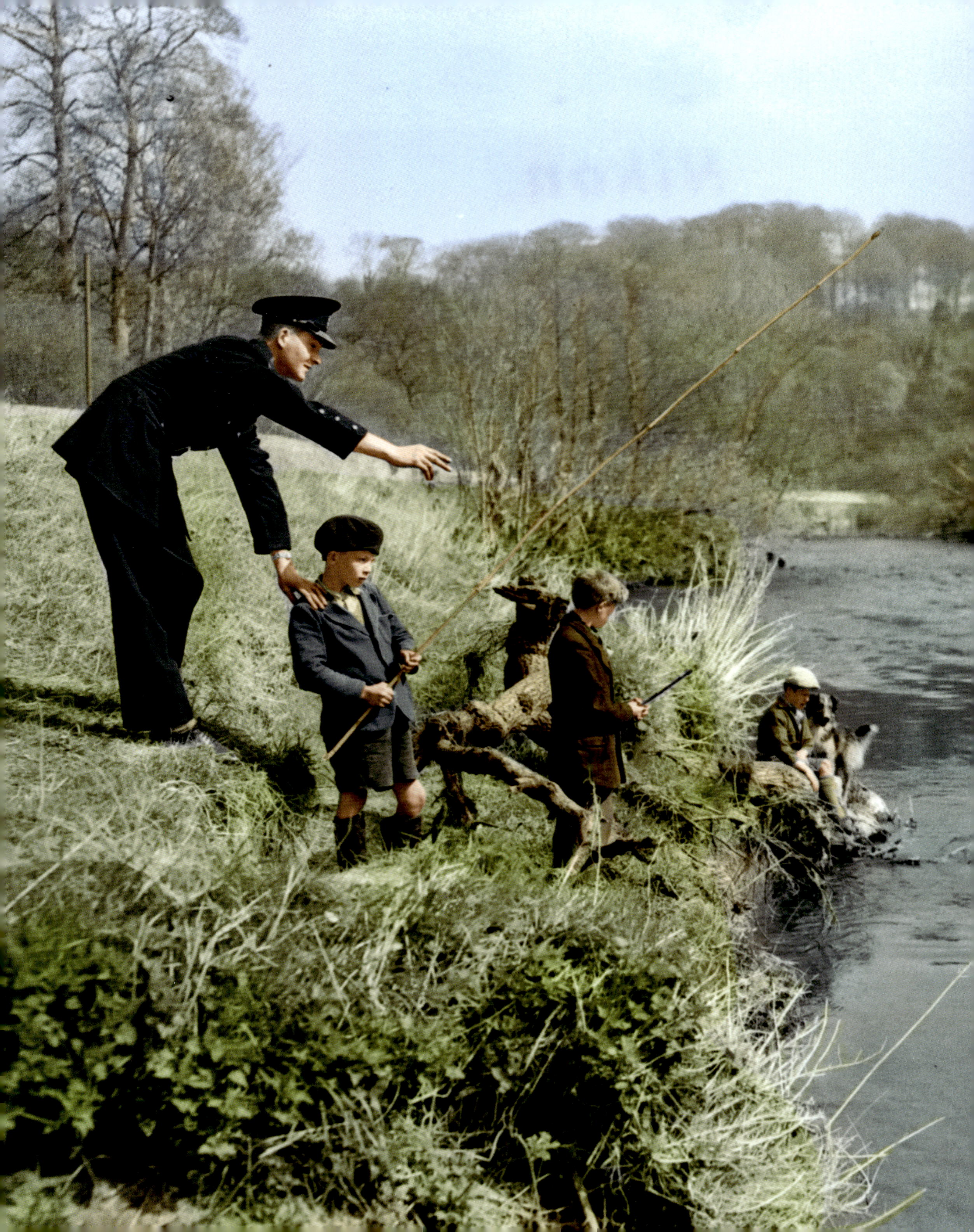

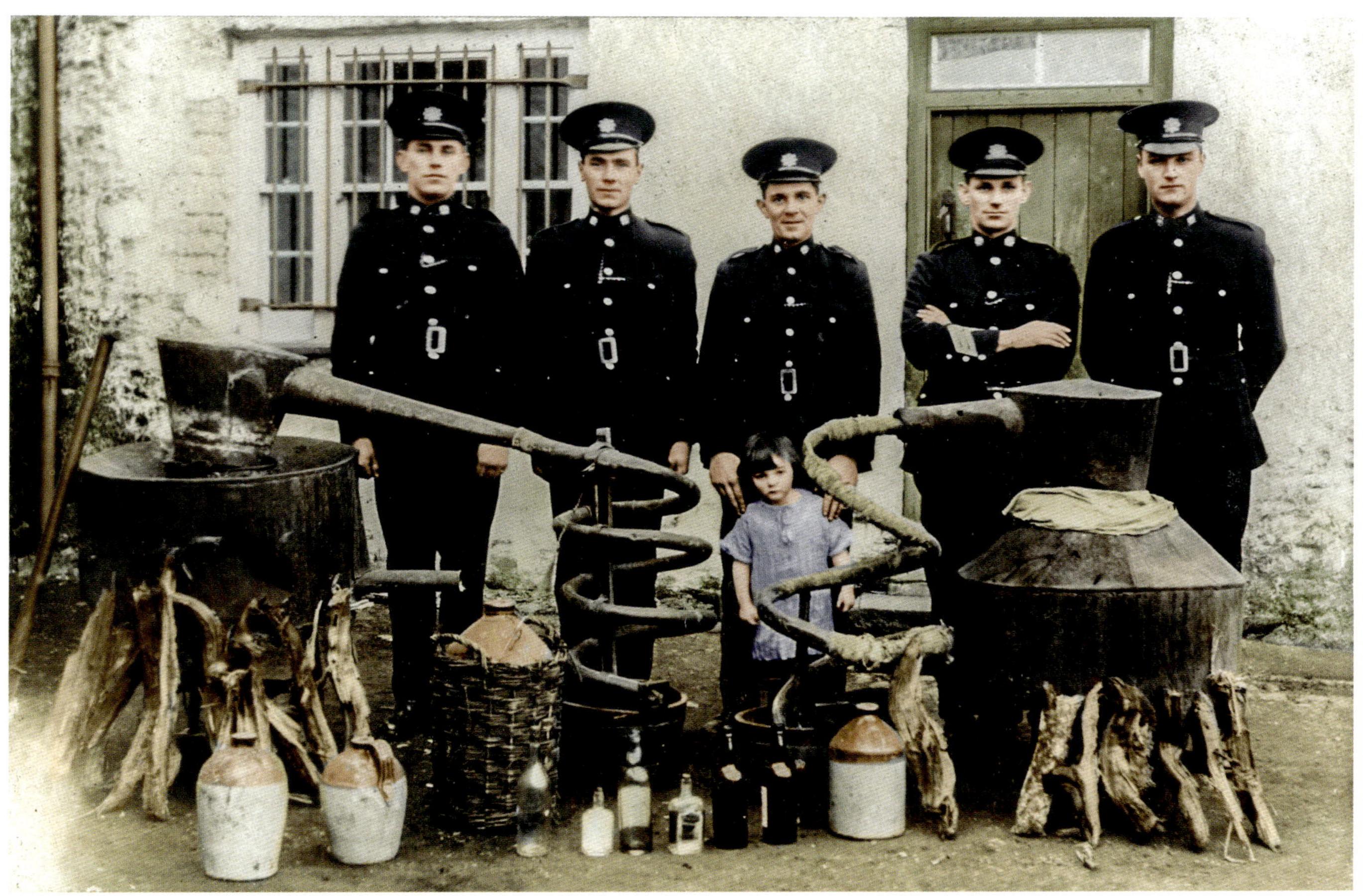

Left: Across Ireland, the unarmed police force, the Garda Síochána, were an established part of the communities they served. During the mid-twentieth century, their duties often focused on minor infractions, like bicycle light violations and ensuring public houses adhered to licensing hours.

Top right: For much of the twentieth century, poteen distilling was widespread across rural Ireland. The liquor had garnered quite a reputation – American troops stationed in the Six Counties during World War II were given a pocket guide to local mores that included the warning: 'Up in the hills, you may be offered an illicit concoction known as "potheen" … a moonshine whiskey made out of potato mash. Watch it. It is dynamite.' In an era marked by low crime, the Garda Síochána conducted annual sweeps of the mountains and remote corners to locate hidden stills. Here, Gardaí at Milford, County Donegal, proudly display their haul.

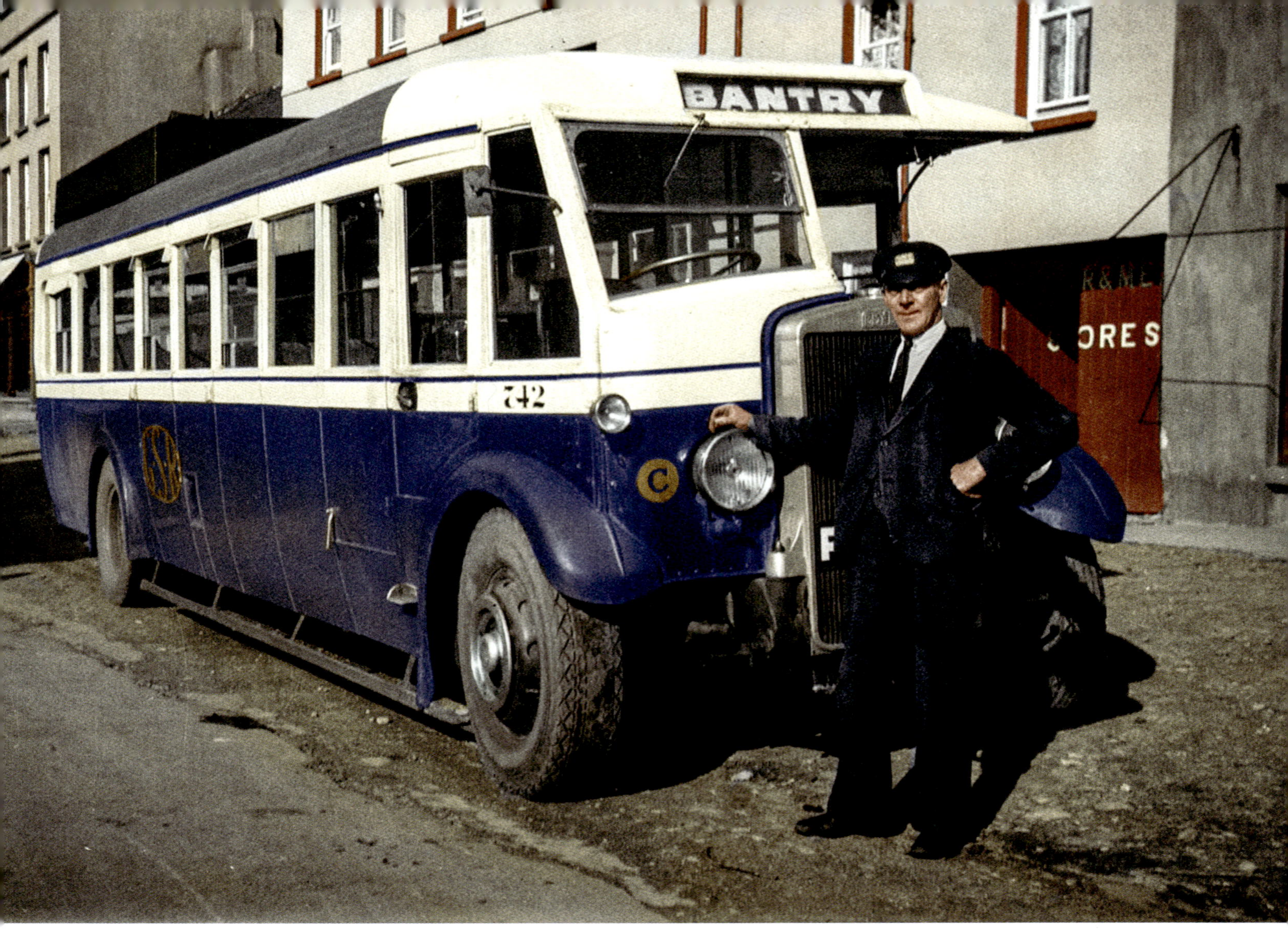

Better roads and vehicles resulted in the Irish railways losing traffic and incurring large losses. By the end of the 1950s, most narrow-gauge railways in Ireland had been closed, while the standard-gauge network had reduced by a quarter from its 1920 peak – with more closures on the way. Bus services took their place. Here at Bantry, County Cork in the early 1950s, the bus still bears the Great Southern Railways logo, soon to be replaced by that of the newly formed CIÉ (Córas Iompair Éireann).

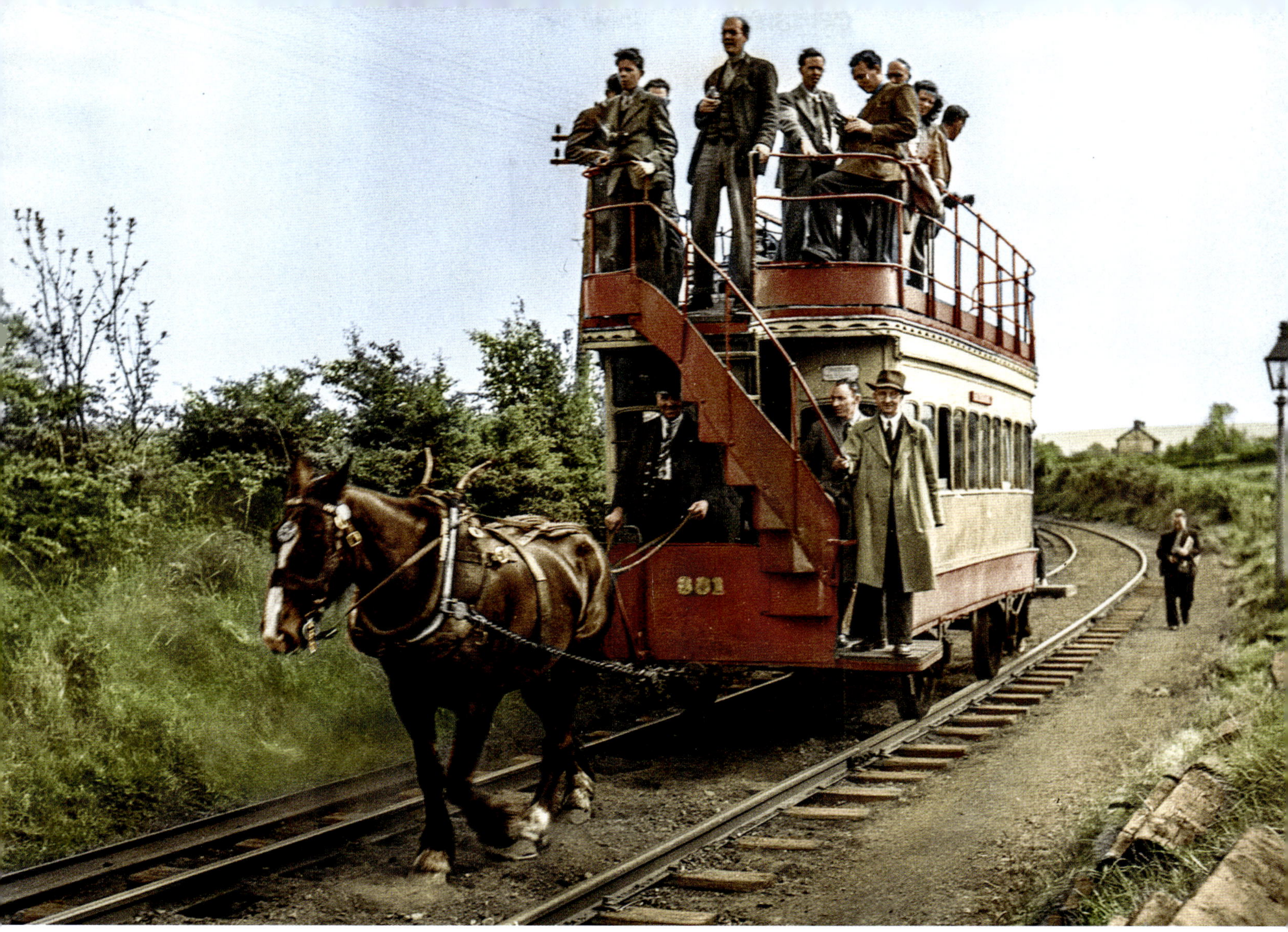

A tiny rural railway: the Fintona railway was a
unique one-kilometre branch line in County
Tyrone, connecting Fintona town to Fintona
Junction. It was noted for its horse-drawn
passenger service, which operated for 104
years, from 1853 to 1957.

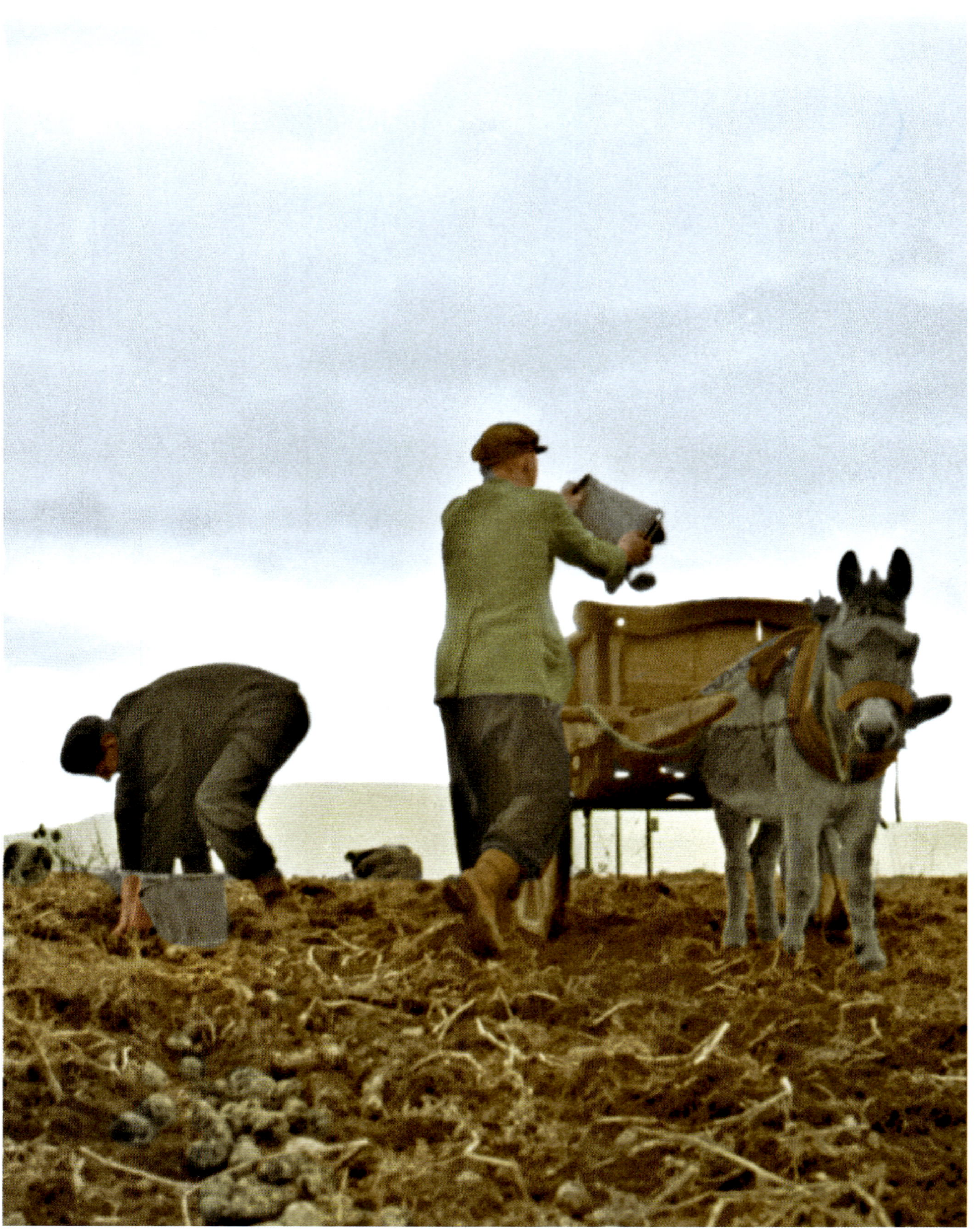

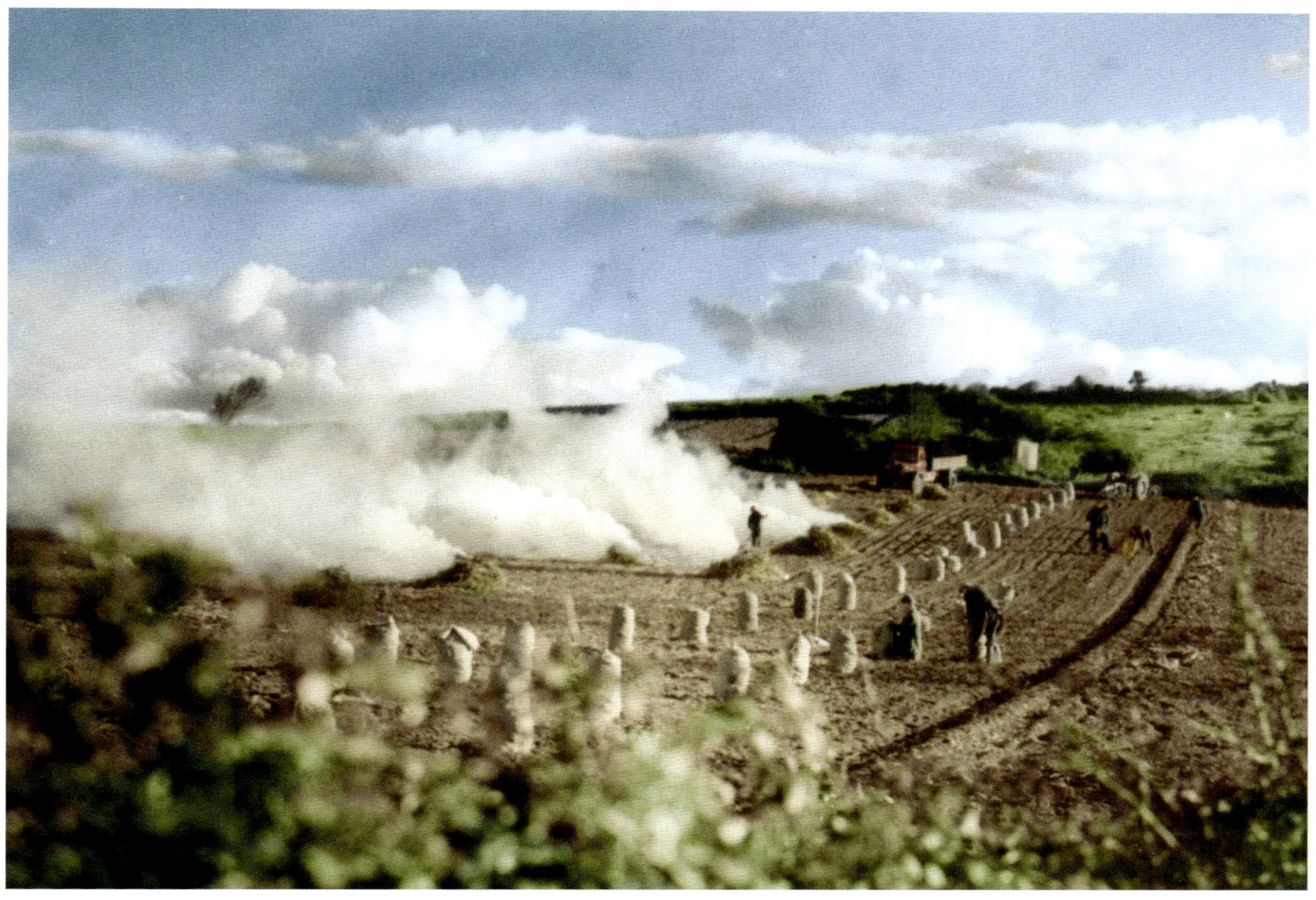

Left: Collecting the potatoes near Kinvara, County Galway. The potato, introduced to Ireland in the late sixteenth century, quickly took hold as its suitability for Ireland's mild, temperate climate made it an ideal crop. With its high yield and caloric value, the potato offered a dependable food source. However, when the potato blight struck Ireland in the mid-nineteenth century, it led to the Great Famine, which claimed the lives of over a million people and forced millions more to emigrate. Nevertheless, cultivation remained strong in the decades that followed, and the potato still holds a place in Irish farming and cuisine today.

Top right: A world away from the west of Ireland, north County Dublin, with its fertile soils and mild coastal climate, was the heart of Ireland's market gardening industry. The region's proximity to the capital ensured a steady demand and growers in the region supplied Dublin city with crops like potatoes, onions and cabbages. Here we see the burning off of potato stalks at Skerries in 1960 – a final step in the harvesting process. After the potatoes had been lifted and bagged, the dried-out stalks were burned off to clear the field.

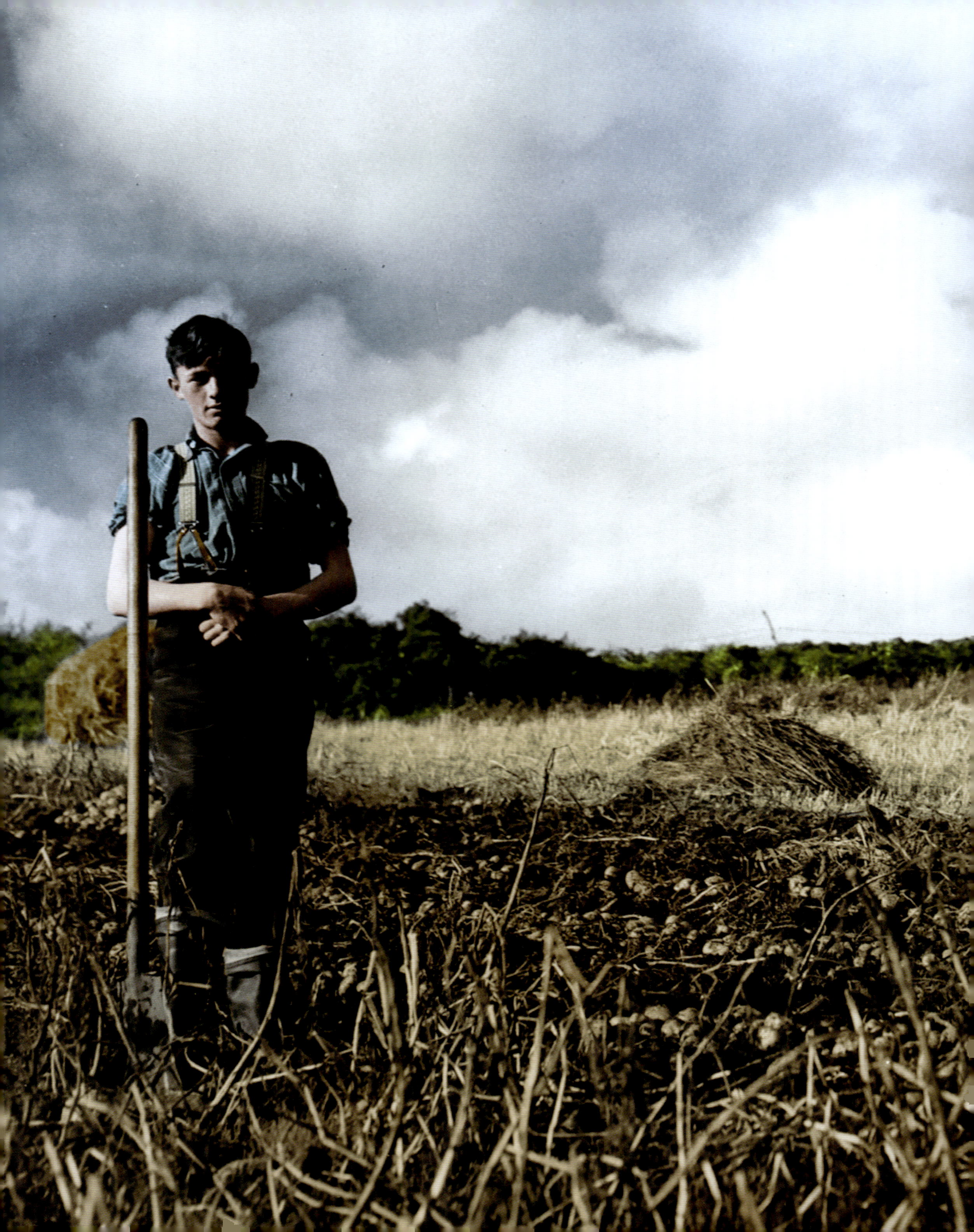

Reminiscent of Jean-François Millet's famous 1859 painting *The Angelus*, this scene unfolds not in France but near Ballina, County Mayo in the 1950s, as a family pauses at midday to say the Angelus.

In the Ireland of that time, Catholicism was deeply woven into daily life, particularly in rural communities. With over 90 per cent of the population in the Republic of Ireland identifying as Catholic, the Church's influence then extended far beyond the parish, shaping government policies, education and social norms. Faith was not just an aspect of life but its foundation, guiding people's routines, values and sense of identity.

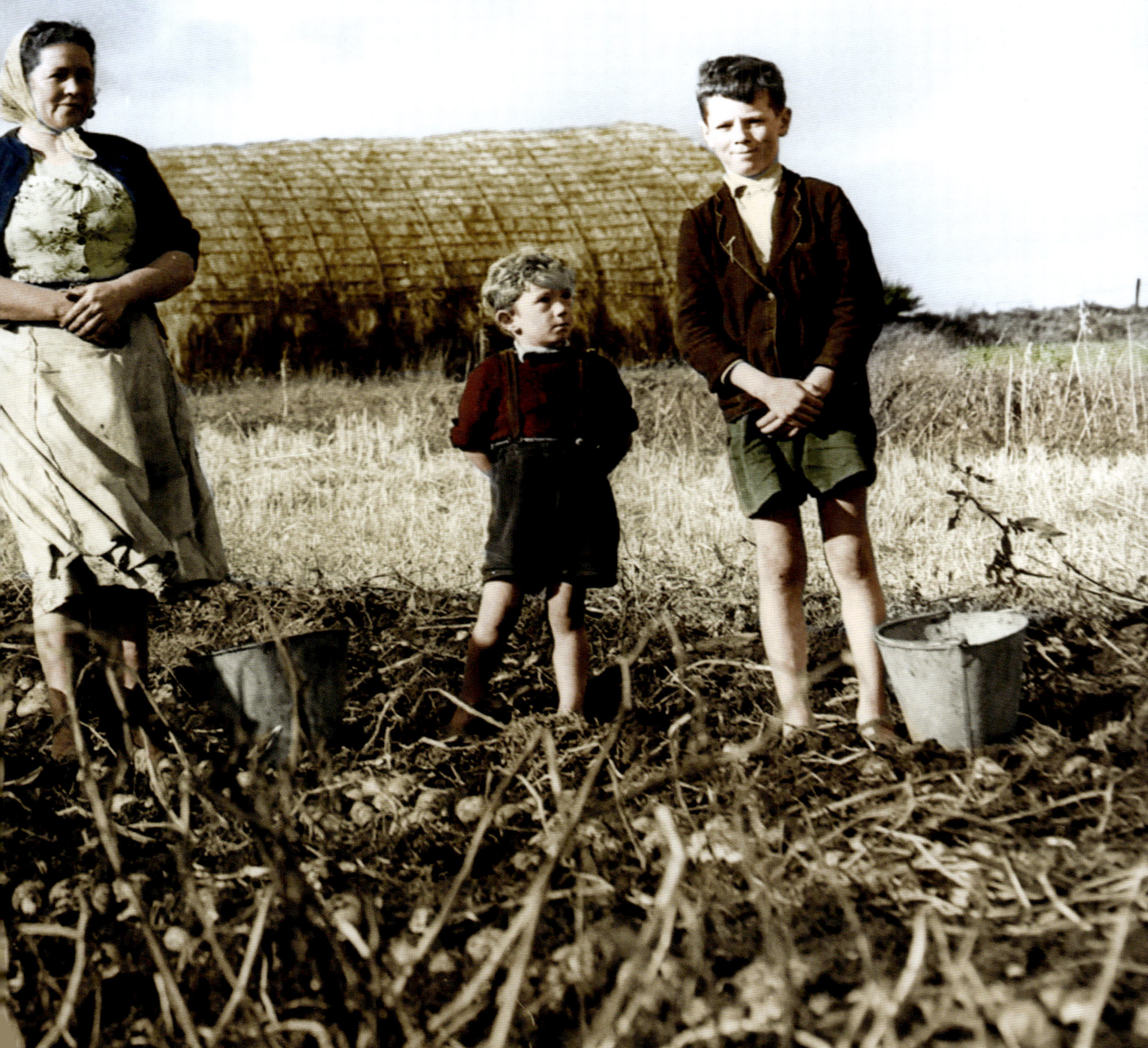

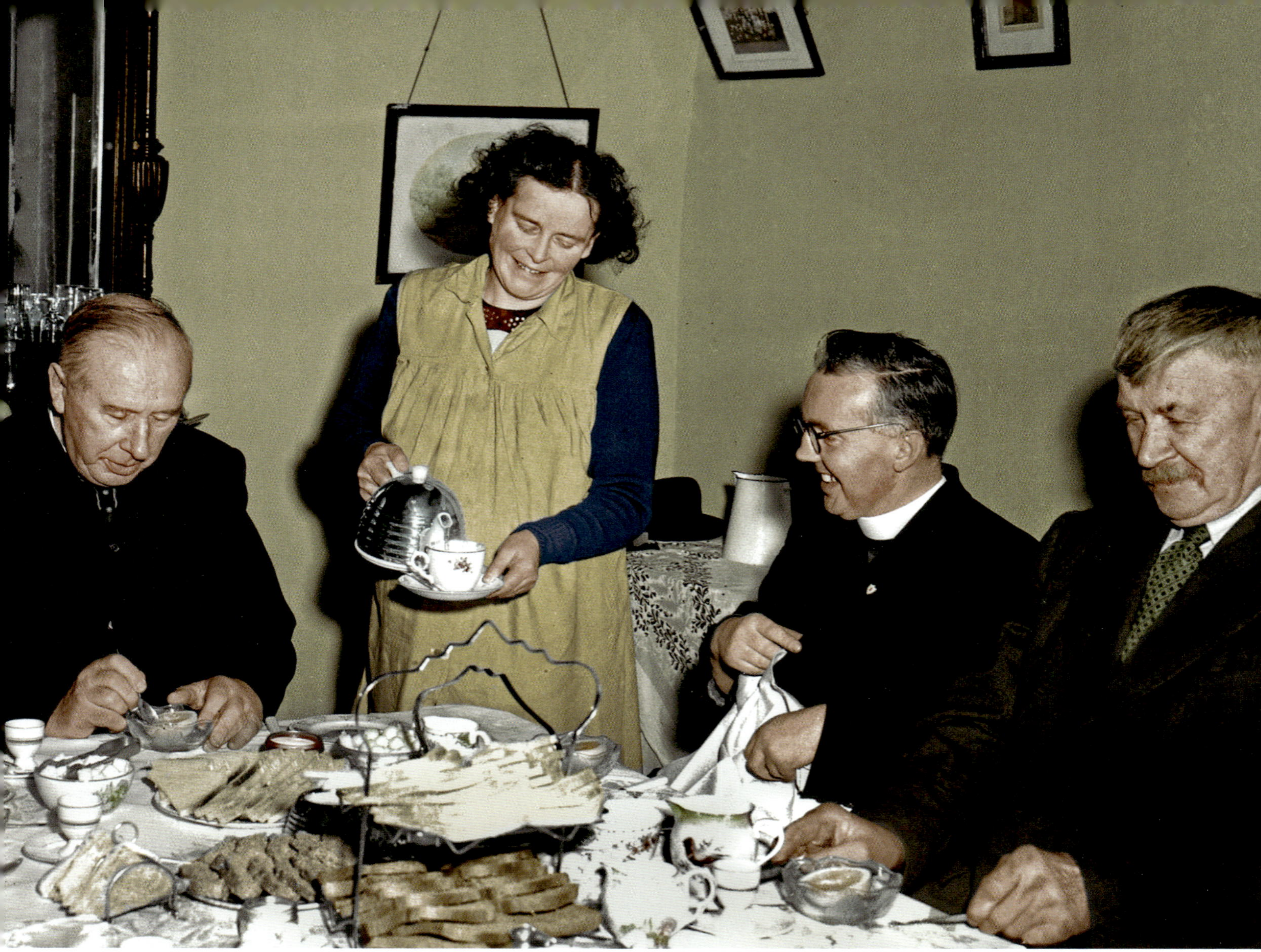

In rural Ireland during the 1950s and 1960s, the 'Stations' were an important religious and social tradition. These were Masses held in family homes, usually on farms. Afterwards, the host family provided food and tea, making it a social occasion as well as a religious one. While the tradition has declined, it still continues in some areas. Here, in Ballinhassig, County Cork, a woman pours tea for a priest during a meal following the Stations, a moment of hospitality that was central to the practice.

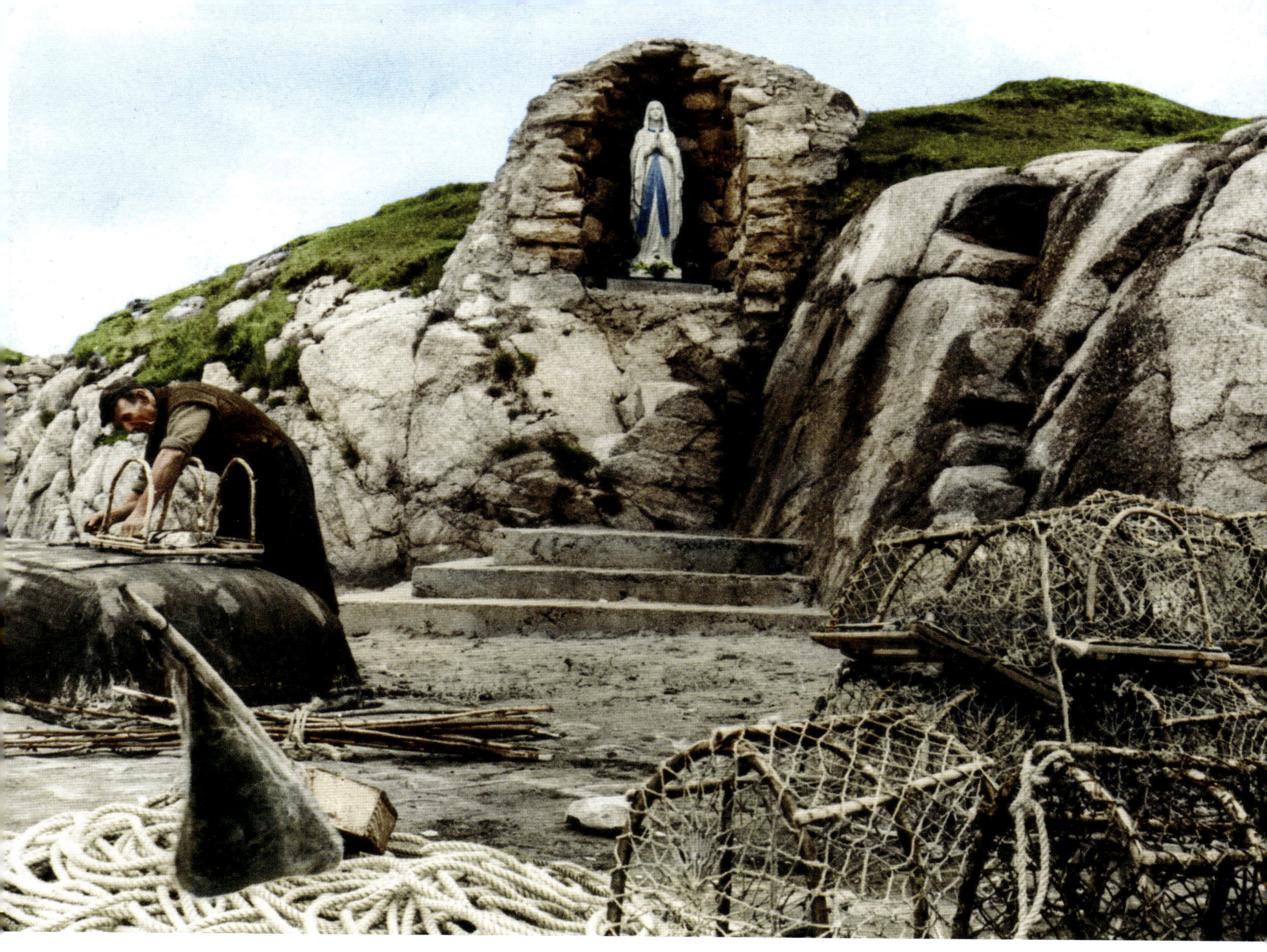

A familiar sight across Ireland, a Blessed
Virgin statue watches over this scene of a man
working on his lobster pots.

In 1950, the Holy Year was marked by
deep religious devotion in Ireland, with
communities across the country taking
part in acts of faith, such as the erection
of crosses on mountain tops. A Holy
Year, declared by the Pope, is a special
year in the Catholic Church marked
by particular religious observances,
indulgences and pilgrimages. The
1950 Holy Year called for renewal and
reflection, while in 1954 the Marian Year,
dedicated to the Virgin Mary, continued
this spirit of devotion.

In this photograph from October
1950 at Enniskeane, County Cork, a
multitude follows men carrying a large
wooden cross as part of the Holy Year
observances. The cross was erected
on a prominent hill in the area. The
practice of erecting crosses remained a
powerful symbol of piety in rural Ireland,
extending into the Marian Year and
beyond.

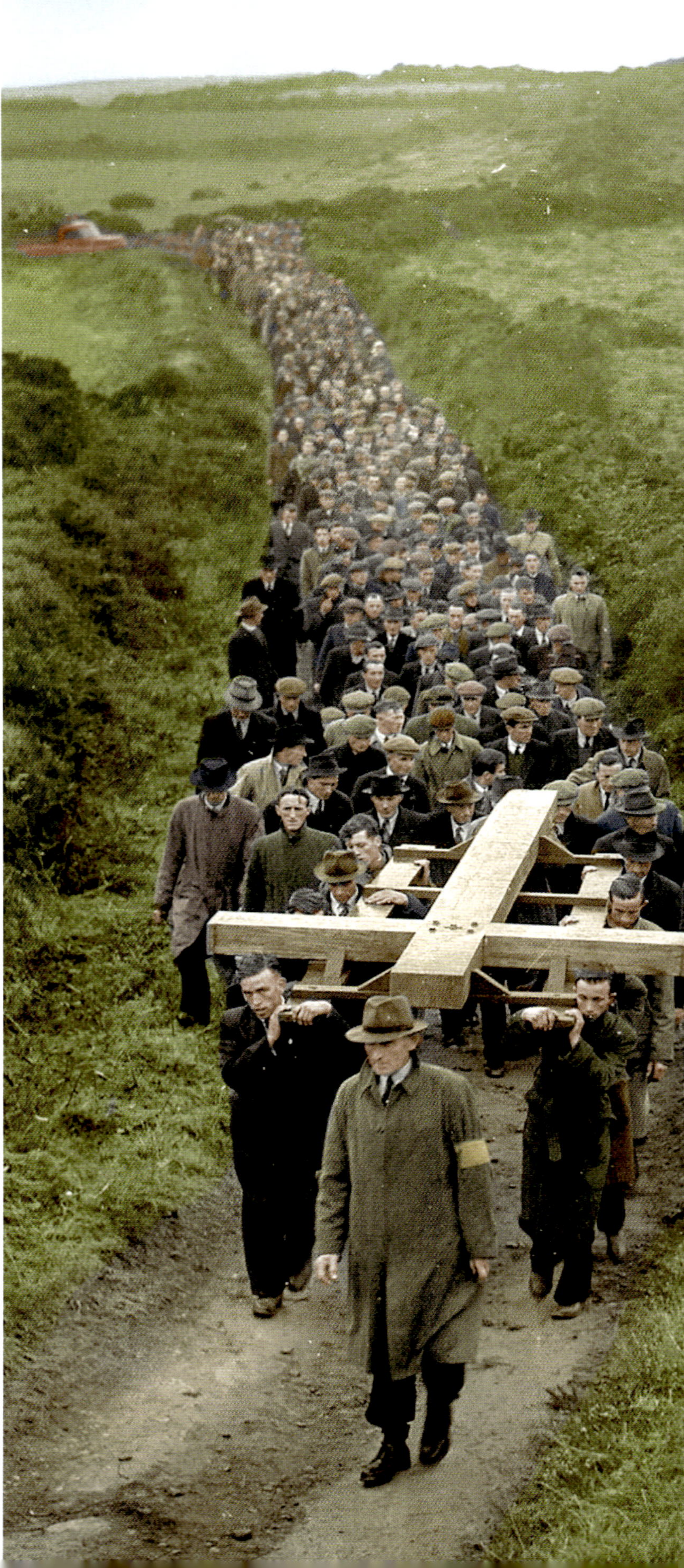

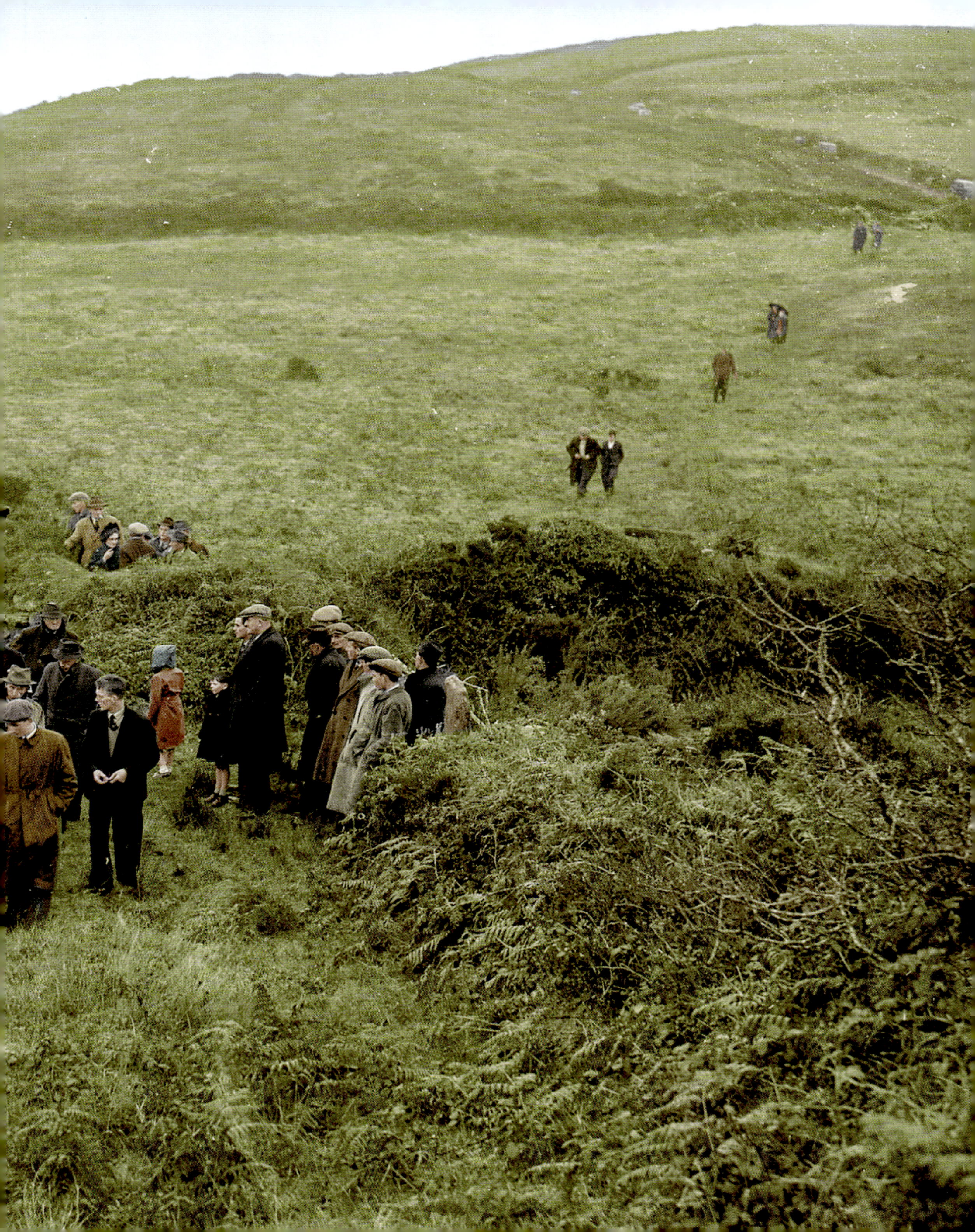

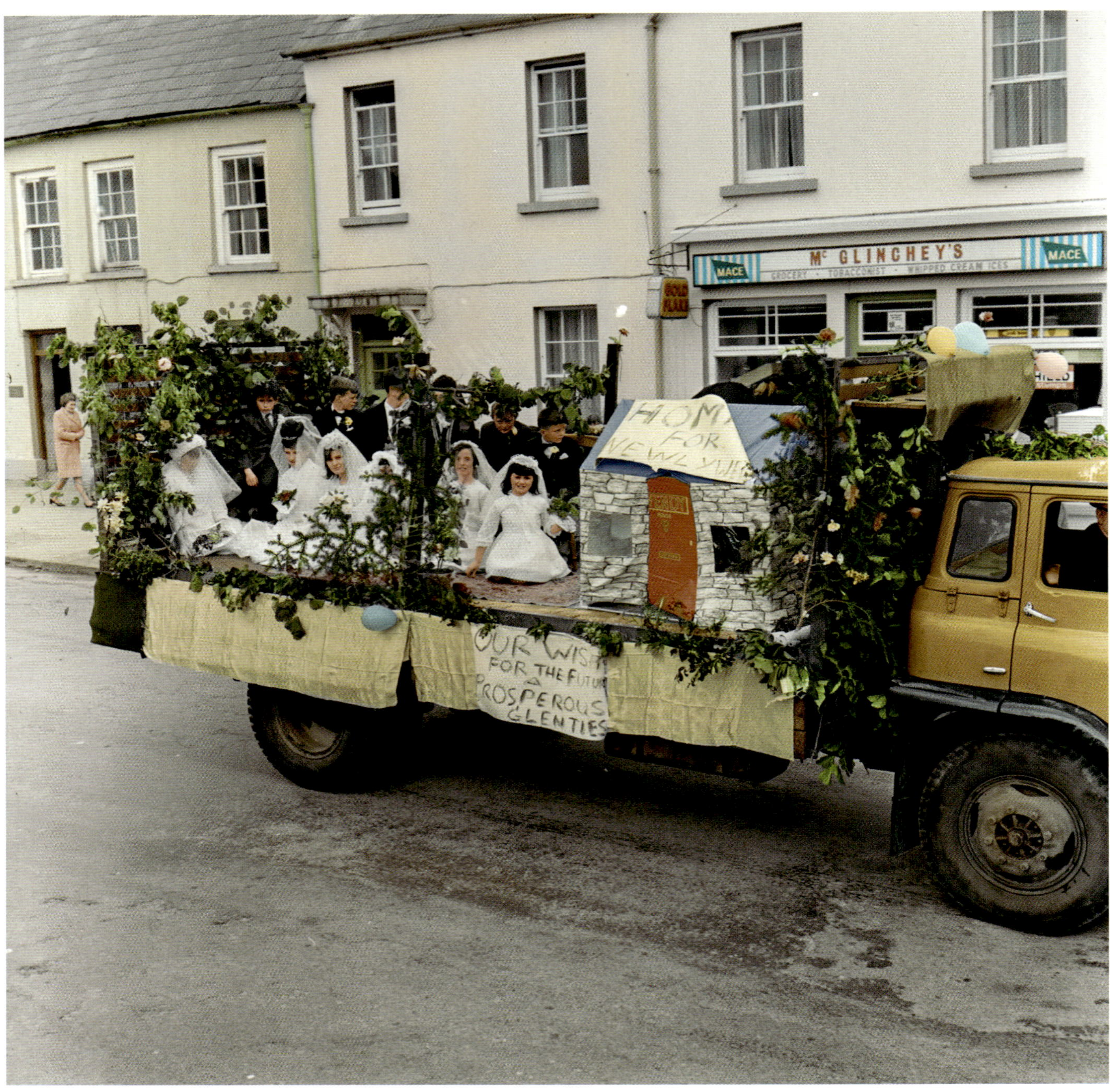

Girls and boys in their best attire are seen
here on a float at a parade in Glenties, County
Donegal.

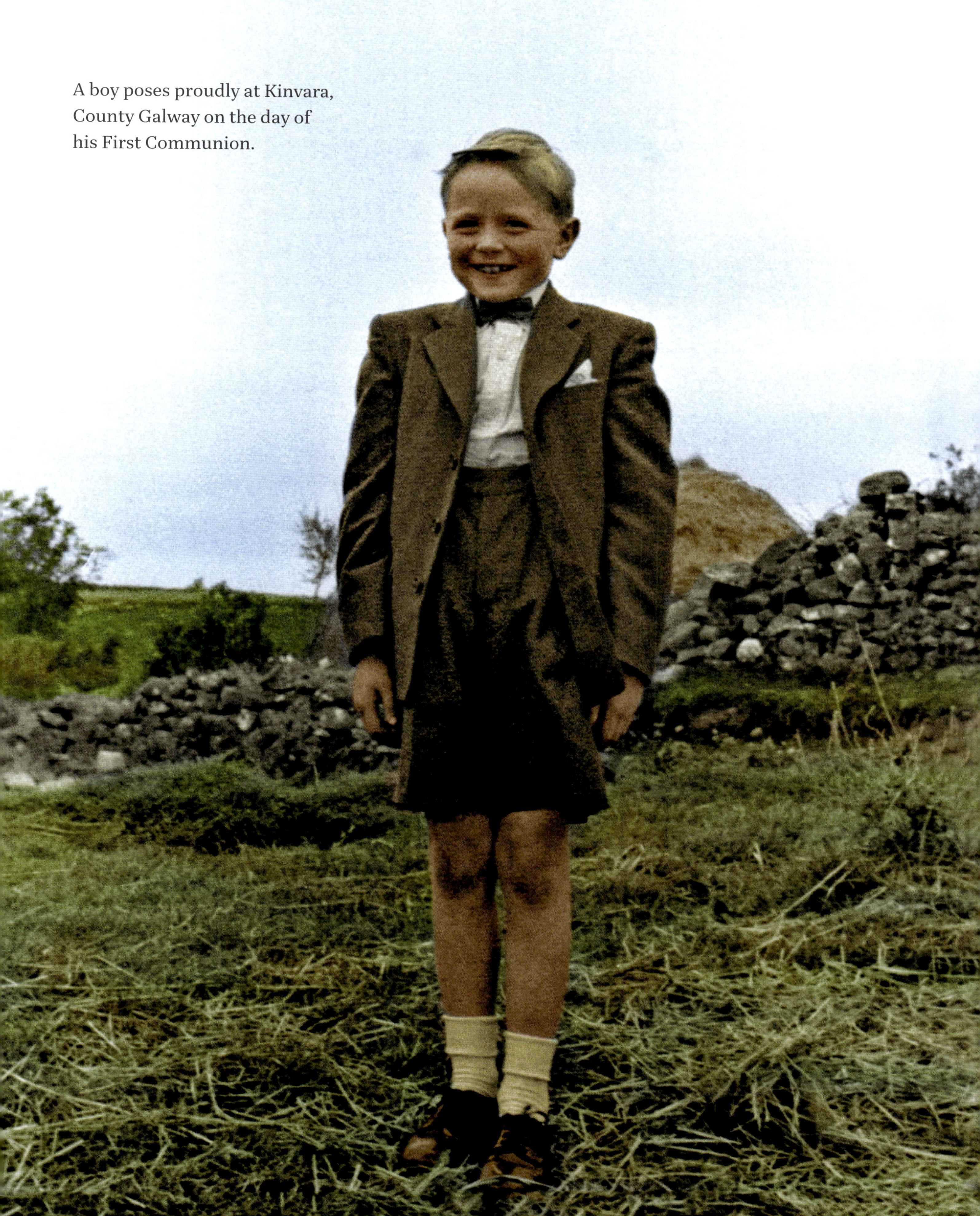

A boy poses proudly at Kinvara, County Galway on the day of his First Communion.

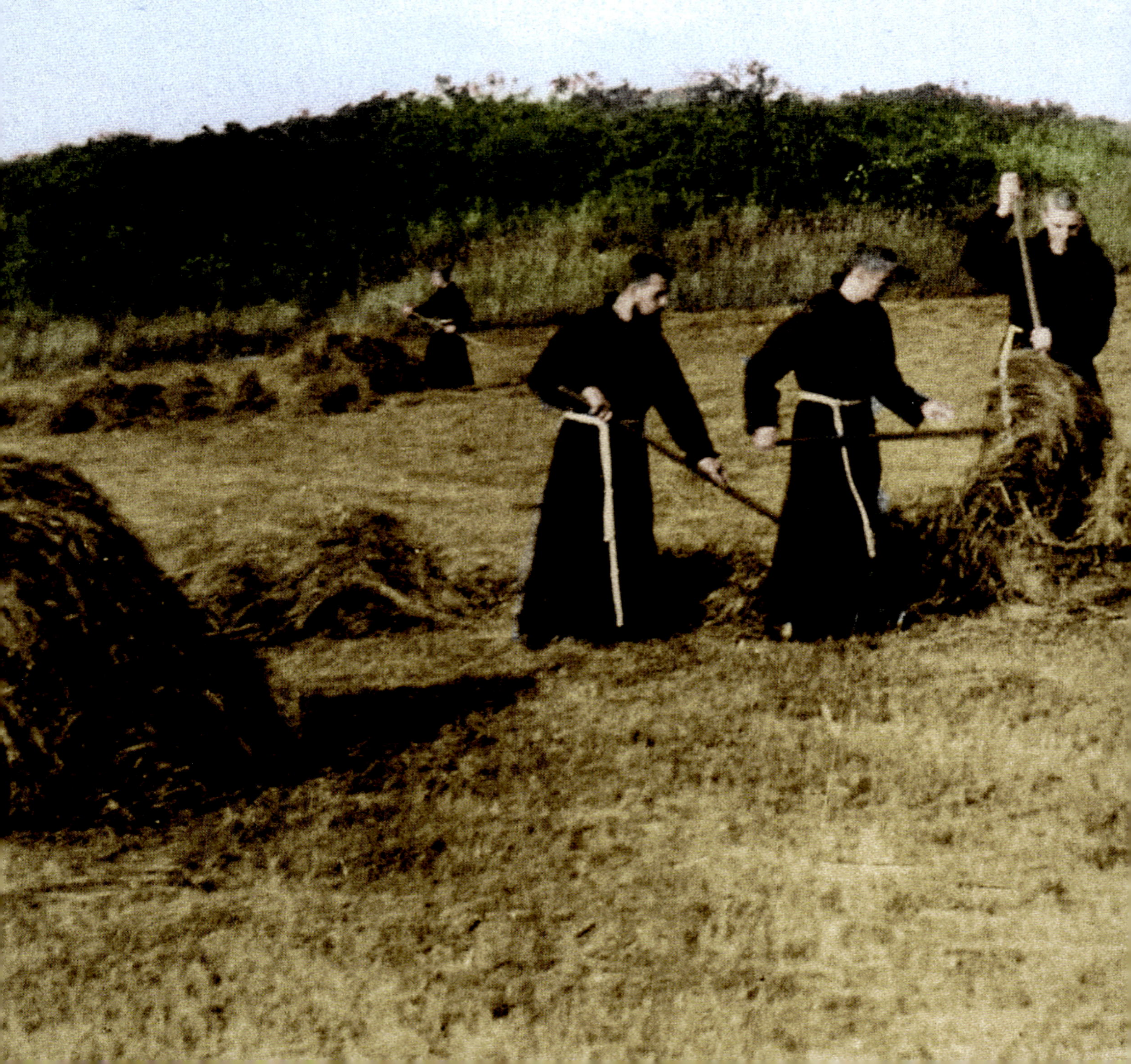

Capuchin Friars piking the hay at Ard Mhuire Friary, located in Creeslough, County Donegal. Opened in 1930, it still functions as a retreat and conference centre for both religious and lay organisations.

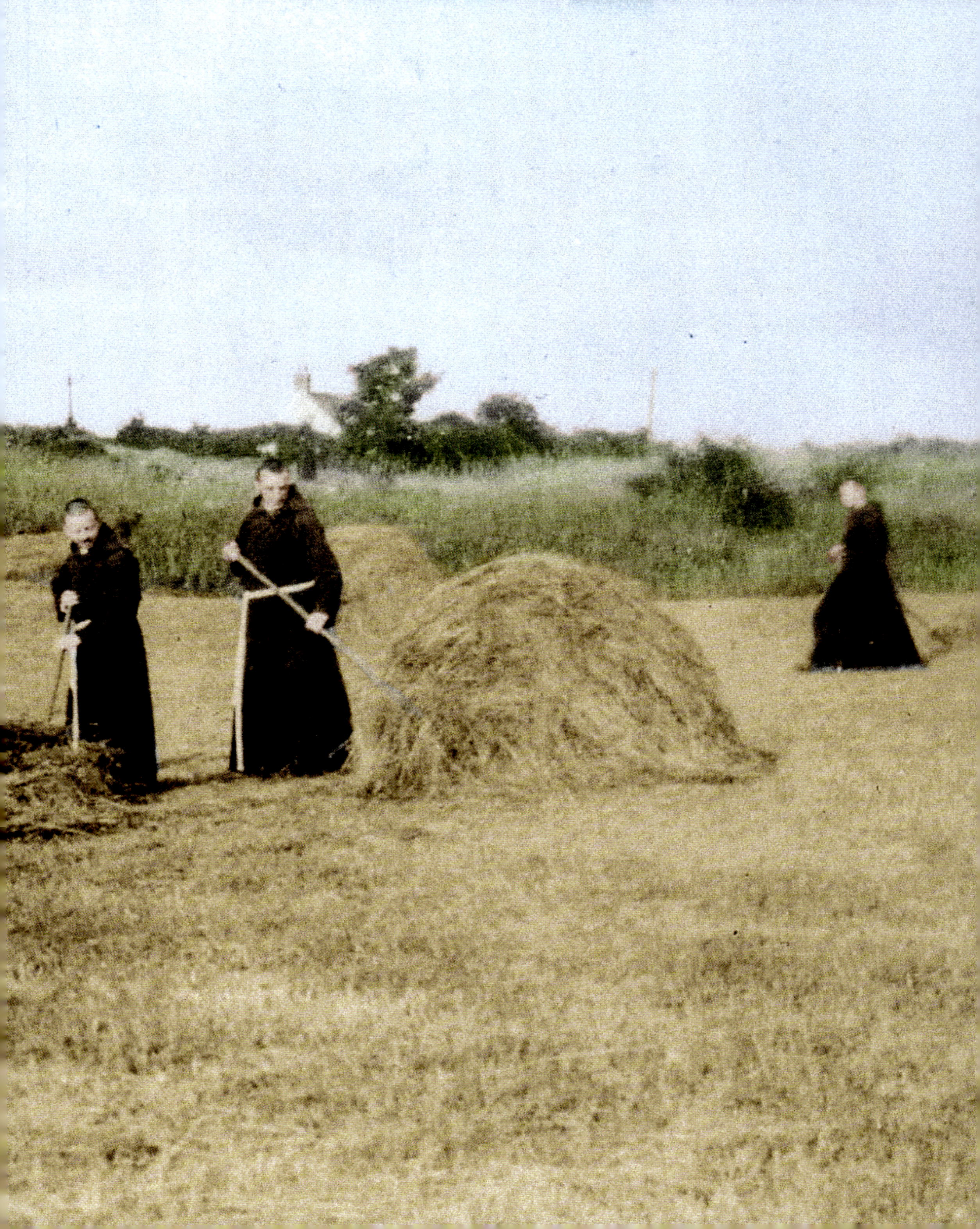

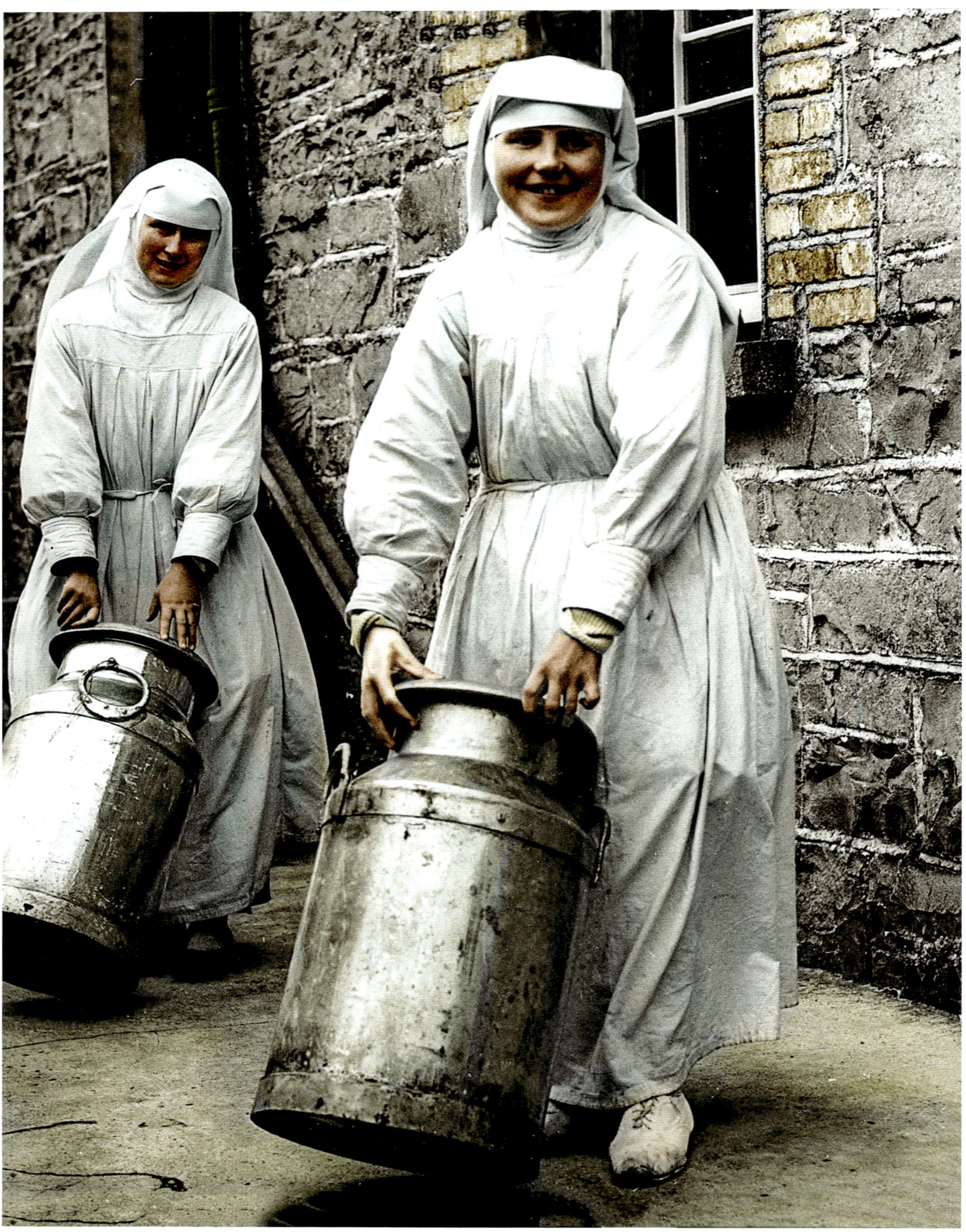

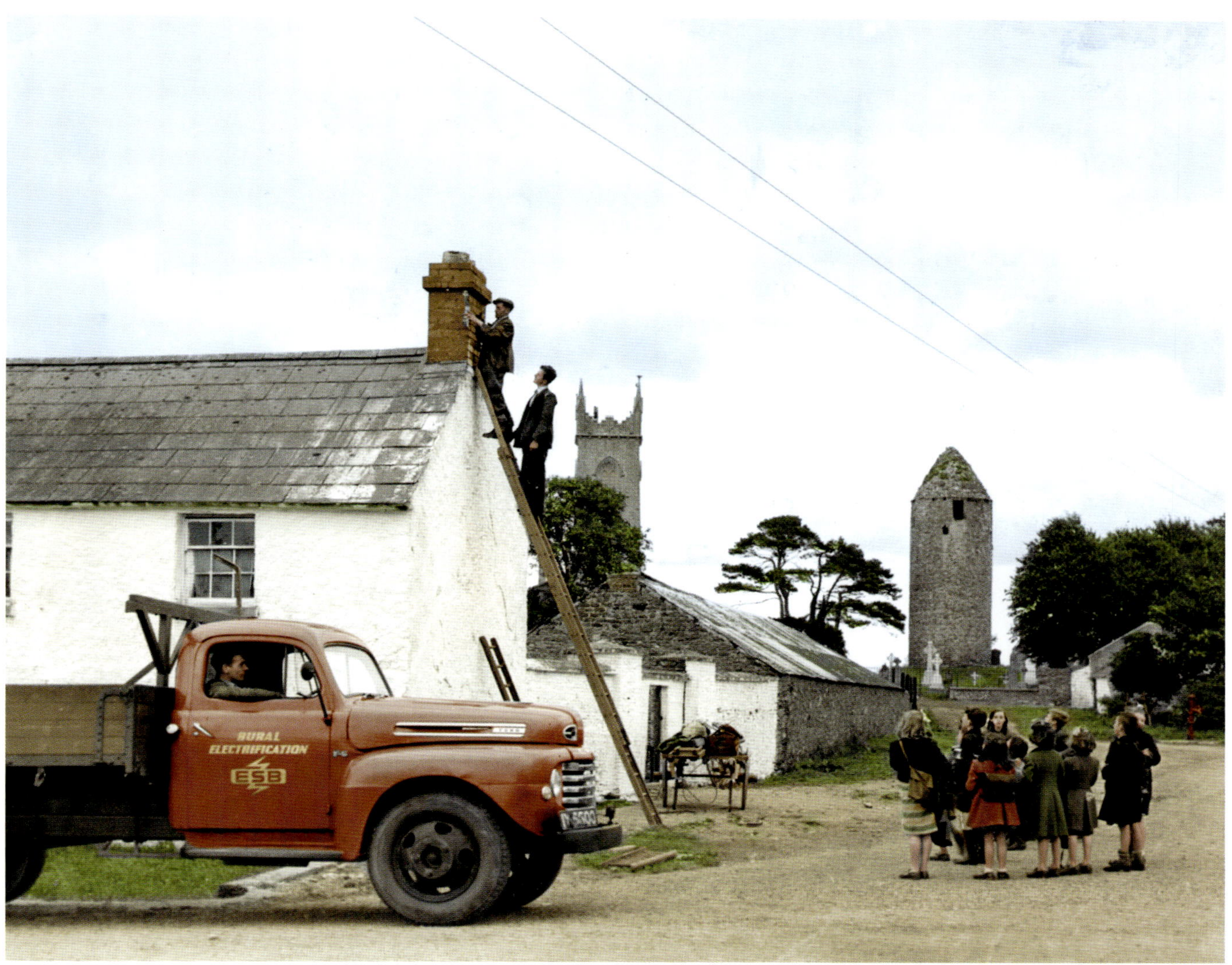

Left: Hauling the churns: the nuns of Loughglynn Convent, County Roscommon, an institution established in 1903. The nuns initially ran a school teaching domestic science and lace making. In turn, they operated a dairy farm up to the 1960s that became renowned for its butter and cheese production.

Top right: Making a connection – work underway at Dromiskin, County Louth. By the end of the war, the Electricity Supply Board (ESB) generating capacity comprised the great hydro station at Ardnacrusha, a few small hydro stations on the River Liffey and the thermal power station at the Pigeon House. As two out of three Irish homes had no electricity, an ambitious rural electrification scheme was commenced in 1946.

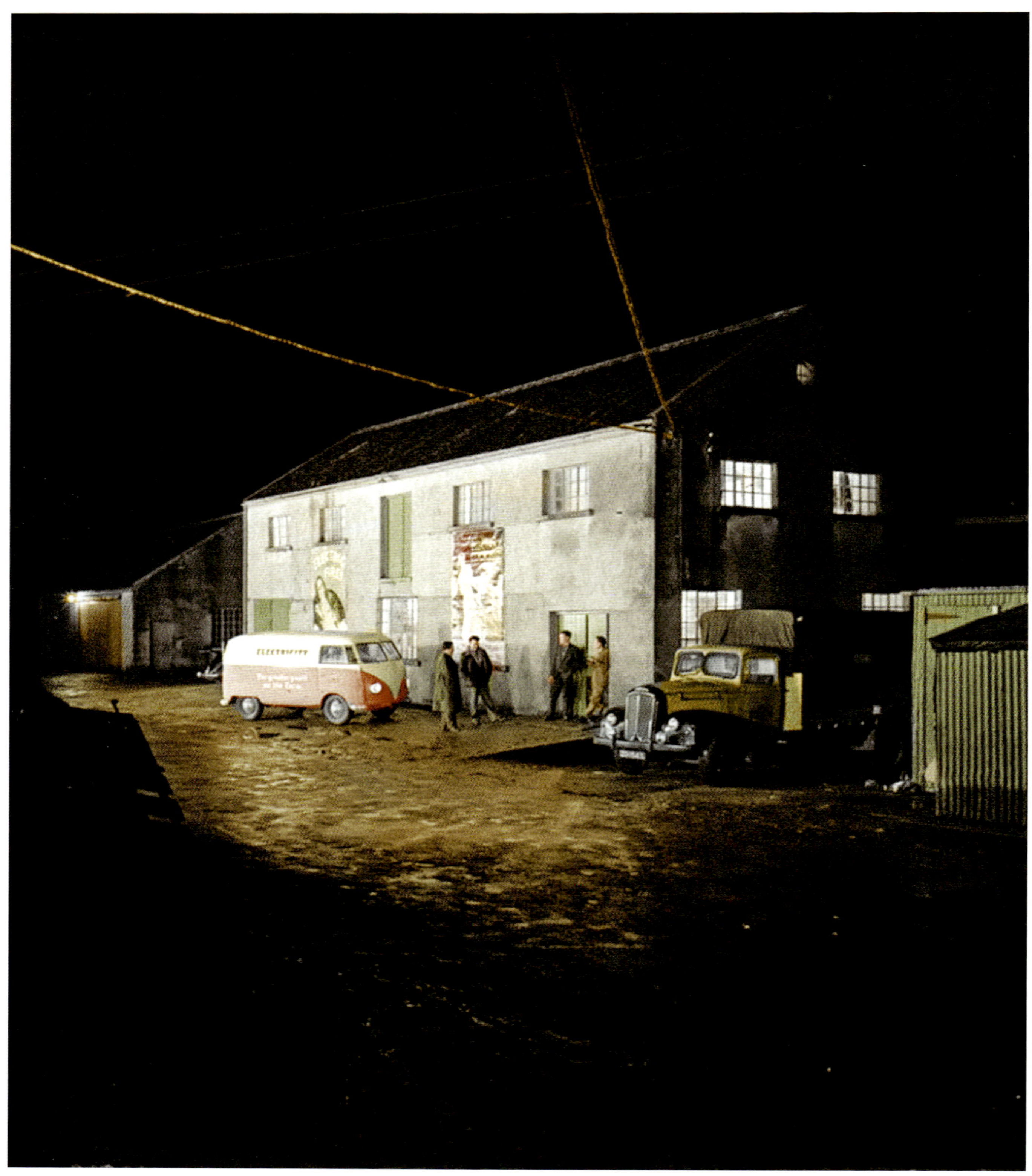

The scheme was rolled out, and electricity was supplied to a sometimes sceptical populace. Here there is light where once was darkness: at the switching-on ceremony at Ballinamult Creamery, the ESB's 100,000th rural consumer.

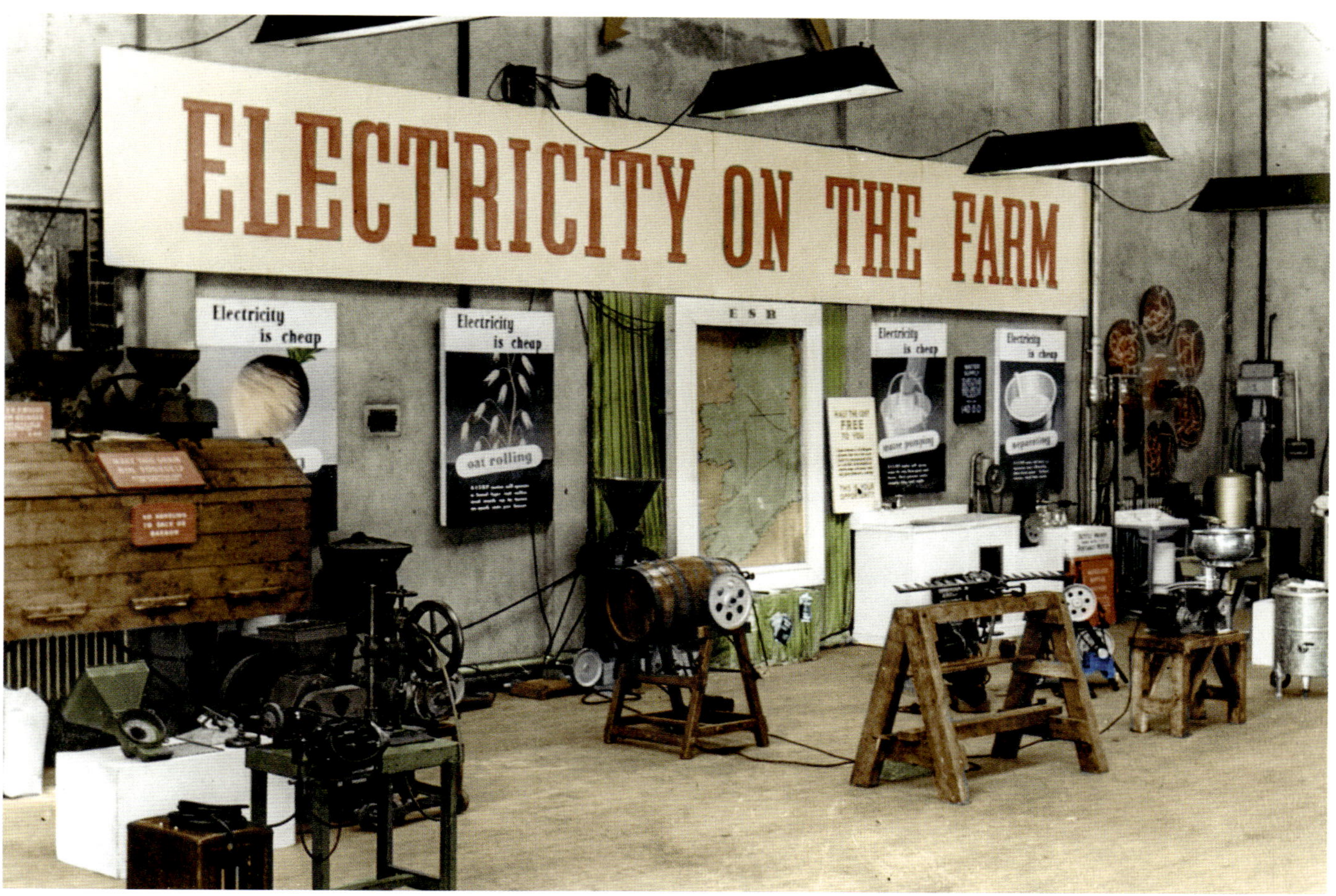

It's hard to imagine now in our connected world, when electricity is so ubiquitous, but in the late 1940s and 1950s, electricity was a new concept in all parts of rural Ireland. The ESB had to work hard to demonstrate what electricity was, how it could be safely used and what benefits it could bring to people. In an exercise almost like proselytising for a new religion, ESB staff canvassed homes in local areas to encourage people to sign up for 'the light'. They worked closely with parish priests – important figures in rural communities – to spread the message of electrification from the pulpit.

Local information meetings and exhibitions like the one seen here, were organised to explain the practical benefits of electricity to farmers. The key message was clear: electricity would make farm work easier, homes brighter and warmer, and the efficiencies gained from using electrical appliances would make the cost of it all well worth the investment.

By the time the scheme finished in 1964, one million poles had been erected and 80,000km of line had been strung. The arrival of electricity brought unprecedented change to rural Ireland – it revolutionised daily life, boosted agricultural productivity, and connected isolated areas to the wider world.

In many ways, it was more than just a technical advancement; it was a cornerstone of modern Irish society. Indeed, as many have noted, the ESB rural electrification scheme stands as the greatest social revolution in rural life since the land reforms of the late nineteenth century.

Pulleys, pipes and an electric motor – the machines offering a promise to transform the tasks of daily toil. As the ESB representative explains their benefits, a group of farmers, each with a cup of tea in hand, listens intently.

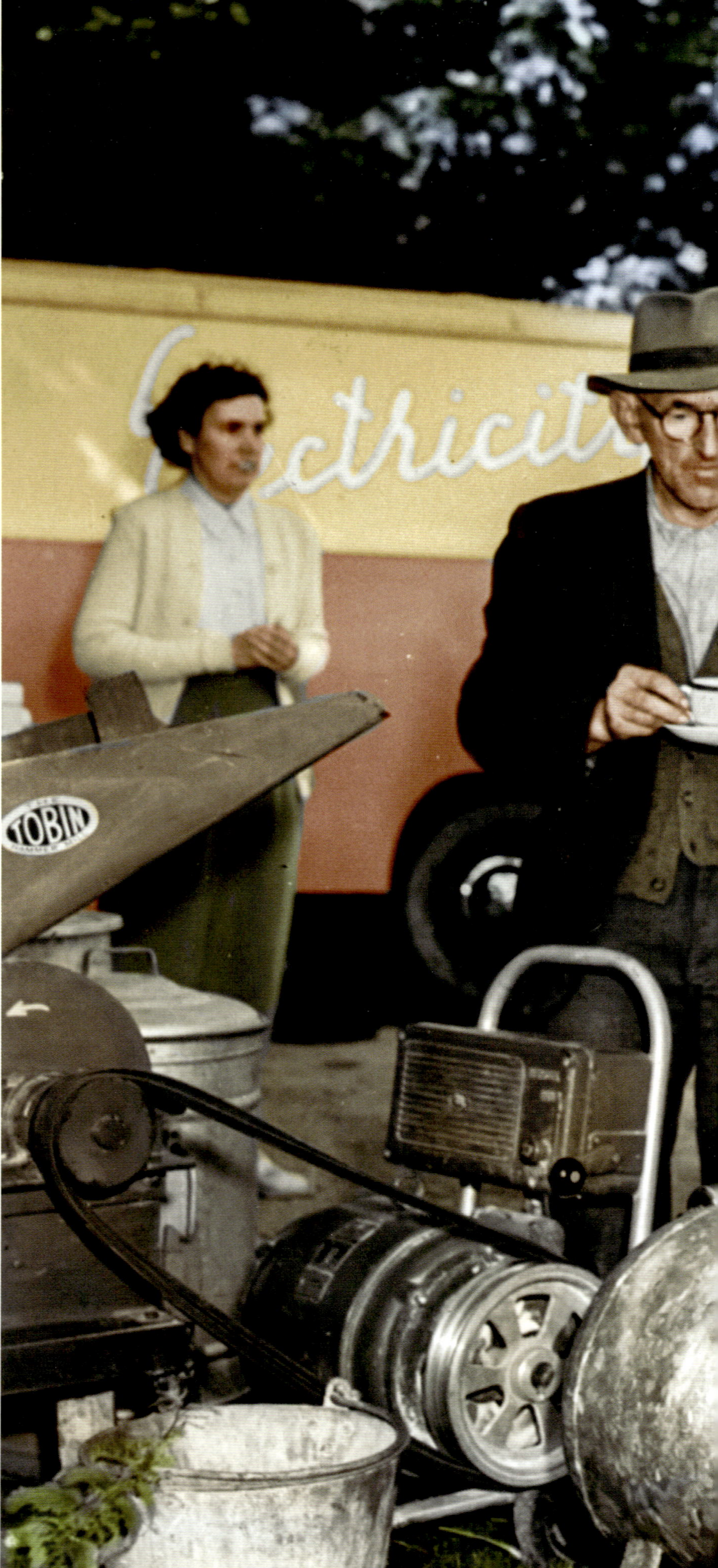

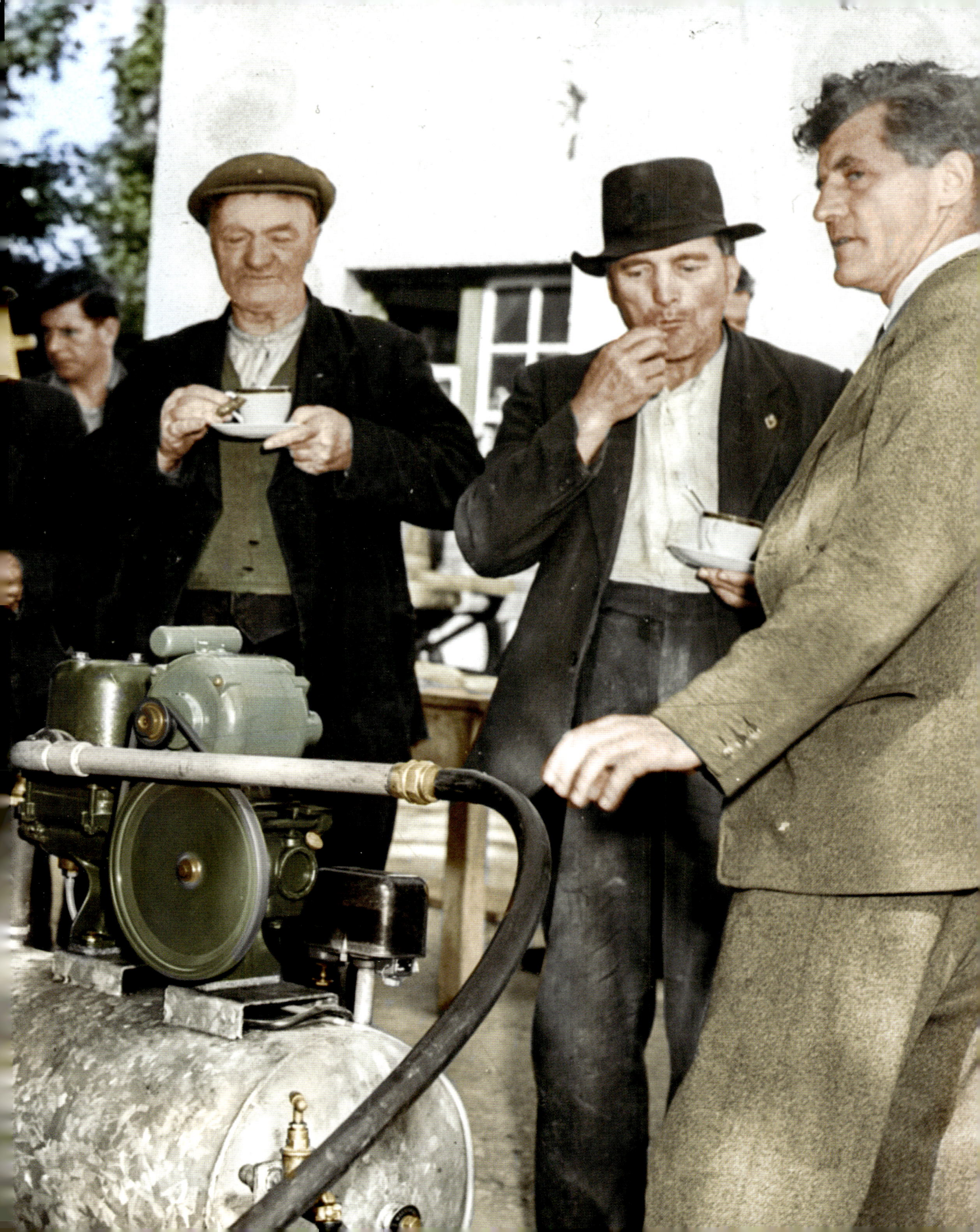

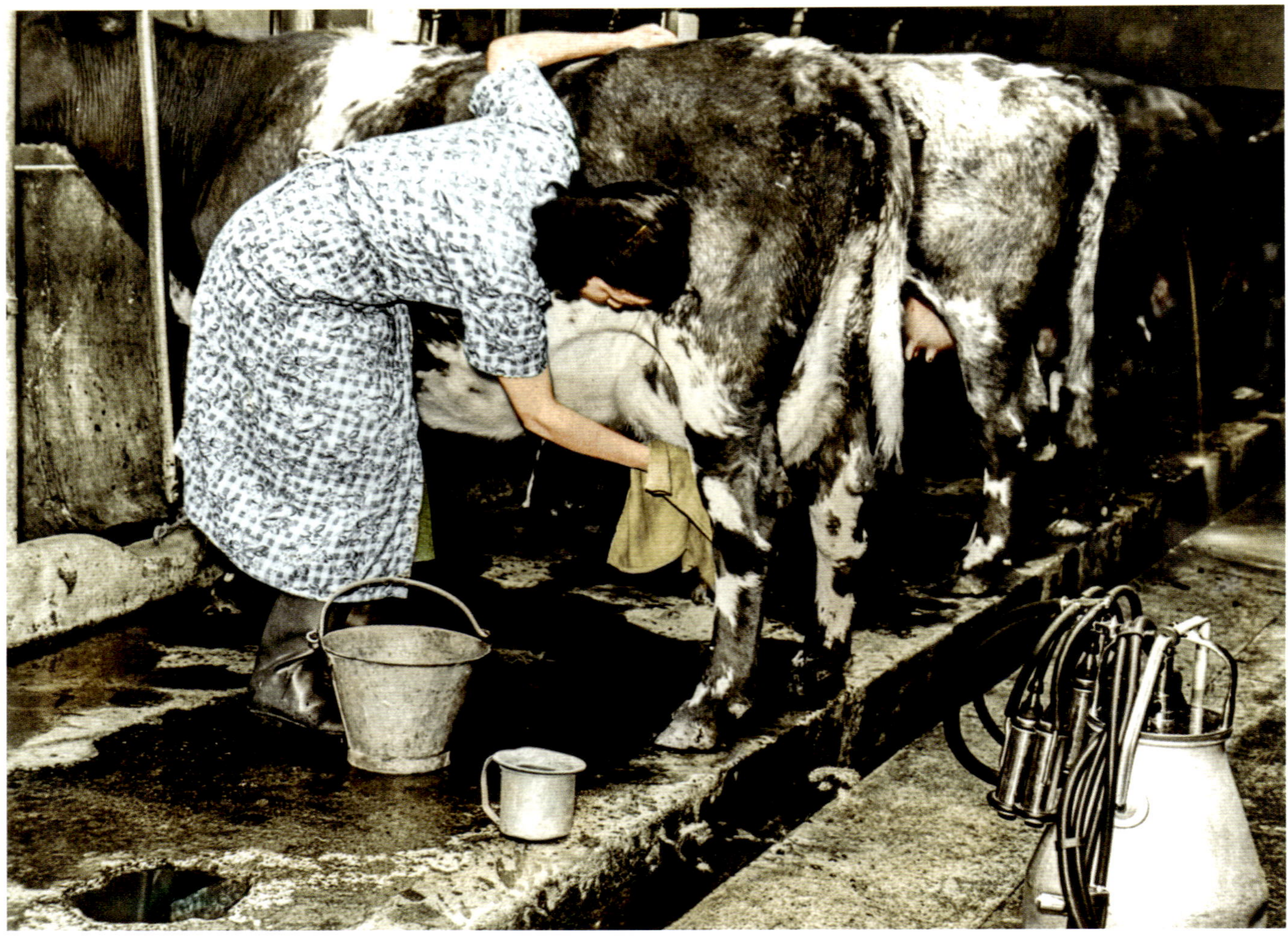

Top left: A woman works in the cowshed, with the new electric milking machine to hand. For generations, the Irish farmwife's day was filled with hard and repetitive tasks – milking cows, drawing water from the well, washing clothes by hand and boiling kettles over an open fire. But with the advent of electricity, her life was about to change. The introduction of electric appliances was truly transformational – these held the promise of easing the burden of everyday chores.

Right: For generations, the kettle sat over what was, in many cases, an open turf fire. Now, with electricity, boiling water took minutes with no effort.

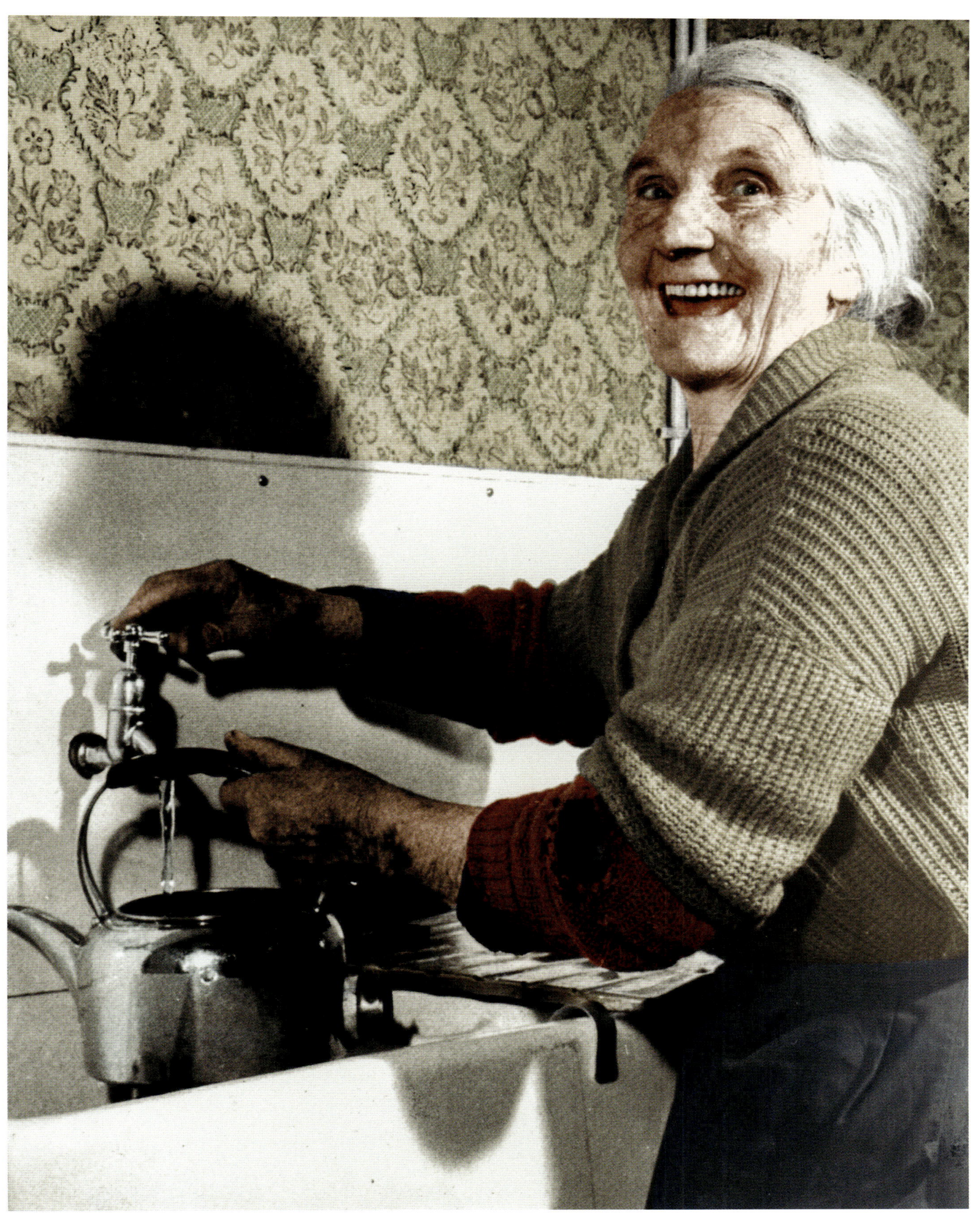

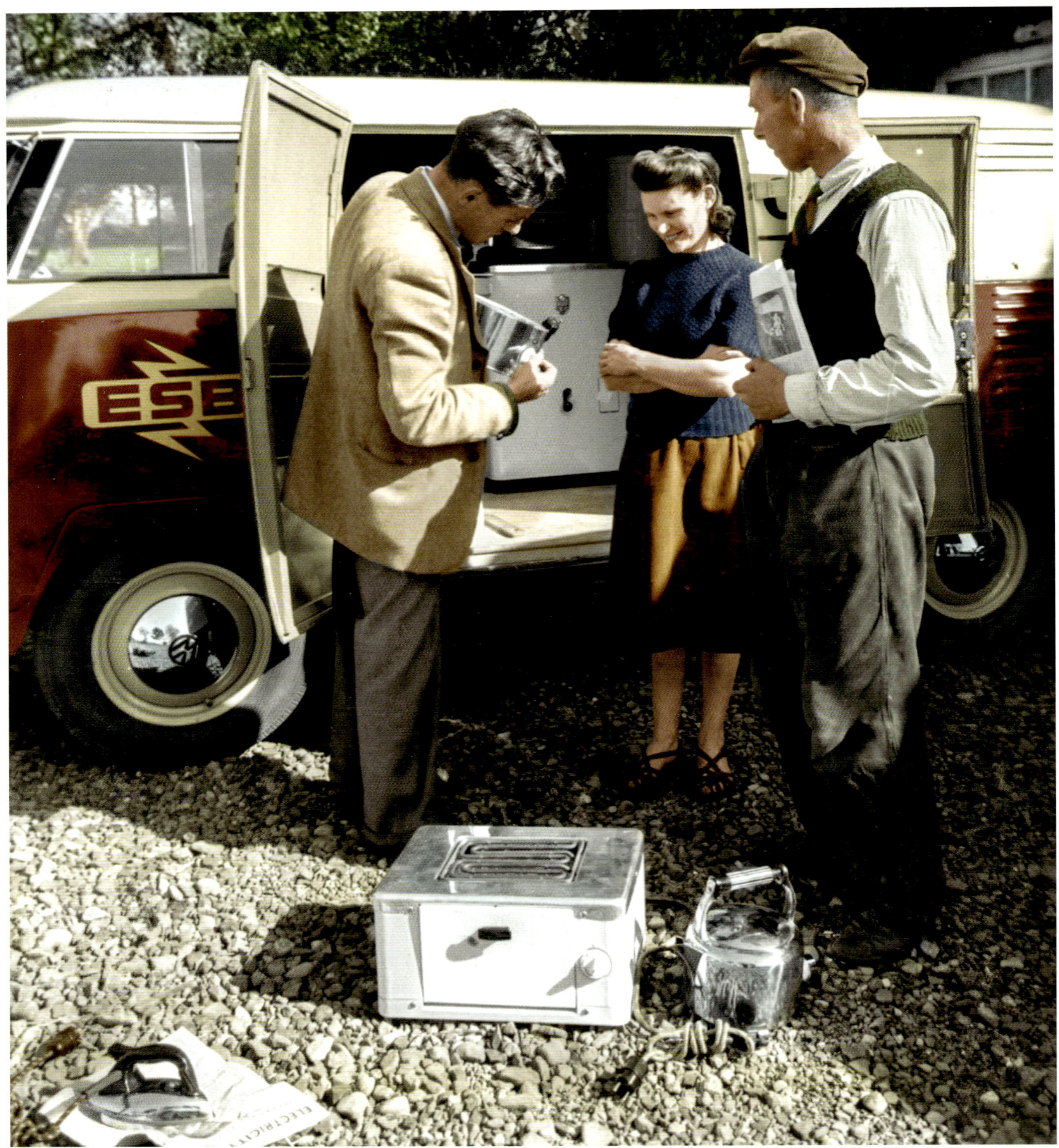

Top left: Modernity was now on the horizon. The ESB man demonstrates the potential of electricity to a farmer and his wife, showcasing a fridge, an iron, a basic oven with a hotplate and an electric kettle.

Right: The ESB installation teams didn't just cross mountains and rivers – they also adapted to local challenges, as seen here with a lineman dealing with a swarm of bees.

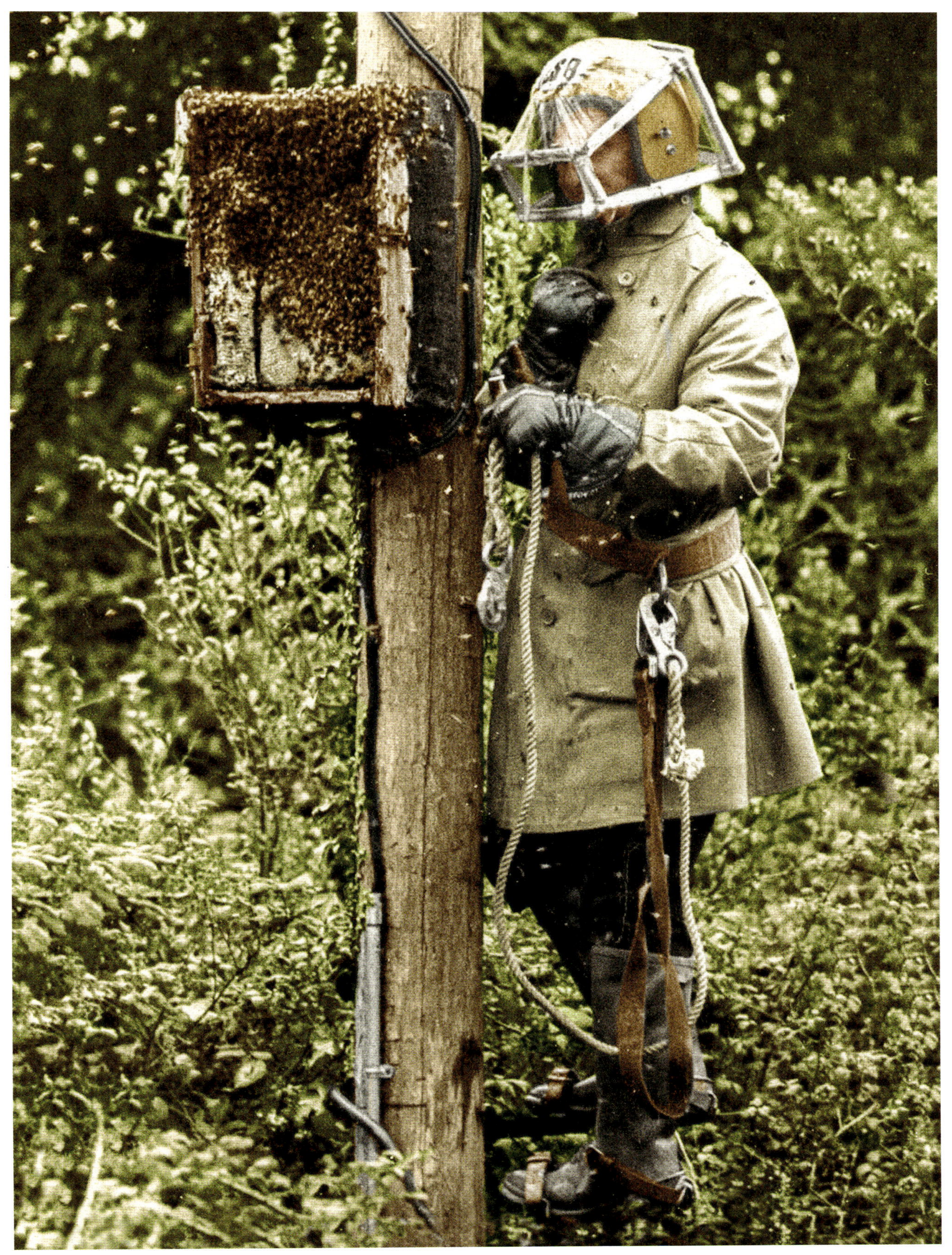

Happy out: Patrick Gahan captures a day trip by the Irish Countrywomen's Association (ICA) to Owenahincha beach, near Rosscarbery, County Cork, in the late 1940s or 1950s. The scene features around two dozen women, accompanied by a few children, all enjoying a lively and cheerful gathering. With a Primus stove steaming away and baskets of food at hand, it's clear that the women were well prepared for a great day out. As the tea is poured, the sound of an accordion adds to an afternoon of relaxation and camaraderie.

The ICA, founded in 1910, plays an important role in the lives of rural women in Ireland, offering them a platform for social and educational development. It is the largest women's organisation in Ireland, with approximately 6,000 members. The ICA seeks to enhance rural and urban life by offering avenues for social engagement and learning, promoting Irish culture and supporting community development.

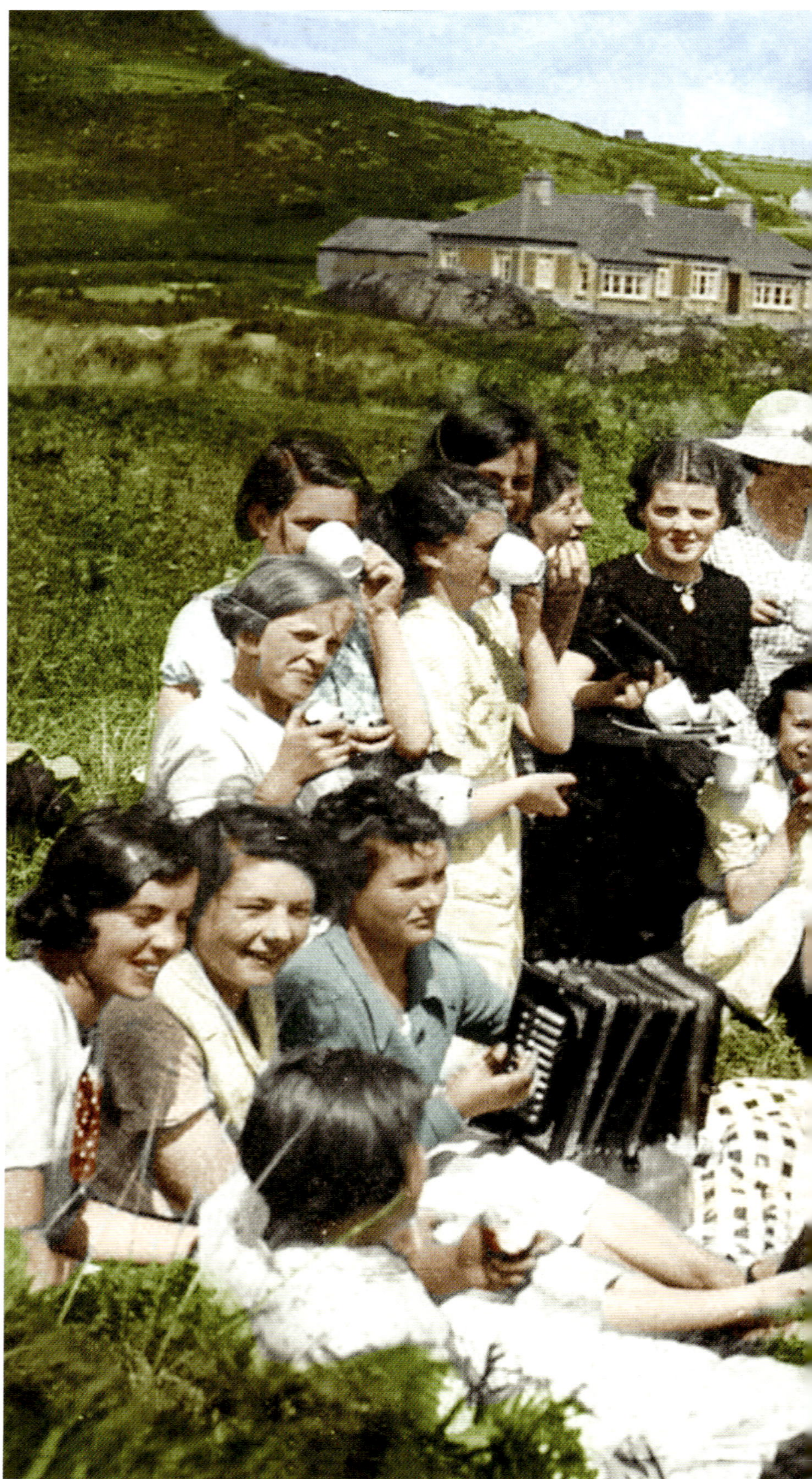

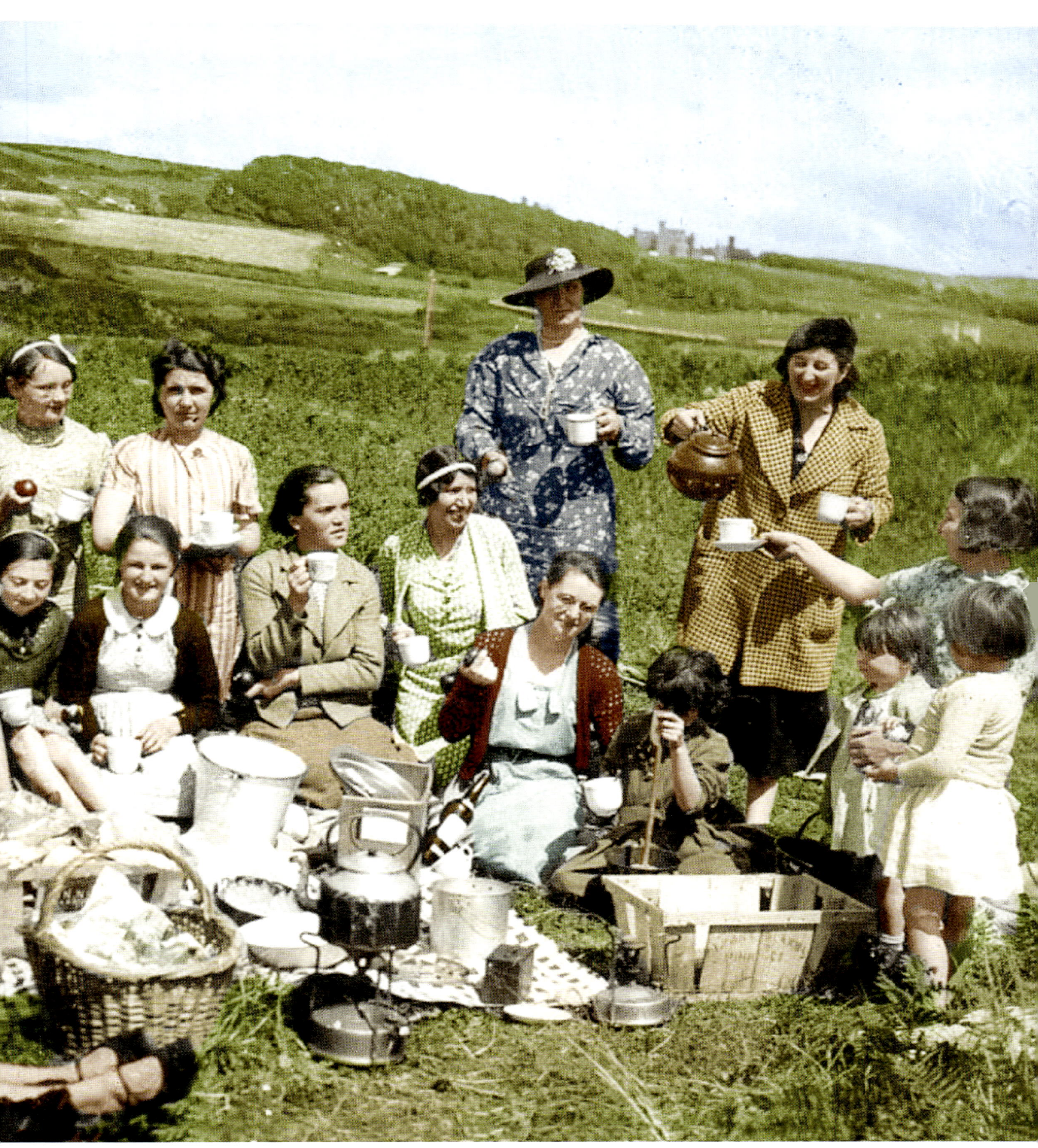

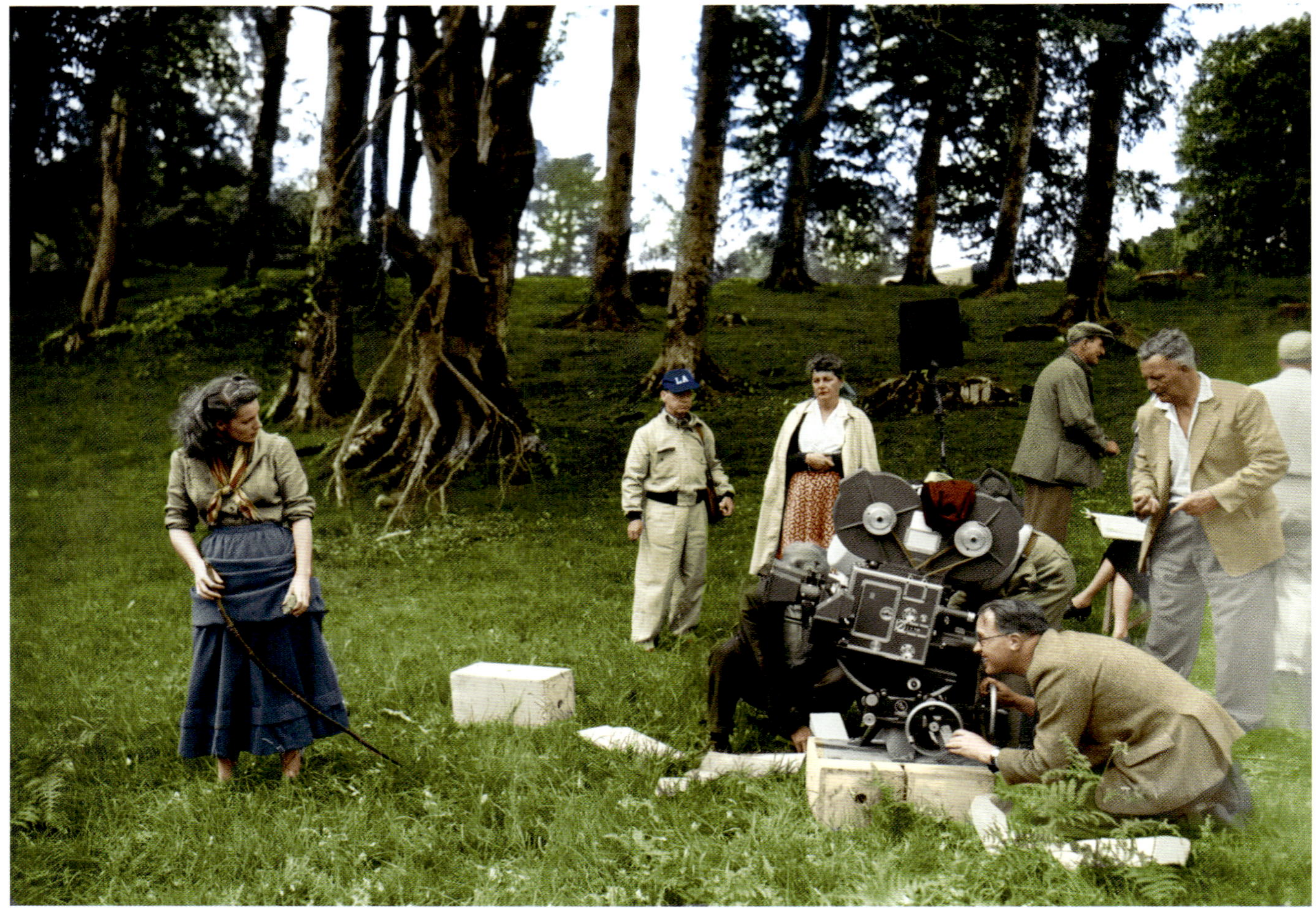

Maureen O'Hara on the set of *The Quiet Man* (1952), the quintessential film depicting rural Irish life. Born in Dublin, O'Hara brought an authentic Irish presence to the role of Mary Kate Danaher, a strong-willed farmer's daughter. Just seen in the background and exiting right is John Wayne, her co-star. In the film he stands as the outsider, an American returning to his ancestral homeland.

Directed by John Ford, whose own Irish heritage deeply influenced the film, *The Quiet Man* offers a romanticised yet nuanced portrayal of Ireland's farming community. Rather than leaning into clichéd depictions (or even the American penchant for featuring leprechauns) often seen in portrayals of Ireland at the time, it emphasises traditions like matchmaking, local festivals and the central importance of land and family.

With scenes of ploughing and working the land, and close-knit relationships among the villagers, it provides a heartfelt and authentic representation of traditional Irish farming life.

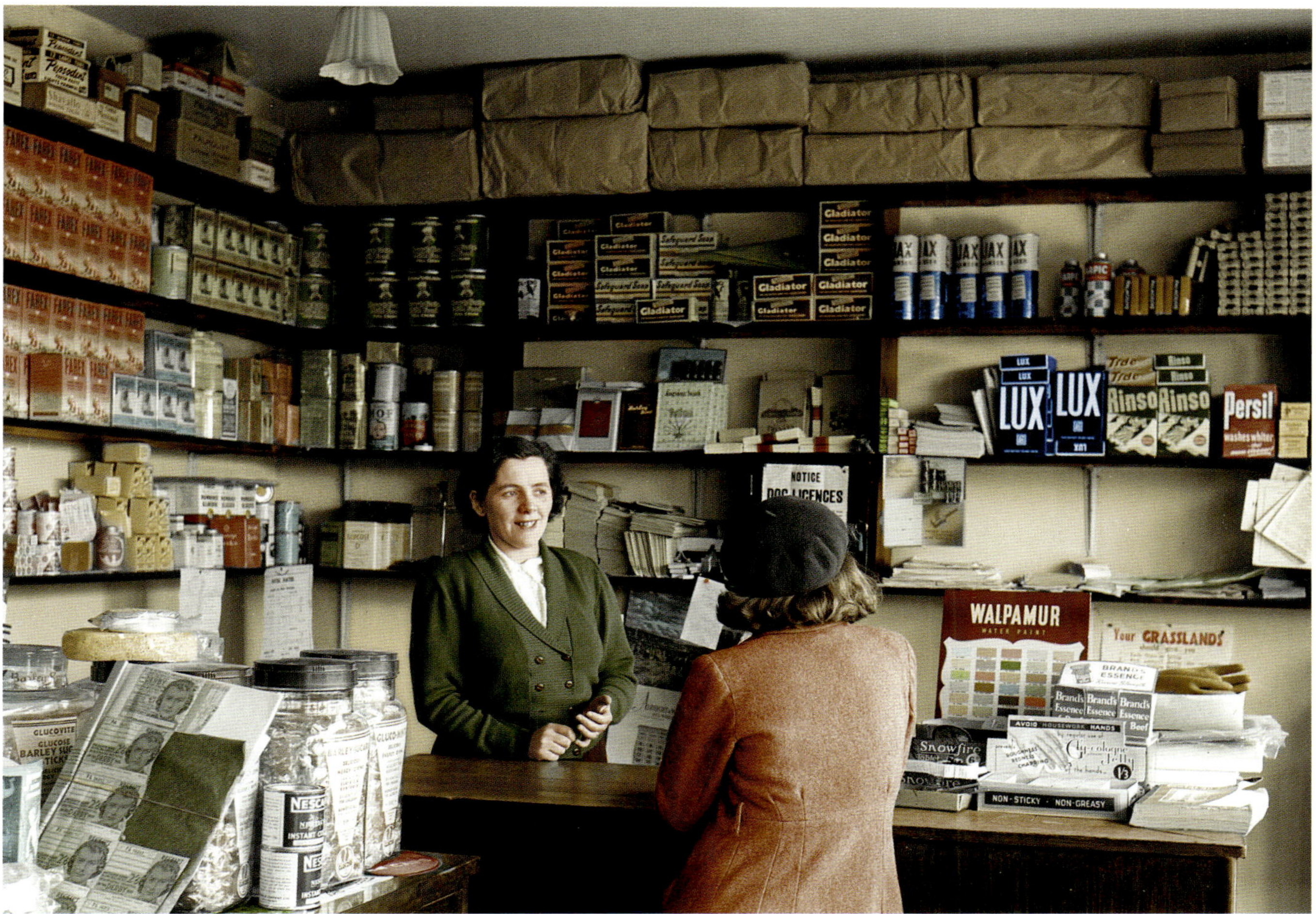

A scene from a typical village shop of the past: shelves lined with an eclectic mix of stock, some brands now lost to history, others still with us. A notice about dog licences hangs on the wall, while a book of Irish sweepstakes tickets for the Derby rests against a jar of barley sugar sweets. The goods range from Farex for the baby to Rinso for washing clothes. Amid the stacked provisions, a customer lingers for a chat with the woman behind the counter. More than just a place of commerce, the village shop was the heart of the community – a space where one could have a conversation.

The air carried the mingled scents of tea (which came in tea chests), tobacco and paraffin oil, while behind the counter, everyday essentials were carefully measured and wrapped by hand. There could be loaves of batch bread, butter in packs – or better still, the tastier 'country butter' direct from the farm. Many shops stocked much more than just groceries, offering essentials such as bolts of cloth, tin buckets and boot polish.

As the adults discussed local news, children, eyes wide with anticipation, could edge closer to the big glass jars of sweets or on occasion get a bar of chocolate, a Black Jack or a lucky bag. If they were fortunate, there was a fridge where they could get a portion of ice cream, cut from a block and wedged between two wafers – anything from a twopenny treat to a sixpenny version, so large one couldn't get one's mouth around it.

A postman pushes his bicycle along a boreen, a scene familiar to generations of Irish people. Through rain and shine, the Irish postman has been a constant and welcome presence in the rural landscape.

The Irish mail service has a long history, stretching from the days of mail coaches to the railways and now motor transport. The post office of the steam era was a marvel of organisation and logistics, with frequent and fast deliveries. The mail always got through to the Irish countryside, including the ubiquitous 'letter from America', containing the dollars that helped sustain many rural households.

While the means of delivery have been modernised (but not necessarily speeded up), the personal touch of the local postman remains. More than just bearers of letters, they play a vital role in rural life – sharing news, looking in on the elderly and even fetching messages from the town – all helping to foster a sense of community.

Today, postmen (and women) are more often seen in their An Post vans, reflecting the changing nature of the service. In an increasingly digital world, with fewer letters being sent, the economics of rural postal delivery are becoming more difficult. As local post offices close and delivery routes shrink, it is to be hoped that government support will help preserve this essential lifeline – one that has long kept rural Ireland connected.

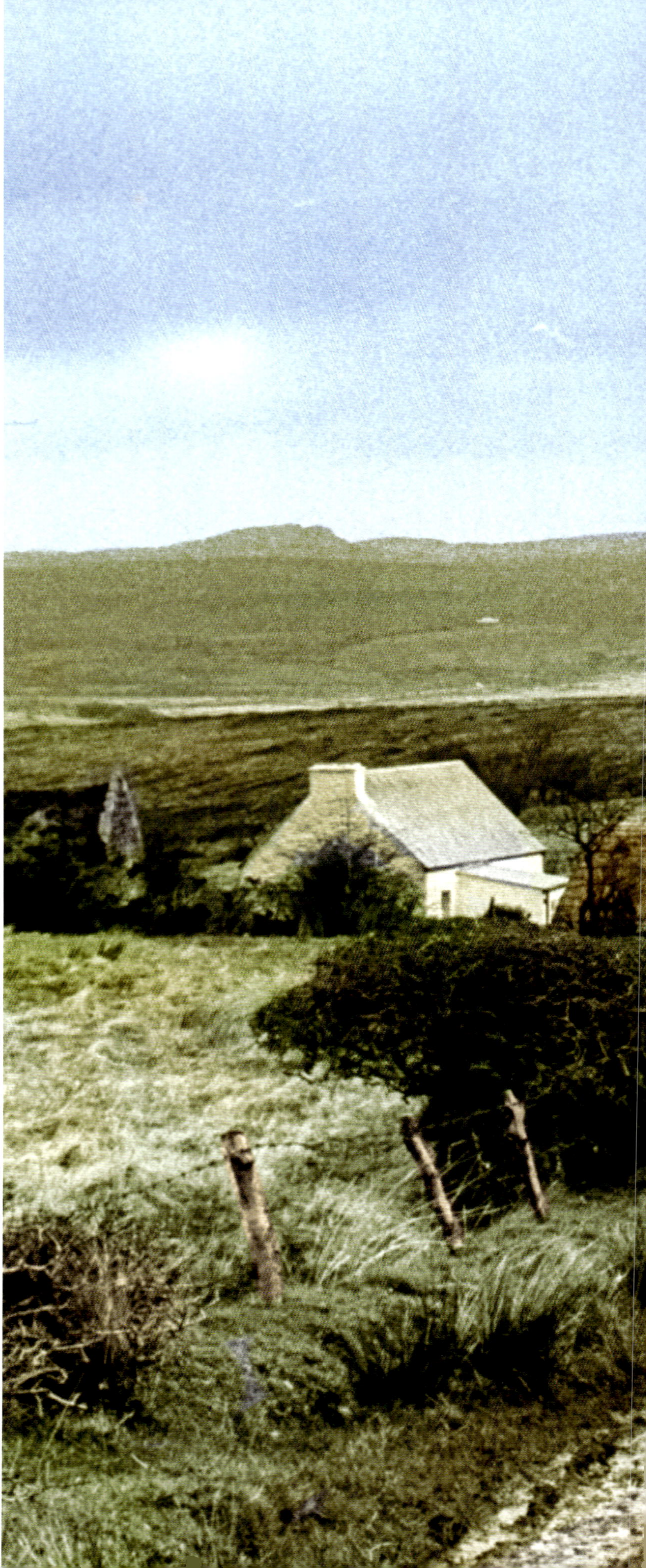

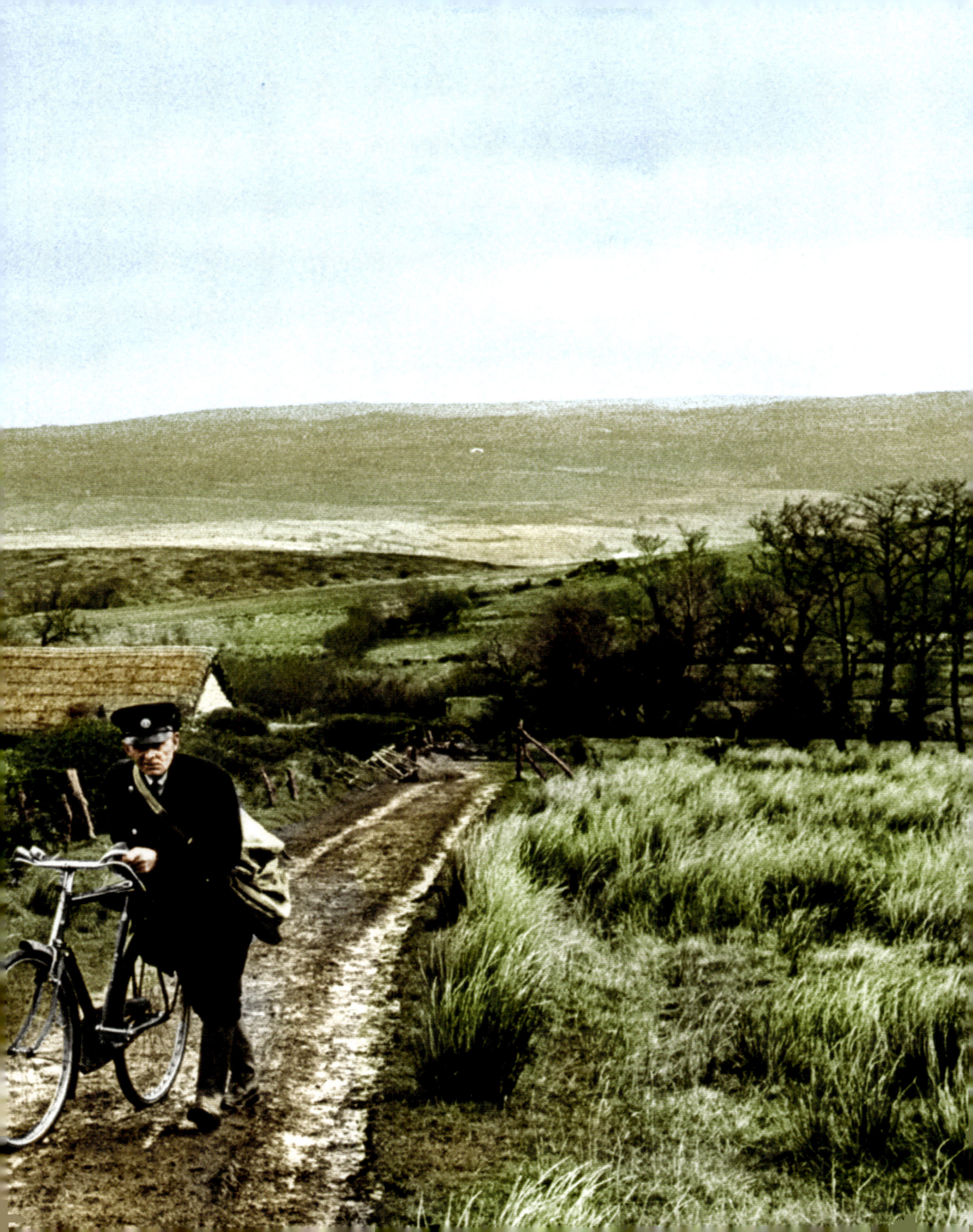

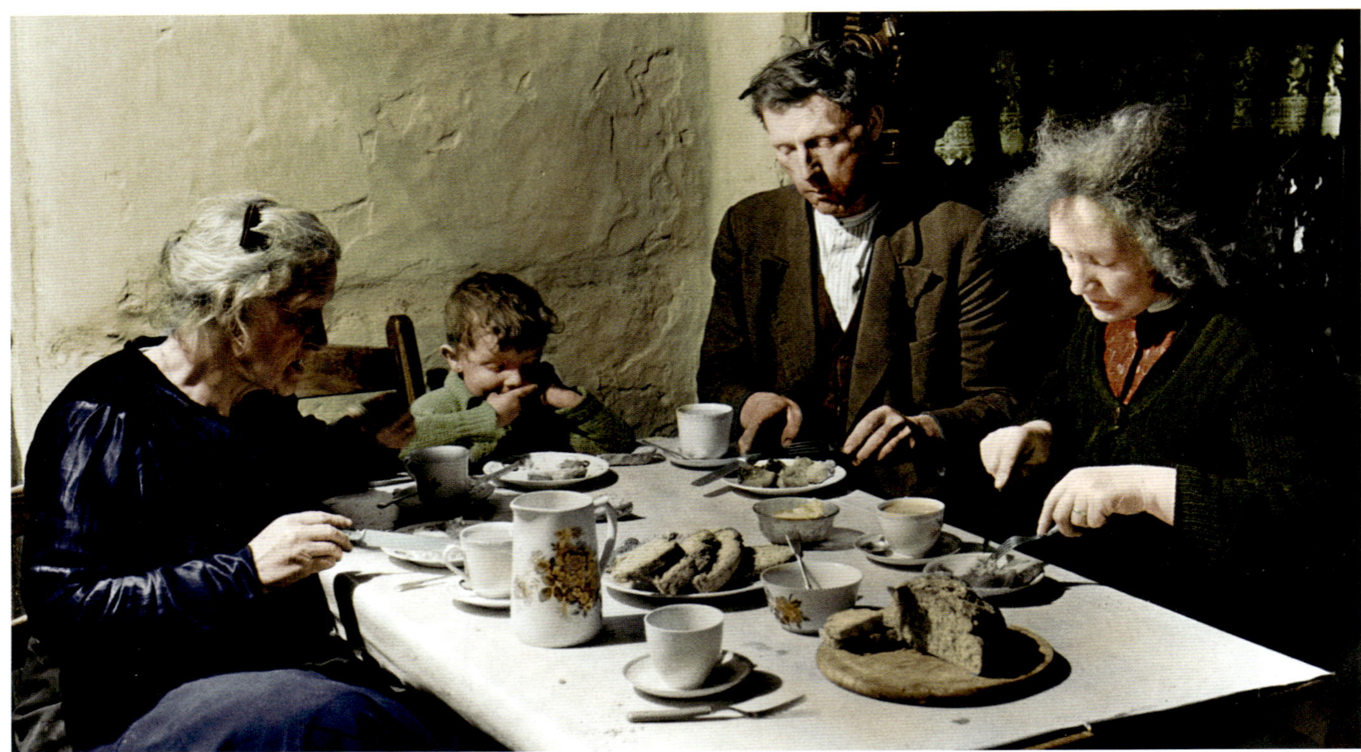

A rural Irish family gathers for what appears to be their evening 'tea'. It is a simple repast – as they cut their slices of meat, they have butter and bread. The bread is soda bread, a staple that dates back to the 1830s, when baking soda was first introduced to Ireland. Traditionally, soda bread required only four basic ingredients: wheat flour, baking soda, salt and soured milk. It was baked in iron pots or on griddles over open hearths.

Nowadays, 'shop' or white bread is (quite rightly, due to the goodness being refined out of it) regarded as unhealthy and lacking in flavour, often compared to blotting paper. However, in the past, white bread was a luxury – its scarcity and expense made it a special treat for many Irish families. Similarly, sweet cakes were not an everyday indulgence but reserved for special occasions, particularly Christmas.

Until the final decades of the twentieth century, the main meal of the day – called 'dinner' – was traditionally eaten after midday, usually around 1 p.m. This was essential for sustaining farmers, who had been working since early morning. The midday dinner, reflecting the traditional Irish diet, often consisted of meat (lamb, beef or pork) and vegetables (commonly cabbage, carrots or peas). Potatoes were a staple in various forms. While pasta and rice are now common in modern Irish cuisine, it is easy to forget how ubiquitous the potato once was and how a floury potato was considered highly desirable.

In the evening, families would gather for a lighter meal known as 'tea' or 'supper'. This meal always included bread. On occasion 'goody' (bread mashed in hot milk with sugar) was served at the end, a favourite treat among children.

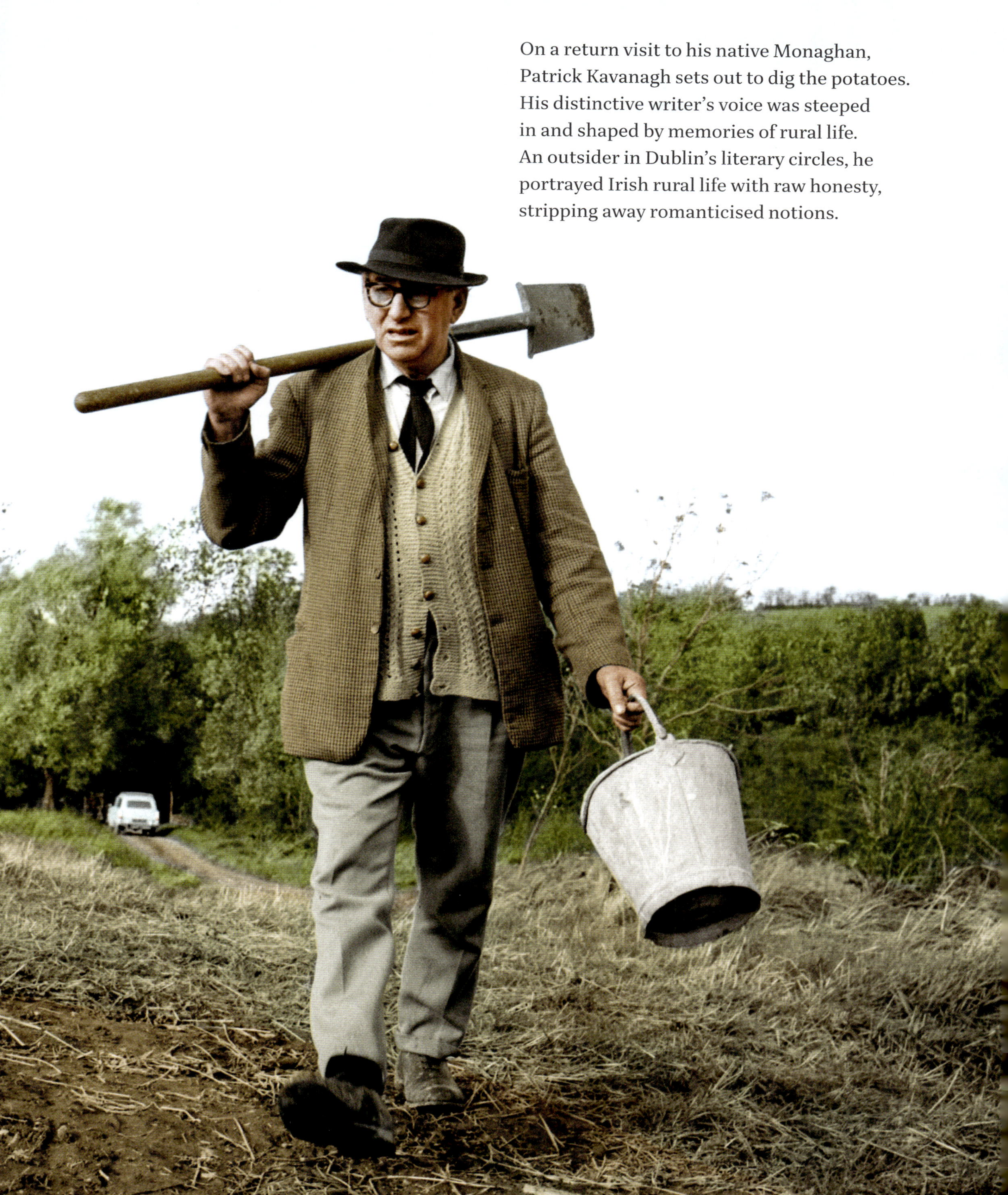

On a return visit to his native Monaghan, Patrick Kavanagh sets out to dig the potatoes. His distinctive writer's voice was steeped in and shaped by memories of rural life. An outsider in Dublin's literary circles, he portrayed Irish rural life with raw honesty, stripping away romanticised notions.

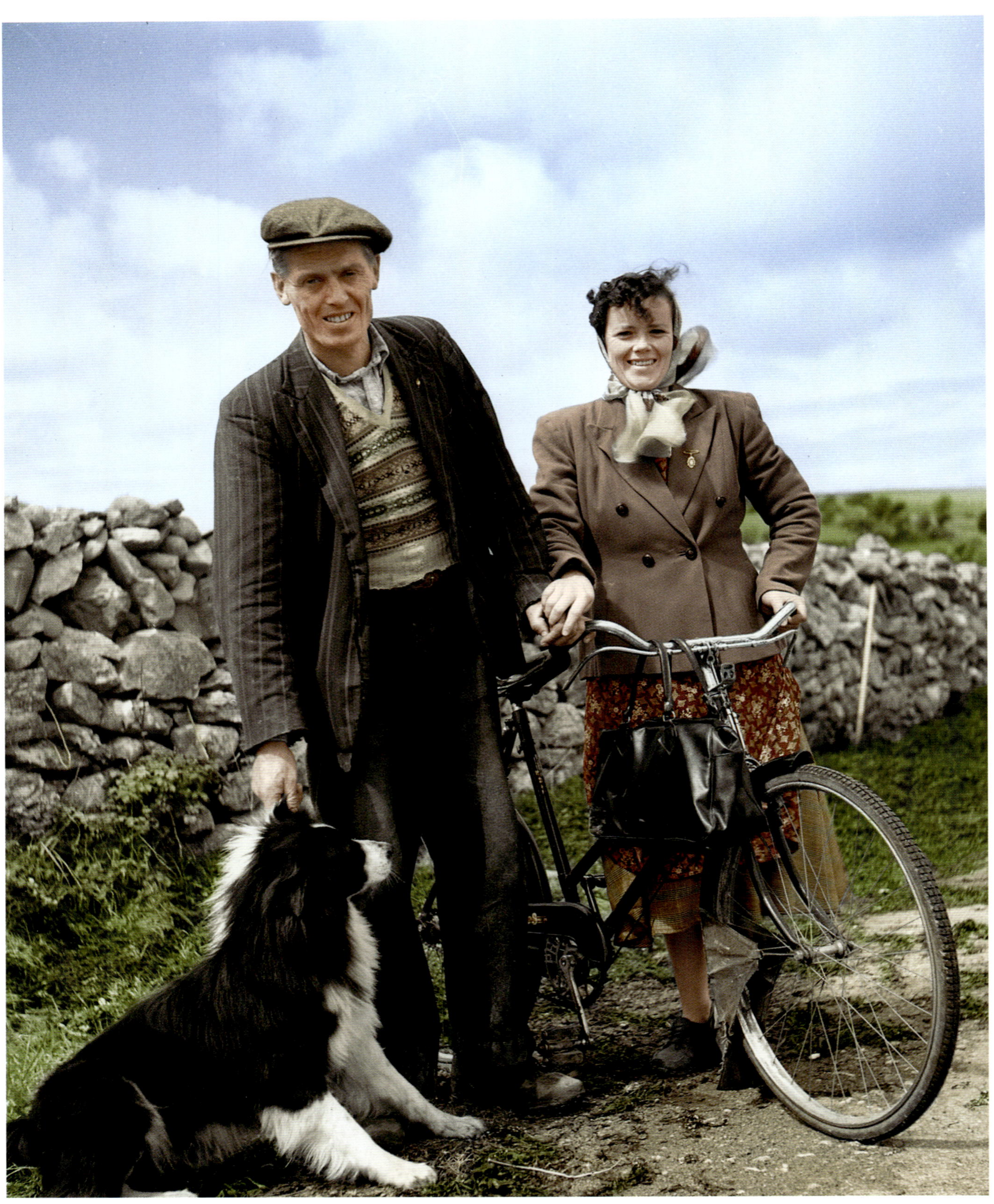

A farmer and his wife, with their sheepdog, pause – a simple portrait of life in the countryside.

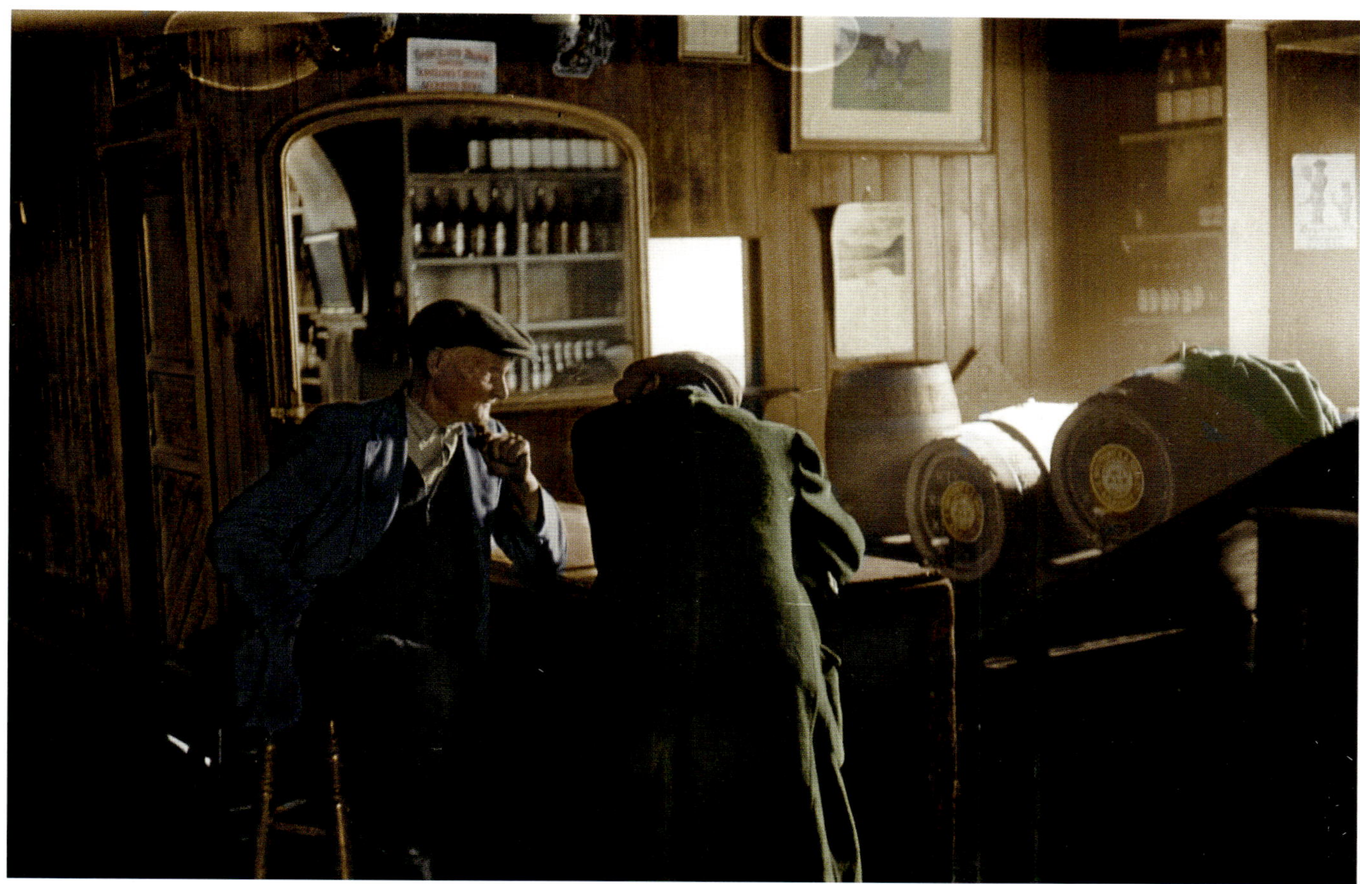

Another simple portrait of life in rural Ireland: in this atmospheric scene, two men sit in a local pub, a fixture of country life. On Sundays they were particularly busy as farmers gathered for a drink after Mass.

The public house, with its mahogany counter and distinct atmosphere, was more than just a place to drink – it was often combined with a grocery shop or sold goods like animal feed. The Guinness, delivered in timber barrels, was hand-pumped and poured with care. The process was slower and more deliberate and gave the beer a different texture and taste.

This world, so different from today's contemporary bars with their lavish furnishings and wide-screen TVs, was steeped in tradition. In the old days, there were snugs – small, intimate rooms where mainly women sat, quietly enjoying a glass of sherry. In an era before Coca-Cola reached rural Ireland, the child might be treated to a glass of red lemonade. The precise licensing hours meant that, on occasion, owners had to be on the *qui vive* for the local 'strict' Garda, who might be on the prowl.

The pub was and is a social cornerstone, where the simple, unhurried rhythms of rural life played out over pints and conversation. Today, however, strict but sensible drink-driving laws have led to a decline in the number of drinkers, and the number of rural pubs has thinned out.

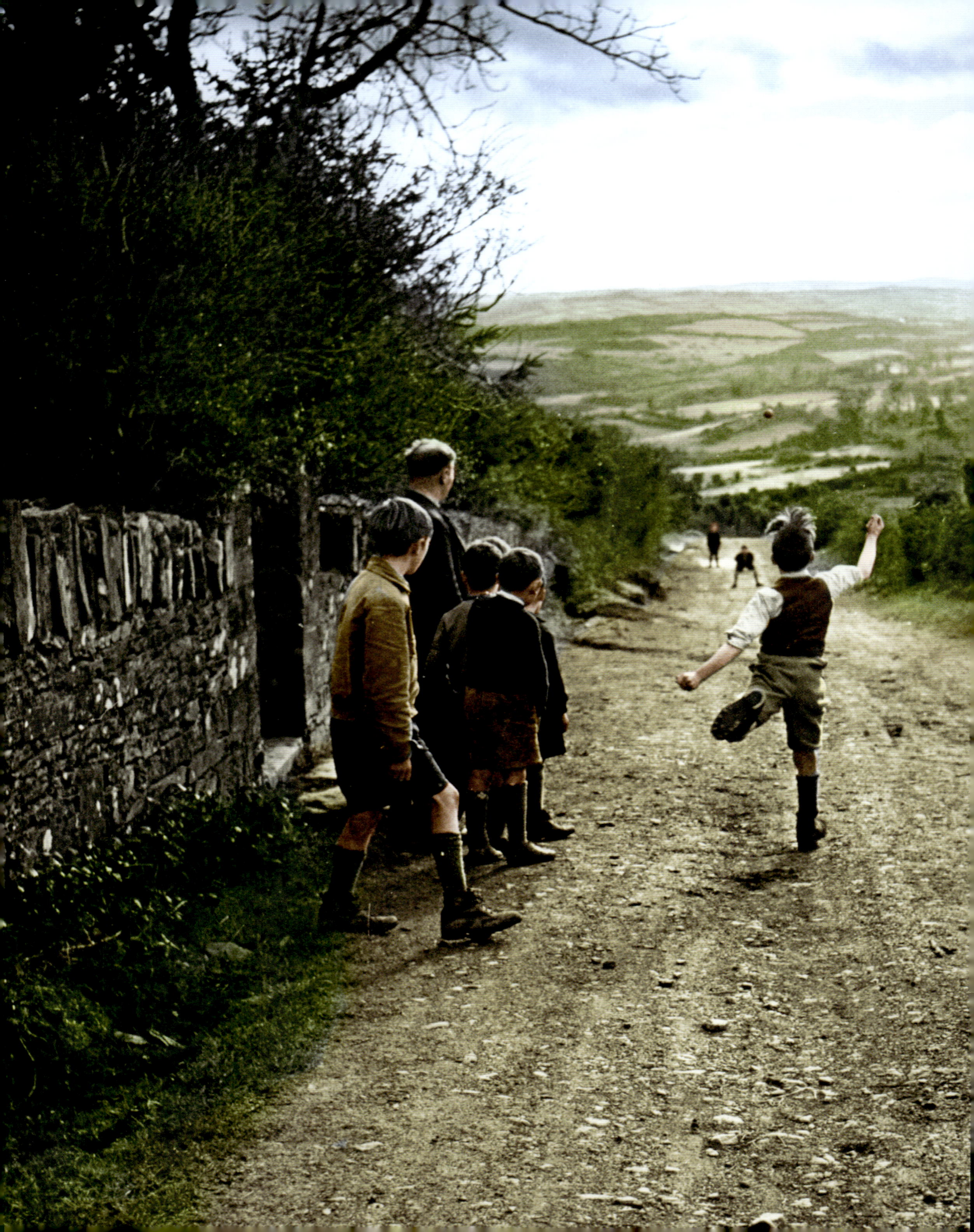

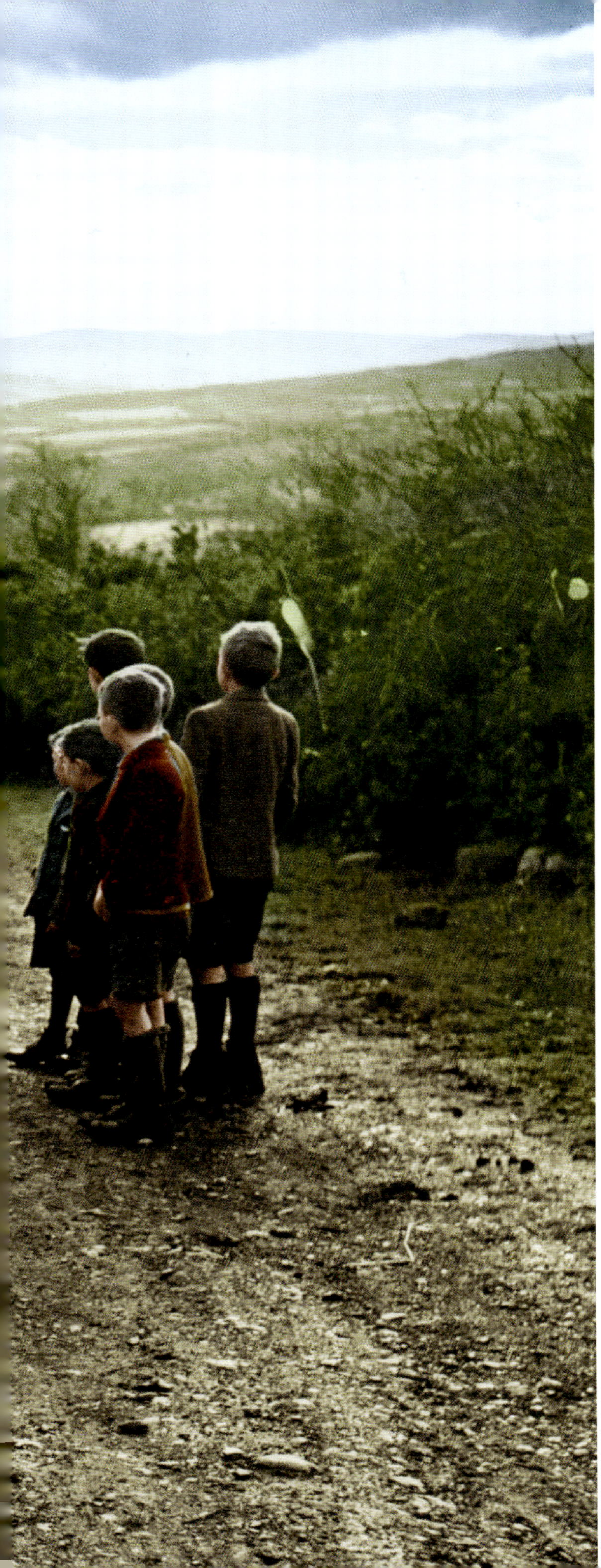

A good throw: a young boy, along with his friends, enjoys a game of road bowling – an Irish sport with a history dating back to at least the seventeenth century.

Players throw an iron ball, a 'bowl' – the standard size weighing around 800 grams – along a rural road. Once thrown, the bowl rolls along the road's natural curves and slopes. The aim is to cover the distance in as few throws as possible, with the winner being the player who uses the least number of throws. The game is most commonly played in counties like Cork and Armagh – and there are players among the Irish diaspora in North America.

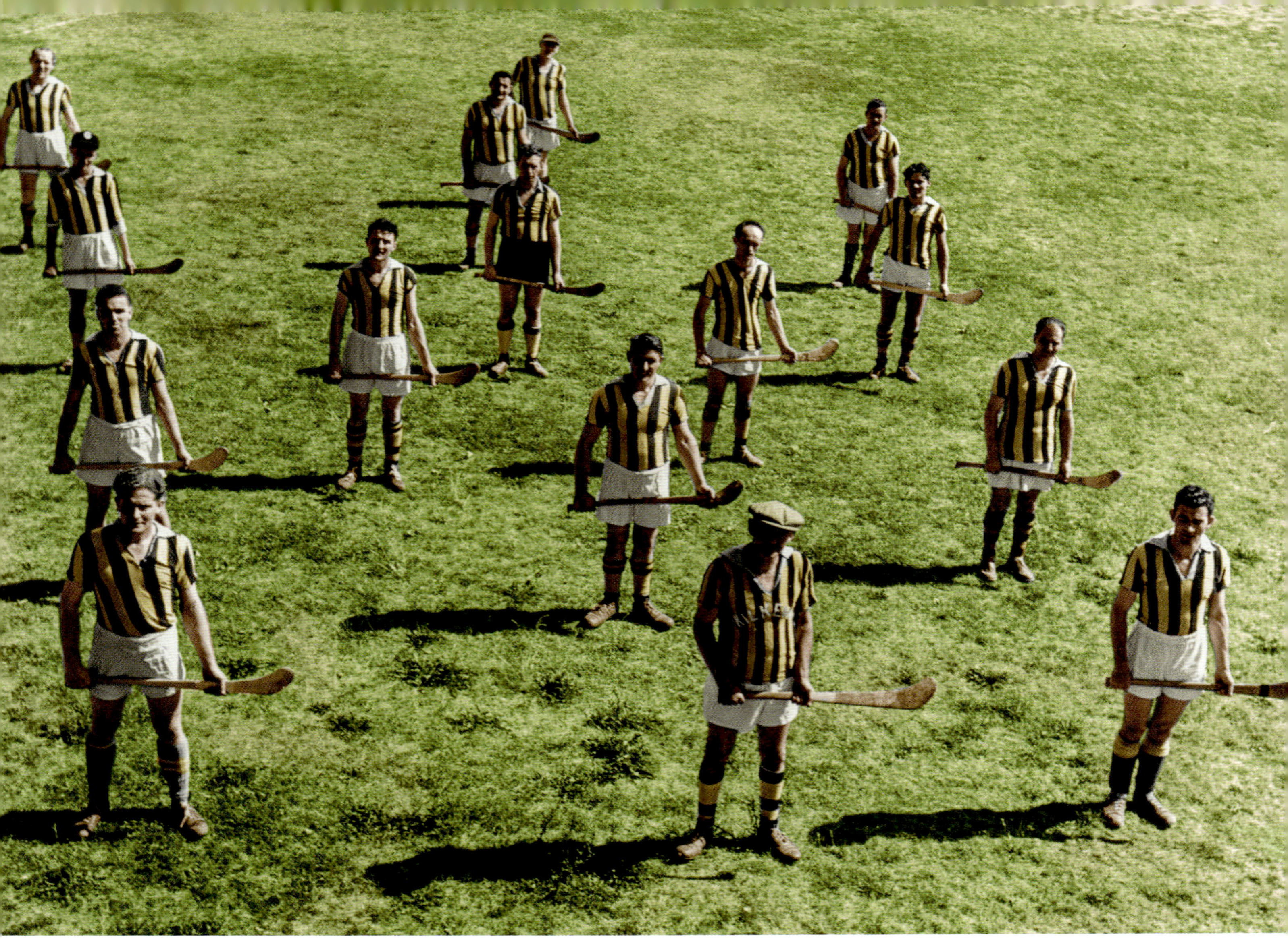

Hurling is often described as the fastest field sport in the world – fiercely competitive and deeply rooted in local pride, it blends speed, skill and physicality. County teams like Kilkenny, pictured here in 1955, have long inspired loyalty and passion. Although this team didn't go on to win the All-Ireland that year – Wexford claimed the title – it remains part of the county's proud hurling tradition and enduring legacy in the game.

The GAA, which oversees Gaelic games, has become deeply woven into the fabric of Irish society, particularly in rural areas. With over 2,200 clubs across all 32 counties, it remains a cornerstone of community life. In towns and villages, young men and women leave their farms and workplaces to train on local pitches, embodying the passion and dedication that define the GAA.

Beyond the sports field, GAA clubs often function as community hubs, hosting social events and offering youth programmes, ensuring their central place in local life. The strong connection to parish and county pride is evident, with both players and supporters exhibiting intense allegiance to their teams and colours.

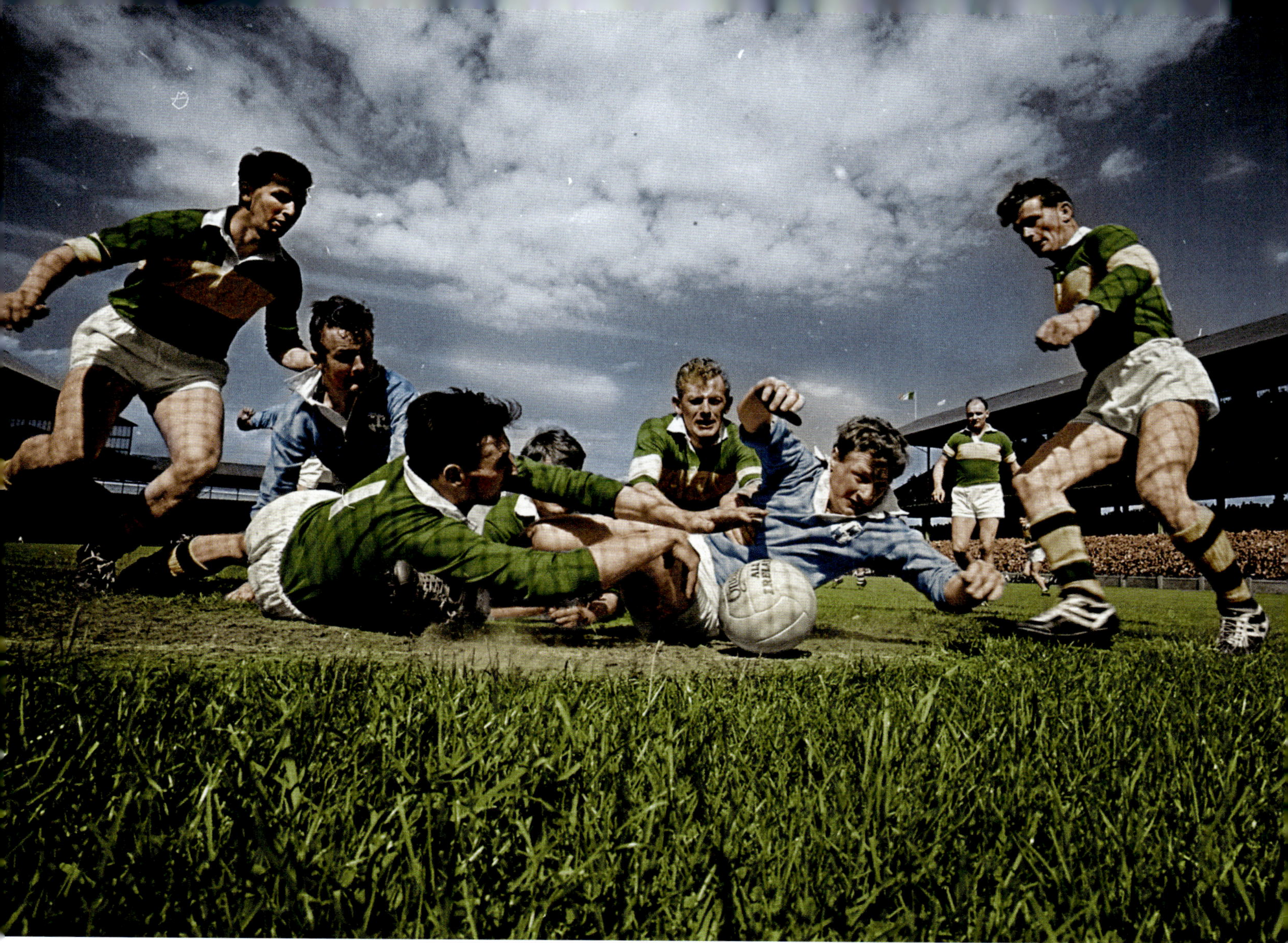

A moment of intense action at the goal during the 1985 All-Ireland Gaelic football semi-final between traditional rivals Kerry and Dublin – where Kerry emerged victorious. The win sparked jubilant celebrations across the county, as one of the sport's most successful counties once again brought All-Ireland glory home.

Gaelic football is the other great Gaelic sport, alongside hurling. One of Ireland's most popular sports, it features teams of 15 players who aim to score points by either kicking the ball over the crossbar to gain one point or into the goal, earning three points. The game is fast-paced and physically demanding, with players using their hands to carry, pass and shoot the ball, while also using their feet to kick it.

Many consider that Gaelic football is far more exciting than soccer due to its continuous flow of play, the use of both hands and feet, and its physical intensity. Unlike soccer, where goals can be infrequent, Gaelic football offers high-scoring action and a blend of strategic complexity.

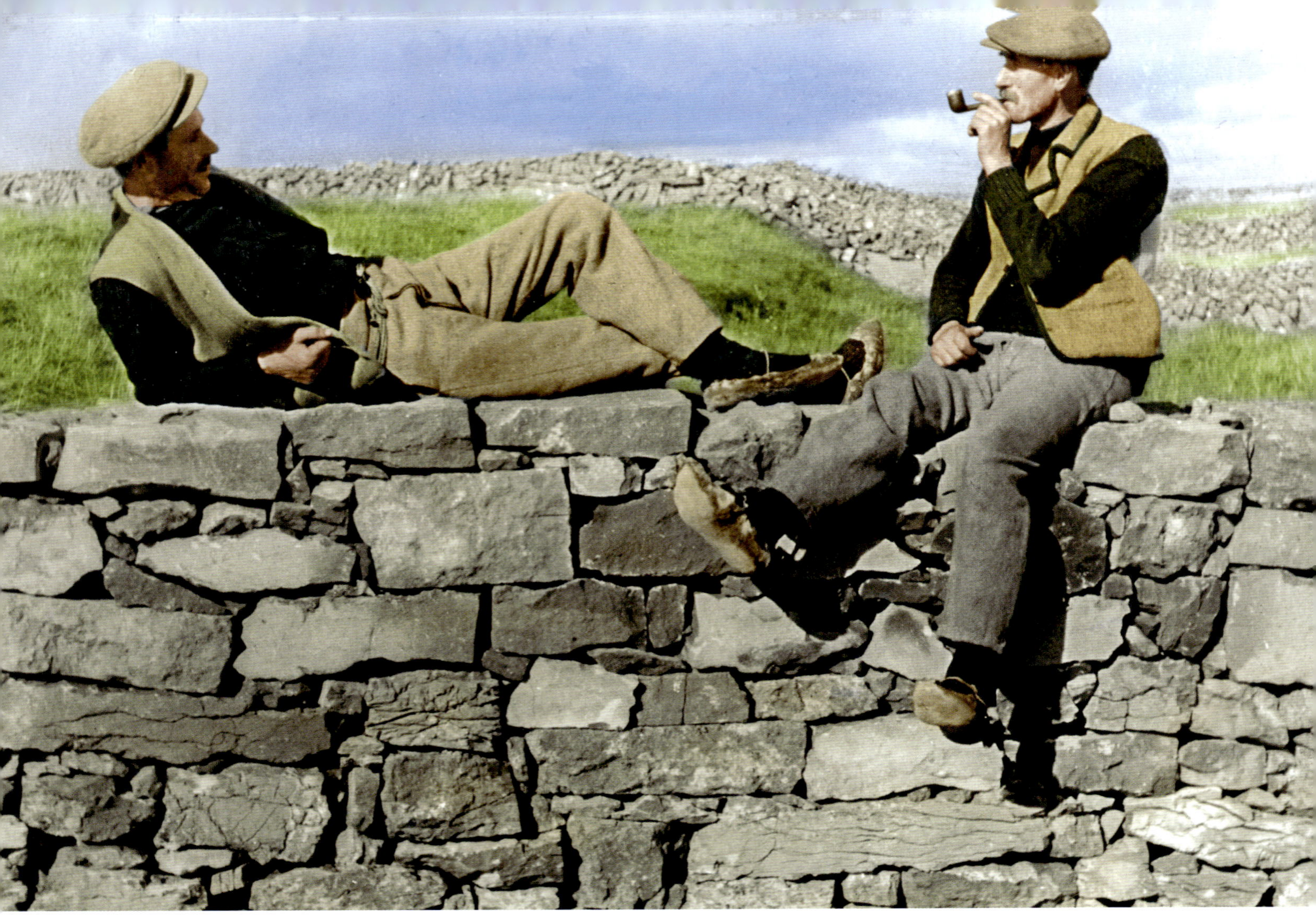

Two *seanchaithe* (storytellers-cum-historians), dressed in traditional clothes, take their ease in the Aran Islands. A *seanchaí* is the inheritor of a millennia-long Gaelic storytelling tradition. It may be difficult to comprehend now in the era of television, internet and mobile devices, but during most of the twentieth century, life was more social and there was a greater sense of community.

Neighbours in the Irish countryside could entertain themselves at home with a story told by a *seanchaí*. There was also a large variety of activities such as impromptu music sessions, traditional dancing, card games like poker and whist, listening to a radio at a friend's house – or simply conversing and socialising by the fireside.

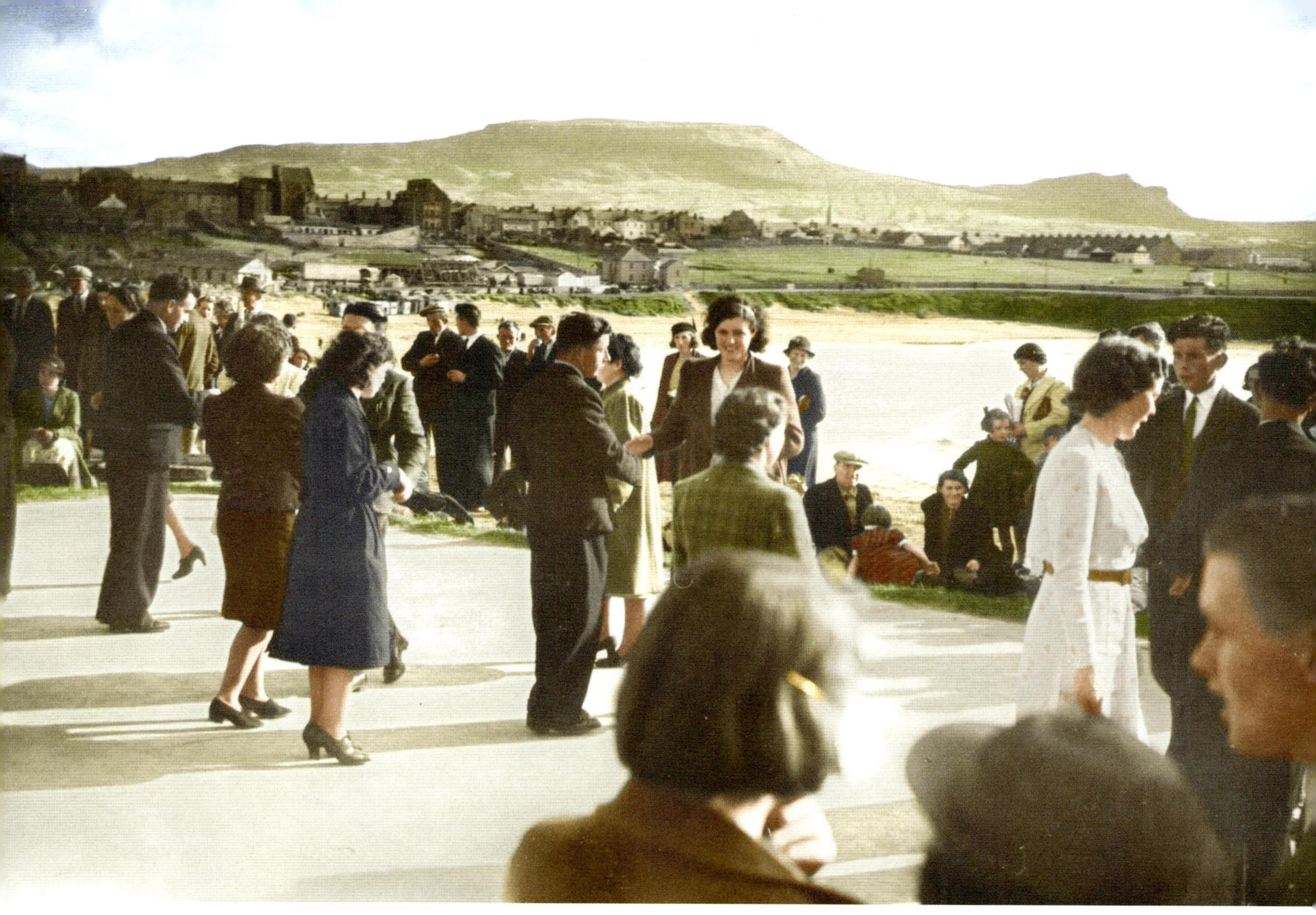

Dancing at Bundoran, County Donegal – here it's not exactly at the crossroads, but there are plenty of what Éamon de Valera might have described as 'comely maidens'. These outdoor events were called 'pattern dances' – all one needed was a fiddle and an accordion or two, and if there was a timber floor with a bit of spring in it, all the better. Romances often blossomed at dances like this, but decades ago, matchmaking was another route to marriage, with local matchmakers (usually known for their wisdom in understanding people and highly skilled in the matter) arranging suitable matches.

There are several traditions of masquerade in Ireland where a group of local friends or family dress up in colourful disguises (frequently with straw costumes), travel to neighbours in the district and give a performance. There are the Strawboys, who perform at weddings, and the Wrenboys, popular in the south, who go hunting the wren (considered a mystical bird in ancient Celtic beliefs) on St Stephen's Day. Another tradition is that of the mummers, popular in northern counties. Seen here in 1955, mummers celebrate with glasses of porter after performing to what was clearly an appreciative audience. Their comic antics during the Twelve Days of Christmas include music, song, dance and sometimes a short folk play.

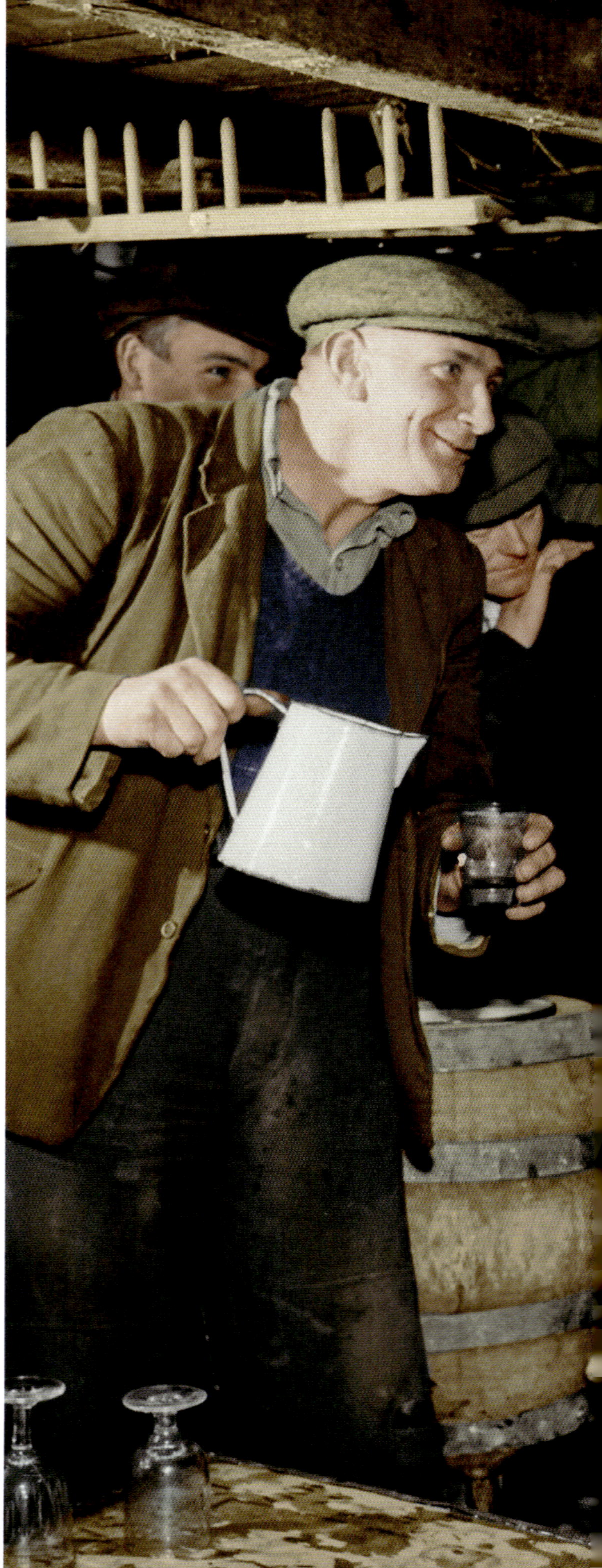

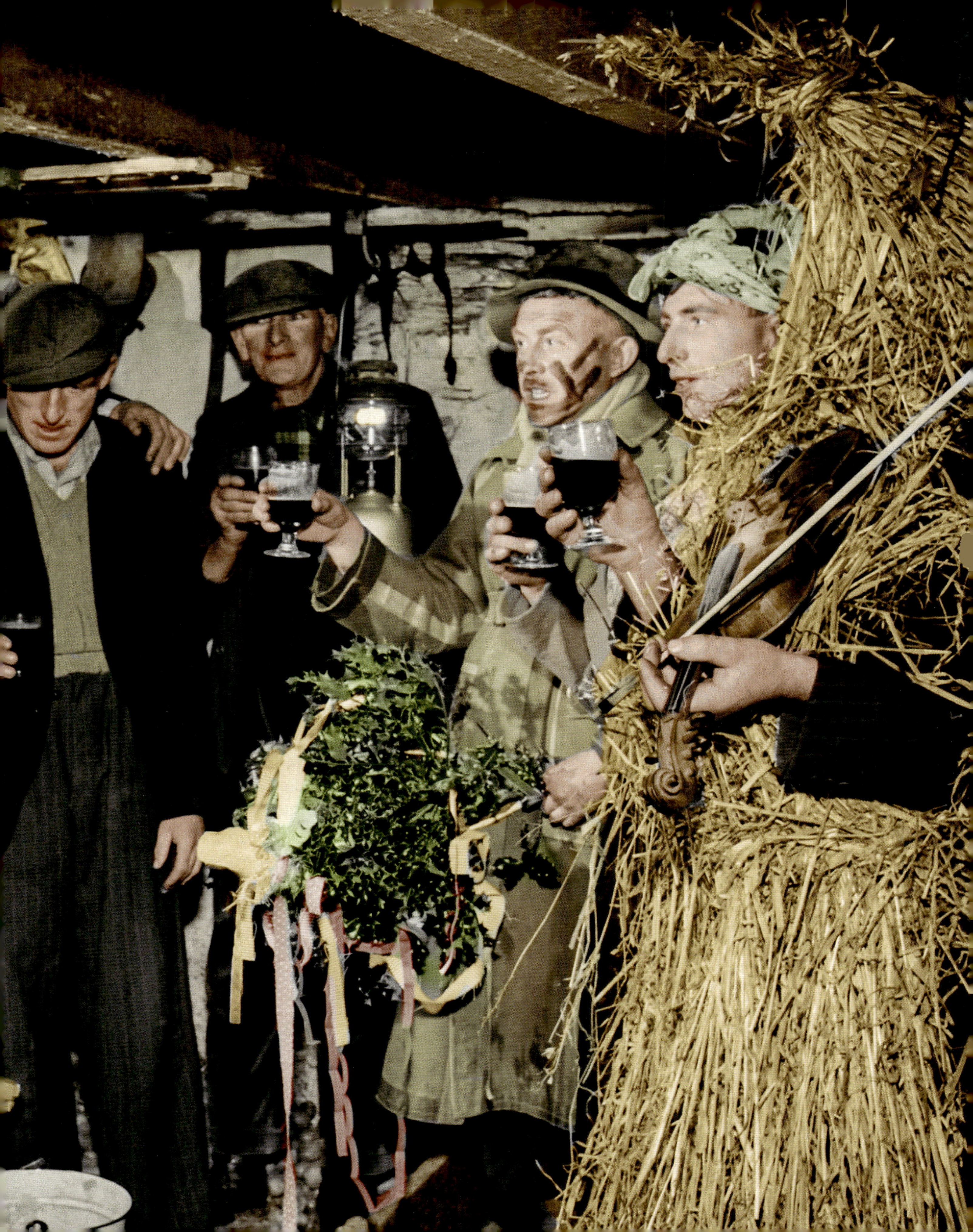

The Fleadh Cheoil at Clones, County
Monaghan, 1964. Looking down on a
lively gathering of musicians playing
fiddles, flutes and accordions, this
scene captures the spirit of Ireland's
national celebration of traditional
music. Organised by Comhaltas
Ceoltóirí Éireann, fleadhs bring
together players and audiences from
across the country – and beyond – to
compete, perform and keep the living
tradition of Irish music thriving.

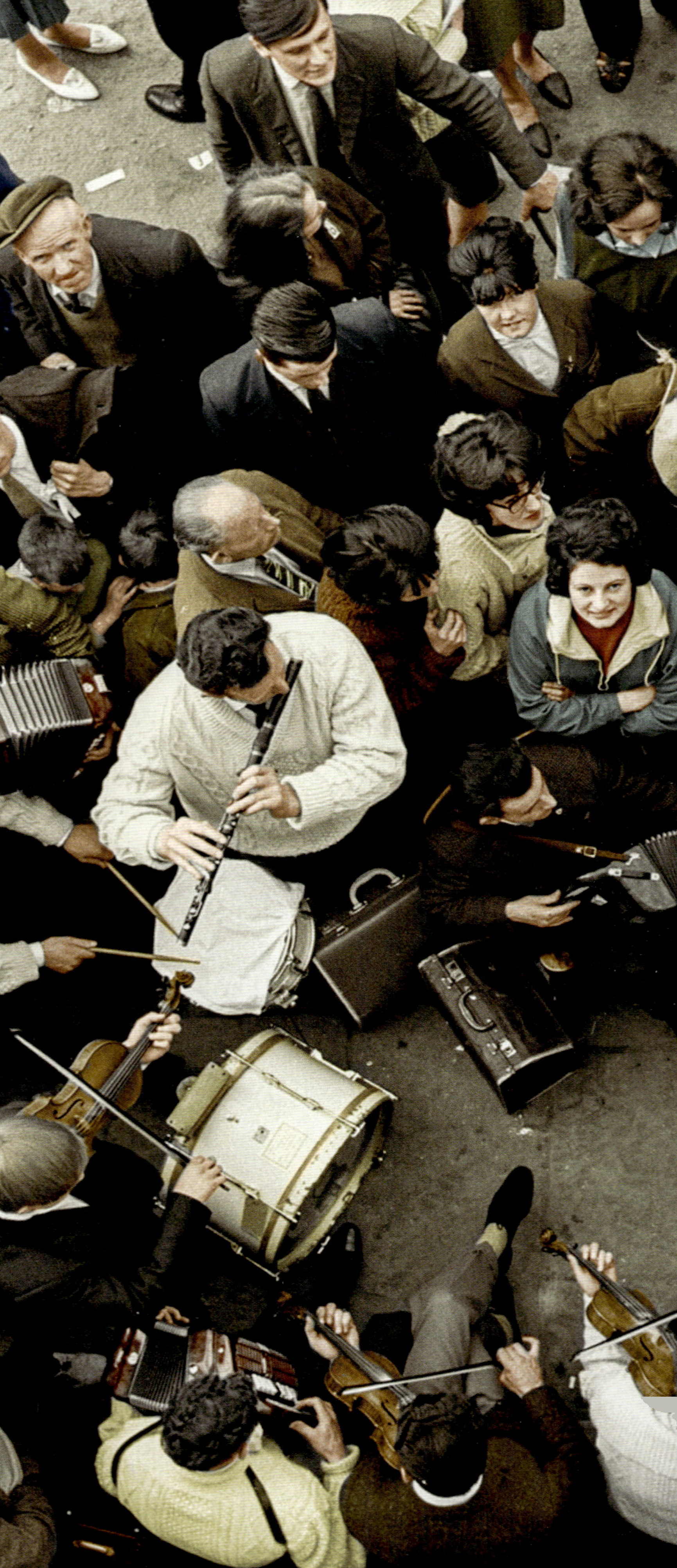

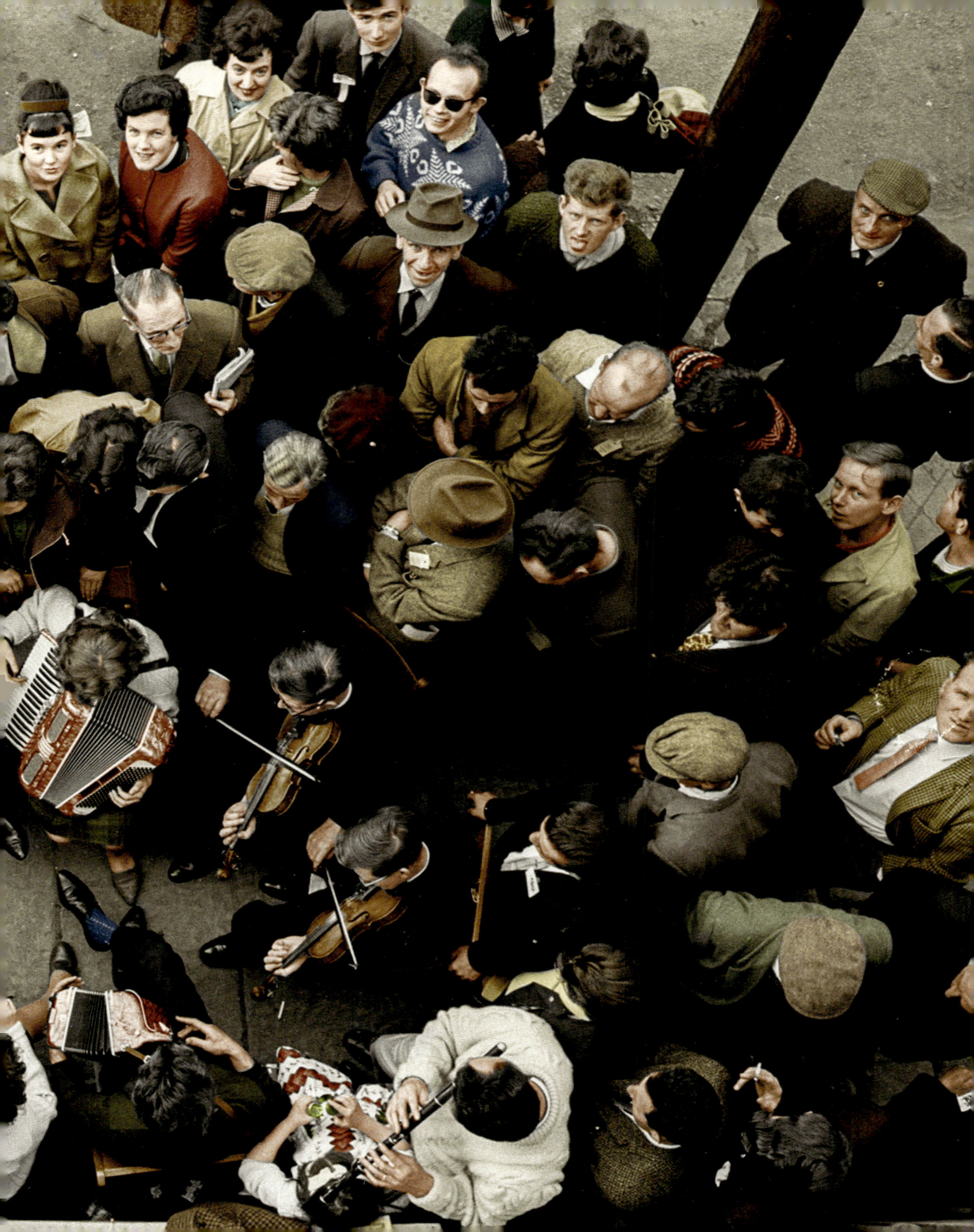

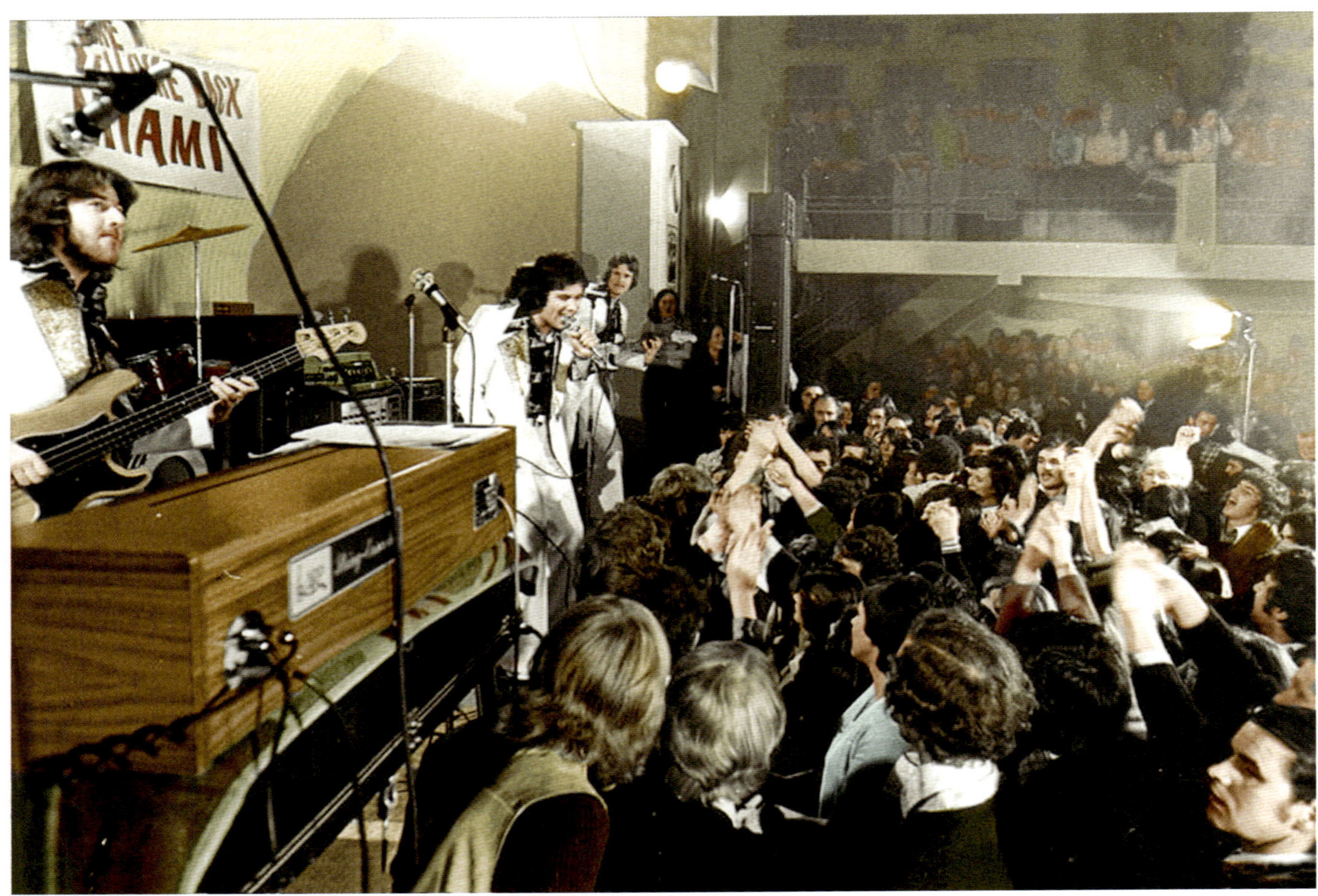

Top left: The temperature rises as the Miami Showband (reformed after the 1975 massacre) belts it out at the Seapoint Ballroom, Galway. Showbands, a uniquely Irish phenomenon, mixed rock, pop and ballads in lively performances. Known for their colourful costumes and stage presence, they were central to Ireland's music scene from the 1960s to the 1980s.

Right: A still from *Ballroom of Romance* (1982) shows a man giving a woman a lift home on his bike, a quiet moment that captures the film's themes of love, longing and the rural Irish experience. The showband era coincided with the rise of dance halls as social hubs, where people found connection, joy and an escape from daily life.

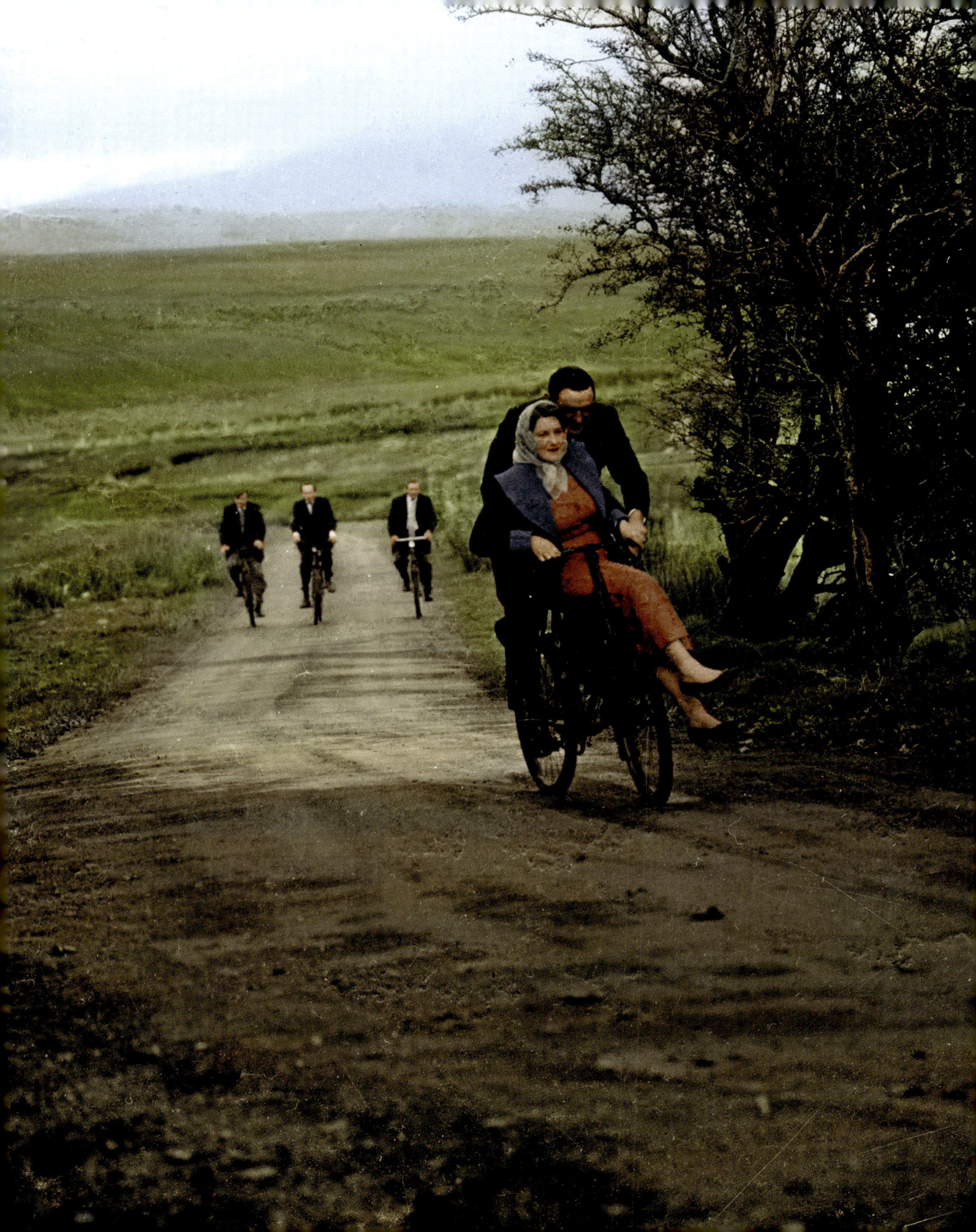

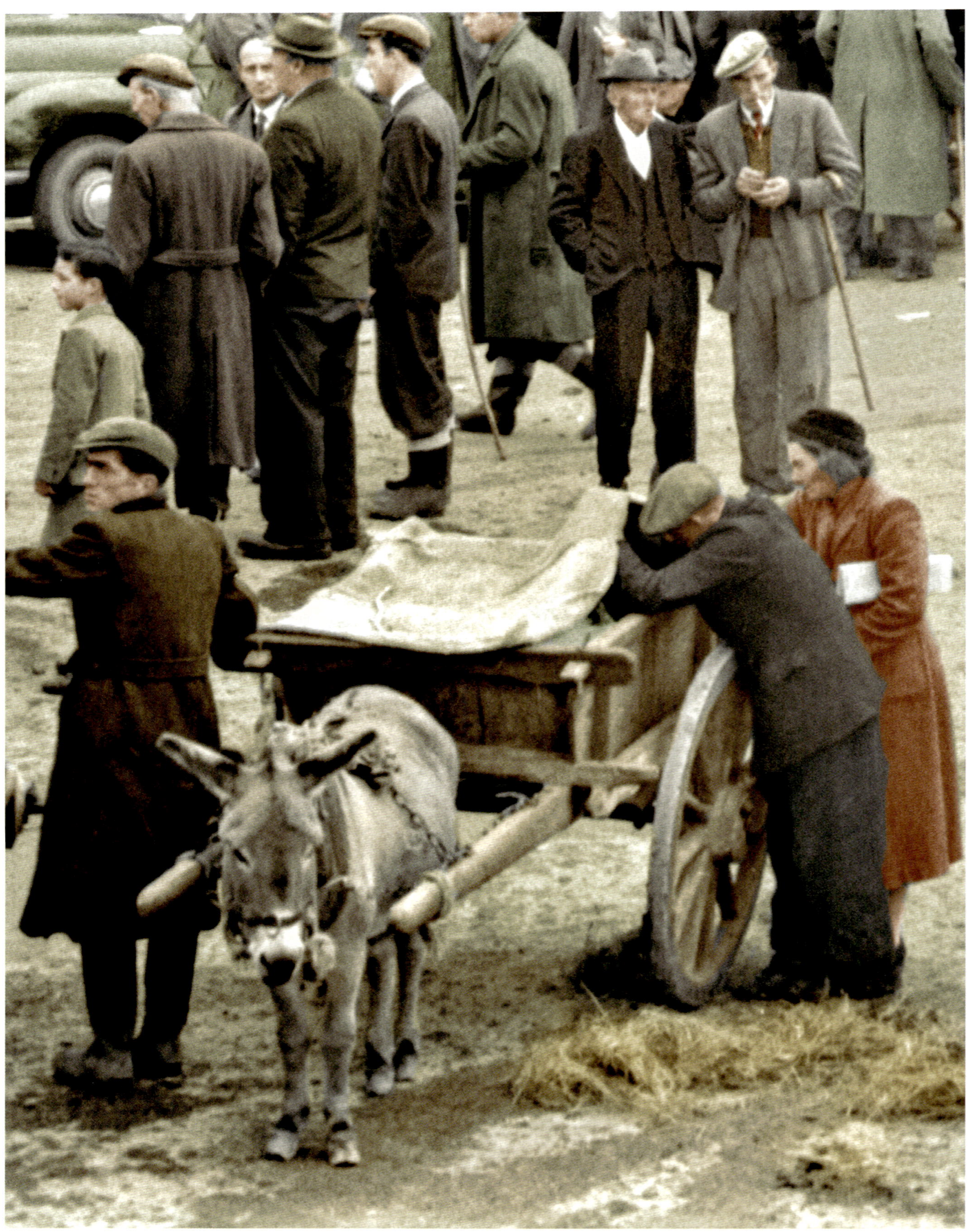

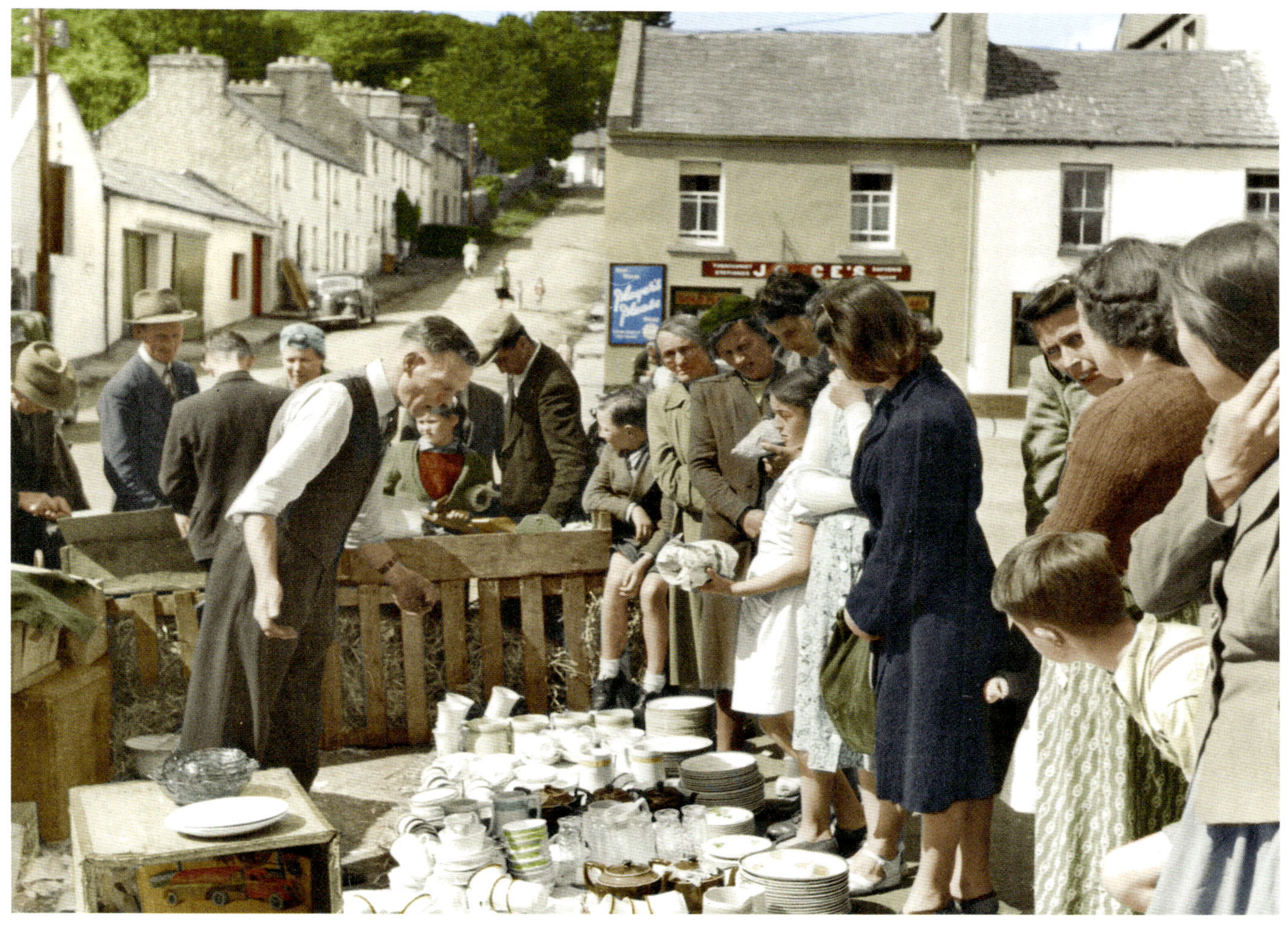

Left: Fair Day at Kinvara, County Galway. A woman makes a careful assessment of the goods on offer in the cart.

Top right: A scene at Clifden Market, County Galway, *c*.1955. Markets like this offered more than just cattle and sheep. Here, women inspect crockery and glassware laid out on the ground.

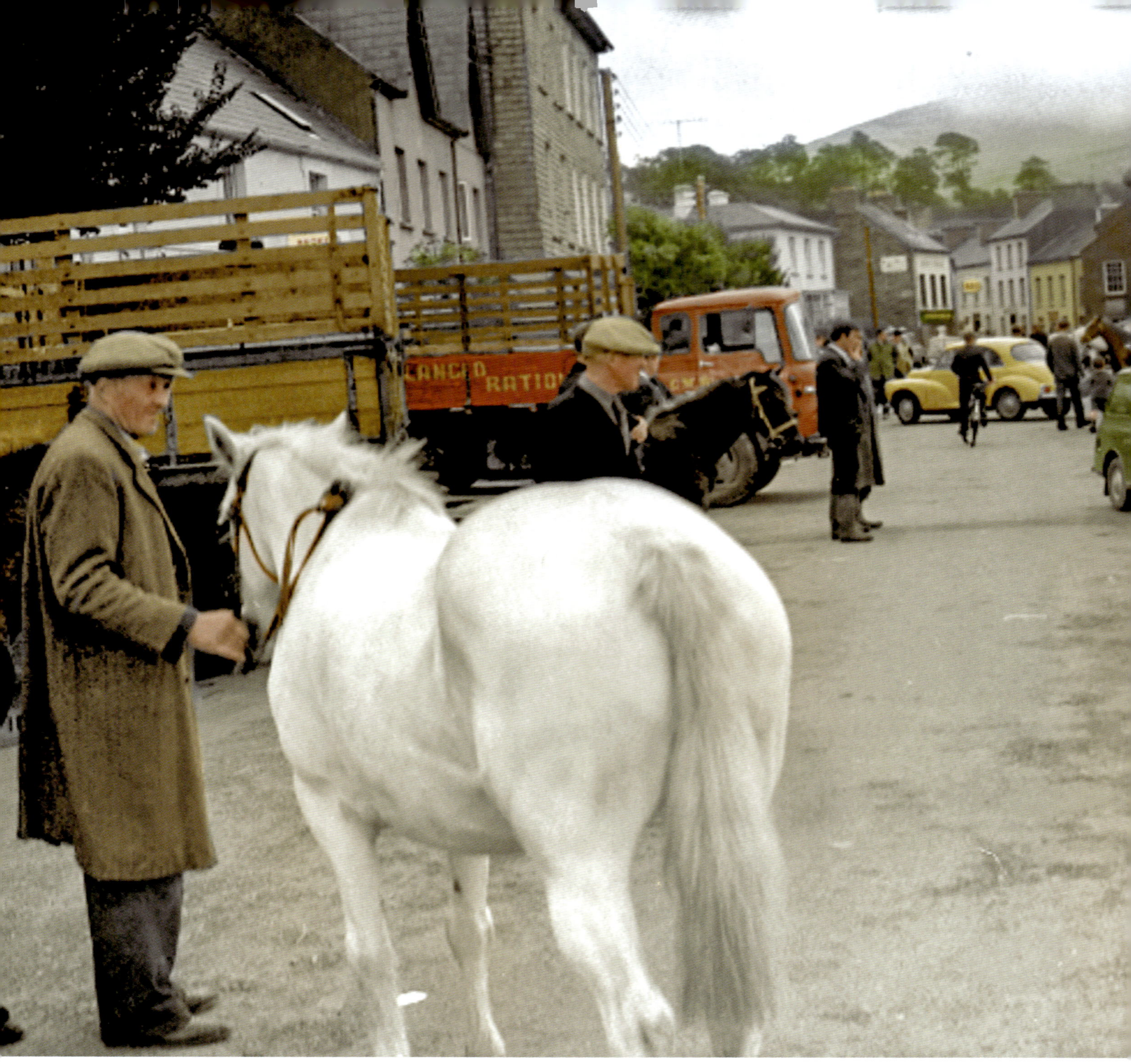

Despite the steady rise of the tractor, there still was a demand for horses, as seen here in 1966 at the Horse Fair in the Square at Bantry, County Cork. In 1921, Ireland had over 400,000 working horses – one of the highest equine densities in Europe relative to arable land. Though the tractor had become increasingly common, with 23,000 in use by 1960, a 1964 survey found that nearly a quarter of smallholders still relied on horses for primary tillage.

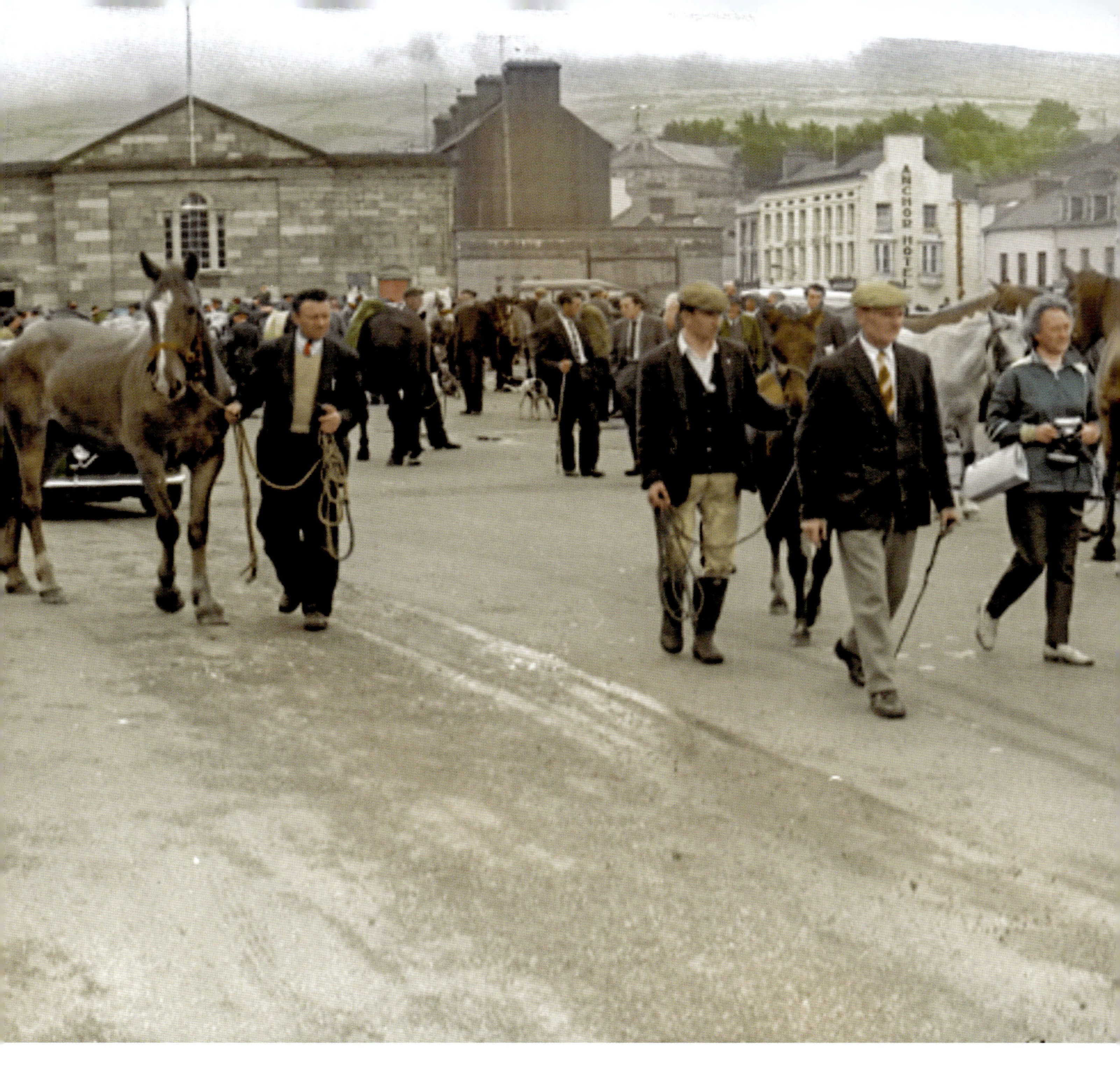

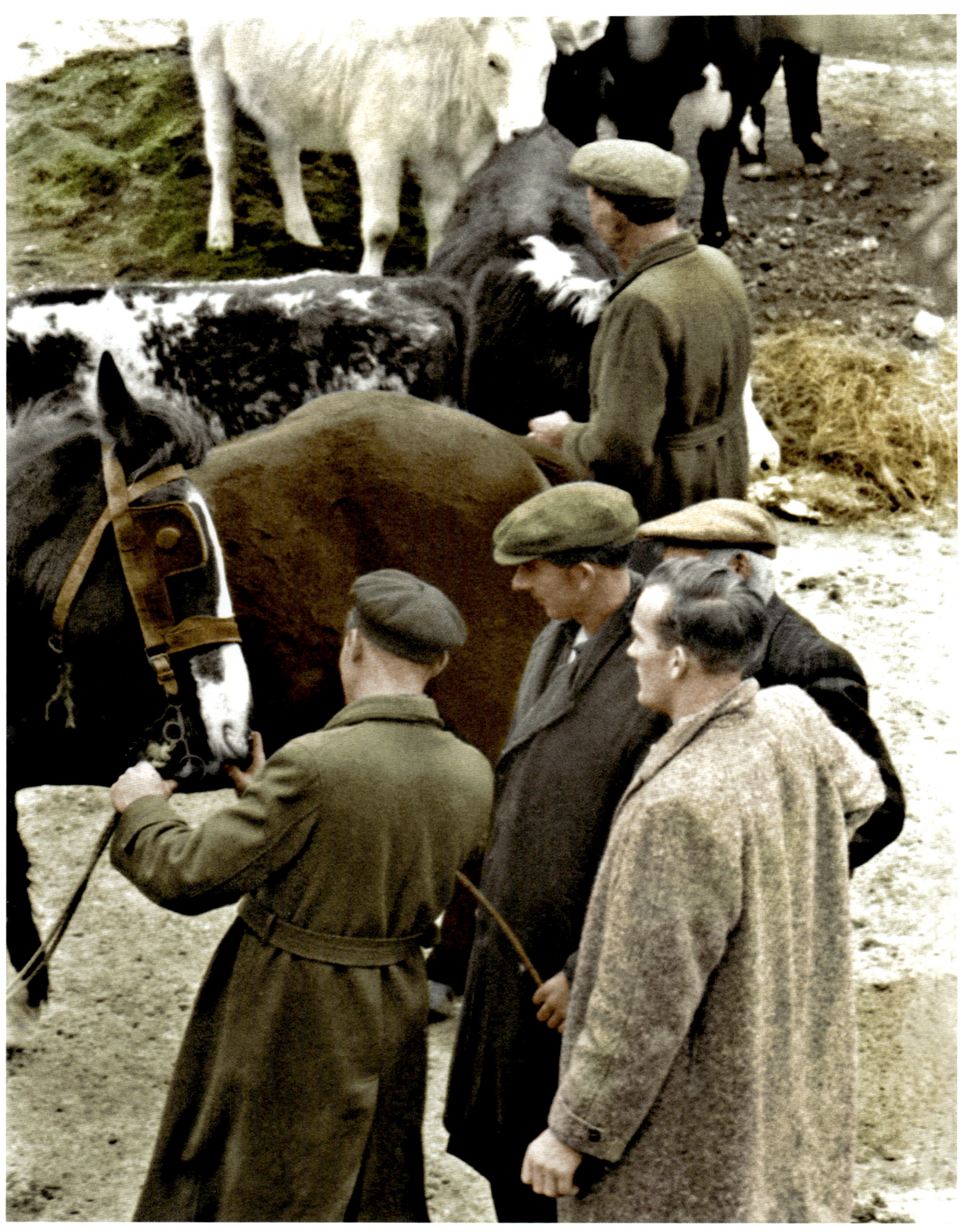

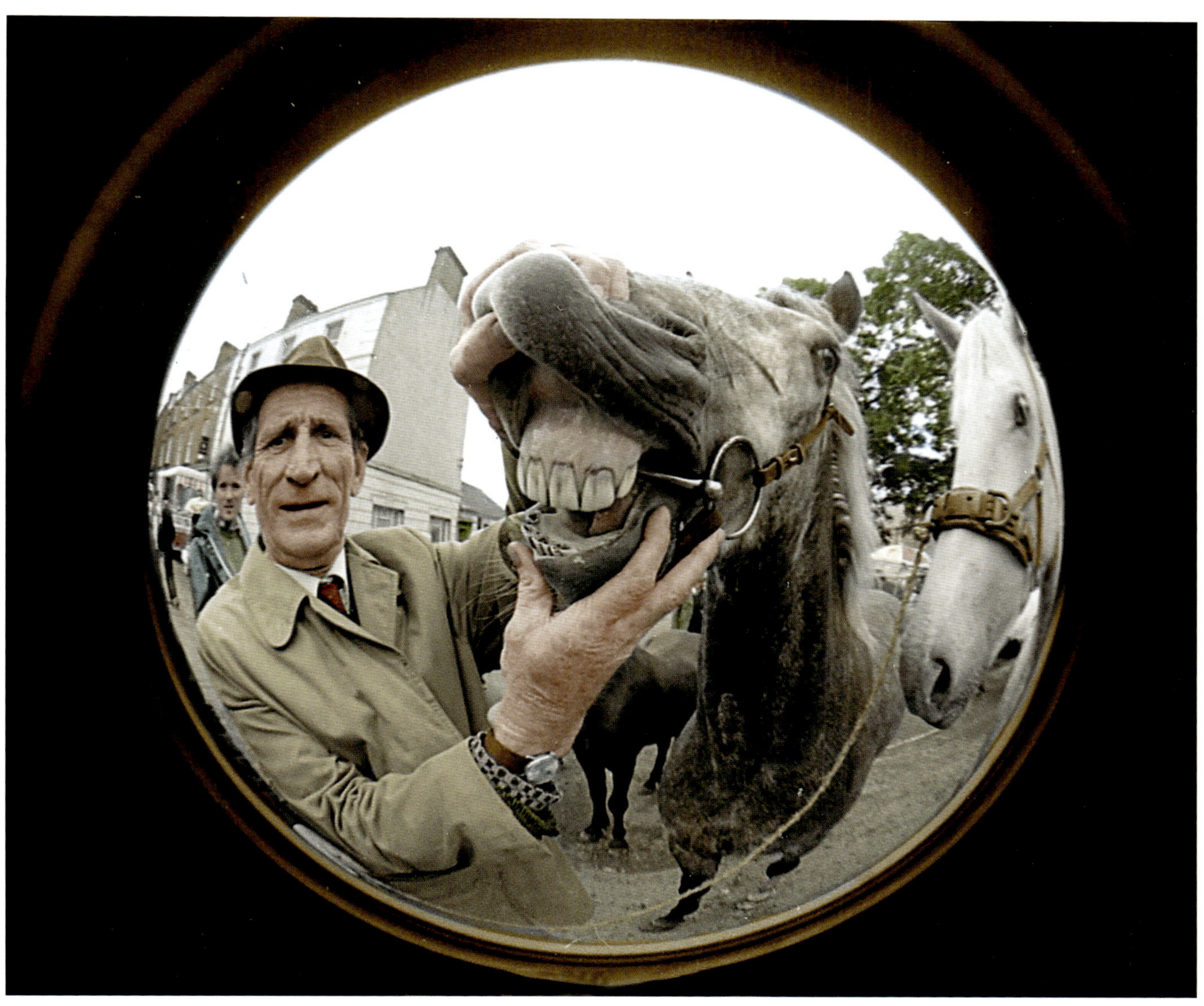

Left: A discerning farmer at Kinvara, County Galway, carefully examines a horse. A seasoned buyer understands the importance of taking the time to assess the animal's build and temperament.

Top right: At Cahirmee Horse Fair in Buttevant, County Cork, a seller bares his horse's teeth for inspection – a time-honoured practice to gauge the animal's age and condition.

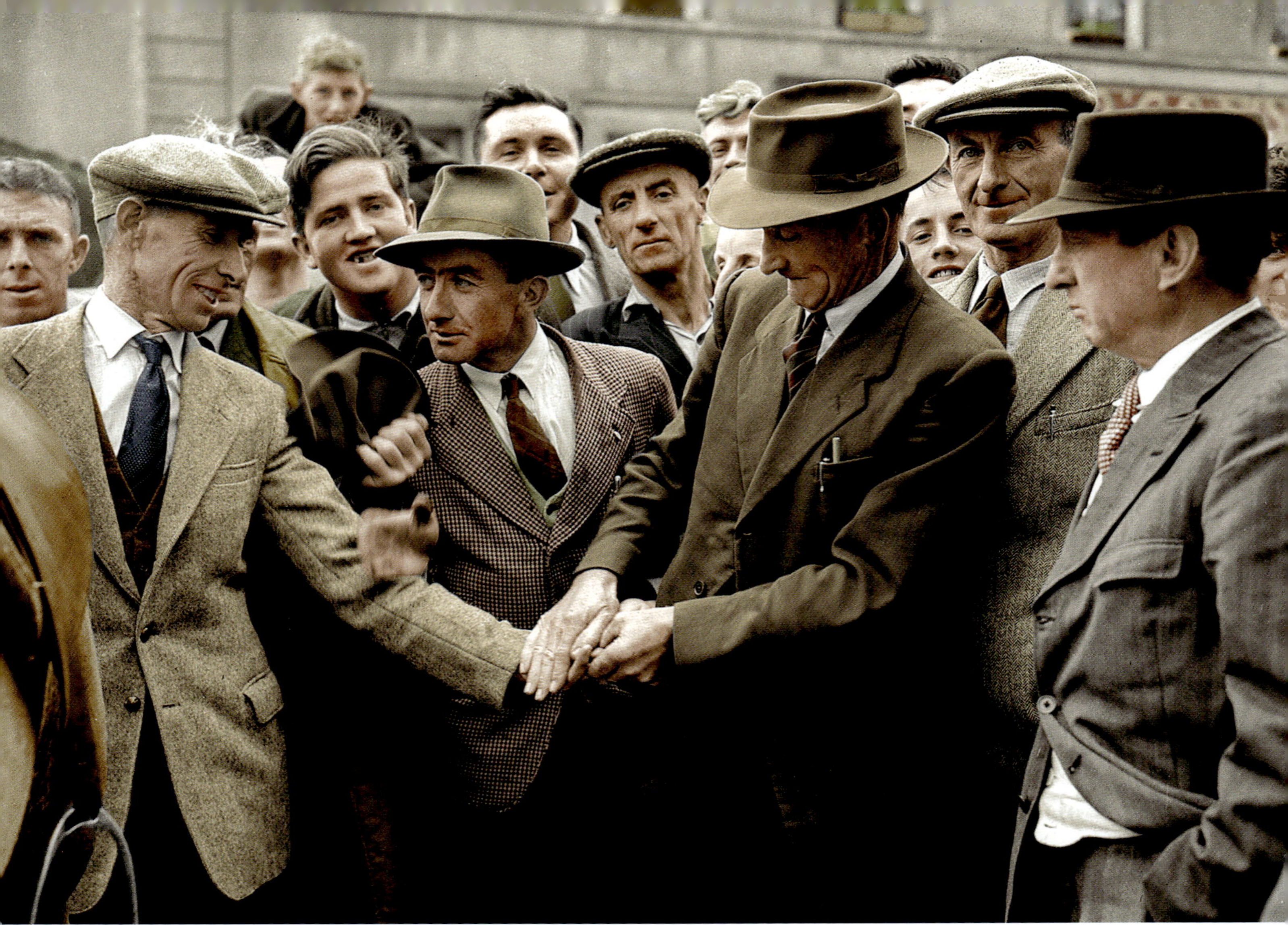

At the Cahirmee Horse Fair, the scene
unfolded in stages: the careful sizing up of
the animal, the back-and-forth of offer and
counter-offer, and, finally, the firm handshake
that sealed the deal. As evidenced by the men
clustered around, these dramatic moments
made these fairs lively and entertaining events.

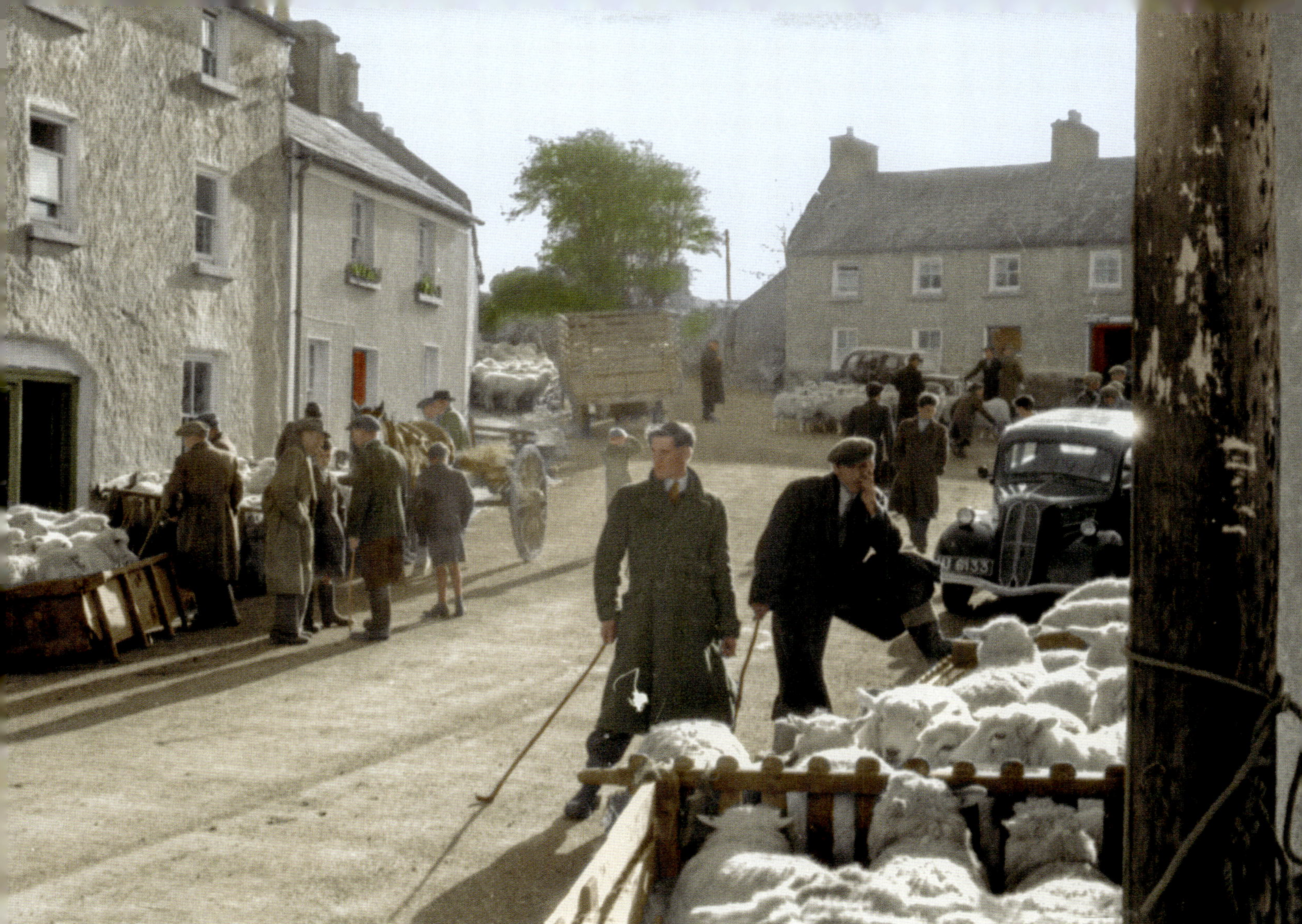

Another market, this time for a different animal. Here at the Fair Day in Kinvara, County Galway, the morning sun shines as local farmers gather to trade their sheep.

In the west of Ireland, sheep farming is influenced by its rugged landscapes, including rocky uplands and less fertile soils. Such conditions are well suited to hardy sheep breeds that thrive on rough grazing lands. Historically, wool and lamb sales have been vital sources of income for small-scale farmers here. These farms are diversified, with sheep raised alongside cattle, pigs and poultry to maximise the flow of income.

This photograph, along with the following two, is part of the remarkable Cresswell Archive. Robert Cresswell, an American anthropologist, lived in Kinvara during the mid-1950s, observing and documenting the everyday life of the rural community. His in-depth study, captured through a large collection of photographs and notes, offers a valuable insight into the social and cultural landscape of the west of Ireland during that era. The collection is now preserved and made accessible through the Kinvara Community Council website: https://kinvara.ie/old-kinvara.

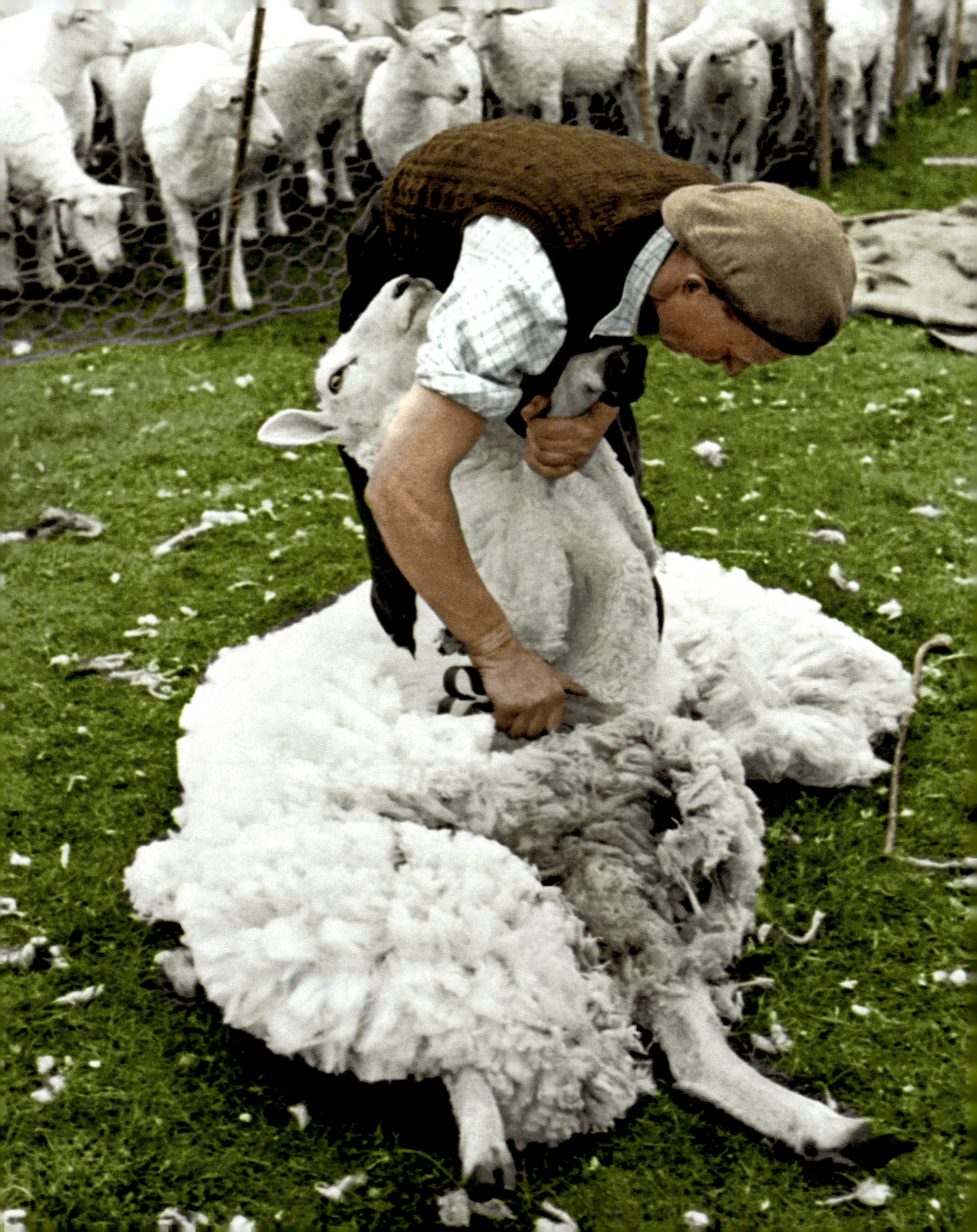

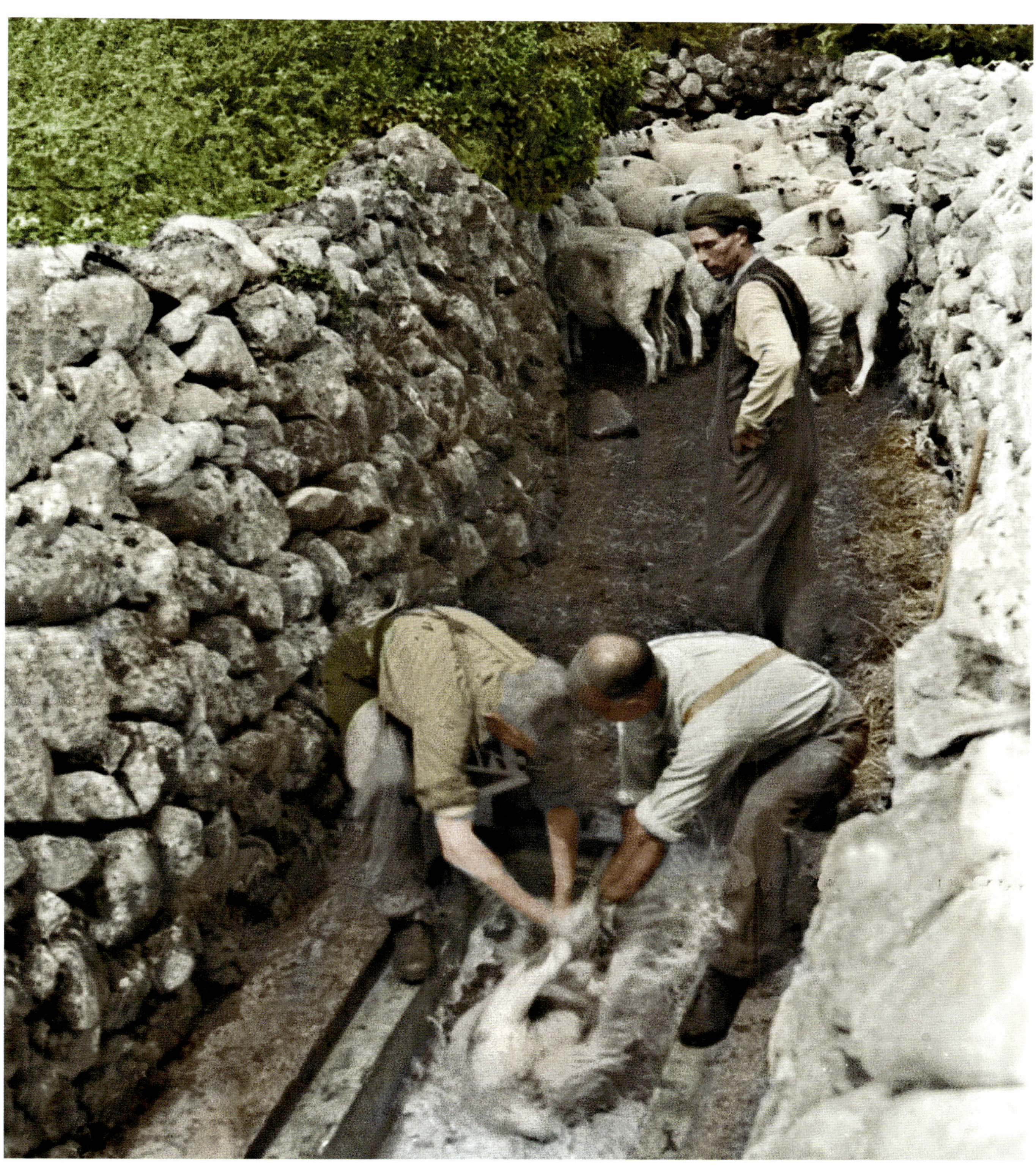

Left: A man shears a sheep at Kinvara, County Galway.

Top right: A sheep dip is underway – the sheep is immersed in a medicated solution to eliminate external pests like lice and mites.

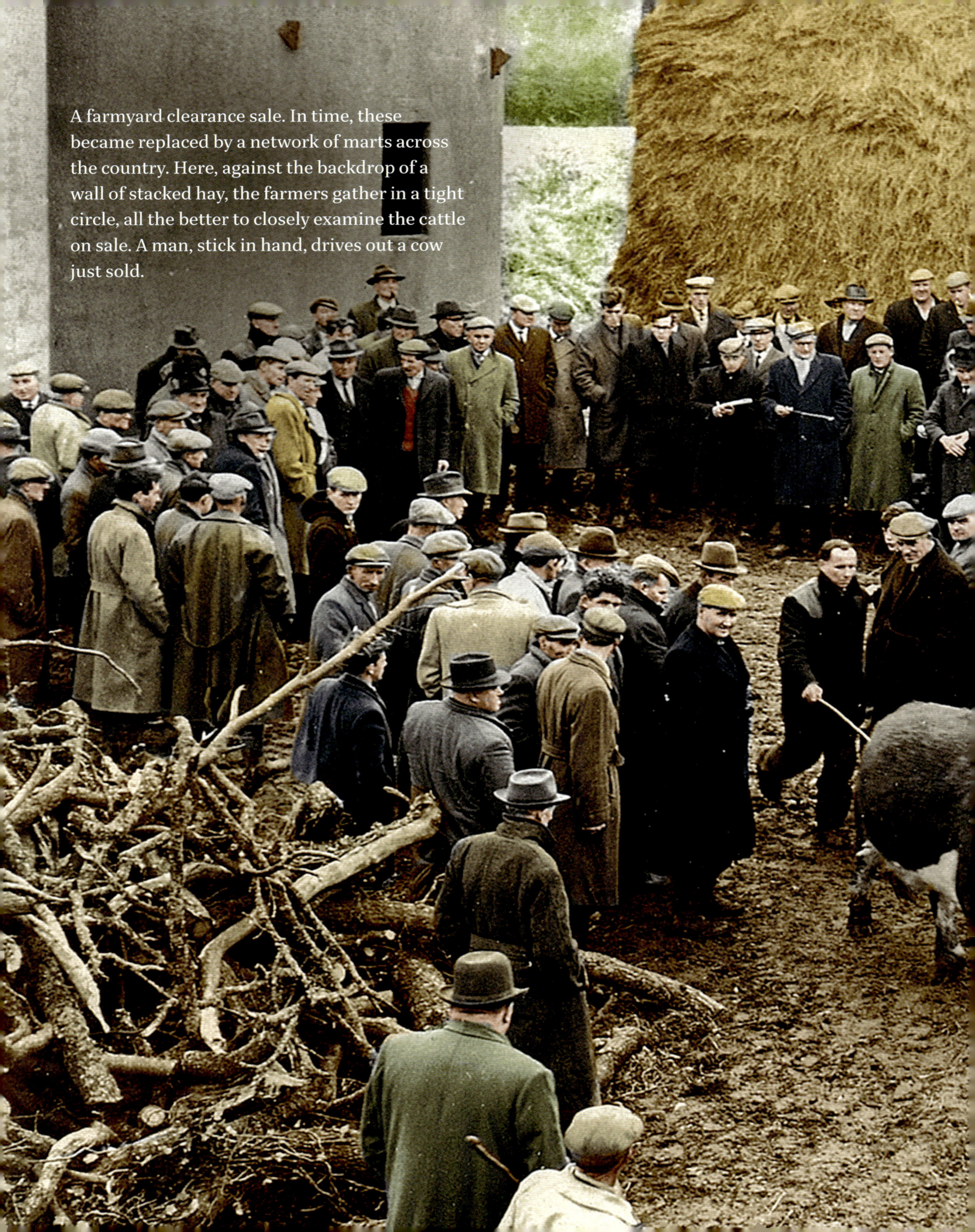

A farmyard clearance sale. In time, these became replaced by a network of marts across the country. Here, against the backdrop of a wall of stacked hay, the farmers gather in a tight circle, all the better to closely examine the cattle on sale. A man, stick in hand, drives out a cow just sold.

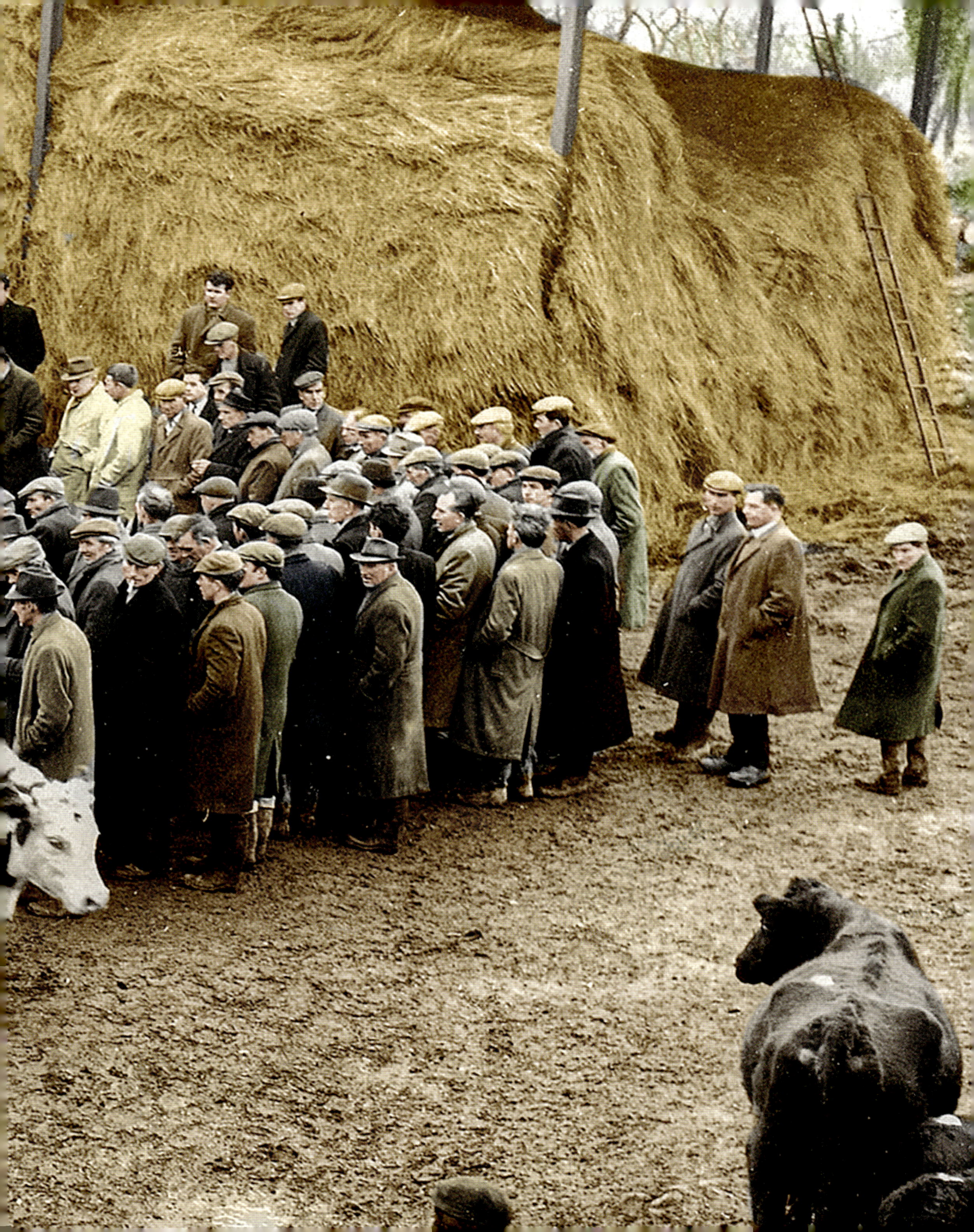

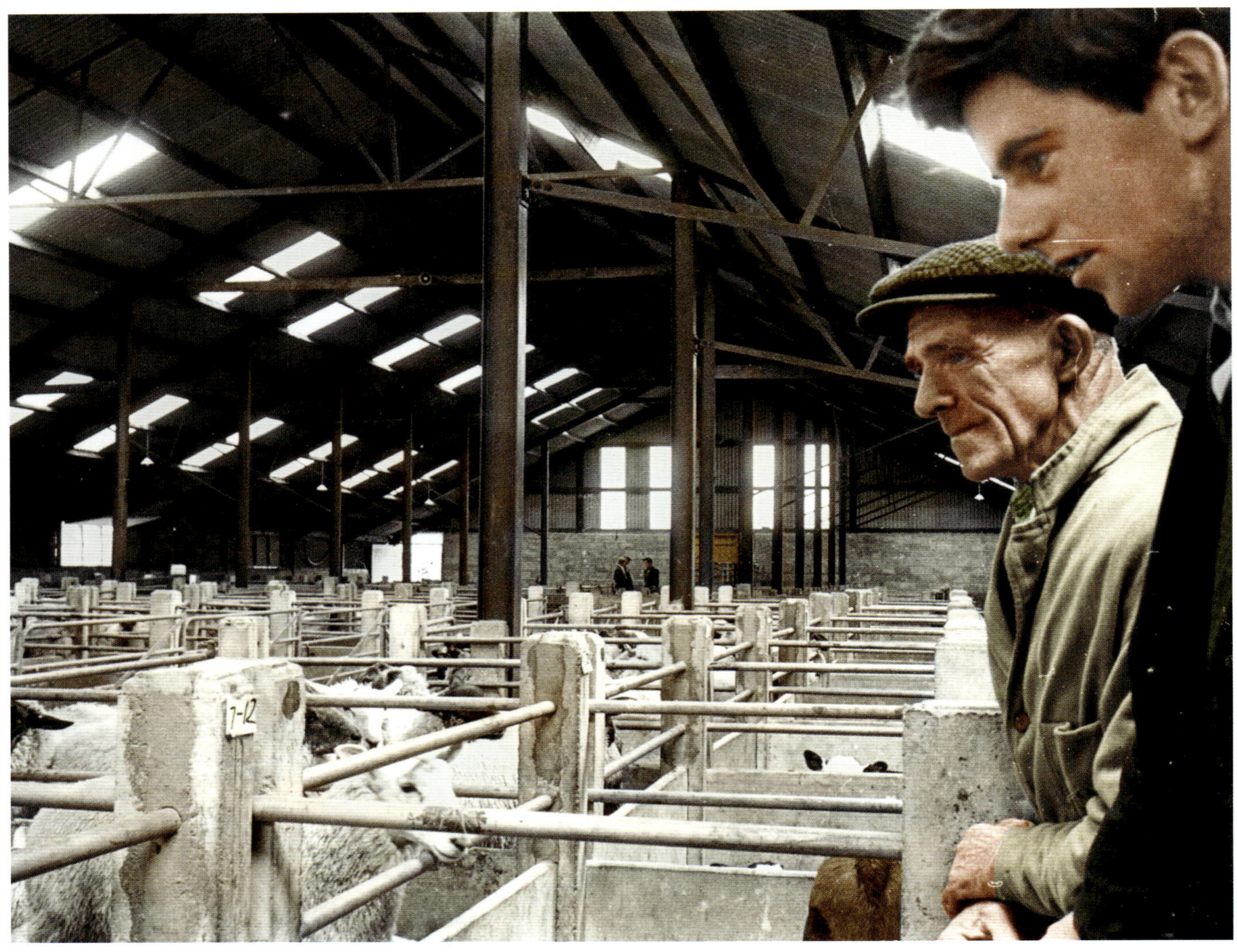

Top left: Sheep are corralled in pens at a Cahir, County Tipperary market in 1969. Fifty years ago, Irish sheep farming was a small-scale, traditional affair, with wool as a valuable product. Today, the sector is supported by modern technology and export-focused meat production, with lamb prices reaching record highs. However, challenges remain, including the decline of the wool market and growing sustainability pressures.

Right: In the 1950s' west of Ireland, a man with his donkey and cart pauses to peer into the window of a small car – a quiet moment that speaks to a country on the cusp of change. For generations, farmers travelled narrow lanes into town for the week's 'messages', their days shaped by the pace of the land and the animal. Today, in some cases in SUVs, they travel on better and faster roads to large supermarkets on the outskirts of expanding towns. The donkey cart, once part of the fabric of everyday life, is now a curiosity – part of an Ireland that moved more slowly, but was in many ways more rooted.

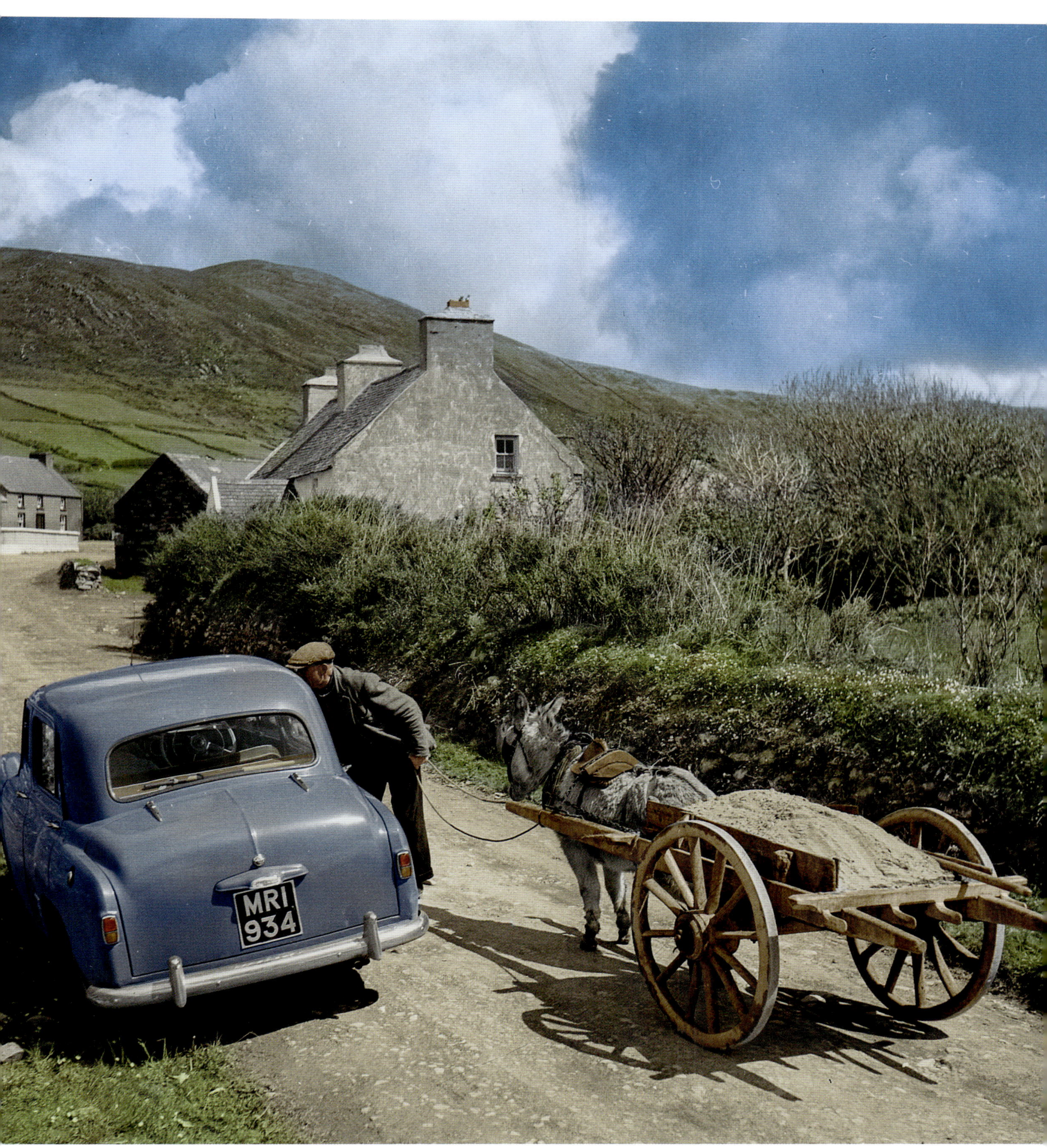

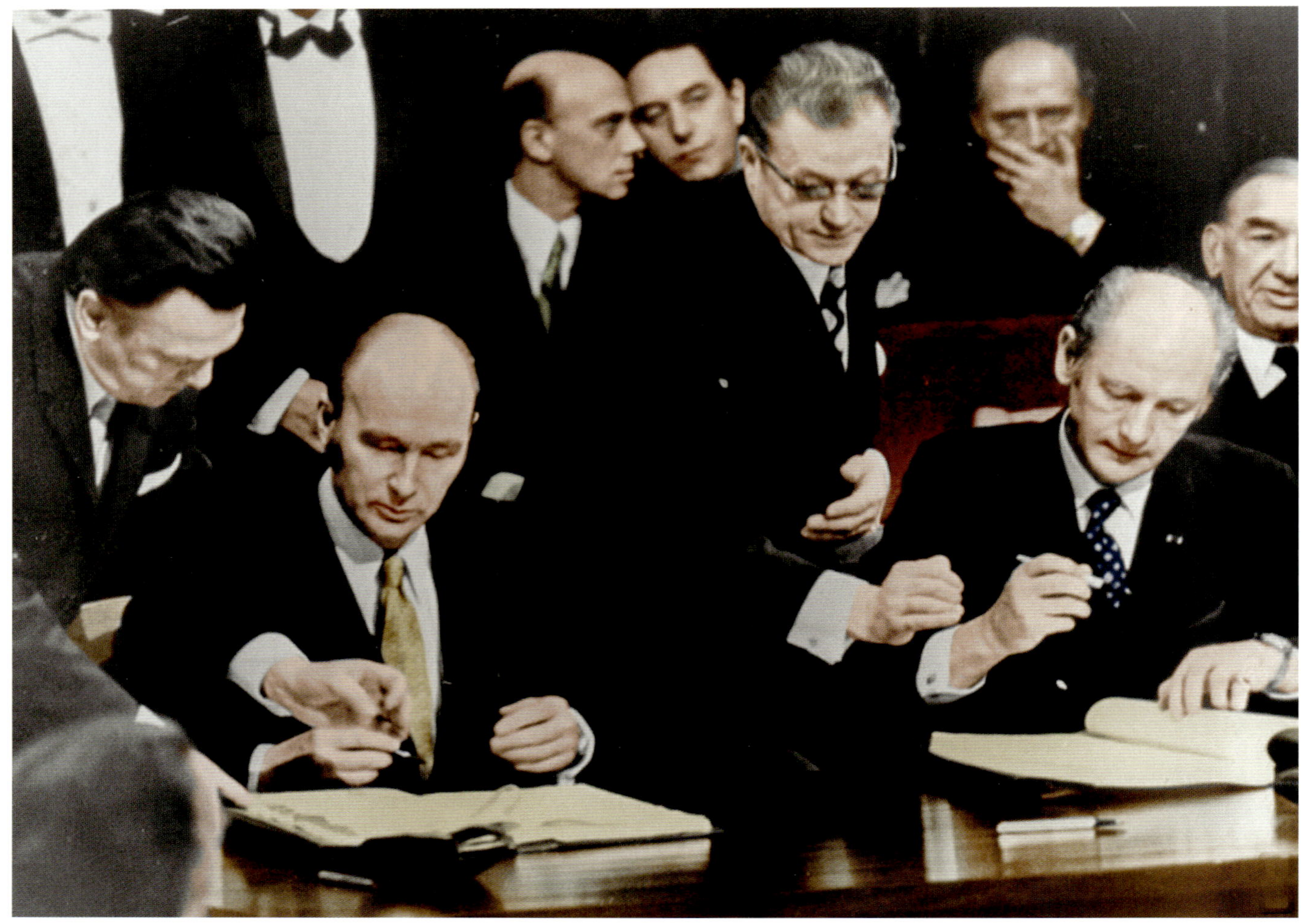

Top left: Patrick Hillery (left), Minister for External Affairs, and Taoiseach Jack Lynch (right) sign the Treaty of Accession in Brussels on 22 January 1972, formally setting Ireland on the path to membership of the European Economic Community (EEC). The country would officially join on 1 January 1973. For farmers, the move symbolised hope – access to larger markets and fairer prices. Yet it also marked a leap into the unknown, as small farms faced the challenge of competing in a vast, modern agricultural landscape.

Right: An Irish Creamery Milk Suppliers Association (ICMSA) delegation heads off to talks with the EEC Commission in 1970.

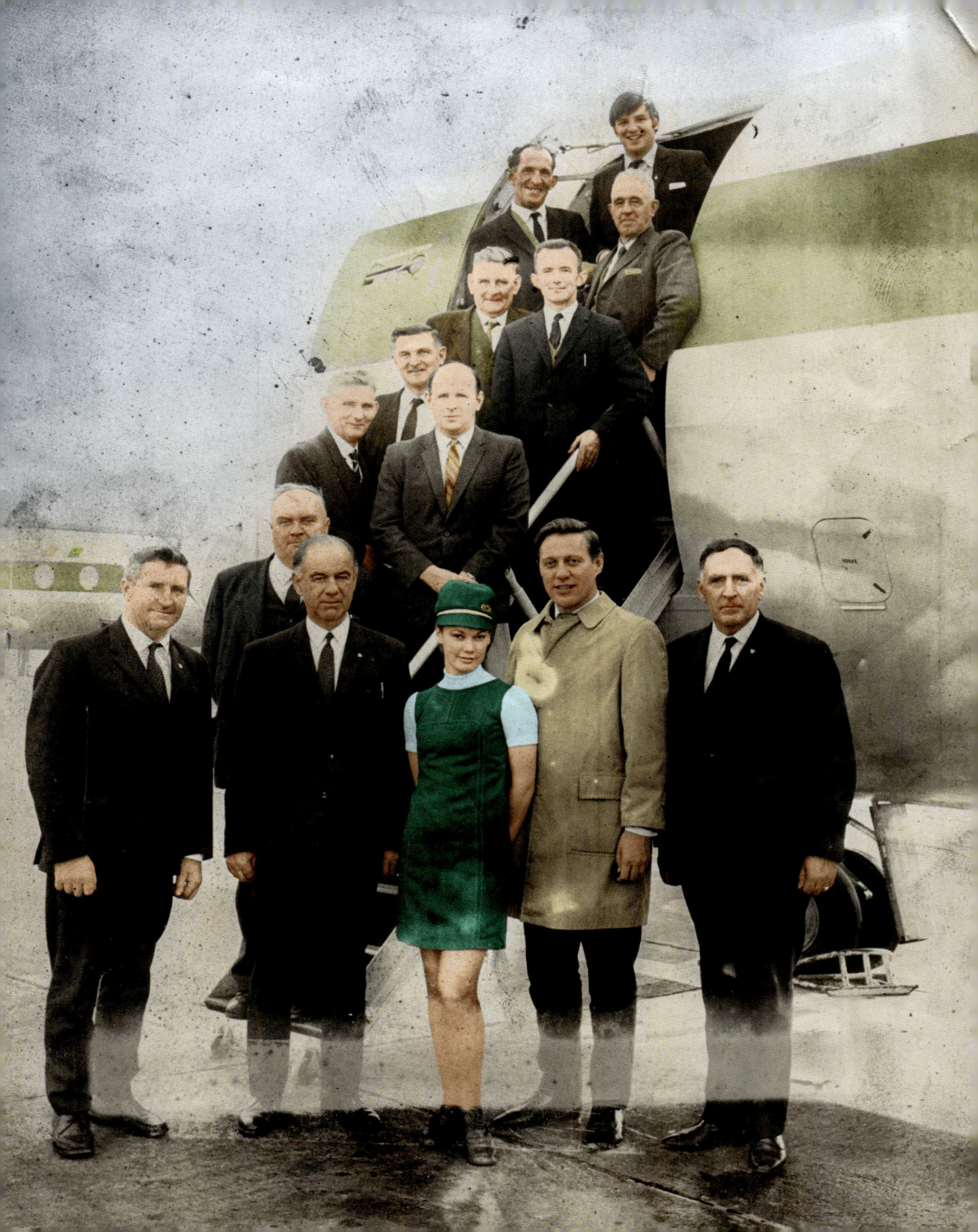

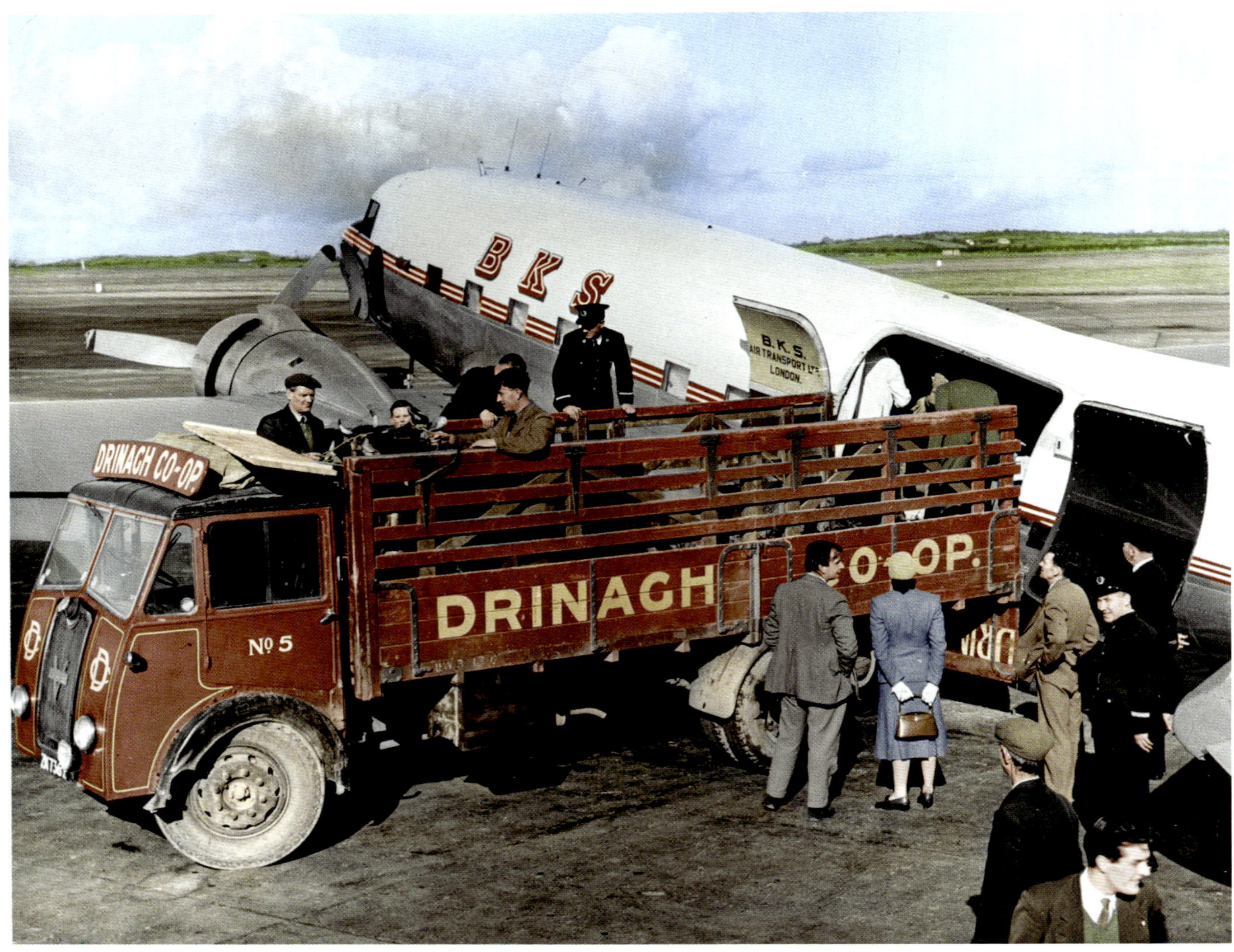

A historic moment at Shannon Airport in 1957: Drinagh Co-op offloaded 11 pure-bred TB-free in-calf Jersey heifers. They had been flown in from the Channel Islands as part of a bold initiative to improve local dairy herds by introducing the Jersey breed, renowned for its rich milk and butterfat production.

Founded in 1923 as a small creamery serving local farmers, Drinagh Co-op has since grown into a dynamic agricultural business. Overcoming the challenges of geography and limited resources, it expanded to many branches across West Cork by the mid-twentieth century and diversified into retail, milling and dairy processing. Today, Drinagh operates 15 outlets and remains firmly rooted in the heart of the community.

By the mid-twentieth century, the Irish co-operative movement had revolutionised agriculture, modernising dairy processing, establishing livestock marts and fostering rural development. Co-ops blended innovation with community values, helping consolidate smaller operations into larger, more efficient entities.

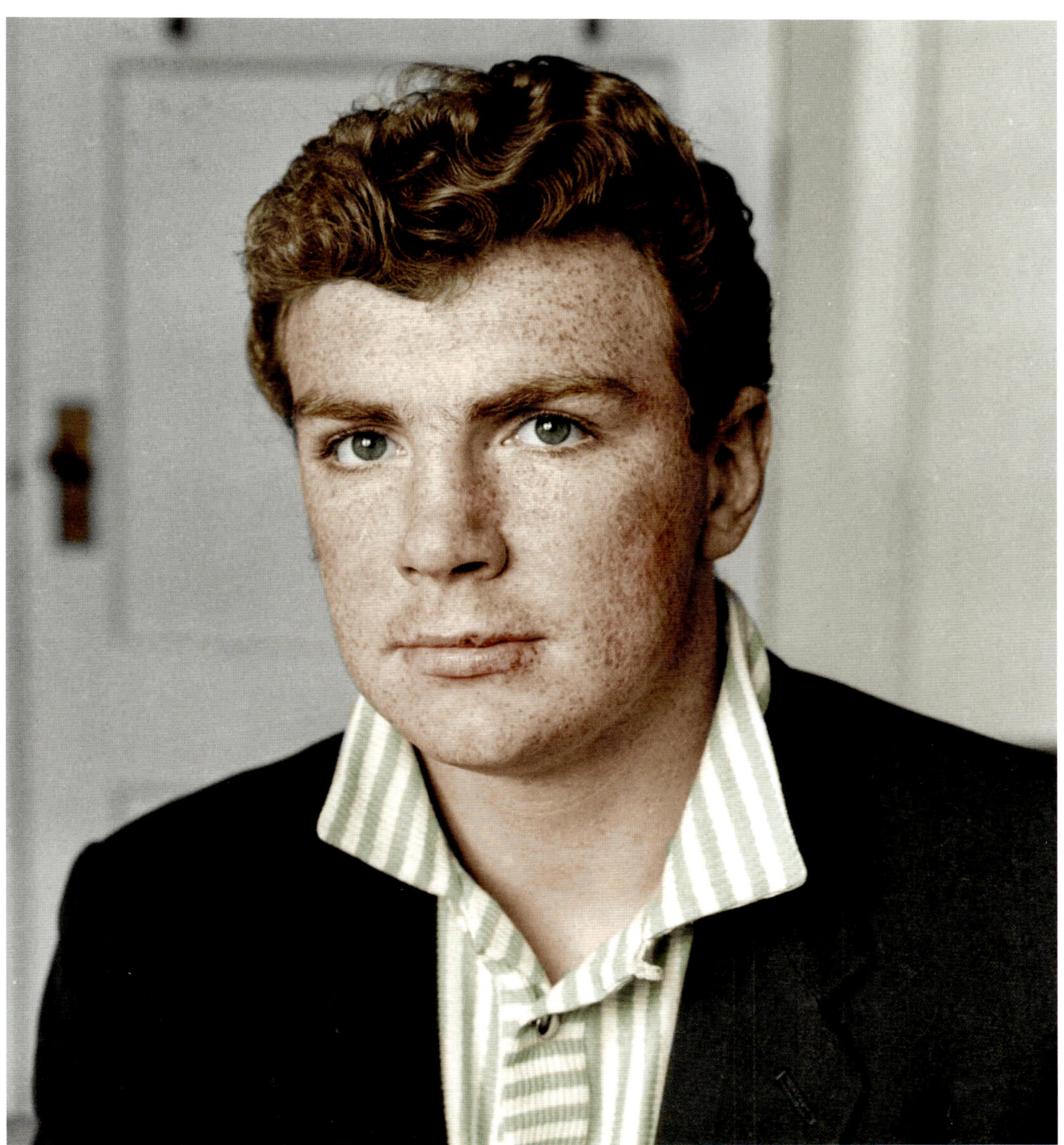

Long before he became a global business magnate, Tony O'Reilly began his remarkable journey with a nascent Bord Bainne in 1962 when, at the age of 26, he masterminded the launch of Kerrygold as Ireland's first national butter brand. Recognising the superior quality of Irish milk, he used his marketing vision to position Kerrygold as a premium product, revolutionising the dairy industry and putting Irish agriculture on the international map.

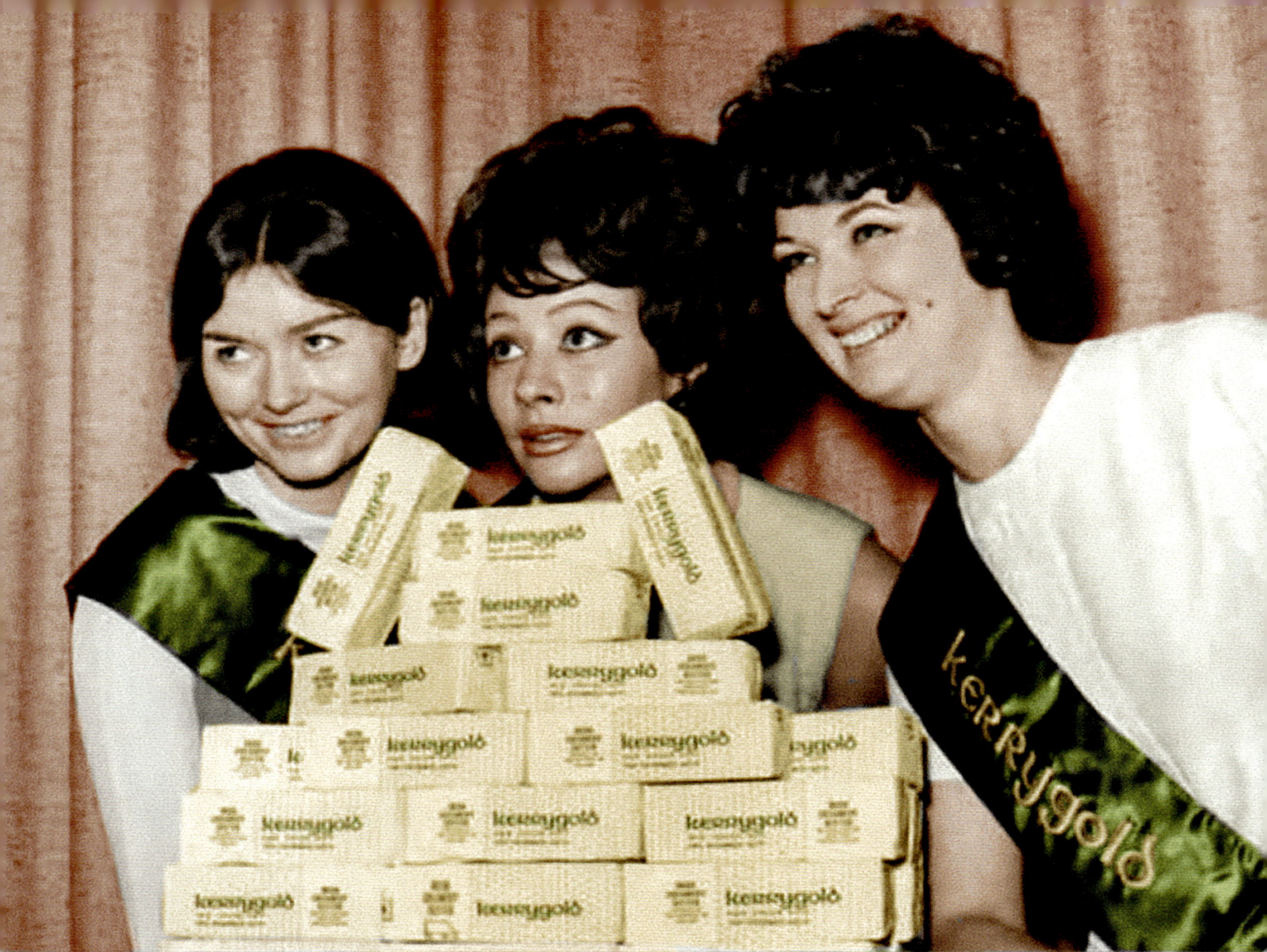

An early marketing promotion of Kerrygold, already in its now-iconic gold packaging. The butter stands out for its quality – unlike the pale, whitish butter common in some countries, Kerrygold's rich yellow colour comes naturally from beta-carotene, a pigment found in fresh grass. Irish cows, grazing on lush pastures for most of the year, produce milk that gives Kerrygold its distinctive taste and colour. Despite being priced at twice the cost of domestic butter – and weathering challenges such as US tariffs – it is up to now the second most popular butter brand in the United States. In Germany, it has seen even greater success, becoming the country's number one butter brand. Kerrygold has established itself as a leader in the global dairy market, with its parent company, Ornua, positioning it to become a €2 billion brand.

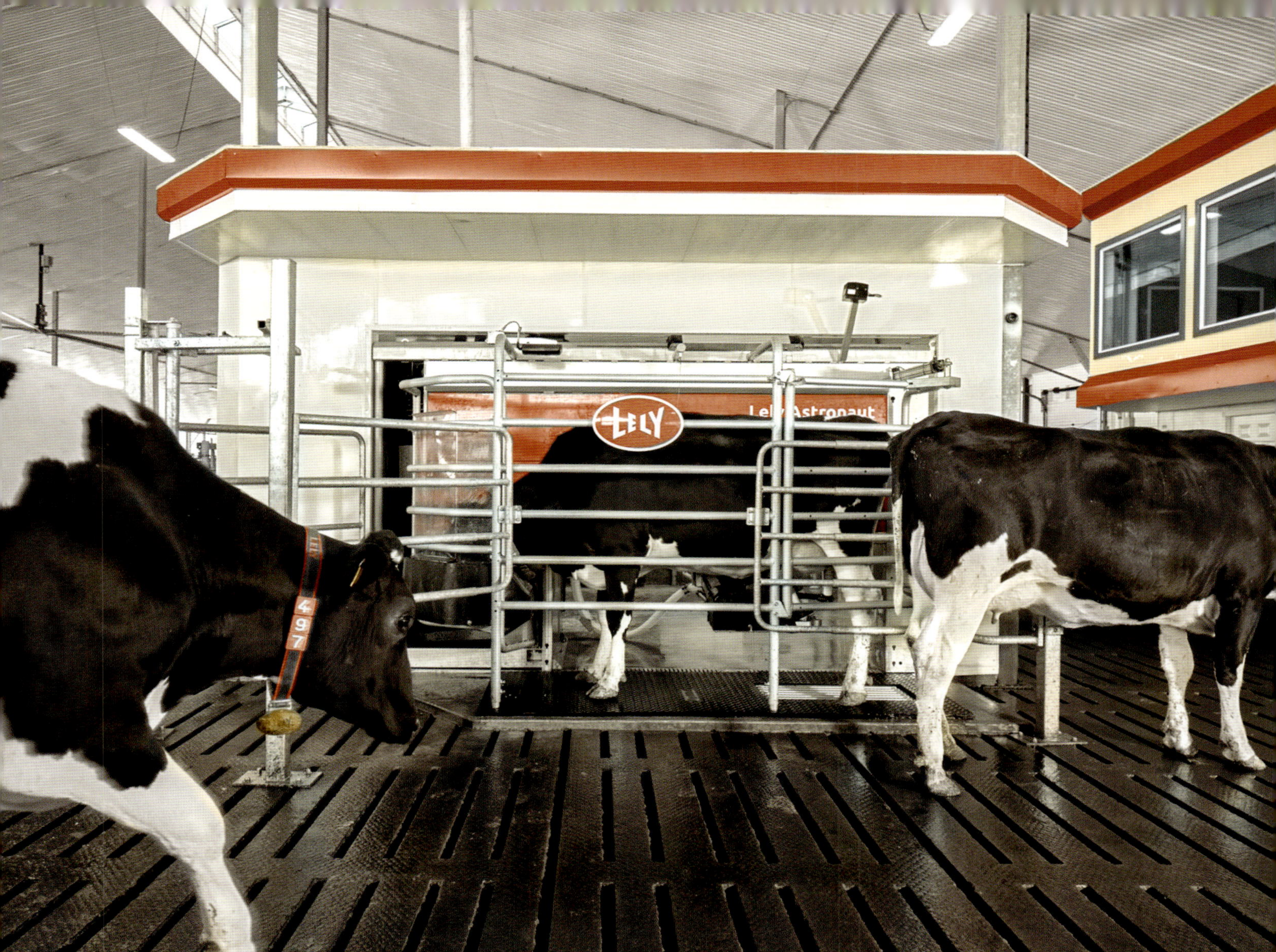

The future? Cows line up to enter a Lely robotic milking system. There are well over 1,000 robotic milking units now in operation across Ireland. The benefits are clear: addressing labour shortages, enabling herd expansion, providing flexibility in milking schedules, and, importantly, freeing up time to allow farmers to have a normal lifestyle. This technology will continue to evolve as artificial intelligence and machine learning improve over time.

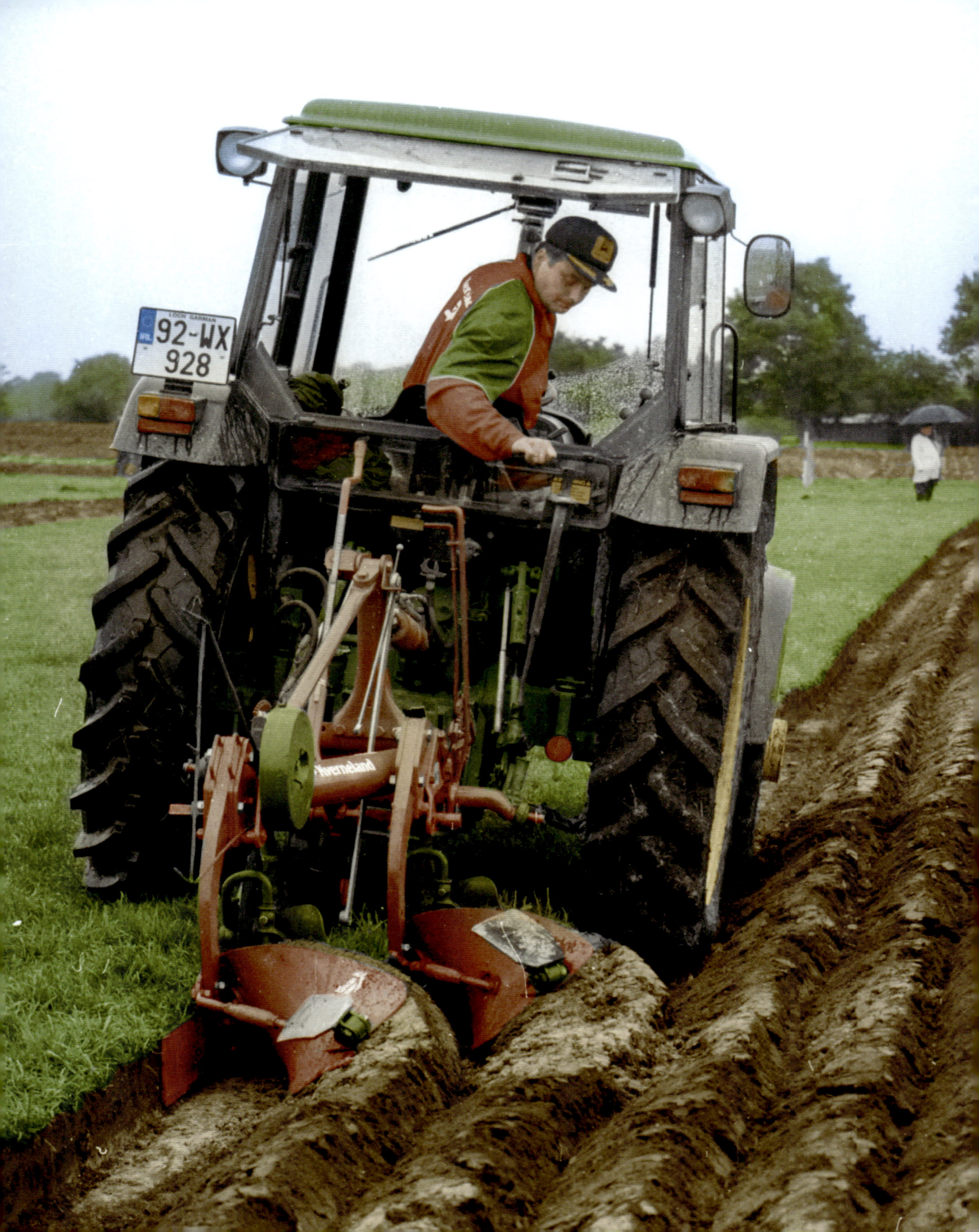
92-WX
928

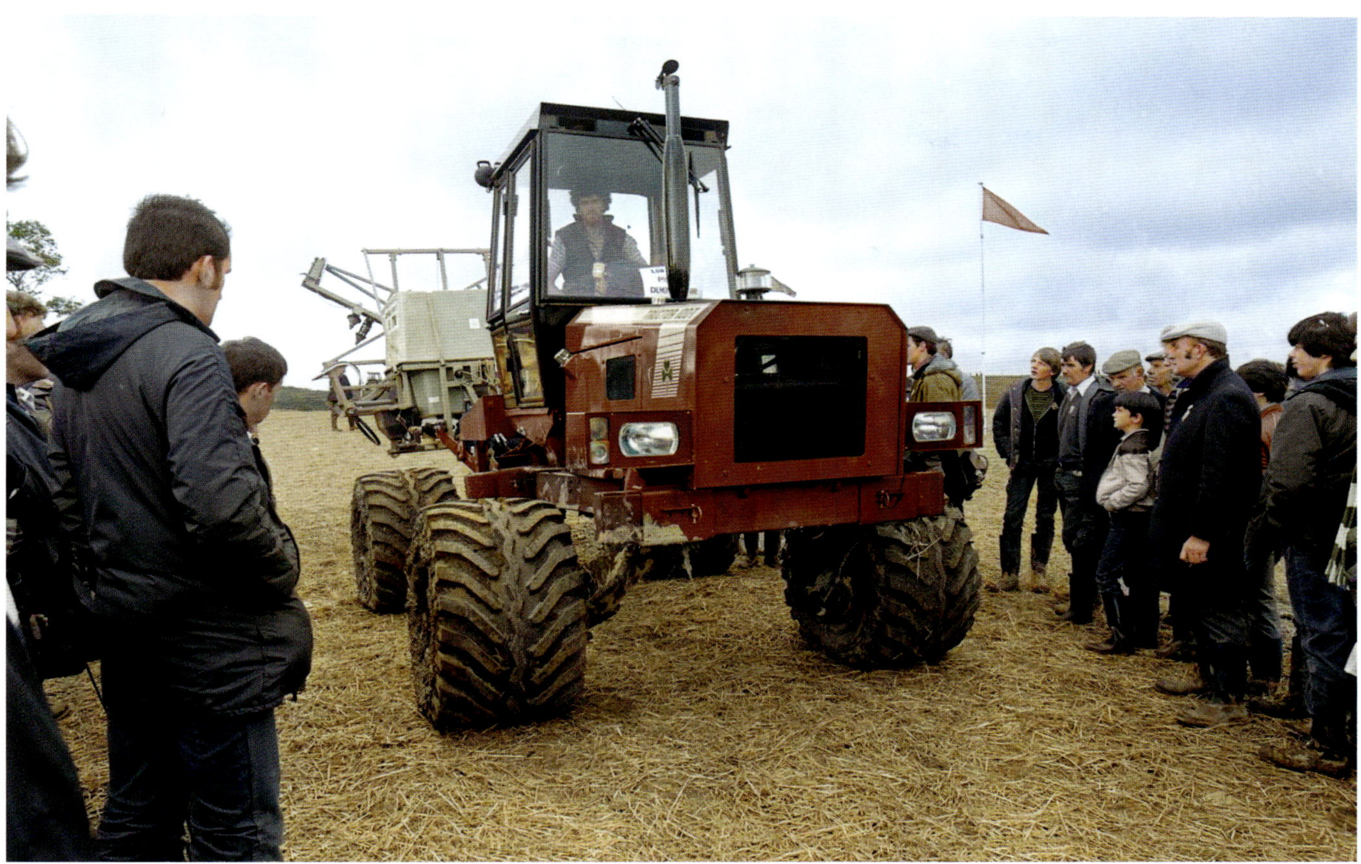

Left: Tillage has long been an enduring part of Irish farming. A contestant demonstrates how to precisely turn over the soil at the National Ploughing Championships, held near Birr, County Offaly in 1997. The National Ploughing Championship is one of the largest agricultural events in Europe. It attracts thousands of visitors annually, with farmers, professionals and anyone with an interest in rural life gathering to showcase ploughing, machinery and farming innovation.

Top right: A large tractor being put through its paces at the National Ploughing Championships at Waterford in 1983 – it's a far cry from the compact, versatile and relatively low-horsepower versions of such makes as Massey Ferguson and Ford that were popular in earlier decades.

While smaller tractors are still sold, Irish farmers have increasingly turned to larger, more powerful machines. This shift toward high-horsepower tractors is driven by the need for greater efficiency and productivity as labour shortages and environmental regulations push farmers to optimise their operations.

Farmers on O'Connell Street, Dublin, October 1956. Over 22,000 dairy farmers, transported by special trains and other means organised by the Irish Creamery Milk Suppliers Association (ICMSA), marched in Dublin to demand the release of a government report on milk costings.

This demonstration was part of a long tradition of Irish farmers mobilising in large numbers for fair pricing and better conditions. Over the decades, their protests – often involving road blockades, sit-ins and tractor convoys – have caused significant disruption, demonstrating their determination. These actions have repeatedly influenced policy, proving farmers' ability to unite and force government responses on agricultural issues.

Ireland has several farming organisations representing different sectors, the largest being the Irish Farmers' Association (IFA) and the ICMSA.

Founded in 1955 as the National Farmers' Association, the IFA adopted its current name in 1971. It is Ireland's largest farming organisation, representing all sectors from dairy and beef to tillage and horticulture. Acting as a powerful lobbying force, it advocates for fair prices, farm incomes and rural development, interacting with the Irish government and EU policymakers. With a strong tradition of grassroots activism, the IFA remains a leading voice for Irish farmers in an evolving agricultural landscape.

Dating from 1950, the ICMSA represents dairy and livestock farmers and promotes fair milk prices, farm incomes and sustainable policies. Focused on protecting family-run dairy farms, it engages with government and EU officials on trade, environmental regulations and the future of Irish agriculture.

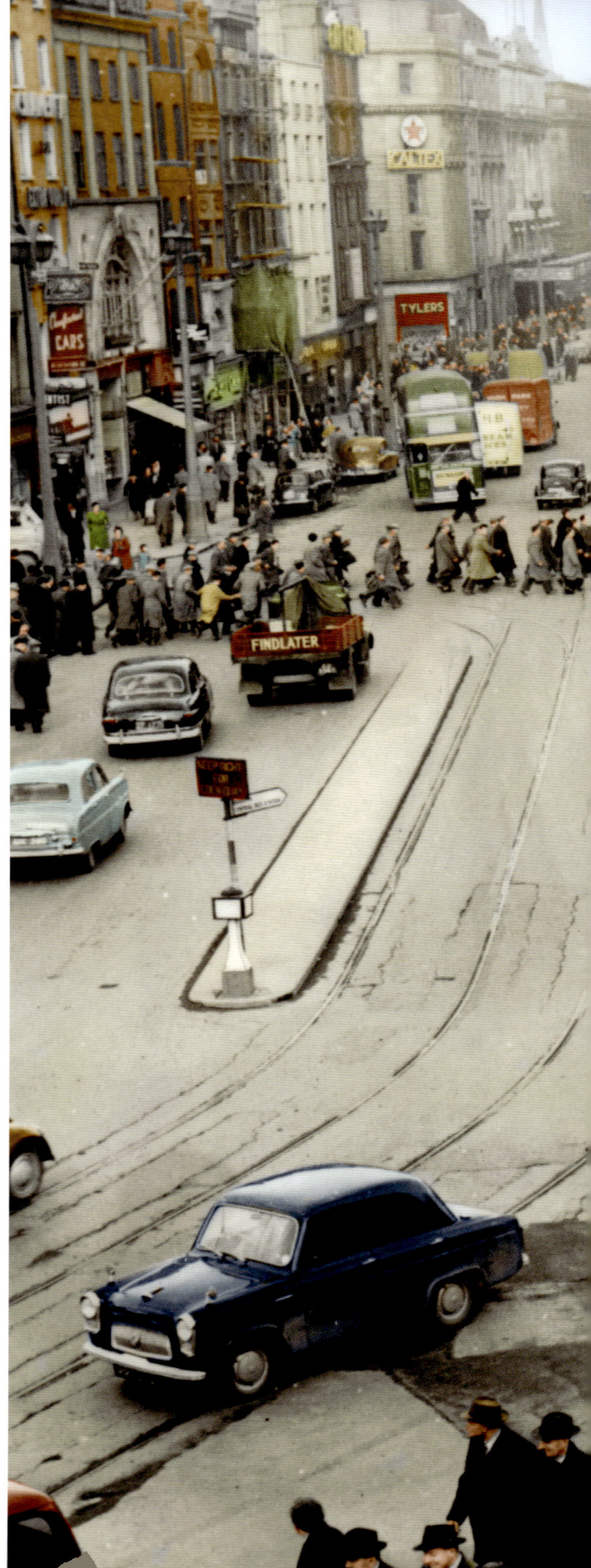

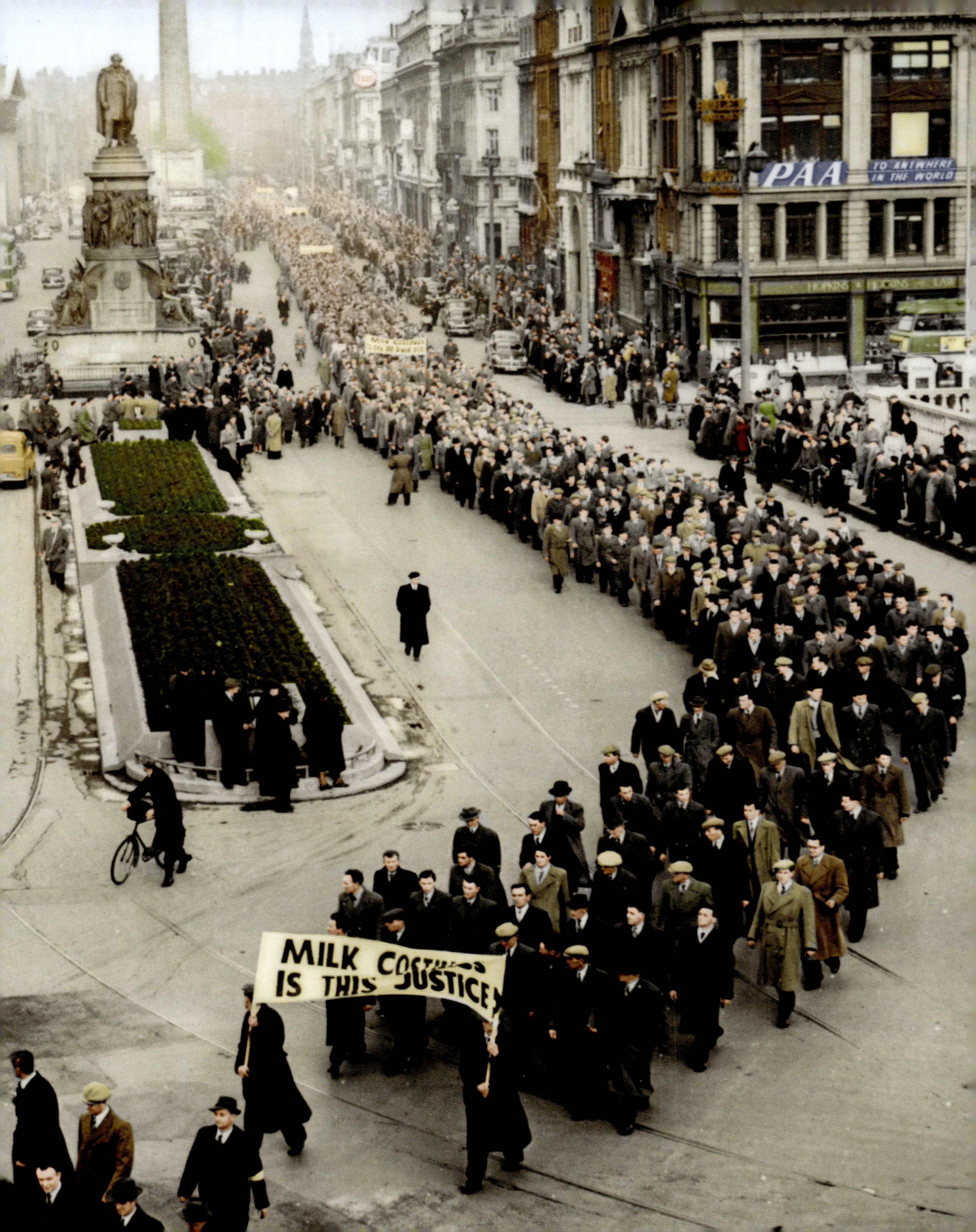

PAA
TO ANYWHERE IN THE WORLD
HOPKINS & HOPKINS
MILK COSTS
IS THIS JUSTICE

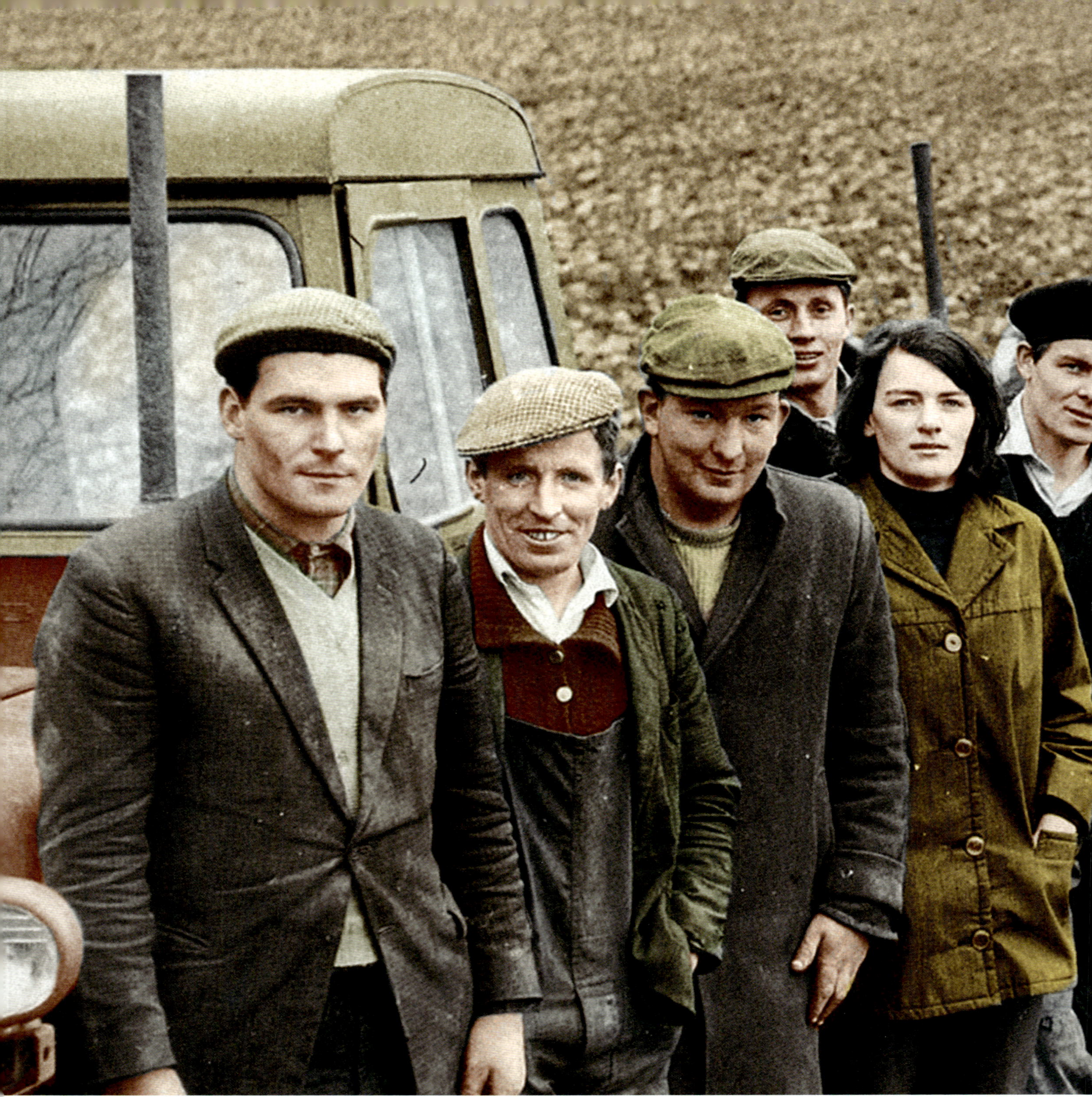

Dedication and solidarity are clear in the faces of these farmers, who came together in 1967 to plough fields in support of a neighbour imprisoned after protests (pages 246–7). Over the decades, farmers have faced economic struggles, policy changes and the fight for fair prices. Today, they face new challenges, from environmental regulations to market volatility, yet the resilience shown in 1967 remains a defining trait of Irish farmers.

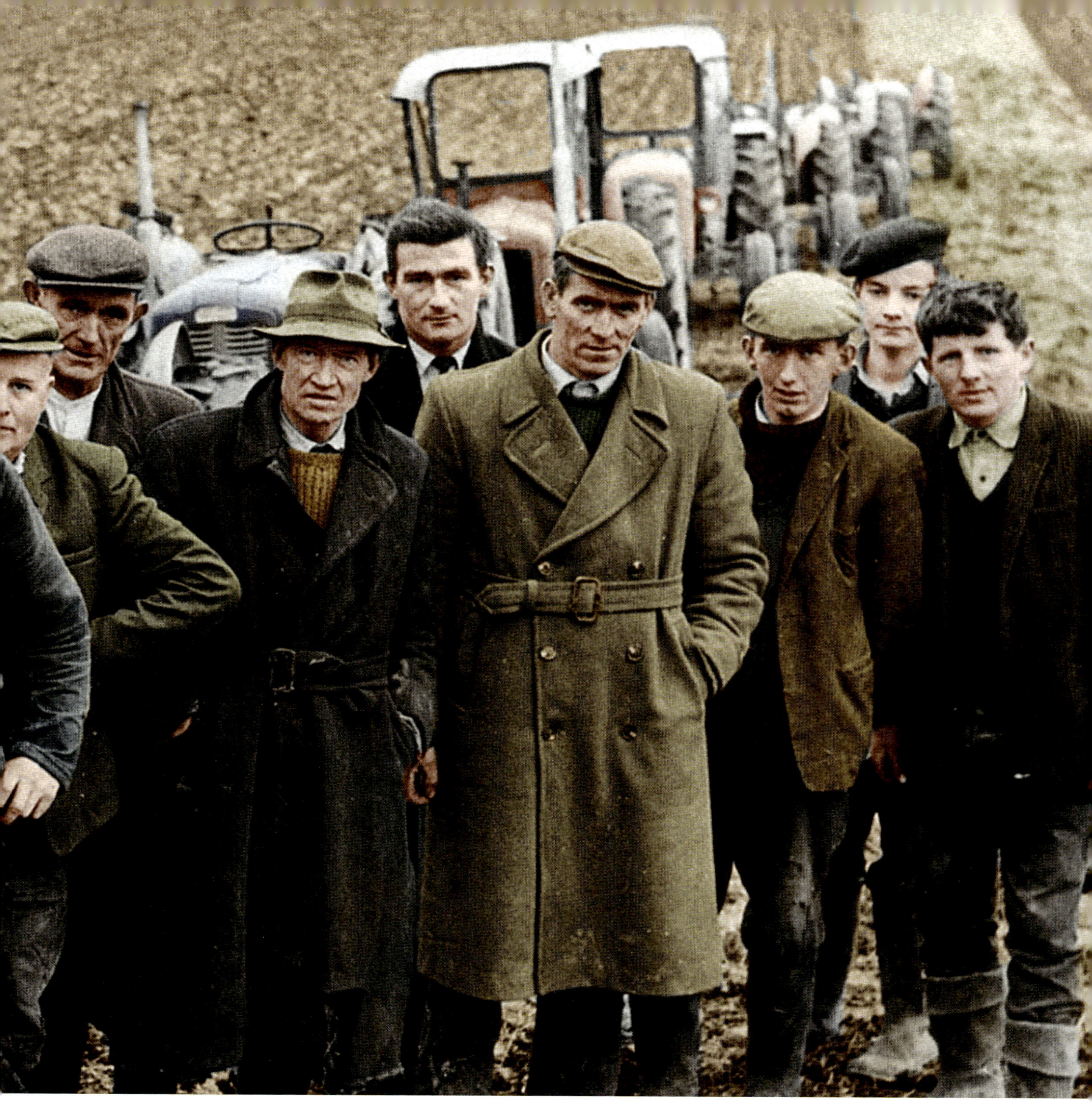

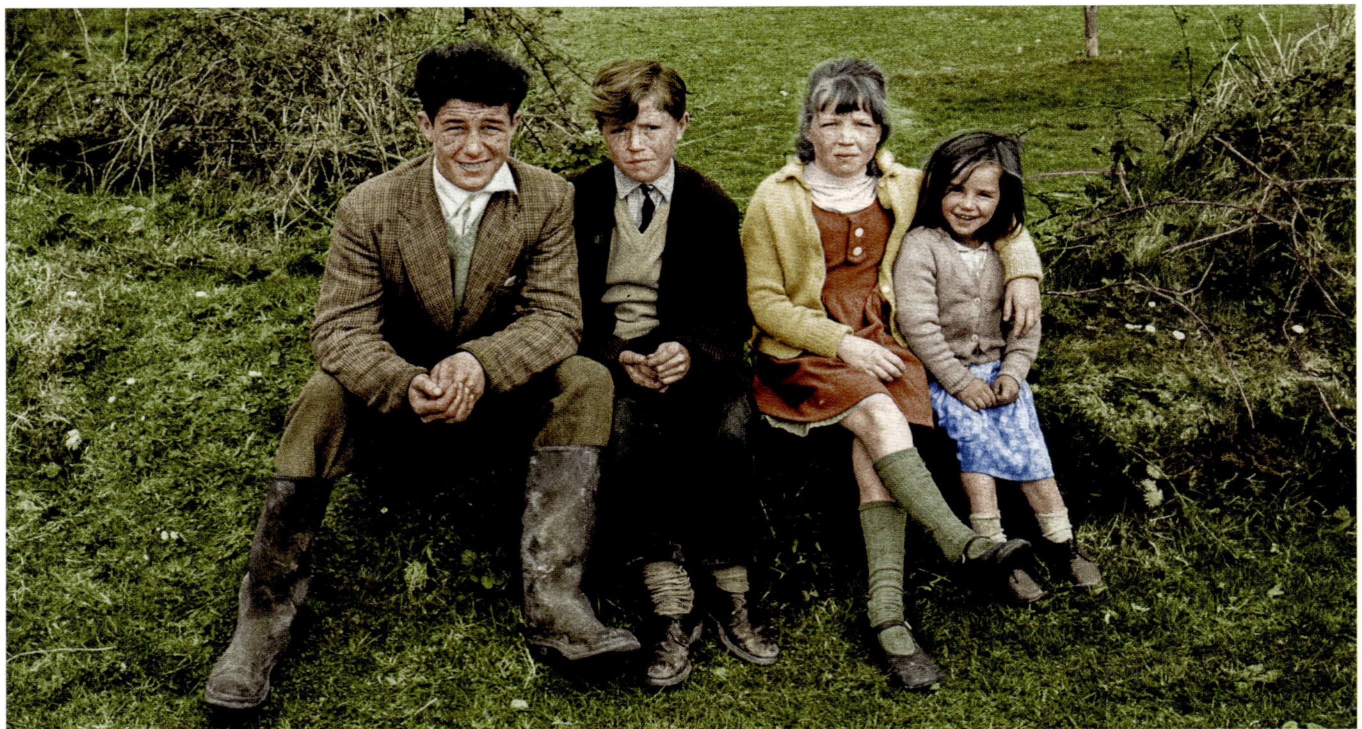

Young people are the future of rural Ireland, and those entering farming will need to tackle the delicate balance between economic survival and environmental responsibility.

There are many challenges. Irish agriculture is heavily export-oriented, with still a strong reliance on the UK market, which exposes farmers to external risks. Farm prices are volatile, influenced by weather patterns and market fluctuations. The EU's Common Agricultural Policy remains a work in progress, as Ireland seeks to steer between efficient agricultural production with fair farmer incomes, stable markets, food security and affordable consumer prices.

Agriculture is a significant contributor to Ireland's greenhouse gas emissions, and there is increasing pressure to reduce emissions and improve sustainability, especially in the meat and dairy sectors. The EU Green Deal's targets for reducing fertiliser use and enhancing biodiversity remain sources of contention.

Structural changes are evident, as the number of farm holdings continues to decline. Fewer young people are entering farming, and small farm sizes – especially in the west and north-west – make it difficult to maintain financially viable operations.

Income from farming remains low compared to other sectors, leading many young farmers to question: why continue with the hard life, when there may be a nine-to-five job just down the road? However, farming offers independence and a connection to the land, allowing individuals to work for themselves and maintain traditions that have been passed down through generations.

History shows that Irish farmers have faced and overcome challenges before. With a growing focus on science, innovation and sustainability, new technologies and approaches offer hope for a more resilient and prosperous future in agriculture.

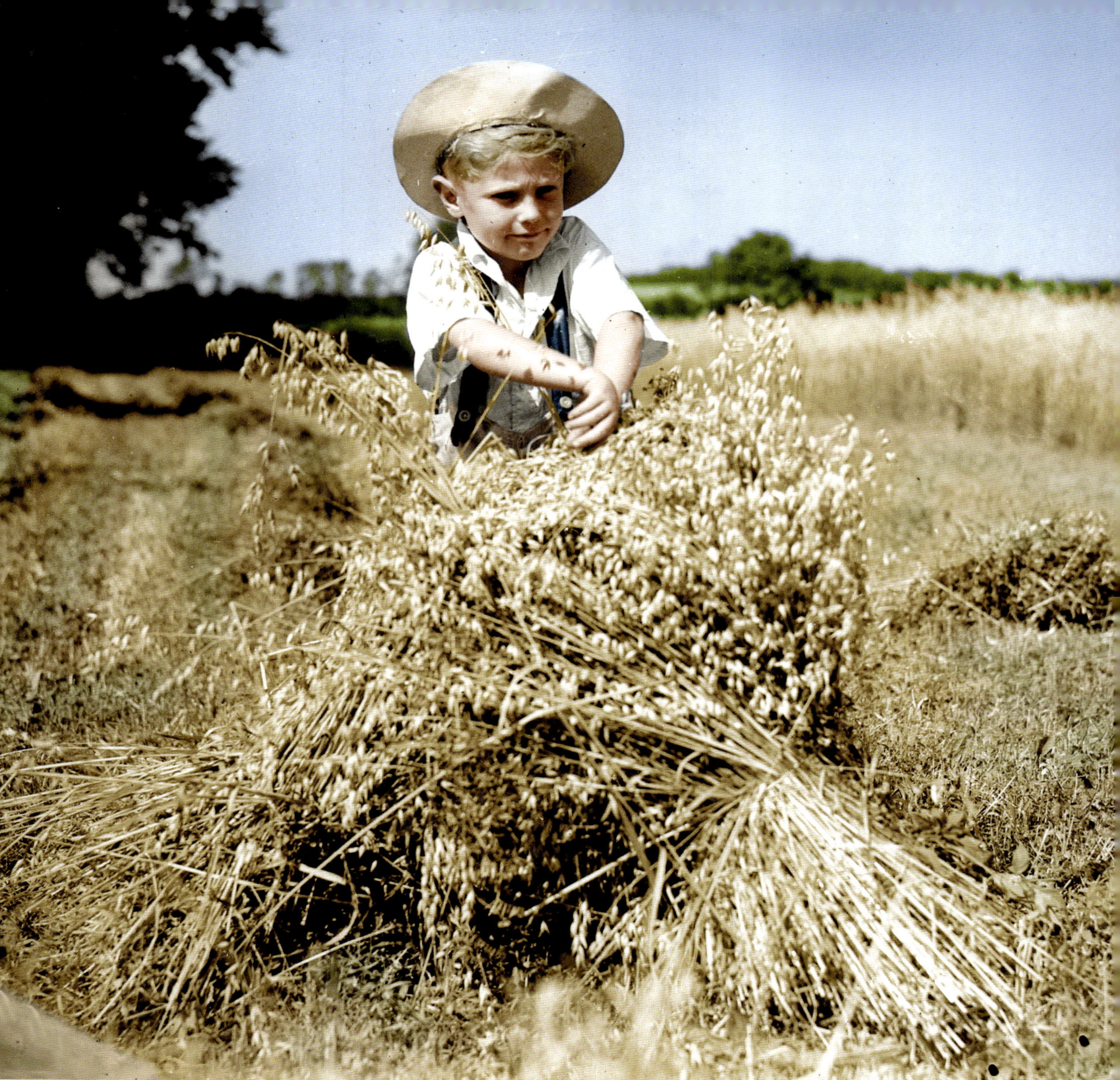

A young boy amidst the golden sheaves. Ireland's farming tradition is rooted in a unique blend of fertile soil, a favourable climate and the continuing connection between farmers and the land. Over the centuries, Irish farmers have demonstrated a remarkable spirit, enduring famine, emigration and ongoing economic challenges. As the next generation steps forward, there is hope that they will continue to build upon the legacy of their forebears, navigating new challenges while preserving our rich heritage.

IMAGE CREDITS

© Alamy Stock Photo: Nearby, 7; Pictorial Press Ltd, 42–43; KGPA Ltd, 75; Trinity Mirror / Mirrorpix, 108, 167, 220–221; Classic Cinema Archive, 204; Allan Cash Picture Library, 171, 205, 210, 237; Sueddeutsche Zeitung Photo, 250; © An Post: 119, 171; © Bibliothèque Nationale de France: 110–111; © Bill Power Collection: 133; © Bord na Móna: 160; © Capuchin Archives: 60, 86, 109, 122, 123, 130, 137, 138–139, 156–157, 181, 185, 216, 217, 225; © Clare Libraries: 35, 62–63, 144, 201; © Cork Public Museum: 112–113; © Drinagh Co-op / Philip O'Regan: 240; © European Commission: 238; © ESB Archives: 193, 194, 195, 196–197, 198, 199, 200; © Irish Examiner: 119, 126–127, 128–129, 146, 147, 153, 168–169, 172–173, 182–183, 184, 186–187, 226–227, 229, 230, 251; © Getty Images: Hulton Deutsch, 125, 208; Keystone, 150; Mirrorpix, 165, 166, 192; Charles Hewitt, 174–175; Terence Spencer/Popperfoto, 206–207; Werner Rings, 211; George Pickow/Three Lions, 212–213, 214, 218–219; Independent News and Media, 245; © Garda Archives: 176, 177; © Guinness Archives: 135; © ICMSA: 132, 236, 239, 246–247; © Irish Farmers' Association: 234–235, 248–249; © Irish Farmer's Journal: 244; © Irish Railway Record Society: 159, 161, 178, 179; © Jim Gahan: 120, 121, 124, 136, 202–203; © Kinvara Community Group: 180, 189, 224, 228, 232, 233; © Library of Congress: VI, 8–9, 10, 16–17, 19, 22–23, 26–27, 29, 42, 50–52, 58, 68–69, 72, 81, 97, 103, 107; © Michael Davitt Museum: 119; © Michael Hinch / IRRS: 159; © Military Archives: 151, 158; © National Library of Ireland: 7, 12–13, 14–15, 18, 20–21, 24–25, 30, 31, 32–33, 34, 36–37, 38, 39, 40–41, 44, 45, 46, 47, 48, 49, 53, 54–55, 59, 61, 64–65, 66–67, 70–71, 76, 77, 78–79, 80, 84–85, 87, 88–89, 90, 91, 96, 98–99, 100, 101, 102, 104–105, 114, 115, 116–117, 131, 134, 140–141, 142, 143, 145, 154–155, 162–163, 164, 188, 209, 215; © National Museum of Northern Ireland: 73, 74, 93; © Ornua: 242; © Deputy Keeper of the Records, the Public Record Office of Northern Ireland: 92; D2886/W/Portrait/27, 94; D2886/W/Portrait/14, 95; D1422_B_17_46-ALL-A, 106; © RDS Archives: 152; © State Library of Victoria: 28; © Stephen Travers: 222; © The Lawrence Collection / Terry O'Brien: 223; © University of Nottingham Manuscripts and Special Collections: 148–149; © Wikimedia Commons: 83, 241.

GLOSSARY

Common Agricultural Policy	An EU framework established in 1962 to support farmers, ensure food security, promote sustainable agriculture and develop rural areas across member states.
Fodder	Food for livestock, especially crops like hay, silage and grains.
Green Deal	A comprehensive EU strategy launched in 2019 to achieve climate neutrality by 2050, transform the economy and promote sustainable growth across all sectors.
ICMSA	Irish Creamery Milk Suppliers Association, a national farm organisation in Ireland representing dairy and livestock farmers and advocating for their interests at local, national and EU level.
IFA	Irish Farmers' Association, Ireland's largest farming organisation, representing farmers across all agricultural sectors and advocating for their interests at national and EU levels since 1955.
Meitheal	A traditional Irish system of communal labour, where neighbours come together to help each other, often seen in harvesting.
National Land League	An organisation founded in 1879 that fought for land reform, ultimately leading to significant changes in Irish land ownership and tenant rights.
Silage	Grass or other forage crops that have been fermented and preserved for feeding animals in winter.
Thresher	A machine used to separate the grain from stalks or husks in crops like oats or barley.
Tillage	The mechanical preparation of soil for planting crops, including ploughing, harrowing and cultivating.

BIBLIOGRAPHY

Archives Consulted

The Capuchin Archives, Dublin; Cork Public Museum; The Military Archives, Dublin; The Library of Congress; The National Library of Ireland, Dublin; The National Museum of Ireland; The National Museum of Northern Ireland, Belfast; The Public Record Office of Northern Ireland.

Periodicals

General Irish and British newspapers; *Irish Farmers Journal*.

Books

Bell, Jonathan, *People and the Land: Farming Life in Nineteenth-Century Ireland*, Friar's Bush Press, 1992.

Bell, Jonathan, *Ulster Farming Families, 1930–1960*, Ulster Historical Foundation, 2006.

Bell, Jonathan and Watson, Mervyn, *Farming in Ulster: Historic Photographs of Ulster Farming and Food*, Friar's Bush Press, 1988.

Bell, Jonathan and Watson, Mervyn, *Irish Farming Life: History and Heritage*, Four Courts Press, 2014.

Cullen, Louis M., *An Economic History of Ireland Since 1660*, Batsford, 1978.

Dempsey, Matt, *The Path to Power: 60 Years of the Irish Farmers' Association*, IFA, 2015.

Dungan, Myles, *Land Is All That Matters: The Struggle That Shaped Irish History*, Bloomsbury, 2024.

ICMSA, *Leaders of Courage: The Story of the ICMSA*, ICMSA, 2000.

Irish Rural Life and Industry, Irish International Exhibition, 1907.

Lee, J.J., *Ireland, 1912–1985: Politics and Society*, Cambridge University Press, 2010.

McElwaine, Alan, *It Really Did Happen: The Changes in Farming Since the 1940s*, Choice Publishing, 2006.

Ó Fathartaigh, Mícheál, *Developing Rural Ireland: A History of the Irish Agricultural Services*, Wordwell, 2021.

Offaly Historical Society, *Farming in Offaly Down the Years*, Offaly Historical Society, 1987.

O'Hagan, John and O'Toole, Francis, *The Economy of Ireland: Policy Making in a Global Context*, Bloomsbury, 2017.

O'Hanlon, Michael, *Hiring Fairs & Farm Workers in North-West Ireland*, Guildhall Press, 1992.

Oram, Hugh, *Old Irish Country Life*, Stenlake Publishing, 2007.

O'Regan, Philip, *Drinagh 1923–2023: 100 Years of Drinagh Co-operative Creamery Limited*, Drinagh, 2023.

O'Reilly, Michael, *Dancehall Days: When Showbands Ruled the Stage*, Gill Books, 2014.

Rynne, Colin, *At the Sign of the Cow: The Cork Butter Market, 1770–1924*, Collins Press, 1998.

Stout, Geraldine and Keane, Margaret, *Farming and the Ancient Countryside*, Teagasc, 1996.

Taylor, Alice, *To School Through the Fields: An Irish Country Childhood*, Brandon, 2016.

Treacy, Steve, *Scythe to Setaside: 30 Years of Agricultural Photography*, IAWS, 1993.

INDEX